INTERNATIONAL RELATIONS

INTERNATIONAL RELATIONS
Contemporary Theory and Practice

George A. Lopez
University of Notre Dame

Michael S. Stohl
Purdue University

A Division of Congressional Quarterly Inc.
1414 22nd Street N.W., Washington, D.C. 20037

Printed in the United States of America

Third Printing

Developed for CQ Press by Irving Rockwood & Associates, Inc.

Library of Congress Cataloging-in-Publication Data

International relations: contemporary theory and practice / [edited by] George A. Lopez, Michael S. Stohl.
    p. cm.
    Bibliography: p.
    Includes index.
    ISBN 0-87187-476-8
    1. International relations. 2. United States—Foreign relations—1945- 3. World politics—1945- I. Lopez, George A. II. Stohl, Michael, 1947- .
JX 1391.I637   1989   88-17043
327'.09'045—dc19   CIP

CONTENTS

Contents

Contents

PREFACE

Twenty-five years of experience teaching the introductory course in international relations have gone into *International Relations: Contemporary Theory and Practice*. What that experience has taught us is that it is not enough simply to tell our students about the events of international politics—however interesting some of those events might be—or to teach the major conceptual tools employed by scholars who study those events.

Our students also have wanted to know how concepts such as deterrence, power, and national security relate to the real world of policy. This book is an attempt to show why and how ideas and theories influence the way policy makers think and, ultimately, act.

The strong and critical relationships among theory, policy, and practice have encouraged us to develop this text with four major pedagogical objectives in mind:

1. To introduce the central concepts and theories of international relations.
2. To demonstrate how these concepts and theories are developed and tested by scholars.
3. To illustrate how these same concepts, theories, and findings then become part of policy formation and practice.
4. To foster an appreciation of the sometimes obvious and sometimes subtle linkages among theory, policy making, and policy implementation.

The eleven chapters that follow are grouped into four parts. The first part deals with the actors and the decision-making context of the international system. The second discusses the tools of policy and the third, policy strategies. The final part is an essay by the editors that summarizes and integrates the material in the preceding chapters.

Each of the middle nine chapters, which constitute the heart of the book, contains an editors' introduction outlining critical concepts and themes and a set of readings—scholarly articles and policy statements—that illustrate how theory, policy, and practice are interrelated. Each chapter concludes with a set of discussion questions and suggestions for further reading.

We believe that the events of international affairs can be understood only when placed in proper context. That context includes not only an understanding of global politics, but a sound conceptual and theoretical foundation in international relations as well. The "policy excerpts" in Chapters 2 through 10 wrestle with real problems and real issues in a way that reveals the connections between theory and policy.

When policy and theory are examined together one can usefully see what happens to the "neatness" of a concept such as deterrence in the real world. Does the concept have utility and meaning when policy makers use it as a framework for decision making? Does the logic of the balance of power theory hold when that theory is translated into policy? It is questions like these that inform and undergird this book.

In the three years it has taken to complete this book, we have amassed many debts to students and colleagues who have read, reacted to, and critiqued the manuscript. They have helped bring the manuscript closer to matching our own best intentions.

In particular we would thank participants in the 1986 course in political violence and world order at Earlham College; with that class George Lopez premiered the first set of chapter commentaries and readings appearing in this volume. Subsequently, the challenges posed by students in Lopez's introductory course in international relations at the University of Notre Dame from 1986 to 1988 helped to develop the blend of readings.

Throughout this process, Irving Rockwood of Irving Rockwood & Associates, Inc., has fulfilled the roles of editor, policy critic, and student-at-large in a manner that has clarified the link between the commentaries and readings and also enhanced our general sensitivity to the needs of the introductory student. It is not just that the text is better due to his contribution; rather, this volume exists because of his role.

As we moved from penultimate to final chapter drafts, we benefited greatly from the critiques of three reviewers—Timothy J. Lomperis of Duke University, B. David Meyers of University of North Carolina at Greensboro, and Donald A. Sylvan of Ohio State University. Although they will notice that we did not heed all of their advice, their careful comments and corrections brought us a broader theoretical and historical sense of the field and an appreciation of the needs of the student and teacher in an introductory course.

At the beginning of this venture and during the rough spots of bringing it to completion, we have enjoyed the quiet but firm support of CQ Press. We are grateful to Joanne Daniels for inviting us to join CQ Press's growing list in international relations. The work of our project editor, Carolyn McGovern, and Kathryn Suárez and Ellen Kresky in marketing reflected commitment and professionalism too rarely experienced in numerous other publishing ventures. We are thankful to each of them.

Throughout the preparation of this volume we have benefited from the support of Velma (Sam) DeBruler of the Social Science Division at Earlham College, Rosemarie Green and Midge Holleman of the Institute for International Peace Studies at Notre Dame, and Kim Orth and Beth Turner of the Department of Political Science at Purdue University. They not only took care of us and the manuscript, they did so in good humor and with the highest professional standards.

As when we began, we are firmly convinced that understanding the dynamic interplay between theory, policy, and practice is essential for the future citizens of the world. Thus, to our children, Thomas, Martin, and Patrick Lopez and Rachel and Ilene Stohl, who are the future, we express appreciation as well. You will help us evolve the setting and context in which the theory, policy, and practice of international relations will unfold.

George A. Lopez
Michael S. Stohl

PERSPECTIVES ON THE NATURE
OF INTERNATIONAL RELATIONS

THEORIES, POLICIES, AND PRACTICE IN INTERNATIONAL RELATIONS   *1*

What are the causes of war? How can nations maintain peace and security? How can nations improve their own international trading positions without causing harm to their trading partners? How, in short, does the international system work, and how does it affect the people who live in it?

These questions have perplexed citizens, diplomats, and scholars alike throughout human history. They do not permit easy answers, and none will be offered here. It is our purpose, instead, to lay the foundation for an improved understanding of such questions. We begin in this chapter with a discussion of the following elements:

1. the definition of international relations;
2. the relationship between theory, policy, and practice in international relations;
3. the evolution of the modern state system;
4. the ways policy makers, scholars, and citizens learn about international relations.

International relations may be defined as a human activity in which individuals or groups from one nation interact, officially or unofficially, with individuals or groups from other nations. International relations involve not only face-to-face or direct physical contact, but also economic transactions, the use of military force, and diplomacy both public and private. The study of international relations then encompasses activities as diverse as war, humanitarian assistance, international trade and investment, tourism, and the Olympic games.

Because some scholars use the terms interchangeably, international relations and international politics are often confused. We understand international relations to mean the broad sphere of international human interaction of which international politics, international economics, international law, and international security affairs are subcategories.

Understanding Contemporary International Relations

Differences of interpretation in the study of international relations often arise because of the different frameworks, or sets of assumptions, used by different analysts. For example, historians often disagree about the meaning of historical events and the motives of the actors involved. As students of international relations, we must be aware that any given policy or action is shaped by the prevailing beliefs of the period and the worldviews of the actors.

We must also understand that these perspectives change over time. Niccolo Machiavelli's sixteenth-century pronouncement that rulers would fare better if they were feared rather than loved by their citizens dominated the philosophy and practice of Western rulers for the next two centuries. Prussian general Karl von Clausewitz's definition of war as "politics by other means" influenced the thinking and behavior of Otto von Bismarck, the leader who unified Germany and reshaped Europe in the late nineteenth century.

In short, the history of international relations demonstrates that theory influences policy, and policy in turn influences theory.

Ironically, although its historical importance is obvious, this linkage between ideas and policies is easily overlooked in the immediacy of the present. We are too close to contemporary events to realize that today, as in the past, there is a clear link between theory, policy, and practice in international relations. Similarly, it remains true today that differences in theoretical assumptions, in worldview, give rise to differences in policy and practice. This last point is easily forgotten in the heat of debate. But what is more important than unanimity among scholars is that a scholarly approach can help us to understand the implications of different theoretical assumptions and policy preferences, and the relationship between the two.

To recognize the interactive nature of theory, policy, and practice is to admit that we cannot understand world affairs without investigating both the policies and events and the way we think about these policies and events. A competent grasp of international relations involves an understanding of (1) the critical concepts and theories that shape the way policy makers view the world; (2) the way a given concept or theory is "played out" in the policies of nations; and (3) the interplay between the success or failure of policy as it unfolds in practice and the continued vitality, demise, or reinterpretation of the theory. The relationship of these three elements is outlined in Figure 1-1.

Studying contemporary international relations, therefore, requires investigating more than just the meaning of concepts such as deterrence or balance of power. We must also consider the way these concepts are applied by real-world policy makers. We must ask if the presumed neatness of the concepts vanishes when national leaders attempt to put them to use. And finally we must ask how the results of policy makers' efforts are likely to influence our view of the concepts or theories in the future.

The State and the Westphalian System

Although there are numerous approaches to the study of international relations, scholars overwhelmingly agree on a number of central propositions.

Figure 1-1   The Interrelationship of Theory, Policy, and Practice

Theory
the set of logically related concepts
and generalizations concerning a
particular area of international
relations and the actions of elites
who conduct foreign affairs

*guides the thinking of those
who make*

*provides the real-world
material for the making
of better*

the way international politics is
actually conducted by policy makers

Practice

Policy
the stated goals and intentions of a
state as expressed by its leaders

becomes implemented as

One of these is the importance of the nation-state. Scholars, statesmen, and the public alike tend to view the state as the major actor in the international system. Indeed, some scholars see states as the only actors who possess and can use power. We will see later that this is not a completely accurate view, but it is nonetheless true that states are the most important actors in contemporary international relations.

The modern nation-state system originated in 1648 with the Treaty of Westphalia, which ended the Thirty Years' War. That European conflict, which began in 1618, arose from the Protestant Reformation. During the Reformation the combatants joined into two great coalitions, thereby starting the first war involving all of Europe. Out of the ashes of the Thirty Years' War came the Treaty of Westphalia and the political basis for the modern international system.

The Thirty Years' War was fought in large part over religion. It was primarily a fight between Catholics, who supported the Roman Catholic church and the Holy Roman Emperor, and the forces of the Reformation. But it was more than a religious war, for such simple and straightforward labels as Protestant and Catholic concealed deep underlying political and economic differences and interests.

Consider, for example, the mid-sixteenth-century controversy over the marriages of Henry VIII. Henry VIII's dispute with the pope and the Catholic church over his right to divorce was more than a struggle over his religious obligations, more than a dramatic saga of lust and personal animosity. Rather, it concerned the power of the church, the wealth it controlled, and its ability to command (and thus divide) the loyalty of Henry's nobles. This contest between the "state" and the "church" for political power and control of elites, grew out of two contemporaneous upheavals: the political and economic changes that accompanied the decline of European feudalism and the extension to the world of the competition among European kings that began the Age of Exploration.

Henry's break with the church led not only to his becoming the "spiritual" leader of the newly formed Church of England but also to his acquisition of the church's wealth and lands and of the right to appoint high church officials. By selling much of the confiscated lands to the newly emerging merchant class, Henry gave this important group a direct interest in the religious question as well. Thus, in England the conflict between church and state was settled in favor of the state before the outbreak of the Thirty Years' War, altering the distribution of both political and economic power. The redistribution of land weakened the landed nobility and strengthened the new commercial and manufacturing class. As a result, the state (represented by the monarch) and the producing class developed a common interest in preserving the state whose economic policies included the stimulation of economic growth through increased trade and production of nonagricultural goods. In this way England became one of the first nation-states to make the transition from a feudal system dominated by the nobility to a capitalist system dominated by commercial and manufacturing interests

The formula agreed upon at Westphalia was *cuius regio eius religio*, that is, whose the region, his the religion. This doctrine effectively elevated the power of the state above that of the Holy Roman Emperor, the Roman Catholic church, and the individual. It made the state the most important political unit in Europe—and, eventually, the most important economic and social unit. These developments coincided with the emergence of capitalism in Europe, the beginning stages of a world economy, and the extension of European power and influence throughout the world. Although the political legacy of the Treaty of Westphalia is the primary focus of the traditional approach to international relations, the emergence of worldwide trade and commercial interaction and the extension of the European capitalist system and colonization were equally significant.

After 1648 the state became the dominant actor on the global stage, and its interactions became the focus of international political analysis. These interests remain economic as well as political. The Treaty of Westphalia made the European state the most important economic actor and the protector of capitalist economic development within Europe. Ultimately the state became the agent whereby capitalism was extended to all corners of the globe.

The State: Concept and Reality

What then is the state, and how does its Westphalian heritage influence contemporary international relations? The *state*, in the modern sense, implies a population that occupies a definite territory, subject to a government that is accorded sovereignty and has a regime recognized as legitimate by other states. In international relations we distinguish between the state and the nation; the *nation* is a large social grouping whose people share common customs, language, heritage, and a sense of group identity. The formation of the first states by the earliest European and Asian nations—England, France, Spain, China, Japan, and Persia—gave rise to the term *nation-state.*

The frequent use of the terms *nation* and *state* as interchangeable is confusing and inaccurate. It is altogether possible for one nation—the social grouping—to reside in or be identified with more than one state or to be represented by no states. Thus in contemporary Africa we have nations split between two or more states (for example, the Yorubas in Benin and Nigeria; the Hausa in Niger and Nigeria; and the Fulani in Mauritania, Nigeria, and Mali) and also nations without states (for example, the Palestinians). Similarly, many modern states are multinational—for example, the United States, the Soviet Union, India, and Yugoslavia. Thus, although the first European states were true nation-states in that the population of each was a nation, the population of the modern state is more likely to be an amalgam of nations as the result of migration, war, colonialism, or a combination of all three.

A map of Africa shows states that have been created by (1) the achievement of independence in former European colonies whose boundaries had been drawn and redrawn, and (2) wars among tribal groups joined or separated by European mapmakers, resulting in vast migrations of war refugees. For example, in what was the Belgian Congo, the establishment of an independent Congo in 1960 was followed by separatist movements, civil war, intervention by the United Nations, and an eventual reunification. Nigerian independence was likewise marked by a subsequent separatist movement in Biafra, civil war, and mass migrations.

Two other terms that need to be defined are *government* and *regime.* *Government* refers to the organizational units that make, enforce, and adjudicate the laws and regulations according to which the state operates and

7

conducts its official relations with other states. A *regime* is the set of individuals who currently inhabit the positions of government. The regime then consists of those who are "in power."

In the Westphalian framework, states (but not the individuals who reside within them) are viewed as the members of an international society. The states that comprise the system are accorded the right and the responsibility to protect their own population and to act on their own behalf. They are said, therefore, to be sovereign.

The sovereignty of the state is central to the Westphalian system. *Sovereignty*, in the words of some observers, is a "legal fiction" that, in principle, grants absolute rights to the state to govern within its own borders and to represent all the people within those borders in dealings with other states. The concept of sovereignty is referred to as a legal fiction, because no state has, or can have, absolute control over its population or can completely close off all outside influences. Further, while sovereignty implies the "equality" of states, some states have always been "more equal than others." As Thucydides wrote more than two thousand years ago, "the strong do what they have the power to do and the weak accept what they must."

For a given regime to function as the legal representative of a sovereign state, empowered to speak and act on the state's behalf, it must be accorded diplomatic recognition by other states. The process has not always been smooth and uncontested, but it generally is accomplished by the exchange of diplomatic representatives. Since 1945, recognition has also entailed a formal vote to seat the regime's representatives in the General Assembly of the United Nations.

Perhaps nothing better illustrates the meaning of sovereignty as a legal fiction than the case of the People's Republic of China from 1949 to 1971. During this period, the Chinese seat in the United Nations was occupied by representatives of the Republic of China, the defeated remnants of the regime that had ruled China prior to 1949 and which since then has governed the island of Taiwan, one hundred miles off the Asian mainland. Thus, although the communist government of the People's Republic of China physically controlled the 800 million inhabitants on the mainland of China, in the eyes of the United Nations the People's Republic did not exist. Although it is unusual for an anomaly of this magnitude to persist for this length of time, China's belated formal recognition by the UN illustrates the "fictive" nature of sovereignty.

Recent Changes in the International System

At least two significant developments since World War II have altered the Westphalian system. The first of these was the establishment of international war crimes tribunals at Nuremberg, Tokyo, and Manila. At Nuremberg, twenty-two German officials were charged with major war crimes, including waging an aggressive war and committing crimes against humanity. Nineteen were convicted, and twelve were sentenced to death. Thus the Nuremberg tribunal established the principle that government leaders could be held accountable to outside authorities for waging an aggressive war and committing crimes against humanity.

At the same time Nuremberg tended to strengthen the principle of state sovereignty over domestic affairs. Charges were brought at Nuremberg only for crimes committed outside the borders of Germany and specifically excluded crimes against humanity (that is, the genocide of Jews) undertaken within those borders. In effect the trials served, perhaps unintentionally, to reaffirm the rights of the state over and above the rights of the individual.

The second major post-World War II development was the establishment of the United Nations. Despite its importance, the UN has not led, as some thought it would, to a reduction in state sovereignty. The United Nations Charter was written by representatives of sovereign states who were interested in creating an institution that would protect the interests of their states. In effect, the UN has served to reaffirm traditional Westphalian principles. In particular, it has ensured the continuing sovereignty of states as "equal" international actors with "absolute" responsibility for the governance of the people of their own states.

Realism and the International System

The Westphalian system removed the remaining vestiges of belief in an absolute authority or overall ruler of the nations of Europe, a role previously played, at least symbolically, by the Catholic church and the Holy Roman Emperor. The successful operation of the new political system depended upon the behavior of its members, the sovereign states. Such systems are referred to as self-help systems because each state assumes the responsibility for its own safety and continued existence.

While there is today wide disagreement over how best to understand such systems, the dominant approach within the American scholarly community for much of this century has been the approach known as realism. Realism is based on the assumption, derived from the English philosopher Thomas Hobbes, that the essence of politics is the "struggle for power" and that international politics is best understood in terms of the conflicts that arise from this struggle. The "realist" view leads its practitioners and students to approach international relations primarily as a series of major disturbances to the world system—wars, revolutions, and natural disasters—and to focus on the causes and consequences of these power struggles. Thus, for many years scholars and practitioners differentiated between the "high politics" of war and security affairs and the "low politics" of economic, social, and cultural interactions.

A second major assumption of realism is that, in the absence of any central authority able to provide for the security of individual states, each state must provide for its own security. Each state must act in its own interest (without regard to any other concerns) and expect other states to behave in the same manner.

For realists, instability within the international system represents a threat to state security. Statesmen reared in this tradition will enter into agreements with other states for outside assistance if needed. In the end, however, they are unlikely to place great faith in such arrangements but will endeavor to develop their own state's ability to protect itself.

This results in the paradox of the "security dilemma." As each state attempts to increase its own power in an effort to ensure its security, other states that are likely to perceive this action as threatening can be expected to respond in a similar manner. This cycle may make a state even less secure.

Nonetheless, the realist vision of the state leads statesmen and scholars to argue not only that the state has the right to do whatever it must, without limit, to preserve its existence but that all states can be expected to behave the same way. In the realist view, standards of personal morality must not be allowed to interfere with actions necessary to ensure national survival. For realists, vigilance on behalf of the national interest is the primary political virtue, and whatever actions may be necessary to ensure national survival must be undertaken without hesitation. To behave otherwise is to display naiveté about the true nature of international politics.

The realist approach draws a clear distinction between the "state of nature" that characterizes the international system and the stable, ordered existence typical of domestic politics. This, indeed, is precisely the idealized view one often finds in textbooks and policy pronouncements. It is a view in which all states are assumed to have governments that are stable, legitimate in the eyes of their citizens, and competent to exercise their authority effectively and equitably. A classic presentation of this view is former secretary of state John Foster Dulles's list of the characteristics of the nation-state:

1. Laws written or unwritten that reflect the moral judgment of the community.
2. Political machinery to change these laws as conditions change.
3. An executive body to administer law.
4. Courts that settle disputes of a justiciable character.
5. Superior public force that deters violence by its ability to apprehend and punish adequately any who break or defy the law.
6. Well-being sufficient so that people are not driven by desperation to follow ways of violence.

Many international relations textbooks assert that all states, because they reside within the same international system, share an interest in preserving the system and its core values, as well as the state's own core values, which are usually said to include protection from invasion and economic security. Although somewhat oversimplified here, this is the realist view of the nation-state in the international system.

Realism: A Brief Critique and Search for Alternatives

Among the shortcomings of the realist approach is that it focuses our attention almost exclusively on the more dramatic aspects of international interaction, the world of "high politics," of conflict and strategic issues. As a result, much of the everyday functioning of the international system goes unnoticed or is relegated to the attention of specialists. However, as the last two decades have demonstrated, many major world crises—the oil crisis of 1973-1974, the collapse of the international monetary system, and the enduring threats to international trade—originate in the world of "low politics." Although the economic and welfare issues of low politics sometimes lack the drama or sense of urgency associated with the security issues of high politics, they are often of great significance. Unfortunately, that significance can remain unnoticed until the issue reaches crisis proportions.

Basic to the realist view is the underlying assumption of a fundamental consensus on the legitimacy of the state and its component parts. Such a consensus, however, has not existed within many states throughout most of the modern era. Most states, in fact, have been very fragile entities. There are few states in which the government has a monopoly on the use of force and fewer still in which the government is perceived as a neutral conflict manager. Hence, the contemporary world has been witness to dozens of civil wars, coups, insurgencies, and separatist movements, all violent indications of the fragility of the modern state's legitimacy in the eyes of its citizens.

Further, most nation-states long ago became "penetrated" political systems. Penetrated political systems are dependent upon or interdependent with external influences. Such influence may take the form of trade, economic aid or investment, or cultural interaction. It may also, however, include disinformation, propaganda, and political or military intervention, either overt or covert. Any of these influences has the potential to create countervailing centers of power, legitimacy, and authority that compete with the "sovereign state" in its exercise of "sovereign authority." So it is that observers of the United States-Mexico relationship have often noted, "Poor Mexico, so far from God, but so near the United States." Or as others have described the European economic relationship with the United States, "When the United States sneezes, Europe catches cold."

For all these reasons, we believe it is worthwhile to look for an approach to international relations that is not based on the conventional, realist distinctions between domestic politics and international relations. Such distinctions are based on "ideal types" that have the virtue of conceptual neatness but do not necessarily fit the real world. This discrepancy represents one of the great limitations of the realist approach to international relations.

Realism is derived from a tradition that has proven vulnerable to criticism. The underlying argument of this tradition is that of the doctrine of "reason of state," which equates state interest with political necessity. This doctrine is often credited to Niccolò Machiavelli, who wrote four centuries ago in *The Prince*, "The rule to preserve the state is the first principle of the Prince's morality." Machiavelli's advice is the best-known example of a widely held doctrine that continues, even now, to influence international policy makers and, on occasion, serves to justify actions that advance the interests of the regime over that of its citizens. Consider, for example, the following language from the introduction of the U.S. Department of State's *Country Reports on Human Rights for 1981*, which states that there are some political leaders who "find it inconvenient or threatening to respect their subjects' rights. For such people there is great temptation to legitimate their own interests by broadening the basic concept of rights to include these interests."

Notwithstanding the near universal tendency of states to pursue their own self-interest within the international arena, some states have at times chosen to take a broader and longer-term interest in the welfare of the international system. This other-directedness has resulted in agreements to provide development aid, health care assistance, and famine relief. A similar interest in cooperation underlies efforts to establish an international postal union and to assign radio frequencies on an international basis. While states have resorted to military force far too often, most disputes between states are resolved through diplomacy.

It can be argued, in fact, that cooperation rather than conflict is the norm in international relations. Even in an apparently Hobbesian world, states band together and cooperate in pursuit of mutual interests. A few examples are the joint scientific adventures of the International Geophysical Year, the fifteen-year effort to create a law of the sea, the treaties on the nonproliferation of nuclear weapons, and the establishment of the Latin American and South Pacific nuclear free zones.

International politics need not inevitably be viewed as a "war of all against all." The international system can instead be viewed as a "primitive" or "developing" political system. Our task becomes one of exploring how that system, like any political system, determines who gets what, when, and how. Studies of primitive political systems indicate that order quite often exists without a monopoly of force and that the role customarily assigned to a central authority is performed by contingent structures that arise as needed. Like primitive political systems, the international system may be seen as one that depends on interaction patterns of implicit and explicit bargaining and customs rather than formal rules. The threat of violence can be used to enforce obligations to achieve objectives when other modes of interaction break down.

The study of international relations, then, can be viewed as more than the study of war and conflict. For example, the international political system can be seen as a society of states that interact according to custom and rules. Among those who have taken this perspective is the Dutch jurist and codifier of international law, Hugo Grotius, a contemporary of Thomas Hobbes.

Whereas the realist approach—derived from Hobbes—assumes that the conflict among nations is the normal state of affairs, the Grotian—or liberal internationalist—approach begins with the assumption that economic and social links between states are predominant. Where Hobbes and the realists see prudence and expediency as the only limits on state action, Grotius and the liberal internationalists view morality and law as integral components of self-interest. In the Hobbesian view, all interactions between states are of the zero sum variety, meaning that there are only winners and losers and the winner's gains always equal the loser's losses. From a Grotian perspective, however, interactions between states can readily result in gains for more than one party, and those gains need not come at the expense of others. Grotians share a variable sum view of international relations.

By looking for alternative approaches to international affairs, we can alert ourselves to other visions of reality. If instead we accept the Hobbesian view, we are all but certain to become preoccupied with the "security dilemma," seeing only threats and never cooperation. By moving beyond the Hobbesian view, we may come to perceive the importance of actors other than the state on the world stage.

International relations becomes more than the activities of governmental elites operating on behalf of states. Instead, it encompasses a variety of actors, customs, and rules developed over the centuries that regulate much of our international life and provide predictability in international interactions.

Life in the international system is not, as Hobbes described it, merely "nasty, brutish and short." It is rather, much as Grotius argued, complex, cooperative, and multidimensional. The enduring concerns of international relations are, in addition to questions of peace and security, the expansion and enhancement of international economic interaction, communication, contact between peoples, and a general concern for joint methods of solving problems that affect all people and all states.

For Further Reading

Bull, Hedley. *The Anarchical Society*. New York: Columbia University Press, 1977. An analysis of the basis of order in international relations that encompasses Hobbes, Kant, and Grotius. A useful and learned challenge to the realist approach.

Dulles, J. F. "The Institutionalizing of Peace," *Department of State Bulletin* 34 (May 7, 1956): 740. A classic contemporary realist statement of the differences between domestic and international politics. Best read in conjunction with C. F. Alger's "Comparison of Intranational and International Politics," *American Political Science Review* 57, No. 2 (June 1963): 414-419, and R. Masters' "World Politics as a Primitive Political System," *World Politics* 16, No. 4 (July 1964): 595-619.

Grotius, Hugo (Hugo Cornets de Groot, 1583-1645). *The Law of War and Peace*, 1625. The classic treatise on international law discusses the origins of international law in customs and rules created by explicit agreement.

Hobbes, Thomas. *Leviathan*. Michael Oakeshott, ed. New York: Collier-Macmillan, 1962. One of the enduring works of political philosophy. First published in 1651, Hobbes's description of the state of nature and the implications that follow from it is central to the realist view of international relations. Hobbes was indebted to Thucydides, whose *Peloponnesian War* he translated, and there is a clear similarity in their understandings of the sources of power.

Hinsley, F. H. *Power and Pursuit of Peace*. London: Cambridge University Press, 1967. Contains an analysis of the contributions to international relations theory made by Rousseau, Kant, and Bentham and diplomatic practices from the eighteenth through the early twentieth centuries. A difficult work but well worth the effort.

Morgenthau, Hans. *Politics Among Nations*. 5th ed. New York: Alfred A. Knopf, 1978. The classic contemporary treatise on realism. It was first published in 1948; the fifth edition was the last written exclusively by Morgenthau. The writing is elegant, and there is no clearer exposition of the realist approach.

Wallerstein, Immanuel. *The Modern World System: Capitalist Agriculture and the Origins of the European World Economy in the Sixteenth Century*. New York: Academic Press, 1974. This difficult work challenges the prevailing view that the key to an understanding of international relations lies in the political realm. Wallerstein contends instead that economics is the driving force of international affairs, and that the appropriate level of analysis is that of the world system itself rather than the nation-state. An excellent introduction to the development of capitalism as both a political and economic process and its relation to the development of the modern nation-state.

THE GREAT GAME OF NATIONS **2**

I nternational relations is often referred to as the "great game of nations." To understand it, we must be able to identify the players, the rules, and the arena in which the game unfolds. Our understanding of the game of international relations, however, is made more complicated by the fact that the players, the rules, and the location of the game are constantly changing.

Some Rules of the Game of Nations

Change, it would seem, is one of the few constants in international relations. The world today has become a very different place from the world of 1900, 1945, 1960, or even 1970. There are more nations, a different set of great powers, many new types of actors, new technologies, and new problems. Similarly, historical trends—many, such as globalism, of relatively recent origin—have altered the international political environment and changed the rules of the game.

But neither recognizing change nor agreeing on its implications is an easy task. Many international relations scholars are concerned, in fact, that our current leaders may not fully understand the rules, the participants, or the objectives of the game. Many of these leaders, analysts note, came of political age during a period when the rules, participants, and playing field were quite different from those we face today. Such leaders may misinterpret much of what is actually occurring, selectively ignoring events or actions that do not fit their own interpretation.

For many current American and European leaders, for example, the formative years were those of World War II and the years immediately preceding and following. Their views of international relations were shaped by events of the late 1930s, such as the appeasement of Hitler at Munich, and postwar events such as the Berlin Blockade of 1948, which marked the emergence of the Cold War. Given their experiences, these leaders often associate the failure to use force with weakness and believe that the containment of aggression requires a willingness to confront aggressive behavior. Likewise, many are convinced that the United States has consistently used its power during the postwar period in a wholly fair and prudent manner.

Leaders born during or just after World War II matured during a much different period. Influenced by the Vietnam War, they view less favorably the history of the use of force by the United States and are less likely to perceive conflict between the superpowers as the main threat to world peace. For them, Third World instability, conflict among—and with—the oil-producing Arab states, and international terrorism have been the major sources of concern. They worry not about rebuilding a shattered world but about maintaining their own place in it.

Clearly, then, the interaction between how we think about the world, how we "see" it—and especially how our leaders see it—and what actually happens is critical to our understanding of contemporary world affairs. But an understanding of some "objective" realities is also crucial

Some of these objective realities become easier to grasp if we think of the world as a global village of 100 people. In this village 70 persons would be unable to read, and only one would have a college education. Over 50 would be suffering from malnutrition, and over 80 would live in what Americans would classify as substandard housing. If the world were a global village of 100 residents, 6 of them would be Americans. These 6 would have half the village's entire income; 24 others—representing the other developed countries—would have more than half of the remaining income, leaving the other 70 to exist on approximately 20 percent of the total village income.

This brief description of the global village is important because it highlights the fact that we, as Americans, do not share the experience or have the same perspective as the vast majority of the world's peoples. Thus, when Americans are asked to identify the most pressing problems in international relations, they generally refer to the arms race; the struggle between the United States and the Soviet Union; conflict in the Middle East or, more recently, in Central America; international terrorism; or other dramatic and violent events.

The same question elicits quite different responses in the Third World, where hunger, malnutrition, mass poverty, disease, population pressures, as well as problems of trade, aid, and debt are likely to be seen as the most pressing problems. In the developed states of the First World, such as the United States, citizens look to the national government to provide for basic needs such as access to food, clothing, and shelter, and protection from physical attack. But in the Third World many citizens look to international actors outside their own country for at least some of their basic needs. For the Sudanese, for example, assistance for the growing proportion of the population that lives at the subsistence level can come only from outside sources. Citizens of the Sudan and similar states are far more dependent on assistance provided by international actors other than their own governments.

The Players

As we indicated in Chapter 1, states have long been considered the primary actors in international affairs, and much scholarly and diplomatic thinking about international relations has indeed been "state centric." Within the last five decades, however, the primacy of the sovereign territorial state, both as the major actor in interstate relations and the sole source of internal and external security in the Westphalian system, has been challenged, both in theory and in practice.

This century has seen a vast increase in the number of state actors, resulting from the breakup of the European empires after two world wars. The breakup of the Austro-Hungarian, Russian, and Ottoman empires after World War I created a large number of new nation-states in the Balkans, the Baltic, the Mediterranean, and Central and Eastern Europe. After the second world war, the division of the remaining colonial empires into new and independent states became a worldwide phenomenon. More than one hundred new states emerged after 1945, mostly in Africa, Asia, Oceania, and the Caribbean. Thus the total number of states in the world has tripled in the past forty years.

There is great divergence in the size and power of the states that now make up the international system. At one extreme lies the People's Republic of China (PRC) with a population of over 1 billion and a territory of just under 3.7 million square miles. (The United States, by comparison, has a population of approximately 250 million and a territory of just over 3.6 million square miles.) At the other extreme lies the island country of Nauru in the Western Pacific, a state of nine thousand persons living on approximately 8 square miles. To be sure, there are very few states as small as Nauru, but there are nine other states with populations of less than one hundred thousand and a total of almost forty whose populations do not exceed 1 million. Although these microstates are states, as China is a state, and may have all the trappings of sovereignty, they clearly are not equal to China. They do not possess China's political, military, or economic power, nor can they possibly have the same needs, opportunities, or concerns as a China or an India—the only other state whose population approaches that of the PRC.

Differences in the relative power and size of contemporary states are nowhere more important than at the top of the power hierarchy. With the advent of nuclear weapons at the close of World War II and the emergence of two superpowers whose military capabilities and nuclear arsenals surpass that of all the other states of the globe put together, a new and historically unique international system came into being. We explore more fully the implications of nuclear weapons for the international system in Chapter 7. Here it is sufficient to recognize (as does John Herz in his selection in this chapter) that the development of nuclear weapons accelerated a long-term trend—dating back at least to the Industrial Revolution—in which the offensive capabilities of the state have outstripped its ability to protect its citizens from attack. So far has this process gone that today it threatens not just the populations of the two superpowers but the entire world's population. All the inhabitants of the system would perish if the two superpowers were to employ their weapons fully.

While much has been made of their great nuclear capabilities, the superpowers are not "super" merely because of their nuclear weapons. Much of their status derives from their massive "conventional" weapon strength and their ability to employ their power worldwide. While their capabilities differ in many respects, the Soviet Union and the United States are the only states that have the capability to intervene directly in virtually every corner of the globe. They are true global powers with superior naval, land, and air forces. Each controls vast quantities of raw materials and possesses massive intelligence, information, and command and communication networks, and each can employ her power far more rapidly and widely than any previous great power.

While other states, such as France and the United Kingdom (former great powers) and India and China, also have independent nuclear capabilities, their ability to employ their power is limited to particular regions. Thus, while the current British prime minister has at her disposal far greater destructive power than the British fleet had when Britannia ruled the waves, British military strength is limited in comparison with that of either superpower, and Britain is today a declining regional power.

States, however, are no longer the only significant actors in the international political arena. During this century, other types of actors have become increasingly prominent. The most conspicuous of these have been the League of Nations, created after World War I, and its successor, the United Nations, established after World War II. Both are "universal" international organizations with membership open to all—or almost all—recognized nation-states. Their creation can be viewed as an attempt by victorious nations to create a viable, ongoing organization within which certain international problems could be addressed and another world war prevented.

In addition, the United Nations has provided the organizational umbrella for a "family" of specialized organizations that deal with areas such as development, health, education, trade, refugees, food, labor, maritime organization, finance, social and scientific research, and weather monitoring. Known as *IGOs—international governmental organizations*—these specialized agencies often provide vital services to their clientele. The World Health Organization (WHO), for example, set out to eradicate smallpox worldwide and by 1976 was able to claim almost complete success. From the perspective of the average U.S. citizen, the end of smallpox may not appear to be a major accomplishment, but viewed from a Third World perspective, it appears far more significant. This example illustrates the relatively greater importance of these agencies for the everyday lives of Third World inhabitants. People in many Third World countries view agencies such as WHO, the Food and Agriculture Organization (FAO), and the United Nations International Children's Emergency Fund (UNICEF) as a source of vital, basic services that their own governments are often unable to supply.

As a general rule, membership in IGOs is composed of states. But, by convention, the term *IGO* also refers to organizations established by states, some or all of whose members may be quasi-official organizations. Thus, the membership of organizations such as the International Telecommunications

Union (ITU) and the International Labour Organisation (ILO), comprises a mix of representatives from the private and public sectors. In all, there are now more than two hundred IGOs. Together these organizations perform a large number of important international tasks and serve to link their nation-state members in a way considered unlikely, if not impossible, sixty years ago.

IGOs, however, are but one type of international organization. In addition, there are at least ten times as many *international nongovernmental organizations* (INGOs), of which about one-tenth have consultative status with the United Nations. These organizations include such groups as Amnesty International, which is concerned with human rights, and the International Federation of Airline Pilots' Associations (IFALPA), which, among other things, promotes safe working conditions for airline pilots. Both of these organizations play a significant role in international relations. Amnesty International's work for political prisoners throughout the world is well known. IFALPA has been an important player in the international response to terrorist incidents, pressuring governments to adopt effective antihijacking measures. IFALPA's threatened boycott of routes to countries unwilling to act to prevent hijacking, for example, contributed greatly to the passage of antihijacking agreements in the 1970s.

There are a variety of other significant types of international organizations, all with confusingly similar acronyms. In addition to IGOs and INGOs, these include BINGOs and RINGOs, or business INGOs and religious INGOs. Among these, business INGOs—more commonly known as *multinational corporations* (MNCs)—are among the most important. Unlike IGOs and most INGOs, MNCs are large, often complex organizations that are hierarchically organized and centrally controlled. Their purpose is to produce profits for their shareholders. During the past four decades, multinationals have proliferated. They have greatly expanded their operations worldwide, becoming major players on the world scene. Some, in fact, control resources far in excess of those controlled by the vast majority of nation-states. The extent of multinationals' power has been controversial. The reading selection by Thomas J. Biersteker included in this chapter directly examines the theoretical and practical dimensions of this issue.

Religious organizations also play a role in world politics. While the Catholic church has less power to influence international politics today than in earlier times—notably during the period of the Holy Roman Empire—it still wields considerable influence. This is true not only because of the large number of Catholics, their broad geographic dispersion, and the church's economic wealth, but also because the church has been both vocal and politically active on such issues as population control, peace, and human rights. Likewise, the steadily increasing influence and visibility of various Islamic groups in the Middle East, Africa, and Asia attests to the continuing importance of RINGOs on the world stage.

Each of the types of actors mentioned thus far—states, international

19

governmental organizations, and the various types of international nongovernmental organizations—have regional counterparts. The most extensive and highly developed set of regional organizations are found in Western Europe, but there are many important Asian, Latin American, African, and Western Hemisphere organizations. A number of military alliances also operate on a regional level. Although we discuss alliances in Chapter 8, here we simply note that alliances have in many cases become much more "permanent" and multifaceted than was anticipated at their founding. In addition to conducting military exercises—with all the associated formal interactions—many alliances, and especially NATO (the North Atlantic Treaty Organization) and WTO (the Warsaw Treaty Organization or Warsaw Pact), have developed permanent infrastructures and command and control centers with bureaucracies of their own.

The Arena

The arena within which this new and larger cast of characters interacts has itself been modified over the past four decades. Advances in transportation, communication, and weaponry have altered the pace of international events. News of international events now reaches decision makers almost instantaneously, while today's military forces can in many instances be transported to the scene of a conflict in a matter of hours, even minutes. The world is at once a much smaller yet more complex system. Even though there are many more actors, and many of the important actors are separated from one another by great distances, they can interact more readily than ever before.

At the same time, another set of changes has enhanced the need for greater regional and global interaction and cooperation. Advances in health care—and the associated improvement in survival rates for children—and longer life spans have dramatically accelerated the world's rate of population growth in the past century. Whereas it took from the beginning of civilization until approximately 1750 for the world's first billion persons to be born, the second billion arrived by 1930, the third billion by 1960, the fourth billion by 1975, and the fifth billion in 1987. Increasingly, this ever-expanding population resides in urban areas. The resulting pressures on agricultural and industrial production and distribution, as well as on the environment, create new problems, many of which can be solved only through regional and global cooperation.

Likewise, the industrial revolution and the subsequent growth in production have led to greatly increased international economic interdependence among nations and contributed to great shifts in the demand for various raw materials and energy resources. The shift from coal to oil and then to uranium as energy-producing "minerals" has in turn altered the relative importance of the various regions in which these materials are found. The Persian Gulf region, the Levant—a name that refers also to the countries bordering on the eastern Mediterranean—and the Near East were strategically important to British prime ministers of the eighteenth and nineteenth centuries because of those areas' location on the trade route to India. In the twentieth century, the oil trapped deep beneath their sands has accorded this same region an enormous importance. Many analysts believe that the industrial West would be virtually compelled to resort to war if its access to these vital supplies were threatened.

With the information revolution in the last quarter of the twentieth century has come the widespread use of computers for command and control purposes, for the virtually instantaneous worldwide trading of stocks and commodities, for intelligence gathering and monitoring, and for information processing. This technology has altered the pattern of interactions and the resources and requirements of decision making. It is no longer the aristocratic diplomat with "old school" ties and the "proper" training and background who represents the interests of his state. Now millions of bureaucrats inside and outside governmental agencies transact the political, financial, industrial, agricultural, and intelligence business of their respective governments. And thousands of citizens in their roles as members of other international organizations, both governmental and nongovernmental, possess capabilities only dreamed of by kings of the past two millennia.

Confronted with a complex and rapidly changing international system, theorists and practitioners have inevitably developed, either implicitly or explicitly, their own models of the international system. The underlying purpose of such models is understanding through simplification. At the same time, these models, particularly those devised by theorists, must and do attempt to capture as much of the reality of the system as possible.

The prevailing model of the international system has been the *balance of power model*. Based on a "narrow" conception of politics, which is to say one that focuses on the distribution of power as the critical variable, the balance of power model is a profoundly "realist" construct. A precise definition is difficult. Analysts have noted that the term *balance of power* has been used in more than twenty different senses in the international relations literature. In general, however, what scholars usually mean by a balance of power system is an international system in which there are at least five "great powers" whose behavior is assumed to be governed by realist premises and each of which seeks to maximize its own power. In the pursuit of power, each of these states will ordinarily enter into alliances with one or more of its counterparts, with each alliance in turn being "balanced" by combinations of other states. The precise membership of these alliances will shift over time as necessary to prevent any single state from gaining hegemony over the system as a whole.

As we discuss in further detail in Chapter 8, formal and informal alliances within a balance of power system are in a relatively constant state of flux because states must continually gauge their relative power positions vis-à-vis one another both as individual states and as blocs. The system often relies on a "balancer," a state whose leaders recognize that maintaining the system is in their own national interest. Hence states engage in a systematic policy of aligning with one alliance or another as seems appropriate.

Ultimately, however, the balance of power system relies not only on the gauging of power and the timely shifting of alliances but also on the threat of war and a belief in the utility of war. When the system has "worked," wars have been averted or have been very brief. When the system has "failed," the wars that resulted have been far more destructive. Each war in turn has marked an end to the system as it had been constituted. This was the case at the end of the second world war when a new system, the bipolar system, emerged.

The *bipolar system* is characterized by two major powers who are able to dominate the remaining members. Each of the major powers seeks to align with itself as many of the remaining states as possible and to maintain the integrity of its own bloc. Such a world is divided in two; the major issues arise from—and are defined by—differences in the interests of the two major powers and their blocs. A gain for one bloc is interpreted as a loss for the other. The interests of a major power essentially become identical to the interests of its bloc as a whole. Within this system there is far less fluidity than in the balance of power system, and alliances and coalitions are far more enduring. In the bipolar system no nation can act as a balancer.

Even such a brief introduction to these two systems should make it clear that failure to identify correctly the type of system within which one is operating could lead to actions that would seriously damage one's own interests and threaten the stability of the system. In a balance of power system, for example, a statesman who refused to ally his country with others in order to balance the threat from an emerging and stronger power would effectively unbalance the system and encourage war. Within a bipolar system that same behavior might well be prudent, for the blocs are much more tightly drawn in such a system and the shifting of states from one bloc to another is inherently dangerous.

The Readings

The readings in this chapter analyze the state system in more detail. In the classic piece that is our first selection, John Herz examines the role of the territorial state, the basic structural and functional unit of the balance of power or Westphalian system. Herz argues that developments in modern warfare, including the use of economic blockade, ideological penetration, air warfare, and nuclear weaponry have threatened the ability of the territorial state to perform its duties. Writing in 1957, Herz foresaw the end of the territorial state as the basic unit of international organization and argued that a new form of political organization was necessary if the international system were to survive.

Herz wrote a decade later in a selection not reprinted here that readers who inferred that he had anticipated the disappearance of the territorial state were wrong (as indeed it appeared was he). This caveat notwithstanding, Herz's analysis here sets forth quite clearly the basic nature of the sovereign state within the Westphalian system and the difficulties confronting states that today seek to protect the integrity of their own territory and citizenry.

The second reading is excerpted from Robert Gilpin's 1981 book, *War and Change in International Politics*. Gilpin examines changes in the international system that threaten the stability of the bipolar world. He is especially concerned with five developments that tend to destabilize bipolar systems: the failure to exercise a balancing role; the rise of a third party; increased polarization; the entanglement of major powers in minor power disputes; and loss of control over economic, political, and social developments. Gilpin alerts us to the importance of such concepts as spheres of influence, hegemony, client states, and the Pax Americana. Gilpin concludes that the United States is the more powerful of the two superpowers due to the range of its commitments and its pivotal role in the international political economy.

In the third selection, Biersteker challenges the thesis of the declining nation-state. In contrast to Herz's article, which focuses on the military defensibility of the territorial state, Biersteker's piece is concerned with international economic developments. In particular, he examines the power of emergent nation-states—in this case Nigeria—to control and limit multinational corporations operating within their borders. Unlike many earlier analysts, Biersteker concludes that there has been a resurgence of state power, even in the Third World. Thus, to paraphrase Mark Twain, the rumored demise of the territorial state appears to have been greatly exaggerated.

Policy makers, too, bring their own visions of the world to their labors, as illustrated by Secretary of State George P. Shultz's speech in London in December 1985. Shultz sees the continued relevance of viewing the world in balance of power terms, noting, however, that today's balance is multidimensional. Thus, in addition to the strategic balance and regional conflicts, Shultz discusses the importance of the democratic revolution (the ideological penetration to which Herz referred), the role of economic progress, and the promise of capitalist expansion. The future, he concludes, appears bright, and the state and the current international system strong and progressive.

Our final reading adopts a very different view of the international system, one closer (at least in terms of structure) to that of Robert Gilpin than to Secretary Shultz's. In "The Octopus" Robin Jenkins compares the international system to an octopus whose tentacles represent the political, military, and economic dimensions of the system. In effect, Jenkins argues for viewing the world as interconnected and dynamic and for considering the importance of economic as well as political and military power in the state system. Like Gilpin, Jenkins concludes that the nonmilitary power of the United States— especially the economic component—is far greater than that of the Soviet Union, and that the United States is, for that reason, a far more dominant player on the world stage.

2.1 ■■■■■

JOHN H. HERZ

Rise and Demise of the Territorial State

Students and practitioners of international politics are at present in a strange predicament. Complex though their problems have been in the past, there was then at least some certainty about the "givens," the basic structure and the basic phenomena of international relations. Today one is neither here nor there. On the one hand, for instance, one is assured—or at least tempted to accept assurance—that for all practical purposes a nuclear stalemate rules out major war as a major means of policy today and in the foreseeable future. On the other hand, one has an uncanny sense of the practicability of the unabated arms race, and a doubt whether reliance can be placed solely on the deterrent purpose of all this preparation. We are no longer sure about the functions of war and peace, nor do we know how to define the national interest and what its defense requires under present conditions. As a matter of fact, the meaning and function of the basic protective unit, the "sovereign" nation-state itself, have become doubtful. On what, then, can policy and planning be built?

In the author's opinion, many of these uncertainties have their more profound cause in certain fundamental changes which have taken place in the structure of international relations and, specifically, in the nature of the units among which these relations occur. This transformation in the "statehood" of nations will be the subject of this article.

Basic Features of the Modern State System

Traditionally, the classical system of international relations, or the modern state system, has been considered "anarchic," because it was based on unequally distributed power and was deficient in higher—that is, supranational—authority. Its units, the independent, sovereign nation-states, were forever threatened by stronger power and survived precariously through the balance-of-power system. Customarily, then, the modern state system has been contrasted with the medieval system, on the one hand, where units of international relations were under higher law and higher authority, and with those more recent international trends, on the other, which seemed to point toward a greater, "collective" security of nations and a "rule of law" that

---

From *World Politics* 9, no. 4 (July 1957). Copyright © 1957 by Princeton University Press. Reprinted by permission of Princeton University Press.

would protect them from the indiscriminate use of force characteristic of the age of power politics.

From the vantage point of the atomic age, we can probe deeper into the basic characteristics of the classical system. What is it that ultimately accounted for the peculiar unity, compactness, coherence of the modern nation-state, setting it off from other nation-states as a separate, independent, and sovereign power? It would seem that this underlying factor is to be found neither in the sphere of law nor in that of politics, but rather in that substratum of statehood where the state unit confronts us, as it were, in its physical, corporeal capacity: as an expanse of territory encircled for its identification and its defense by a "hard shell" of fortifications. In this lies what will here be referred to as the "impermeability," or "impenetrability," or simply the "territoriality," of the modern state. The fact that it was surrounded by a hard shell rendered it to some extent secure from foreign penetration, and thus made it an ultimate unit of protection for those within its boundaries. Throughout history, that unit which affords protection and security to human beings has tended to become the basic political unit; people, in the long run, will recognize that authority, any authority, which possesses the power of protection.

Some similarity perhaps prevails between an international structure consisting of impenetrable units with an ensuing measurability of power and comparability of power relations, and the system of classical physics with its measurable forces and the (then) impenetrable atom as its basic unit. And as that system has given way to relativity and to what nuclear science has uncovered, the impenetrability of the political atom, the nation-state, is giving way to a permeability which tends to obliterate the very meaning of unit and unity, power and power relations, sovereignty and independence. The possibility of "hydrogenization" merely represents the culmination of a development which has rendered the traditional defense structure of nations obsolete through the power to by-pass the shell protecting a two-dimensional territory and thus to destroy—vertically, as it were—even the most powerful ones. Paradoxically, utmost strength now coincides in the same unit with utmost vulnerability, absolute power with utter impotence.

This development must inevitably affect traditional power concepts. Considering power units as politically independent and legally sovereign made sense when power, measurable, graded, calculable, served as a standard of comparison between units which, in the sense indicated above, could be described as impermeable. Under those conditions, then, power indicated the strategic aspect, independence the political aspect, sovereignty the legal aspect of this selfsame impermeability. With the passing of the age of territoriality, the usefulness of these concepts must now be questioned.

Thus the Great Divide does not separate "international anarchy," or "balance of power," or "power politics," from incipient international interdependence, or from "collective security"; all these remain within the realm of the territorial structure of states and can therefore be considered as trends or stages *within* the classical system of "hard shell" power units. Rather, the Divide occurs where the basis of territorial power and defensibility vanishes. It is here and now. But in order to understand the present, we must study more closely the origin and nature of the classical system itself. . . .

The Decline of the Territorial State

Beginning with the nineteenth century, certain trends became visible which tended to endanger the functioning of the classical system. Directly or indirectly, all of them had a bearing upon that feature of the territorial state which was the strongest guarantee of its independent coexistence with other states of like nature: its hard shell—that is, its defensibility in case of war.

Naturally, many of these trends concerned war itself and the way in which it was conducted. But they were not related to the shift from the limited, duel-type contests of the eighteenth century to the more or less unlimited wars that developed in the nineteenth century with conscription, "nations in arms," and increasing destructiveness of weapons. By themselves, these developments were not inconsistent with the classical function of war. Enhancing a nation's defensive capacity, instituting universal military service, putting the economy on a war footing, and similar measures tended to bolster the territorial state rather than to endanger it.

Total war in a quite different sense is tied up with developments in warfare which enable the belligerents to overlap or by-pass the traditional hard-shell defense of states. When this happens, the traditional relationship between war, on the one hand, and territorial power and sovereignty, on the other, is altered decisively. Arranged in order of increasing effectiveness, these new factors may be listed under the following headings: (a) possibility of economic blockade; (b) ideological-political penetration; (c) air warfare; and (d) atomic warfare.

(a) *Economic warfare.* It should be said from the outset that so far economic blockade has never enabled one belligerent to force another into surrender through starvation alone. Although in World War I Germany and her allies were seriously endangered when the Western allies cut them off from overseas supplies, a very real effort was still required to defeat them on the military fronts. The same thing applies to World War II. Blockade was an important contributing factor, however. Its importance for the present analysis lies in its unconventional nature, permitting belligerents to by-pass the hard shell of the enemy. Its effect is due to the changed economic status of industrialized nations.

Prior to the industrial age, the territorial state was largely self-contained economically. Although one of the customary means of conducting limited war was starving fortresses into surrender, this applied merely to these individual portions of the hard shell, and not to entire nations. Attempts to starve a belligerent nation in order to avoid having to breach the shell proved rather ineffective, as witness the Continental Blockade and its counterpart in the Napoleonic era. The Industrial Revolution made countries like Britain and Germany increasingly dependent on imports. In war, this meant that they could survive only by controlling areas larger than their own territory. In peacetime, economic dependency became one of the causes of a phenomenon which itself contributed to the transformation of the old state system: imperialism. Anticipating war, with its new danger of blockade, countries strove to become more self-sufficient through enlargement of their areas of control. To the extent that the industrialized nations lost self-sufficiency, they were driven into expansion in a (futile) effort to regain it. Today, if at all, only control of entire continents enables major nations to survive economically in major wars. This implies that hard-shell military defense must be a matter of defending more than a single nation; it must extend around half the world.

(b) *Psychological warfare,* the attempt to undermine the morale of an enemy population, or to subvert its loyalty, shares with economic warfare a by-passing effect on old-style territorial defensibility. It was formerly practiced, and practicable, only under quite exceptional circumstances. Short periods of genuine world revolutionary propaganda, such as the early stages of the French Revolution, scarcely affected a general practice under which dynasties, and later governments, fought each other with little ideological involvement on the part of larger masses or classes. Only in rare cases—for instance, where national groups enclosed in and hostile to multinational empires could be appealed to—was there an opening wedge for "fifth column" strategies.

With the emergence of political belief-systems, however, nations became more susceptible to undermining from within. Although wars have not yet been won solely by subversion of loyalties, the threat involved has affected the inner coherence of the territorial state ever since the rise to power of a regime that claims to represent, not the cause of a particular nation, but that of mankind, or at least of its suppressed and exploited portions. Bolshevism from 1917 on has provided the second instance in modern history of world revolutionary propaganda. Communist penetration tactics subsequently were imitated by the Nazi and Fascist regimes and, eventually, by the democracies. In this way, new lines of division, cutting horizontally through state units instead of leaving them separated vertically from each other at their frontiers, have now become possible.

(c) *Air warfare* and (d) *nuclear warfare.* Of all the new developments, air warfare, up to the atomic age, has been the one that affected the territoriality of nations most radically. With its coming, the bottom dropped out—or, rather, the roof blew off—the relative security of the territorial state. True, even this new kind of warfare, up to and including the Second World War, did not by itself account for the defeat of a belligerent, as some of the more enthusiastic prophets of the air age had predicted it would. Undoubtedly, however, it had a massive contributory effect. And this effect was due to strategic action in the *hinterland* rather than to tactical use at the front. It came at least close to defeating one side by direct action against the "soft" interior of the country, by-passing outer defenses and thus foreshadowing the end of the frontier—that is, the demise of the traditional impermeability of even the militarily most powerful states. Warfare now changed "from a fight to a process of devastation."

That air warfare was considered as something entirely unconventional is seen from the initial reaction to it. Revolutionary transition from an old to a new system has always affected moral standards. In the classical age of the modern state system, the "new morality" of shooting at human beings from a distance had finally come to be accepted, but the standards of the age clearly distinguished "lawful combatants" at the front or in fortifications from the civilian remainder of the population. When air war came, reactions thus differed significantly in the cases of air fighting at the front and of air war carried behind the front. City bombing was felt to constitute "illegitimate" warfare, and populations were inclined to treat airmen engaging in it as "war criminals." This feeling continued into World War II, with its large-scale area bombing. Such sentiments reflected the general feeling of helplessness in the face of a war which threatened to render obsolete the concept of territorial power, together with its ancient implication of protection.

The process has now been completed with the advent of nuclear weapons. For it is more than doubtful that the processes of scientific invention and technological discovery, which not only have created and perfected the fission and fusion weapons themselves but have brought in their wake guided missiles with nuclear warheads, jet aircraft with intercontinental range and supersonic speed, and the prospect of nuclear-powered planes or rockets with unlimited range and with automatic guidance to specific targets anywhere in the world, can in any meaningful way be likened to previous new inventions, however revolutionary. These processes add up to an uncanny absoluteness of effect which previous innovations could not achieve. The latter might render power units of a certain type (for instance, castles or cities) obsolete and enlarge the realm of defensible power units from city-state to territorial state or even large-area empire. They might involve destruction, in war, of entire populations. But there still remained the seemingly inexhaustible reservoir of the rest of mankind. Today, when not even two halves of the globe remain impermeable, it can no longer be a question of enlarging an area of protection and of substituting one unit of security for another. Since we are inhabitants of a planet of limited (and, as it now seems, insufficient) size, we have reached the limit within which the effect of the means of destruction has become absolute. Whatever remained of the impermeability of states seems to have gone for good.

What has been lost can be seen from two statements by thinkers separated by thousands of years and half the world; both reflect the condition of territorial security. Mencius, in ancient China, when asked for guidance in matters of defense and foreign policy by the ruler of a small state, is said to have counseled: "Dig deeper your moats; build higher your walls; guard them along with your people." This remained the classical posture up to our age, when a Western sage, Bertrand Russell, in the interwar period could still define power as something radiating from one center and growing less with distance from that center until it finds an equilibrium with that of similar geographically anchored units. Now that power can destroy power from center to center, everything is different.

Outlook and Conclusion

It is beyond the compass of this article to ask what the change in the statehood of nations implies for present and future world relations; whether, indeed, international relations in the traditional sense of the term, dependent as they have been on a number of basic data (existence of the nation-state, measurable power, etc.) and interpreted as they were with the aid of certain concepts (sovereignty, independence, etc.), can survive at all; and, if not, what might take their place. Suffice it to remark that this question is vastly complex. We cannot even be sure that one and only one set of conclusions derives from what has happened or is in the process of happening. For, in J. Robert Oppenheimer's words, one of the characteristics of the present is "the prevalence of newness, the changing scale and scope of change itself. . . ." In the field of military policy, this means that since World War II half a dozen military innovations "have followed each other so rapidly that efforts at adaptation are hardly begun before they must be scrapped." The scientific revolution has been "so fast-moving as to make almost impossible the task of military men whose responsibility it is to anticipate the future. Military planning cannot make the facts of this future stay long enough to analyze them."

If this applies to military planning, it must apply equally to foreign policy planning, and, indeed, the newness of the new is perhaps the most significant and the most exasperating aspect of present world relations. Hardly has a bipolar world replaced the multipower world of classical territoriality than there loom new and unpredictable multipower constellations on the international horizon. However, the possible rise of new powers does not seem to affect bipolarity in the sense of a mere return to traditional multipower relations; since rising powers are likely to be nuclear powers, their effect must be an entirely novel one. What international relations would (or will) look like, once nuclear power is possessed by a larger number of power units, is not only extremely unpleasant to contemplate but almost impossible to anticipate, using any familiar concepts. Or, to use another example: We have hardly drawn the military and political conclusions from the new weapons developments, which at one point seemed to indicate the necessity of basing defense on the formation and maintenance of pacts like NATO and the establishment of a network of bases on allied territory from which to launch nuclear weapons "in case" (or whose existence was to deter the opponent from doing so on his part),

29

and already further scientific and technological developments seem to render entire defense blocs, with all their new "hard shells" of bases and similar installations, obsolete.

To complicate matters even more, the change-over is not even uniform and unilinear. On the contrary, in concepts as well as in policies, we witness the juxtaposition of old and new (or several new) factors, a coexistence in theory and practice of conventional and new concepts, of traditional and new policies. Part of a nation's (or a bloc's) defense policy, then, may proceed on pre-atomic assumptions, while another part is based on the assumption of a preponderantly nuclear contest. And a compounding trouble is that the future depends on what the present anticipates, on what powers now think and how they intend to act on the basis of their present thinking; and on the fact that each of the actors on the scene must take into consideration the assumptions of the others.

There then evolves the necessity of multilevel concepts and of multilevel policies in the new era. In this we have, perhaps, the chief cause of the confusion and bewilderment of countries and publics. A good deal in recent foreign policies, with their violent swings from one extreme to another, from appeasement or apathy to truculence and threats of war, and also much in internal policies, with their suspicions and hysterias, may be reflections of world-political uncertainties. Confusion, despair, or easy optimism have been rampant; desire to give in, keep out, or get it over with underlies advocacy of appeasement, neutralism, or preventive war; mutually exclusive attitudes follow each other in rapid succession.

One radical conclusion to be drawn from the new condition of permeability would seem to be that nothing short of global rule can ultimately satisfy the security interest of any one power, and particularly any superpower. For only through elimination of the single competitor who really counts can one feel safe from the threat of annihilation. And since elimination without war is hardly imaginable, destruction of the other power by preventive war would therefore seem to be the logical objective of each superpower. But—and here the security dilemma encounters the other great dilemma of our time—such an aim is no longer practical. Since thermonuclear war would in all likelihood involve one's own destruction together with the opponent's, the means through which the end would have to be attained defeats the end itself. Pursuance of the "logical" security objective would result in mutual annihilation rather than in one unit's global control of a pacified world.

If this is so, the short-term objective must surely be mutual accommodation, a drawing of demarcation lines, geographical and otherwise, between East and West which would at least serve as a stopgap policy, a holding operation pending the creation of an atmosphere in which, perhaps in consequence of a prolonged period of "cold peace," tensions may abate and the impact of the ideologies presently dividing the world diminish. May we then expect, or hope, that radically new attitudes, in accordance with a radically transformed structure of nationhood and international relations, may ultimately gain the upper hand over the inherited ones based on familiar concepts of old-style national security, power, and power competition? Until recently, advocacy of policies based on internationalism instead of power politics, on substituting the observance of universal interests for the prevalence of national interests, was considered utopian, and correctly so. National interests were still tied up with nation-states as units of power and with their security as impermeable units; internationalist ideals, while possibly recognized as ethically valid, ran counter to what nations were able to afford if they wanted to survive and prosper. But the dichotomy between "national self-interest" and "internationalist ideals" no longer fits a situation in which sovereignty and ever so absolute power cannot protect nations from annihilation.

What used to be a dichotomy of interests and ideals now emerges as a dichotomy between two sets of interests. For the former ideal has become a compelling interest itself. In former times, the lives of people, their goods and possessions, their hopes and their happiness, were tied up with the affairs of the country in which they lived, and interests thus centered around nation and national issues. Now that destruction threatens everybody, in every one of his most intimate, personal interests, national interests are bound to recede behind—or at least compete with—the common interest of all mankind in sheer survival. And if we add to this the universal interest in the common solution of other great world problems, such as those posed by the population-resources dilemma (exhaustion of vital resources coupled with the "population explosion" throughout the world), or, indeed, that of "peacetime" planetary pollution through radio-active fallout, it is perhaps not entirely utopian to expect the ultimate spread of an attitude of "universalism" through which a rational approach to world problems would at last become possible.

It may be fitting to conclude this article by quoting two men, one a contemporary scientist whose words on nuclear problems may well apply to other problems of world relations, the second a philosopher whose statement on the revolutionary impact of attitude changes seems as valid today as when it was first made: "It is a practical thing to recognize as a common responsibility, wholly incapable of unilateral solution, the complete common peril that atomic weapons constitute for the world, to recognize that only by a community of responsibility is there any hope of meeting the peril. It would seem to me visionary in the extreme, and not practical, to hope that methods which have so sadly failed in the past to avert war will succeed in the face of this far greater peril. It would in my opinion be most dangerous to regard, in these shattering times, a radical solution less practical than a conventional one" (J. Robert Oppenheimer). And: "Thought achieves more in the world than practice; for, once the realm of imagination has been revolutionized, reality cannot resist" (Hegel).

ROBERT GILPIN

War and Change in World Politics

. . . The purpose of this epilogue is to assess the world situation at the beginning of the decade of the 1980s in terms of the ideas on international political change advanced in this study and to consider whether or not events and the fundamental forces at work suggest a world once again out of control and on the verge of another global hegemonic struggle. Although no one can predict the future, the fact is that both statesmen and the public act on assessments of the trend of events, and prognostications frequently become self-fulfilling prophecies. It is therefore prudent to turn to the past and to seek an understanding of the dynamics of world politics for guidance. It is important to appreciate the real dangers as well as the possible unappreciated opportunities of the present moment. Dispassionate analysis in an era of rapid change is needed to help avoid cataclysmic war.

Using the terminology of the model of international political change set forth in this study, we may say that a disequilibrium has developed between the existing governance of the international system and the underlying distribution of power in the system. Although the United States continues to be the dominant and most prestigious state in the system, it no longer has the power to "govern" the system as it did in the past. It is decreasingly able to maintain the existing distribution of territory, the spheres of influence, and the rules of the world economy. The redistribution of economic and military power in the system to the disadvantage of the United States has meant that the costs to the United States of governing the system have increased relative to the economic capacity of the United States to support the international status quo. The classic symptoms of a declining power characterize the United States in the early 1980s: rampant inflation, chronic balance-of-payments difficulties, and high taxation.

Responding to this disequilibrium and a severe fiscal crisis, the United States has employed the traditional techniques for reestablishing equilibrium between the costs and the benefits of the existing international system. The United States has retrenched its forces and withdrawn from exposed positions in Southeast Asia, the Far East, Latin America, and the Middle East, frequently leaving a vacuum for the Soviet Union or other powers to occupy. It has formally recognized the Soviet sphere of influence in eastern Europe and negotiated a rapprochement with China, and it is reluctantly acceding to the wishes and ambitions of growing regional powers: India, Brazil, Nigeria, etc. It has accepted strategic nuclear parity with the Soviet Union, as well as loss of control over the world petroleum industry, and it finds itself unable to prevent the continued proliferation of nuclear weapons. It no longer unilaterally sets the rules regarding international trade, money, and investment. In brief, the United States, through political and military retrenchment, has sought to reduce its international commitments much as Great Britain did in the decades immediately preceding the outbreak of World War I.

At the same time, the United States also has attempted to generate new resources to support its reduced but still-dominant international position. It has urged its European and Japanese allies to increase their contributions to the common defense. It has increased its own defense expenditures and has moved toward a quasi-alliance with China to resist Soviet "hegemonism." Perhaps most significant of all, the United States, on August 15, 1971, announced a new foreign economic policy and forced changes in the rules governing international trading and monetary affairs that would benefit the American economy, especially to improve America's declining trade position. In addition, decreasing the public-sector consumption and increasing domestic investment in order to increase productivity and the reindustrialization of the American economy have become major preoccupations of political and economic leadership. President Ronald Reagan, in his inaugural address, called for "a national renewal." Finally, the United States has told "client" states around the globe that they will have to increase their contributions to their own defense (Nixon doctrine). Thus, through traditional techniques the United States is also attempting to increase its resources in order to maintain its dominant international position.

It is obviously too early to determine if the United States can or will retrench to a more modest but secure position, if it can generate additional resources to maintain its global hegemony, and if, through some combination of both responses, it can restore a favorable equilibrium between its power and commitments. This will depend not only on specific policy initiatives of the United States but also on those of other governments in the years ahead. The thrust of political, economic, and technological forces creates challenges and opportunities; domestic politics and political leadership create the responses of states to these challenges and opportunities. The course of history is indeterminant; only in retrospect does it appear otherwise.

In the meantime, the contemporary era has been aptly described as one of "eroding hegemony." Such a condition in world politics has, of course, existed in the past. The interregnum between British dominance and American dominance of international economics and politics, what E. H. Carr called the "twenty years' crisis" (1919-39), was such a period; the former hegemonic power could no longer set the rules, and the rising hegemonic power had neither the will nor the power to assume this responsibility. In the absence of rejuvenation by the old hegemony or the triumph of its successor or the establishment of some other basis of governance, the pressing issues of world order (rules governing trade, the future of the international monetary system, a new regime for the oceans, etc.) remain unresolved. Progress toward the formulation of new rules and regimes for an international system to follow the Pax Americana has been slow or nonexistent.

Yet, on the basis of the analysis of political change advanced in this study, there are reasons for believing that the present disequilibrium in the international system can be resolved without resort to hegemonic war. Although the danger of hegemonic war is very real, what is known about such wars provides grounds for guarded optimism. Whereas the contemporary world displays some of the preconditions for hegemonic conflict, other preconditions appear to be totally or partially lacking. An evaluation of the current international situation reinforces the hope that a gradual process of peaceful change, rather than war, may characterize the present era of world politics.

An extremely important reason for guarded optimism is the relative stability of the existing bipolar structure. As [Kenneth N.] Waltz argued, the present bipolar system appears to be relatively stable. Historically, however, as this study has shown, five types of developments tend to destabilize bipolar systems and trigger hegemonic conflict. Fortunately, none of these destabilizing developments appears imminent in the contemporary world (1980), at least for the immediate future.

The first potentially destabilizing factor is the danger that one of the pair (like Sparta prior to the outbreak of the Peloponnesian War) will fail to play its balancing role. Through neglect, it permits a dangerous shift in the balance of power to take place. As long as the United States and the Soviet Union maintain a system of mutual nuclear deterrence, this is unlikely to happen. Although many Americans and others fear that the United States has permitted a dangerous shift in the military balance to take place in favor of the Soviet Union, the strategic nuclear relationship continues to be one based firmly on the presumption of "mutually assured destruction" in the event of hegemonic war; each superpower has the capability to devastate the other. Yet, it must be added that a continuing deterioration in the American military position could remove this constraint on the system of mutual deterrence; at the least it could encourage Soviet leadership to exploit politically the belief that the Soviet Union has become the reigning hegemon.

The second potentially destabilizing factor is the danger of the rise of a third party to upset the bipolar balance. Although students of international relations disagree on the relative stability of bipolar systems versus multipolar systems, almost all agree that a tripolar system is the most unstable configuration. As long as western Europe lacks political unity, Japan remains weak militarily, and China continues in a backward state, this danger is minimized, though by no means eliminated. Certainly the Soviet Union has a genuine fear of an encircling alliance composed of these neighboring powers and the United

States. The United States, for its part, would regard the loss of one of these powers or the loss of the oil fields of the Middle East as a major setback. Thus, although the contemporary bipolar distribution of power is basically stable, it does contain the potential for dangerous tripolar structures of power.

The third potentially destabilizing factor is the danger of polarization of the international system as a whole into two hostile camps. In such a situation, international relations become a zero-sum game in which a gain to one camp or bloc is a loss to the other. This was the case prior to the outbreak of World War I, when minor tensions in the Balkans flared up into a major conflagration. Such a polarization has not yet developed (1980). To repeat an earlier metaphor, political space is not closing in. On the contrary, the world is becoming more pluralistic, with the emergence of a number of regional actors and issues. The outcomes of political conflicts in Asia, Africa, and elsewhere do not necessarily advantage one or another of the two superpowers so as to force the other to take decisive counteraction. Yet the emergence of frequently unstable new powers in the so-called Third World, the proliferation of nuclear weapons to these states, and the conflicts among them could involve the superpowers in highly volatile situations.

The fourth potentially destabilizing factor is the danger of entanglement of the major powers in the ambitions and difficulties of minor allies. It was the ambitions of Sparta's ally, Corinth, and its provocations of Athens that precipitated the great war between the Peloponnesian and Delian leagues. The difficulties of Germany's ally, Austria, beset with a decaying multiethnic empire, escalated into World War I. In neither of these cases could the major power tolerate the defeat or disintegration of its minor ally. Fortunately, these dangers do not appear imminent today. Even though particular allies of both superpowers have unfulfilled ambitions and/or serious political problems of their own, it is unlikely that they could or would set in motion a series of untoward events that would precipitate conflict among the two superpowers; this is because these allies are insufficiently independent and the superpowers are sufficiently self-reliant. Again, however, one must not too quickly dismiss this potential danger. A Sino-Soviet confrontation, workers' revolts in eastern Europe, or political instability among America's allies in western Europe and the Middle East could pose dangers for the international system.

The fifth potentially destabilizing factor is the danger of loss of control over economic, political, and social developments. Eras of rapid and revolutionary change within and among nations create dangerous uncertainties and anxieties that lead political elites in great powers to miscalculate. Hegemonic wars signal not merely changes in political relations among states but frequently social and economic upheavals as well; World War I, as [Elie] Halévy showed, represented a collapse of the decaying European social and economic order. The crisis of world capitalism in the 1980s (high rate of inflation, rising level of unemployment, and low rate of economic growth) and the equally severe crisis of world communism (as represented by the workers' revolt in Poland) signal major strains in both systems.

Although the decades following World War II frequently have been called an age of political turbulence, the international system in that period has actually been characterized by remarkable resilience. It has accommodated a number of major developments: an unprecedented process of decolonization, rapid technological changes, the emergence of new powers (India, Brazil, China), sociopolitical revolutions in developing countries, massive shocks to the world economy, and the resurgence of non-Western civilizations. Yet the basic framework of an international system composed of two central blocs and a large nonaligned periphery has remained essentially intact.

This relative stability of the system has been strengthened by the domestic stability of the two dominant powers themselves. In contrast to the situations prevailing before World Wars I and II, neither power has been torn by powerful class or national conflicts. Although racial strife in the United States and ethnic problems in Russia are causing tensions in both societies, these internal difficulties pale in comparison with the nationalistic struggles of the Austro-Hungarian Empire in 1914 and the intense class conflicts of the European powers in the 1930s. The basic domestic stability of the United States and the Soviet Union today helps to ensure that revolutionary upheavals in these societies will not disrupt the international system.

Yet it would be foolish to be complacent regarding the underlying social stability of the system. A prolonged period of restricted economic growth could erode the political stability of the United States and the Soviet Union. A more probable threat to world stability would be untoward developments in important peripheral areas, in particular eastern Europe and the Middle East. The dependence of Soviet security on the subservient eastern European bloc and the dependence of the West on Middle Eastern petroleum constitute worrisome factors in contemporary world politics. The maintenance of stable conditions in these areas over the long term is a formidable challenge. Another continuing danger is that one or both of the superpowers might engage in foreign adventures in order to dampen internal dissent and promote political unity.

Another reason for guarded optimism regarding the avoidance of hegemonic war is that in the closing decades of the twentieth century, economic, political, and ideological cleavages are not coalescing but instead are running counter to one another. In the past, a precondition for hegemonic war in many cases has been the coalescence of political, economic, and ideological issues. In periods prior to the outbreak of hegemonic war, conflict has intensified because the contending parties have been at odds with one another on all fronts and have had few interests in common to moderate the antagonism. In such situations, compromise in one issue area becomes increasingly difficult because of its linkage to other issue areas. As a consequence, disputes in one area easily spill over into other areas, and the joining of issues leads to escalation of the conflict. The great wars of world history have tended to be at once political, economic, and ideological struggles.

In the 1980s, however, although the United States and the Soviet Union find themselves in political and ideological conflict, they share a powerful interest in avoiding nuclear war and stopping the proliferation of nuclear weapons. Moreover, they also share certain economic interests, and both countries have numerous economic conflicts with their political and economic allies. This intermingling of interests and conflicts is thus a source of stability. Ironically, a less autarkic Soviet Union challenging the United States in world markets and competing for scarce resources would be, and might very well become, a destabilizing factor. A decline in Soviet production of petroleum or Soviet entry into world markets may change this situation and increase the level of economic tensions.

The contemporary situation is somewhat anomalous in the multiple nature of the challenge to the dominant power in the system. On the one hand, the position of the United States is challenged economically by Japan, western Europe, and the members of OPEC. On the other hand, the military and political challenge comes principally from the Soviet Union. Although there are those writers who believe that the economic confrontation between the United States and its allies is threatening to world peace, the position of this book is that the worst danger to international stability is the Soviet-American confrontation. From this perspective, the primary consequence of the economic competition between the United States and its allies has been to undermine the capacity of the United States to meet the Soviet challenge; however, if Japan and West Germany were to convert their military potential into actual capability, then the balance of military and political power could be changed dramatically, probably with important unforeseen consequences. At best, therefore, one can say that the long-term significance of contemporary developments for the future of the system is ambiguous.

Finally, and most important of all, hegemonic wars are preceded by an important psychological change in the temporal outlook of peoples. The outbreaks of hegemonic struggles have most frequently been triggered by the fear of ultimate decline and the perceived erosion of power. The desire to preserve what one has while the advantage is still on one's side has caused insecure and declining powers to precipitate great wars. The purpose of such war frequently has been to minimize potential losses rather than to maximize any particular set of gains.

Here, perhaps, is the greatest cause for anxiety in the years immediately ahead. What would be the reaction of the United States if the balance of power is seen to be shifting irrevocably to the Soviet advantage? What would be the Soviet response to a perceived threat of encirclement by a resurgent United States, an industrialized China, a dynamic Japan, a hostile Islam, an unstable eastern Europe, and a modernized NATO? How might one or another of these powers (the United States today, Russia tomorrow) respond to the continuing redistribution of world power?

Robert Gilpin

A generally unappreciated factor in the preservation of world peace over the past few decades has involved the ideological perspectives of the United States and the Soviet Union. Each rival power subscribes to an ideology that promises inevitable victory to its own system of values and assures it that history is on its side. For the United States, freedom, democracy, and national independence are the most powerful forces in the world; for the Soviet Union, communism is the "wave of the future." These rival belief systems have been sources of conflict but also of reassurance for both nations. Despite their clashes and struggles, neither side has experienced the panic that has preceded the great wars of history, a panic that arises from fear that time has begun to run against one. Neither nation has felt the need to risk everything in the present in order to prevent inevitable defeat in the future. Fortunately for world peace, both the United States and the Soviet Union have believed the logic of historical development to be working for them. Each power has believed the twentieth century to be its century. But the foundations of both of these faiths are experiencing strain.

At the end of World War II, the United States held a position of unparalleled preeminence in the international system. During the first decades of the postwar period, its power and influence expanded until it was finally checked in the jungles of Southeast Asia and by more fundamental changes in the international distribution of economic and military power. The administration of Richard Nixon constituted a watershed in that it was the first to deal with the challenge posed by the increasing disequilibrium between America's international position and America's capacity to finance it. The United States has worked to meet this challenge through political retrenchment, efforts toward detente with the Soviet Union, rapprochement with China, and the generation of additional resources through changes in its domestic and foreign economic policies.

The fundamental task of the United States in the realm of foreign affairs has become one of responding to its changed position in the world as new powers arise on the world scene. It must bring its power and commitments into balance, either through increasing the former or reducing the latter or by some combination of both strategies. Although this is a serious challenge, it need not be a source of alarm. Other great powers have succeeded in this task and have survived, maintaining their vital interests and values intact. There is danger, however, that the military challenge of the Soviet Union and the changing economic fortunes of the United States might generate severe anxiety in the American public. Although there is certainly cause for concern in these matters, exaggerated rhetoric over the relative decline of American power and wealth can itself give rise to panic and irrational actions.

Despite its relative decline, the American economy remains the most powerful in the world and dwarfs that of the Soviet Union. However, American society has placed on its economy consumption demands (both public and private) and protection demands beyond its capabilities at the same

38

time that productive investment and economic productivity have slackened. Although the Reagan administration can greatly increase defense expenditures to meet the Soviet challenge in an era of restricted economic growth, it could do so only at high cost to consumption or investment or both. The inherent danger in a massive expansion of defense expenditures is that it will be inflationary and will further undermine the productivity of the economy. The long-term well-being and security of the United States necessitate judicious allocation of national resources among the areas of consumption, protection, and investment.

The Soviet Union is, of course, the rising challenger, and it appears to be the one power that in the years to come could supplant the American dominance over the inter-national system. Although the growth and expansion of Russian power have deep historical roots, the acceleration in the development of Soviet industrial and military might in recent decades has been formidable. The Soviet Union has fashioned a powerful military machine from a state that was near defeat and collapse during World War II. Further, it occupies a central position on the Eurasian land mass and enjoys conventional military superiority over the United States in important areas. A major question for the future is whether or not the Soviets can translate and are willing to translate these expanding military capabilities into decisive political gains in Europe, Asia, and elsewhere in the world.

Meanwhile, the relative decline in American power and the continuing restraint on the use of military force has given rise to an era of uneasy coexistence between the superpowers. The erratic process of detente, if ultimately successful, may turn out to be an unprecedented example of peaceful change. What it could well signify is a change from an America-centered global system to a more nearly equal bipolar system, and, perhaps eventually, a multipolar global system. The apparent settlement of the German and central European questions has stabilized, at least for the moment, the outstanding territorial issue dividing the two superpowers. The fundamental issue in the strategic-arms-limitation talks has been the stabilization of the nuclear arms race on the basis of strategic parity. Both powers favor steps to discourage further proliferation of nuclear weapons. There remain, however, many other issues about which the two superpowers continue to have antagonistic interests that could destabilize their relations. The Soviet aggression in Afghanistan is a case in point, and, of course, the rise of other powers could undermine this emergent bipolar structure over the longer term.

At the present juncture, it is the United States whose position is threatened by the rise of Soviet power. In the decades ahead, however, the Soviet Union also must adjust to the differential growth of power among states. For the Soviet Union, the burden of adjusting to the transformation of the international system from a bipolar system to a tripolar or even multipolar system could be even more severe than it would prove to be for the United States. In the wake of the collapse of Communist ideological unity and the rise of a rival ideological center in Peking, the Soviet Union finds itself surrounded by potentially threatening and growing centers of industrial power. Although it possesses unprecedented military strength, it could lose the reassurance of its ideology, and it is sluggish with respect to economic growth and technological development. If its neighboring powers (Japan, western Europe, and China) continue to grow in economic power and military potential, Russia's logistical advantage of occupying a central position on the Eurasian continent is also a political liability. On all sides, centrifugal forces could pull at this last of the great multiethnic empires as neighbors make demands for revision of the territorial status quo and as subordinate non-Russian peoples seek greater equality and autonomy. Such external and internal challenges could give rise to powerful defensive reactions on the part of the Soviet governing elite.

Several years ago, Ernest Mandel, a leading European Marxist, ascribed the changing fortunes of the United States to the law of uneven development: "After having benefited from the law of unequal development for a century, the United States is now becoming its victim." Similarly, one may make the same observation regarding the future of the Soviet Union; this law plays no favorites between capitalists and communists. Observing the growing challenge of a unified and developing Communist China, an Indian political scientist writes that the uneven development of socialism is creating contradictions in the system today. [Partha] Chatterjee put it best: "In the long run, the law of uneven socialist development may pose a greater threat to the Soviet Union than does the law of uneven capitalist development to the United States. In the years ahead, both nations may need to adjust to a world in which power is diffusing at an unprecedented rate to a plurality of powers."

We conclude this epilogue on a cautiously optimistic note. Although there are powerful forces that could lead to hegemonic war between the superpowers, the historic conditions for such a war are only partially present. The redistribution of military power in favor of Russia as the rising state in the international system and the possibility of further redistributions of power to other states pose serious threats to the stability of the system; in response the superpowers might precipitate a course of events over which they could lose control. However, these potentially destabilizing developments are balanced by the restraint imposed by the existence of nuclear weapons, the plurality of the system, and the mutual benefits of economic cooperation. The supreme task for statesmen in the final decades of the twentieth century is to build on the positive forces of our age in the creation of a new and more stable international order.

■■■■■■■ **2.3**

THOMAS J. BIERSTEKER

The Illusion of State Power

Although they have disagreed about nearly every aspect of the contemporary world economy, liberal economists and dependency writers have historically shared at least one important observation. They have agreed that the global expansion of transnational corporations has constrained the exercise of state power in the Third World. That is, they have agreed that the ability of independent states to formulate *and execute* policies (their effective authority, not their jurisdictional authority) has been reduced or even undermined by the operations of large, transnational corporations within their national boundaries.

For most liberal economists, the expansion of transnational corporations after World War II further entangled the state in a "web of interdependence" already initiated by "increasing economic interdependence and technological advances in communication and transportation" (Gilpin 1975a). Charles Kindleberger declared the nation-state "just about through as an economic unit" (Kindleberger 1969), Harry Johnson described world government as "the only rational method for coping with the world's economic problems" (Johnson 1970), and Raymond Vernon went even further to proclaim "sovereignty at bay" (Vernon 1971).

For most dependency writers, transnational corporations have constrained the exercise of state power by reinforcing transnational class alliances that link domestic compradores directly to the centers of international capitalism. As Fernando Cardoso and Enzo Faletto described the situation confronting most states, "some of the mechanisms controlling the national economy are beyond the control of the country concerned; the international market sets certain universal standards for the modern production system that allow no alternatives" (Cardoso and Faletto 1978).

By the early 1970s this convergence of assessments of the ability of transnational corporations to constrain state power had virtually become an orthodoxy in the growing literature on international political economy. It was not long, however, before major challenges to this orthodoxy arose from both within and from outside these rival traditions. Variously described as "neomercantilism" or the "rediscovery of the state," scholars, statesmen, and

From "The Illusion of State Power: Transnational Corporations and the Neutralization of Host-Country Legislation," *Journal of Peace Research*, Vol. 17 (1980), pp. 207-221, by permission of Norwegian University Press, Oslo.

events began to challenge the contention that transnational corporations have constrained the exercise of state power in the developing world.

The Resurgence of the State

C. Fred Bergsten introduced one of the first challenges to the idea of an erosion of state power with his influential warnings about the "threat from the third world" (Bergsten 1973). At a time when the successful cartelization of petroleum was being emulated by other producer organizations, the "Group of 77" had attained unprecedented levels of cooperation, and policies of economic nationalism (nationalization and indigenization) were widespread, Bergsten wrote "host country efforts are now far more likely to succeed because of fundamental shifts in the world economic and political environment that have put many host countries in a far stronger position than before" (Bergsten 1974). Rather than constraining state power, the power of transnational corporations is increasingly constrained:

> Virtually every country in the world which receives direct investment . . .
> is levying increasingly stringent requirements on foreign firms. (Bergsten 1974)

According to Bergsten, "firms can no longer dictate, or even heavily influence, host-country policies as they may have done in the past. . . . In short, sovereignty is no longer at bay in host countries" (Bergsten 1974).

This change in the relationship between transnational corporations and the state is said to have developed from a number of important changes in the contemporary international system. Since virtually all host countries have begun to adopt policies designed to maximize national returns, transnational corporations can no longer play off one host-country against another in search of the most lucrative investment climate. In addition, host-country policies have become more explicit, and their policy objectives have broadened considerably. Host-countries also have more choices available to them as a result of increased competition between American, European, and Japanese transnationals and the increased availability of other alternatives to direct foreign investment (such as licensing, consulting, and turn key arrangements) (Bergsten 1974). Bergsten qualifies his assessment of this shift in power between states and transnational corporations, suggesting that its degree differs from country to country and from industry to industry. Yet he concludes, "the trend appears inexorable" (Bergsten 1974).

Bergsten's assessment of the growing threat from the Third World has been echoed by a number of neo-conservative scholars, such as Daniel P. Moynihan (Moynihan 1975) and Robert W. Tucker (Tucker 1975), who view this trend with alarm. As one scholar characterized these assessments of the changing configuration of power:

It thus appears that many observers feel that the events of the early 1970s have essentially completed the decolonization process begun after World War II. Economic has come to complement political sovereignty. (Smith 1977)

The ability of transnational corporations to constrain the exercise of state power was therefore under serious challenge by the mid-1970s.

Another challenge to the idea of the erosion of state power has been presented by advocates of a neo-mercantilist approach to international political economy. Neo-mercantilists criticize both liberal economists and dependency writers for having underestimated the significance of the nation-state. As Stephen Krasner described the situation:

> In recent years, students of international relations have multinationalized, transnationalized, bureaucratized, and transgovernmentalized the state until it has virtually ceased to exist as an analytic construct. (Krasner 1976)

Neo-mercantilists want state power reintroduced as the central focus of international political economy.

Robert Gilpin has emphasized the significance of state power in creating international economic regimes, from the gold standard to the Bretton Woods (Gilpin 1975b). According to Gilpin, the essence of neo-mercantilism "is the priority of *national* economic and political objectives over considerations of *global* economic efficiency" (Gilpin 1975a). States should not be treated as dependent variables, responding to changes in the movement of global forces. Rather, they should be treated as independent variables, responsible for creating and maintaining the structure of the world economy.

According to the neo-mercantilist perspective, the existence and relative significance of nonstate actors such as the transnational corporation "can only be understood within the context of a broader structure that ultimately rests upon the power and interests of states" (Krasner 1976). The phenomenal expansion of U.S. based transnational corporations must therefore be understood as having taken place within the structure of a world economy created and maintained by an unchallenged U.S. economic power (manifested in the form of the post World War II Bretton Woods system). As this system has begun to break down, so too has the position of the transnational corporation within it:

> In the wake of the relative decline of American power and of growing conflicts among the capitalist economies, a new international political order less favorable to the multinational corporation is coming into existence. Whether it is former President Nixon's five-power world (US, USSR, China, the EEC, and Japan), a triangular world (US, USSR, and China), or some form of American-Soviet condominium, the emergent world order will be characterized by intense international economic competition for markets, investment outlets, and sources of raw materials. (Gilpin 1975a)

Within this emergent world order the relative power of transnational corporations vis-à-vis state power will inevitably change. As more governments attempt and succeed to construct policies designed to maximize their own interests, the operations of transnational corporations will increasingly be constrained.

The growing literature concerned with the balance of bargaining power between transnationals and host countries has presented a third major challenge to the assertion that transnational corporations have constrained state power. The relative negotiating strength of states and transnationals is determined by a number of factors, including the characteristics of the project under negotiation (such as its size, or technology choice), the characteristics of the host country (such as its local market size or its rate of growth), and exogenous factors (such as the extent of competition in the international market) (Moran 1978). Accordingly, the relative bargaining position of transnational corporations and host countries will vary from case to case. Transnationals will be able to constrain the exercise of state power when they have very little investment at stake in the host country, or when the host country has a very limited domestic market to offer, or when the transnational corporation is not threatened by serious international competition. However, most scholars concerned with the dynamics of bargaining relationship between transnationals and host countries have begun to assert that the balance is beginning to shift away from the transnational corporation.

Theodore H. Moran has suggested that this change in relative bargaining power has taken place in part because of the increasing competition between transnational corporations of diverse national origins. This development "strengthens, rather than weakens, the position of the Third World countries because it gives them more alternatives to choose from" (Moran 1978). Moran has also stressed the significance of the amount of learning and increased sophistication that has occurred among Third World bureaucrats in recent years, citing the "continued growth in host-country skill in monitoring and analyzing multinational corporate activities" as a factor contributing to host country strength (Bergsten, Horst, and Moran 1978).

The increased frequency with which host countries are willing to cooperate with each other by pooling information, coordinating foreign investment policies, or presenting a unified position in North-South negotiations (such as in the case of the Andean Common Market) has prompted some observers to comment that their new power "will not easily be eroded" (Smith 1977).

Thus, although there are still a large number of cases in which the balance of bargaining power is heavily tilted toward the transnational corporation, "one would expect the benefits from foreign investment in the aggregate to be rising and the cost of securing those benefits to be falling, over time" (Moran 1978). There is a gradual, evolutionary, and inevitable trend toward a reassertion of state power. State power is not severely threatened or constrained, because in the long run, transnational corporations are all dead.

The most recent challenge to the general assertion that transnational corporations have constrained state power is contained in the literature emphasizing the increased role of the state in political and economic affairs. Alfred Stepan begins his study of state and society in Peru with the observation:

> A major, nearly worldwide trend since the 1930s has been the steady growth of the role of the state in political life. (Stepan 1978)

All national states have increasingly taken on regulative and welfare functions, while in the Third World "most development plans call for the state to play a major role in structuring economic and social systems" (Stepan 1978). Peter Evans makes the same general point in his recent work on dependent development in Brazil in which he emphasizes the growing significance of state corporations in Brazilian development (Evans 1979).

Stepan asserts that the strong and visible presence of transnational corporations will often stimulate a response in the form of an increased state role in the management of the economy:

> There is also the very real possibility that the growth of multinationals will stimulate the appearance of multistate planning and bargaining organizations such as the Andean Pact and OPEC. There is thus reason to think that the multinational corporations may well encourage the rise of countervailing bureaucracies in which the state will play a key role. (Stepan 1978)

According to this view, the state will not only play a more active role, it will also play a more effective role as well. In spite of the power disparities between Third World states and foreign capital, "the state has the potential to construct policies for almost every one of the relevant variables (affecting its capacity to control foreign capital) in order to increase its bargaining position vis-à-vis foreign capital" (Stepan 1978).

Peter Evans pursues this line of argument in his examination of the growth of state capital in Brazil. He asserts that the direct role of the Brazilian state in the process of industrialization "has given the state a new position of power from which to bargain with the multinationals" (Evans 1979). Because of the experience the state bourgeoisie is gaining from its cooperation with multinational and local capital in Brazil's emerging "triple alliance," it will become "a more formidable opponent for the multinational managers" (Evans 1979). From his examination of nationalist pressures from the Brazilian state and the response of transnational corporations to them, Evans concludes "even modest successes are useful from the nationalist point of view in that they provide a base upon which future changes can be built incrementally" (Evans 1979). Thus, the apparently inexorable trend toward the reassertion of state power is accomplished incrementally.

Like their predecessors in the "threat from the Third World," "neomercantilist," and "bargaining" literatures, the "rise of the state" literature attacks the notion that transnationals have the capacity to constrain state power. Stepan declares:

> To the proposition that multinational corporations contribute to the erosion of the nation state I offer a counter-hypothesis: the growth of

multinationals may well help generate in some countries normative and administrative aspirations to create mechanisms to control multinationals. (Stepan 1978)

Evans agrees when he writes:

Some chroniclers of the growth of the multinationals leave the impression that geographic boundaries and the governments organized around them are becoming anachronisms ... my own view is quite the reverse. (Evans 1979)

The New Orthodoxy

Thus, the attack on the "sovereignty at bay" notion is quite complete. Criticisms of the idea had become so widespread and so thorough that by the late 1970s the original formulators of the notion offered revisions. Raymond Vernon, who regretted ever titling his influential 1971 book *Sovereignty at Bay*, began writing about the ways in which transnational corporations behave as directed by host countries (Vernon 1979), and initiated a project examining the operations of state corporations. Similarly, in the postscript added to their 1978 English edition of *Dependency and Development in Latin America*, Fernando Cardoso and Enzo Faletto wrote about the changes that have "led local states, despite the capitalist ideology they defend, to expand their functions and thereby create a national basis from which to bargain with the multinationals" (Cardoso and Faletto 1978). Thus, we have the emergence of a new orthodoxy.

It is no longer fashionable to discuss the ability of transnational corporations to place limits on the exercise of state power. If anything, the transnational corporation is "at bay," a sentiment increasingly echoed by the public relations officers of corporations concerned about the growth of host country regulation. The major challenges to the "constrained power of the state" idea were all formulated in response to changes in events during the 1970s and the inability of the conventional arguments of liberal economists and dependency writers to take account of those changes. Thus, the neo-conservatives, the neo-mercantilists, the bargaining writers, and the statists are all struck by the growth of producer cartels modeled after OPEC, South-South cooperation in regional arrangements and in the Group of 77, competition between advanced capitalist economies, the emergence of state corporations, and the frequency and extent of host country regulation (especially nationalization and indigenization).

It is clear that this new orthodoxy on the relationship between states and transnational corporations is an improvement over its predecessor. The major challenges to the sovereignty at bay thesis have improved on its logical shortcomings and have been better able to take account of major changes in events or "empirical reality." The re-introduction of the state into discussions of international political economy has been a very important contribution. However, most of these challenges to the old orthodoxy have tended to underestimate the ability of transnational corporations to respond to this changing global environment. The survival of transnational corporations is based on their ability to respond to changing environments. Given even a short amount of stability in host country policy, they are able to adjust to new requirements.

There are three major assumptions made in much of the literature of the new orthodoxy that require further examination. First, there is a tendency to assume that the increase in the frequency of state action designed to control transnational corporations is equivalent to an increase in the frequency of *effective* state actions. This assumption is most apparent in the writings of C. Fred Bergsten and most of the neo-conservative writers. Bergsten asserts that host country efforts are far more likely to succeed in the contemporary world environment and cites the dramatic increase in the number of nationalizations and indigenization policies during the 1970s as evidence of the growing "threat" from the Third World (Bergsten 1973). Bergsten, Horst, and Moran similarly argue that although not all host-country demands are met, "even from the failures, host countries learn how best to get foreign investors to serve host-country needs" and that the many successful nationalistic actions "generate a clear demonstration effect" (Bergsten, Horst, and Moran 1978).

Second, and more important, there is a tendency in much of the recent literature of the new orthodoxy to equate the sharing of equity with the sharing of control of transnational corporations. For example, Peter Evans is well aware that local partners are sometimes without influence in joint ventures in which they share equity with transnational corporations. Nevertheless, he maintains that joint ventures (operationally defined by the sharing of equity) "are still the best indication of shared control" (Evans 1979). Like many other writers in this tradition, Evans assumes that each partner in a joint venture possesses voting power or control over decision making that is commensurate with its equity participation.

Effective control requires more than the holding of a simple majority of the equity share capital. It requires an ability to use equity or other means to determine with regularity the outcomes of decisions on the "most important" questions confronting the management of the firm (i.e. questions concerning production output, technology choice, re-investment, local-content use, export promotion, profits and dividends, local research and development, etc.). Thus, control is defined in terms of managerial responsibility for financial, technical, and commercial aspects of production, rather than in terms of responsibility for non-critical functions such as labor relations, product distribution, and advertising.

Third, and finally, there is a tendency in much of the recent literature to assert that the balance of bargaining power is shifting in the direction of host countries in a gradual, incremental, but inexorable way. The actions of states are examined in great detail, while the responses of transnational corporations are largely ignored. Significantly, Moran omits any mention of the capacity of transnational corporations to counteract host country regulation in his classification of three major sets of hypotheses to try to account for relative negotiating strength of states and transnationals (Moran 1978). Similarly, Stepan's variables affecting the capacity of the state to control foreign capital concentrate exclusively on *state* capacities (Stepan 1978). Since there is no examination of the transnational's responses to state pressures, only a part of the bargaining relationship is captured. Any change in the balance of bargaining power must take account of the dynamics of change within each of the major protagonists, both the state's actions and the transnational corporation's responses to them.

The extent to which this new orthodoxy about the resurgence of the state has underestimated the ability of transnational corporations to respond to changing business environments can be illustrated with an examination of the responses of transnational corporations to specific host country policies. Responses to Nigeria's recent indigenization efforts provide a good illustration of the deficiencies of some of the arguments prevailing among writers expounding the new orthodoxy about the relationship between states and transnational corporations. . . .

Conclusions

The range of strategies available to transnational corporations is impressive. By employing benignly legal methods (such as encouraging a wide distribution of shares) or blatantly illegal ones (such as bribery), transnational corporations have had little difficulty in retaining effective managerial control over their Nigerian operations in the face of the "resurgence of state power." Even though Nigeria may appear to fit that model, transnational corporations show no signs of being held "at bay" in the country.

Several of the assumptions prevalent in much of the "resurgence of the state" literature require some modification based on the Nigerian example. First, it is clear from this example that an increase in the frequency of state actions and the extent of state intervention is by no means equivalent to an increase in the effectiveness of state actions. Despite the fact that Nigeria has gone through all the motions of a reassertion of state power, it has not made very much progress in its efforts to obtain control over the major economic actors operating in its economy.

Second, it should be quite apparent that the sharing of equity is a long way from the sharing of control in joint ventures with transnational corporations. Nearly every scholar writing about transnational corporations is aware of this fact, but it is striking how frequently it is overlooked.

Finally, it is apparent that any assessment of the balance of bargaining power between states and transnationals must take account of the dynamics of change within each of the major protagonists. Too much of the bargaining literature focuses primarily on the capacities of states. Certainly, Nigeria lacks some of the characteristics of a strong state, but its inability to acquire control over transnational corporations also has a great deal to do with the responsive capacities of those firms. Although in the long run the balance may be shifting in the direction of the state, it is not likely to be the smooth, gradual, or incremental process described in much of the literature. Rather, it is likely to proceed along a more discontinuous path, with each innovative state action being answered with innovative defensive responses by transnational corporations.

Changes have certainly taken place in the relations between states and transnational corporations during the 1970s, with the emergence of state corporations, more joint ventures, and increasingly stringent host-country regulations. Nigeria is no exception to this general trend. However, the balance of bargaining power between host-countries and transnational corporations has not shifted either as far or as quickly as most of the advocates of the "resurgence of the state" literature maintain. Transnational corporations are still able to constrain the exercise of state power in the Third World.

Some of these conclusions are contextually specific to the Nigerian case and cannot be readily generalized to other examples of the relationship between states and transnational corporations. This is certainly true of some of the specific strategies employed by transnational corporations in Nigeria, since they are responses to specific aspects of Nigerian policy (e.g. the two-company strategy). However, similar conclusions have been reached in other studies of the relationship between states and transnational corporations (Weinstein 1976, Lall & Bibile 1977, and Sanchez forthcoming). Given a comparable amount of access to transnational corporations, it would be possible to reach similar kinds of conclusions about nearly all Third World countries in the contemporary world economy.

The rediscovery of the state as an independent actor is an important contribution to the international political economy debate. However, it is important that we do not confuse the illusion of state power with the reality of state power. As long as transnational corporations continue to respond to state policies as they have in the past (and there is every indication that they will), efforts by states to obtain effective control of their operations will prove extraordinarily difficult, and transnationals will therefore continue to limit the exercise of state power.

References

Akeredolu-Ale, E. O., 1975. *The Underdevelopment of Indigenous Entrepreneurship in Nigeria*. Ibadan: Ibadan University Press.

Bergsten, C. Fred, 1973. "The Threat from the Third World," *Foreign Policy*, No. 11.

Bergsten, C. Fred, 1974. "Coming Investment Wars?" *Foreign Affairs*, Vol. 53, No. 1.

Bergsten, C. Fred, Thomas Horst, and Theodore H. Moran, 1978. *American Multinationals and American Interests.* Washington: The Brookings Institution.

Biersteker, Thomas J., 1978. *Distortion or Development? Contending Perspectives on the Multinational Corporation.* Cambridge: The MIT Press.

Cardoso, Fernando H. and Enzo Faletto, 1978. *Dependency and Development in Latin America.* Berkeley: University of California Press.

Evans, Peter, 1979. *Dependent Development: The Alliance of Multinational, State and Local Capital in Brazil.* Princeton: Princeton University Press.

Federal Government of Nigeria, 1977. "Nigerian Enterprises Promotion Decree, 1977," *Supplement to Official Gazette,* Vol. 64, No. 2, Part A. Lagos: Ministry of Information, Printing Division.

Gilpin, Robert, 1975a. "Three models of the future," *International Organization,* Vol. 29, No. 1.

Gilpin, Robert, 1975b. *U.S. Power and the Multinational Corporation.* New York: Basic Books.

International Monetary Fund, 1979. *Balance of Payments Yearbook.* Washington: IMF.

Johnson, Harry G., 1970. *International Economic Questions Facing Britain, the United States, and Canada in the 70s.* British-North American Research Association.

Kindleberger, Charles, 1969. *American Business Abroad.* New Haven: Yale University Press.

Krasner, Stephen D., 1976. "State Power and the Structure of International Trade," *World Politics,* Vol. XXVIII, No. 3.

Lall, Sanjaya and Senaka Bibile, 1977. "The Political Economy of Controlling Transnationals: The Pharmaceutical Industry in Sri Lanka (1972-1976)," *World Development,* Vol. 5, No. 8.

Moran, Theodore H., 1974. *Multinational Corporations and the Politics of Dependence: Copper in Chile.* Princeton: Princeton University Press.

Moran, Theodore H., 1978. "Multinational corporations and dependency: a dialogue for dependentistas and non-dependentistas," *International Organization,* Vol. 32, No. 1.

Moynihan, Daniel P., 1975. "The United States in Opposition," *Commentary,* March 1975.

Sanchez, David, forthcoming. "Denationalization and Local Capital in Brazil," Ph.D. Dissertation, Department of Political Science, Yale University.

Smith, Tony, 1977. "Changing configurations of power in North-South relations since 1945," *International Organization,* Vol. 31, No. 1.

Stepan, Alfred, 1978. *The State and Society: Peru in Comparative Perspective.* Princeton: Princeton University Press.

Tucker, Robert W., 1975, "Egalitarianism and International Politics," *Commentary,* September 1975.

Vernon, Raymond, 1971. *Sovereignty at Bay.* New York: Basic Books.

Vernon, Raymond, 1979. "Multinationals: No Strings Attached," *Foreign Policy*, No. 33.

Weinstein, Franklin B., 1976. "Multinational Corporations and the Third World: The Case of Japan and Southeast Asia," *International Organization*, Vol. 30, No. 3.

2.4 ■■■■■

GEORGE P. SHULTZ

The New International Era: An American Perspective

I am very delighted to be here. As it turns out, I am a member of, what I've learned is known as, a sister organization in the United States. And so, I take particular pleasure in appearing at this luncheon.

Of course, there has been a great deal of talk about the Geneva meeting. For a long time, we insisted on calling it a meeting, and that was the word out of the White House. But as it seemed to have been a success, we now call it a summit. And we are even beginning to talk about the next summit. But choice of words is very important in all of these things, as we all know. I was alarmed in Geneva, when we were there before the meeting started. I wandered into a room and there were a bunch of White House people who were plotting things, and they were talking about arranging a tete-a-tete between the President and General Secretary Gorbachev. And I barged in and said, "You have got to knock this off. It's a one-on-one. You keep using these French words, and the next thing you know, you'll be talking about detente."

So much for the summit. A month ago, Washington was charmed by a visit from the Prince and Princess of Wales. We were also pleased and impressed that His Royal Highness visited our Library of Congress and attended a seminar on our Constitution with our Chief Justice and legal scholars. This noble document, of course, was a product of our rebellion against his ancestor; but it was also, we all know, a product of the British political heritage. We have a written constitution; yours is unwritten. But the principle of constitutionalism is the same: government limited by the rule of law to protect the freedom of the individual against arbitrary power.

One of the striking features of today's world is how durable and relevant this ideal is. The principle of liberty turns out to be a hardy and powerful idea

---

Address before the Pilgrims of Great Britain, London, December 10, 1985.

with a compelling attraction to peoples around the globe. The notion of restraints on power, of course, has its international application, as statesmen struggle to build stability and balance into the international order.

Yet today, we all know, the world order has been challenged by a host of developments that yesterday's thinkers could not have foreseen. We face new strategic realities, new evidence of the power of ideas, new understanding of economic realities, and a new revolution in technology that will have profound political consequences. Each of these forces has posed a philosophical challenge to established orthodoxy, to conventional wisdom about strategic, political, and economic relations among nations.

The United States approaches this challenge confident that the free nations together are in a strong position to shape the course of events in accordance with our ideals. Perhaps it's just American brashness to feel this way. But in any case, let me describe how America views these new trends—in strategy, ideology, economics, and technology—and why we feel confident about what the future will bring.

The Classical Conception of International Order

Among the ideas that have been decisively altered in the postwar era is our conception of the balance of power. As a British audience knows, the classical conception served well as a functional description of international order. The idea of national sovereignty was born in Europe, and thus the problem of peace was to nurture some kind of equilibrium among sovereign states. Sometimes the balance was stable; sometimes not. When some continental power seemed bent on dominance, Britain would join others in restoring the balance.

Today, the classical conception still serves, to a degree. When faced with Soviet expansionism after World War II, for example, the West had no choice but to unite to deter and resist Soviet ambitions.

But the strategic realities of the postwar era demanded new modes of resistance and deterrence. In the classical or European model, the balance of power tended to be one-dimensional; its objective was the maintenance of equilibrium between the states in question. The balance of power in the contemporary world is, by contrast, multidimensional.

Multidimensional character could not be better illustrated than by the variety of topics on the agenda of the President's recent meetings with Mr. Gorbachev. As the classical conception of the balance of power would imply, the two sides discussed the strategic military balance. But we also discussed regional conflicts, in a world where ideology sometimes reflects and sometimes exploits the turbulence of vast regions of the globe. We discussed human rights, the irrepressible yearning of men and women everywhere for freedom and democracy, an issue which, in fact, lies at the heart of a number of conflicts in the world. And we discussed bilateral issues, seeking more open exchanges as a corrective to the self-isolation and rigidity which Soviet ideology imposes on the Soviet system.

The New Strategic Balance: Offense, Defense, and Stability

In the strategic dimension, the stability of the balance is literally the main focus of American efforts in arms control. Strategic stability, of course, is not just an American concern but an alliance concern. Stability means preventing war.

Sometimes you hear Soviet claims that the danger of war in Europe has been growing. That's nonsense. Since the late 1940s, Europe has faced on its doorstep the most heavily armed power on earth. Yet in a century that saw two European cataclysms in one generation, Europe has known unprecedented peace in the last four decades. The military balance in Europe is stable because the alliance has maintained the strength to deter attack. We have made clear that a threat to any of us is a threat to all of us. Any would-be aggressor knows in advance that an attack will fail.

The ultimate deterrent to any such threat has been, and continues to be, U.S. strategic forces. Therefore, the Soviet strategic buildup in recent years that threatened to upset the balance had to be met by an American program of strategic modernization. This is essential to Europe's security as well as to our own. For any Soviet perception of a decisive strategic advantage over the United States would only encourage the Soviets to think they had an intimidating advantage over Western Europe. A war might never take place. But European nations would surely find their confidence in American protection diminished, the shadow of Soviet power looming larger, and their control over their own sovereign destiny reduced.

The main danger to strategic stability has come from the Soviet advantage in heavy, accurate ICBMs [intercontinental ballistic missiles] with multiple warheads that could threaten the survival of the land-based portion of U.S. forces. This category of strategic weapons—this *offensive* threat—has been one of our central concerns in arms control for many years. These offensive weapons menace deterrence; these offensive weapons represent a serious imbalance; these offensive weapons pose the danger of surprise attack. Therefore, American proposals for arms control have emphasized radical, equitable, verifiable reductions in these strategically significant systems.

The Soviet response, until very recently, was to ignore the problem. Their most recent proposals now embrace our idea of radical reductions, though not adequately. Their main contribution to arms control was continual denunciation of the President's Strategic Defense Initiative (SDI)—a research program into potential defense systems that don't yet exist—while slighting the threat from menacing offensive weapons that already exist in excessive numbers.

SDI represents a conceptual leap into the future. If it proves feasible, it will enhance deterrence. It will supplement Western nuclear strategy with the prospect of being able to block or at least blunt an attack, reinforcing the traditional deterrence through retaliation; it will rest defense policy on a kind of mutual assured security instead of mutual assured destruction. The global system will be more stable if the U.S.-Soviet strategic relationship is more stable.

You have heard these points before. But I would stress here the relevance of SDI to Europe's security. First of all, if it proves feasible, it can blunt the threat of SS-20s and other missiles against Europe. It can only enhance the credibility of America's pledge to risk its own safety on behalf of yours. And a structure of deterrence *and* defense, coupled with radical offensive reductions, is likely to be the most stable environment of all, offering hope of a diminished danger of war into the next century.

The revolution in technology is already underway, and prudence clearly requires that we examine all new possibilities. Certainly the Soviets are doing so. Technology doesn't stop; history doesn't stop; the balance of power keeps changing its form. All of us who care about avoiding war and preserving peace must adapt our thinking to new conditions—especially when the new conditions offer a hopeful opportunity and a positive vision of a safer future.

Ideology and Regional Conflicts

The President and Mr. Gorbachev, as I noted earlier, spoke also about conflicts in the developing world that affect the stability of the international system.

It goes without saying that not all of these conflicts represent the division between East and West in miniature. But if there is any real danger of U.S.-Soviet confrontation, it is likely to originate in some crisis in the developing world—precisely because the central military balance in Europe is stable. Angola, Afghanistan, Nicaragua, Ethiopia, Cambodia—remember how these interventions fed the disillusionment with detente in the 1970s, disrupting the arms control process and shattering hopes for better East-West relations.

The problem of our time is to try to contain these regional conflicts—to help resolve them—and to understand what such a diplomacy requires in a turbulent world.

We live in an ideological age, when the international order is challenged by movements and passions that transcend national boundaries. Whatever theory one subscribes to about the true source of Soviet motivation—whether communist ideology or traditional Russian expansionism—it is not difficult to see the advantage to Soviet foreign policy of its alliance with radical movements throughout the developing world. Indeed, until the rise of revolutionary Islam, almost all of these radical forces were left-wing, claiming "socialist" aspirations and seeing the Soviet Union as a natural partner. And even revolutionary Islam shares with other radical forces a profound anti-Western impulse born of historical resentments, local social tensions, and a reflexive resort to force against the established order. This impulse clearly works to the geopolitical advantage of the Soviet Union—threatening moderate pro-Western governments, menacing the West's oil supply, spreading the evil of terrorism and the gospel of upheaval.

All of us in the West favor political solutions to such conflicts. We believe that peoples have a right to choose their own systems and their own leaders; that conflicts should be resolved whenever possible by negotiation and compromise; that a world of diversity and tolerance is a world compatible with our interests. We can live with any political solution that reflects the will of the parties and resolves their differences. Whether there is an important East-West dimension, as in the conflicts I have mentioned, or where there is less of an East-West dimension, as in the Arab-Israeli conflict, the United States adheres strongly to the view that negotiated political solutions represent the best hope for lasting peace. And this is our policy.

But it is important to understand what negotiated solutions depend upon. And here I want to address an issue that has been on my mind for some time, on which we and our European friends have occasionally had tactical differences. And that is the relation between power and diplomacy.

Negotiated solutions require two things. First, we, or the friends we support, must be willing to negotiate a fair solution. Whether we speak of Israel or our friends in Central America or in Africa or Southwest or Southeast Asia, we or our friends must pursue negotiation and compromise in good faith and with dedication. Such an attitude strengthens moderates on the other side, helps defuse radicalism, and offers hope for a solution.

But this is only half the story. Almost always, it is the willingness of the other side to negotiate that is far more problematic. And thus a firm policy on our part, or our friends' part, is usually a prerequisite for good-faith negotiation on the other side. Only when they see the futility of their military "solutions" and the resolve of opposing strength will real compromise become possible.

Occasionally, the immediate problem we face is, regrettably, openly military—a Soviet invasion of Afghanistan, a Vietnamese occupation of Cambodia, a massive Soviet and Cuban military intervention in Africa, a Nicaraguan attempt to subvert neighboring countries, and Cuban combatants using Soviet weapons in Nicaragua. Diplomacy is unlikely to work unless there is effective resistance. In many of these countries, there is resistance. It is a tribute to the courage of brave peoples who somehow never heard that communism is the wave of the future, peoples who reject the Brezhnev doctrine and its claims of permanence for communist tyranny.

What the West should do in these situations varies with the circumstances. Sometimes we should give military and economic assistance to neighboring states that are threatened; sometimes we should extend moral or humanitarian or other kinds of support to those resisting. Sometimes help may be better given without open acknowledgment; covert action has been part of the arsenal of states since time immemorial, providing a means of influence short of outright confrontation. We should be prudent, realistic, and always cognizant of the political dimension of the problem. Nevertheless, the factor of power is inescapable.

In the 1980s and beyond, most likely we will never see a world in a total state of peace—or a state of total war. The West is relatively well prepared to deter an all-out war, and we have to stay that way, or a Soviet attack on Western Europe or Japan; that's why these are the least likely contingencies. But day in and day out, we will continue to see a wide range of conflicts in a gray area between major war and millennial peace. Some of them—not all—will affect Western interests. Terrorism, particularly state-sponsored terrorism, is already a weapon increasingly resorted to by those seeking to undermine Western nations and friends of the West in the developing world. We must be equally well prepared and organized for this intermediate range of challenges.

We must recognize, as well, that we encourage moderate solutions not only by our own good faith but by denying success to those who seek radical solutions. In the Middle East, for example, the Arab world is divided: Moderates like Egypt and Jordan work actively for peace. But radicals oppose it. Sometimes it is said that the slowness of the peace process is a source of radicalism because it builds frustration. Partly true. But the violence comes from the enemies of peace, from those who would be more angry if the peace process were making rapid progress. These extremists must be resisted, not appeased. They must be shown that military options don't exist, that blackmail and pressures will get nowhere, and that negotiation is the only possible hope for achievement of legitimate Arab objectives.

We differ with some of our European friends over the role of the PLO [Palestine Liberation Organization]. To us it seems obvious that the PLO excludes itself as a player so long as it rejects UN Security Council Resolutions 242 and 338 and Israel's right to exist. Is the PLO becoming a more moderate organization? We shall see. Meanwhile, the PLO is not entitled to any payment in advance so long as it rejects what are, after all, the basic premises of the peace process. A country cannot be expected to make concessions to those who resort to terrorism and who treat negotiation as only a way-station on the road to its ultimate destruction. If PLO policy changes, that fact will be acknowledged. We have always said this. Unlike some of our European friends, however, we feel that gestures toward the PLO, while it has not accepted 242 and 338, only mislead its leaders into thinking their present inadequate policy is gaining them international acceptance and stature.

For diplomacy does not depend on good will alone; it does not depend on good intentions alone. Sometimes it depends on single-mindedness and will. In Lebanon two years ago, the Syrians, listening to the debate in the United States, concluded we were, in their words, "short of breath"; the rationale of our diplomacy—that the May 17 agreement was the way to bring Israeli withdrawal—was itself undercut when Israel pulled back.

Today, in Central America, by contrast, we do have staying power; it comes from bipartisan backing in the Congress for our program. In Central America, we are aiding moderates; we are supporting democratic governments like those of El Salvador, Costa Rica, and Honduras, with Guatemala about to form a civilian elected government—all threatened by Nicaragua. I might say that the role of the M-19 in its relationship to Nicaragua has been dramatized in the battle, in the Palace of Justice, in Colombia. So the threat of what Nicaragua supports is seen on a broader scale. Three-quarters of our aid to the region has been economic aid. We are supporting the Contadora process in pursuit of a diplomatic solution, and we are supporting the democratic opposition within Nicaragua, for they need our help to defend themselves against Soviet weapons and Cuban troops.

In the turbulent developing world, a balanced and realistic program of political objectives, leverage, and staying power—these are the ingredients of an effective diplomacy for global peace.

The Democratic Revolution

The course of regional conflict has required adjustments in our thinking about East-West relations and the developing world. But one of these adjustments is a happy one for the West: We must make room in our theories for the new vigor and vitality of the idea of democracy. As the battle rages between moderates and radicals in many regions of the globe, we should never underestimate the longing for peace or the new strength of the moderate center that rejects extremism of both right and left. This too is altering the global balance.

There was a time, not long ago, when it was fashionable to be pessimistic about the fate of democracy in the world at large. Democracy was thought to be culture-bound, a precious family heirloom of the industrialized West—with its prospects somewhat shaky even in parts of southern Europe. The developing world, in any case, seemed an inhospitable soil for democratic habits to take root. The massive social and economic problems that developing nations faced seemed to call for strong central authority; they could hardly afford the "luxury" of limited government; their passionate politics seemed ill-suited to constitutional restraints.

But today, it looks different. We should have known better. We have seen democracy flourish in non-European societies as diverse as Japan, India, and Costa Rica. And today in our own Western Hemisphere, we see the dramatic resurgence of domestic government after a long period of rule by military juntas and dictatorships. Over 90% of the people of Latin America now live under governments that are democratic or are in transition to democracy—in contrast to only one-third in 1979. In the last 6 years, elected civilian leaders have replaced authoritarian regimes in Argentina, Bolivia, Brazil, Ecuador, El Salvador, Grenada, Guatemala, Honduras, Peru, and Uruguay. In Brazil—as well as India—we have seen the tragic death of an elected leader followed by a peaceful constitutional transition to a new democratic leader. With all the problems that many of these countries have, this trend is an inspiring display of people's faith in themselves and of the power of the democratic ideal.

From the perspective of the United States, this means that a belief in democracy is not just a Wilsonian dream, or a naive crusade; it is a reflection of hard reality. Consider too the reemergence of human rights as a legitimate subject of international discourse—especially since the Helsinki Final Act 10 years ago.

As the Helsinki process reminds us, these are not only issues for the developing world but issues quite relevant to Europe—to the eastern half of Europe whose aspirations for freedom remain artificially suppressed.

I will be visiting Eastern Europe in a few days' time. We have all learned a great deal over the postwar period about both the opportunities and the limits of our influence in Eastern Europe. There is a new reality since Helsinki—an even more unmistakable yearning among these peoples for something better. This is a powerful force whose significance should never be underestimated.

Some day, the Soviet Union under wise leadership may learn that its own security needs can be met without suppressing the freedom of its neighbors. In the meantime, we do what we can to foster greater openness in these countries. We differentiate among them, and between them and the Soviet Union, to encourage more independent foreign policies, greater respect for human rights, and economic and social reforms. Governments that show such positive trends receive our reinforcing acknowledgment.

The Future: The Economic Dimension

Finally, I want to speak of another kind of revolution that is altering the world balance of forces—a reawakening of economic thought and a new era in the technology of communication.

The future of the world economy will do much to shape the world's political future—much more, indeed, than some conventional theorists of the balance of power may recognize. I say this not because of a Marxist belief in economic determinism, but because it is obvious that the basic conditions of life can affect the cohesion and goals of societies. In a world of nations less and less dominated by authoritarian structures and political elites, the basic needs of citizens will be all the more compelling in national policies. In the democratic world, growth is a key to social equity and also to societies' ability to look after essential defense needs; in times of slow growth, investment in defense always comes under budgetary strain. In the developing world, democratic or moderate governments are under stress as they struggle to overcome economic problems.

Economic problems are not new in history. What is new in recent history is the intellectual shift taking place about how to remedy these problems. Lord Keynes's point about practical men being in thrall to some defunct economist may be less true now than in the past. Or perhaps the wise perceptions of Adam Smith two centuries ago are once again gaining practical prominence. At any rate, reality is intruding on some long-held notions about economic policy.

There is a new skepticism about statist solutions, central planning, and government control. Perhaps the extraordinary vigor of the American recovery has made the point: 10 million new jobs created in 3 years, with low inflation and declining interest rates. We have much more work to do. We have to do something about our fiscal deficit. But we have revised our tax system to provide more incentives to work, to save, to invest, to be efficient, to take risks. We have reduced government regulation, intervention, and control. And we think it has paid off.

And this economic wisdom isn't culture-bound either. We see on every continent—Western Europe, East Asia, Latin America, and Africa—movement to decentralize, to deregulate, to denationalize, to reduce rigidities in labor markets, and to enlarge the scope for individual producers and consumers to interact freely in open markets. At the Bonn economic summit last May, the leaders of the industrial democracies stressed the importance of moving in that direction. This insight is revolutionizing agricultural productivity across the globe. It explains the extraordinary growth rates in noncommunist East and Southeast Asia, and it explains the extraordinary effort underway in China to liberate the creative energies of a billion talented people.

This reawakening in economic thinking itself coincides with a revolution in the technological base of the global economy. Microchip computers, advanced telecommunications, and an accelerating process of innovation are transforming the world we live in.

By no coincidence, this creativity is coming from the societies of the democratic world that let ideas, people, and capital resources flow freely across boundaries, that encourage entrepreneurship and experiment. These societies have grasped the plain fact that the source of economic vitality is individual creativity and not the state. The advance of these technologies is bound to challenge many traditional notions of sovereignty. But the West has the advantage because the free flow of information is intrinsic to our political system and principles.

The industrial age is coming to an end. The age when economic power was symbolized by the steel mill and the assembly line is passed. In some places, this age is completely over. The economy of the future will be based more and more on information technologies. And the flow of information requires freedom—freedom of thought and communication. Ideology has nothing to do with this: it's just a fact of life.

The communist rulers thus face an excruciating problem. They remember the power of the Ayatollah's message on tape cassettes in Iran; they fear the photocopying machine as a dangerous instrument to be kept under lock and key. The more they try to stifle these technologies, the more they are likely to fall behind in this movement from the industrial to the information age; but

59

the more they permit these new technologies, the more they risk their monopoly of control over information and communication. In the end, though, they don't really have a choice, because they cannot reverse the tide of technological advance.

Facing the Future

One of the great qualities of America, I think, is its readiness for change, its willingness—indeed, eagerness—to adapt to new conditions. But all the industrial democracies have the same advantages and the same opportunities. We are not *status-quo* powers holding the line against the forces of change: We are the pioneers of change, the champions of the idea of freedom, accustomed to innovating and adapting, strong enough to resist threats to our interests and ideals, and skilled at helping shape positive solutions to international problems.

That is why we can be confident about the future of the West. I do not envy Mr. Gorbachev and the challenge he faces in trying to defy the laws of economics and squeeze more productivity out of a system of imposed discipline and bureaucracy. He must come to realize that he must loosen up. And he will find, as he no doubt fears, that he has whetted the appetites of his people, and the diverse peoples of Eastern Europe, for more freedom. Change is certain.

The West will undoubtedly suffer setbacks. The democracies have not always met their responsibilities—either in deterring aggression or in managing their economies wisely. But we have a precious advantage. We draw strength from our freedom, from one another, and from the newly democratic nations that are joining our ranks inspired by our heritage.

Britain, and America, and all the free nations face an exhilarating challenge, and we are readier for it than many people realize.

2.5 ▰▰▰

ROBIN JENKINS

The Octopus: A Summary of the Relations Between Nations

... A symmetrical model of the world, one which assumes a similarity of interests between the powerful nations, each of which dominates a sphere of influence which together encompass the rest of the world, fails to stand up to empirical examination on any count.

From *Exploitation* (London: MacGibbon & Key), 1970, by Robin Jenkins. Reprinted by permission of the author.

The cold war was not a symmetrical arms race between the USA and the USSR but an attempt to dominate the world by the USA, which produced its reaction in the USSR. The poor nations are not uniformly exploited by the rich nations but by the rich capitalist nations. . . . The octopus in [the diagram] does not have eight equal tentacles; the spheres of influence of the five nuclear nations are only superficially similar. The GNP of the USA is forty per cent of the total GNP of all nations in the world. On top of this, United States' corporations own foreign interests equal to forty per cent of the gross domestic product of the USA. This means that at the very most conservative estimate, the United States owns well over half the world's realized wealth although it has only six per cent of the world's population—and it should be added that ac-cording to official US estimates, twenty-five per cent of its own population lives in poverty. The octopus has one extremely long and tenacious tentacle for a start. There are no similar statistics for Britain and France, but the highest estimate gives Britain as owning seven per cent of the world's realized wealth while France has rather over five per cent.[1] These are small tentacles by comparison and in addition, US capital is increasingly dominating the British economy, even if the French are managing to avoid large American take-overs for the time being.

Figure 2-1   The Octopus—A Model of the Politico-Economic Structure of the World

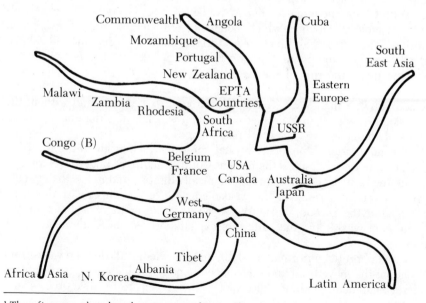

---

[1] These figures are based on the assumption that British and French owned interests abroad are not a higher percentage of their gross domestic product than forty per cent.

When it comes to the USSR, which, with its East European satellites, owns some fifteen per cent of the world's realized wealth, the tentacle has considerable shortcomings as an analogy. The legacy of Russian imperialism over the states of Asia still exists within the USSR, where wealth tends to accumulate in the Russian Republic to the detriment of the other members of the Union. In Eastern Europe, the USSR has played a more or less predatory role since the end of the Second World War, even to the extent of distorting the industrialized economies of Czechoslovakia and Eastern Germany to the production of goods for the USSR alone. As a result, Eastern Europe has been underdeveloped by the USSR, though this underdevelopment is on an entirely different level and scale from the underdevelopment of Latin America by the USA or the underdevelopment of Africa by all the rich capitalist nations combined. While the American tentacle is increasingly reaching out to every corner of the globe despite setbacks in Cuba and Vietnam, and the French and British tentacles are becoming more and more subservient to American capital, the USSR tentacle is in no way expansionist at present. Soviet investment in Cuba, or India or Pakistan, does not serve the same functions as US foreign investment and Cuba at least is of no economic benefit to the USSR, which buys its sugar at a guaranteed rate which is three times greater than the world market price. However, there is plenty of evidence that the USSR is slowly traversing the road back to some form of state capitalism and the very fact that the USSR gives aid to reactionary dictatorships like the Pakistani and Peruvian regimes is evidence of a potential for expansionist imperialism abroad.

With China, the tentacle analogy is plain wrong. The only state closely allied to China is Albania, which benefits from Chinese aid. The Tibetan invasion, which restored Tibet to its former status as a province of China, gained overwhelming popular support from the people who had been liberated from the theocratic rule of the Lamas.[2]

China accounts for some four per cent of the world's realized wealth, considerably less than West Germany, at around six per cent, and without the expansionist tendency of West German capital which is now dominating major sectors of the economy of several poor nations.

It is international monopoly capital, most of which originates in the USA, which creates and maintains the present world structure of underdevelopment. Despite the fact that colonialism has practically disappeared in less than twenty years—largely as a result of the weakened state of the imperialist European nations after the Second World War—the structure of the world system, the allocation of wealth and the pattern of exploitation remain fundamentally the same.

Capital, profits, information, skills, and knowledge all flow upwards from the nations that have been underdeveloped to nations which brought about that underdevelopment. The socialist bloc has escaped from this process and

---

[2] Since this article was written, Albania has ceased to be an ally of China. Ed.

becomes simply a residual category in world capitalism, at times emulating the more conspicuous and prestigious forms of wasting surplus in which the United States is the leading entrepreneur. Mankind's surplus value tends to end up in the United States because it is US capital that owns the major part of the world. Inside the United States, this surplus value is used (a) to maintain the system that produced it[3] and (b) to litter the moon and other solar bodies with plastic copies of the stars and stripes. In return for extracting the surplus from man's labour throughout the capitalist world,[4] the USA renames the oppressed nations and calls them "developing countries," exports models of development which emphasize the moral prerequisites for the accumulation of capital, like frugality and a need for achievement, and ignores the fundamental reasons for the division of the world into rich and poor. Some nations are poor because they lack the resources that are necessary to become rich, but for the majority of poor nations, this is not the case: they are poor because their surplus is expropriated. Some nations are rich because they have the resources that are necessary to become rich but for the majority of rich nations that is not the case either: they are rich because now or in the past, they were imperialist. . . .

Discussion Questions

1. At the beginning of this chapter, we note that the perspectives and attitudes of world political leaders are shaped by the historical events and experiences of their formative years. What historical events have influenced your worldview? In what way?

2. The principal actors in international politics are described and discussed in the introduction to this chapter. With which, if any, of these types of actors do you have any contact, involvement, membership, or influence? In what way, if at all, does that involvement link you to the world of international politics?

3. Based on your reading of this chapter, what do you believe will be the nation-state's role in the international system by the year 2050? The multinational corporation's role?

4. Several of the readings, and especially the Biersteker piece, describe the ways nations have come to influence or penetrate one another's internal affairs. What are the predominant types of such penetration today? Is there a pattern as to which states are involved? What are the positive and negative outcomes associated with such penetration?

---

[3] The 1969 US military budget amounted to more than £33,850,000,000, two-thirds the GNP of China.

[4] The capitalist world includes the third world, which is the economic appendage of the capitalist states.

For Further Reading

Classic Studies of the State System

Calvocoressi, Peter. *World Politics Since 1945.* 5th ed. London and White Plains, N.Y.: Longman, 1987. A widely used, concise history of the postwar world. It discusses changes and events on a region-by-region basis.

Herz, John H. *The Nation-State and the Crisis of World Politics.* New York: David McKay Company, 1976. A celebrated collection of essays in which Herz examines the implications for the nation-state system of modern developments in technology, power, and nuclear weapons.

Russett, Bruce M. *Trends in World Politics.* New York: Macmillan, 1969. A short survey of international affairs from the end of World War II through the late sixties. Although focusing on the Atlantic nations, this work also examines the global political economy and the role and future of international organizations generally.

Seton-Watson, Hugh. *Nations and States: An Enquiry into the Origins of Nations and the Politics of Nationalism.* Boulder, Colo.: Westview Press, 1977. A major study by a well-known British historian that examines the very different histories of nationalism, national development, and national identity and their contributions to today's international society.

Studies of Current International Relations

Annual Editions. *World Politics.* Guilford, Conn.: Dushkin Publishing Group. An annual collection of essays taken from the best foreign affairs and opinion journals, primarily U.S. publications. It is organized by topic—for example, human rights, terrorism, and U.S.-Soviet relations.

Brown, Lester R. *State of the World.* New York: W. W. Norton, 1987. Now issued annually by the Worldwatch Institute, this volume reports on the condition of the world in areas such as energy, food production and distribution, and population growth.

Kegley, Charles W., Jr., and Eugene R. Wittkopf, eds. *The Global Agenda: Issues and Perspectives.* 2d ed. New York: Random House, 1988. A collection of noteworthy essays that focus on issues such as arms and influence, discord and collaboration, politics and markets, and politics and ecology.

Kidron, Michael, and Ronald Segal. *The New State of the World Atlas.* New York: Simon & Schuster, 1984. A unique collection of full-color maps that depict the relative standing of nation-states on nearly sixty different variables, including indicators of economic, military, and environmental resources.

Spiegel, Steven L., ed. *At Issue: Politics in the World Arena.* 5th ed. New York: St. Martin's, 1988. A wide-ranging and popular collection of essays arranged by topic, this work examines such issues as the problems of revolutionary change in Central America and the crisis of international institutions.

DETERMINANTS OF DECISION MAKING 3

As we discussed in Chapter 1, the Peace of Westphalia (1648), which brought to a close the Thirty Years' War, also marked the beginning of the modern international system. In this system large geographic entities called nation-states are the primary political units.

A critical element in this system is the manner in which these nation-states conduct their international political affairs. The need to conduct a wise and effective foreign policy places a heavy burden upon political leaders. It is not surprising, then, that foreign policy decision making is an area in which controversies about events past and present abound.

Consider, for example, the following historical controversies:

☐ Why was Neville Chamberlain unwilling to challenge Hitler's early expansion into southeastern Europe?
☐ Why did Hitler renounce the nonaggression pact and make war on the Soviet Union in 1941?
☐ What influenced President Harry Truman to drop the first atomic bomb on Hiroshima? Or to drop a second bomb on Nagasaki?
☐ How were Nikita Khrushchev and John Kennedy able to resolve the Cuban missile crisis without starting World War III?

Or the following more recent controversies:

☐ What prompted Lyndon B. Johnson to continue U.S. involvement in the Vietnam War?
☐ Richard Nixon to forge détente with the Soviet Union?
☐ Jimmy Carter to advocate a great emphasis on human rights in the conduct of U.S. foreign policy?
☐ Ronald Reagan to bomb Libya in 1986?

In their efforts to address these perplexing questions, students of foreign policy have devoted much of their energy to examining the factors that influence the choices presidents and prime ministers ultimately make. These policy determinants include (1) the particular *perceptions* of the world that the leaders themselves bring to the task of decision making; (2) the manner in which the *process* of information gathering, goal setting, and discussing alternative policy options occurs; and (3) the *wider political environment* in which the decision is pondered and finally made.

In this chapter, we consider these policy determinants. We also examine the special dilemma of foreign policy decisions made during crises. Finally, we provide a set of readings that illustrate the roles played by perceptions, process, and the wider political environment in selected prominent foreign policy cases and in contemporary discussions of foreign policy.

Perceptions as Policy Determinants

For purposes of discussing foreign policy, we can define a *perception* as a mental image of how international affairs operates. National leaders make decisions on the basis of their perceptions of particular situations, rather than on the basis of some ascertainable or "objective" reality. Short of delving into a complex philosophical discussion about the nature of reality, we can say that those matters we call "the facts" and our interpretation of specific events that we label "reality" will often differ from the facts and reality as seen by others.

So it is with decision makers, each of whom is likely to employ a unique perceptual lens and thus to perceive a reality that differs in one or more critical ways from the perceptions of others. Like other individuals, decision makers perceive and assess the information and alternatives available to them on the basis of their own experiences and frameworks. These perceptions, experiences, and frameworks will, in turn, influence their decision making.

Although the content and structure of human perceptions is a controversial area of study within the social sciences, we can identify three dimensions of perception—the cognitive, the affective, and the evaluative—that are particularly relevant to an understanding of foreign policy.

The first of these is the *cognitive* dimension, which refers to how decision makers sort through, retain, and assimilate new information. This sorting, retention, and (especially) assimilation of new information is necessarily influenced by the context in which it occurs—namely, what the individual already knows and thus believes to be true.

Both history and social science theory suggest that foreign policy decision making is effective when decision makers' perceptions of the world evolve over time—in short, when decision makers are able to adjust their worldviews to take account of new information. Poor foreign policy decisions, on the other hand, are often the result of decision makers' inability or unwillingness to adjust their worldviews to new and changed circumstances. Such results are particularly likely when the new information involved contradicts the existing beliefs of the decision makers. Consider the following examples.

The 1962 Cuban missile crisis is generally thought to be an example of good foreign policy decision making. As the article by Graham T. Allison in this chapter points out, President Kennedy's actions during this crisis demonstrated that he had learned from his experience with the Bay of Pigs debacle. Thus, he was reasonably sure that the Soviet Union would be willing and able to back away from a confrontation if provided the opportunity to do so *and* that the Soviets would dismantle their missile sites if faced with a blockade. Further, he took possible Soviet reactions into account in rejecting an air strike as a policy option. He knew such an action would be too costly from the Soviet perspective, making it difficult for them to back down gracefully.

But history also contains examples of poor foreign policy decisions resulting from the cognitive rigidity of decision makers. The U.S. command in Hawaii in 1941, for example, realized that a military confrontation with Japan was imminent. But despite various indications to the contrary, they believed the confrontation would not occur while diplomatic negotiations were still underway and that it would not involve an attack on Pearl Harbor. Again, in 1951, despite various signals from the Chinese that they would intervene in Korea should UN forces under General Douglas MacArthur cross the 38th parallel, the UN (and U.S.) command failed to process these messages. Shortly thereafter MacArthur was confronted with a major Chinese counterattack on his overextended forces and the UN (and the United States) were involved in a fundamentally different and much larger conflict than the one that had sparked the UN intervention. Thirty years later, the Argentines would also dramatically misread British intentions concerning the Falklands, with the result being the Falklands/Malvinas war.

The second dimension of perception is the *affective* dimension, which refers to the basic values of the individual decision maker. In the context of foreign policy, the affective dimension comes into play when a decision maker forecloses various policy options that conflict with his or her basic values and moral sentiments—or interprets events unfolding on the international scene in light of these values. When different leaders advocate or pursue mutually exclusive foreign policies in a given area, each claiming steadfastly that their own policy reflects "the public good," neither leader is necessarily being deceitful. Rather, the explanation often lies in the affective domain, in fundamentally different sets of personal values.

The importance of the affective component of a leader's perceptions can be illustrated by the different values placed on human rights in the foreign policies of the Carter and Reagan administrations. Upon entering the White House in 1977, President Jimmy Carter advocated a greater emphasis on human rights in the conduct of U.S. foreign policy, especially with respect to foreign aid. This approach clearly reflected his own personal and deep commitment to improving human rights throughout the world. But Carter's view of human rights was far broader than that of many U.S. leaders who saw security issues as paramount. Thus, Carter chose to make the renegotiation of the Panama Canal treaty a cornerstone of U.S. Latin American policy, arguing that the ownership of resources located within a nation's own borders represented a fundamental human right.

Throughout the late 1970s, Carter continued to assert—in the face of slowly mounting criticism—that an active human rights stance was part of an effective foreign policy. When a number of authoritarian governments, although traditional supporters of U.S. policies and long-term recipients of U.S. aid, failed to respond to his urging for internal reform, he suspended foreign aid. Carter's rhetoric raised expectations, at home and abroad, that the United States' relationships with other nations would be determined in part by extent of the human rights abuse in those countries. Such a policy offered hope to victims of human rights abuses throughout the world.

Ultimately, however, Carter's policy proved difficult to implement when security interests were also at issue. Such was the case in the late 1970s, when the Shah's regime in Iran began to crumble and when Somoza's rule in Nicaragua was threatened. In both instances, the United States was forced to choose between abandoning long-time U.S. supporters and continuing to ignore their abuses of human rights. The choices proved difficult, but in the end security issues came to outweigh the president's human rights agenda with, it may be argued, unfortunate results.

President Ronald Reagan has had priorities markedly different from Carter's on human rights. As a presidential candidate, Reagan took the position that the major issues involved in the Panama Canal treaty process were those of U.S. nationalism and national security, rather than Panamanian human rights. Said Reagan, "We built it, we paid for it and we're not going to give it away."

In unveiling his human rights policy to the Congress early in his administration, the new president claimed there was no greater threat to individual human rights than the violent actions of international terrorists. Thus, a strong counterterrorist stance was the basis for a strong human rights policy. Secretary of State Alexander Haig further argued that because the Soviet Union both aided and benefited from terrorist activities against the Western democracies, a firm anti-Soviet policy would enhance human rights.

The differences in the affective dimensions of the Carter and Reagan perceptions may best be seen, however, in the criticisms of Carter's human rights policies by Reagan's ambassador to the United Nations, Jeane Kirkpatrick. Carter's values in the human rights area, Kirkpatrick argued, may have been correct, but he failed to recognize (1) those instances in which improvement in human rights could be expected to occur in the "normal" course of events—and thus no action was necessary, and (2) those instances in which an aggressive human rights posture weakened our friends and thus damaged U.S. security.

Left to their own devices, Kirkpatrick argued, authoritarian leaders can be expected to improve their performance on human rights issues. Suspending aid was unwise, because it made improvement in human rights more difficult and increased the vulnerability of these nations to subversion by their (and our) enemies. Carter should have taken the battle directly to the Soviet Union and other communist states that continually abuse such rights, according to Kirkpatrick.

The final perceptual dimension influencing foreign policy decision making is the *evaluative* dimension. Whereas the cognitive dimension deals with what the leader knows and the affective with what the leader values, the evaluative dimension is a measure of how the leader judges alternatives and policy priorities vis-à-vis one another. For example, although their methods have varied, American leaders since Truman have consistently evaluated national security policy options in terms of their likely effect on deterring potential Soviet aggression in Europe. And despite general agreement among most elites that barriers to international trade should be minimized, decision makers are nonetheless always wary of the potential cost of economic alliances designed to lower those barriers, especially if one of the costs involved is a potential increase in domestic unemployment.

In reaching these judgments, elites are often influenced by their cognition of past experience or events, such as the rise of Hitler or the bombing of Pearl Harbor. This combination of knowledge and judgment represents the cognitive dimension of their decision making. Their decisions also have an affective component in that they reflect the decision makers' basic values. Finally, the way elites evaluate the "lessons of history"—the evaluative dimension of their decisions—will also vary.

Three generalizations emerge from this examination of perception. First, the wider the parameters of the decision maker's cognitive perception, the more likely that wise and prudent foreign policy decisions will be made. Ideally, a leader's cognitive capacity and flexibility would continue to grow as new and different information about events and circumstances becomes available. Second, the influence of the affective or value component of the perceptions should not be underestimated. Foreign policy decision making often involves moral claims, and the decision maker's own values inevitably come into play in such cases, leading to forceful advocacy for particular actions. Finally, foreign affairs leaders evaluate the world in terms of predetermined goals and policy priorities, as well as in terms of what they know and value.

If too narrowly circumscribed or rigid, both the affective and evaluative dimensions of a leader's perception can result in a predisposition to prejudge possible foreign policy options. A political cartoon of a few years ago depicted a U.S. official behind a podium, obviously about to field questions from the reporters gathered in front of him. He begins by saying, "The answer is, 'More weapons.' Now what is the question?"

Process as a Determinant of Policy

The history of foreign affairs provides numerous examples of poor policies that resulted from inaccurate perceptions of international events. We also know that any single individual's perceptions, even those of government leaders, will be inadequate in some respects. In short, left to their own devices, individual decision makers may rightly feel less than prepared to make a wise, moral, and effective foreign policy decision.

Leaders often have surrounded themselves with advisers whom they believed to be "the best and the brightest." The logic of this practice rests, in part, on the notion that since individual perceptions differ, having access to a variety of opinions should help a decision maker avoid errors of perception. In matters as complex as foreign policy, too many cooks do not necessarily spoil the broth.

The manner in which advice is provided and the structural arrangements involved vary from nation to nation. Textbooks on American foreign policy are often filled with organizational charts illustrating how expert advice from the White House staff, the National Security Council (NSC), the State Department, and other foreign affairs agencies flows to the president. These organizational details matter because, as the Allison article in the readings illustrates, the substance and impact of an advisory group's recommendations may, in large part, be determined by the extent of the group's participation in the decision-making process.

There is a considerable and fascinating literature on this subject, and excerpts from two widely respected studies on this issue—by Allison and by Irving L. Janis—are included in the readings in this chapter. Among the most important generalizations about the effect of process on foreign policy decision making are the following:

1. Advisory groups involved in foreign policy decision making have a tendency to fall victim to *groupthink*, a condition in which groups engaged in a shared task fail to use their individual critical judgment to its fullest for fear of disturbing the good feeling and harmony within the group. In so doing, they build illusions for themselves about their world and themselves. This situation often isolates the leader from critical information and advice.

2. Leaders play a major role in structuring the decisional setting of their advisers. The more the leader seeks to "keep everyone on board, so no one rocks the boat," the more the individuals in the group will refuse to engage in critical questioning and dissent. The more the leader encourages a wide-ranging exploration of the issue in all its aspects (exercising what Janis calls "vigilance"), the more likely the group will be to air broad-ranging opinions.

3. Advisers and leaders, even when doing their best to avoid groupthink symptoms, may adopt a particular style of providing advice. Advisers may choose to reflect the point of view of their own staffs and agencies. Or advisers may assume the role of problem solvers and seek solutions as rational as possible. Or, finally, the advisory group may consider decision making a bargaining environment in which the best advice provided to a leader is a result of various compromises among alternative viewpoints and policy recommendations.

The Wider Political Environment
as a Determinant of Policy

A few years ago the political satirist Art Buchwald commented about the demise of the Carter administration's foreign policy emphasis on human rights, "I always suspected that the United States wouldn't stay with human rights too long. It never did play in Peoria."

Buchwald's remark illustrates a fundamental truism about foreign policy decision making: many foreign policy decisions are the result of domestic political considerations. Still others represent an effort to support other nations or, at the very least, to present a show of support on shared concerns. These factors external to the immediate context of a particular decision make up the wider political environment that affects foreign policy decision making.

In many democracies, the ongoing examination of public satisfaction with and support for foreign policy has become a major industry. Two decades ago the Gallup organization and major newspaper pollsters kept Americans abreast of the "popularity" of the Vietnam War, and especially of the president, Lyndon B. Johnson, who presided over the war's progress. More recently, the Watergate scandal during Nixon's presidency, the Iran hostage crisis late in the Carter administration, and the Iran-contra scandal during the presidency of Ronald Reagan all affected presidential power and prestige. In each case, the loss of public confidence in the president appears to have narrowed what each believed he could attempt and what he, in fact, did attempt in subsequent situations.

Watergate had an adverse effect on détente and slowed the pace of the Strategic Arms Limitation Talks (SALT) with the Soviets. The plight of the Tehran hostages during the last year of the Carter presidency came to overshadow virtually all other foreign policy issues. Although the significance of the Iran-contra scandal is still unfolding as of this writing, historical experience suggests that it will weaken domestic support for other Reagan administration initiatives.

The impact of domestic politics on foreign policy is not confined to the United States or even to democracies. In less open societies, such as the Soviet Union, foreign policy also has a marked domestic content. Constraints or opportunities at home influence a leader's choices in the international arena. This is precisely the situation that General Secretary Mikhail Gorbachev faced in early 1987 as he undertook *glasnost,* or an "opening" of political expression in the Soviet Union. This initiative, as well as his proposed political and economic reforms, *perestroika,* were criticized by some Soviet officials. But in achieving a major agreement with the United States to eliminate intermediate-range nuclear missiles in Europe, the Soviet leader produced a foreign policy victory that silenced, at least temporarily, his domestic critics.

Facing its own political crisis in 1986-1987, the Reagan administration also appeared much more willing to seek an arms accord with the Soviets than in its first six years in office. This odd combination of factors meant that by early 1987 both national leaders "needed" an arms agreement. Thus, the desire to enhance their domestic political support pushed Reagan and Gorbachev to make greater efforts on arms control than they otherwise might have.

The relationship between domestic politics and foreign policy is, in fact, often most obvious when political leaders are faced with dwindling domestic support. At such times, they often find it convenient to divert the public's attention from domestic difficulties by focusing on international events. This seems to have been precisely the type of thinking that motivated the Argentine government when, confronted with severe domestic economic and political difficulties, it undertook the actions that led to the 1982 Falklands/Malvinas war with the United Kingdom. Of course such a strategy need not always result in war. Always, however, the objectives are to reduce the level of domestic dissent, enhance the government's popularity, and unify the nation against an unpopular enemy.

The environment of foreign policy decision making has a nondomestic component as well. Some policies, however much they may advance the "national interest," are politically unacceptable because of their impact on respected friends and allies. Allison's account of National Security Council discussions during the Cuban missile crisis makes it clear that U.S. policy makers ruled out some actions because of such constraints. Similarly, Secretary of State George P. Shultz, in the policy statement in this chapter, notes that decision makers' expectations of how other nations will interpret a given action is a continuing constraint on policy making.

As the international political environment has changed since World War II, so too have the opportunities and constraints it places on foreign policy decision makers. In fact, the nature of the entire international system has been considerably altered, as we saw in Chapter 2, by a marked increase in both the number of nations and an increasingly diverse set of nonstate actors. In addition, the norms governing the use of force have liberalized considerably in recent years. In the decade immediately after World War II, states were extremely self-conscious about the use of force, and there was considerable pressure to submit disputes to international organizations for mediation or adjudication. This disinclination to use force had substantially eroded by the 1970s, when the prevailing ethos favored unilateral action as a means for settling differences (see Chapters 9 and 10).

That a leader's reading of the domestic and international political environment is critical to successful foreign policy action ought to be apparent. The link between a decision maker's perceptions and his or her view of the environment also becomes clear. The mutually interactive nature of perception, the decision-making process, and the wider context or environment of that process makes foreign policy decision making an especially difficult enterprise. It also explains why the decision-making nexus has been subjected to such intense scrutiny by scholars and policy makers alike.

Decision Making in Times of Crisis

Thus far in this chapter we have discussed the major determinants of foreign policy decision making. Whether a policy maker is engaged in routine decisions, such as signing a trade bill or appointing an ambassador, or reacting to an act of war, the leader's perceptions, the structure of the decisional process, and the wider political environment play a role in shaping the final decision.

If foreign policy decision making is inherently difficult, it is even more so during times of crisis. A foreign policy *crisis* may be said to exist when the issue at hand is very important to the nation, the decision time is perceived as short, and the issues involved place foreign policy elites under unusually great pressure. It is under such circumstances that the phenomenon of groupthink described by Janis is most likely to arise and to impair the critical judgment of decision makers.

If a crisis is by definition a special type of situation, one that places unusual pressure on decision makers and the decision-making process, then it follows that crises tend to be associated with certain kinds of behavior not typical of "normal" situations. In fact, the literature on international crisis is one of the richest literatures in international relations. Some of the more interesting findings in that literature may be summarized as follows:

1. In crises, decision makers tend to perceive their own range of choices as narrow (and narrowing over time) but those of their opponents as much broader (and widening over time).
2. Although decision makers under crisis do not necessarily narrow their own alternatives, they tend to choose poorly among alternatives compared to their performance in noncrisis situations.
3. In crises, leaders tend to create new, ad hoc committees as part of the foreign policy decision-making structure.
4. In crises, decision makers tend to appeal more readily to the inherent morality of their own position and to view their opponent's position as immoral.
5. As stress in crises increases, decision makers reduce their search for more information from the external environment and from advisers.
6. As stress in crises increases, decision makers focus more on immediate issues, questions, and goals than on longer-term or broader issues and goals.
7. The more prolonged the crisis, the greater the anxiety about the quality of information received.

All of these findings suggest the tension and uncertainty associated with crisis decision making. And the history of crises, as well as the experience of more routine foreign policy making, verifies the role of perceptions, process, and the wider environment as major determinants of decision making.

The Readings

In choosing the reading selections in this chapter, we have paid particular attention to the concepts and themes developed in this chapter introduction. Our first selection is an influential article by Robert Jervis entitled "Hypotheses on Misperception." Jervis, the premier analyst of the psychological aspects of perception in foreign policy making discusses the factors that influence what goes on in "the heads" of elites as they grapple with the demands of foreign policy making. In the second article, by Ole R. Holsti, Robert C. North, and Richard A. Brody, we see the processes described by Jervis at work in a case study of World War I. This classic study also demonstrates the importance of perceptions and misperceptions as causes of war.

Whereas Jervis provides the theory, and the outbreak of World War I the illustration of the importance of perceptions to foreign policy making under crisis, the next two pieces discuss methods for averting a foreign policy debacle in response to crisis. The article by social psychologist Irving L. Janis describes the phenomenon of groupthink, summarizes the conditions under which it develops, and suggests how the advisory process can be structured so as to limit its impact. The Janis piece is followed by Allison's study of the Cuban missile crisis. Among other things, the Allison article explains how groupthink was successfully avoided by President Kennedy and his advisers.

We conclude our readings section with two policy excerpts, "Moralism and Realism" by George Shultz and "Losing Moral Ground" by Richard Barnet. These two pieces present directly contrasting perspectives on foreign policy. Together they illustrate the manner in which different perceptions of the external environment influence a decision maker's perceptions of the available options. More important, the pieces embody contrasting perspectives and distinctive value frameworks from which to view international affairs.

ROBERT JERVIS

Hypotheses on Misperception

In determining how he will behave, an actor must try to predict how many others will act and how their actions will affect his values. The actor must therefore develop an image of others and of their intentions. This image may, however, turn out to be an inaccurate one; the actor may, for a number of reasons, misperceive both others' actions and their intentions. In this research note I wish to discuss the types of misperceptions of other states' intentions which states tend to make. The concept of intention is complex, but here we can consider it to comprise the ways in which the state feels it will act in a wide range of future contingencies. These ways of acting usually are not specific and well-developed plans. For many reasons a national or individual actor may not know how he will act under given conditions, but this problem cannot be dealt with here. . . .

The evidence from both psychology and history overwhelmingly supports the view (which may be labeled Hypothesis 1) that decision-makers tend to fit incoming information into their existing theories and images. Indeed, their theories and images play a large part in determining what they notice. In other words, actors tend to perceive what they expect. Furthermore (Hypothesis 1a), a theory will have greater impact on an actor's interpretation of data (a) the greater the ambiguity of the data and (b) the higher the degree of confidence with which the actor holds the theory.

For many purposes we can use the concept of differing levels of perceptual thresholds to deal with the fact that it takes more, and more unambiguous, information for an actor to recognize an unexpected phenomenon than an expected one. An experiment by [Jerome] Bruner and [Leo] Postman determined "that the recognition threshold for . . . incongruous playing cards (those with suits and color reversed) is significantly higher than the threshold of normal cards." Not only are people able to identify normal (and therefore expected) cards more quickly and easily than incongruous (and therefore unexpected) ones, but also they may at first take incongruous cards for normal ones. . . .

The question of the relations among particular beliefs and cognitions can often be seen as part of the general topic of the relation of incoming bits of information to the receivers' already established images. The need to fit data into a wider framework of beliefs, even if doing so does not seem to do justice to individual facts, is not, or at least is not only, a psychological drive that decreases the accuracy of our perceptions of the world, but is "essential to the logic of inquiry." . . .

Hypothesis 2: scholars and decision-makers are apt to err by being too wedded to the established view and too closed to new information, as opposed to being too willing to alter their theories. Another way of making this point is to argue that actors tend to establish their theories and expectations prematurely. In politics, of course, this is often necessary because of the need for action. But experimental evidence indicates that the same tendency also occurs on the unconscious level. . . .

. . . Scholars have often been too unsympathetic with the people who were proved wrong. On closer examination, it is frequently difficult to point to differences between those who were right and those who were wrong with respect to their openness to new information and willingness to modify their views. Winston Churchill, for example, did not open-mindedly view each Nazi action to see if the explanations provided by the appeasers accounted for the data better than his own beliefs. Instead, like Chamberlain, he fitted each bit of ambiguous information into his own hypotheses. That he was correct should not lead us to overlook the fact that his methods of analysis and use of theory to produce cognitive consistency did not basically differ from those of the appeasers.

A consideration of the importance of expectations in influencing perception also indicates that the widespread belief in the prevalence of "wishful thinking" may be incorrect, or at least may be based on inadequate data. The psychological literature on the interaction between affect and perception is immense and cannot be treated here, but it should be noted that phenomena that at first were considered strong evidence for the impact of affect on perception often can be better treated as demonstrating the influence of expectations. Thus, in international relations, cases like the United States' misestimation of the political climate in Cuba in April 1961, which may seem at first glance to have been instances of wishful thinking, may instead be more adequately explained by the theories held by the decision-makers (e.g., Communist governments are unpopular). Of course, desires may have an impact on perception by influencing expectations, but since so many other factors affect expectations, the net influence of desires may not be great.

There is evidence from both psychology and international relations that when expectations and desires clash, expectations seem to be more important. The United States would like to believe that North Vietnam is about to negotiate or that the USSR is ready to give up what the United States believes is its goal of world domination, but ambiguous evidence is seen to confirm the opposite conclusion, which conforms to the United States' expectations. Actors are apt to be especially sensitive to evidence of grave danger if they think they can take action to protect themselves against the menace once it has been detected. . . .

An actor's perceptual thresholds—and thus the images that ambiguous information is apt to produce—are influenced by what he has experienced and learned about. If one actor is to perceive that another fits in a given category he must first have, or develop, a concept for that category. . . .

Three main sources contribute to decision-makers' concepts of international relations and of other states and influence the level of their perceptual thresholds for various phenomena. First, an actor's beliefs about his own domestic political system are apt to be important. In some cases, like that of the USSR, the decision-makers' concepts are tied to an ideology that explicitly provides a frame of reference for viewing foreign affairs. Even where this is not the case, experience with his own system will partly determine what the actor is familiar with and what he is apt to perceive in others. Louis Hartz claims, "It is the absence of the experience of social revolution which is at the heart of the whole American dilemma. . . . In a whole series of specific ways it enters into our difficulty of communication with the rest of the world. We find it difficult to understand Europe's 'social question'. . . . We are not familiar with the deeper social struggles of Asia and hence tend to interpret even reactionary regimes as 'democratic.'" Similarly, George Kennan argues that in World War I the Allied powers, and especially America, could not understand the bitterness and violence of others' internal conflicts: ". . . The inability of the Allied statesmen to picture to themselves the passions of the Russian civil war [was partly caused by the fact that] we represent . . . a society in which the manifestations of evil have been carefully buried and sublimated in the social behavior of people, as in their very consciousness. For this reason, probably, despite our widely traveled and outwardly cosmopolitan lives, the mainsprings of political behavior in such a country as Russia tend to remain concealed from our vision."

Second, concepts will be supplied by the actor's previous experiences. An experiment from another field illustrates this. [DeWitt] Dearborn and [Herbert] Simon presented business executives from various divisions (e.g., sales, accounting, production) with the same hypothetical data and asked them for an analysis and recommendations from the standpoint of what would be best for the company as a whole. The executives' views heavily reflected their departmental perspectives. William W. Kaufmann shows how the perceptions of Ambassador Joseph Kennedy were affected by his past: "As befitted a former chairman of the Securities Exchange and Maritime Commissions, his primary interest lay in economic matters. . . . The revolutionary character of the Nazi regime was not a phenomenon that he could easily grasp. . . . It was far simpler, and more in accord with his own premises, to explain German aggressiveness in economic terms. The Third Reich was dissatisfied, authoritarian, and expansive largely because her economy was unsound." Similarly it has been argued that Chamberlain was slow to recognize Hitler's intentions partly because of the limiting nature of his personal background and business experiences. The impact of training and experience seems to be demonstrated when the background of the appeasers is compared to that of their opponents. One difference stands out: "A substantially higher percentage of the anti-appeasers (irrespective of class origins) had the kind of knowledge which comes from close acquaintance, mainly professional, with foreign affairs." Since members of the diplomatic corps are responsible for meeting threats to the nation's security before these grow to major proportions and since they have learned about cases in which aggressive states were not recognized as such until very late, they may be prone to interpret ambiguous data as showing that others are aggressive. It should be stressed that we cannot say that the professionals of the 1930's were more apt to make accurate judgments of other states. Rather, they may have been more sensitive to the chance that others were aggressive. They would then rarely take an aggressor for a status-quo power, but would more often make the opposite error. Thus in the years before World War I the permanent officials in the British Foreign Office overestimated German aggressiveness. . . .

A third source of concepts, which frequently will be the most directly relevant to a decision-maker's perception of international relations, is international history. As Henry Kissinger points out, one reason why statesmen were so slow to recognize the threat posed by Napoleon was that previous events had accustomed them only to actors who wanted to modify the existing system, not overthrow it. The other side of the coin is even more striking: historical traumas can heavily influence future perceptions. They can either establish a state's image of the other state involved or can be used as analogies. An example of the former case is provided by the fact that for at least ten years after the Franco-Prussian War most of Europe's statesmen felt that Bismarck had aggressive plans when in fact his main goal was to protect the status quo. Of course the evidence was ambiguous. The post-1871 Bismarckian maneuvers, which were designed to keep peace, looked not unlike the pre-1871 maneuvers designed to set the stage for war. But that the post-1871 maneuvers were seen as indicating aggressive plans is largely attributable to the impact of Bismarck's earliest actions on the statemen's image of him.

A state's previous unfortunate experience with a type of danger can sensitize it to other examples of that danger. While this sensitivity may lead the state to avoid the mistake it committed in the past, it may also lead it mistakenly to believe that the present situation is like the past one. Santayana's maxim could be turned around: "Those who remember the past are condemned to make the opposite mistakes." As Paul Kecskemeti shows, both defenders and critics of the unconditional surrender plan of the Second World War thought in terms of the conditions of World War I. Annette Baker Fox found that the Scandinavian countries' neutrality policies in World War II were strongly influenced by their experiences in the previous war, even though vital aspects of the two situations were different. Thus "Norway's success [during the First World War] in remaining non-belligerent though pro-Allied gave the Norwegians confidence that their country could again stay out of war." And the lesson drawn from the unfortunate results of this policy was an important fact in Norway's decision to join NATO.

The application of the Munich analogy to various contemporary events has been much commented on, and I do not wish to argue the substantive points at stake. But it seems clear that the probabilities that any state is facing an aggressor who has to be met by force are not altered by the career of Hitler and the history of the 1930's. Similarly the probability of an aggressor's announcing his plans is not increased (if anything, it is decreased) by the fact that Hitler wrote *Mein Kampf.* Yet decision-makers are more sensitive to these possibilities, and thus more apt to perceive ambiguous evidence as indicating they apply to a given case, than they would have been had there been no Nazi Germany.

Historical analogies often precede, rather than follow, a careful analysis of a situation (e.g., Truman's initial reaction to the news of the invasion of South Korea was to think of the Japanese invasion of Manchuria). Noting this precedence, however, does not show us which of many analogies will come to a decision-maker's mind. . . .

The way people perceive data is influenced not only by their cognitive structure and theories about other actors but also by what they are concerned with at the time they receive the information. Information is evaluated in light of the small part of the person's memory that is presently active—the "evoked set." My perceptions of the dark streets I pass walking home from the movies will be different if the film I saw had dealt with spies than if it had been a comedy. If I am working on aiding a country's education system and I hear someone talk about the need for economic development in that state, I am apt to think he is concerned with education, whereas if I had been working on, say, trying to achieve political stability in that country, I would have placed his remarks in that framework.

Thus Hypothesis 5 states that when messages are sent from a different background of concerns and information than is possessed by the receiver, misunderstanding is likely. Person A and person B will read the same message quite differently if A has seen several related messages that B does not know about. The difference will be compounded if, as is frequently the case, A and B each assume that the other has the same background he does. This means that misperception can occur even when deception is neither intended nor expected. Thus Roberta Wohlstetter found not only that different parts of the United States government had different perceptions of data about Japan's intentions and messages partly because they saw the incoming information in very different contexts, but also that officers in the field misunderstood warnings from Washington: "Washington advised General Short [in Pearl Harbor] on November 27 to expect 'hostile action' at any moment, by which it meant 'attack on American possessions from without,' but General Short understood this phrase to mean 'sabotage.'" Washington did not realize the extent to which Pearl Harbor considered the danger of sabotage to be primary, and furthermore it incorrectly believed that General Short had received the intercepts of the secret Japanese diplomatic messages available in Washington which indicated that surprise attack was a distinct possibility. Another implication of this hypothesis is that if important information is known to only part of the government of state A and part of the government of state B, international messages may be misunderstood by those parts of the receiver's government that do not match, in the information they have, the part of the sender's government that dispatched the message. . . .

From the perspective of the perceiver several other hypotheses seem to hold. Hypothesis 8 is that there is an overall tendency for decision-makers to see other states as more hostile than they are. There seem to be more cases of statesmen incorrectly believing others are planning major acts against their interest than of statesmen being lulled by a potential aggressor. There are many reasons for this which are too complex to be treated here (e.g., some parts of the bureaucracy feel it is their responsibility to be suspicious of all other states; decision-makers often feel they are "playing it safe" to believe and act as though the other state were hostile in questionable cases; and often, when people do not feel they are a threat to others, they find it difficult to believe that others may see them as a threat). It should be noted, however, that decision-makers whose perceptions are described by this hypothesis would not necessarily further their own values by trying to correct for this tendency. The values of possible outcomes as well as their probabilities must be considered, and it may be that the probability of an unnecessary arms-tension cycle arising out of misperceptions, multiplied by the costs of such a cycle, may seem less to decision-makers than the probability of incorrectly believing another state is friendly, multiplied by the costs of this eventuality.

Hypothesis 9 states that actors tend to see the behavior of others as more centralized, disciplined, and coordinated than it is. This hypothesis holds true in related ways. Frequently, too many complex events are squeezed into a perceived pattern. Actors are hesitant to admit or even see that particular incidents cannot be explained by their theories. Those events not caused by factors that are important parts of the perceiver's image are often seen as though they were. Further, actors see others as more internally united than they in fact are and generally overestimate the degree to which others are following a coherent policy. The degree to which the other side's policies are the product of internal bargaining, internal misunderstandings, or subordinates' not following instructions is underestimated. This is the case partly because actors tend to be unfamiliar with the details of another state's policy-making processes. Seeing only the finished product, they find it simpler to try to construct a rational explanation for the policies, even though they know that such an analysis could not explain their own policies.

Familiarity also accounts for Hypothesis 10: because a state gets most of its information about the other state's policies from the other's foreign office, it tends to take the foreign office's position for the stand of the other government as a whole. In many cases this perception will be an accurate one, but when the other government is divided or when the other foreign office is acting without specific authorization, misperception may result. For example, part of the reason why in 1918 Allied governments incorrectly thought "that the Japanese were preparing to take action [in Siberia], if need be, with agreement with the British and French alone, disregarding the absence of American consent," was that Allied ambassadors had talked mostly with Foreign Minister Motono, who was among the minority of the Japanese favoring this policy. Similarly, America's NATO allies may have gained an inaccurate picture of the degree to which the American government was committed to the MLF because they had greatest contact with parts of the government that strongly favored the MLF. And states that tried to get information about Nazi foreign policy from German diplomats were often misled because these officials were generally ignorant of or out of sympathy with Hitler's plans. The Germans and the Japanese sometimes purposely misinformed their own ambassadors in order to deceive their enemies more effectively.

Hypothesis 11 states that actors tend to overestimate the degree to which others are acting in response to what they themselves do when the others behave in accordance with the actor's desires; but when the behavior of the other is undesired, it is usually seen as derived from internal forces. If the *effect* of another's action is to injure or threaten the first side, the first side is apt to believe that such was the other's *purpose*. An example of the first part of the hypothesis is provided by Kennan's account of the activities of official and unofficial American representatives who protested to the new Bolshevik government against several of its actions. When the Soviets changed their position, these representatives felt it was largely because of their influence. This sort of interpretation can be explained not only by the fact that it is gratifying to the individual making it, but also, taking the other side of the coin mentioned in Hypothesis 9, by the fact that the actor is most familiar with his own input into the other's decision and has less knowledge of other influences. The second part of Hypothesis 11 is illustrated by the tendency of actors to believe that the hostile behavior of others is to be explained by the other side's motives and not by its reaction to the first side. Thus Chamberlain did not see that Hitler's behavior was related in part to his belief that the British were weak. More common is the failure to see that the other side is reacting out of fear of the first side, which can lead to self-fulfilling prophecies and spirals of misperception and hostility.

This difficulty is often compounded by an implication of Hypothesis 12: when actors have intentions that they do not try to conceal from others, they tend to assume that others accurately perceive these intentions. Only rarely do they believe that others may be reacting to a much less favorable image of themselves than they think they are projecting.

For state A to understand how state B perceives A's policy is often difficult because such understanding may involve a conflict with A's image of itself. Raymond Sontag argues that Anglo-German relations before World War I deteriorated partly because "the British did not like to think of themselves as selfish, or unwilling to tolerate 'legitimate' German expansion. The Germans did not like to think of themselves as aggressive, or unwilling to recognize 'legitimate' British vested interest."

Hypothesis 13 suggests that if it is hard for an actor to believe the other can see him as a menace, it is often even harder for him to see that issues important to him are not important to others. While he may know that another actor is on an opposing team, it may be more difficult for him to realize that the other is playing an entirely different game. This is especially true when the game he is playing seems vital to him.

The final hypothesis, Hypothesis 14, is as follows: actors tend to overlook the fact that evidence consistent with their theories may also be consistent with other views. When choosing between two theories we have to pay attention only to data that cannot be accounted for by one of the theories. But it is common to find people claiming as proof of their theories data that could also support alternative views. This phenomenon is related to the point made earlier that any single bit of information can be interpreted only within a framework of hypotheses and theories. And while it is true that "we may without a vicious circularity accept some datum as a fact because it conforms to the very law for which it counts as another confirming instance, and reject an allegation of fact because it is already excluded by law," we should be careful lest we forget that a piece of information seems in many cases to confirm a certain hypothesis only because we already believe that hypothesis to be correct and that the information can with as much validity support a different hypothesis. For example, one of the reasons why the German attack on Norway took both that country and England by surprise, even though they had detected German ships moving toward Norway, was that they expected not an attack but an attempt by the Germans to break through the British blockade and reach the Atlantic. The initial course of the ships was consistent with either plan, but the British and Norwegians took this course to mean that their predictions were being borne out. This is not to imply that the interpretation made was foolish, but only that the decision-makers should have been aware that the evidence was also consistent with an invasion and should have had a bit less confidence in their views.

The longer the ships would have to travel the same route whether they were going to one or another of two destinations, the more information would be needed to determine their plans. Taken as a metaphor, this incident applies generally to the treatment of evidence. Thus as long as Hitler made demands for control only of ethnically German areas, his actions could be explained either by the hypothesis that he had unlimited ambitions or by the hypothesis that he wanted to unite all the Germans. But actions against non-Germans (e.g., the takeover of Czechoslovakia in March 1938) could not be accounted for by the latter hypothesis. And it was this action that convinced the appeasers that Hitler had to be stopped. It is interesting to speculate on what the British reaction would have been had Hitler left Czechoslovakia alone for a while and instead made demands on Poland similar to those he eventually made in the summer of 1939. The two paths would then still not have diverged, and further misperception could have occurred.

 **3.2**

OLE R. HOLSTI
ROBERT C. NORTH
RICHARD A. BRODY

Perception and Action in the 1914 Crisis

Introduction

The Archduke Francis Ferdinand, heir apparent to the throne of Austria-Hungary, was assassinated June 28, 1914, in Sarajevo by a young Serbian nationalist. Within a week, imperial Germany had promised "blank check" support of the Vienna government in its policy to punish Serbia for the crime. On July 23 the Austro-Hungarians presented Serbia with an ultimatum, and five days later Vienna declared war against its neighbor. On July 29, the day following the declaration of war, imperial Russia—acting to support a small, fellow Slav nation and to "deter" Austria-Hungary—ordered and then cancelled a general mobilization. Efforts were made to shape a mobilization clearly directed against Austria-Hungary, but technical difficulties of communication intervened, and on July 30, St. Petersburg reversed its decision in favor of general mobilization—in spite of German warnings and misgivings. The Berlin government then proclaimed a "state of threatening danger of war" on July 31 and dispatched to St. Petersburg a twelve-hour ultimatum demanding a cessation of Russian preparations on the German frontier. On the following day Germany ordered mobilization, and at 7:00 P.M. declared war on Russia, which had not replied to Berlin's ultimatum.

Foreseeing a two-front war, in the east with Russia and in the west with France, the Berlin government tried to gain an initial advantage by invading Luxembourg and demanding permission of Belgium to cross Belgian territory. On August 3, Germany declared war against France, and the following day Great Britain declared war against Germany. Within three weeks what began as a local Balkan dispute—a "limited" war—had exploded into a major

Reprinted with permission of The Free Press, a division of Macmillan, Inc. from *Quantitative International Politics*, J. David Singer, Editor. Copyright © 1968 by The Free Press.

European war, and in the years that followed a large part of the world became involved. When the fighting finally stopped in the latter part of 1918, the Austro-Hungarian Empire was in dissolution and imperial Germany was on the edge of collapse. Essentially, then, two wars began in the summer of 1914: a war between Austria-Hungary and Serbia, which most European statesmen of the time hoped to keep localized, and a major "world war," which escalated from the smaller conflict in spite of universal intentions to the contrary.

What purpose if any, can be served by a re-examination of a situation that, from at least some perspectives, can be considered a part of "ancient"— that is, pre-nuclear—history? What relevance does such a historical crisis have for the present? Clearly the circumstances are different, the nations and leaders are different, and the weapons are different. Why dig into the half-forgotten past?

Like many historical situations, the events culminating in World War I have been studied for a multitude of purposes. Early studies were largely characterized by single-minded searches for a culprit or culprits upon whom to lay full blame for the war. Among the most important of these were the analyses made by Lenin and Hitler, each of whom was using history in order to support the necessity for activist political movements. Whatever the shortcomings of their analyses in terms of scientific objectivity and rigor, their practical effect cannot be denied; our present world has been shaped in large part by the movements led by Lenin and Hitler.

As archives containing the documentary evidence were opened and the passions aroused by the war subsided, historians searching for scapegoats were largely superseded by scholars who were more concerned with determining "what really happened" rather than "who was to blame." Here the work of Sydney B. Fay (1928) and Luigi Albertini (1953) stands out.

More recently the events of 1914 have been re-examined with the purpose of discovering possible recurring patterns of decision-making behavior in crisis (Abel, 1941; Russett, 1962). These social science approaches to historical situations are based upon the fundamental assumption that there are patterns, repetitions, and close analogies throughout the history of human affairs. The circumstances and paraphernalia will differ between the Peloponnesian War and World War II, but the patterns of human fears and anxieties and perceptions of threat and injury may not be dissimilar. A fundamental part of the problem lies in identifying the levels of abstraction at which problems or events that are widely separated in time and space are found to be similar.

There are important advantages in using historical situations for this kind of research. With the whole sweep of human history to choose from, the scholar can select situations where the archives are open and documentation is relatively complete and illuminating. Clearly, in view of security restrictions, it is impossible to obtain materials of this quality in a more contemporary situation. Attempts at developing a theory of international behavior will almost of necessity, then, depend on the examination of historical evidence.

Beyond this, historical situations offer the advantages of an algebra book with the answers in the back. A scholar thus enjoys the possibility of working at a problem—even making a "prediction"—and comparing his "answer" with the way things really turned out. In this way he can compare in most minute detail what statesmen have said with what they have actually done—and determine what perceptions have shaped their decisions.

History provides the sole key we have into the future: "The only way to judge what will happen in the future is by what has happened in the past" (Horst, 1963). Wisdom about the present and future is derived wholly from what we have experienced—or learned about—in the past. It is by comparing new problems with old experiences, by looking for similarities and differences, that we move into the future. "Other things being equal, the more frequently things have happened in the past, the more sure you can be they will happen in the future" (*ibid.*). As human beings without occult pre-vision, we have no other way of assessing, judging, and deciding.

Essentially, then, it is by projecting past experience into the future that human beings make decisions; and statesmen, in this respect, are not exceptions. Foreign policy decisions, like other human decisions, imply not only an abstraction from history, but also the making of "predictions"—the assessment of probable outcomes. These two operations may be undertaken almost unconsciously, but they are nonetheless real and inescapable. The Marshall Plan was based upon a prediction, derived from some combination of experience, that systematic aid to European nations would bring about certain consequences. Viewed in retrospect, this prediction seems to have been generally sound. The basic prediction inherent in Khrushchev's decision to establish long-range missiles in Cuba, on the other hand, was much less accurate.

The weeks just prior to the outbreak of war in 1914 offer a particularly useful setting for studying the behavior of states, the processes of international conflict, and the escalation of limited war into major war. Embedded in archival data lies something close to a prototype of crisis against which a contemporary crisis—or future crisis—can be measured profitably. A primary goal throughout this study has been to develop an empirical model of interstate behavior. The relatively complete nature of the 1914 data makes it an ideal situation in which to undertake initial testing and modification of such a model.

When we study transactions between nation-states we are focusing on decisions which are arrived at and initially implemented by a small group of leaders who have reached high status and are performing their roles as an outcome of an elective, appointive, or some other highly differentiating selective process. In systemic terms this group may be viewed as a specialized, functional sub-system or component of the national system. In fact, the sub-system is still a collection of individuals, however, and thus decision makers remain the fundamental unit of analysis.

The individual decision maker within any large organization, including a nation-state, is embedded, of course, in a considerable number of more or less nesting and overlapping groups each with its own roles, statuses, expectations, and preferences. He also has carried with him into office a complex of personal habits, memories, attitudes, inclinations, and predispositions. In performing his decision-making role he is to one degree or another aware of pressures and limitations emanating from these sources, and also from public opinion and expectation; the interests and policies of other components of his government; advice from military, scientific, and other specialized advisers; institutional memories; and the history and traditions of the organization. Essentially, then, the behavior of a decision maker cannot be considered without reference to the organization of which he is a part.

The Importance of Perceptions

Foreign-policy-making may be viewed as a search for satisfactory alternatives from among the range of those perceived by leaders who choose for their respective nation-states. The key concept in this approach is the *perception*, the process by which decision makers detect and assign meaning to inputs from their environment and formulate their own purposes or intents. For an individual to respond to a person, object, or event, there must first be the *detection* of signals, which is a function of our senses. In addition, however, we must have some code—a set of concepts or images—which permits us to *interpret* the meaning of the stimulus.

For all human beings these codes are largely a product of experience and training. The infant with normal hearing can detect the sound waves created by human voices. But there is little understanding, and therefore limited influence on the behavior of the child, until he learns the code (language) which permits him to organize and interpret the sound waves into meaningful patterns. These concepts become the "lenses" through which each of us makes sense of the otherwise unmanageable number of signals from the environment with which we are bombarded. Some concepts are relatively simple and may be subject to little variation across individuals or time. Other concepts are more complex and open to misinterpretation or disagreement. And, as Richard Snyder (1962) has pointed out, complexity, ambiguity, and lack of stability are a few of the characteristics which tend to be more pronounced in foreign policy decision-making than in other settings. Perceptions appear to be equally crucial to studies of conflict and studies of coalition, organization, federation, or unification.

Our studies to date have also reinforced our belief in the necessity of taking perceptual variables into account and for correlating them with more "objective" indices. For human beings do not always respond to the same stimuli in the same way. A phenomenon may be perceived by one actor as positive (acceptable, rewarding) and by another as negative (unacceptable, punishing). Similarly, the same actor may view the same stimulus as positive in one situation—that is, when associated with one set of accompanying stimuli—and negative in another situation. In any case, the essential point is that the actor's response will be shaped *by his perception* of the stimulus and not necessarily by qualities objectively inherent in it. This means that my behavior—in terms of my perceptions—may appear perfectly rational and appropriate to me (subjective rationality), whereas you—*in terms of your perceptions*—may consider my behavior utterly mad. This is a major reason why the rights and wrongs in conflicts on all levels—between husband and wife, between labor and management, and between opponents in the cold war—are frequently so difficult to establish.

Relating Perceptions to Behavior:
The Interaction Model

We are interested not only in what national decision makers *perceive*—or say they perceive—about themselves and others. We are also interested in what they actually *do*. How are these perceptual and action elements to be brought together systematically and correlated for meaningful analysis? Basically, we are interested in inter-nation "communication" in the sense that this concept can be used to characterize all transactions between nations. This indicates that both the verbal *and* the physical acts have information potential. The acts of one nation can be considered as inputs to other nations. The basic problem is this: given some input to a nation, what additional information do we need to account for the nation's foreign policy response?

The conceptual framework we have selected for such analysis is a two-step mediated stimulus-response ($S\text{-}r : s\text{-}R$) model. These elements are as follows: A stimulus (S) is an event in the environment which may or may not be perceived by a given actor, and which two or more actors may perceive and evaluate differently. A stimulus may be a physical event or a verbal act. The stimuli relevant to international politics tend to originate with the acts of other nations (or are perceived as) directed toward a nation in question. This is not to say that domestic problems (for example, pressure for tariffs) have no relevance. Rather, it is to assert that the impetus for most decisions, especially in crisis, is extra-national. Input behavior (S) can be described in terms of the clarity and salience of the stimulus. Clarity is a function of both the nature of the act, and its intensity. Is the act physical or verbal? Is it at a high or low level of intensity? These characteristics may play a considerable part in determining the manner in which the nation-state responds (R). On the other hand, physical acts of moderate to high intensity may have a low level of salience; even a very clear stimulus may find the actors focused elsewhere. For example, during the early weeks of the 1914 crisis, British decision makers were primarily concerned with the Ulster situation rather than the events on the Continent.

Figure 3-1   The Interaction Model

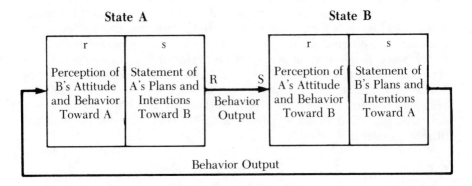

A response (R) is an action of an actor, without respect to his intent or how either he or other actors may perceive it. Both S's and R's are non-evaluative and non-affective. For example, on July 29, 1914, Russia, in response to the declaration of war, ordered a partial mobilization of the southern district (R). Although the intention behind it was only to deter Austria-Hungary from invading Serbia, this action served as a stimulus (S) to Germany, which, within hours, responded by threatening a mobilization of its own (R).

In the model, the perception (r) of the stimulus (S) within the national decision system corresponds to the "definition of the situation" in the decision-making literature (Snyder, et al., 1962; March and Simon, 1958). For example, during the crisis leading up to World War I, Germany perceived that Russia was threatening German borders. Finally, (s) represents the actor's expressions of his own intentions, plans, actions, or attitude toward another actor; for example, Germany asserted an intention of supporting Austria-Hungary. Both (r) and (s) carry evaluative and affective loadings. In the case of the Russian partial mobilization (R), although the intent behind it (s) was aimed solely at Austria-Hungary, it was perceived (r) as a serious threat by German decision makers, who expressed their own intent (s) to take similar action. Three days later Germany ordered a general mobilization (R).

Operationally, it would be much simpler, of course, to confine oneself only to S and R, as do many traditional theories of international politics. In many situations and for many decision makers the best predictor of state A's action response to state B will be the nature of state B's action. If the latter were unambiguously dangerous, one would expect them to be negatively valued by almost any individual or group in a decision-making role. Predicting President Roosevelt's response to the attack on Pearl Harbor would not be difficult. However, not all—or even most—inter-nation actions are so unambiguous. Consider, for example, Chamberlain's and Churchill's perceptions of Hitler's invitation to confer at Munich on the fate of Czechoslovakia.

Collecting the Perceptual Data

The selection of the 1914 crisis as the initial case in which to attempt rigorous quantitative analyses of conflict at the international level was based on several considerations. The available documentation relating to the outbreak of World War I surpasses that of any crisis of similar magnitude. Among the major nations involved, only the Serbian archives have remained relatively inaccessible to the investigator. Moreover, a generation of careful scholarship has produced published and readily accessible document collections of unquestioned authenticity, including those of Austria-Hungary (1930), France (1936), Great Britain (1926), Germany (Montgelas and Schücking, 1924), and Russia (1934). The forged, altered, or incomplete collections—produced by the various governments while passions and charges of "war guilt" still ran high—have been superseded. Finally, the crisis is a classic example of war through escalation. The minor war between Austria-Hungary and Serbia—which crisis-hardened European diplomats expected to remain localized—engulfed nearly the entire continent within ten days. The existing international system—still referred to by many as the classic example of a functioning "balance of power" system—was unable to cope with the situation as it had previously done in the recurring Balkan crises. While extensive war plans had been drawn up by the various general staffs, there is little evidence that any European decision maker wanted or expected a general war—at least in 1914.

The perceptual data were derived in whole from documents authored by selected British, French, Russian, German, and Austro-Hungarian decision makers. Those persons filling key roles such as head of state, head of government, or foreign minister were selected, unless there was a clear indication—from such standard sources as Fay (1928) or Albertini (1935)—that the person had no part whatsoever in the formulation of decisions. In addition, certain other persons who played a prominent part in the events were added. The complete list of decision makers whose messages were subjected to content analysis is found in Table 3-1.

The initial step in the exploitation of these documents was to devise perceptual units that could be defined, recognized by separate investigators, counted, and ranked along scales of more-to-less intensity. The units used in these analyses of international crisis—the *perceptions*—have been abstracted from the documents in terms of the following elements: *the perceiving party or actor; the perceived party or actors; the action or attitude; and the target party or actor.* For example, the assertion by a Russian decision maker that "The Austrian, as well as German, hope is for the ultimate annihilation of Serbia," was coded as follows:

Perceiver	*Perceived*	*Action or Attitude*	*Target*
Russia	Austrian	hope is for the ultimate annihilation of	Serbia
Russia	German	hope is for the ultimate annihilation of	Serbia

Ole R. Holsti, Robert C. North, and Richard A. Brody

Table 3-1 1914 Decision Makers Selected for Documentary Content Analysis

Position[a]	Austria-Hungary	Germany	England	France	Russia
Head of State	Franz Joseph	Wilhelm II	George V	Poincaré	Nicholas II
Head of Government	Stürgkh[b] Tisza	Bethmann-Hollweg	Asquith	Viviani	
Secretary for Foreign Affairs	Berchtold	Jagow	Grey	Viviani	Sazonov
Undersecretary for Foreign Affairs	Forgach Macchio Hoyos	Zimmer-mann Stumm	Nicolson	Bienvenu-Martin Berthelot Ferry	
Minister of War/Chief of General Staff	Conrad	Moltke		Messimy	Sukhom-linov
Others			Haldane[c]		

[a] Position refers to functionally equivalent roles, not to formal titles, which vary from nation to nation.
[b] Stürgkh was Austro-Hungarian Minister-President; Tisza was Hungarian Prime Minister.
[c] Lord Chancellor.

The 1914 documents yielded over 5,000 such cognitive and affective perceptions.

The analysis of these data has gone through three fairly distinctive states: (1) the use of only *frequency* of perceptions; (2) the recoding of the documents, and scaling of the perceptions for the *intensity* of various attributes; and (3) correlational analyses between perceptions and the various types of *"hard"* and *action* data.

After the complete recoding and scaling of the 1914 documents, the hypotheses relating perceptions of capability and injury were re-examined. It was found that decision makers of each nation most strongly felt themselves to be the victims of injury precisely at that time when its leaders were making policy decisions of the most crucial nature (Holsti and North, 1965). As mentioned, perceptions of its inferior capability did not deter a nation such as Germany from going to war. The Kaiser's desperate reaction to the events which were engulfing him—perhaps most characterized by his assertion, "If we are to bleed to death, England shall at least lose India" (Montgelas and Schücking, 1924)—is the reaction of a decision maker under such severe stress that any action is preferable to the burden of the sustained tension.

90

This reaction in the face of an adversary's greater capabilities—a reaction strikingly familiar to instances in the Peloponnesian Wars, the wars between Spain and England during the sixteenth century, and the Japanese decision to strike at Pearl Harbor (Holsti, 1963)—are not unrelated to the dilemmas of our own age of missiles and nuclear warheads. These findings underscore the need for re-examining that "common sense" and almost irresistible "conventional wisdom" which argues that deterrence is merely a matter of piling up more and/or better weapons than the opponent can amass.

Relating Perception and Military Action

The next step was to test the basic interaction (S-r : s-R) model with the data. Students of conflict have frequently asserted that parties acting in crisis situations reveal more or less consistent patterns of rising tensions and escalation leading to violence (Boulding, 1962; Richardson, 1960a). Within the context of international politics, the line of reasoning can be summarized as follows: If state A—correctly or incorrectly—perceives itself threatened by state B, there is a high probability that A will respond with threats of hostile action. As state B begins to perceive this hostility directed toward itself, it is probable that B, too, will behave in a hostile (and defensive) fashion. This threatening behavior by B will confirm for A that its initial perceptions were correct, and A will be inclined to increase its hostile (and defensive) activity. Thereafter, the exchanges between the two parties will become increasingly negative, threatening, and injurious (North, 1962).

An initial and partial test of this sequence of interaction was carried out by correlating perceptual, or affective, data from 1914 with the spiral of military mobilizations just prior to the outbreak of World War I (North, *et al.*, 1964). The findings suggest that mobilizations accounted for a considerable part—but by no means all—of the variance in hostility. There was a steady rise in hostility *prior to* any acts of mobilization, and thus, to some degree, the decision makers were responding to verbal threats and diplomatic moves, rather than to troop movements, in earlier phases of the crisis. This study thus revealed the necessity of correlating perceptual data with other types of action data. It also underscored the importance of testing hypotheses in other crisis situations, since there was little in the 1914 data to suggest under what conditions the exchange of threats leads to "de-escalation," as appears to have happened in the October, 1962, Cuban crisis, rather than to a conflict spiral.

The action data (S and R in the model) were expanded to include all events of a military character involving nations in the 1914 crisis either as agents or targets of actions. These were gathered from standard military histories of the period (Edmunds, 1937; McEntee, 1937; Frothingham, 1924) and such usually reliable newspapers as the *New York Times*, *Times* (London), and *Le Temps* (Paris). Wherever possible the reports were verified in an authoritative history of the crisis (Albertini, 1953). If serious doubt existed about the accuracy of an item—in the closing days of the crisis newspapers were filled with many unsubstantiated charges and countercharges—the item was discarded. As with the documentary data, the action data were coded in a uniform format; that is, according to the *agent* of action, the *action*, and the *target* of action. Unless the target of action was *explicit*, it was coded as general. The coding yielded three hundred and fifty-four military actions, of which the following are examples:

Agent	*Action*	*Target*
French Chamber	approves a 3-year military law	(general)
German fleet	leaves Norway for home ports	(general)
Austrian army	bombarded	Belgrade
Churchill (Britain)	orders shadowing in Mediterranean of	two German battle-cruisers
Germany	declares war on	France

For purposes of combining action and perceptual data in the S-r : s-R model, both the *s* and *r* stages in the model are operationalized solely in terms of the hostility variable. Previous studies involving multivariant analysis, which have revealed hostility to be the best predictor of action, are supported in the present study. With violence of action as the dependent variable, only the rank-order correlation coefficient for hostility ($r_s = .66$) is statistically significant. A convenient starting point is to assume congruence across the S-r : s-R model. In these terms it is postulated—however tentatively—that a given amount of violence (or any other quality which the investigator wishes to measure) in an environmental stimulus (S) will yield an appropriate level of expressed affective response (r) which, in turn, will stimulate an expressed "intent" (s) of like affective loading and a response (R) at about the same level of violence as the original stimulus (S). Where data from historical crisis situations provide incongruent patterns across the model, other sources of variance must be sought to account for the discrepancy between the expected and obtained relationship.

Perceptual and action data are divided to correspond to two coalitions for the purposes of testing hypotheses across the S-r : s-R model: the Triple Entente (England, France, Russia) and the Dual Alliance (Austria-Hungary, Germany). An examination of the data . . . raises some questions about the classical theories of international relations which are built on a simple S-R model: There is a rather consistent lack of congruence in the actions of the two alliances. Under certain circumstances we may be able to predict any nation's reactions quite accurately if we know the behavior input it experiences. There is an extremely high probability that a full-scale nuclear attack by the United States or the Soviet Union on the other would elicit a similar response. Unfortunately, as Kenneth Boulding has pointed out, we are far less certain that the use of *rewards* at the international level will lead to reciprocation (Boulding, 1959).

Previous studies have suggested that in situations where two or more actor-nations are minimally engaged or involved in an interaction, the environmental stimulus (S) may yield an accurate prediction of an actor-nation's response (R). Stated somewhat differently, S may be the best predictor of R in circumstances where the actor-nations perceive that neither the penalties nor the rewards are likely to be of any great significance (Zaninovich, 1964).

The first hypothesis specifies the conditions under which the degree of congruence between S and R is high or low.

> The correlation between input action (S) and policy response (R) will be better in a situation of low involvement than in one of high involvement.

This suggests that in the *low* involvement situation, the analysis of perceptions (s and r) may be less crucial, and that "objective" criteria may give the analyst adequate information. Rummel's (1964a) findings that domestic data predict state behavior fairly well—except under conditions of high conflict—can be interpreted as lending support to this hypothesis.

Of the two coalitions engaged in the crisis, the Triple Entente was engaged for a much shorter period. During the month between June 27 and July 27, that coalition revealed a total of only 40 perceptions of hostility compared to 171 for the Dual Alliance; in the late period (July 28 to August 4) the figures were 229 and 270 respectively. This certainly coincides with the historians' consensus.

As suggested by the hypothesis, the degree of congruence between S and R for the less-engaged coalition, the Triple Entente, is considerably lower ($r_s = .463$) than that for the Dual Alliance ($r_s = .678$). Several explanations are possible. First, at least two members of the Triple Entente—England and France—acted (R) with a high level of violence only relatively late in the crisis period, withholding action until the threat (S) from the Dual Alliance was quite clearly defined.

On the other hand, the actions of the Dual Alliance—and particularly Austria-Hungary's actions in the early and middle part of the crisis period leading to a hoped-for local war—were not commensurate with the level of violence displayed by either Serbia or other members of the Triple Entente. There were two overlapping crises which became one at midnight August 4. The first was the result of a rather deliberately planned local war that had little to do with the actions of the other major powers and in which the members of the Triple Entente were only minimally engaged; the second resulted in an unplanned escalation into general war, engulfing all the nations.

A second hypothesis including the S and R (action) stages of the model is concerned not only with congruence or lack of congruence, but with the direction of differences.

> In a situation of low involvement, policy response (R) will tend to be at a lower level of violence than the input action (S), whereas in a high-involvement situation, the policy response (R) will tend to be at a higher level of violence than the input action (S).

In terms of the events of 1914, the hypothesis suggests that the nations of the Triple Entente would under-respond to actions from the other side, whereas those of the Dual Alliance would be over-reacting to the threat from the Triple Entente. A Mann-Whitney U Test (Siegel, 1956) to compare the magnitude of the difference between input (S) and output (R) action reveals that the values for the Dual Alliance are indeed consistently negative (indicating over-reaction), whereas those of the Triple Entente are positive (under-reaction) on balance.

The inability to predict reactions (R) solely on the basis of action (S) suggests an examination of the relationship between action, perceptual, and situational variables.

Where such lack of congruence between input and output action exists, the intervening perceptions may perform either an accelerating or decelerating function. This suggests the hypothesis that

In the low-involvement situation, r will tend to be at a lower level than S, whereas in the high-involvement situation, R will tend to be higher than S.

Intuitively the hypothesis makes sense. In a period of relative calm and low involvement, perceptual distortion will probably tend in the direction of underperception; one may even be lulled into a false sense of security by failing to perceive a real threat. The British and French reaction to Nazi Germany— until the aggressive actions of Hitler became so unambiguous that even Chamberlain and Daladier perceived the danger—is a case in point. During a period of intense stress, on the other hand, when all fingers are near or on the trigger, even the most innocent action may be perceived as a threat of great magnitude. This pattern is much like that exhibited by Kaiser Wilhelm during the intense crisis leading up to World War I. Although possessor of the world's second ranking navy, at one point he perceived the presence of a few Russian torpedo boats in the Baltic as adequate cause for alerting the entire German fleet (Montgelas and Schücking, 1924).

The hypothesis is supported by the 1914 data [, which reveal] the difference between the level of input action (S) and perceptions of those actions (r). The leaders of the Dual Alliance consistently overperceived the level of violence in the actions of the Triple Entente. On the other hand, the Triple Entente tended to underperceive the actions of the other coalition.

The same hypothesis can also be tested in a somewhat different way. The first six periods (June 27-July 27) have been described as those in which the members of the Dual Alliance were highly involved with the events in the Balkans, whereas those of the Triple Entente were not. On the other hand, during the culminating periods of the crisis (July 28-August 4), nations in both alliances were being drawn into war. Thus, if the hypothesis is correct, differences in the way in which actions (S) are perceived (r) by nations of the two coalitions should be greatest during the early stages of the crisis. When the data ... are re-analyzed in this manner, the hypothesis is again supported. The difference between the two coalitions in regard to the S-r link during the early period is statistically significant $(U = 4, \ p = .013)$, whereas in the later period it is not ($U = 11$, $p =$ n.s.).

A further hypothesis within the model relates perceptions of one's own intent with perceptions of the intent of others. Boulding (1959), Osgood (1962), and many others have pointed to the propensity of nations to perceive their own intentions in the best light possible, while attributing more hostile motives to those of others.

> To the extent that there is a difference between perceptions of the other's policy (r) and statements of own intent (s), perceptions of hostility in r will tend to be higher than in s in *both* the low-involvement and the high-involvement situations.

The figures ... support the hypothesis both in that the level of perceived hostility for (r) is consistently higher than for (s), and in that there is no significant difference between the two coalitions.

The final intervening perceptual link in the model is that between the perception of one's own behavior (s) and the level of violence in the actual response (R). The hypothesis is that

> In the situation of low involvement, statements of intent (s) will tend to be higher than action responses (R), whereas in the high-involvement situation, s will tend to be lower than R.

Again there is at least intuitive support for the hypothesis. In a situation of high involvement, whether the action is essentially cooperative or conflictual, the effort one makes often far surpasses stated intent. The efforts of war-torn Western European nations after 1945 toward rebuilding economies, establishing supranational organizations, and contributing to the defense of Europe during the period of most severe Soviet threat undoubtedly exceeds the plans and intentions of most leaders. In the case where one feels little stress, on the other hand, the propensity of promises to run ahead of performance appears enhanced. The subsequent European unwillingness to raise NATO divisions, even to the promised and planned level can, at least in part, be attributed to a situation of less likelihood of massive Soviet invasion of Western Europe.

... [H]owever, ... there is, in fact, no difference between the two coalitions in regard to the *s-R* linkage. In both cases, R is consistently higher than s; that is, the states in both coalitions tended to react at a higher level of violence than suggested by the statements of intent by their various leaders.

Summary of Findings

The analysis of the 1914 crisis began with an assumption basic to most traditional theories of international politics—that is, the assumption of congruence between input (S) and output (R) action. The data revealed, however, a significant difference between the two coalitions corresponding to the different levels of involvement in the situation. Congruence between (S) and (R) was high for the members of the Triple Entente, which became involved only very late in the crisis. The level of congruence was much lower for the nations of the

Dual Alliance, which were engaged for essentially the entire crisis period.

Having failed to account for the escalation from a local incident to a general war with only the action variables, the perceptual variables (r) and (s) were analyzed. The various links across the model were examined and no significant difference between the two coalitions in regard to the s-R step was found: (R) was higher than (s) in both cases. As predicted, there was little difference between the Triple Entente and Dual Alliance in the r-s link, both perceiving themselves as less hostile than the other coalition. A significant difference did appear at the S-r step, however. The leaders of the Dual Alliance consistently overperceived the actions of the Triple Entente. Thus the S-r link served a "magnifying" function. The decision makers of the Triple Entente, on the other hand, tended to underperceive the actions of the Dual Alliance. This difference in perceiving the environment (the S-r link) is consistent with the pronounced tendency of the Dual Alliance to respond at a higher level of violence than the Triple Entente.

The present study of the 1914 crisis has encompassed—within the context of developing an empirical theory—an analysis of the process of escalation from a single incident through a planned war to an unplanned world war. To what extent are the findings, and the analytical framework employed here, relevant for the study of situations removed both in time and space?

In general there are indications that, the more intense the interaction between the parties, the more important it is to incorporate perceptual data into the analysis. Or, to state this somewhat differently, in a situation of low involvement, one may be able to predict a nation's action responses to environmental stimuli rather accurately without recourse to the perceptions of its decision makers. On the other hand, in a period of crisis marked by high involvement and rising intensity—as in the weeks prior to August 1914—the role of perception becomes increasingly important.

More specifically, it was found that the manner in which one party—or, as in this case, one coalition—perceived the actions of the other party was the crucial link between perception and action. The findings from the study of the Cuban missile crisis are relevant in this respect. In comparing the events of October 1962 with those in the summer of 1914, some important differences emerge. The members of the Dual Alliance—the more highly involved coalition—in 1914 consistently overperceived the level of violence in actions taken by members of the Triple Entente. British, French, and Russian decision makers, on the other hand, underperceived the level of violence in the actions of the Dual Alliance. Moreover, whereas there was a significant difference between the two coalitions during the early phase of the crisis—when members of the Dual Alliance were more highly involved with the events in the Balkans than were members of the Triple Entente—this difference disappeared as *all* nations were being drawn into war. In terms of the S-r : s-R model, this relationship between one coalition's actions, the other coalition's perceptions of those actions, and the resulting policies was apparently the crucial one.

In the Cuban crisis, however, both sides tended to perceive rather accurately the nature of the adversary's actions, and then proceeded to act at an "appropriate" level; that is, as the level of violence or potential violence in the adversary's actions diminished, perceptions of those actions increased in positive affect and decreased in negative affect, and the level of violence in the resulting policies also decreased. Thus, unlike the situation in 1914, efforts by either party to delay or reverse the escalation were generally perceived as such, and were responded to in like manner. Whether the different patterns of action and perception found in the 1914 and Cuban cases will consistently be found to distinguish crises that escalate and de-escalate, of course, can only be determined through continuing research.

████████ **3.3**

IRVING L. JANIS

The Groupthink Syndrome

Symptoms of Groupthink

The first step in developing a theory about the causes and consequences of groupthink is to anchor the concept of groupthink in observables by describing the symptoms to which it refers. Eight main symptoms run through the case studies of historic fiascoes and are seldom present in the case studies of the nongroupthink decisions. Each symptom can be identified by a variety of indicators, derived from historical records, observers' accounts of conversations, and participants' memoirs. The eight symptoms of groupthink include group products and processes that reinforce each other, as can be seen most clearly in the case study of the Bay of Pigs invasion plan. The symptoms can be divided into three main types, which are familiar features of many (although not all) cohesive groups observed in research on group dynamics.

Type I: Overestimations of the group—its power and morality

    1. An illusion of invulnerability, shared by most or all the members, which creates excessive optimism and encourages taking extreme risks

    2. An unquestioned belief in the group's inherent morality, inclining the members to ignore the ethical or moral consequences of their decisions

Type II: Closed-mindedness

    3. Collective efforts to rationalize in order to discount warnings or other information that might lead the members to reconsider their

assumptions before they recommit themselves to their past policy decisions

4. Stereotyped views of enemy leaders as too evil to warrant genuine attempts to negotiate, or as too weak and stupid to counter whatever risky attempts are made to defeat their purposes

Type III: Pressures toward uniformity

5. Self-censorship of deviations from the apparent group consensus, reflecting each member's inclination to minimize to himself the importance of his doubts and counterarguments

6. A shared illusion of unanimity concerning judgments conforming to the majority view (partly resulting from self-censorship of deviations, augmented by the false assumption that silence means consent)

7. Direct pressure on any member who expresses strong arguments against any of the group's stereotypes, illusions, or commitments, making clear that this type of dissent is contrary to what is expected of all loyal members

8. The emergence of self-appointed mindguards—members who protect the group from adverse information that might shatter their shared complacency about the effectiveness and morality of their decisions

Consequences

When a policy-making group displays most or all of the symptoms in each of the three categories, the members perform their collective tasks ineffectively and are likely to fail to attain their collective objectives as a result of concurrence-seeking. In rare instances, concurrence-seeking may have predominantly positive effects for their members and their enterprises. For example, it may make a crucial contribution to maintaining morale after a defeat and to muddling through a crisis when prospects for a successful outcome look bleak. But the positive effects are generally outweighed by the poor quality of the group's decision-making. My assumption is that the more frequently a group displays the symptoms, the worse will be the quality of its decisions, on the average. Even when some symptoms are absent, the others may be so pronounced that we can expect all the unfortunate consequences of groupthink. . . .

Are Cohesive Groups Doomed to Be Victims?

Cohesiveness of the policy-making group is a major antecedent condition that has been emphasized throughout this book. In the very first chapter I stated as the central theme the following generalization: The more amiability and esprit de corps among the members of an in-group of policy-makers, the greater is the danger that independent critical thinking will be replaced by groupthink, which is likely to result in irrational and dehumanizing actions directed at out-groups. Yet when we recall the case studies of the Cuban missile crisis and the Marshall Plan, we surmise that some caveats about applying this generalization are in order. A high degree of "amiability and esprit de corps among the members" are manifestations of the high degree to which the members value their membership in one group and want to continue to be affiliated—that is, group cohesiveness. But, as I have stated in earlier chapters, group cohesiveness does not invariably lead to symptoms of groupthink. It is a necessary condition, but it is not a sufficient condition. Taking this into account, I have introduced an explicit proviso in the wording of the generalization, asserting that the greater the cohesiveness of the group, "the greater is the danger" of a groupthink type of decision. Dangers do not always materialize and can sometimes be prevented by precautionary measures. Structural features of the group and situational context factors play a crucial role in determining whether a moderately or highly cohesive group will develop symptoms of groupthink. It follows that the positive relationship between cohesiveness and groupthink cannot be regarded as an iron law of executive behavior that dooms the members of every cohesive group to become victims of groupthink every time they make a collective decision. Rather, we should expect high cohesiveness to be conducive to groupthink only when certain additional determining conditions are present but not under other conditions, such as when special precautions are taken to set up norms for vigilant search and appraisal that counteract collective uncritical thinking and premature consensus.

When appropriate precautions are taken, a group that has become moderately or highly cohesive probably can do a much better job on its decision-making tasks than if it had remained noncohesive. Compliance out of fear of recrimination is likely to be strongest when there is little or no sense of solidarity among the group members. In order to overcome this fear, each participant in the group's deliberations needs to have a great deal of confidence that he is a member in good standing and that the others will continue to value his role in the group, whether or not he argues with them about the issue under discussion. Social psychological studies indicate that as a member of a group is made to feel more accepted by the others—a feature that is usually associated with increased group cohesiveness—he acquires greater freedom to say what he really thinks. Dittes and Kelley, for example, discovered in a social psychological experiment that when individuals in a group were given information indicating that they were highly accepted by their fellow members, they became more willing to express opinions that deviated from the group consensus. Members who were made to feel that they were not accepted by their colleagues became subdued. After being informed about the low acceptance ratings, they participated in the group discussions only half as often as they had before. When they did speak, they showed much more conformity with the group consensus than the other participants did. However, these conformists had developed an attitude of inner detachment from the group. This was revealed in their answers to questions that elicited their private views, which showed little conformity to the group's norms and low valuation of membership in the group. Their superficial conformity appears to have been motivated by a fear of being humiliated by being expelled from the group altogether.

The unaccepted members in the Dittes and Kelley study probably reacted the way most people do in a group of high-status people who are strangers, before cohesiveness and feelings of security have developed. The highly accepted members probably reacted like members of cohesive groups who feel secure about their status as members. In the Dittes and Kelley study, the accepted members were more responsive than unaccepted members to new information that contradicted the group's earlier assumptions and more freely expressed opinions differing from the group consensus. This pattern of relatively independent thinking is probably characteristic of group members who have developed a relationship of mutual acceptance in which each person assumes that the others in the group want to know what he really thinks and will want him to continue as a member regardless of what he says.

When a group has a low degree of cohesiveness, there are, of course, sources of error in decision-making in addition to deliberate conformity out of fear of recrimination. One that is especially likely to plague a noncohesive group of politicians or administrators is a win-lose fighting stance, which inclines each participant to fight hard for his own point of view (or the point of view of his organization), without much regard for the real issue at stake. When unlike-minded people who are political opponents are forced to meet together in a group, they can be expected to behave like couples in olden times who were forced to live together by a shotgun marriage. The incompatible members of a shotgun committee often indulge in painfully repetitious debates, frequently punctuated with invective, mutual ridicule, and maneuvers of one-upmanship in a continuous struggle for power that is not at all conducive to decisions of high quality. This is another reason for expecting that policy-making groups lacking amiability and esprit de corps, even though spared the unfavorable symptoms of groupthink, will sometimes show more symptoms of defective decision-making and produce worse fiascoes than groups that are moderately or highly cohesive. When we consider the two major sources of error that beset noncohesive groups—deliberate conformity out of fear of recrimination and a win-lose fighting stance—we see that cohesive groups can have great advantages if groupthink tendencies can be kept from becoming dominant.

As the members of a decision-making group develop bonds of friendship and esprit de corps, they become less likely to use deceitful arguments or to play safe by dancing around the issues with vapid or conventional comments. We expect that the more cohesive a group becomes, the less the members will deliberately censor what they say because of fear of being socially punished for antagonizing the leader or any of their fellow members. But the outcome is complicated because the more cohesive a group becomes, the more each member is likely to censor what he or she thinks because of the newly acquired motivation to preserve the unity of the group and to adhere to its norms. Thus, although the members of a highly cohesive group feel much freer to deviate from the majority, their desire for genuine concurrence on all important issues—to match their opinions with each other and to conduct themselves in acordance with each other's wishes—often inclines them not to use this freedom. In a cohesive group of policy-makers the danger is not that each individual will fail to reveal his strong objections to a proposal favored by the majority but that he will think the proposal is a good one, without attempting to carry out a critical scrutiny that could lead him to see that there are grounds for strong objections. When groupthink dominates, suppression of deviant thoughts takes the form of each person's deciding that his misgivings are not relevant, that the benefit of any doubt should be given to the group consensus. A member of a cohesive group will rarely be subjected to direct group pressures from the majority because he or she will rarely take a position that threatens the unity of the group.

Prior research on group dynamics indicates that at least three different types of social rewards tend to increase group cohesiveness—friendship, prestige, and enhanced competence. Concurrence-seeking tendencies probably are stronger when high cohesiveness is based primarily on the rewards of being in a pleasant "clubby" atmosphere or of gaining prestige from being a member of an elite group than when it is based primarily on the opportunity to function competently on work tasks with effective co-workers. In a cohesive policy-making group of the latter type, careful appraisal of policy alternatives is likely to become a group norm to which the members conscientiously adhere; this helps to counteract groupthink. But even when the basis of high cohesiveness is enhancement of task-oriented values in a well-functioning group whose members trust each other sufficiently to tolerate disagreements, there is still the danger that groupthink will become a dominant tendency. Each member develops a strong motivation to preserve the rewards of group solidarity, an inner compulsion to avoid creating disunity, which inclines him or her to believe in the soundness of the proposals promoted by the leader or by a majority of the group's members.

A cohesive group that on one occasion suffers from groupthink is capable on other occasions of gaining the advantages of high morale and free expression of dissent, depending on whether special conditions that promote groupthink are present. The duality of cohesiveness may explain some of the inconsistencies in research results on group effectiveness. For example, Marvin Shaw in his textbook, *Group Dynamics*, presents as a plausible hypothesis the proposition, "High-cohesive groups are more effective than low-cohesive groups in achieving their respective goals," but he acknowledges that the evidence "is not altogether consistent." A major source of inconsistency may be attributed to concurrence-seeking tendencies: Sometimes the groupthink syndrome occurs in highly cohesive groups when the members are working on certain kinds of decision-making tasks, which reduces their effectiveness; when working on other kinds of decision-making tasks (and also on a variety of other tasks that do not involve decision-making) the members of highly cohesive groups show increased effectiveness. This is how I interpret the difference between the ineffective Bay of Pigs decision and the effective Cuban missile crisis decision made by nearly cohesive groups of policy-makers headed by the same leader.

For most groups, optimal functioning in decision-making tasks may prove to be at a moderate level of cohesiveness, avoiding the disadvantages of conformity out of fear of recrimination when cohesiveness is low and the disadvantages of strong concurrence-seeking tendencies when cohesiveness is high. If, however, the latter disadvantages can be held to a minimum by administrative practices that prevent groupthink tendencies from becoming dominant, then the optimal level of cohesiveness for effective decision-making could prove to be much higher. . . .

Rudiments of an Explanatory Theory

The problem of *why* groupthink occurs is more difficult to investigate than the problem of *who* is vulnerable and *when*. But *why* is the heart of the matter if we want to explain the observed phenomena of concurrence-seeking. An adequate explanation would specify the main incentives for engaging in the types of behavior that constitute the groupthink syndrome. It would account for the known conditions that promote concurrence-seeking tendencies and would enable us to predict the effects of conditions that we do not yet know about.

The search for an explanation forces us to tread through a morass of complicated theoretical issues in still largely uncharted areas of human motivation. For many years, psychologists have been trying to formulate general psychological principles that would apply to all the observed phenomena of group dynamics, but no well-established theory is generally accepted by behavioral scientists. However, promising leads extracted from recent social psychological research may point the way to an explanation of the groupthink syndrome.

The central explanatory concept I have in mind involves viewing concurrence-seeking as a form of striving for mutual support based on a powerful motivation in all group members to cope with the external or internal stresses of decision-making. When the source of stress is an *external* threat, such as being defeated in a struggle with a rival group or being caught and punished for illegal actions, the concurrence-seeking tendency, as we have just seen, is expected to increase, provided that the members have little hope of finding a better way to deal with the impending dangers than the solution favored by the leader. Under conditions of high external stress, the main incentive for the members to rely on the leader's wisdom and to try to maintain group harmony is their motivation to relieve the anxieties generated by the salient external threats.

Even when the members are not particularly concerned about risks of material losses for themselves or their organization, so that the level of external stress is low, they may nevertheless be subjected to *internal* sources of stress, which cannot be handled in quite the same way. This source of stress involves a temporary lowering of self-esteem as a result of situational provocations. The most frequent provocations are (1) recent failures, such as an unanticipated poor outcome resulting from a prior decision for which the members of the policy-making group feel responsible, which makes the members keenly aware of their personal inadequacies; (2) a current complicated and perplexing choice requiring the members of the policy-making group to carry out extremely difficult decision-making tasks that they perceive as being beyond their level of competence, which lowers each member's sense of self-efficacy; and (3) a moral dilemma posed by the necessity to make a vital decision when the members of the policy-making group perceive a lack of any feasible alternatives except ones that violate their ethical standards of conduct. The third type of provocation will occur most frequently, of course, when the policy-makers have been selected for their top-level positions not only for their competence and practical wisdom but also as standard bearers of humanitarian and ethical values. Such policy-makers are more likely than others to be confronted with moral dilemmas that generate an intense conflict between humanitarian or ethical values on the one hand and the utilitarian demands of national or organizational goals, practical politics, and economics on the other. The participants may try to reassure themselves with the platitudinous thought that "you can't make an omelet without breaking some eggs." Nevertheless, each time they realize they are sacrificing moral values in order to arrive at a viable policy, they will be burdened with anticipatory feelings of shame, guilt, and related feelings of self-depreciation, which lower their self-esteem. Even those policy-makers who pride themselves on their capacity to play the game of "hardball" politics without any qualms may have to contend from time to time with anticipatory shame or guilt arising from "super-ego" conflicts of which they are not fully aware. The point is that no one is likely to be exempt from undergoing a temporary lowering of self-esteem occasionally as a result of being exposed to any one of the three types of situational provocations. For all such sources of internal stress, participating in a unanimous consensus along with the respected fellow members of a congenial group will bolster the decision-maker's self-esteem.

Some individuals are extraordinarily self-confident practically all the time and may seldom need the support of a cohesive group when their decisions are subject to social criticism and self-disapproval. For example, the spirited symphony orchestra conductor Sir Thomas Beecham once said, "I have made just one mistake in my entire life and that was one time when I thought I was wrong but actually I was right." Very few people who are required to put it on the line as decision-makers are able to maintain such an unassailable sense of self-assurance.

Psychological Functions of the Eight Symptoms

Concurrence-seeking and the various symptoms of groupthink to which it gives rise might be best understood as a mutual effort among the members of a group to maintain emotional equanimity in the face of external and internal sources of stress arising when they share responsibility for making vital decisions that pose threats of failure, social disapproval, and self-disapproval. The eight symptoms of groupthink form a coherent pattern if viewed in the context of this explanatory hypothesis. The symptoms may function in somewhat different ways to produce the same result.

A shared illusion of invulnerability and shared rationalizations can alleviate incipient fears of failure and prevent unnerving feelings of personal inadequacy, especially during a crisis. Even during noncrisis periods, whenever the members foresee great gains from taking a dangerous, a socially disapproved, or an unethical course of action, they may be seeking some way of disregarding the disturbing threats and welcome the optimistic views of the members who argue for the attractive but risky course of action. At such times, as well as during distressing crises, if the threat of failure is salient, the members are likely to convey to each other the attitude that "we needn't worry, everything will go our way." By pooling their intellectual resources to develop rationalizations, the members build up each other's confidence and feel reassured about unfamiliar risks, which, if taken seriously, would be dealt with by applying standard operating procedures to obtain additional information and to carry out careful planning.

The members' firm belief in the inherent morality of their group and their use of undifferentiated negative stereotypes of opponents would enable them to minimize decision conflicts between ethical values and expediency, especially when they are inclined to resort to violence. The shared belief that "we are a good and wise group" inclines them to use group concurrence as a major criterion to judge the morality as well as the efficacy of any policy under discussion. "Since our group's objectives are good," the members feel, "any means we decide to use must be good." This shared assumption helps the members avoid feelings of shame or guilt about decisions that may violate their personal code of ethical behavior. Shared negative stereotypes that feature the evil nature of the enemy would enhance their sense of moral righteousness as well as their pride in the lofty mission of the in-group. Shared stereotypes that feature the weakness of the enemy would alleviate their incipient fears of being defeated.

Every cohesive group that is required to make policy decisions tends to develop a set of policy doctrines, derived from the members' subculture, that provides the members with a cognitive map for conceptualizing the intentions and reactions of opponents, allies, and neutrals. But to be effective decision-makers, the members need to exercise a certain flexibility in the use of those doctrines in order to take account of new information and their own feelings of empathy. They can then evolve sophisticated concepts that enable them to weigh the prospects for negotiations in the light of fresh evidence about their opponents' current objectives and strategies. During a confrontation involving the threat of open hostilities, the loss of flexibility is the price a cohesive group pays to gain the greater sense of confidence and moral righteousness from sharing an image of the enemy as weak, intractable, and deserving of punishment. Stereotypes that dehumanize out-groups alleviate guilt by legitimizing destructive and inhumane acts against them. As Donald Campbell says, "The out-group's opprobrious characteristics seem [to the in-grouper] to fully justify the hostility and rejection he shows toward it." Focusing hostility on out-groups probably also serves the psychological function of displacing aggression away from the in-group, thereby reducing stress arising from latent jealousies and antagonisms within the group.

When most members fall back upon the familiar forms of social pressure directed against a member who questions the group's wisdom or morality, they are in effect protecting psychological defenses that help them to keep anxiety, shame, and guilt to a minimum. If subtle pressures fail, stronger efforts are made to limit the extent of his deviation, to make him a domesticated dissenter. We have seen this clearly in the case of President Johnson's in-group when one or two of the members disagreed with the majority's position that air attacks against North Vietnam should be increased. A doubter who accepts the role is no longer a problem because his objections are confined to issues that do not threaten to shake the confidence of the group members in the reasonableness and righteousness of their collective judgments. At the same time, the doubter's tamed presentation of an opposing viewpoint permits the others to think that their group is strong-minded enough to tolerate dissent. If the domestication efforts do not succeed, the dissenter is ultimately ostracized, so that the relatively tranquil emotional atmosphere of a homogeneous group is restored.

When a member is dependent on the group for bolstering his feelings of confidence and self-esteem, he tends to exercise self-censorship over his misgivings. The greater the dependence, the stronger will be the motivation to adhere to the group's norms. One of the norms that is likely to become dominant under conditions of high external or internal stress involves living up to a mutual nonaggression pact. Each individual in the group feels himself to be under an injunction to avoid making penetrating criticisms that might bring on a clash with fellow members and destroy the unity of the group. Adhering to this norm promotes a sense of collective strength and also eliminates the threat of damage to each member's self-esteem from hearing his or her own judgments on vital issues criticized by respected associates. We have seen how much painful emotion was generated in Kennan's group of critical thinkers working on the Marshall Plan and in Kennedy's Executive Committee debating alternative ways to get rid of the Soviet missiles in Cuba. In contrast, the emotional state of those who participated in the groupthink-dominated deliberations that led to fiascoes was relatively placid. When the mutual nonaggression pact and other related norms for preserving the unity of the group are internalized, each member avoids interfering with an emerging consensus by assuring himself that the opposing arguments he had in mind must be erroneous or that his misgivings are too unimportant to be worth mentioning.

The various devices to enhance confidence and self-esteem require an illusion of unanimity about all important judgments. Without it, the sense of group unity would be lost, gnawing doubts would start to grow, confidence in the group's problem-solving capacity would shrink, and soon the full emotional impact of all the internal and external sources of stress generated by making a difficult decision would be aroused. Preserving the sense of unity can do more than keep anxiety, shame, and guilt to a minimum; it can induce pleasant feelings of elation. Members of a group sometimes enjoy an exhilarating sense of omnipotence from participating in a crisis decision with a group that displays solidarity against an evil enemy and complete unanimity about everything that needs to be done.

Self-appointed mindguards help to preserve the shared sense of complacency by making sure that the leader and other members are not exposed to information that might challenge their self-confidence. If the mindguard were to transmit the potentially distressing information, he and the others might become discouraged by the apparent defects in their cherished policy and find themselves impelled to initiate a painful reevaluation in an unpleasant state of emotional tension.

The explanatory hypothesis about why groupthink occurs gives preeminence to provocative situational factors. According to this hypothesis, the crucial incentives that induce the groupthink syndrome occur when members of a cohesive group are confronted by a situation that evokes either (1) a high level of stress from external threats combined with low hope of a better solution than the one favored by the leader or (2) a marked lowering of self-esteem (constituting an *internal* source of stress) induced by recent failures, excessive difficulties on current decision-making tasks, or moral dilemmas.

Until the explanation of groupthink in terms of mutual support to cope with external or internal sources of stress and all the various antecedent factors are substantially confirmed by systematic research, it is risky to make huge inferential leaps from theory to the practical sphere of prevention. Ultimately, a well-substantiated theoretical analysis should have valuable practical applications to the formulation of effective prescriptions. As Kurt Lewin pointed out, "Nothing is so practical as a good theory." But until we know we have a good theory—one that is well supported by controlled experiments and systematic correlational research, as well as by case studies—we must recognize that any prescriptions we draw up are speculative inferences based on what little we know, or think we know, about when and why groupthink occurs. Still, we should not be inhibited from drawing tentative inferences in order to call attention to potentially useful means of prevention—as long as we label them as presumptions, or, to use Michael Scriven's term, "significant possibilities":

> We can . . . answer the question, what do we learn from history, without having to produce absurd or trivial laws, or bare particulars about the past, or murmur mysteriously about deepening our understanding of man. What we most importantly learn from history is a range of possibilities—not of probabilities, not of certainties. And of course these are not mere possibilities, of the kind that one has in mind when one says, Oh, anything is possible! They are significant possibilities, ones that have shaken empires or cabinets before and may do so again for all that we know to the contrary. They are thus most deserving of our respect, and with our knowledge of them we can plan more rationally for the future. If we wish to make a certain outcome more likely, then we can try to bring about those conditions which on previous occasions, not demonstrably irrelevant to the present case, [apparently] did bring about that outcome. If we wish to prevent an outcome, what we can do is to make it less likely; we try to eliminate those circumstances which [seem to] have in the relevant past brought about those circumstances that [seem to] have previously frustrated it.

Perhaps the worst consequences can be prevented if we take steps to avoid the circumstances in which groupthink seems to flourish.

████████ **3.4**

GRAHAM T. ALLISON

Conceptual Models and the Cuban Missile Crisis

The Cuban missile crisis is a seminal event. For thirteen days of October 1962, there was a higher probability that more human lives would end suddenly than ever before in history. Had the worst occurred, the death of 100 million Americans, over 100 million Russians, and millions of Europeans as well would make previous natural calamities and inhumanities appear insignificant. Given the probability of disaster—which President Kennedy estimated as "between 1 out of 3 and even"—our escape seems awesome. . . .

. . . This study proceeds from the premise that marked improvement in our understanding of such events depends critically on more self-consciousness about what observers bring to the analysis. What each analyst sees and judges to be important is a function not only of the evidence about what happened but

From *American Political Science Review* (September 1969). Copyright © 1969 by the American Political Science Association. Reprinted by permission.

also of the "conceptual lenses" through which he looks at the evidence. The principal purpose of this essay is to explore some of the fundamental assumptions and categories employed by analysts in thinking about problems of government behavior, especially in foreign and military affairs.

The general argument can be summarized in three propositions:

1. Analysts think about problems of foreign and military policy in terms of largely implicit conceptual models that have significant consequences for the content of their thought. . . .

2. Most analysts explain (and predict) the behavior of national governments in terms of various forms of one basic conceptual model, here entitled the Rational Policy Model (Model I). . . .

3. Two "alternative" conceptual models, here labeled an Organizational Process Model (Model II) and a Bureaucratic Politics Model (Model III) provide a base for improved explanation and prediction. . . .

Model I: A Rational Policy

. . . How do analysts attempt to explain the Soviet emplacement of missiles in Cuba? The most widely cited explanation of this occurrence has been produced by two RAND Sovietologists, Arnold Horelick and Myron Rush. They conclude that "the introduction of strategic missiles into Cuba was motivated chiefly by the Soviet leaders' desire to overcome . . . the existing large margin of U.S. strategic superiority." How do they reach this conclusion? In Sherlock Holmes style, they seize several salient characteristics of this action and use these features as criteria against which to test alternative hypotheses about Soviet objectives. For example, the size of the Soviet deployment, and the simultaneous emplacement of more expensive, more visible intermediate range missiles as well as medium range missiles, it is argued, exclude an explanation of the action in terms of Cuban defense—since that objective could have been secured with a much smaller number of medium range missiles alone. Their explanation presents an argument for one objective that permits interpretation of the details of Soviet behavior as a value-maximizing choice.

How do analysts account for the coming of the First World War? According to Hans Morgenthau, "the first World War had its origin exclusively in the fear of a disturbance of the European balance of power." In the period preceding World War I, the Triple Alliance precariously balanced the Triple Entente. If either power combination could gain a decisive advantage in the Balkans, it would achieve a decisive advantage in the balance of power. "It was this fear," Morgenthau asserts, "that motivated Austria in July 1914 to settle its accounts with Serbia once and for all, and that induced Germany to support Austria unconditionally. It was the same fear that brought Russia to the support of Serbia, and France to the support of Russia." How is Morgenthau able to resolve this problem so confidently? By imposing on the data a "rational outline."

The value of this method, according to Morgenthau, is that "it provides for rational discipline in action and creates astounding continuity in foreign policy which makes American, British, or Russian foreign policy appear as an intelligent, rational continuum . . . regardless of the different motives, preferences, and intellectual and moral qualities of successive statesmen." . . .

What is striking about these examples from the literature of foreign policy and international relations are the similarities among analysts of various styles when they are called upon to produce explanations. Each assumes that what must be explained is an action, i.e., the realization of some purpose or intention. Each assumes that the actor is the national government. Each assumes that the action is chosen as a calculated response to a strategic problem. For each, explanation consists of showing what goal the government was pursuing in committing the act and how this action was a reasonable choice, given the nation's objectives. This set of assumptions characterizes the rational policy model. . . .

Most contemporary analysts (as well as laymen) proceed predominantly—albeit most often implicitly—in terms of this model when attempting to explain happenings in foreign affairs. Indeed, that occurrences in foreign affairs are the *acts* of *nations* seems so fundamental to thinking about such problems that this underlying model has rarely been recognized: to explain an occurrence in foreign policy simply means to show how the government could have rationally chosen that action. . . .

Rational Policy Paradigm

Basic Unit of Analysis: Policy as National Choice

Happenings in foreign affairs are conceived as actions chosen by the nation or national government. Governments select the action that will maximize strategic goals and objectives. These "solutions" to strategic problems are the fundamental categories in terms of which the analyst perceives what is to be explained. . . .

Dominant Inference Pattern

This paradigm leads analysts to rely on the following pattern of inference: if a nation performed a particular action, that nation must have had ends towards which the action constituted an optimal means. The rational policy model's explanatory power stems from this inference pattern. Puzzlement is relieved by revealing the purposive pattern within which the occurrence can be located as a value-maximizing means.

General Propositions

The disgrace of political science is the infrequency with which propositions of any generality are formulated and tested. "Paradigmatic analysis" argues for explictness about the terms in which analysis proceeds, and seriousness about the logic of explanation. Simply to illustrate the kind of propositions on which analysts who employ this model rely, the formulation includes several.

The basic assumption of value-maximizing behavior produces propositions central to most explanations. The general principle can be formulated as follows: the likelihood of any particular action results from a combination of the nation's (1) relevant values and objectives, (2) perceived alternative courses of action, (3) estimates of various sets of consequences (which will follow from each alternative), and (4) net valuation of each set of consequences. This yields two propositions.

A. An increase in the cost of an alternative, i.e., a reduction in the value of the set of consequences which will follow from that action, or a reduction in the probability of attaining fixed consequences, reduces the likelihood of that alternative being chosen.

B. A decrease in the costs of an alternative, i.e., an increase in the value of the set of consequences which will follow from that alternative, or an increase in the probability of attaining fixed consequences, increases the likelihood of that action being chosen. . . .

The U.S. Blockade of Cuba: A First Cut

The U.S. response to the Soviet Union's emplacement of missiles in Cuba must be understood in strategic terms as simple value-maximizing escalation. American nuclear superiority could be counted on to paralyze Soviet nuclear power; Soviet trangression of the nuclear threshold in response to an American use of lower levels of violence would be wildly irrational since it would mean virtual destruction of the Soviet Communist system and Russian nation. American local superiority was overwhelming: it could be initiated at a low level while threatening with high credibility an ascending sequence of steps short of the nuclear threshold. All that was required was for the United States to bring to bear its strategic and local superiority in such a way that American determination to see the missiles removed would be demonstrated, while at the same time allowing Moscow time and room to retreat without humiliation. The naval blockade—euphemistically named a "quarantine" in order to circumvent the niceties of international law—did just that.

The U.S. government's selection of the blockade followed this logic. Apprised of the presence of Soviet missiles in Cuba, the President assembled an Executive Committee (ExCom) of the National Security Council and directed them to "set aside all other tasks to make a prompt and intense survey of the dangers and all possible courses of action." This group functioned as "fifteen individuals on our own, representing the President and not different departments." As one of the participants recalls, "The remarkable aspect of those meetings was a sense of complete equality." Most of the time during the week that followed was spent canvassing all the possible tracks and weighing the arguments for and against each. Six major categories of action were considered.

1. Do nothing. U.S. vulnerability to Soviet missiles was no new thing. Since the U.S. already lived under the gun of missiles based in Russia, a Soviet capability to strike from Cuba too made little real difference. The real danger stemmed from the possiblity of U.S. over-reaction. The U.S. should announce the Soviet action in a calm, casual manner thereby deflating whatever political capital Khrushchev hoped to make of the missiles.

This argument fails on two counts. First, it grossly underestimates the military importance of the Soviet move. Not only would the Soviet Union's missile capability be doubled and the U.S. early warning system outflanked. The Soviet Union would have an opportunity to reverse the strategic balance by further installations, and indeed, in the longer run, to invest in cheaper, shorter-range rather than more expensive longer-range missiles. Second, the political importance of this move was undeniable. The Soviet Union's act challenged the American President's most solemn warning. If the U.S. failed to respond, no American commitment would be credible.

2. Diplomatic pressures. Several forms were considered: an appeal to the U.N. or O.A.S. for an inspection team, a secret approach to Khrushchev, and a direct approach to Khrushchev, perhaps at a summit meeting. The United States would demand that the missiles be removed, but the final settlement might include neutralization of Cuba, U.S. withdrawal from Guantanamo base, and withdrawal of U.S. Jupiter missiles from Turkey or Italy.

Each form of the diplomatic approach had its own drawbacks. To arraign the Soviet Union before the U.N. Security Council held little promise since the Russians could veto any proposed action. While the diplomats argued, the missiles would be operational. To send a secret emissary to Khrushchev demanding that the missiles be withdrawn would be to pose untenable alternatives. On the one hand, this would invite Khrushchev to seize the diplomatic initiative, perhaps committing himself to strategic retaliation in response to an attack on Cuba. On the other hand, this would tender an ultimatum that no great power could accept. To confront Khrushchev at a summit would guarantee demands for U.S. concessions, and the analogy between U.S. missiles in Turkey and Russian missiles in Cuba could not be erased.

But why not trade U.S. Jupiters in Turkey and Italy, which the President had previously ordered withdrawn, for the missiles in Cuba? The U.S. had chosen to withdraw these missiles in order to replace them with superior, less vulnerable Mediterranean Polaris submarines. But the middle of the crisis was no time for concessions. The offer of such a deal might suggest to the Soviets that the West would yield and thus tempt them to demand more. It would certainly confirm European suspicions about American willingness to sacrifice European interests when the chips were down. Finally, the basic issue should be kept clear. As the President stated in reply to Bertrand Russell, "I think your attention might well be directed to the burglars rather than to those who have caught the burglars."

3. A secret approach to Castro. The crisis provided an opportunity to separate Cuba and Soviet Communism by offering Castro the alternatives, "split or fall." But Soviet troops transported, constructed, guarded, and controlled the missiles. Their removal would thus depend on a Soviet decision.

4. Invasion. The United States could take this occasion not only to remove the missiles but also to rid itself of Castro. A Navy exercise had long been scheduled in which Marines, ferried from Florida in naval vessels, would liberate the imaginary island of Vieques. Why not simply shift the point of disembarkment? (The Pentagon's foresight in planning this operation would be an appropriate antidote to the CIA's Bay of Pigs!)

Preparations were made for an invasion, but as a last resort. American troops would be forced to confront 20,000 Soviets in the first Cold War case of direct contact between the troops of the super powers. Such brinksmanship courted nuclear disaster, practically guaranteeing an equivalent Soviet move against Berlin.

5. Surgical air strike. The missile sites should be removed by a clean, swift conventional attack. This was the effective counter-action which the attempted deception deserved. A surgical strike would remove the missiles and thus eliminate both the danger that the missiles might become operational and the fear that the Soviets would discover the American discovery and act first.

The initial attractiveness of this alternative was dulled by several difficulties. First, could the strike really be "surgical"? The Air Force could not guarantee destruction of all the missiles. Some might be fired during the attack; some might not have been identified. In order to assure destruction of Soviet and Cuban means of retaliating, what was required was not a surgical but rather a massive attack—of at least 500 sorties. Second, a surprise air attack would of course kill Russians at the missile sites. Pressures on the Soviet Union to retaliate would be so strong that an attack on Berlin or Turkey was highly probable. Third, the key problem with this program was that of advance warning. Could the President of the United States, with his memory of Pearl Harbor and his vision of future U.S. responsibility, order a "Pearl Harbor in reverse"? For 175 years, unannounced Sunday morning attacks had been an anathema to our tradition.

6. Blockade. Indirect military action in the form of a blockade became more attractive as the ExCom dissected the other alternatives. An embargo on military shipments to Cuba enforced by a naval blockade was not without flaws, however. Could the U.S. blockade Cuba without inviting Soviet reprisal in Berlin? The likely solution to joint blockades would be the lifting of both blockades, restoring the new *status quo*, and allowing the Soviets additional time to complete the missiles. Second, the possible consequences of the blockade resembled the drawbacks which disqualified the air strike. If Soviet ships did not stop, the United States would be forced to fire the first shot, invit-

ing retaliation. Third, a blockade would deny the traditional freedom of the seas demanded by several of our close allies and might be held illegal, in violation of the U.N. Charter and international law, unless the United States could obtain a two-thirds vote in the O.A.S. Finally, how could a blockade be related to the problem, namely, some 75 missiles on the island of Cuba, approaching operational readiness daily? A blockade offered the Soviets a spectrum of delaying tactics with which to buy time to complete the missile installations. Was a *fait accompli* not required?

In spite of these enormous difficulties the blockade had comparative advantages: (1) It was a middle course between inaction and attack, aggressive enough to communicate firmness of intention, but nevertheless not so precipitous as a strike. (2) It placed on Khrushchev the burden of choice concerning the next step. He could avoid a direct military clash by keeping his ships away. His was the last clear chance. (3) No possible military confrontation could be more acceptable to the U.S. than a naval engagement in the Caribbean. (4) This move permitted the U.S., by flexing its conventional muscle, to exploit the threat of subsequent non-nuclear steps in each of which the U.S. would have significant superiority.

Particular arguments about advantages and disadvantages were powerful. The explanation of the American choice of the blockade lies in a more general principle, however. As President Kennedy stated in drawing the moral of the crisis:

> Above all, while defending our own vital interests, nuclear powers must avert those confrontations which bring an adversary to a choice of either a humiliating retreat or a nuclear war. To adopt that kind of course in the nuclear age would be evidence only of the bankruptcy of our policy—of a collective death wish for the world.

The blockade was the United States' only real option.

Model II: Organizational Process

For some purposes, governmental behavior can be usefully summarized as action chosen by a unitary, rational decisionmaker: centrally controlled, completely informed, and value maximizing. But this simplification must not be allowed to conceal the fact that a "government" consists of a conglomerate of semi-feudal, loosely allied organizations, each with a substantial life of its own. Government leaders do sit formally, and to some extent in fact, on top of this conglomerate. But governments perceive problems through organizational sensors. Governments define alternatives and estimate consequences as organizations process information. Governments act as these organizations enact routines. Government behavior can therefore be understood according to a second conceptual model, less as deliberate choices of leaders and more as *outputs* of large organizations functioning according to standard patterns of behavior.

113

To be responsive to a broad spectrum of problems, governments consist of large organizations among which primary responsibility for particular areas is divided. Each organization attends to a special set of problems and acts in quasi-independence on these problems. But few important problems fall exclusively within the domain of a single organization. Thus government behavior relevant to any important problem reflects the independent output of several organizations, partially coordinated by government leaders. Government leaders can substantially disturb, but not substantially control, the behavior of these organizations.

To perform complex routines, the behavior of large numbers of individuals must be coordinated. Coordination requires standard operating procedures: rules according to which things are done. Assured capability for reliable performance of action that depends upon the behavior of hundreds of persons requires established "programs." Indeed, if the eleven members of a football team are to perform adequately on any particular down, each player must not "do what he thinks needs to be done" or "do what the quarterback tells him to do." Rather, each player must perform the maneuvers specified by a previously established play which the quarterback has simply called in this situation.

At any given time, a government consists of *existing* organizations, each with a *fixed* set of standard operating procedures and programs. The behavior of these organizations—and consequently of the government—relevant to an issue in any particular instance is, therefore, determined primarily by routines established in these organizations prior to that instance. But organizations do change. Learning occurs gradually, over time. Dramatic organizational change occurs in response to major crises. Both learning and change are influenced by existing organizational capabilities.

Borrowed from studies of organizations, these loosely formulated propositions amount simply to *tendencies*. Each must be hedged by modifiers like "other things being equal" and "under certain conditions." In particular instances, tendencies hold—more or less. In specific situations, the relevant question is: more or less? But this is as it should be. For, on the one hand, "organizations" are no more homogeneous a class than "solids." When scientists tried to generalize about "solids," they achieved similar results. Solids tend to expand when heated, but some do and some don't. More adequate categorization of the various elements now lumped under the rubric "organizations" is thus required. On the other hand, the behavior of particular organizations seems considerably more complex than the behavior of solids. Additional information about a particular organization is required for further specification of the tendency statements. In spite of these two caveats, the characterization of government action as organizational output differs distinctly from Model I. Attempts to understand problems of foreign affairs in terms of this frame of reference should produce quite different explanations.

Organizational Process Paradigm

Basic Unit of Analysis: Policy as Organizational Output

The happenings of international politics are, in three critical senses, outputs of organizational processes. First, the actual occurrences are organizational outputs. . . .

Government leaders can trim the edges of this output and exercise some choice in combining outputs. But the mass of behavior is determined by previously established procedures. Second, existing organizational routines for employing present physical capabilities constitute the effective options open to government leaders confronted with any problem. The fact that fixed programs (equipment, men, and routines which exist at the particular time) exhaust the range of buttons that leaders can push is not always perceived by these leaders. But in every case it is critical for an understanding of what is actually done. Third, organizational outputs structure the situation within the narrow constraints of which leaders must contribute their "decision" concerning an issue. Outputs raise the problem, provide the information, and make the initial moves that color the face of the issue that is turned to the leaders. As Theodore Sorensen has observed: "Presidents rarely, if ever, make decisions—particularly in foreign affairs—in the sense of writing their conclusions on a clean slate. . . . The basic decisions, which confine their choices, have all too often been previously made." If one understands the structure of the situation and the face of the issue—which are determined by the organizational outputs—the formal choice of the leaders is frequently anti-climactic. . . .

General Propositions

A number of general propositions have been stated above. In order to illustrate clearly the type of proposition employed by Model II analysts, this section formulates several more precisely.

A. *Organizational Action.* Activity according to SOPs and programs does not constitute far-sighted, flexible adaptation to "the issue" (as it is conceived by the analyst). Detail and nuance of actions by organizations are determined predominantly by organizational routines, not government leaders' directions.

1. SOPs constitute routines for dealing with *standard* situations. Routines allow large numbers of ordinary individuals to deal with numerous instances, day after day, without considerable thought, by responding to basic stimuli. But this regularized capability for adequate performance is purchased at the price of standardization. If the SOPs are appropriate, average performance, i.e., performance averaged over the range of cases, is better than it would be if each instance were approached individually (given fixed talent, timing, and resource constraints). But specific instances, particularly critical instances that typically do not have "standard" characteristics, are often handled sluggishly or inappropriately.

2. A program, i.e., a complex action chosen from a short list of programs in a repertoire, is rarely tailored to the specific situation in which it is executed. Rather, the program is (at best) the most appropriate of the programs in a previously developed repertoire.

3. Since repertoires are developed by parochial organizations for standard scenarios defined by that organization, programs available for dealing with a particular situation are often ill-suited.

B. *Limited Flexibility and Incremental Change.* Major lines of organizational action are straight, i.e., behavior at one time is marginally different from that behavior at $t - 1$. Simple-minded predictions work best: Behavior at $t + 1$ will be marginally different from behavior at the present time.

1. Organizational budgets change incrementally—both with respect to totals and with respect to intra-organizational splits. Though organizations could divide the money available each year by carving up the pie anew (in the light of changes in objectives or environment), in practice, organizations take last year's budget as a base and adjust incrementally. Predictions that require large budgetary shifts in a single year between organizations or between units within an organization should be hedged.

2. Once undertaken, an organizational investment is not dropped at the point where "objective" costs outweigh benefits. Organizational stakes in adopted projects carry them quite beyond the loss point.

C. *Administrative Feasibility.* Adequate explanation, analysis, and prediction must include administrative feasibility as a major dimension. A considerable gap separates what leaders choose (or might rationally have chosen) and what organizations implement.

1. Organizations are blunt instruments. Projects that require several organizations to act with high degrees of precision and coordination are not likely to succeed.

2. Projects that demand that existing organizational units depart from their accustomed functions and perform previously unprogrammed tasks are rarely accomplished in their designed form.

3. Government leaders can expect that each organization will do its "part" in terms of what the organization knows how to do.

4. Government leaders can expect incomplete and distorted information from each organization concerning its part of the problem.

5. Where an assigned piece of a problem is contrary to the existing goals of an organization, resistance to implementation of that piece will be encountered. . . .

The U.S. Blockade of Cuba: A Second Cut

Organizational Intelligence. At 7:00 P.M. on October 22, 1962, President Kennedy disclosed the American discovery of the presence of Soviet strategic missiles in Cuba, declared a "strict quarantine on all offensive military equipment under shipment to Cuba," and demanded that "Chairman Khrushchev halt and eliminate this clandestine, reckless, and provocative threat to world peace." This decision was reached at the pinnacle of the U.S. Government after a critical week of deliberation. What initiated that precious week were photographs of Soviet missile sites in Cuba taken on October 14. These pictures might not have been taken until a week later. In that case, the President speculated, "I don't think probably we would have chosen as prudently as we finally did." U.S. leaders might have received this information three weeks earlier—if a U-2 had flown over San Cristobal in the last week of September. What determined the context in which American leaders came to choose the blockade was the discovery of missiles on October 14.

There has been considerable debate over alleged American "intelligence failures" in the Cuban missile crisis. But what both critics and defenders have neglected is the fact that the discovery took place on October 14, rather than three weeks earlier or a week later, as a consequence of the established routines and procedures of the organizations which constitute the U.S. intelligence community. These organizations were neither more nor less successful than they had been the previous month or were to be in the months to follow.

The notorious "September estimate," approved by the United States Intelligence Board (USIB) on September 19, concluded that the Soviet Union would not introduce offensive missiles into Cuba. No U-2 flight was directed over the western end of Cuba (after September 5) before October 4. No U-2 flew over the western end of Cuba until the flight that discovered the Soviet missiles on October 14. Can these "failures" be accounted for in organizational terms?

On September 19 when USIB met to consider the question of Cuba, the "system" contained the following information: (1) shipping intelligence had noted the arrival in Cuba of two large-hatch Soviet lumber ships, which were riding high in the water; (2) refugee reports of countless sightings of missiles, but also a report that Castro's private pilot, after a night of drinking in Havana, had boasted: "We will fight to the death and perhaps we can win because we have everything, including atomic weapons"; (3) a sighting by a CIA agent of the rear profile of a strategic missile; (4) U-2 photos produced by flights of August 29, September 5 and 17 showing the construction of a number of SAM sites and other defensive missiles. Not all of this information was on the desk of the estimators, however. Shipping intelligence experts note the fact that large-hatch ships were riding high in the water and spelled out the inference: the ships must be carrying "space consuming" cargo. These facts were carefully included in the catalogue of intelligence concerning shipping. For experts sensitive to the Soviets' shortage of ships, however, these facts carried no special signal. The refugee report of Castro's private pilot's remark had been received at Opa Locka, Florida, along with vast reams of inaccurate reports generated by the refugee community. This report and a thousand others had to be checked and compared before being sent to Washington. The two weeks required for initial processing could have been shortened by a large increase in resources, but the yield of this source was already quite marginal. The CIA agent's sighting of the rear profile of a strategic missile had occurred on September 12; transmission time from agent sighting to arrival in Washington typically took 9 to 12 days. Shortening this transmission time would impose severe cost in terms of danger to sub-agents, agents, and communication networks.

On the information available, the intelligence chiefs who predicted that the Soviet Union would not introduce offensive missiles into Cuba made a reasonable and defensible judgment. Moreover, in the light of the fact that these organizations were gathering intelligence not only about Cuba but about potential occurrences in all parts of the worlds, the informational base available to the estimators involved nothing out of the ordinary. Nor, from an organizational perspective, is there anything startling about the gradual accumulation of evidence that led to the formulation of the hypothesis that the Soviets were installing missiles in Cuba and the decision on October 4 to direct a special flight over western Cuba.

The ten-day delay between that decision and the flight is another organizational story. At the October 4 meeting, the Defense Department took the opportunity to raise an issue important to its concerns. Given the increased danger that a U-2 would be downed, it would be better if the pilot were an officer in uniform rather than a CIA agent. Thus the Air Force should assume responsibility for U-2 flights over Cuba. To the contrary, the CIA argued that this was an intelligence operation and thus within the CIA's jurisdiction. Moreover, CIA U-2's had been modified in certain ways which gave them advantages over Air Force U-2's in averting Soviet SAM's. Five days passed while the State Department pressed for less risky alternatives such as drones and the Air Force (in Department of Defense guise) and CIA engaged in territorial disputes. On October 9 a flight plan over San Cristobal was approved by COMOR, but to the CIA's dismay, Air Force pilots rather than CIA agents would take charge of the mission. At this point details become sketchy, but several members of the intelligence community have speculated that an Air Force pilot in an Air Force U-2 attempted a high altitude overflight on October 9 that "flamed out," i.e., lost power, and thus had to descend in order to restart its engine. A second round between Air Force and CIA followed, as a result of which Air Force pilots were trained to fly CIA U-2's. A successful overflight took place on October 14.

This ten-day delay constitutes some form of "failure." In the face of well-founded suspicions concerning offensive Soviet missiles in Cuba that posed a critical threat to the United States' most vital interest, squabbling between organizations whose job it is to produce this information seems entirely inappropriate. But for each of these organizations, the question involved the issue: "*Whose* job was it to be?" Moreover, the issue was not simply, which organization would control U-2 flights over Cuba, but rather the broader issue of ownership of U-2 intelligence activities—a very long standing territorial dispute. Thus though this delay was in one sense a "failure," it was also a nearly inevitable consequence of two facts: many jobs do not fall neatly into precisely defined organizational jurisdictions; and vigorous organizations are imperialistic.

Organizational Options. Deliberations of leaders in ExCom meetings produced broad outlines of alternatives. Details of these alternatives and blueprints for their implementation had to be specified by the organizations that would perform these tasks. These organizational outputs answered the question: What, specifically, *could* be done?

Discussion in the ExCom quickly narrowed the live options to two: an air strike and a blockade. The choice of the blockade instead of the air strike turned on two points: (1) the argument from morality and tradition that the United States could not perpetrate a "Pearl Harbor in reverse"; (2) the belief that a "surgical" air strike was impossible. Whether the United States *might* strike first was a question not of capability but of morality. Whether the United States *could* perform the surgical strike was a factual question concerning capabilities. The majority of the members of the ExCom, including the President, initially preferred the air strike. What effectively foreclosed this option, however, was the fact that the air strike they wanted could not be chosen with high confidence of success. After having tentatively chosen the course of prudence—given that the surgical air strike was not an option—Kennedy reconsidered. On Sunday morning, October 21, he called the Air Force experts to a special meeting in his living quarters where he probed once more for the option of a *"surgical"* air strike. General Walter C. Sweeny, Commander of Tactical Air Forces, asserted again that the Air Force could guarantee no higher than ninety percent effectiveness in a surgical air strike. That "fact" was false.

The air strike alternative provides a classic case of military estimates. One of the alternatives outlined by the ExCom was named "air strike." Specification of the details of this alternative was delegated to the Air Force. Starting from an existing plan for massive U.S. military action against Cuba (prepared for contingencies like a response to a Soviet Berlin grab), Air Force estimators produced an attack to guarantee success. This plan called for extensive bombardment of all missile sites, storage depots, airports, and, in deference to the Navy, the artillery batteries opposite the naval base at Guantanamo. Members of the ExCom repeatedly expressed bewilderment at military estimates of the number of sorties required, likely casualties, and collateral damage. But the "surgical" air strike that the political leaders had in mind was never carefully examined during the first week of the crisis. Rather, this option was simply excluded on the grounds that since the Soviet MRBM's in Cuba were classified "mobile" in U.S. manuals, extensive bombing was required. During the second week of the crisis, careful examination revealed that the missiles were mobile, in the sense that small houses are mobile: that is, they

119

could be moved and reassembled in 6 days. After the missiles were reclassified "movable" and detailed plans for surgical air strikes specified, this action was added to the list of live options for the end of the second week.

Organizational Implementation. Ex-Com members separated several types of blockade: offensive weapons only, all armaments, and all strategic goods including POL (petroleum, oil, and lubricants). But the "*details*" of the operation were left to the Navy. Before the President announced the blockade on Monday evening, the first stage of the Navy's blueprint was in motion, and a problem loomed on the horizon. The Navy had a detailed plan for the blockade. The President had several less precise but equally determined notions concerning what should be done, when, and how. For the Navy the issue was one of effective implementation of the Navy's blockade—without the meddling and interference of political leaders. For the President, the problem was to pace and manage events in such a way that the Soviet leaders would have time to see, think, and blink.

A careful reading of available sources uncovers an instructive incident. On Tuesday the British Ambassador, Ormsby-Gore, after having attended a briefing on the details of the blockade, suggested to the President that the plan for intercepting Soviet ships far out of reach of Cuban jets did not facilitate Khrushchev's hard decision. Why not make the interception much closer to Cuba and thus give the Russian leader more time? According to the public account and the recollection of a number of individuals involved, Kennedy "agreed immediately," called McNamara, and over emotional Navy protest, issued the appropriate instructions." As Sorensen records, "in a sharp clash with the Navy, he made certain his will prevailed." The Navy's plan for the blockade was thus changed by drawing the blockade much closer to Cuba.

A serious organizational orientation makes one suspicious of this account. More careful examination of the available evidence confirms these suspicions, though alternative accounts must be somewhat speculative. According to the public chronology, a quarantine drawn close to Cuba became effective on Wednesday morning, the first Soviet ship was contacted on Thursday morning, and the first boarding of a ship occurred on Friday. According to the statement by the Department of Defense, boarding of the *Marcula* by a party from the *John R. Pierce* "took place at 7:50 A.M., E.D.T., 180 miles northeast of Nassau." The *Marcula* had been trailed since about 10:30 the previous evening. Simple calculations suggest that the *Pierce* must have been stationed along the Navy's original arc which extended 500 miles out to sea from Cape Magsi, Cuba's eastern most tip. The blockade line was *not* moved as the President ordered, and the accounts report. What happened is not entirely clear. One can be certain, however, that Soviet ships passed through the line along which American destroyers had posted themselves before the official "first contact" with the Soviet ship. On October 26 a Soviet tanker arrived in Havana and was honored by a dockside rally for "running the blockade." Photographs of this vessel show the name *Vinnitsa* on the side of the vessel in

Cyrillic letters. But according to the official U.S. position, the first tanker to pass through the blockade was the *Bucharest*, which was hailed by the Navy on the morning of October 25. Again simple mathematical calculation excludes the possibility that the *Bucharest* and *Vinnitsa* were the same ship. It seems probable that the Navy's resistance to the President's order that the blockade be drawn in closer to Cuba forced him to allow one or several Soviet ships to pass through the blockade after it was officially operative.

This attempt to leash the Navy's blockade had a price. On Wednesday morning, October 24, what the President had been awaiting occurred. The 18 dry cargo ships heading towards the quarantine stopped dead in the water. This was the occasion of Dean Rusk's remark, "We are eyeball to eyeball and I think the other fellow just blinked." But the Navy had another interpretation. The ships had simply stopped to pick up Soviet submarine escorts. The President became quite concerned lest the Navy—already riled because of Presidential meddling in its affairs—blunder into an incident. Sensing the President's fears, McNamara became suspicious of the Navy's procedures and routines for making the first interception. Calling on the Chief of Naval Operations in the Navy's inner sanctum, the Navy Flag Plot, McNamara put his questions harshly. Who would make the first interception? Were Russian-speaking officers on board? How would submarines be dealt with? At one point McNamara asked Anderson what he would do if a Soviet ship's captain refused to answer questions about his cargo. Picking up the Manual of Navy Regulations the Navy man waved it in McNamara's face and shouted, "It's all in there." To which McNamara replied, "I don't give a damn what John Paul Jones would have done; I want to know what you are going to do, now." The encounter ended on Anderson's remark: "Now, Mr. Secretary, if you and your Deputy will go back to your office the Navy will run the blockade."

Model III: Bureaucratic Politics

The leaders who sit on top of organizations are not a monolithic group. Rather, each is, in his own right, a player in a central, competitive game. The name of the game is bureaucratic politics: bargaining along regularized channels among players positioned hierarchically within the government. Government behavior can thus be understood according to a third conceptual model not as organizational outputs, but as outcomes of bargaining games. In contrast with Model I, the bureaucratic politics model sees no unitary actor but rather many actors as players, who focus not on a single strategic issue but on many diverse intra-national problems as well, in terms of no consistent set of strategic objectives but rather according to various conceptions of national, organizational, and personal goals, making government decisions not by rational choice but by the pulling and hauling that is politics.

The apparatus of each national government constitutes a complex arena for the intra-national game. Political leaders at the top of this apparatus plus the men who occupy positions on top of the critical organizations form the circle of central players. Ascendancy to this circle assures some independent standing. The necessary decentralization of decisions required for action on the broad range of foreign policy problems guarantees that each player has considerable discretion. Thus power is shared.

Men share power. Men differ concerning what must be done. The differences matter. This milieu necessitates that policy be resolved by politics. What the nation does is sometimes the result of the triumph of one group over others. More often, however, different groups pulling in different directions yield a resultant distinct from what anyone intended. What moves the chess pieces is not simply the reasons which support a course of action, nor the routines of organizations which enact an alternative, but the power and skill of proponents and opponents of the action in question.

This characterization captures the thrust of the bureaucratic politics orientation. If problems of foreign policy arose as discreet issues, and decisions were determined one game at a time, this account would suffice. But most "issues," e.g., Vietnam or the proliferation of nuclear weapons, emerge piecemeal, over time, one lump in one context, a second in another. Hundreds of issues compete for players' attention every day. Each player is forced to fix upon his issues for that day, fight them on their own terms, and rush on to the next. Thus the character of emerging issues and the pace at which the game is played converge to yield government "decisions" and "actions" as collages. Choices by one player, outcomes of minor games, outcomes of central games, and "foul-ups"—these pieces, when stuck to the same canvas, constitute government behavior relevant to an issue.

The concept of national security policy as political outcome contradicts both public imagery and academic orthodoxy. Issues vital to national security, it is said, are too important to be settled by political games. They must be "above" politics. To accuse someone of "playing politics with national security" is a most serious charge. What public convention demands, the academic penchant for intellectual elegance reinforces. Internal politics is messy; moreover, according to prevailing doctrine, politicking lacks intellectual content. As such, it constitutes gossip for journalists rather than a subject for serious investigation. Occasional memoirs, anecdotes in historical accounts, and several detailed case studies to the contrary, most of the literature of foreign policy avoids bureaucratic politics. The gap between academic literature and the experience of participants in government is nowhere wider than at this point.

Bureaucratic Politics Paradigm

. . . Individuals become players in the national security policy game by occupying a critical position in an administration. For example, in the U.S. government the players include "Chiefs": the President, Secretaries of State, Defense, and Treasury, Director of the CIA, Joint Chiefs of Staff, and, since

1961, the Special Assistant for National Security Affairs; "Staffers": the immediate staff of each Chief; "Indians": the political appointees and permanent government officials within each of the departments and agencies; and *"Ad Hoc* Players": actors in the wider government game (especially "Congressional Influentials"), members of the press, spokesmen for important interest groups (especially the "bipartisan foreign policy establishment" in and out of Congress), and surrogates for each of these groups. Other members of the Congress, press, interest groups, and public form concentric circles around the central arena—circles which demarcate the permissive limits within which the game is played.

Positions define what players both may and must do. The advantages and handicaps with which each player can enter and play in various games stems from his position. So does a cluster of obligations for the performance of certain tasks. The two sides of this coin are illustrated by the position of the modern Secretary of State. First, in form and usually in fact, he is the primary repository of political judgment on the political-military issues that are the stuff of contemporary foreign policy; consequently, he is a senior personal advisor to the President. Second, he is the colleague of the President's other senior advisers on the problems of foreign policy, the Secretaries of Defense and Treasury, and the Special Assistant for National Security Affairs. Third, he is the ranking U.S. diplomat for serious negotiation. Fourth, he serves as an Administration voice to Congress, the country, and the world. Finally, he is "Mr. State Department" or "Mr. Foreign Office," "leader of officials, spokesman for their causes, guardian of their interests, judge of their disputes, superintendent of their work, master of their careers." But he is not first one, and then the other. All of these obligations are his simultaneously. His performance in one affects his credit and power in the others. The perspective stemming from the daily work which he must oversee—the cable traffic by which his department maintains relations with other foreign offices—conflicts with the President's requirement that he serve as a generalist and coordinator of contrasting perspectives. The necessity that he be close to the President restricts the extent to which, and the force with which, he can front for his department. When he defers to the Secretary of Defense rather than fighting for his department's position—as he often must—he strains the loyalty of his officialdom. The Secretary's resolution of these conflicts depends not only upon the position, but also upon the player who occupies the position.

For players are also people. Men's metabolisms differ. The core of the bureaucratic politics mix is personality. How each man manages to stand the heat in his kitchen, each player's basic operating style, and the complementarity or contradiction among personalities and styles in the inner circles are irreducible pieces of the policy blend. Moreover, each person comes to his position with baggage in tow, including sensitivities to certain issues, commitments to various programs, and personal standing and debts with groups in the society. . . .

... "Solutions" to strategic problems are not derived by detached analysts focusing coolly on *the* problem. Instead, deadlines and events raise issues in games, and demand decisions of busy players in contexts that influence the face the issue wears. The problems for the players are both narrower and broader than *the* strategic problem. For each player focuses not on the total strategic problem but rather on the decision that must be made now. But each decision has critical consequences not only for the strategic problem but for each player's organizational, reputational, and personal stakes. Thus the gap between the problems the player was solving and the problem upon which the analyst focuses is often very wide.

... Bargaining games do not proceed randomly. Action-channels, i.e., regularized ways of producing action concerning types of issues, structure the game by pre-selecting the major players, determining their points of entrance into the game, and distributing particular advantages and disadvantages for each game. Most critically, channels determine "who's got the action," that is, which department's Indians actually do whatever is chosen. Weapon procurement decisions are made within the annual budgeting process; embassies' demands for action cables are answered according to routines of consultation and clearance from State to Defense and White House; requests for instructions from military groups (concerning assistance all the time, concerning operations during war) are composed by the military in consultation with the Office of the Secretary of Defense, State, and White House; crisis responses are debated among White House, State, Defense, CIA, and Ad Hoc players; major political speeches, especially by the President but also by other Chiefs, are cleared through established channels.

... Government decisions are made and government actions emerge neither as the calculated choice of a unified group, nor as a formal summary of leaders' preferences. Rather the context of shared power but separate judgments concerning important choices, determines that politics is the mechanism of choice. Note the *environment* in which the game is played: inordinate uncertainty about what must be done, the necessity that something be done, and crucial consequences of whatever is done. These features force responsible men to become active players. The *pace of the game*—hundreds of issues, numerous games, and multiple channels—compels players to fight to "get others' attention," to make them "see the facts," to assure that they "take the time to think seriously about the broader issue." The *structure of the game*—power shared by individuals with separate responsibilities—validates each player's feeling that "others don't see my problem," and "others must be persuaded to look at the issue from a less parochial perspective." The *rules of the game*—he who hesitates loses his chance to play at that point, and he who is uncertain about his recommendation is overpowered by others who are sure—pressures players to come down on one side of a 51-49 issue and play. The *rewards of the game*—effectiveness, i.e., impact on outcomes, as the immediate measure of performance—encourages hard play. Thus, most players come to fight to "make the government do what is right." The strategies and tactics employed are quite similar to those formalized by theorists of international relations.

. . . Important government decisions or actions emerge as collages composed of individual acts, outcomes of minor and major games, and foul-ups. Outcomes which could never have been chosen by an actor and would never have emerged from bargaining in a single game over the issue are fabricated piece by piece. Understanding of the outcome requires that it be disaggregated.

. . . If a nation performed an action, that action was the *outcome* of bargaining among individuals and groups within the government. That outcome included *results* achieved by groups committed to a decision or action, *resultants* which emerged from bargaining among groups with quite different positions and *foul-ups*. Model III's explanatory power is achieved by revealing the pulling and hauling of various players, with different perceptions and priorities, focusing on separate problems, which yielded the outcomes that constitute the action in question.

General Propositions

1. *Action and Intention.* Action does not presuppose intention. The sum of behavior of representatives of a government relevant to an issue was rarely intended by any individual or group. Rather separate individuals with different intentions contributed pieces which compose an outcome distinct from what anyone would have chosen.

2. *Where you stand depends on where you sit.* Horizontally, the diverse demands upon each player shape his priorities, perceptions, and issues. For large classes of issues, e.g., budgets and procurement decisions, the stance of a particular player can be predicted with high reliability from information concerning his seat. In the notorious B-36 controversy, no one was surprised by Admiral Radford's testimony that "the B-36 under any theory of war, is a bad gamble with national security," as opposed to Air Force Secretary Symington's claim that "a B-36 with an A-bomb can destroy distant objectives which might require ground armies years to take."

3. *Chiefs and Indians.* The aphorism "where you stand depends on where you sit" has vertical as well as horizontal application. Vertically, the demands upon the President, Chiefs, Staffers, and Indians are quite distinct.

The foreign policy issues with which the President can deal are limited primarily by his crowded schedule: the necessity of dealing first with what comes next. His problem is to probe the special face worn by issues that come to his attention, to preserve his leeway until time has clarified the uncertainties, and to assess the relevant risks.

Foreign policy Chiefs deal most often with the hottest issue *de jour*, though they can get the attention of the President and other members of the government for other issues which they judge important. What they cannot guarantee is that "the President will pay the price" or that "the others will get on board." They must build a coalition of the relevant powers that be. They must "give the President confidence" in the right course of action.

Most problems are framed, alternatives specified, and proposals pushed, however, by Indians. Indians fight with Indians of other departments; for example, struggles between International Security Affairs of the Department of Defense and Pol· ·cal-Military of the State Department are a microcosm of the action at higher levels. But the Indian's major problem is how to get the *attention* of Chiefs, how to get an issue decided, how to get the government "to do what is right."

In policy making then, the issue looking *down* is options: how to preserve my leeway until time clarifies uncertainties. The issue looking *sideways* is commitment: how to get others committed to my coalition. The issue looking *upwards* is confidence; how to give the boss confidence in doing what must be done. To paraphrase one of [Richard E.] Neustadt's assertions which can be applied down the length of the ladder, the essence of a responsible official's task is to induce others to see that what needs to be done is what their own appraisal of their own responsibilities requires them to do in their own interests.

Specific Propositions

. . . The probability of nuclear attack depends primarily on the probability of attack emerging as an outcome of the bureaucratic politics of the attacking government. First, which players can decide to launch an attack? Whether the effective power over action is controlled by an individual, a minor game, or the central game is critical. Second, though Model I's confidence in nuclear deterrence stems from an assertion that, in the end, governments will not commit suicide, Model III recalls historical precedents. Admiral Yamamoto, who designed the Japanese attack on Pearl Harbor, estimated accurately: "In the first six months to a year of war against the U.S. and England I will run wild, and I will show you an uninterrupted succession of victories; I must also tell you that, should the war be prolonged for two or three years, I have no confidence in our ultimate victory." But Japan attacked. Thus, three questions might be considered. One: Could any member of the government solve his problem by attack? What patterns of bargaining could yield attack as an outcome? The major difference between a stable balance of terror and a questionable balance may simply be that in the first case most members of the government appreciate fully the consequences of attack and are thus on guard against the emergence of this outcome. Two: what stream of outcomes might lead to an attack? At what point in that stream is the potential attacker's politics? If members of the U.S. government had been sensitive to the stream of decisions from which the Japanese attack on Pearl Harbor emerged, they would have been aware of a considerable probability of that attack. Three: how might miscalculation and confusion generate foul-ups that yield attack as an outcome? For example, in a crisis or after the beginning of conventional war, what happens to the information available to, and the effective power of, members of the central game.

The U.S. Blockade of Cuba: A Third Cut

The Politics of Discovery. A series of overlapping bargaining games determined both the *date* of the discovery of the Soviet missiles and the *impact* of this discovery on the Administration. An explanation of the politics of the discovery is consequently a considerable piece of the explanation of the U.S. blockade.

Cuba was the Kennedy Administration's "political Achilles' heel." The months preceding the crisis were also months before the Congressional elections, and the Republican Senatorial and Congressional Campaign Committee had announced that Cuba would be "the dominant issue of the 1962 campaign." What the administration billed as a "more positive and indirect approach of isolating Castro from developing, democratic Latin America," Senators Keating, Goldwater, Capehart, Thurmond, and others attacked as a "do-nothing" policy. In statements on the floor of the House and Senate, campaign speeches across the country, and interviews and articles carried by national news media, Cuba—particularly the Soviet program of increased arms aid—served as a stick for stirring the domestic political scene.

These attacks drew blood. Prudence demanded a vigorous reaction. The President decided to meet the issue head-on. The Administration mounted a forceful campaign of denial designed to discredit critics' claims. The President himself manned the front line of this offensive, though almost all Administration officials participated. In his news conference on August 19, President Kennedy attacked as "irresponsible" calls for an invasion of Cuba, stressing rather "the totality of our obligations" and promising to "watch what happens in Cuba with the closest attention." On September 4, he issued a strong statement denying any provocative Soviet action in Cuba. On September 13 he lashed out at "loose talk" calling for an invasion of Cuba. The day before the flight of the U-2 which discovered the missiles, he campaigned in Capehart's Indiana against those "self-appointed generals and admirals who want to send someone else's sons to war."

On Sunday, October 14, just as a U-2 was taking the first pictures of Soviet missiles, McGeorge Bundy was asserting:

> I *know* that there is no present evidence, and I think that there is no present likelihood that the Cuban government and the Soviet government would, in combination, attempt to install a major offensive capability.

In this campaign to puncture the critics' charges, the Administration discovered that the public needed positive slogans. Thus, Kennedy fell into a tenuous semantic distinction between "offensive" and "defensive" weapons. This distinction orginated in his September 4 statement that there was no evidence of "offensive ground to ground missiles" and warned "were it to be otherwise, the gravest issues would arise." His September 13 statement turned on this distinction between "defensive" and "offensive" weapons and announced a firm commitment to action if the Soviet Union attempted to introduce the latter into Cuba. Congressional committees elicited from administration officials testimony which read this distinction and the President's commitment into the *Congressional Record*.

What the President wanted to hear, the CIA was most hesitant to say plainly. On August 22 John McCone met privately with the President and voiced suspicions that the Soviets were preparing to introduce offensive missiles into Cuba. Kennedy heard this as what it was: the suspicion of a hawk. McCone left Washington for a month's honeymoon on the Riviera. Fretting at Cap Ferrat, he bombarded his deputy, General Marshall Carter, with telegrams, but Carter, knowing that McCone had informed the President of his suspicions and received a cold reception, was reluctant to distribute these telegrams outside the CIA. On September 9 a U-2 "on loan" to the Chinese Nationalists was downed over mainland China. The Committee on Overhead Reconnaissance (COMOR) convened on September 10 with a sense of urgency. Loss of another U-2 might incite world opinion to demand cancellation of U-2 flights. The President's campaign against those who asserted that the Soviets were acting provocatively in Cuba had begun. To risk downing a U-2 over Cuba was to risk chopping off the limb on which the President was sitting. That meeting decided to shy away from the western end of Cuba (where SAMs were becoming operational) and modify the flight pattern of the U-2s in order to reduce the probability that a U-2 would be lost. USIB's unanimous approval of the September estimate reflects similar sensitivities. On September 13 the President had asserted that there were no Soviet offensive missiles in Cuba and committed his Administration to act if offensive missiles were discovered. Before Congressional committees, Administration officials were denying that there was any evidence whatever of offensive missiles in Cuba. The implications of a National Intelligence estimate which concluded that the Soviets were introducing offensive missiles into Cuba were not lost on the men who constituted America's highest intelligence assembly.

The October 4 COMOR decision to direct a flight over the western end of Cuba in effect "overturned" the September estimate, but without officially raising that issue. The decision represented McCone's victory for which he had lobbied with the President before the September 10 decision, in telegrams before the September 19 estimate, and in person after his return to Washington. Though the politics of the intelligence community is closely guarded, several pieces of the story can be told. By September 27, Colonel Wright and others in DIA [Defense Intelligence Agency] believed that the Soviet Union was placing missiles in the San Cristobal area. This area was marked suspicious by the CIA on September 29 and certified top priority on October 3. By October 4 McCone had the evidence required to raise the issue officially. The members of

COMOR heard McCone's argument, but were reluctant to make the hard decision he demanded. The significant probability that a U-2 would be downed made overflight of western Cuba a matter of real concern.

The Politics of Issues. The U-2 photographs presented incontrovertible evidence of Soviet offensive missiles in Cuba. This revelation fell upon politicized players in a complex context. As one high official recalled, Khrushchev had caught us "with our pants down." What each of the central participants saw, and what each did to cover both his own and the Administration's nakedness, created the spectrum of issues and answers.

At approximately 9:00 A.M., Tuesday morning, October 16, McGeorge Bundy went to the President's living quarters with the message: "Mr. President, there is now hard photographic evidence that the Russians have offensive missiles in Cuba." Much has been made of Kennedy's "expression of surprise," but "surprise" fails to capture the character of his initial reaction. Rather, it was one of startled anger, most adequately covered by the exclamation, "He can't do that to *me!*" In terms of the President's attention and priorities at that moment, Khrushchev had chosen the most unhelpful act of all. Kennedy had staked his full Presidential authority on the assertion that the Soviets would not place offensive weapons in Cuba. Moreover, Khrushchev had assured the President through the most direct and personal channels that he was aware of the President's domestic political problem and that nothing would be done to exacerbate this problem. The Chairman had *lied* to the President. Kennedy's initial reaction entailed action. The missiles must be removed. The alternatives of "doing nothing" or "taking a diplomatic approach" could not have been less relevant to *his* problem.

These two tracks—doing nothing and taking a diplomatic approach—were the solutions advocated by two of his principal advisors. For Secretary of Defense McNamara, the missiles raised the spectre of nuclear war. He first framed the issue as a straightforward strategic problem. To understand the issue, one had to grasp two obvious but difficult points. First, the missiles represented an inevitable occurrence: narrowing of the missile gap. It simply happened sooner rather than later. Second, the United States could accept this occurrence since its consequences were minor: "seven-to-one missile 'superiority,' one-to-one missile 'equality,' one-to-seven missile 'inferiority'—the three postures are identical." McNamara's statement of this argument at the first meeting of the ExCom was summed up in the phrase, "a missile is a missile." "It makes no great difference," he maintained, "whether you are killed by a missile from the Soviet Union or Cuba." The implication was clear. The United States should not initiate a crisis with the Soviet Union, risking a significant probability of nuclear war over an occurrence which had such small strategic implications.

The perceptions of McGeorge Bundy, the President's Assistant for National Security Affairs, are the most difficult of all to reconstruct. There is no question that he initially argued for a diplomatic track. But was Bundy laboring under his acknowledged burden of responsibility in Cuba I? Or was he playing the role of devil's advocate in order to make the President probe his own initial reaction and consider other options?

The President's brother, Robert Kennedy, saw most clearly the political wall against which Khrushchev had backed the President. But he, like McNamara, saw the prospect of nuclear doom. Was Khrushchev going to force the President to an insane act? At the first meeting of the ExCom, he scribbled a note, "Now I know how Tojo felt when he was planning Pearl Harbor." From the outset he searched for an alternative that would prevent the air strike.

The initial reaction of Theodore Sorensen, the President's Special Counsel and "alter ego," fell somewhere between that of the President and his brother. Like the President, Sorensen felt the poignancy of betrayal. If the President had been the architect of the policy which the missiles punctured, Sorensen was the draftsman. Khrushchev's deceitful move demanded a strong counter-move. But like Robert Kennedy, Sorensen feared lest the shock and disgrace lead to disaster.

To the Joint Chiefs of Staff the issue was clear. *Now* was the time to do the job for which they had prepared contingency plans. Cuba I had been badly done; Cuba II would not be. The missiles provided the *occasion* to deal with the issue: cleansing the Western Hemisphere of Castro's Communism. As the President recalled on the day the crisis ended, "An invasion would have been a mistake—a wrong use of our power. But the military are mad. They wanted to do this. It's lucky for us that we have McNamara over there."

McCone's perceptions flowed from his confirmed prediction. As the Cassandra of the incident, he argued forcefully that the Soviets had installed the missiles in a daring political probe which the United States must meet with force. The time for an air strike was now.

The Politics of Choice. The process by which the blockade emerged is a story of the most subtle and intricate probing, pulling, and hauling; leading, guiding, and spurring. Reconstruction of this process can only be tentative. Initially the President and most of his advisers wanted the clean, surgical air strike. On the first day of the crisis, when informing Stevenson of the missiles, the President mentioned only two alternatives: "I suppose the alternatives are to go in by air and wipe them out, or to take other steps to render them inoperable." At the end of the week a sizeable minority still favored an air strike. As Robert Kennedy recalled: "The fourteen people involved were very significant. . . . If six of them had been President of the U.S., I think that the world might have been blown up." What prevented the air strike was a fortuitous coincidence of a number of factors—the absence of any one of which might have permitted that option to prevail.

First, McNamara's vision of holocaust set him firmly against the air strike. His initial attempt to frame the issue in strategic terms struck Kennedy as particularly inappropriate. Once McNamara realized that the name of the game was a strong response, however, he and his deputy Gilpatric chose the blockade as a fallback. When the Secretary of Defense—whose department had the action, whose reputation in the Cabinet was unequaled, in whom the President demonstrated full confidence—marshalled the arguments for the blockade and refused to be moved, the blockade became a formidable alternative.

Second, Robert Kennedy—the President's closest confidant—was unwilling to see his brother become a "Tojo." His arguments against the air strike on moral grounds struck a chord in the President. Moreover, once his brother had stated these arguments so forcefully, the President could not have chosen his initially preferred course without, in effect, agreeing to become what RFK had condemned.

The President learned of the missiles on Tuesday morning. On Wednesday morning, in order to mask our discovery from the Russians, the President flew to Connecticut to keep a campaign commitment, leaving RFK as the unofficial chairman of the group. By the time the President returned on Wednesday evening, a critical third piece had been added to the picture. McNamara had presented his argument for the blockade. Robert Kennedy and Sorensen had joined McNamara. A powerful coalition of the advisers in whom the President had the greatest confidence, and with whom his style was most compatible, had emerged.

Fourth, the coalition that had formed behind the President's initial preference gave him reason to pause. *Who* supported the air strike—the Chiefs, McCone, Rusk, Nitze, and Acheson—as much as *how* they supported it, counted. Fifth, a piece of inaccurate information, which no one probed, permitted the blockade advocates to fuel (potential) uncertainties in the President's mind. When the President returned to Washington Wednesday evening, RFK and Sorensen met him at the airport. Sorensen gave the President a four-page memorandum outlining the areas of agreement and disagreement. The strongest argument was that the air strike simply could not be surgical. After a day of prodding and questioning, the Air Force had asserted that it could not guarantee the success of a surgical air strike limited to the missiles alone.

Thursday evening, the President convened the ExCom at the White House. He declared his tentative choice of the blockade and directed that preparations be made to put it into effect by Monday morning. Though he raised a question about the possibility of a surgical air strike subsequently, he seems to have accepted the experts' opinion that this was no live option. (Acceptance of this estimate suggests that he may have learned the lesson of the Bay of Pigs—"Never rely on experts"—less well than he supposed.) But this information was incorrect. That no one probed this estimate during the first week of the crisis poses an interesting question for further investigation.

A coalition, including the President, thus emerged from the President's initial decision that something had to be done; McNamara, Robert Kennedy, and Sorensen's resistance to the air strike; incompatibility between the

President and the air strike advocates; and an inaccurate piece of information.

Conclusion

This essay had obviously bitten off more than it has chewed. For further developments and synthesis of these arguments the reader is referred to the larger study. In spite of the limits of space, however, it would be inappropriate to stop without spelling out several implications of the argument and addressing the question of relations among the models and extensions of them to activity beyond explanation.

At a minimum, the intended implications of the argument presented here are four. First, formulation of alternative frames of reference and demonstration that different analysts, relying predominantly on different models, produce quite different explanations should encourage the analyst's self-consciousness about the nets he employs. The effect of these "spectacles" in sensitizing him to particular aspects of what is going on—framing the puzzle in one way rather than another, encouraging him to examine the problem in terms of certain categories rather than others, directing him to particular kinds of evidence, and relieving puzzlement by one procedure rather than another—must be recognized and explored.

Second, the argument implies a position on the problem of "the state of the art." While accepting the commonplace characterization of the present condition of foreign policy analysis—personalistic, non-cumulative, and sometimes insightful—this essay rejects both the counsel of despair's justification of this condition as a consequence of the character of the enterprise, and the "new frontiersmen's" demand for *a priori* theorizing on the frontiers and *ad hoc* appropriation of "new techniques." What is required as a first step is non-casual examination of the present product: inspection of existing explanations, articulation of the conceptual models employed in producing them, formulation of the propositions relied upon, specification of the logic of the various intellectual enterprises, and reflection on the questions being asked. Though it is difficult to overemphasize the need for more systematic processing of more data, these preliminary matters of formulating questions with clarity and sensitivity to categories and assumptions so that fruitful acquisition of large quantities of data is possible are still a major hurdle in considering most important problems.

GEORGE P. SHULTZ

Morality and Realism in American Foreign Policy

I deeply appreciate this marvelous award because of the greatness of the man in whose honor it was established. My appreciation is doubly reinforced because of the greatness of the man [Dr. Henry Kissinger] who has just made this presentation.

Hans Morgenthau's Legacy

Hans Morgenthau was a pioneer in the study of international relations. He, perhaps more than anyone else, gave it intellectual respectability as an academic discipline. His work transformed our thinking about international relations and about America's role in the postwar world. In fundamental ways, he set the terms of the modern debate, and it is hard to imagine what our policies would be like today had we not had the benefit of his wisdom and the clarity of his thinking.

As a professor at the University of Chicago—and I was once a professor at the University of Chicago and a colleague of his—in 1948 he published the first edition of his epoch-making text, *Politics Among Nations.* Its impact was immediate—and alarming to many. It focused on the reality of so-called power politics and the balance of power—the evils of the Old World conflicts that immigrants had come to this country to escape and which Wilsonian idealism had sought to eradicate.

Morgenthau's critics, however, tended to miss what he was really saying about international morality and ethics. The choice, he insisted, is not between moral principles and the national interest, devoid of moral dignity, but between moral principles divorced from political reality and moral principles derived from political reality. And he called on Americans to relearn the principles of statecraft and political morality that had guided the Founding Fathers.

Hans Morgenthau was right in this. Our Declaration of Independence set forth principles, after all, that we believed to be universal. And throughout our history, Americans as individuals—and, sometimes, as a nation— have frequently expressed our hopes for a world based on those principles. The very nature of our society makes us a people with a moral vision, not

Address before the National Committee on American Foreign Policy on the occasion of receiving the Hans J. Morgenthau Memorial Award, New York City, October 2, 1985.

only for ourselves but for the world.

At the same time, however, we Americans have had to accept that our passionate commitment to moral principles could be no substitute for a sound foreign policy in a world of hard realities and complex choices. Our Founding Fathers, in fact, understood this very well.

Hans Morgenthau wrote that "the intoxication with moral abstractions . . . is one of the great sources of weakness and failure in American foreign policy." He was assailing the tendency among Americans at many periods in our later history to hold ourselves above power politics and to believe that moral principles alone could guide us in our relations with the rest of the world. He correctly worried that our moral impulse, noble as it might be, could lead either to futile and perhaps dangerous global crusades, on the one hand, or to escapism and isolationism, equally dangerous, on the other.

The challenge we have always faced has been to forge policies that could combine morality and realism that would be in keeping with our ideals without doing damage to our national interests. Hans Morgenthau's work shaped our national debate about this challenge with an unprecedented intensity and clarity.

Ideals and Interests Today

That debate still continues today. But today there is a new reality.

The reality today is that our moral principles and our national interests may be converging, by necessity, more than ever before. The revolutions in communications and transportation have made the world a smaller place. Events in one part of the world have a more far-reaching impact than ever before on the international environment and on our national security. Even individual acts of violence by terrorists can affect us in ways never possible before the advent of international electronic media.

Yesterday, outside of Tunis, violence struck yet again in the Middle East. In the face of rising terrorist acts of violence against the citizens of Israel, yesterday saw Israel's response in its attack on the facilities of the PLO [Palestine Liberation Organization] in Tunis. Terrorism is terrorism. It deserves no sanctuary, and it must be stopped.

But where do we go from here? Do we go toward more and more violence, or do we go toward peace? I say, it is time to say, "Enough. Enough to violence in the Middle East." We have heard the exclamation point of violence. Let us now follow it with a period, a period that signifies an end to armed struggle and a commitment to find a negotiated way to peace and justice.

Let us reject the radicals and the haters. Let us turn toward and support and encourage those who stand for reason and statesmanship, like President Bourguiba of Tunisia. President Bourguiba leads a country which has long been a close friend of the United States, and he shares our dedication to a more peaceful world. President Bourguiba is, indeed, one of those farseeing and wise statesmen, who was among the very first to urge a negotiated settlement of the Arab-Israeli conflict.

And let us rally in support of those who display the courage to move toward peace. We have had, in recent days, intensive talks with King Hussein of Jordan, aimed at our joint goal of advancing the peace process and the day when negotiations can start. We support his efforts. We admire his wisdom and courage and pray that we may soon see the opening of a new chapter in the expansion of the peace process.

And let us recognize a leader whose commitment to peace is unequivocal and beyond question: Prime Minister Shimon Peres. The truth is unavoidable. There will be no justice for the Middle East unless it is understood that there is no military option and that the only road to peace and justice lies through direct negotiations between Israel and each of its Arab neighbors.

In our world, our ideals and our interests thus are intimately connected. In the long run, the survival of America and American democracy is essential if freedom itself is to survive. No one who cherishes freedom and democracy could argue that these ideals can be gained through policies that weaken this nation.

We are the strongest free nation on earth. Our closest allies are democracies and depend on us for their security. And our security and well-being are enhanced in a world where democracy flourishes and where the global economic system is open and free. We could not hope to survive long if our fellow democracies succumbed to totalitarianism. Thus, we have a vital stake in the direction the world takes—whether it be toward greater freedom or toward dictatorship.

All of this requires that we engage ourselves in the politics of the real world, for both moral and strategic reasons. And the more we engage ourselves in the world, the more we must grapple with the difficult moral choices that the real world presents to us.

We have friends and allies who do not always live up to our standards of freedom and democratic government, yet we cannot abandon them. Our adversaries are the worst offenders of the principles we cherish, yet in the nuclear age, we have no choice but to seek solutions by political means. We are vulnerable to terrorism because we are a free and law-abiding society, yet we must find a way to respond that is consistent with our ideals as a free and law-abiding society.

The challenge of pursuing policies that reflect our ideals and yet protect our national interests is, for all the difficulties, one that we must meet. The political reality of our time is that America's strategic interests require that we support our ideals abroad.

Consider the example of Nicaragua. We oppose the efforts of the communist leaders in Nicaragua to consolidate a totalitarian regime on the mainland of Central America—on both moral and strategic grounds. Few in the United States would deny today that the Managua regime is a moral disaster. The communists have brutally repressed the Nicaraguan people's yearning for freedom and self-government, the same yearning that had earlier made possible the overthrow of the Somoza tyranny. But there are some in this country who would deny that America has a strategic stake in the outcome of the ideological struggle underway in Nicaragua today. Can we not, they ask, accept the existence of this regime in our hemisphere even if we find its ideology abhorrent? Must we oppose it simply because it is communist?

The answer is we must oppose the Nicaraguan dictators not simply because they are communists but because they are communists who serve the interests of the Soviet Union and its Cuban client and who threaten peace in this hemisphere. The facts are indisputable. Had the communists adopted even a neutral international posture after their revolution; had they not threatened their neighbors, our friends and allies in the region, with subversion and aggression; had they not lent logistical and material support to the Marxist-Leninist guerrillas in El Salvador—in short, had they not become instruments of Soviet global strategy, the United States would have had a less clear strategic interest in opposing them.

Our relations with China and Yugoslavia show that we are prepared for constructive relations with communist countries regardless of ideological differences. Yet, as a general principle in the postwar world, the United States has and does oppose communist expansionism, most particularly as practiced by the Soviet Union and its surrogates. We do so not because we are crusaders in the grip of ideological or messianic fervor, but because our strategic interests, by any cool and rational analysis, require us to do so.

Our interests, however, also require something more. It is not enough to know only what we are against. We must also know what we are for. And in the modern world, our national interests require us to be on the side of freedom and democratic change everywhere—and no less in such areas of strategic importance to us as Central America, South Africa, the Philippines, and South Korea.

We understood this important lesson in Western Europe almost 40 years ago, with the Truman Doctrine, the Marshall Plan, and NATO; and we learned the lesson again in just the last 4 years in El Salvador: the best defense against the threat of communist takeover is the strengthening of freedom and democracy. The most stable friends and allies of the United States are invariably the democratic nations. They are stable because they exist to serve the needs of the people and because they give every segment of society a chance to influence, peacefully and legally, the course their nation takes. They are stable because no one can question their fundamental legitimacy. No would-be revolutionary can claim to represent the people against some ruling oligarchy because the people can speak for themselves. And the people never "choose" communism.

One of the most difficult challenges we face today is in South Africa. Americans naturally find apartheid totally reprehensible. It must go. But how shall it go? Our influence is limited. Shall we try to undermine the South African economy in an effort to topple the white regime, even if that would hurt the very people we are trying to help as well as neighboring black countries whose economies are heavily dependent on South Africa? Do we want to see the country become so unstable that there is a violent revolution? History teaches that the black majority might likely wind up exchanging one set of oppressors for another and, yes, could be worse off.

The premise of the President's policy is that we cannot wash our hands of the problem or strike moralistic poses. The only course consistent with American principles is to stay engaged as a force for peaceful change. Our interests and our values are parallel because the present system is doomed, and the only alternative to a radical, violent outcome is a political accommodation now, before it is too late.

The moral—and the practical—policy is to use our influence to encourage a peaceful transition to a just society. It is not our job to cheer on, from the sidelines, a race war in southern Africa or to accelerate trends that will inexorably produce the same result.

Therefore, the centerpiece of our policy is a call for political dialogue and negotiation between the government and representative black leaders. Such an effort requires that we keep in contact with all parties, black and white; it means encouraging the South African Government to go further and faster on a course on which it has already haltingly embarked. The President's Executive order a month ago, therefore, was directed against the machinery of apartheid, but in a way that did not magnify the hardship of the victims of apartheid. This approach may suffer the obloquy of the moral absolutists—of those opposed to change and of those demanding violent change. But we will stick to this course because it is right.

The Importance of Realism

A foreign policy based on realism, therefore, cannot ignore the importance of either ideology or morality. But realism *does* require that we avoid foreign policies based exclusively on moral absolutes divorced from political reality. Hans Morgenthau was right to warn against the dangers of such moral crusades or escapism.

We know that the spread of communism is inimical to our interests, but we also know that we are not omnipotent and that we must set priorities. We cannot send American troops to every region of the world threatened by Soviet-backed communist insurgents, though there may be times when that is the right choice and the only choice, as in Grenada. The wide range of challenges we face requires that we choose from an equally wide range of responses: from economic and security assistance to aid for freedom fighters to direct military action when necessary. We must discriminate; we must be prudent; we must use all the tools at our disposal and respond in ways appropriate to the challenge. Realism, as Hans Morgenthau understood it, is also a counsel of restraint and healthy common sense.

We also know that supporting democratic progress is a difficult task. Our influence in fostering democracy is often limited in those nations where it has never before taken root, where rulers are reluctant to give up their privileged status, where civil strife is rampant, where extreme poverty and inequality pose obstacles to social and political progress.

Moral posturing is no substitute for effective policies. Nor can we afford to distance ourselves from all the difficult and ambiguous moral choices of the real world. We may often have to accept the reality that advances toward democracy and greater freedom in some important pro-Western nations may be slow and will require patience.

If we use our power to push our nondemocratic allies too far and too fast, we may, in fact, destroy the hope for greater freedom; and we may also find that the regimes we inadvertently bring into power are the worst of both worlds: they may be both hostile to our interests *and* more repressive and dictatorial than those we sought to change. We need only remember what happened in Iran and Nicaragua. The fall of a strategically located, friendly country can strengthen Soviet power and, thus, set back the cause of freedom regionally and globally.

But we must also remember what happened in El Salvador and throughout Latin America in the past 5 years—and, for that matter, what is happening today in Nicaragua, Cambodia, Afghanistan, and Angola, where people are fighting and dying for independence and freedom. What we do in each case must vary according to the circumstances, but there should not be any doubt of whose side we are on.

Our Ideals as a Source of Strength

Over 20 years ago, President Kennedy pledged that the United States would "pay any price, bear any burden, meet any hardship, support any friend, oppose any foe, in order to assure the survival and the success of liberty." We know now that the scope of that commitment was too broad, even though it reflected a keen understanding of the relevance of our ideals to our foreign policy. More recently, another administration took the position that our fear of communism was inordinate and emphasized that there were severe limits to America's ability or right to influence world events. I believe this was a council of despair, a sign that we had lost faith in ourselves and in our values.

Somewhere between these two poles lies the natural and sensible scope of American foreign policy. Our ideals must be a source of strength—not paralysis—in our struggle against aggression, international lawlessness, and terrorism. We have learned that our moral convictions must be tempered and tested in daily grappling with the realities of the modern world. But we have also learned that our ideals have value and relevance, that the idea of freedom is a powerful force. Our ideals have a concrete, practical meaning today. They not only point the way to a better world, they reflect some of the most powerful currents at work in the contemporary world. The striving for justice, freedom, progress, and peace is an ever-present reality that is today, more than ever, impressing itself on international politics.

As Hans Morgenthau understood, the conduct of a realistic and principled foreign policy is an honorable endeavor and an inescapable responsibility. We draw strength from our ideals and principles, and we and our friends among the free nations will not shrink from using our strength to defend and further the values and principles that have made us great.

███████ **3.6**

RICHARD J. BARNET

Losing Moral Ground:
The Foundations of U.S. Foreign Policy

These days the world of morals and the world of politics seem poles part. Political leaders secure the approval—or at least the passive acquiescence—of large majorities of citizens by appealing to the worst within us. President Reagan won overwhelming reelection by resorting to coded racist messages ("the South will rise again"), by inspirational jingoism (the United States is "back standing tall," having wiped away the stain of humiliating defeat in Vietnam and Iran by trouncing Grenada), and by celebrating selfishness in its many guises.

Orwellian words to soothe aching consciences come off the assembly line faster than the missiles. Good anti-communist, authoritarian governments such as Marcos' regime in the Philippines and Pinochet's Chile don't "kill" people any more. They engage in the "unlawful or arbitrary deprivation of life," according to the State Department. In the Pentagon, peace is known as "permanent pre-hostility," combat as "violence processing," and the Grenada invasion as a "predawn vertical insertion."

The appearance of being moral, as Henry Kissinger once put it, is more important than being moral. The U.S. government is resorting to ever more sophisticated techniques to defuse the moral qualms of citizens about what it does in their name. And at the same time, its policies diverge ever more sharply from the best moral traditions of the nation: encouragement of democracy, tolerance of ideological diversity, dedication to international law, and promotion of Third World development.

From *Sojourners*, March 1985. Reprinted with permission from *Sojourners*, Box 29272, Washington, D.C. 20017.

The principles are still professed, but the policies negate the principles. South Africa, Chile, the Philippines, and Pakistan receive support. A regime declared "Marxist-Leninist"—a designation that a former Reagan administration ambassador to Nicaragua considered an inaccurate description of the Sandinista government—is targeted for destruction. After placing mines in the harbors of Nicaragua, the United States defies its international obligations by ignoring the World Court's jurisdiction over the matter. The vice president celebrates religious liberty in El Salvador, where the archbishop was murdered while saying Mass, and condemns religious repression in Nicaragua, where the archbishop attacks the government from the pulpit each week.

Official rhetoric still proclaims our dedication to a world in which the weak have rights as well as the strong, but the operative policy is that enunciated by the Athenian generals who subdued the island of Melos: the strong exact what they wish and the weak yield what they must.

As the foreign policy of the United States becomes increasingly isolationist and nationalistic, the American people appear to approve of the show of raw power abroad. The election results lead to the conclusion that jingoist rhetoric, demonstrations of force in the Caribbean, the Middle East, and Central America; and heavy increases in the military budget that sacrifice essential health and social services make large numbers of Americans feel better about their country and themselves. It is critical to ask why this is so.

Even as the returns were being counted, the Reagan administration staged a crisis about non-existent MiGs in Nicaragua that a high official characterized as an "exercise in perception management." It is now commonplace to note that image has crowded out substance.

"New ideas" are advertised but not explained or defended. It is now widely assumed that crafted TV spots, scurrilous direct mail appeals, and presidential news management are the irresistible secret weapons of reactionary politics. Any stain left on a candidate by his own mudslinging TV messages is carefully expunged by professional image polishers. As he bowed out of public life, Walter Mondale apologized for being a lackluster TV performer.

Much of the reporting on the cynical exercise of power reflects the same cynicism. Instances of official trickery are not always suppressed. Sometimes they make the front pages. Thus, for example, the Scowcroft Commission appointed by Reagan found that the "window of vulnerability"—on which the president had campaigned for office two years earlier—was non-existent, continuing a long tradition in which the bomber gaps and the missile gaps of election time disappear once the alarmists take power.

Commentators usually point this out in a spirit of wry resignation. That's the way it is. They sure fooled us that time.

By acquiescing in policies that flagrantly violate their professed religious and political beliefs, the American people lend moral authority to what the government does in their name. The pressures to conform to a prepackaged, market-tested view of the world are considerable. Hate and fear are simpler emotions than love. The search for truth requires the recognition of complexity, logical inconsistencies, and the dialectical nature of reality. Packaged truth dispenses with it all and offers the voters a Manichean drama of good and evil.

There are few clear voices holding up an alternative vision. Liberal politics has deliberately eschewed that role. Politics is presented as a series of problems to be solved, and government is offered as the pragmatic tinkerer that can solve or manage them. It is not surprising that that view has been decisively rejected by the American people in the last four elections. The political Right has offered people a moral angle of vision through which to view the world, but that view is partial, and because it sees only what it wants to see, it is dangerous.

It has been a long time since a national leader dedicated to ending the arms race and addressing the urgent planetary problems of hunger, wretchedness, environmental pollution, and massive unemployment has articulated the moral basis of American foreign policy. Moralistic rhetoric is not the same as a moral analysis. Indeed, moralism is the indispensable wrapping for immoral policies. Ritualistic liberal hand-wringing about support for dictators, massive arms budgets, subsidized torture, and the like are shrugged aside as long as people are convinced that the world cannot be different.

The Italian statesman Cavour once said that if we did for ourselves what we do for our country we would all be scoundrels. The state gives medals for precisely the same activities for which it would imprison the heroes if they were acting on their own behalf. As long as the American voters believe in the inverted morality that divides the world of international relations and the world of human relations into two totally separate domains, each with a set of rules almost exactly opposite that of the other, they will continue to acquiesce in a policy of escalating militarism.

There are many social and political pressures and traditions operating on leaders in political parties, churches, unions, indeed in all institutions, that help reinforce moral blindness, particularly in international relations. As a people we are allergic to preachiness in politics unless the preacher is telling us how good we are or how rich God wants us to be. It goes less against the grain to forget morals and to argue for good works on grounds of enlightened self-interest.

In the 1950s liberals used to argue that foreign aid was an insurance policy on peace; the wretched of the earth who "want what we have," as Lyndon Johnson once put it, will come and take it away from us if we cannot be a little generous. Mindless anti-communism in the Third World, it was argued, will produce more Cubas. Military expenditures are bad for the economy and keep us from being competitive in civilian markets. If we behave in a militaristic manner, we forfeit the decent opinion of humankind, and our allies will turn on us.

In the sweep of history, all those arguments, I am persuaded, will prove to be correct. But in the short-term, reality looks different. People on the edge of starvation in far-off places pose no military threat to the territory of the United

States. A tough U.S. stance in the hemisphere seems to have induced caution about experimenting with the export of revolution in the manner of Ché Guevara, especially since those experiments of many years ago were failures in and of themselves.

The Reagan recovery was fueled to a significant extent by military expenditures, a method of creating budget deficits that is closest to Lord Keynes' recommendation that, if necessary, we should prime the economic pump by digging holes in the ground and filling them up again. The importance of the dollar as the world currency is still sufficient to give the other industrial nations pause when they are tempted to oppose U.S. policies in, say, Latin America.

There is far more friction between the allies and more open opposition than in the past, but there are limits. The United States lacks the power to run most of the world as it largely did at the end of World War II, but it retains enough power to keep international relations effectively paralyzed because, so far at least, other nations dare not confront the number-one nation except at the margins.

The pragmatic arguments in favor of decency are not instantly compelling. It takes a little thought, for example, to recognize the flaw in a policy that calls for the massive subsidization of El Salvador and the systematic destruction of Nicaragua at the same time. You would have to know that in economic terms Central America is a single region and that the policy is self-defeating, indeed guaranteed to keep the whole region poor and in turmoil.

Most people in the United States don't know that and do not see much reason to learn. So enlightened self-interest gives way to emotional appeals to hate and fear unless it is firmly grounded in a moral vision.

The official view of the moral sensibilities of the American people is as cynical as the policies themselves. The public will support invasions of foreign countries if they are quick, like Grenada, and won't if they are prolonged, like Vietnam. They will support food aid policies that withhold timely food shipments to Ethiopia because that government is "Marxist-Leninist" even as they watch Ethiopian babies die on the nightly news. Meanwhile the politically correct babies of Somalia are saved with U.S. grain.

As secrecy has become more difficult as a practical matter—despite being sanctioned by ever tougher laws—we have entered the world of overt covert operations. Today the size and power of the news-gathering industry makes it impossible to hide a large secret war like that being carried out by the *contras* in Nicaragua. Twenty-five years ago the CIA's secret war in Laos could be kept off the front pages, but much innocence has been lost since then. Today's undeclared war against Nicaragua is discussed openly by U.S. officials without admitting responsibility for it. The operation is deliberately overt in order to put maximum pressure on the Sandinistas. It is also covert in order to avoid the constitutional processes of deliberation with respect to war-making.

Thus our most basic foreign policies are carried out without examination of their moral content. No politician asks: what does it do to a people to hear their government year after year dramatize the threat to kill hundreds of millions of innocent people?

Politicians prate about the perils of big government, but none even allude to the development that has totally transformed the relationship of the citizen and the state. The decision about war and peace has been surrendered to one man. Supported only by machines and a few advisers, he decides in the moment of crisis whether to blow up the planet. (That is, if the system works as it is supposed to work. Otherwise that person could be a confused nuclear submarine commander.)

This power is beyond the wildest dreams of tyrants. But the profound implications for democracy of what has happened to us are not discussed within the political process. No one asks how the people can get back some of the power they have turned over to the small-town lawyers, the peanut farmer, and movie actor whom they have anointed with God-like might.

This overriding argument for making our number-one priority the effort to denuclearize and demilitarize our security policy is not considered respectable. Anyone aspiring to office who would make that argument would be perceived by the professional king-makers and opinion molders as a bit hysterical, naive, certainly lacking in the *gravitás* we expect of men with fingers on or near the button. But no one seems to notice that once citizens have surrendered the most basic decision over the lives, progeny, and property to this anointed leader all lesser decisions are affected.

Powers of all sorts flow relentlessly into the same hands. The terrible stakes, the need for swift decision, and the necessary secrecy are all adduced as arguments for concentrating ever greater power in the presidency. Ten years ago during the Watergate scandal, there was much talk of the "imperial presidency." But the president has more power today than he had then to censor, to conduct surveillance on U.S. citizens, and to circumvent the will of Congress—all in the name of "national security."

Moral examination is critical to the idea of informed consent, the only sort of consent that the law recognizes. If, without even realizing it, citizens consent to policies that violate the moral precepts by which they wish to live, their integrity as moral beings is undermined, and the integrity of the political community for which they sacrifice their personal moral principles is also undermined.

There is a difference between the consent of free men and women that is based on understanding, access to information, deliberation, and real, rather than symbolic, participation in the political process and what I would call consumer's consent, the familiar reflex conditioned by advertising that causes the shopper to reach for one brand of toothpaste rather than another. Informed consent requires that the actual consequences of policy be examined.

Moralistic justifications for unexamined policies abound. A few thousand more missiles should be targeted on 250 million men, women, and children because the Soviet Union is the focus of evil in the world. The Soviet leaders repress Baptists and Jews, and they could have even tried to kill the pope. Look what's happening in Poland. The Nicaraguans deserve everything they get; look what they did to the Miskito Indians. Rome had a similar bill of particulars about Carthage to justify its destruction. Joseph Goebbels shook with moral outrage as he explained Hitler's declaration of war against the plutocrats and Jews in the United States. Instant moral outrage is easily manufactured.

But the actual moral content of our own policies—which can be ascertained only by the testing of policy by the standards of either religious faith, ethical principles, or constitutional tradition—gets little attention. As Jesus' metaphor about beams and motes makes clear, members of our species are amazingly tolerant of their own actions. Just by originating with us, acts take on a moral coloration that would never be there had they been undertaken by anyone else.

The anti-war movement and the movement against imperialist adventures must be rooted in a deeper understanding of the moral implications of militarism. We need to ask why we are doing things collectively that we would never do individually. Most of us would never dream of taking hostages. Yet we pay with our taxes for hostage-taking on a gigantic scale.

The official policy is to "deter" Soviet behavior—not just nuclear war because we insist on reserving the right to use nuclear weapons *first*—by threatening to evaporate, burn, mutilate, and poison millions of Soviet citizens who have no control whatever over what their government does. We employ the language of strategy to obscure this moral madness; we should be using the language of crime, for if it is not a crime to destroy the world, even to attempt to destroy it, even to consider destroying it, then the word has no meaning.

Yet by our actions, the American people through their government have systematically shucked the feeble moral and legal restraints that have been put into place over the past three centuries. Always honored in the breach, to be sure, international law has rules limiting reprisals on innocent civilians in time of war. In World War II, with the air raids on Coventry, London, Hamburg, Dresden, and Tokyo, the rules barely applied. But never before the era of so-called "deterrence" have governments explicitly based their national security on the promise to murder civilians.

Supposedly our nuclear weapons are aimed at "military targets." In the century of total war, that can be anything. But even if the term were narrowly defined, the distinction between military and civilian ceases to exist once weapons are dropped in large numbers.

According to a 1978 study by the Arms Control and Disarmament Agency, a typical U.S. second strike would involve striking Moscow with 60 weapons of megaton or near-megaton strength, Leningrad with more than 40, and the next eight largest cities with an average of 13 weapons each. Over the rest of the Soviet Union, 14.4 warheads would be allocated for every million men, women, and children. The Pentagon has identified

40,000 targets in the Soviet Union.

What does it say about our nation that we can plan such a holocaust? Even if one were to accept the "necessity" of this sort of mass murder, why do we overlook the moral imperative to find a way out? Why is the search for a non-criminal system of national security not the number-one priority of the government?

The moral cost of the deterrence system is enormous: the overthrow of the most basic principles at the heart of our religious faiths, our professed ideas of civilization, and the corruption of the noble impulses that gave birth to this nation.

On another level, deterrence cannot be proved to have worked if the event to be deterred does not occur. The Soviets have neither bombed Washington, nor marched on Paris, either because of their fear of nuclear incineration, or for an almost infinite number of other reasons, including the rather plausible reason that they saw no advantage in doing so. We do know that nuclear weapons did not deter a number of challenges that, according to the theory, they were supposed to deter. Nuclear weapons did not keep Soviet forces from converting eastern Europe into satellite states over the opposition of the United States—though the United States had a monopoly of nuclear weapons at the time—and did not keep a Soviet army out of Afghanistan.

The Armageddon theorists who seem half in love with violent planetary death have abandoned the moral responsibility that God has placed upon us. One aspect of that responsibility is to be creators, not destroyers. The injunction to love your neighbors is a call to create and affirm a social order. The only alternative to getting along with co-inhabitants of the planet, to seeing them as human beings, to empathizing with their needs, their fears, and their dreams is fratricidal war, social decay, and personal despair. Nowhere is it said that the neighbors are easy to get along with. And nowhere is it said that blowing up the world is an option to avoid the dilemma of loving unlovable neighbors.

The sick hope that God will soon blow up the world to rescue us from the moral duty of growing up and figuring out how to coexist with the people of the Soviet Union and 150 other countries offers a theological justification for human-initiated holocaust. God is planning to destroy the world. So when we blow it up, we are doing God's will. In a world in which multimegaton weapons have made hash of the just war doctrine—there are no moral ends to be served by a war that can spell the death of everything—the frightful heresy that we are being faithful by destroying God's creation serves as absolution for the theory and practice of annihilation.

More and more the arms race is theater, but the evidence is powerful that the audience reaction is perverse; consciously engendered fear in the adversary produces aggressive behavior as well as caution. In any particular situation, it is quite unpredictable which it will be.

The moral implications seem clear. To close one's eyes deliberately to the warning signs that the abstract theory (for which we are asked to make ourselves mortal enemies of people we have never met) may be wildly wrong violates the most basic moral obligations. As a people we are easily manipulated by all the latest techniques of television and direct mail, not because the magic of the image-makers is all-powerful, but because it is less uncomfortable to listen to the siren song than to probe the moral basis of policies that bring comfort, money, prestige, and false cheer.

There are many other aspects of national policy besides nuclear policy where the moral issues at stake are ignored because they make us uncomfortable. Our indifference to these questions, which comes easily in any event, is carefully cultivated by sophisticated propaganda. As a people we are susceptible to believing lies because they make us feel better than the truth. Lies, because they obscure what is happening, make acceptable to the American people policies that actually violate their most basic conception of themselves.

Most of us do not think of ourselves as people who would systematically lie to constituted authorities or subsidize criminal activities, including murder and torture. Even the awareness that other people do such things would not justify abandoning our own principles. But here is a sampling of some of the falsehoods included in official testimony of the Reagan administration to support its policies in Central America:

□ Despite repeated testimony that U.S. advisers in El Salvador would not "accompany combat operations" but would be confined to "the most secure areas," U.S. military personnel have come under fire at least eight times. This includes the June 1983 sweep by the Salvadoran army of San Vicente province when U.S. military personnel were present during the attack on this guerrilla stronghold.

□ In April 1981 a Salvadoran army captain with 16 years of service testified that the death squads were made up of members of the security forces and acts of terrorism "are planned by high-ranking military officers. . . ." Despite this and much other testimony, Assistant Secretary of State Elliot Abrams told the House Committee on Western Hemisphere Affairs in August 1983 that "we really don't know who the death squads are."

□ Four times the Reagan administration certified to the Congress that the Salvadoran government "is making a concerted and significant effort to comply with internationally recognized human rights" and "is achieving substantial control over all elements of its armed forces, so as to bring to an end the indiscriminate torture and murder. . . ." Internal U.S. government documents that have come to light point out that intelligence agencies were aware that violence was not down by the time of the second certification. By the third and fourth certifications, the U.S. ambassador in El Salvador was in possession of an International Red Cross cable citing increasing instances of routine torture.

□ President Reagan wrote Howard Baker, then U.S. Senate majority leader, on April 4, 1984, that the United States "does not seek to destabilize or overthrow the Government of Nicaragua. . . ." The CIA manual distributed to the *contras, Psychological Operations and Guerrilla War*, outlines a strategy that "will literally be able to shake up the Sandinista structure, and replace it. . . ."

The more morally dubious a foreign adventure, the more it is certain to be wrapped in lies. What is shocking is the equanimity with which the exposure of lies is received. "National security" has been invoked so often over the past 40 years to justify making affairs of state "clearer than the truth," and resistance has been so belated, feeble, and ineffective that we have come to the point when citizens, even congresspersons, expect to be lied to on important matters of foreign policy. But once lies are accepted, even if accompanied by some fuss in Congress, such acquiescence renders inoperative legislation such as the War Powers Act, human rights amendments, and the like that represent the clear will of Congress and the people.

More important than outright lies in making us comfortable with turning upside down the moral code that operates, however imperfectly, in our personal, civic, and business life are the deadly abstractions. It is safe to assume that in foreign policy any word of three syllables or more obscures more truth than it reveals.

We have already looked at deterrence. Austerity is another. It is a word evoking monkish virtues that actually describes economic processes for paying the "haves" by taking resources away from the "have-nots."

Countries such as Mexico, Venezuela, Zaire, and others have incurred about $800 billion of debts, mostly to a relatively small number of large banks in the United States and Europe. In the high-growth years, these banks aggressively sought the loans; in many cases governments covered the risk. Now the International Monetary Fund conditions its help in staving off bankruptcy by demanding that recipient governments cut basic services and tighten money to the point that unemployment reaches a staggering figure.

The poor keep paying for the miscalculations of banks and high officials. The human toll—children without milk, schools and clinics closed, no drinkable water, no jobs—is hidden in that one sensible-sounding word: austerity.

The development of the rich countries now depends even more on the impoverishment of the world's majority. The same principles are being rapidly enacted into law at home. And the so-called conservatives, under their pro-life banner, are seeking a new prosperity for the middle class by driving more and more of our fellow citizens into poverty and cutting off the funds to feed them, to give them shelter or heat or medical care.

The integrity of a nation, no less than of a man or woman, is measured by how it treats the weak and the powerless. There are costs in comfort, advantage, and easy cheer in facing the moral issues at the root of politics. But until citizens themselves take the lead in demanding and shaping a moral vision of what the nation can be, our politicians will not dare transcend the terrible cynicism that hangs over the waning years of the 20th century.

Discussion Questions

1. This chapter has devoted a great deal of attention to the perceptions of political leaders and foreign policy elites. But leaders are not the only political actors with perceptions that affect foreign policy. You are a political actor with the potential to affect some aspects of policy. Describe the cognitive, affective, and evaluative dimensions of your perceptions as they would apply to foreign affairs.

2. As best you can, describe what you believe to be the current president's most important perceptions about the world of international and domestic politics. Then describe the equivalent perceptions of the current leader of the Soviet Union. What are the major differences between the two sets of perceptions, particularly those that have to do with war and peace? How would you suggest that the differences between the two sets of perceptions might be narrowed?

3. Let us assume, for the moment, that you have been asked by the secretary of state to chair a special White House task force on negotiating a broad-ranging arms control treaty with the Soviet Union. The secretary appears to have selected you, not because you happen to be an expert on nuclear issues and strategy (this does not occur until after you have read Chapter 7), but because your expertise in the perceptual aspects of group process will save the group from making a poor decision. Based on your reading of Chapter 3, what advice would you give the secretary on how to reach a good foreign policy decision?

4. The two readings, Secretary of State George P. Shultz's "Moralism and Realism in American Foreign Policy" and Richard Barnet's "Losing Moral Ground," present directly contrasting views of the role and importance of morality in foreign affairs decision making. In your view, which of the two views is correct or most nearly correct? Why?

For Further Reading

Classic Studies of the Foreign Policy

Allison, Graham T. *The Essence of Decision: Explaining the Cuban Missile Crisis*. Boston: Little, Brown, 1971. The book-length investigation from which the article excerpted in this chapter was drawn. A first-rate case study and test of alternative theories.

Frankel, Joseph. *The Making of Foreign Policy: An Analysis of Decision-Making*. New York: Oxford University Press, 1963. Another early study that distinguishes clearly between the manner in which individual variables affect policy outcomes as compared with the larger environment of the decisional process.

Holsti, Ole R. "The Belief System and National Images: A Case Study." *Journal of Conflict Resolution* (September 1962): 244-252. The often-cited study of John Foster Dulles in which Holsti examines (through a content analysis of Dulles's speeches and testimonies) Dulles's image of the Soviet Union. That strongly negative image is found to preclude any acceptance of new information or change.

Lindblom, Charles. "The Science of Muddling Through." *Public Administration Review* (Spring 1959): 79-88. Influential because of its title and because of its thesis that bureaucratic and personal learning, adaptation, and compromises tend to weigh heavily in the outcome of public policy making.

Snyder, Richard C., H. W. Bruck, and Burton Sapin, eds. *Foreign Policy Decision-Making*. New York: Free Press, 1963. This volume ushered in the analytical study of foreign policy. The editors were especially interested in decision-making theory as a reference point for understanding international relations generally.

Studies of Crisis Decision Making

Hermann, Charles F., ed. *International Crises: Insights from Behavioral Research*. New York: Free Press, 1972. A wide-ranging set of essays that examines the contributions of a number of social science theories and disciplines to the study of crises.

Holsti, Ole R. "The 1914 Case." *American Political Science Review* (June 1965): 365-378. A classic study of decision making during international crisis in the tradition of Paige, Snyder, and others.

International Studies Quarterly. (March 1977). A special issue on international crises that includes some of the best work available.

Charles McClelland, "Access to Berlin: The Quality and Variety of Events, 1948-1963." in J. D. Singer, ed. *Quantitative International Politics*. New York: Free Press, 1968. A detailed analysis of U.S.-Soviet policies on Berlin over a fifteen-year period.

Paige, Glenn D. *The Korean Decision, June 24-30, 1950*. New York: Free Press, 1958. The first detailed analysis of crisis decision making that set the stage for the case studies (for example, that of Allison) and quantitative work (for example, that of Holsti, North, and Brody) to come.

Other Influential Sources

Allison, Graham T., and Morton H. Halperin, "Bureaucratic Politics: A Paradigm and Some Policy Considerations." *World Politics* (Spring 1972): 40-79. A classic theoretical article about the dimensions of bureaucracy and its impact on foreign policy making.

Etheredge, Lloyd S. *Can Governments Learn? American Foreign Policy and Central American Revolutions*. New York: Pergamon Press, 1985. An examination of an important question against the background of the past thirty years of U.S. interventionism in Central America. Well-researched study with implications for much of the decision-making literature.

Gelb, Leslie, with Richard Betts. *The Irony of Vietnam: The System Worked*. Washington, D.C.: Brookings Institution, 1978. An exceptional case study in which the authors examine alternative explanations of how the United States entered the Vietnam War and why it remained.

Janis, Irving L. *Groupthink: Psychological Studies of Policy Decisions and Fiascoes*. Boston: Houghton Mifflin, 1982. The most recent version of the provocative set of comparative case studies in which Janis defines groupthink and describes its influence on a number of well-known foreign policy decisions.

Jervis, Robert. *Perception and Misperception in International Politics*. Princeton, N.J.: Princeton University Press, 1976. A major theoretical study which examines the psychology of decision making and the importance of accurate readings of events and messages to sound foreign policy decision making.

McGowan, Patrick J., and Howard Shapiro. *The Comparative Study of Foreign Policy: A Survey of the Scientific Findings*. Beverly Hills, Calif.: Sage Publications, 1973. A compilation of the major propositions and findings of international relations research on foreign policy through the early seventies.

Stoessinger, John G. *Why Nations Go to War*. 4th ed. New York: St. Martin's Press, 1985. A short case study of six wars of this century. The author explores the perceptual and national dynamics which lead decision makers to go to war.

THE GLOBAL POLITICAL ECONOMY   *4*

The role of economics in international affairs has only recently been acknowledged. While the importance of the economic consequences of political events has been long recognized, politics and economics were for many years treated—by policy makers and by analysts—as altogether separate disciplines. Further, for much of this century, many scholars assumed that politics determined economics, that what happened in the economic arena—while important—was a function of political decisions. In the last decade, however, these assumptions have been called into question by developments such as the rise of the Organization of Petroleum Exporting Countries (OPEC), growing international trade problems, the global debt crisis, and weaknesses in the international monetary system. These events have coincided with shifts in scholarly thinking about the relationship between economics and politics. One result has been the reappearance of political economy on the agenda of statesmen, scholars, and students.

The Development of the Bretton Woods Political Economy

The underlying assumptions of the architects of the post-World War II international economic order were those of neoclassical economics and liberalism. As Robert Gilpin discusses in the second article in this chapter, these assumptions included the notion that politics and economics are relatively separate and autonomous spheres and that the goal of international economic activity is the maximization of global (rather than national) welfare. Many American policy makers also believed that what was good for the U.S. economy was good for the international economy and that an expanding global economy was consistent with the American national interest. As the address by George P. Shultz included in this chapter suggests, this view is still influential among American policy makers—a circumstance that explains much of American political and economic policy of the past five decades.

The defeat of the Axis powers (Germany, Japan, and Italy) in 1945 drastically altered the international political system. It also destroyed the economic structures that had linked almost all of the major participants in the war. The balance of power system was replaced with a bipolar system dominated by two superpowers, the United States and the Soviet Union. This new world order meant that political struggles for power and influence characteristic of state behavior would now feature two major actors and their allies rather than six or eight major actors.

The destruction resulting from World War II radically transformed the "world's economic power structure" and left the United States with three-quarters of the world's invested capital and two-thirds of its industrial capacity. Thus, the second world war, so disastrous for millions of people, had in many ways a positive impact on the U.S. economy, the only major economy to grow dramatically during the war.

The war also afforded the United States the opportunity to forge a new international political economy. Determined first and foremost to avert a repetition of the Great Depression, American economic and political elites were generally agreed that a new economic world order was required. The new order they envisioned would be based on principles of free trade and free access to raw materials vital to industrial production. They also hoped for an "open door" for American private investment overseas.

During the last years of the war and the early postwar period U.S. policy makers thus orchestrated the creation not only of new world political institutions such as the United Nations but also of the new international economic institutions subsequently known as the Bretton Woods system.

The *Bretton Woods agreements* of 1944 provided for the creation of the *International Monetary Fund* (IMF) and the *International Bank for Reconstruction and Development* (IBRD), now known as the World Bank. The IMF was designed to stabilize *exchange rates* (the ratio of the value of the currency of one country to that of another country) and to provide short-term loans to countries with *balance of payments* problems (imbalances between expenditures on imports and revenues from the sale of exports). The World Bank was to provide long-term loans and to guarantee loans secured by governments through private sources. Both institutions were dominated by the United States and its closest allies, because voting rights were based on holdings of the organization's capital stock, which in the American case was approximately 40 percent at the time of the Bretton Woods agreement. (Because the share of U.S. investment has declined vis-à-vis the other industrial powers, its voting rights have been reduced in the late 1980s to about 20 percent.)

IMF policies were based on the dollar as the world's *reserve currency*. In this capacity, the dollar became a medium of exchange among nations, filling the same role as gold in earlier years. The dollar's status as the world's reserve currency, its overall strength, and the vitality of the American economy after World War II soon made the dollar the universal currency. At the same time, American money, both public and private, became the world's major source of foreign assistance while the United States dominated the World Bank's operations.

The status of the dollar and the overall strength of the American economy constituted a great advantage for U.S. policy makers. The United States became, in effect, the world's central banker. Virtually all important international financial transactions flowed through the United States, and U.S. policy makers were able to exert great influence over the nature of these transactions, determining the patterns and recipients of foreign assistance and shaping trade arrangements and investment opportunities to suit U.S. interests. New York became the world's financial capital.

Another major economic institution that contributed to the creation of the new world political-economic order was the *General Agreement on Tariffs and Trade* (GATT). Established in 1947 by the major Western trading states, GATT's purpose was to encourage international trade by providing a forum in which to limit or reduce political and economic trade barriers. According to the *most-favored-nation principle* (MFN), all member states were to grant each other equal access to their domestic markets. The underlying objective of the MFN principle was the gradual deregulation of trade in order to produce a free world market.

Over the ensuing years, GATT has effectively reduced tariffs and other restraints on international trade (such as quota systems and controls on the use of foreign exchanges by importers), especially among the wealthier states. However, numerous restrictions on free trade have remained, and many of these have applied to trade between the richer, industrial states and the poorer, generally agricultural states. Restrictions on the importation of agricultural products from Third World countries have been a particularly persistent problem. Many industrial nations, for example, levy substantially greater tariffs on processed foodstuffs than on raw agricultural materials, the net effect of which is to discourage the development of a processed food industry in the Third World.

GATT has also allowed regional economic groups such as the European Community (EC) to limit access by outside competitors to their internal markets and thus to protect their domestic industries in selected areas. Further, the emergence of Europe and Japan as major challengers to U.S. economic hegemony in the 1960s has increased demands within the United States—and in Europe—for government protection from foreign competition. "Voluntary" export limits on Japanese products, enacted by the United States and European governments in response to these pressures, have been accompanied by threats of more serious actions and have raised the prospect of a reappearance of the extensive tariff barriers and "beggar-thy-neighbor" U.S. and European economic policies of the 1930s.

Foreign Assistance

In the early postwar years, U.S. foreign economic policy was based upon large quantities of foreign assistance. The largest, most successful, and most important of these programs was the European Recovery Program, better known as the *Marshall Plan*.

The Marshall Plan was a response to the postwar economic plight of

Europe. When it became clear in 1946-1947 that even countries such as Britain, France, and Italy, which had initially begun to recover from the war, were not likely to achieve sustained progress without additional assistance, the United States undertook to provide Europe with massive doses of economic assistance. The new policy was announced on June 5, 1947, by then secretary of state George C. Marshall, after extensive consultation with European leaders, State Department personnel, business leaders, and politicians.

The Marshall Plan became operational in 1948 following the appropriation of an initial $4 billion in funding by the U.S. Congress. An American agency, the Economic Cooperation Administration, was created to administer funds, while the recipient countries established the Organization for European Economic Cooperation (OEEC) to implement the program. Over time, total U.S. expenditures under the Marshall Plan exceeded $17 billion.

The net effect of the Marshall Plan—and related political developments discussed later—was to integrate the European nations into a rejuvenated global economic system dominated by the United States. The IMF, World Bank, and GATT established the institutional parameters for international economic interchange, based—however loosely—on free trade principles. It also helped to ensure American access to markets throughout the noncommunist world, tending, for example, to encourage the evolution of European economic systems structured in ways conducive to American investment and trade.

The OEEC eventually was transformed into the Organization for Economic Cooperation and Development (OECD) and is now often known as the "Rich Man's Club." The OECD became the most important organizational forum for policy discussions among the advanced capitalist states. Its working groups discussed aid, trade, and investment strategies of concern to its members. In addition to attempting to coordinate its members' foreign and domestic economic policies, OECD also became the forum for formulating and discussing First World responses to Third World proposals.

The Marshall Plan pattern was replicated in U.S. economic and military assistance to Third World countries of Asia, Africa, and Latin America over the next forty years. The first U.S. postwar commitment to foreign assistance to non-European countries took the form of President Truman's Point Four Program announced in 1949 and funded by Congress in 1950. The thrust of the program was the provision of technical assistance to Third World countries, and the initial authorization was $35.4 million. Point Four was followed by relatively larger appropriations of U.S. foreign economic assistance that have slowly declined in size from 1950 to the present. Approximately half of all such assistance from 1950 until the mid-1960s was allocated for military purposes.

As with the earlier European programs, U.S. aid to Third World countries was designed to accomplish several goals. First, such aid provided less developed countries with dollars with which to buy goods produced in the United States. Second, some aid was earmarked for technical assistance projects primarily designed to improve the economic infrastructure of recipient countries. Such aid was primarily used for the construction of roads and highways, railroads, harbors, communication networks, and electric power plants—projects that facilitated the production and transportation of goods by American multinationals operating in these countries. In effect, such programs resulted in American taxpayers' providing funds to create new markets and reduce production costs for the largest U.S.-based international firms. As the European and Japanese economies recovered and as the wave of decolonization swept Africa and Asia, the Europeans and Japanese followed the American path, establishing their own economic spheres of influence.

Such aid had political purposes as well. Deliberately or otherwise, it often supported the growth and development in the Third World of powerful—and often highly conservative—political and economic elites that became junior partners in the global economic system. Generous amounts of U.S. military assistance were provided to train and equip domestic police forces and armies that could be used, and in numerous instances were used, by local elites to repress domestic political opposition. In this fashion, U.S. policy in the postwar period tended to link recipient nations economically and politically to the United States and to provide trade and investment opportunities for U.S. multinationals.

Agricultural assistance has also been an important component of U.S. foreign aid. Most of this aid has been dispensed under Public Law 480 (PL 480), passed in 1954 and since 1961 designated the Food for Peace Program. Generally perceived by American taxpayers as humanitarian assistance for hungry people, PL 480 also absorbed cumbersome surpluses of agricultural commodities in the United States. Such commodities, purchased by the American government to support domestic farm prices, were then sold to Third World countries in exchange for local currency. These local currencies were held by the United States and used to make selected purchases within the recipient country.

The annual dollar value of Food for Peace shipments was approximately $.5 billion during the period 1953 to 1957, $1 billion from 1958 to 1962, over $1.5 billion from 1962 to 1967, and $1 billion from 1968 to 1972. PL 480 shipments declined markedly in the 1970s when farm prices began to rise, and the United States began to sell large quantities of commodities overseas. Because of the volume of shipments involved during the peak years of the PL 480 and Food for Peace programs, these programs resulted in major U.S. purchases of foreign currencies and represented a significant source of U.S. economic leverage.

The economics of commodity surpluses illustrate the growing economic interdependence between foreign aid programs and other developments in domestic and international trade. Throughout the postwar period, American foreign assistance, and later that of the other advanced capitalist nations, served the dual purposes of maintaining the international market shares of firms based in the donor country and influencing the internal politics of other nations. In Europe, U.S. aid served both to create a market for America's surplus production and investment capital and to support European efforts to recreate their economic and political order. In the Third World, American, European, and Japanese assistance programs to their respective client states were used for a variety of purposes, including the repression of liberation movements and the maintenance of dependent economic relationships between the donor and recipient countries.

Foreign aid programs, then, served a multitude of purposes, including the provision of a viable infrastructure to facilitate corporate investments in the Third World and the assurance of the continued availability of ready supplies of raw materials and agricultural commodities. The collective impact of these programs, however, was also to stimulate the growth and development of the world economy. This growth was accompanied by yet greater levels of foreign trade, aid, investment, and, ultimately, higher levels of both dependence and interdependence between First and Third World societies.

Foreign Investment

Foreign trade programs and international investment were not invented in the twentieth century. However, the magnitude of these investments and changes in the size and nature of the firms involved during the postwar period has created a new set of actors and political-economic relationships. The Bretton Woods agreements, with their underlying philosophy of free trade, led to an enormous movement of capital and a steady increase in direct overseas investment by the private sector. In the early postwar period, the United States was the dominant player in this arena, but British, Japanese, West German, and other European corporations have greatly expanded their overseas investments efforts in recent years. The lion's share of First World direct investments has gone to other First World nations, but large sums have also been invested in the Third World. The largest shares of direct foreign investment were in both cases made in manufacturing industries. In the last decade, multinational firms based in Third World nations have emerged, and they too have expanded their operations, following in the footsteps of their First World predecessors.

Likewise, the scale of international banking operations in the postwar period has transformed the global financial network. International banking provides funds for multinational corporations, international agencies, and nations in the First, Second, and Third Worlds. In the past decade Third World countries have become increasingly reliant on private banks, rather than international agencies like the International Monetary Fund, as sources of much-needed loans. Much like the IMF loans of the 1950s and 1960s, such loans often come with strict economic requirements, including monetary devaluation, deflationary fiscal policies, and dramatic reductions in the level of governmental funding for food, housing, transportation, education, and health care facilities.

The Debt Crisis

In the Third World, as elsewhere, it is by now abundantly clear that economics affects politics and that the interrelationship between the two has global ramifications. One of these ramifications is the current "debt crisis."

That crisis arises in part from the shift to private funding noted earlier. It also results from the economic weakness of Third World countries that are struggling to integrate their economies into the international economic system. Often energy-poor and resource-deficient, many of these countries are unable to pay for the cost of needed imports—such as machinery and oil—from current earnings. Particularly in the wake of the two "oil shocks" of the 1970s, many Third World countries have suffered from larger and larger balance of payments deficits. Forced to borrow to cover these deficits, many Third World nations found themselves with such high levels of indebtedness that they required even larger new loans to make payments on their earlier ones or simply to finance interest payments.

It is at precisely this point, of course, that creditors—an increasing proportion of whom are private banks—are most likely to make demands for policy changes and reductions in governmental spending, conditions which often cause domestic hardship and are, therefore, likely to be politically unpopular. Thus, financial penetration of the Third World has been accompanied by economic and political penetration as well. The current debt crisis is, therefore, a serious problem for the citizens of the debt-ridden nations whose efforts to maintain credit-worthiness often lead to economic constraints on development and additional hardships.

But the debt crisis is also an important problem for creditor nations, international banks, and the international monetary system. The magnitude of the debt and the extension of credit to Third World nations far beyond their capacity to pay has created a potential for default that could cause the collapse of major international financial institutions. Further, the need to make debt payments reduces the debtor nations' ability to purchase goods from the United States and other First World nations, thereby reducing First World exports.

In today's world, the flow of money—particularly in dollars, marks, yen, pounds, and Swiss francs—is controlled not by governments but by the world's largest private banks. One result is that international lending practices are more likely to be governed by profit considerations than by broader concerns, such as the risk that an ever-increasing money supply may fuel inflation. The Eurocurrency system, for example—which along with the dollar is now at the core of international finance—is unfettered by controls from any nation-state and often operates in a manner contrary to the needs of the individual states where the member banks are based.

Summary

The Bretton Woods system was established in 1945 at a time when the United States was the dominant economic and political power, Europe was economically devastated, the socialist world was in its infancy, and many of today's Third World nations were successfully throwing off the political—although not necessarily the economic—shackles of the colonial era. Domestic and international changes brought this system to the brink of crisis in the 1970s and 1980s. The free movement of capital, the increasing interdependence of the First World, and the multinational corporations' continued dominance of direct private investment in the Third World have led to the development of a new international economic pattern and new strains on the international economic system. By the late 1980s, that system was facing a debt crisis of serious proportions.

Changes and Contradictions
in the First World Political Economy

One obvious change in the world system since 1945 has been the relative decline in U.S. economic power. The United States, as the only major economic power to emerge from World War II not only intact but with a booming economy, enjoyed a virtually unparalleled position of world economic leadership and dominance. The American position was, however, essentially artificial and destined to be temporary. Further, by acting to speed the recovery of its traditional major trading partners, the United States in effect deliberately hastened the day when it would no longer dominate the international economic system. That day, however, came even earlier than anticipated because of the dynamic growth of the European and Japanese economies. By the 1970s, the United States was no longer in a position to control or restore an increasingly unstable international economic system.

The U.S. Economic Decline

In 1947 the United States produced 50 percent of the world's gross national product (GNP), in 1955 36 percent, and in 1980 22 percent. The nine major West European nations' share of world GNP during this period was 18 percent in 1955 and 22 percent in 1980, while Japan's share increased from 2 percent to 10 percent. Similarly, the U.S. share of world exports declined from 16.7 percent in 1950 to 11 percent in 1984, while the European Community's share increased from 15.4 percent to 28.6 percent and Japan's from 2 to 8 percent. In 1950, the United States held 49.8 percent of the world's reserve currency; in 1970 it held 15.9 percent, and in 1984 8 percent. The European Community, on the other hand, held 6.1 percent in 1950 and 33 percent by 1970—before declining to 29 percent in 1984. Japan's share increased from 2 percent in 1955 to 6 percent in 1984.

It is in trade that the U.S. decline has been perhaps most noticeable. During the 1980s the U.S. trade deficit has risen dramatically—from roughly $40 billion annually at the beginning of the decade to over $150 billion by 1985. During these years the European trade deficit has declined from $60 billion annually to under $20 billion, and Japan has consistently enjoyed huge surpluses.

As U.S. economic power has declined, so has its ability to dominate the global economy. As the statistics suggest, the Marshall Plan (and related programs) and the operations of American multinationals transformed America's European allies and Japan from poverty-stricken dependencies in the 1940s to major competitors who—particularly in the case of Europe—held enormous quantities of American dollars by the 1960s.

Soviet and East Bloc Development

A second change involves the economic development of the Soviet Union. In 1945, the Soviet Union was still hopeful of maintaining a partnership with the West and securing U.S. assistance for its own economic recovery. After the onset of the Cold War in 1945-1947 and Soviet rejection of the conditions for economic integration contained in the Marshall Plan, the Soviet Union and its socialist allies within Eastern European countries chose instead to pursue an independent economic course. This in turn led to the creation of a socialist bloc in Europe and an attempt to limit economic interactions with nonsocialist nations. Thus the Soviet Union sought, in its economic interactions with Eastern Europe and a relatively small number of Third World socialist states (for example, Burma, Vietnam, Tanzania, Cuba, and China), to create an essentially closed alternative international economy that would engage in trade with nonsocialist nations only for items not available from socialist sources. This proved difficult to carry off, however, and within the past decade and a half the economies of most of the socialist nations have been gradually integrated into the larger world economy. The Soviet Union remains the major exception; it still buys relatively little from Western sources, restricting its purchases primarily to food and technological goods.

Third World Challenges

A third major change has come in the form of a call from the Third World nations of Africa, Asia, and Latin America for a *new international economic order* (NIEO) to replace the Bretton Woods system. By the 1960s most of the remaining colonial territories had been granted political independence, with the result that membership in the United Nations tripled between 1945 and 1970. Yet, even as political independence was achieved, the new nations of the Third World confronted a new form of domination, neocolonialism, in which their economies were effectively dominated by multinational corporations, banks, and international institutions.

The stability of the Bretton Woods system was thus ultimately jeopardized by fundamental changes in the nature of the world economy, changes unleashed in part by the very nature of the system itself. The free movement of capital led U.S., European, and Japanese manufacturing firms to locate an increasing proportion of their production facilities in the Third World. Thus American, European, and Japanese firms began to produce transistor radios in Taiwan, Singapore, Korea, and other Asian states, manufacturing and assembling their brand-name radios outside the United States. Almost the entire American consumer electronics industry relocated its manufacturing facilities in this manner. The same pattern occurred in other industries, notably the European textiles industry and the automobile industry. Both General Motors and Volkswagen, for example, established automobile plants in Brazil. All this was made possible by the emergence of "standardized product lines" designed for worldwide consumption and the simplification—or decomposition—of complex production operations. Control over the new production facilities, however, remained securely in the hands of the First World parent firms.

Increasingly, then, direct foreign investment in the "periphery" nations has been centered in manufacturing rather than in raw materials and agriculture, with a resulting shift in trade patterns. Third World countries, no longer mere suppliers of raw materials and agricultural products, are becoming producers of manufactured goods. The more successful of these efforts have come in the "export platforms"—also known as the newly industrializing countries, NICs (for example, Taiwan, South Korea, Singapore, and Malaysia).

The praise heaped on these "development success stories" tells much about the shift in development theory during recent decades. Built almost without exception on a combination of low wages; significant American assistance, often for security purposes; and massive U.S., European, and Japanese multinational investment, the economies involved are more often than not dominated or controlled by outside states or corporations. Furthermore, virtually all of these nations have authoritarian governments that have sought to encourage the relocation of multinational firms by taking measures— including the judicious use of force—to ensure the continued availability of a relatively low-cost work force. Profits for the firms involved, however, have often come at the expense of First World production workers, many of whom—their jobs having effectively been "exported" to the Third World—are left with the prospect of employment in lower paying "service industries."

In due course, however, came economic crisis. A major contributing factor was the inherently anarchical nature of capitalism, which normally experiences periods of expansion and contraction. During periods of sustained growth, such as that experienced by Western economies during the late 1940s and 1950s, the production of goods increases, investment rises, wages increase, unemployment declines, and the political position of workers improves. So does pressure on profits, which typically shrink in the face of rising wages, competition, and technological innovation. When profit margins decline, capitalists begin to invest and produce less, unemployment rises, and consumption declines along with wages and benefits. The result is recession.

The recession that followed the long expansion of the 1950s and 1960s was particularly severe. Coupled with severe inflation resulting from monopoly pricing and high levels of government spending, particularly for military goods, the recession resulted in economic crisis within the capitalist world in the 1970s. This crisis, which extended to the Third World, brought increased joblessness, enormous increases in the prices of basic commodities, and reduced production of goods. It called into question the basic vitality of the economic system itself and bred political crisis. Thus, the international economic order faced challenges from within as well as without the First World.

The worldwide economic crisis of the 1970s presented a major challenge to U.S. policy makers who found themselves under increasing domestic pressure to protect U.S. workers and industry from foreign competition at precisely the same time that their ability to manage the international system had declined. It was during this period, for example, that other First World nations within the OECD challenged the United States for economic leadership. The 1970s also saw the rise of and subsequent decline of OPEC, two major worldwide recessions (in 1974-1975 and 1980) that proved resistant to standard economic cures and were accompanied by persistent inflation, the emergence of structural unemployment, and a decline in the competitiveness of key First World industries.

One result of these developments has been the now annual economic summits of the leaders of the seven major capitalist nations—the United States, the United Kingdom, Japan, West Germany, France, Canada, and Italy. These meetings, designed to discuss monetary and trade issues, have been only minimally successful in coordinating economic policy. Nonetheless, they are likely to continue, if only as a symbol of First World awareness of the need to cooperate economically in order to avoid the beggar-thy-neighbor policies associated with many past international economic disasters.

The Third World and a New International Economic Order

From a Third World perspective, one of the most significant international developments of the 1970s was the developing countries' persistent attempts to alter the structure of international economic interaction so as to enhance their own prospects for development and establish their economic independence. That effort effectively began with the creation of the United Nations Conference on Trade and Development (UNCTAD) in 1964. If nothing else, UNCTAD served as institutional evidence of longstanding Third World dissatisfaction with their economic and political status vis-à-vis the First World. The failure of that initial effort was implicitly acknowledged when the United

Nations called for a Second Development Decade at the beginning of the 1970s. The first serious challenge to the First World, however, was issued at the Sixth Special Session of the United Nations General Assembly in 1974 by the *Group of 77* (in the late 1980s comprising 122 nations) in the form of a call for the creation of a new international economic order (NIEO).

The call for NIEO had a number of purposes: (1) to increase the profitability and volume of Third World exports, (2) to increase the benefits accruing to Third World countries from direct foreign investment, (3) to increase development aid to the Third World, (4) to provide debt relief, (5) to establish new rules for the international monetary system, and (6) to modify the institutions involved in such a way as to give the more numerous Third World nations an increased voice in, if not control over, international political-economic decision making.

The subsequent series of negotiations conducted during several special sessions of the United Nations General Assembly and other international meetings such as UNCTAD and the Conference on International Economic Cooperation (CIEC) were not successful. The nations of the First World—the "North"—were far more interested in discussing energy-related issues than the issues of development, trade, and aid of greatest interest to the Third World. Similarly, the Second World, or socialist nations, whose role was of relatively minor importance, displayed little more than rhetorical interest in increasing their contributions to the Third World.

Among the few concrete results of the meetings were the establishment of the Integrated Program for Commodities (the IPC)—an attempt to stabilize prices of key agricultural raw material exports—and some movement by First World nations to provide debt relief on a case-by-case basis. But the First World blocked all Third World attempts to restructure the current international economic system in directions that would significantly reduce First World advantages. As these talks entered the 1980s—amid discussions of a Third United Nations Development Decade and preparatory meetings for a North-South summit—there was difficulty in even establishing agendas. First World nations, primarily concerned about their relationships with one another, lost interest in negotiations, and no significant institutional changes in North-South relations have actually occurred. The old order teeters on from crisis to crisis, thus far averting disaster. The First World nations, now under more conservative leadership, have throughout the 1980s pursued policies more clearly and openly designed to serve their own interests and to preserve the existing order.

The Readings

At the beginning of this chapter we noted that the study of political economy had only recently reentered the international relations curriculum. In the first two readings in this chapter, Joan Spero and Robert Gilpin discuss the reasons for the longstanding divorce between the study of politics and the study of economics and the nature of the global relationships between the two spheres. Spero shows that different historical periods have been characterized not only by differences in the structure of the relationship between politics and economics but also by differences in modes of thinking about that relationship.

Robert Gilpin's piece focuses on a comparison of the needs and interests of nation-states and large corporations and on the possible contradictions between the profit-oriented interests of corporations and the strategic and political concerns of the nation-states under whose banner the corporations operate. Thus, Gilpin is interested in the tension between the production of wealth and the political determinants of production, distribution, and consumption. Gilpin also introduces, describes, and compares the underlying assumptions and approaches associated with three prevailing conceptions of political economy— liberalism, Marxism, and mercantilism. In the process, he demonstrates how each leads to a distinctly different understanding of the nature and functioning of the international political economy, thus explaining why scholars—and policy makers—from different traditions are at times not only unable to agree on policy but also unable to comprehend each other's understanding of "reality."

Our third selection, by R. Peter Dewitt, employs the three theoretical frameworks identified by Gilpin to analyze a contentious real-world policy issue—the impact of U.S. foreign investment on the U.S. economy. In so doing, Dewitt illustrates some of the tensions between the "national interest" and the "corporate interest," as well as the differences in interpretation resulting from the analysis of the same set of data from the three different theoretical traditions.

The final two selections offer a clear contrast between competing visions. Secretary of State George P. Shultz, defending and promoting the Reagan administration's foreign and domestic economic policy, portrays such policies as having dramatically increased U.S. economic performance and having a positive impact on the global system. He bases much of his argument on the benefits and value of free trade, the perils of protectionism, the nature of competition among the industrial powers, the role of exchange rates and balance of payments issues, and the interrelationship of foreign and domestic economic performance.

Investment banker Felix Rohatyn argues that these same policies have virtually ensured a major economic crisis. He also discusses the growing interdependence of the national and global political economies and the future implications of internal and external national debt and trade imbalances. Mr. Rohatyn argues that a new Bretton Woods conference is needed to reestablish a stable international monetary system, and he discusses the implications of U.S. tax policy for international financial and economic stability.

4.1 ▰▰▰▰

JOAN SPERO

The Link Between Economics and Politics

The interaction of politics and economics is an old theme in the study of international relations. From seventeenth-century mercantilists to twentieth-century Marxists, students of relations among states have dealt with the problems of international political economy. Yet in the twentieth century the study of international political economy has been neglected. Politics and economics have been divorced from each other and isolated in the analysis and theory, if not in the reality, of international relations.

One reason for this divorce is to be found in the theoretical heritage of modern Western academe. The heritage that has shaped much of the modern study of politics and economics—and that is responsible for the artificial separation of economics and politics—is liberalism. Liberal theorists rejected the age-old concept of a unified political and economic order and replaced it with two separate orders.

First, argued the liberals, an economic system is based on the production, distribution, and consumption of goods and services; these economic processes operate under natural laws. Furthermore, they maintained, there is a harmony in these laws and in the economic system, and such natural harmony operates best and to the benefit of all when political authority interferes least with its automatic operation. The liberals considered economic activity to be the preserve of private enterprise, not of government.

Second, they contended that the political system consists of power, influence, and public decision making. Politics, they asserted, unlike economics, does not obey natural laws or harmony. Politics is unavoidable and government is necessary for essential services—defense, law and order. But, for them, government and politics should not interfere with the natural economic order. Indeed, in an international system, the liberals' only hope for peace and harmony is for politics to be isolated from economics and for the natural and harmonious processes of free trade to operate among nations, bringing not only prosperity but also peace to all.

Such theoretical separation has led to, and has been reinforced by, the specializations of modern academe. Since the nineteenth century, economics and political science have developed as separate disciplines, focusing on separate processes; and each to a great extent ignores the common ground where the two overlap and interrelate. Consequently, international political economy has been fragmented into international politics and international economics. Economists have, for the most part, ignored the role of political factors in international economic process and policy, whereas students of international politics tended to ignore economic issues in relations among states.

Two political and economic developments following World War II have reinforced this formal division of analysis. In the early postwar years, the major world powers reached an agreement on postwar international economic relations. In the West, the Bretton Woods system of international economic management established the rules for commercial and financial relations among the major industrial states. In the East, Soviet hegemony in Eastern Europe provided the foundation for a separate and stable international economic system. Finally, during the first postwar decade, the greater part of the Third World remained politically and economically subordinate. Linked with the developed countries of the West in formal and informal imperial relations, these states had little choice but to acquiesce to the international economic system established for them. As a result of the agreed-upon structures and rules of international economic interaction, conflict over economic issues was minimized, and the significance of the economic aspect of international relations seemed to recede. Although certain developments such as the European Economic Community and the problem of the British pound surfaced from time to time, international economic interaction was relegated to the level of "low" politics.

Another postwar development that caused international economic relations to recede was the emergence of the Cold War. The problems of international relations that preoccupied decision makers and observers alike were security issues: the Soviet Union's domination of Eastern Europe and the development of Soviet nuclear capability, the division of Germany, the forging of the North Atlantic Treaty Organization (NATO) and American nuclear strategy, the Korean conflict, Vietnam, and the problems of limited war. Thus, analysis of international relations focused on what seemed to be the subjects of "high" politics, on security and security-related issues. Systems analysis, decision-making theory, strategy and game theory, simulation, conflict resolution—all were based on the primacy of security issues.

The current reality of international relations has undermined the separation of economics from the study of international politics. The givens of the postwar decades that shaped the study of international politics—economic consensus and constant military tension—have changed. The Sino-Soviet split and the loosening of ties within the Atlantic alliance have helped replace the bipolar standoff of the 1950s with a more flexible international system. Although East-West détente waxes and wanes, the United States and Western Europe are no longer preoccupied with their military security. In the 1970s, the United States and the Soviet Union demonstrated a willingness and an ability to reach agreements on security issues, thus alleviating some of the tension of the Cold War. West Germany's Eastern policy, or *Ostpolitik*, and the agreements reached at the 1975 Helsinki Conference on European Security, have helped reduce a great source of instability in Eastern Europe. Finally, the long war in Vietnam ended, and the European countries completed the wrenching task of freeing their colonies. The developed countries are now at peace.

At the same time, the broad agreement on economic rules established after World War II has collapsed under the weight of powerful new forces. In the West, the Bretton Woods system of management has broken down. The renewed economic vigor of Western Europe and Japan, the strain on the United States' balance of payments, the oil crisis, inflation, and the growth of freewheeling international capital markets have led to the disintegration of the international monetary system developed after World War II. The growth of the European Economic Community as an economic power, the dynamics of Japanese trade, recurrent recessions, and soaring inflation threaten established commercial relations. New international patterns of production pose a multifaceted challenge to the traditional economic and political order. In the East, the Soviet Union and the Communist states of Eastern Europe have found their closed system too restrictive for economic development and are turning to the West for trade and technology. China has also signaled its willingness to increase its economic ties with the developed countries. In the South, the now independent Third World countries, with new economic problems and new economic demands, have entered the world arena. The principal political concerns of these countries are economic: development, aid, trade, foreign investment, and ultimate independence. How they will be integrated into the world economy has become a major issue. Some less-developed countries—Brazil, Mexico, and South Korea, for example—have more robust economies which threaten sensitive sectors in the industrialized states. A few Southern countries have burst onto the international economic scene with their newfound oil wealth. The majority of Third World countries, many themselves feeling the victims of the present international economic system, face numerous obstacles to development. The Third World as a group is demanding a new international economic order, a restructuring of the international relations between the haves and have-nots. Therefore, as the postwar economic consensus disintegrates, economic issues are reemerging alongside security issues as a focus of international relations.

Thus, if theory and analysis are to maintain touch with reality, it will be necessary to bridge the gap between economics and politics, to explore the interface between economics and politics in the international system. This study will examine one aspect of that interface: the way in which international politics shapes international economics.

The Political Dynamics of International Politics

Those students of international politics who have examined the interaction between economics and politics have almost always examined the way in which economic reality has affected politics. There is, for example, a body of thought that maintains that economic resources determine strategic and diplomatic power. Analysts have pointed out the ways in which a country's gross national product, the quantity and quality of its resources, and its international trade and financial position determine its military strength. The literature demonstrates that the impact of economics on politics is quite important. The early industrialization of Great Britain in the nineteenth century, for example, was a significant resource base for British political power and an important factor in Great Britain's domination of that century's international economic and political structure. Similarly, the United States' economic power was important in creating America's military and political dominance in the twentieth century.

Just as economic factors influence political outcomes, so political factors influence economic outcomes. Students of international politics, however, often overlook the political determinants of international economic relations. Though not denying the effect of economics on politics, this book will be concerned with that other side of the coin that has been frequently ignored: the political dynamics of international economics.

There are three ways in which political factors affect economic outcomes. *First, the political system shapes the economic system*, because the structure and operation of the international economic system is, to a great extent, determined by the structure and operation of the international political system. *Second, political concerns often shape economic policy*, because economic policies are frequently dictated by overriding political interests. *Third, international economic relations themselves are political relations*, because international economic interaction, like international political interaction, is a process by which state and nonstate actors manage, or fail to manage, their conflicts and by which they cooperate, or fail to cooperate, to achieve common goals. Let us now look in more detail at these three political dimensions of international economics.

The Political System and the Economic System

The structure and operation of the international economic system are to a great extent determined by the structure and operation of the international political system. Production, distribution, and consumption have throughout modern history been affected by diplomatic and strategic factors.

During the mercantilistic period between the fifteenth and eighteenth centuries, economic interaction had two principal political characteristics. First was the rise of powerful nation states from the ruins of medieval universalism and local particularism: the emergence of new centralized political units—England, France, Spain, Sweden, Prussia, Russia—whose policy was the consolidation of power, both internally, vis-à-vis local power structures, and externally, vis-à-vis other states. Second, in the mercantile political system, was the competition among these many nearly equal states. Because power was distributed fairly equally, relatively minor changes could be important to a state's overall power position. But despite the competition for power, there were certain limits to competition. There was a common political culture, including a consensus on royal legitimacy. There were also limits to state capability. State administration was weak, armies were small and mercenary, and, therefore, military and diplomatic objectives were limited.

The impact of the political structure on the economic structure of mercantilism was profound. The economic realm became the main arena for political conflict. The pursuit of state power was carried out through the pursuit of national economic power and wealth, and the process of competition, limited by political reality, was translated into economic competition. All international economic transactions were regulated for the purpose of state power.

Because mercantilists believed that wealth and power were closely associated with the possession of so-called precious metals, governments organized their international trading structures for the purpose of maintaining a favorable balance of trade to accumulate these metals. There were controls on exchange markets and the international movement of precious metals, along with regulation of individual and general commercial transactions through tariffs, quotas, and prohibitions of some transactions. States gave subsidies to export and import substitution industries and sometimes engaged in production or trade.

Mercantilist states also acquired colonies for the purpose of favorable trade balances and for the political goal of self-sufficiency. Colonies existed to accommodate the mercantile interests of the metropole, and strict state regulation of the colonial economy existed to serve these ends. It was the reaction to such mercantilist policies—the regulation of production and exports and imports and the control of shipping—that led the American colonies to rebel against England.

Thus in the mercantile period, it was the nature of the emerging state and the state system that in large part determined economic interaction—and when that political structure changed, when Great Britain rose to political dominance, the economic system also changed.

In the nineteenth century, the political system was characterized by the balance of power on the continent and by Great Britain's power overseas. On the continent, Russia and France were constrained by the territorial realignments of the Congress of Vienna, and the four major continental powers were controlled through their own rivalries. This enabled Great Britain to play a balancing and mediating role. With its geographic position off the European continent and its predominance on the seas, Great Britain was able to control Europe's access to the rest of the world by denying overseas colonies to continental states. This naval power combined with the decline of the continental powers meant that the greater part of the non-European world was independent or under British rule.

Because of this political system of a balance of power on the continent and British power overseas, Great Britain achieved a head start in economic development and was able to establish an international economic system that centered on Britain. The basis of this system was free trade.

The political roots of free trade may be traced back to the Napoleonic period, when the French emperor imposed the continental system: an economic embargo on Great Britain. The Napoleonic embargo encouraged a transformation of the British economy from trade with the Continent to trade overseas. After the defeat of France and the end of the embargo, Britain continued on the established path. With the repeal of the Corn Laws, the navigation laws, and the gradual removal of tariffs, however, Britain devised an exchange system of domestic manufactures for overseas raw materials. Treaties with and among other European states expanded the system to the Continent, and trading dominance was reinforced by British investment overseas. In the nineteenth century, vast amounts of capital flowed out of Great Britain to the United States, Canada, Latin America, and the nontropical areas of the empire, and the city of London emerged as the world's financial center.

Thus in the nineteenth century, military and political dominance enabled Britain to adopt and internationalize a liberal economic system. But once again, when the political system began to change at the end of the nineteenth century—when British power waned—the liberal economic system also began to decline, and a new imperialist system emerged.

The roots of nineteenth-century imperialism are complex and elusive, but two political factors were crucial to its growth. The first was the decline of British dominance that stemmed from the rise of rival political, military, and economic powers, in particular, the United States and Germany. And second, the disruptive influence of these new powers was reinforced by the emergence of modern nationalism. The increasingly powerful rival states, and Britain as well, were motivated by the unruly forces of national identity, national pride, and the quest for national self-fulfillment and power. More nearly equal power relations and the new nationalism led to a highly competitive international system, one increasingly less constrained by Great Britain's balancing and overseas domination, which had stabilized the earlier nineteenth-century system.

These political changes permitted the operation of other forces: the political pressures of a newly powerful capitalist class, along with the military; the escapades of various adventurers (explorers and fortune hunters); technological and communications developments, which facilitated control of overseas territories; and the action and reaction dynamic of imperial competition.

International political conflict increased, but often it was acted out not in Europe—at least not until 1914—but, rather, in Asia and Africa. In only a few decades, much of Asia and virtually all of Africa were divided up by Western Europe and the United States.

This new imperialism was the basis for a new international economic system. European political domination led to economic domination and exploitation. As in the days of mercantilism, colonies were integrated into an international economic system designed to serve the economic interest of the metropole. The political victors controlled investment and trade, regulated currency and production, and manipulated labor, thus establishing structures of economic dependency in their colonies that endured far longer than their actual political authority.

The imperialist system and the residual domination of the United Kingdom in the West finally collapsed under the strain of World Wars I and II. In the post-World War II period, a new political and economic system emerged based on the hostile confrontation of the two superpowers. Politically, the new system was bipolar. In the West, there was a hierarchy, with the United States as the dominant political and military power over a weakened Europe and Japan; in the Third World, most of the nations remained politically subordinate to the old imperial powers; and in the East, the Soviet Union was the overwhelmingly dominant political and military power. And finally, East and West confronted each other in the Cold War.

This international political system determined the postwar international economic system. For political reasons, the East and West were isolated into two separate economic systems. In the East, the Soviet Union imposed a Communist international economic system based on the concept of a socialist commonwealth and, for political reasons, sought to make the other members of the socialist commonwealth economically dependent on the Soviet Union and economically isolated from the West. In the West, U.S. military and political dominance was matched by U.S. economic dominance. America's liberal vision shaped the economic order in the West. The principles of the international economic system were again as in the period of British hegemony: free-trade and free-capital movements. With such a system, American trade, American investment, and the American dollar predominated. Thus, politics shaped economics in the postwar era. And in the 1970s, as before, it was to a great extent the changing political scene that caused the breakdown of the postwar economic system. The decline of American power and increasing pluralism in the West, a superpower détente, and a new political consensus in the underdeveloped countries transformed the international economic system.

Political Concerns and Economic Policy

In addition to influencing economic systems, political factors also influence economic policies. Throughout history, as we have seen, national policy has shaped international economics. In the mercantile period, governments regulated economic activity and acquired colonies. In the nineteenth century, the British repealed the Corn Laws and the navigation acts and turned to free trade. At the end of that century, public policy turned to the annexation of territory in Asia and Africa. In the years since World War II, American foreign policy has focused on a multilateral, free-trading system.

These national policies were, in turn, determined by internal political processes. Economic policy is the outcome of a political bargaining process in which different groups representing different interests conflict over different preferred policy outcomes. Group conflict occurs, for example, between groups favoring low tariff barriers and those advocating protection, between advocates of foreign economic assistance and its opponents, and between those favoring energy independence and those advocating reliance on foreign sources of energy. The outcome of political conflict is determined by power. The different strengths of the competing groups affect the outcomes of foreign economic policy. Thus mercantilism may be viewed as the outcome of a political conflict between particularist local powers and the rising power of the central government; free trade was the product of a conflict between the landed class, which advocated protection, and the rising bourgeois class, which supported free trade; imperialism reflected the political power of the ascendant military and capitalist classes; and U.S. liberalism was determined by the support it enjoyed among powerful business and labor groups.

Very often, what determines the political bargaining process are overriding strategic and diplomatic interests. Economic policy is frequently either shaped by political concerns or becomes an explicit tool of national strategic and diplomatic policy. Trade policy is often linked with political goals. Embargo has been an economic tool of political warfare throughout history. France applied an embargo to weaken Great Britain during the Napoleonic wars; the League of Nations called for an embargo of Italy after its invasion of Ethiopia in an effort to end that aggression in 1935; the United States since 1949 has frequently embargoed trade with Communist countries in an effort to weaken military capability; the 1973 Arab oil embargo of the United States and the Netherlands was an effort to alter their pro-Israeli foreign policy; and in 1980, the United States tried to use economic pressure to force Iran to release its American hostages.

Trade policy has also been used for defensive military purposes. Alexander Hamilton argued that the fledgling United States should establish a domestic manufacturing system through trade protection to avoid dependence on foreign sources of supply that could be cut off in time of political conflict or war. Recently, there have been calls for the United States to develop its domestic energy resources in order to avoid the consequences, both economic and political, of dependence on foreign sources of supply.

Foreign aid is another familiar economic tool used for strategic and diplomatic ends. The Marshall Plan, under which the United States gave $17 billion in outright grants to Western European countries to rebuild their economies after World War II, was designed to make Western Europe impervious to aggression by the Soviet Union. Foreign economic assistance to underdeveloped countries has been used to win friends for the West or the East during the Cold War. Foreign aid has also been used by former colonial powers to retain political influence in those newly independent former colonies.

International Economics as International Politics

Finally, international economic relations, in and of themselves, constitute political relations. International politics may be defined as the "patterns of political interaction between and among states." And as with all politics, international politics involves goal-seeking behavior and a process of deciding who gets what, when, and how. Thus international relations is political when it involves the interaction of different groups in goal-seeking pursuits.

Interaction among groups in the international system ranges from conflict to cooperation. At one extreme is pure conflict, as when the interests of the groups involved are diametrically opposed: if one group realizes its goal, the other cannot achieve its objective. For example, in a conflict over territory, one state will gain the territory and the other will lose it. At the other extreme is cooperation. In such a situation, groups have a common interest, and all benefit from the pursuit of this shared interest. For example, allies have a common interest in ensuring their common defense, or colonies have a common interest in achieving independence, or trading partners have a common interest in maintaining beneficial trading relations.

Most international interaction contains elements of both conflict and cooperation. Even in situations of extreme conflict, there is often an element of cooperation. For example, despite the confrontation between the United States and the Soviet Union over placing missiles in Cuba in 1962 or over the Middle East war of 1973, both superpowers' interest in preventing the escalation of these conflicts into nuclear war and holocaust led to cooperation as their resolution. Conversely, in situations involving high levels of cooperation, there is often an element of conflict; and even when groups share interests, there is usually conflict over specific interests and specific solutions. For example, all states may want to establish and maintain a stable international monetary system; but some of these states may prefer a particular type of monetary system, such as a fixed exchange rate or a floating exchange rate regime, which satisfies their more specific national interests. Thus within a framework of common goals, states disagree over the best means to achieve their common end.

In domestic politics, goal-seeking behavior is regulated by government, which has the authority to make decisions for a society and the power to enforce those decisions. The characteristic that distinguishes international politics from internal politics is the absence of government. In the international system, no legitimate body has the authority to manage conflict or achieve common goals by making and enforcing decisions for the system; instead, decision-making authority is dispersed among many governmental, intergovernmental, and nongovernmental groups.

Because there is no international government, the central problems of international politics are the adjustment or management of conflict and the achievement of cooperation. The means by which state and nonstate actors manage, or fail to manage, their conflicts and the ways in which they cooperate, or fail to cooperate, to achieve common goals are the central subject of international politics. Over the centuries, actors have deliberately or inadvertently devised rules, institutions, and procedures to manage international conflict and cooperation. These forms of managing international order have varied over time, space, and issues. They range from balances of power to alliances to international organizations, from hegemony to colonialism to international law. When there are effective rules, institutions, and procedures, conflict takes place within agreed-upon limits, and cooperation is facilitated. But when there are no effective rules, institutions, and procedures, conflict may be unregulated and cooperation may be impossible to achieve. In such a situation, therefore, international conflict may escalate into war.

The subject of international economic relations may also be viewed as the management of conflict and cooperation in the absence of government. As with all international political interaction, economic interaction ranges from pure conflict to pure cooperation. Some economic relations lead to high levels of conflict. Wealth is an important goal of groups in international politics, and the pursuit of wealth in the presence of scarce resources leads to conflict—over access to markets, the control of raw materials, and the control of the means of production. Such conflict often is linked to conflicts over power and sovereignty. The confrontation of producers and consumers over the price of oil, for example, is a challenge by the producers to the power of both the developed countries and the oil companies. The concern in Canada, Europe, and the Third World about multinational corporations is, in part, a reaction to the infringement of their sovereignty. Much international economic interaction, however, has a high level of cooperation. Many states share the goals of a stable monetary system, expanding trade relations, and rising production, though they differ over the means of achieving these ends. Some favor fixed exchange rates, whereas others prefer a float. Some advocate tariff reductions on textiles, whereas others forcefully oppose them. Some favor growth through free trade, whereas others feel that free trade inhibits growth. Some consider multinational corporations to be a vital new road to economic growth, whereas others believe that they perpetuate underdevelopment.

As with all international politics, states have deliberately or inadvertently established rules, institutions, and procedures to manage international conflict and cooperation. International economic management thus varies with the time, place, and issue. Mercantilism, free trade, and imperialism have been different historical forms of trade management. At different times, the gold standard and the dollar system have regulated international monetary relations. Sometimes, as during the nineteenth-century gold standard or the twentieth-century dollar system, the management is effective. But at other times, as during the Great Depression of the 1930s or the monetary crisis of 1971-1973, the management breaks down. In some relations, such as those among the developed market economies, there are complex and effective management rules, institutions, and procedures. In other relations, such as those between developed and less-developed countries, there either are no rules, institutions, and procedures, or they are the subject of great disagreement. Finally, in some areas, such as international trade, complex rules have been formally established, international organizations created, and informal procedures devised. In other areas, such as international production, international management relies on more rudimentary forms of control. . . .

4.2 ■■■■■■■

ROBERT GILPIN

The Nature of Political Economy

The international corporations have evidently declared ideological war on the "antiquated" nation state. . . . The charge that materialism, modernization and internationalism is the new liberal creed of corporate capitalism is a valid one. The implication is clear: the nation state as a political unit of democratic decision-making must, in the interest of "progress," yield control to the new mercantile mini-powers.

While the structure of the multinational corporation is a modern concept, designed to meet the requirements of a modern age, the nation state is a very old-fashioned idea and badly adapted to serve the needs of our present complex world.

These two statements—the first by Kari Levitt, a Canadian nationalist, the second by George Ball, a former United States undersecretary of state—express a dominant theme of contemporary writings on international relations. International society, we are told, is increasingly rent between its economic and its political organization. On the one hand, powerful economic and technological forces are creating a highly interdependent world economy, thus diminishing the traditional significance of national boundaries. On the other hand, the

From *U.S. Power and the Multinational Corporation: The Political Economy of Foreign Direct Investment,* by Robert Gilpin. Copyright © 1975 by Basic Books, Inc. Reprinted by permission of the publisher.

nation-state continues to command men's loyalties and to be the basic unit of political decision making. As one writer has put the issue, "The conflict of our era is between ethnocentric nationalism and geocentric technology."

Ball and Levitt represent two contending positions with respect to this conflict. Whereas Ball advocates the diminution of the power of the nation-state in order to give full rein to the productive potentialities of the multinational corporation, Levitt argues for a powerful nationalism which could counterbalance American corporate domination. What appears to one as the logical and desirable consequence of economic rationality seems to the other to be an effort on the part of American imperialism to eliminate all contending centers of power.

Although the advent of the multinational corporation has put the question of the relationship between economics and politics in a new guise, it is an old issue. In the nineteenth century, for example, it was this issue that divided classical liberals like John Stuart Mill from economic nationalists, represented by Georg Friedrich List. Whereas the former gave primacy in the organization of society to economics and the production of wealth, the latter emphasized the political determination of economic relations. As this issue is central both to the contemporary debate on the multinational corporation and to the argument of this study, this chapter analyzes the three major treatments of the relationship between economics and politics—that is, the three major ideologies of political economy.

The Meaning of Political Economy

The argument of this study is that the relationship between economics and politics, at least in the modern world, is a reciprocal one. On the one hand, politics largely determines the framework of economic activity and channels it in directions intended to serve the interests of dominant groups; the exercise of power in all its forms is a major determinant of the nature of an economic system. On the other hand, the economic process itself tends to redistribute power and wealth; it transforms the power relationships among groups. This in turn leads to a transformation of the political system, thereby giving rise to a new structure of economic relationships. Thus, the dynamics of international relations in the modern world is largely a function of the reciprocal interaction between economics and politics.

First of all, what do I mean by "politics" or "economics"? Charles Kindleberger speaks of economics and politics as two different methods of allocating scarce resources: the first through a market mechanism, the latter through a budget. Robert Keohane and Joseph Nye, in an excellent analysis of international political economy, define economics and politics in terms of two levels of analysis: those of structure and of process. Politics is the domain "having to do with the establishment of an order of relations, a structure. . . ." Economics deals with "short-term allocative behavior (i.e., holding institutions, fundamental assumptions, and expectations constant). . . ." Like Kindleberger's definition, however, this definition tends to isolate economic and political phenomena except under certain conditions, which Keohane and Nye define as the "politicization" of the economic system. Neither formulation comes to terms adequately with the dynamic and intimate nature of the relationship between the two.

In this study, the issue of the relationship between economics and politics translates into that between wealth and power. According to this statement of the problem, economics takes as its province the creation and distribution of wealth; politics is the realm of power. . . .

. . . In the real world, wealth and power are ultimately joined. This, in fact, is the basic rationale for a political economy of international relations. But in order to develop the argument of this study, wealth and power will be treated, at least for the moment, as analytically distinct.

To provide a perspective on the nature of political economy, the next section of the chapter will discuss the three prevailing conceptions of political economy: liberalism, Marxism, and mercantilism. Liberalism regards politics and economics as relatively separable and autonomous spheres of activities; I associate most professional economists as well as many other academics, businessmen, and American officials with this outlook. Marxism refers to the radical critique of capitalism identified with Karl Marx and his contemporary disciples; according to this conception, economics determines politics and political structure. Mercantilism is a more questionable term because of its historical association with the desire of nation-states for a trade surplus and for treasure (money). One must distinguish, however, between the specific form mercantilism took in the seventeenth and eighteenth centuries and the general outlook of mercantilistic thought. The essence of the mercantilistic perspective, whether it is labeled economic nationalism, protectionism, or the doctrine of the German Historical School, is the subservience of the economy to the state and its interests—interests that range from matters of domestic welfare to those of international security. It is this more general meaning of mercantilism that is implied by the use of the term in this study. . . .

Three Conceptions of Political Economy

The three prevailing conceptions of political economy differ on many points. Several critical differences will be examined in this brief comparison. (See Table 4-1.)

The Nature of Economic Relations

The basic assumption of liberalism is that the nature of international economic relations is essentially harmonious. Herein lay the great intellectual innovation of Adam Smith. Disputing his mercantilist predecessors, Smith

Table 4-1 Comparison of the Three Conceptions of Political Economy

	Liberalism	Marxism	Mercantilism
Nature of economic relations	Harmonious	Conflictual	Conflictual
Nature of the actors	Households	Economic classes	Nation-states
Goal of economic activity	Maximization of global welfare	Maximization of class interests	Maximization of national interest
Relationship between economics and politics	Economics *should* determine politics	Economics *does* determine politics	Politics determines economics
Theory of change	Dynamic equilibrium	Tendency toward disequilibrium	Shifts in the distribution of power

argued that international economic relations could be made a positive-sum game; that is to say, everyone could gain, and no one need lose, from a proper ordering of economic relations, albeit the distribution of these gains may not be equal. Following Smith, liberalism assumes that there is a basic harmony between true national interest and cosmopolitan economic interest. Thus, a prominent member of this school of thought has written, in response to a radical critique, that the economic efficiency of the sterling standard in the nineteenth century and that of the dollar standard in the twentieth century serve "the cosmopolitan interest in a national form." Although Great Britain and the United States gained the most from the international role of their respective currencies, everyone else gained as well.

Liberals argue that, given this underlying identity of national and cosmopolitan interests in a free market, the state should not interfere with economic transactions across national boundaries. Through free exchange of commodities, removal of restrictions on the flow of investment, and an international division of labor, everyone will benefit in the long run as a result of a more efficient utilization of the world's scarce resources. The national interest is therefore best served, liberals maintain, by a generous and cooperative attitude regarding economic relations with other countries. In essence, the pursuit of self-interest in a free, competitive economy achieves the greatest good for the greatest number in international no less than in the national society.

Both mercantilists and Marxists, on the other hand, begin with the premise that the essence of economic relations is conflictual. There is no underlying harmony; indeed, one group's gain is another's loss. Thus, in the language of game theory, whereas liberals regard economic relations as a non-zero-sum game, Marxists and mercantilists view economic relations as essentially a zero-sum game.

The Goal of Economic Activity

For the liberal, the goal of economic activity is the optimum or efficient use of the world's scarce resources and the maximization of world welfare. While most liberals refuse to make value judgments regarding income distribution, Marxists and mercantilists stress the distributive effects of economic relations. For the Marxist the distribution of wealth among social classes is central; for the mercantilist it is the distribution of employment, industry, and military power among nation-states that is most significant. Thus, the goal of economic (and political) activity for both Marxists and mercantilists is the redistribution of wealth and power.

The State and Public Policy

These three perspectives differ precisely in their views regarding the nature of the economic actors. In Marxist analysis, the basic actors in both domestic and international relations are economic classes; the interests of the dominant class determine the foreign policy of the state. For mercantilists, the real actors in international economic relations are nation-states; national interest determines foreign policy. National interest may at times be influenced by the peculiar economic interests of classes, elites, or other subgroups of the society; but factors of geography, external configurations of power, and the exigencies of national survival are primary in determining foreign policy. Thus, whereas liberals speak of world welfare and Marxists of class interests, mercantilists recognize only the interests of particular nation-states.

Although liberal economists such as David Ricardo and Joseph Schumpeter recognized the importance of class conflict and neoclassical liberals analyze economic growth and policy in terms of national economies, the liberal emphasis is on the individual consumer, firm, or entrepreneur. The liberal ideal is summarized in the view of Harry Johnson that the nation-state has no meaning as an economic entity.

Underlying these contrasting views are differing conceptions of the nature of the state and public policy. For liberals, the state represents an aggregation of private interests: public policy is but the outcome of a pluralistic struggle among interest groups. Marxists, on the other hand, regard the state as simply the "executive committee of the ruling class," and public policy reflects its interests. Mercantilists, however, regard the state as an organic unit in its own right: the whole is greater than the sum of its parts. Public policy, therefore, embodies the national interest or Rousseau's "general will" as conceived by the political elite.

The Relationship Between Economics and Politics; Theories of Change

Liberalism, Marxism, and mercantilism also have differing views on the relationship between economics and politics. And their differences on this issue are directly relevant to their contrasting theories of international political change.

Although the liberal ideal is the separation of economics from politics in the interest of maximizing world welfare, the fulfillment of this ideal would have important political implications. The classical statement of these implications was that of Adam Smith in *The Wealth of Nations*. Economic growth, Smith argued, is primarily a function of the extent of the division of labor, which in turn is dependent upon the scale of the market. Thus he attacked the barriers erected by feudal principalities and mercantilistic states against the exchange of goods and the enlargement of markets. If men were to multiply their wealth, Smith argued, the contradiction between political organization and economic rationality had to be resolved in favor of the latter. That is, the pursuit of wealth should determine the nature of the political order.

Subsequently, from nineteenth-century economic liberals to twentieth-century writers on economic integration, there has existed "the dream . . . of a great republic of world commerce, in which national boundaries would cease to have any great economic importance and the web of trade would bind all the people of the world in the prosperity of peace." For liberals the long-term trend is toward world integration, wherein functions, authority, and loyalties will be transferred from "smaller units to larger ones; from states to federalism; from federalism to supranational unions and from these to superstates." The logic of economic and technological development, it is argued, has set mankind on an inexorable course toward global political unification and world peace.

In Marxism, the concept of the contradiction between economic and political relations was enacted into historical law. Whereas classical liberals—although Smith less than others—held that the requirements of economic rationality *ought* to determine political relations, the Marxist position was that the mode of production does in fact determine the superstructure of political relations. Therefore, it is argued, history can be understood as the product of the dialectical process—the contradiction between the evolving techniques of production and the resistant sociopolitical system.

Although Marx and Engels wrote remarkably little on international economics, Engels, in his famous polemic, *Anti-Duhring*, explicitly considers whether economics or politics is primary in determining the structure of international relations. E. K. Duhring, a minor figure in the German Historical

School, had argued, in contradiction to Marxism, that property and market relations resulted less from the economic logic of capitalism than from extraeconomic political factors: "The basis of the exploitation of man by man was an historical act of force which created an exploitative economic system for the benefit of the stronger man or class." Since Engels, in his attack on Duhring, used the example of the unification of Germany through the Zollverein or customs union of 1833, his analysis is directly relevant to this discussion of the relationship between economics and political organization.

Engels argued that when contradictions arise between economic and political structures, political power adapts itself to the changes in the balance of economic forces; politics yields to the dictates of economic development. Thus, in the case of nineteenth-century Germany, the requirements of industrial production had become incompatible with its feudal, politically fragmented structure. "Though political reaction was victorious in 1815 and again in 1848," he argued, "it was unable to prevent the growth of large-scale industry in Germany and the growing participation of German commerce in the world market." In summary, Engels wrote, "German unity had become an economic necessity."

In the view of both Smith and Engels, the nation-state represented a progressive stage in human development, because it enlarged the political realm of economic activity. In each successive economic epoch, advances in technology and an increasing scale of production necessitate an enlargement of political organization. Because the city-state feudalism restricted the scale of production and the division of labor made possible by the Industrial Revolution, they prevented the efficient utilization of resources and were, therefore, superseded by larger political units. Smith considered this to be a desirable objective; for Engels it was an historical necessity. Thus, in the opinion of liberals, the establishment of the Zollverein was a movement toward maximizing world economic welfare; for Marxists it was the unavoidable triumph of the German industrialists over the feudal aristocracy.

Mercantilist writers from Alexander Hamilton to Frederich List to Charles de Gaulle, on the other hand, have emphasized the primacy of politics; politics, in this view, determines economic organization. Whereas Marxists and liberals have pointed to the production of wealth as the basic determinant of social and political organization, the mercantilists of the German Historical School, for example, stressed the primacy of national security, industrial development, and national sentiment in international political and economic dynamics.

In response to Engels's interpretation of the unification of Germany, mercantilists would no doubt agree with Jacob Viner that "Prussia engineered the customs union primarily for political reasons, in order to gain hegemony or at least influence over the lesser German states. It was largely in order to make certain that the hegemony should be Prussian and not Austrian that Prussia continually opposed Austrian entry into the Union, either openly or by pressing for a customs union tariff lower than highly protectionist Austria could stomach." In pursuit of this strategic interest, it was "Prussian might, rather than a common zeal for political unification arising out of economic partnership, (that) . . . played the major role."

In contrast to Marxism, neither liberalism nor mercantilism has a developed theory of dynamics. The basic assumption of orthodox economic analysis (liberalism) is the tendency toward equilibrium; liberalism takes for granted the existing social order and given institutions. Change is assumed to be gradual and adaptive—a continuous process of dynamic equilibrium. There is no necessary connection between such political phenomena as war and revolution and the evolution of the economic system, although they would not deny that misguided statesmen can blunder into war over economic issues or that revolutions are conflicts over the distribution of wealth; but neither is inevitably linked to the evolution of the productive system. As for mercantilism, it sees change as taking place owing to shifts in the balance of power; yet, mercantilist writers such as members of the German Historical School and contemporary political realists have not developed a systematic theory of how this shift occurs.

On the other hand, dynamics is central to Marxism; indeed Marxism is essentially a theory of social *change*. It emphasizes the tendency toward *dis*equilibrium owing to changes in the means of production and the consequent effects on the ever-present class conflict. When these tendencies can no longer be contained, the sociopolitical system breaks down through violent upheaval. Thus war and revolution are seen as an integral part of the economic process. Politics and economics are intimately joined.

Why an International Economy?

From these differences among the three ideologies, one can get a sense of their respective explanations for the existence and functioning of the international economy.

An interdependent world economy constitutes the normal state of affairs for most liberal economists. Responding to technological advances in transportation and communications, the scope of the market mechanism, according to this analysis, continuously expands. Thus, despite temporary setbacks, the long-term trend is toward global economic integration. The functioning of the international economy is determined primarily by considerations of efficiency. The role of the dollar as the basis of the international monetary system, for example, is explained by the preference for it among traders and nations as the vehicle of international commerce. The system is maintained by the mutuality of the benefits provided by trade, monetary arrangements, and investment.

A second view—one shared by Marxists and mercantilists alike—is that every interdependent international economy is essentially an imperial or hierarchical system. The imperial or hegemonic power organizes trade, monetary, and investment relations in order to advance its own economic and

181

political interests. In the absence of the economic and especially the political influence of the hegemonic power, the system would fragment into autarkic
economies or regional blocs. Whereas for liberalism maintenance of harmonious international market relations is the norm, for Marxism and mercantilism
conflicts of class or national interests are the norm. . . .

4.3 ■■■■■■

R. PETER DeWITT, JR.

The Multinational Corporations, State Policy and
Its Impact on the United States Economy

The topic of the multinational corporation has been one of increasing
popular discussion. Much of this discussion has focused on the external
influence of multinational corporations while ignoring largely their internal
impact on their sponsoring nations. U.S. multinational corporations and MNCs
from other developed nations have been criticized for being beyond sovereignty and national jurisdiction. At the same time considerable criticism has
been leveled at the role of multinational corporations in host nations and at the
disruptive effect that MNCs are having on those societies and economies. Such
discussion of multinational enterprise while not without veracity skirts several
major issues which are of national importance for the United States.

The first issue is that of the uncontrolled nature of multinational enterprise
vis-à-vis the nation-state. While many scholars have discussed the essential
nature of the tension between business and the state, in many cases I believe
that this issue of the MNCs has been overstated. Contrary to the popular notion
that the U.S. multinational corporations are unbridled and beyond the
sovereign jurisdiction of the state, I believe that the nation state is a prime vehicle for the expansion of multinational corporations. Indeed as Adam Smith
noted in *The Wealth of Nations* that governments have always been the silent
partners of business and private property would probably not exist a "single
night" without government. My own findings seem to support Adam Smith's
notion that the state protects business and in the case of the MNCs promotes its
expansion abroad with incentives for foreign investment.

A second aspect of current scholarship on the multinational corporations
has provided many important insights into the operations of multinational
enterprise in the developing world. However, by focusing on the Third World,
we have often times neglected the important impact that the growth of
multinational enterprise is having on the United States and other major

From *Social Praxis* 5 (3-4). Reprinted by permission of the publisher.

Table 4-2   Top Ten U.S. Multinational Corporations

Company	Total 1971 sales (billions of dollars)	Foreign sales as percentage of total	Number of countries in which subsidiaries are located
General Motors	$28.3	19%	21
Exxon	18.7	50	25
Ford	16.4	26	30
General Electric	9.4	16	32
IBM	8.3	39	80
Mobil Oil	8.2	45	62
Chrysler	8.0	24	26
Texaco	7.5	40	30
ITT	7.3	42	40
Gulf Oil	5.9	45	61

national sponsors of multinational corporations in the developed world.

A discussion, therefore, of the role of the state in promoting the expansion of U.S. multinational enterprise abroad and the impact of the MNCs on the United States economy and society, I believe will assist in supplementing the literature on the relationship between the MNCs and their sponsoring nations.

A history of the expansion abroad of U.S. multinational corporations since World War II provides the basis for an initial analysis of the problem. The largest U.S. corporations have been going multinational with increasing speed since World War II. They have been expanding their operations abroad, taking their newest technology, plants and equipment as well as a significant percentage of American production and jobs with them. Some of the biggest U.S. multinational corporations now have almost half their total sales overseas.

Table 4-2 illustrates foreign sales as a percentage of total sales for U.S. multinational corporations.

As a result of the shift in the production base of the American economy away from domestic production for export to foreign production, foreign sales by 1968 exceeded domestic exports 4 : 1. This shift in the U.S. economy from trade to an emphasis on foreign production is analyzed below in an attempt to provide an explanation of the changing nature of the economy and its impact on the social structure in the United States. . . .

Theories of Foreign Investment

The expansion of U.S. multinational investment is most often described with one of the following explanations. The first explanation is that which I characterize as the technical-economic view. This viewpoint explains the expansion of multinational investment abroad largely in terms of technical-economic factors such as the need to expand in order to compete with larger economies of scale businesses, the cost differences between domestic and foreign production, the need to expand in order not to lose a potential market abroad to a foreign competitor, and the virtues of vertical integration *et cetera*. Such rationales for the expansion of multinational enterprise are typically advanced by American schools of international business and are reflected in the works of Phatak, Behrman, Jacoby and Vernon. This viewpoint, which emphasized economic and technological factors would also be identical with the liberal school of thought on the expansion of foreign investment. This outlook de-emphasizes the relationship between politics and economics and sees the expansion of the multinational corporations eroding national sovereignty and nationalism thereby contributing to world harmony. The expansion of multinational investment is seen according to this model as an outgrowth of Vernon's, so-called, product life-cycle theory rather than of political-economic factors.

Another explanation is the Marxist or Neo-Marxist one which discusses the expansion of multinational enterprise by analyzing the dynamics of capitalism. More simply stated this theory is an adaption of Lenin's theory of imperialism and attempts to link the expansion of multinational investment to the dynamic need in capitalism to export and reinvest surplus capital. The Marxist explanation merges the following ideas which assist in explaining the expansion of the multinational corporations: (1) the internal contradictions in American capitalism forces firms to expand outward in search of new markets, investment opportunities and sources of raw materials; and (2) this expansion is furthered by the expansionist interests of the dominant economic classes as reflected in U.S. foreign policy. While many theorists have advanced this thesis, Barnet and Müller, Hymer, and Magdoff best apply this argument to the multinational corporations. The difficulty of this thesis is its global nature and the failure of most analysts to translate with empirical evidence how the contradictions in capitalism or the economic interests of the capitalist classes contribute to the expansion of U.S. foreign investment.

While the above theories certainly provide some explanations of the expansion of multinational investment abroad, a more convincing and in-depth argument can be made based on political-economic factors. Both the technical economic or liberal view and the Marxist explanations are insufficient in explaining the tremendous post-war expansion of the multinational corporation. Both neglect to consider the very instrumental role of public economic and foreign policy decisions and the public institutions that reflect these decisions in shifting the thrust of the U.S. economy abroad. The internal dynamics of capitalism in terms of a product life cycle concept or the contradiction in the system provide only a partial explanation for the rise and expansion of U.S. multinational enterprise abroad.

The public policy explanation is important because it recognizes that the dramatic expansion of U.S. foreign investment abroad in the 1950s and 1960s may not have been solely the result of the internal dynamics of capitalism or fear of foreign competition but rather was also the conscious result of public choice and public policy decisions which included both political and economic considerations. The public policy argument, therefore, seems to provide a more meaningful explanation of the relationship between the multinational firm and the U.S. government than does either the technical economic or Marxist view. Indeed the public policy position is a neo-mercantilist position which emphasizes the close identity of interest between the multinational corporations and their home governments. This political-economic perspective in my view is far more insightful than either the technical-economic (liberal) or Marxist position. The historical patterns of U.S. investment abroad seem to support these conclusions. . . .

Impact on the U.S. Economy

The impact of U.S. foreign direct investment on the U.S. economy and society in recent years has become a matter of serious concern. The area of the most outspoken concern has been on the part of American labor in protesting the loss of jobs. U.S. multinational corporations have exported American jobs abroad in ever-increasing numbers. The United States Tariff Commission computed the number of U.S. jobs lost due to multinational corporate foreign expansion employing several different assumptions. Considering the impact of U.S.-based multinationals alone, the estimates ranged from 142,000 to 1.7 million jobs lost. A more recent study by Robert H. Frank and Richard T. Freeman measures the job losses in the United States resulting from multinational overseas investments annually from 1966-1973. Frank and Freeman took into consideration the estimated jobs gained in the United States in supporting the multinational foreign production facilties, U.S. jobs providing partially finished goods, other components shipped abroad and other factors that might contribute to an increase in American jobs. After subtracting jobs gained from jobs lost the Frank and Freeman study made a net estimate that annual losses of jobs and employment opportunities in the United States from 1966-1973 ranged between 115,900 and 160,377 jobs per year due to the expansion of U.S. multinational business abroad. The net employment loss for those eight years equaling approximately 1,062,577. These losses were distributed across 15 industries as illustrated in Table 4-3.

As the figures above clearly indicate the loss of jobs to American workers as a result of the expansion of U.S. multinational business abroad has been substantial. This job loss not only is a financial hardship on the individual workers directly affected but it increases the social costs in our society of unemployment, welfare and increases tax revenue [lost] as American jobs are exported abroad. Foreign production means not only a loss of jobs and U.S. tax revenue but also a loss of revenue for domestic business as consumer income

Table 4-3 Estimated U.S. Job Losses from MNCs Abroad

All manufacturing	735,283
Food products	57,425
Paper and allied products	62,244
Chemicals and allied products	120,763
Rubber and plastic products	44,200
Primary and fabricated metals	58,064
Non-electrical machinery	194,721
Transportation equipment	48,782
Electrical machinery	113,619
Other manufacturing	33,457
Agriculture, forestry and fisheries	33,189
Mining and smelting	894
Petroleum	5,374
Transportation, communication and public utilities	29,282
Retail and wholesale trade	159,339
Federal, state and local government	6,748
Total jobs lost, 1966-1973	1,062,577

declines as a result of underemployment and unemployment. Moreover, it can be calculated that loss to U.S. domestic production due to the export of businesses and jobs abroad in 1973 alone would have amounted to more than $70 billion in exports. The negative impact of foreign production is even more dramatic as Peggy Musgrave has pointed out that one dollar invested in domestic exports generates much more foreign exchange than does one dollar invested in foreign production.

The loss of public revenues is a serious consequence of U.S. direct foreign investment. The loss to the U.S. Treasury has been substantial. In 1972 the United States Treasury collected only about 5 percent of the entire foreign income accruing to U.S. multinational corporations of $24 billion in that year. This revenue loss which equals the difference between the statutory rate of 46 percent and 5 percent collected was largely attributable to the combination of tax deferral on unrepatriated profits and foreign tax credit. The revenue losses will be reflected in higher taxes to the American public or a significantly lower level of governmental expenditure. Since, the exportation of jobs means increased social welfare costs the likelihood of reduced governmental expenditures is small. The alternative, of course, is increased taxes, the major part of the burden of which will not be on U.S. corporations but individual members of the U.S. labor force as 85 percent of the U.S. tax base is borne by the wages and salaries of working individuals.

The national economic loss to the United States is therefore quite substantial. Unlike U.S. domestic taxes lost to tax loopholes, which from a national point of view can be considered a transfer from the public sector to the private sector, tax revenue lost on foreign income which is avoided due to the tax loopholes must be considered a loss to the national economy. In other words there is no trickle down effect. One has no assurance that these tax savings will be reinvested or spent in the domestic economy. The loss to the U.S. Treasury in 1974 alone was significant, with an effective tax rate of only 3.2 percent, U.S. multinational corporations paid $1.4 billion in taxes on an income of $53.6 billion. It is interesting also to note that according to U.S. Treasury data, petroleum companies reported $29.8 billion in foreign source incomes on which no taxes were paid.

Another major tax loophole is the DISC program, Domestic International Sales Corporation enacted in 1971. DISC allows U.S.-based corporations to set up dummy corporations to handle their export activities. DISCs which pay taxes on only 50 percent of their profits until such profits are turned over to the parent corporation, cost the U.S. Treasury an estimated $1.6 billion a year. Tax incentives such as the above create only a trickle out effect with substantial loss to the U.S. economy and society.

The export of technology by U.S. multinational corporations accounts for another substantial loss to the American economy. Technology has become the United States' fastest growing export. U.S. multinational firms have been selling off America's technological advantage at an ever-increasing pace. Receipts from the sale of technology in the form of licensing, royalty and management fees rose from $650 million in 1960 to $3.6 billion in 1974. U.S. firms currently account for between 50 and 60 percent of the world's technology exports. This exportation of our best technology means perhaps that we are trading future domestic manufacturing growth and our global economic position for present profits.

A recent study by the U.S. Department of Commerce suggests that imports often from foreign subsidiaries of U.S. multinational corporations have increasingly invaded American markets and decreased our share of the world export market for manufactured goods. A most critical component for the creation of foreign competition is of course the export of technology along with labor and capital. According to the U.S. Department of Commerce Study, between 1958 and 1973 our share of manufactured exports in the world market dropped from 27.7 to 18.2 percent. Table 4-4 illustrates the loss to particular export sectors of the U.S. economy.

The loss to the U.S. economy then from these tax loopholes, the exportation of jobs, capital and technology has been substantial as the above discussion indicates. Foreign investment, therefore, on the part of U.S. multinational firms has most decidedly had a negative effect on the U.S. economy and society in recent years. The question then becomes whether we would be better off without foreign investment. The matter is not of foreign investment versus domestic investment but rather what the balance should be

Table 4-4 Percentage of U.S. Share of Manufactured Exports
in World Market

	1958	1973
Electrical machinery	32.8	18.2
Chemicals	29.6	18.1
Transportation equipment	35.3	25.2
Non-electrical machinery	35	24
Other manufactures	19.7	11.7

between the two. The existing public policy incentives to U.S. foreign investment do not give any consideration to such a balance and seem to be the result of very limited economic and political interests within our society. Public policy incentives certainly in the future must give some consideration to the need of domestic production, employment patterns and the use of our best technology. Secondly, beyond these changing economic and social needs of the United States, the role of the United States in the world economy is changing, the dollar is no longer the central currency of world trade as mandated by Bretton Woods. These changes may mitigate against a continuing emphasis on a strategy of foreign investment. These changing circumstances in the world economy are reflected in Figure 4-1, which analyzes recent trends in domestic capital formation in relationship to the Gross National Product (GNP).

Clearly the declining capacity of capital formation suggests that the continuing export of domestic capital for foreign investment may even be displacing domestic investments in the short run. The 1977 trade deficit, for example, is estimated at about $27 billion and [that] it could be that high this year and next is suggestive of the magnitude of the problem. In the long run, of course, this chart may be foreboding of our diminished capacity to export capital for foreign investment. The impact of this eroding process is having even broader effects on the U.S. economy and society as a whole.

Overall Effect on the U.S. Economy and Society

The loss of American jobs and tax revenues as a result of U.S. public policies encouraging foreign direct investment is only part of the problem that the expansion of the multinational corporation is having on the U.S. economy and society. One must also question the unregulated activities of the multinational corporation from a national economic point of view. Many economists believe that investments at home are far more productive of jobs and capital than excessive investment abroad. U.S. multinational investments abroad ripple through the foreign economy providing capital and jobs. A recent survey of 111 United States multinational manufacturing corporations conducted by the

Figure 4-1   Real Private Fixed Capital Formation in Relation to GNP

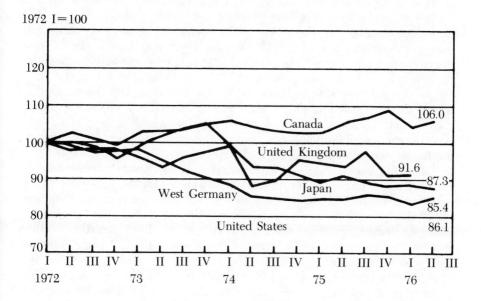

1972 I=100

Business International Corporation—a multinational business group—produced statistics which demonstrate that these companies are increasing employment outside the United States at a rate that far exceeded their employment creation here at home. These firms expanded their employment in the United States by 90,283 jobs in a four-year period, for a 3.3 percent increase, while the foreign subsidiaries of these same 111 multinational firms increased their employment abroad by 360,373 jobs during the same period, a growth of 31.5 percent abroad. The growth of jobs abroad, therefore, was 9.5 times higher than in the home firms. However, while U.S. multinational corporations maximize profits abroad, U.S. labor and U.S. economy suffer a net loss in other ways. Peggy Musgrave in testimony before the Subcommittee on Multinational Corporations noted that,

> The material rate of return on U.S. investment abroad [—] i.e., gross return minus foreign taxes—has been over the recent decade, consistently below the return of domestic investment with the short fall ranging between 25-50 percent.

In the wake of this argument that foreign investment would be better spent at home the multinationals have countered that foreign investment does not displace domestic investment. They argue that the capital that they invest abroad would not be invested in the U.S. domestic economy in the first place due to the lack of investment opportunities at home. This contention on the part of multinationals seems to fly in the face of the capital formation figures for 1972-1976 presented in Figure 4-1 which suggest that capital shortages along with the continuing trade deficit of $27 billion for 1977 may mean that foreign investment will displace domestic investment. Indeed recent studies have demonstrated that there is an interdependence between domestic and foreign investment. Severn (1972), Stevens (1969) and Kwack (1972) have shown foreign investment to be affected positively by domestic cash flow and negatively by domestic sales, the overall debt-equity ratio and domestic plant and equipment expenditures. These results are consistent with the notion that foreign investment is a substitute for domestic investment. Foreign investment, therefore, does seem to displace domestic investment and be the detriment to the U.S. economy, by diminishing our export capacity and thereby, contributing to the trade deficit.

The displacement of domestic investment by foreign investment has changed the global character of the U.S. economy. The United States which achieved economic hegemony as a domestic producing and trading nation now places first priority on foreign production. Currently U.S. foreign production out-ranks domestic production for export four to one. I have noted previously that this fact has contributed to a loss of tax revenues, the U.S. trade deficit as well as having other serious impacts on the character of the U.S. economy. The change in the production of the U.S. economy from one of domestic to foreign production increasingly moves the American economy toward a service orientation rather than its traditional production base. As our manufacturing base continues to wither, we will become more and more dependent on foreign manufactured products. It only follows that we also will become increasingly a service-oriented economy. Already the United States has the highest rate of unemployment of any major industrialized country in the world. Investments in agro-business and agricultural exports which help to offset the U.S. trade deficit are labor extensive, provide few jobs and will not help to reverse this pattern.

This change in the character of the American economy has been forecast by such post industrialists as Daniel Bell in *The Coming of Post Industrial Society*. The dominant feature of the post industrial society is that the preponderance of economic activity is located in the "tertiary" or service sector of the economy. Table 4-5 illustrates this point of the post industrialists in dramatic terms.

The growth in the service sector from 1947-1968 as the table illustrates has far outranked the growth of the production sector. The tremendous expansion in the service sector interestingly enough coincides with the period in which our economy was transformed to a production base abroad that by 1968 was four times as great as domestic production for export.

This dramatic change in the structure of the U.S. economy has far reaching economic political and social effects. For instance, United States public policy decisions which have encouraged U.S. foreign investment also have contributed to shifting wealth away from the working classes. . . . With

Table 4-5 Sector Distribution of Employment by Goods and Services, 1947-1968, Projected to 1980 (in thousands)

	1947	1968	1980	Percentage change	
				1947-1968	1968-1980
Total	51,770	800,780	99,600	56	23
Goods-producing total	26,370	28,975	21,600	9.8	9
Agriculture, forestry, and fisheries	7,890	4,150	3,180	(−48)	(−23)
Mining	955	640	590	(−33)	(−9)
Construction	1,980	4,050	5,480	10	35
Manufacturing	15,540	20,125	22,358	29	11
Durable	8,385	11,850	13,275	41	12
Non-durable	7,160	8,270	9,100	15.5	10
Service-producing total	25,400	51,800	67,980	104	31
Transportation and utilities	4,160	4,500	5,000	8	10
Trade (wholesale and retail)	8,950	16,600	20,500	85.5	23
Finance, insurance, and real estate	1,750	3,725	4,640	113	24
Services (personal, professional, business)	5,050	15,000	21,000	135	40
Government	5,470	11,850	16,800	117	42
Federal	1,890	2,735	3,000	45	10
State and local	3,580	9,110	13,800	150	52

over $133 billion in United States direct foreign investment and with so many countries demanding better terms on these investments or demanding nationalization or expropriation of U.S. property abroad, the words of Lord Keynes offer sage advice to public policy makers that encourage U.S. multinational investment abroad.

From a national economic viewpoint the costs of foreign investment are quite high. A 1976 study indicated that 1,840,000 American jobs have been lost to U.S. multinational investment abroad. U.S. public policy analysts will have to strike a balance between domestic and foreign investment and reconsider the strong incentives to U.S. investment abroad. Failure to consider these important questions will certainly mean an expanded service economy and continued erosion of the dollar.

The above analysis illustrates the importance of adopting a public policy perspective for analyzing the impact of the multinational corporations on their sponsoring nations. Only by recognizing the intricate relationship between politics and economics can we begin to comprehend the far-reaching significance of the multinational corporations on society.

4.4 ▬▬▬

GEORGE P. SHULTZ

National Policies and Global Prosperity

My theme today is simple: the American economy is a success story—a dramatic success story. But success brings with it new challenges, which we must address with great energy in order to preserve and build on the success we have achieved.

We face a paradox. In the past 2 years, our economy has made the strongest recovery of any in the last three decades, and the expansion remains robust. Yet we also see, in our domestic and international economic relations, some unusually large and important imbalances:

- ☐ A large net capital inflow;
- ☐ An exceptionally strong dollar;
- ☐ The largest trade deficit in our history; and
- ☐ Large and continuing deficits in the U.S. Federal budget.

What relationship is there, if any, between our clear economic success and these equally clear imbalances? How do these imbalances relate to each other? What are our prospects if the imbalances continue? And what conclusions follow for economic policy—in this country and in other countries? These are the issues I would like to discuss with you today.

The economic policies of this administration—reducing the role of government, promoting private initiative, and encouraging free trade—have led the United States out of recession and toward prosperity. We can be proud of our economic performance. Our expansion has led to export-induced recoveries abroad—underscoring the interdependence among the world's economies.

In large part, the imbalances I mentioned have contributed to our economic success; some are partly the result of it. To a degree, they have been exacerbated by the economic policies of other nations. Whatever their source,

An address before the Woodrow Wilson School of Public and International Affairs, Princeton University, Princeton, New Jersey, April 11, 1985.

my main conclusion can be stated up front: these imbalances are interrelated, and they must be corrected if we are to maintain the momentum of our economic success. We—and other countries—share a responsibility to make some hard political decisions.

Let me focus on these imbalances, first as they impact on the American economy and then as they are mirrored in other countries. Then I will lay out the policy responses I see as necessary—responses by all nations—to keep the world economy on the path of sustained, noninflationary growth.

Capital Flows

First, the large net capital inflows into the United States.

An impressive investment boom has driven American economic expansion in the past 3 years. To a large extent, this boom reflects the new investment incentives the administration provided in its first term—including incentives for vital research and development, which is the source of future investment. Gross saving by individuals, business, and state and local governments also recovered from its recession low of 18% of GNP [gross national product] in 1982 to 20% in 1984.

But with the Federal deficit, gross national saving alone could not finance this higher level of investment. In 1984, gross saving in the United States by individuals, businesses, and state and local governments ran about $730 billion. On a net basis of capital consumption, the figure was $325 billion. These are healthy amounts by recent standards. After taking account of the large Federal deficit, however, total national saving amounted to only about $150 billion on a net basis or $555 billion on a gross basis—considerably less than the $635 billion recorded in gross private domestic investment in 1984.

As measured by our current account deficit, net capital inflows into the United States were about $100 billion last year. This is almost one-fifth the size of our gross national saving—and two-thirds the size of our net national saving—and has been an important factor in financing the expansion of our investment and, therefore, of our economy.

These inflows have come about largely because of the health and vigor of our own economy, in contrast with the less attractive conditions for lending and investment in other countries. But they come, to some degree, at the expense of building up foreign claims on the United States. On the basis of current trends, the United States will soon become a large net debtor nation—our foreign liabilities could exceed our foreign assets by $100 billion by the end of the year.

And underlying conditions are bound to change in the future. As opportunities to invest improve in other countries, capital inflows into the United States will slow down and outflows will increase. In other words, even if we are prepared to finance investment in the United States through a continuing net inflow of funds, we cannot count on attracting adequate funds indefinitely. Without a compensating increase in domestic saving to support our own investment—and if our federal deficit continues to preempt a large portion of domestic saving—lower capital inflows could force a decline in our investment and impair the long-term growth of the American economy.

The Strong Dollar

These large net capital inflows into the United States have produced an extraordinarily strong dollar. Although the dollar has receded somewhat in the last month, it is still, on a trade-weighted basis, about 80% above its 1980 average in nominal terms.

The exchange value of the dollar today is determined far more by capital movements than by trade balances. Many factors have contributed. The restoration of America's economic vitality and leadership on the world scene has had an important effect on investment decisions. Our economic success— and our bright prospects—cause investments in dollar assets to be judged more attractive and less risky than others despite the dollar's high value. The dollar market also offers the widest selection and greatest liquidity. And dollar assets are serving not only as a store of value but as a political safehaven as well. Exchange markets reflect all these considerations, particularly as they contrast with the poor growth performance in Europe, the financial problems of the developing world, and the large excess of saving over domestic investment in Japan.

The net inflows of foreign capital, and the resulting high dollar, have certain advantages. By reducing the cost of imports and forcing domestic suppliers to compete more effectively, the strong dollar has helped restrain inflation in the United States. The net capital inflows have helped moderate interest rates as well. Abroad, the growth of American imports and slower growth of American exports have stimulated export-related jobs and generated economies of scale for foreign producers. The high value of the dollar also makes offshore procurement, tourism, and American foreign direct investment in other countries all less expensive.

But the extraordinarily high dollar also has important disadvantages.

- ☐ It reduces the competitiveness of our exports and the potential for their growth. Even though our exports have increased and the United States is still the world's largest exporter, our share of the world market for exports of manufactured goods in volume terms is estimated to have declined by 25% since 1980.
- ☐ Because of increased domestic demand, economic activity in the United States has not yet been appreciably restricted. But that may change.
- ☐ The dollar's strength is causing painful structural adjustments in many of our export-related industries; it is altering the character of the American economy in a basic and, in my view, undesirable way. Lower

costs in other countries—due to exchange rates—are leading many American firms to locate abroad production facilities that would otherwise be competitive in the United States. Such decisions to locate or expand abroad would be both difficult and costly to reverse if the dollar's exchange value came down.

☐ The large decline in the value of other currencies against the dollar has also eroded the value of existing foreign investments, sales, and earnings denominated in foreign currencies.

☐ In the meantime, the growth of our imports is spurring protectionist demands for tariffs, nontariff barriers, and export subsidies. Whatever short-term relief for specific industries such measures might provide, the overall long-term cost to the mettle of the American economy, to the American consumer, and to the world economy would be devastating. Let us never forget the catastrophic effects of protection in the 1930s and the exhilarating impact of more open trade in the decades following World War II.

The Trade Account

This leads me to the most visible international consequence of the strong dollar: its role in our huge and growing trade deficit, which reached a record $123 billion in 1984.

Despite the strong dollar, our exports, in fact, grew last year by 9% to a total of $218 billion—demonstrating the underlying strength of the American economy and reflecting adjustments in efficiency occurring within the market place. Nevertheless, the growth of imports overwhelmed the growth of exports, increasing 24% in volume terms and 26% in value terms. Over half of the $85 billion deterioration in the U.S. trade account since 1980 has been attributed to the strong dollar.

I have already mentioned the growing demands for protectionism. The Administration is resisting these pressures, and I will have more to say about our approach to trade policy in a moment. But one point is crucial here: we should not delude ourselves into thinking that a lowering of foreign barriers will have a decisive or even substantial impact on the trade deficit.

We can break the back of the trade deficit only through a combination of, first, a stronger worldwide recovery and, second, a strengthening of other currencies in relation to the dollar as the performance and prospects of other economies improve and as these prospects are recognized by the markets. Even with movement on these fronts, the effects on the trade deficit will be gradual.

With depreciation of the dollar, U.S. imports would become more expensive and there would be some increase in inflationary pressure, at least initially. The growth of imports should slow down but probably with a lag. Purchases of raw materials, energy products and petroleum, specialized capital goods, and many consumer goods do not respond quickly when their prices rise.

The growth of our export sales will depend on several factors: on our ability to remain competitive; on a faster pace of economic recovery in other nations, notably Europe; on the success of adjustment efforts in developing countries; and on long overdue action by Japan to open its markets. Exports to the developing countries, particularly to those in Latin America burdened by debt, will still depend upon their ability to expand their exports to pay for our goods. This means our markets and those of other industrialized countries must remain open to their products. And many American exporters have already lost major foreign markets, recoverable only with a major effort.

The U.S. Federal Deficit

I have discussed the large net capital inflows, the strong dollar, and the huge trade deficit. It is no coincidence that these imbalances are accompanied by huge Federal budget deficits.

As long as there are ample unused resources in our economy, the federal budget deficit does not cause major immediate problems for the United States. But current deficits are simply not sustainable indefinitely. These deficits can become a habit and weaken an essential discipline over Federal spending and over the size of the Federal Government. They drain off national savings, leading to increased reliance on foreign capital or curtailment of needed investment. And, as our expansion begins to stretch our resources, continued large deficits pose an increasing danger to that very expansion.

We can all continue to debate what combination of policies is best designed to deal with all the imbalances I have discussed—budget deficits, large capital inflows, the dollar on a financial high, and trade deficits. But a consensus has emerged that action to reduce the Federal budget deficit is an essential part of our response. The President has shown the way with his proposals and in his negotiations with the Congress. Special interests must give way to the general interest.

Control of government spending, coupled with vigorous growth, must be the key to our effort. We must cut spending in a way that does the least harm to the economy's investment and growth potential and to basic national security. But significant cuts *must* be made *now*. Tax rate increases are not the answer. To the contrary, the recent Reagan tax cuts, like the Kennedy cuts two decades earlier, have stimulated investment, fueling the recovery and contributing to the future productive potential of the economy. In fact, further tax simplification and reform could be very helpful in reducing tax-induced distortions in economic activity and in stimulating additional growth.

Other Industrialized Countries

So far I have focused primarily on the American economy. But in our interdependent world, the impact of domestic policies and performance on the economies of other nations is a two-way street. Other countries face challenges in their own domestic policies. They, too, must meet their challenges if the world economy is to correct the imbalances that cloud our common future. The imbalances can do harm also to important political relationships. We all have a job to do.

The major industrialized countries are recovering from the 1980-82 world recession at different rates. Whereas the United States and, to a lesser degree, Japan and Canada have expanded vigorously, Western Europe still lags. Average real growth in the four major European economies (Germany, France, the United Kingdom, and Italy) accelerated in 1984, but only to a year-over-year annual rate of 2.4%. This rise represented less than half the average of the American, Japanese, and Canadian rates. The Japanese and Canadian expansions, however, have depended heavily on the stimulus of exports to the U.S. market. The increase in Canadian exports to the United States amounted to over half the increase in Canadian GNP in current prices between 1982 and 1984, while the increase in Japanese exports to the U.S. market was over 10% of the increase in current-price GNP over the same period.

The slowness of recovery in Europe results from conditions that stifle investment, particularly structural problems in labor markets and government disincentives to adjustment and growth. The rigidities in European labor rates and conditions also tend to bias investment toward capital-intensive technologies—further inhibiting the growth of employment. There has been essentially no net job creation in Europe since 1970, compared with the American record of over 26 million new jobs during the same period. Over 7.5 million net new jobs have been created in this country since the trough of the recession in 1982.

Expressed as a share of output, gross investment in Europe has declined steadily since the first oil shock in 1973 and is now well below its share in the 1960s. Since investment opportunities in Europe have been less attractive than elsewhere, capital has flowed elsewhere. Much of the capital has come to the United States, either as investment in U.S. assets by foreigners, disinvestment by American investors abroad, or a reduction in the previous rate of foreign lending by U.S. banks. At the same time, it is estimated that half of Western Europe's growth in 1984 came from export sales to the United States. These exports amounted to $75 billion or nearly 22% of total U.S. imports last year.

Capital outflows from Europe and a dependence on exports to the United States—like the other imbalances I have mentioned—cannot be expected to continue indefinitely. Other OECD [Organization for Economic Cooperation and Development] governments must find ways to stimulate growth-oriented investment, thereby making their investment opportunities attractive to domestic and international capital. At stake is an efficient allocation of global resources—a system which responds to economic potential. This will require sound economic policies and hard political decisions—but the result will be sustained growth, job creation, and a brighter economic future.

Japan is a special case. The $37 billion U.S. trade deficit with Japan, as we all know, is a source of intense friction in our bilateral relationship and the cause of much of the growing demand for protectionism in this country. But the more meaningful measure of Japan's external imbalance is not our bilateral imbalance but Japan's overall trade surplus, estimated at $44 billion in 1984.

The Japanese could reduce their trade surplus with the world by pursuing policies to offset the impact of their high savings rate. Gross private saving in Japan is over 30% of GNP, about 50% higher than the average of other OECD countries. This high rate of saving means low consumption. The excess of production over private and public consumption is not being used in domestic investment. It, therefore, appears as net exports. Or, to put it another way, under current conditions, Japan relies on a large excess of exports over imports to maintain full employment.

Opening up investment opportunities within Japan would be one way to use such resources and reduce the pressure to export. The needed decisions are more difficult for Japan politically than economically. The structural rigidities in the Japanese economy restrict access by even Japanese firms and investors. If the Japanese Government would improve incentives and reduce restrictions that currently restrain domestic and foreign firms from investing in Japan, all nations, especially Japan, would benefit. Steps are already underway to liberalize the Japanese capital market so as to channel Japanese savings more efficiently to both foreign and domestic uses and to widen the financial opportunities facing Japanese firms. As this proceeds, and as the international role of the yen expands, we would expect the value of the yen more fully to reflect the strength of the Japanese economy.

On the trade side, the removal of barriers to the sale of foreign goods and services in Japan would expand market opportunities for foreign suppliers, increasing Japan's imports. Prime Minister Nakasone's recent speech and the Japanese Government's package of measures to lower trade barriers and encourage imports are a laudable and encouraging beginning. More specifics must come.

All these steps would help defuse protectionist pressures in other countries. But Japan must deal with its savings-investment imbalance if its chronic imbalance in trade is to be corrected.

The Developing Countries

The external accounts of the developing countries, like those of the European countries, help make up the mirror image of ours. The United States takes nearly 60% of all manufactured exports of developing countries to the industrial world. At the same time, our capital inflows from the developing nations are, in part, the result of American investors bringing their money home or of American banks reducing their foreign lending as opportunities in those countries appear less attractive.

Despite the progress made since the 1982-84 debt crisis, many developing countries still face the need for fundamental changes in their economies and economic strategies.

Several high-debt countries have successfully tackled the job of stabilizing their economies. They have cut public sector spending to more nearly match their resources, priced currencies to reflect better their market value, and set interest rates to encourage saving. They now face the need to get away from massive price subsidies or public sector dominance of investment resources and economic activity.

The emphasis should be on the positive. Austerity is not an end in itself. For difficult adjustments to be undertaken and sustained, a country's citizens must be able to see real prospects for future growth. Economic expansion, fueled by increased investment and exports, is the only way these countries can raise living standards for their people.

This is a theme that applies to many of the issues I have discussed today. Adjustments such as these are more difficult politically than economically—requiring new ways of thinking even more than they require resources. The cuts we must make in our own Federal spending are painful, but they are justified because they safeguard the continued growth of the productive private sector of our economy. The structural reforms in Europe that will ensure an attractive investment climate for domestic savings and international capital are necessary to restore Europe's own growth and technological advance. For the Third World, structural adjustment is the key to economic development.

The developing countries will clearly need financing as they go through this process. But where will this financing come from? No one can realistically expect that official development assistance, bilateral and multilateral, is likely to expand; the net flows are already very large—around $34 billion from official donors. And it is a fact of life that commercial bank lending will not return to the high levels of the past decade. Even increases from current levels are unlikely until developing countries improve their creditworthiness and offer productive investment opportunities. In any case, most developing countries already have more debt than they can readily handle.

There is no escaping this hard conclusion: domestic saving and private foreign equity investment will be the main sources of funds available to finance development and stimulate growth. Development and growth will come only to countries with sound domestic policies that stimulate domestic savings, promote trade, and attract external resources.

□ India is a striking example of a country that finances 92% of its investment needs from domestic savings. India's recent growth has been impressive and its prospects are bright.

□ Protectionism in the developing world can be a further drag on growth. The barriers to trade among developing countries are a hindrance to

Third World expansion, and the barriers to outside trade and investment also retard development.

☐ The value of foreign equity investment cannot be measured by the volume of funds alone. Foreign investors often bring technological and management skills that cannot be easily obtained in other ways. The enterprises of such investors tend to grow more rapidly and export more of their output than the economy as a whole. Moreover, there is no conflict between what needs to be done to stimulate foreign and domestic investment; both respond to a stable and predictable regulatory environment and to an expectation that they will be treated fairly.

Many developing countries seem reluctant to encourage foreign investment. It is their decision to make. But a number of countries have shed once fashionable mythology and recognized the opportunity. Now, after consistent application of sound policies, they are reaping the benefits.

International Trade

For developed and developing countries alike, economic growth clearly depends also on the continued openness of the world trading system and, indeed, on a further liberalization of world trade. This is a collective international responsibility.

Protectionism is not the remedy to an illness. It is itself an illness. It is a hidden tax on the consumer, often an extremely regressive tax. Hold onto your pocketbooks when politicians start trying to "protect" you against buying what you want to buy. Even in the relatively open U.S. market, one estimate is that U.S. protectionist policies cost American consumers directly almost $60 billion in 1980. That was over $250 for every man, woman, and child in the country. Protectionism keeps prices up, reduces living standards, and stifles growth.

Trade promotes the flow not only of goods and services but also of ideas. All countries benefit from the further division of labor that permits a broadening of the international marketplace. Those developing countries will grow the fastest that reduce impediments to trade and exploit their comparative advantage. Nor can developed countries repeal the laws of economics and defy the principle of comparative advantage; they must be prepared, over time, to phase out industries in which they are no longer competitive.

The ninefold growth in the volume of international trade since World War II reflects the success of the world trading system. During this period, world trade increased considerably more than world production. In the prewar period, by contrast, protectionism and a decline in world trade thrust the world into depression. A new initiative is needed to sustain what has been achieved.

The United States has proposed—and strongly urges—a new round of multilateral negotiations early next year to liberalize trade, particularly to eliminate nontariff barriers such as quotas, voluntary export restraints, and subsidies. We want the GATT [General Agreement on Tariffs and Trade] to extend its coverage to trade in services, agriculture, and high technology and to strengthen its system of safeguards and dispute settlement. Progress in these areas will provide new opportunities and new markets, bringing tangible benefits to both developed and developing nations. It will also contribute to the fight against protectionism. In the absence of progress on the multilateral front, pressures for protection and a retreat to reciprocal bilateral arrangements will mount.

From a global perspective, a splintering of the multilateral trading system into a multitude of bilateral arrangements would be a backward step. Bilateral free trade agreements, however, such as we have negotiated with Israel and have offered to discuss with other countries, need not have this result; they can stimulate trade and strengthen the multilateral system. Free trade agreements are sanctioned by the international rules and involve a tighter trade discipline; they can promote freer trade than the multilateral system is currently prepared to accommodate. Our hope, nonetheless, is that the example of greater liberalization—and the recognition that the United States can pursue another course—will help motivate a larger group of nations to tackle the job of expanding trade on a global basis.

But we cannot forget our responsibility here at home. We in the United States are today more affected by the health of the global economic system than we have ever been before. And as the world's largest economy, we cannot escape the reality that any protectionist action here can do enormous harm to the global economic system. So in our own long-term self-interest, we must remain loyal to our long-standing tradition—our proud commitment to free and open trade.

A Program for Sustained Global Growth

Let me conclude with a message and a program that emerge from my analysis. The message is twofold: first, the main objective, and the key to success, is to accelerate growth in the world economy. That's what this is all about. And second, growth in the world economy is the result of interaction among sound national policies. That is the most important common ingredient in the policy steps that nations must take to correct the imbalances I have discussed.

Together, these steps are a program of international action to protect the current recovery and move us decisively onto the path of sustained, noninflationary growth.

First, for our own part, and even for purely domestic reasons, the United States must—and will—substantially reduce its Federal spending and deficit.

Second, the West Europeans should adopt policies that reduce the obstacles to change and innovation, that attract capital, and that stimulate domestic investment.

Third, in addition to opening its markets to foreign products, Japan should reduce the impact of its high rate of domestic saving on its trade surplus. This could be done by a combination of steps, including liberalized capital markets that internationalize the yen and measures to stimulate investment in Japan by Japanese and foreigners alike.

Fourth, the developing nations, especially those heavily indebted, should continue to make the structural adjustments needed to stabilize their economies, reduce the economic burden of government, expand their trade, and stimulate growth. They should encourage domestic savings and foreign equity investment.

Fifth, all nations should support freer international trade and prepare for early commencement of a new international trade round. We must reject a surtax on imports; other countries must contain political pressures that threaten trade.

Finally, our approach to the strength of the dollar should concentrate on the fundamental market forces at work. Intervention in exchange markets addresses only the symptoms of the dollar's strength—and not at all successfully. An easy monetary policy, undertaken in an illusory effort to reduce interest rates, would only reignite fears of inflation, raise interest rates, and weaken economic prospects. Instead, we should maintain consistent, noninflationary growth in monetary aggregates to accommodate economic growth while continuing the trend to lower inflation.

This program of action calls for many hard decisions. But they are the right decisions. We stand at the threshold of what can be, if all governments meet their responsibilities, a long period of global economic expansion and a new era of unprecedented prosperity.

The benefits that economic growth can bring to all the world's people transcend the purely material—though for the world's poor and hungry, this alone would be a monumental blessing. A strong and growing global economy will help advance all of America's most fundamental goals: a world of cooperation, peace, stability, and progress, a world where human rights are respected and freedom flourishes. We have great opportunities to help build such a world, but we will succeed only if we have the will and the wisdom to recognize the dangers and confront them. We know what must be done. But we must act on that knowledge if our hopes for a better world are to become a reality.

███████ **4.5**

FELIX ROHATYN

On the Brink

The United States today is headed for a financial and economic crisis. What appeared to be only a possibility five or six years ago became a probability more recently, and has now become a virtual certainty. The only real questions are when and how. In addition, when the crisis occurs, it will entail, quite possibly, a worldwide recession. How can such a statement be made when the Dow Jones index is at 2300 and unemployment has edged further and further down?

The facts are that the US has been guilty of the most irresponsible fiscal behavior in its history during the last seven years. American fiscal folly, coupled with the inability to coordinate economic policies with Europe and Japan, has created an ever-increasing worldwide pyramid of debt that cannot withstand a major recession. The US is on its way to becoming the world's largest international borrower, and since the worldwide financial markets are interconnected, a serious US economic downturn automatically has worldwide repercussions.

The United States, and the rest of the world, will pay a heavy price for the fact that we have committed $2 trillion for a defense program of dubious value; that we have been unwilling to limit the growth of entitlement programs like Social Security and Medicare regardless of the need of the recipient or of his ability to shoulder some of the costs; and that, in an act of the ultimate financial cowardice, we have attempted to pass on to our children the cost of this behavior by borrowing from tomorrow instead of taxing today.

There are several results of this behavior, many of which are not always visible. The first, and perhaps the least noticed, is that when it comes to our economy we are no longer an independent country. For the first time in our history, we depend on foreign capital to finance day-to-day operations of our government. In 1986, almost half of our budget deficit of about $180 billion was financed by foreign purchases of treasury securities, mainly by the Japanese. From a financial point of view, we are being colonized.

Second, in order to provide Japan and Germany with the funds that we need to borrow, we have allowed our domestic markets to absorb an ever-increasing amount of foreign goods, largely as a result of a gross overevaluation of the dollar during the years between 1980 and 1984. Even though we have dramatically changed course since 1985, collapsing the value of the dollar with other dangerous consequences, our trade deficit reached $160 billion last year and seems to be locked in for years to come. It is worth noting that, even if we were able to reduce our trade deficit by $20 billion per year, by 1995 our external debt would be about $1.5 trillion and the interest on that debt about $120 billion annually.

Third, our domestic national debt has doubled over the last five years and is well over $2 trillion. Interest on the debt alone will be about $125 billion. Corporate debt, partly as a result of unbridled takeover activity fueled by the new phenomenon of the junk bond market, is at its highest level in twenty-five years. By the end of 1986, the total long- and short-term debt of nonfinancial institutions was about $1.6 trillion.

Fourth, the debt of the less-developed countries (LDCs) to governments and banks is now more than $1 trillion as a result of year-after-year rollovers, whereby debtor countries borrow the interest on their debt and add it on to the principal amount.

There is no purely American solution to any of our major economic problems. The US cannot afford a recession that would drive our deficits to more than $300 billion and possibly cause a crash in the value of the dollar as well as in the stock and bond markets. The result could be extensive domestic and international banking defaults, a world recession, and political instability in large parts of the globe. Avoiding such an outcome, if it is possible, would involve a delicate combination of coordinated domestic and international efforts:

- ☐ The US would cut its budget deficit, through a combination of new taxes and reductions in spending. This will inevitably mean a temporary reduction in the standard of living.
- ☐ To counteract the risk of recession, we would reduce interest rates and run an easier monetary policy.
- ☐ To avoid a collapse of the dollar, Japan and Europe would have to stimulate growth, cut taxes, and increase spending.
- ☐ And to promote growth in the third world, the US, Japan, and Western Europe would have to agree on an aggressive plan of debt restructuring and on providing significant amounts of new capital for the debtor countries.

It is hard to see how any of this can happen in a US presidential election year. Under normal circumstances, even if the next president were willing to embrace such programs, they probably would not be enacted until 1990. That may well be too late.

We need a coherent economic strategy; we do not have one. The government's only active policy is to drive down the value of the dollar with everything else "on hold"; no serious action is being taken to reduce the budget deficits, and there is no real change in the debt structure of the less-developed countries. A few tariffs have been imposed on some Japanese products. The administration simply seems to be hoping for a "soft landing"—a dangerous strategy and one likely to fail. Here are some of the risks involved:

(1) We have now had six years of economic growth, fueled by consumer spending, military buildup, and borrowing. The likelihood of a recession in the next two years becomes greater and greater as consumers reach the limits of their borrowing capacity and domestic investment remains soft.

(2) The coming weakness in the US economy must be replaced with growth in foreign economies. As the dollar collapses, the German and Japanese economies will slow down considerably, for both countries depend significantly on sales to the US. Combined with the inability of less-developed countries to grow as a result of crushing debt service, we are coming close to causing a worldwide economic slowdown without helping ourselves in any real way.

(3) There is no precedent or analogy for the worldwide financial structure that has been created in recent years. The amounts of capital that are ricocheting around the world dwarf anything that has been experienced. One and a half trillion dollars *per day* now flows through New York's Clearing House Interbank Payment System (CHIPS), which processes all the domestic and foreign payments passing through New York banks. This amounts to one third of our *annual* Gross National Product. The relationships between exchange rates and trade, between interest rates and economic activities, between fiscal and monetary policies, have become less and less predictable. The potential for a major shock in the credit system and the securities markets gets greater and greater.

The fallout from some of these problems goes considerably beyond the economic sphere. The ability of democratic governments in Mexico, Brazil, Argentina, the Philippines, etc., to survive in the face of continued reductions in the standard of living is questionable. Radical political movements will spring up, calling for the repudiation of debts to the Western banks; whether or not they succeed, they could bring on right-wing military dictatorships that may follow similar debt-related policies. The problems that would be created for the US by a radicalized Mexico are obvious. Whether the radicalization is left-wing or right-wing, the result may be the same: virulent anti-Americanism and an increasingly unstable southern border. The problem of illegal immigration, already extremely serious, will become even greater. The racial and political tensions in the US, especially if we are in the throes of a recession, will heighten considerably. And no one has made any kind of estimate of the additional military cost of having to maintain tighter security on the US-Mexican border.

In our own country, we have combined runaway borrowing and deficits with neglect for our domestic needs and a climate of deregulation pushed to dangerous extremes. For the sake of competition, we have broken up AT&T, and the result has been both bad service and higher prices. We have deregulated the airlines and the resulting price wars did, indeed, lower fares. However, one airline after another is on its way to bankruptcy or to being acquired by another. The result will be a few huge airlines, with questionable financial structures, poor service with possibly higher prices, and worrisome safety factors. Deregulation of the financial markets has resulted in an explosion of private debt, unprecedented market speculation, and the sordid abuses in the financial industry that have been coming to light in recent months. Deregulation, as with most things in life, has to be done in moderation; it has been carried too far. The free market is not always right; it surely is not always fair. It should not be turned into a religion.

Our budget priorities have also been misconceived. The continued military buildup, together with the growth in entitlements, cannot be sustained in the light of our other needs. The recent collapse of a bridge in upstate New York was a small reminder of a major problem, the immense need to rebuild our domestic infrastructure. It is estimated that $50 billion may be required nationally for bridges alone, which does not seem unreasonable in light of New York City's $15 billion commitment to mass transit in the decade of the 1980s. A major domestic reconstruction program for such facilities as railroads, bridges, waterworks, roads, and school buildings must be undertaken soon. It will be more labor-intensive than a continued military buildup and will be a better long-run investment for the country. It cannot be financed without changes in our priorities.

Contrary to some predictions, the productivity of American industry has increased significantly during the last decade. However, no amount of improvement in productivity will make up for wild swings in the value of the dollar which have driven vast amounts of US manufacturing permanently abroad. No amount of productivity will survive competition with the Korean, Malaysian, or Taiwanese standard of living. To create jobs and businesses that add high values to raw materials through skill and technology we need an educated work force. We are not creating one. Our primary and secondary education system is a disgrace, particularly in our large cities. Future generations of inner-city students are condemned to spending unproductive lives. The human cost in crime, misery, and racial tensions is unacceptable, the financial cost to the country's economic capacity is equally great. It is absurd to think of the US as a worldwide economic power unless it can undertake a major effort in education, together with the investment in infrastructure that has to go with it.

Our renewed dependence on imported oil for our domestic energy needs should also be a source of concern. The collapse in oil prices, coupled with the dramatic deterioration of the financial position of many large US oil companies has caused operating rigs to be reduced from over 4000 in 1982 to about 600 today. Imported oil will again supply over 50 percent of our requirements and it may supply a significantly greater proportion by the early 1990s. We cannot once again become hostages to the Middle East for our energy needs. The region is becoming increasingly unstable and we cannot afford the risk of a sharp rise in energy prices in the midst of a 1989 or 1990 recession.

At the same time, a major opportunity may be open to us. Whatever problems we may have, the Soviet Union has many more. It is impossible for a rigid, bureaucratic, totalitarian system to survive competitively in the advanced, industrial, global environment of the late twentieth century. The Soviet system, if it is to adapt to modern telecommunications and data processing, and other new technologies, without which it cannot compete, may have to open itself up politically, provide greater benefits to its population, and limit its imperial ambitions. Its ability to physically control the life of its neighbors in Central Europe may become more limited.

General Secretary Gorbachev seems to understand this reality. The next few years may provide the opportunity for large changes in the relationships between the Soviet Union and the US. Both our countries need to make major investments in defense. In addition, the Soviet Union will need credits and technology from the West. No doubt there is a risk that a more successful Soviet economy will result in a more aggressive Soviet state. There is, however, a greater risk that a continued, uncontrolled arms race, coupled with rising political tensions, will lead not only to ruinous expenditures but to armed confrontation.

Of course arms control agreements with the Soviets must be carefully monitored. But the notion that anything that is good for the Soviets is automatically bad for us is absurd. Our present vacillations about Soviet proposals on nuclear arms reductions in Europe are an example. Some prominent officials and commentators in the US and Europe are worried that eliminating short-range missiles, together with medium-range missiles, will leave Europe at the mercy of Soviet conventional forces. First, the notion that the Soviets will invade Western Europe is far-fetched, given NATO's strategic and tactical nuclear capacities on the one hand, and the fact, on the other, that the Soviets have continuing difficulty in controlling Eastern Europe. Second, the Soviets have indicated a willingness to discuss conventional force reductions. Third, if such reductions do not take place, we should suggest to our European friends that they build up their own conventional forces. Our allies are clearly not carrying their fair share of the defense load. But there is no valid reason not to begin the process of nuclear arms reduction, and we may never see a better opportunity for doing so.

As for long-term global economic strategies, the advanced countries must look for ways to create new, large-scale demand from regions other than Western Europe, North America, and Japan. The main economic risk to the West is not inflation but deflation. Too much capacity has been built up throughout the world with insufficient demand to absorb it. During the next few decades, such additional demand could be encouraged to come from the less-developed countries, and the Soviet bloc. Our long-term international economic strategy should include the following:

(1) Major commitments of Japanese and West German capital to finance the future growth of the less developed countries while we negotiate to restructure their existing debt, enabling those countries to meet

the demands of their people.

(2) Step-by-step arms control agreements and parallel economic cooperation with the Soviet Union and the Soviet bloc countries aimed at their
becoming a major factor in creating additional demand for the world's
economy.

(3) A new Bretton Woods conference to try to evolve a more stable
international monetary system. This is long overdue. This should be the main
item for consideration on the next economic summit in Venice in June 1987.
Such a conference should take up the subjects of exchange rates and debt.
They cannot be separated. Concerning currencies, the conference should
deal with both near-term and long-term objectives. For the near term, the
conference should aim to establish "target zones" for the dollar, the Deutsche
mark, sterling, and yen—ranges in which exchange rates would be permitted
to fluctuate under an agreement to keep the rates from breaking through either
end of the range. At the same time, large-scale interventions in the markets
to defeat speculative runs on the main currencies must be backed by a sizable
and credible intervention fund. The main central banks should as soon as
possible establish a $20 to $30 billion exchange stabilization fund for this
purpose.

The recent series of agreements among the Group of Five—the US, UK,
Japan, Germany, and France—has succeeded in collapsing the dollar but in
little else, since there has been no real coordination of economic policies among
the OECD nations. For the long term, an expansion of the European Monetary
System to include sterling, dollars, and yen should be considered. The EMS on
the whole has been successful in maintaining a level of cooperation and
coordination among its members. Devaluations and reevaluations have occurred, but as part of an orderly, gradual process.

It is time to study how the system can be expanded. In order to do so,
however, the obvious fact to be faced is that the dollar now accounts for
some 80 percent of the world's currency reserves—the currency that governments and international agencies hold to finance international trade; this
disproportion must be counterbalanced by larger volumes of other currencies
than are available today. The European Currency Unit (ECU)—which is based
on a "basket" of European currencies—and the yen offer the best possibilities.

In the long run, currencies cannot be stabilized without considerably
closer coordination between nations and in some cases, integration of their
economic policies. Central to both goals will be the creation of currencies or
baskets of currencies in sufficient volume to counterbalance the dollar.

Such a long-term strategy would still involve major efforts to reorganize
our own economy and to avoid the major economic crisis which is almost upon
us, notwithstanding the difficulties of pursuing difficult changes in economic
and political policy during an election year. Politicians have a tendency to
recreate the last election just as generals have a tendency to fight the last war.
If they follow the conventional wisdom, the Democratic presidential candidates

will refuse to discuss any increase in taxes and the Republican candidates will duck the issue of possible cutbacks in Social Security and other entitlements. That will doom any serious action on the budget deficit until 1990. Neither Democrats nor Republicans, moreover, will want to propose a restructuring of third world debt—extending repayment periods and writing off loans—while the farm sector, the energy sector, and other parts of the US economy are in difficulty. As for American ties with the Soviets, we may expect that prominent Republicans will compete to show they are more hawkish and tough-minded than their colleagues; and Democrats will fear being perceived as "soft on communism."

The presidential candidates in 1988 thus confront implicit choices. If they discuss the country's economic situation realistically and truthfully, they risk political suicide. If they make promises about taxes, entitlements, and energy policy that they cannot possibly keep, they risk being unable to govern if they are elected.

One way to avoid what will be seen as self-defeating choices would be to try to create a consensus among moderate Republican and Democratic leaders on some of the fundamental economic constraints that will face the next president. This could be done by establishing a bipartisan congressional commission modeled on the Temporary National Economic Commission set up by Franklin Roosevelt in 1938 to study the country's economic problems. The commission would consist of members of Congress, business and labor leaders, and academic experts. They would be evenly split between Republicans and Democrats and would represent ideologically moderate wings of their parties. Their task would be to identify the main issues and principal ways of dealing with them responsibly. Even if the commission did not reach a consensus on how to solve the major economic problems, it could frankly lay out the choices—and the limits on them—in analyses that could strongly influence campaign debate.

With respect to the deficit, the options of higher income taxes or new types of consumption taxes, such as energy taxes, would leave much room for argument—as would mechanisms to make certain that new taxes do not become translated into new spending programs. When it comes to trade, the options would include a further lowering of the dollar, temporary tariffs, or some forms of limited industrial policies. As for interest rates and the Federal Reserve, the commission could analyze the differing approaches to monetary policy, for instance directly controlling interest rates, on the one hand, or, on the other, aiming at stability based on the price of gold or the value of some basket of selected commodities. (It could also, I hope, arrive at a unanimous recommendation to continue Paul Volcker for another term.)

With respect to entitlements, the possibilities of applying a means test or of taxing well-to-do recipients should both be examined. And as for third world debt, the options to be considered would include government involvement as part of a major restructuring program of the type recommended by Senator

Bradley of New Jeresy, or the continuation of rollovers together with some version of the current Baker plan under which the debtor countries would be eligible for additional credits if they undertake economic reforms emphasizing the workings of the market.

A commission would provide a coherent frame for debate of the economic alternatives. Its very existence would not only infuse some realism into the national debate but also give candidates courage to state unpalatable truths. It would also provide the domestic background for considering the critical foreign policy issue of the 1988 campaign, namely America's long-term relationship with the Soviet Union.

It may well be too late in the day for such a commission. But even if some kind of economic crisis is now inevitable, the issues I have mentioned will still have to be dealt with, and how we do so may determine the depth and severity of the crisis. Facing reality now will require sacrifice on the part of everyone as well as bipartisanship and cooperation between business and labor. It will call, finally, for leaders who are willing to make it plain that if we are not capable of exercising restraint in our financial expectations, we will find ourselves in great danger.

Discussion Questions

1. What do we mean by political economy? What are the differences in the liberal, mercantilist, and Marxist responses to that question?

2. What is the international economic order? How has it changed since the end of World War II? Why has it changed?

3. What were the political considerations (domestic and international) underlying the creation of the postwar political economy?

4. What were the sources of the decline of the Bretton Woods system?

5. What are the major international economic and political concerns of the developed states? Of the less developed states? How do these concerns shape the attitudes of the two groups toward proposals for a new international economic order?

For Further Reading

Introductory and General Approaches

Adams, John. *International Economics: A Self-Teaching Guide to the Basic Concepts.* 2d ed. New York: St. Martin's, 1985. A programmed text for the student with a limited knowledge of economics. A good complement to any of the three volumes listed below.

Blake, David H., and Robert S. Walters. *The Politics of Global Economic Relations*. 3d ed. Englewood Cliffs, N.J.: Prentice-Hall, 1987. The popularity of this text and the Spero volume listed below is indicative of the increasing attention being given political economy in undergraduate courses in international relations. Both are readable and provide a survey of the field.

Frieden, Jeffrey A., and David A. Lake, eds. *International Political Economy: Perspectives on Global Power and Wealth*. New York: St. Martin's, 1987. A fine essay collection that emphasizes a number of themes echoed in this chapter: the importance of a historical perspective on international political economy, the different views held by various states as to the nature of that economy, and the U.S. role in the global marketplace.

Spero, Joan. *The Politics of International Economic Relations*. 3d ed. New York: St. Martin's Press, 1985.

More Advanced Approaches

Adams, John, ed. *The Contemporary International Economy: A Reader*. 2d ed. New York: St. Martin's Press, 1985. An up-to-date and sophisticated reader that examines theoretical and policy issues in the areas of trade, investment, monetary reform, and the global debt.

Richardson, John D. *Understanding International Economics: Theory and Practice*. Boston: Little, Brown, 1984. A basic text that is sensitive to the various policy dimensions involved in the management of international economics.

The Development of the Postwar World Economy

Block, Fred. *The Origins of International Economic Disorder*. Berkeley, Calif.: University of California Press, 1977. An examination of the major actors who dominate the international marketplace in trade, investment, and finance.

Dam, Kenneth W. *The Rules of the Game: Reform and Evolution in the International Monetary System*. Chicago: University of Chicago Press, 1982. A thorough examination of the monetary system prior to World War II, the rise of the Bretton Woods system, and postwar international economic crises through the 1970s.

Gilpin, Robert. *War and Change in International Politics*. New York: Cambridge University Press, 1982. An important work—and the source of one of the readings in Chapter 2—that contains both a theory of equilibrium in international affairs and an analysis of the way the political economy of great powers in decline becomes a major source of international conflict.

Katzenstein, Peter, ed. *Between Power and Plenty*. Madison, Wis.: University of Wisconsin Press, 1977. A rich collection of essays that examines a number of the political and power dimensions of international economic relations.

Krasner, Stephen. *Defending the National Interest*. Princeton, N.J.: Princeton University Press, 1978. Explores the U.S. role in creating an international economic system favorable to its interests that then necessitated a further investment in the political, economic, and military resources necessary to protect and maintain it.

Wallerstein, Immanuel. *The Politics of the World Economy*. New York: Cambridge University Press, 1984. A brief but influential analysis of the long cycle of capitalist development and the dominance of the international economic order by large and wealthy states from the most cogent critic in the field.

The Collapse of the Postwar Economic System

Claudon, Michael P., ed. *World Debt Crisis: International Lending on Trial*. Cambridge, Mass.: Ballinger, 1986.

Eskridge, William N., ed. *A Dance Along the Precipice: The Political and Economic Dimensions of the Debt Problem*. Lexington, Mass.: Lexington Books, 1985.

Hartland-Thunberg, Penelope, and Charles K. Ebinger, eds. *Banks, Petrodollars and Sovereign Debtors*. Lexington, Mass.: Lexington Books, 1985.

These three collections of essays are among the many recent additions to the literature on the international debt crisis. Each offers a range of perspectives on the debt issue.

Keohane, Robert. *After Hegemony: Cooperation and Discord in the World Economy*. Princeton, N.J.: Princeton University Press, 1984. An enticing study, somewhat similar in approach to Gilpin's, that examines the challenges facing economic powers like the United States when shifts in global patterns of trade, investment, and economic hegemony begin to undermine their historic dominance.

Krasner, Stephen. *Structural Conflict: The Third World Against Global Liberalism*. Berkeley, Calif.: University of California Press, 1985. A wide-ranging discussion of the factors that led the Group of 77 to advocate a new international economic order. Includes a particularly useful analysis of the inequities inherent in relations between the nations of the First and Third Worlds.

II

FUNDAMENTAL PROCESSES
OF INTERNATIONAL RELATIONS

DIPLOMACY, BARGAINING, AND COERCION 5

A few years ago we attended a major conference on preventing war. The conference brought together "theoreticians" of international relations and "practitioners" from the foreign policy-making community to analyze this important topic. After yet another session on crisis decision making, a U.S. foreign service officer in the audience rose and observed that international relations experts spent far too much time analyzing crises and crisis decision making while ignoring the critical 90 percent of international relations—crisis prevention through diplomacy and negotiation. In many ways, the U.S. diplomat was correct. As on the evening news, what "sells" in the study of international relations is often the spectacular, even the gruesome event: war, famine, foreign policy failure, the abuse of power, terrorist violence, and economic collapse. These are important realities, to be sure, but the everyday world of international relations is far less dramatic. It is a world of routine activities often unnoticed—except by the officials immediately involved—a world of diplomacy, bargaining, and coercive pressure.

Diplomacy

Diplomacy is the process through which governments manage their relations with other nations. It is clear from the writings of diplomatic historians, personal memoirs of diplomats, and case studies by international relations scholars that "managing" is an inclusive term indeed. The tasks facing the modern diplomat are many, and the skills necessary to succeed diverse.

First and foremost, diplomats must be a "quick study." That is, they must have the ability to ferret out and absorb a great deal of information about a situation or locale in a short amount of time. Such information includes substantive knowledge of a country or policy issue and a working knowledge of which agency or officer in one's own bureaucracy should be consulted. In short, a key element of good diplomacy is the ability to ascertain quickly what you know, what else you need to know, what you should act upon, and what you should refer to others. (The infamous "in basket-out basket" component of the U.S. Foreign Service examination and screening process is designed to evaluate these skills.) The modern foreign service is simply not the place for the slow, reflective, or indecisive individual, no matter how brilliant.

At the same time, diplomacy requires an intellect of high quality.

Diplomats are called upon to master the language, culture, politics, and society of the nation to which they are assigned, no small feat in light of the numerous country assignments a diplomat may have during a career. Further, successful diplomacy often requires a grasp of knowledge from many different fields. In today's world, an understanding of culture and language is by itself often insufficient. During the course of a typical assignment, a diplomat may be called upon to resolve issues that require a familiarity with science (agricultural or environmental problems, for example), economics, development problems, or international finance (debt payment or international trade problems, for instance).

Successful diplomacy also requires an aptitude for what might be called active listening. Active listening includes the ability (1) to hear and absorb the speaker's view of the facts as distinct from one's own; (2) to push for further clarification through critical questioning; and (3) to process what has been heard in terms of the larger context of the situation and the issues of the moment. Such skills are essential to successful diplomacy in many areas. Diplomats must, for example, be able to "hear" their government and reflect its views to others. Conversely, diplomats must be able to communicate effectively the views of foreigners to their superiors. And whether in bilateral negotiations, international conferences, or times of crisis, a diplomat must be keenly attuned to nuances in wording, format, communication methods, or even body language that may signal an opportunity for conflict resolution.

Finally, successful diplomats possess patience and persistence. That patience is tried and perfected in many ways. Sometimes the diplomat's own government fails to agree with his or her recommendation; the government of the nation to which the diplomat is assigned may change its mind after the diplomat has finally succeeded in convincing his or her own government to accept that point of view; or the diplomat may be assigned to explain and defend to another government a policy decision with which he or she disagrees!

Persistence is equally important. Diplomats learn quickly that a government and its basic views change ever so slowly, if at all. Effective diplomats have both the resolve to continue to push for the acceptance of their ideas and the creativity to develop new ways to educate or persuade ill-informed or skeptical colleagues. We have known foreign service officers and diplomats who labored for years on behalf of policy changes in human rights and arms control. The reward for such labor, often involving years of behind-the-scenes work, comes in the form of an eventual change in their government's position—for example, the U.S. government's willingness to use the term "death squad" in government documents discussing El Salvador. The personal disposition to stick with it through thick and thin is a reflection of individual maturity and dedication to one's nation and one's own ideas and values.

Bargaining

Bargaining is a task that places heavy demands on a diplomat's skills. The setting for bargaining may vary from informal discussions of relatively minor issues over tea to angry, long, near-crisis exchanges regarding the most delicate issues of national security policy. Often, working with teams of colleagues, diplomats must assemble, digest, and evaluate background information and prepare position papers on particular issues for their government. Such efforts are critical to successful bargaining, whether the negotiation at hand is an annual tariff reduction through GATT or an arms control conference.

Also essential to any successful negotiation is the observance of certain basic principles concerning ways of achieving lasting agreements acceptable to all parties. The application of these principles by diplomats who must reflect the interests of their governments while finding workable solutions to disputes has, in fact, until recently been one of the less explored areas of international relations. Five of the more important guidelines are discussed below. For each we offer a brief explanation followed by an example.

1. *International conflict should be considered an exercise in joint problem solving.* The states involved need to be tough on the shared problem but to deal gently with the other parties.

Our first principle has several components and implications. At one level, it means simply that states must realize that, whatever the intensity of their rivalry, they are "in it" (that is, in the crisis) together. In the case of serious disputes, this recognition may well involve downplaying the significance of which state initiated the conflict and focusing on ways to extricate the parties from the situation without major or increased violence.

The importance of this principle lies in the options created by focusing on the problem instead of on the other party to the dispute. A government that views its rival, rather than the rival's actions, as the problem is likely to think only in terms of eliminating or weakening the opponent as a means of solving the problem. Such an approach greatly increases the risk of war. The purpose of bargaining, however, is to resolve disputes short of war. Viewing the other party or parties as potential, indeed essential, collaborators in any proposed solution tends to restrain rhetoric and focus the discussion on tasks to be accomplished.

Nowhere may the utility of this principle be seen more clearly than in the past twenty-five years of U.S.-Soviet arms control discussions. After the 1962 Cuban missile crisis, the leaders of the two nations, John F. Kennedy and Nikita S. Khrushchev, ended a long era of public accusation and entered into a dialogue that culminated in the limited test ban treaty of 1963. Similarly, the SALT I and SALT II agreements of the late 1960s and early 1970s were preceded by a lull in inflammatory rhetoric.

A more recent example is the intermediate nuclear forces treaty signed in

Washington by the United States and the Soviet Union in late 1987. The signing of this treaty was all the more remarkable because it followed six years of the toughest and most accusatory U.S. rhetoric directed at the Soviet Union since the early days of the Cold War. The period immediately prior to the signing of the treaty, however, was one in which the Reagan administration had begun to speak of "our shared agenda" in relation to the two countries' ongoing negotiations on reductions in short- and medium-range nuclear missiles in Europe. To be sure, the change in tone was the result of other factors, notably a recognition that both countries had an interest in the removal of these systems from Europe. Nonetheless, the change in tone was itself a precondition of any agreement.

2. *Although states often present their conditions for ending a conflict as demands, the best prospect for resolution lies in focusing on the underlying needs of the parties.*

Most analysts recognize that conflict originates in the efforts of the actors to satisfy basic needs. Whether the issue is the need for a port with access to a valued naval or trade route, for more favorable trading conditions, or for more clearly defined security arrangements, conflict arises from the quest to meet needs. The irony of this becomes recognizable when one examines the differences between what governments often demand when entering negotiations and what they in fact need. "Return to us the Sinai Peninsula," was the continual Egyptian demand of Israel as a condition for peace after the 1973 war. To this, the Israeli response was "We will hold the Sinai forever as a reminder to Egypt of the futility of war." Because the two positions, so clearly and definitively stated, were mutually exclusive, direct dialogue, let alone compromise or peace, appeared impossible.

And yet grounds for compromise were ultimately found by U.S. negotiators, particularly Henry Kissinger, whose personal travels between the two capital cities during this period gave rise to the term "shuttle diplomacy." Repeated questioning of each side about its hopes, fears, and needs helped the two sides to articulate more clearly their long-term security needs. The new Egyptian position became "We need the Sinai in order to restore to us what was lost in war. For the repairing of our prestige, we will promise not to invade, and we will recognize Israel's right to exist." Similarly, the Israeli stance was softened: "We need recognition and a guarantee that the Egyptian tanks will no longer roll across our borders. If we are recognized and promised nonaggression that can be guaranteed by a state other than Egypt, we can part with the Sinai."

By focusing on basic needs and encouraging the parties to back away from overstated and extreme single-sentence policy positions (which were not, it is clear, optimal expressions of actual needs), the United States was able to help Egypt and Israel forge the Camp David accords in 1978. Israel renounced control of the Sinai and was granted recognition by Egypt. The United States implanted electronic sensors in the Sinai desert to provide Israel with advance warning of any violation of the agreement. Meeting basic needs produced agreement where none had seemed possible.

3. *When confronted with force by another state, a state should be firm in meeting the challenge, but permit the other side to back away from the dispute without losing prestige.*

There are two components to this principle. The first, described by Russell J. Leng and Hugh J. Wheeler in the readings as the "firm but fair" strategy, is that of meeting force with a proportionate level of force but resisting the urge to escalate. The second involves making a conscious effort to avoid backing the other party into a corner, that is, placing the other party in a position where the only options appear to be war or surrender. The objective here is to construct alternatives that provide the other side with a way to save face.

As noted in Chapter 3, this was the basic principle employed by Kennedy in the Cuban missile crisis of 1962. By opting for a naval blockade, rather than an air strike at one extreme or diplomatic protest at the other, and by leaving open for discussion other issues such as the future of U.S. missiles in Turkey and the possibility of cooperative U.S.-Soviet agreements on nuclear weapons, Kennedy permitted Khrushchev the next move. Yet Kennedy made abundantly clear the U.S. demand that Soviet missiles be removed from Cuba.

4. *In bargaining among states of unequal power, a nation should sometimes lose in order to win.*

This is a principle that parents of teenagers have known for years, but it is equally relevant to the world of international affairs. Stronger nations that wish to avoid alienating their smaller and less powerful counterparts must carefully weigh the importance of issues that appear to stand in the way of an agreement. The underlying logic here is that there may be times when the larger state's interest in maintaining a permanent and stable relationship with the smaller nation may be more important than "winning" on the issue at hand. Recognizing this requires, of course, that the larger state be sufficiently enlightened to recognize and act on the basis of its long-term goals, in the process exhibiting a willingness to "give" the smaller state a victory—which it may badly need for any number of political reasons—on the issue at hand.

Contemporary illustrations of the application of this principle abound. The United Kingdom often observed this rule in the course of granting independence to its colonies. Wishing to preserve their political and economic ties with their former colonies and to solidify their leadership position within the new Commonwealth of Nations, the British were willing to let their new partners claim a certain number of diplomatic and economic "victories."

The principle is no less valid in economic matters, especially in bargaining between nonstate and state actors. Over the past two decades, for example, a number of multinational corporations have found that learning to "lose in order to win" is sometimes sound business strategy. Where earlier efforts by MNCs to maximize profits often led to nationalization, current practice calls for the MNC to present to the host government a long-term investment plan that provides for steady—although less than maximum—profits for the MNC and a clear return for the host nation. Both parties gain from this arrangement.

5. *Each party should look for ways to increase the costs of continuing or initiating the conflict and to increase the benefits received from resolution.*

Much of the early literature on bargaining in international affairs was developed with the aid of a tool known as *game theory.* Although heavily mathematical in its more advanced forms, game theory's underlying principles are quite straightforward. The basic approach involves an analysis of conflict by assigning costs and benefits to the various choices available to the parties. (The article by Anatol Rapaport describes a particular type of game known as the prisoner's dilemma.) The value of this approach is that one can apply it to determine which outcomes have which values for the parties to a conflict. If each party to a conflict wishes both to avoid war *and* to maximize their interests, game theory can help determine which choices will come closest to providing the desired outcomes for the most parties.

Recent history indicates that this principle is difficult to apply in two-party conflicts and may prove equally elusive in conflicts where a third party attempts to mediate. Throughout much of the history of the arms race between the United States and the Soviet Union, for example, it has been very difficult for either of the two superpowers to enter into serious negotiations over arms reduction. For both, the perceived costs of such an effort—in terms of the gains accruing to the other in the event of miscalculation—have seemed prohibitive.

Similarly, Secretary of State Alexander Haig's efforts to mediate the 1982 dispute between Britain and Argentina over the Falklands/Malvinas were unsuccessful. Despite his various attempts to provide Argentina with incentives to refrain from unilateral action—including a promise of U.S. involvement in the effort to resolve Argentina's territorial claims—Haig was unable to dissuade the Buenos Aires government from occupying the Malvinas. Nor was he able to dissuade Britain from retaking the islands by force. From the British perspective, the incentives that Haig had to offer were simply insufficient to outweigh the potential benefits of reoccupying the islands.

Coercion

When negotiation and bargaining fail, the next available diplomatic tool is usually coercion. By *coercion* we mean the systematic, incremental, and controlled application of a nation's power against an opponent in a manner intended to induce the opponent to agree to a termination of the conflict. (Power is defined further in the next chapter.) The intent is to demonstrate to the opponent that noncompliance will result in costs "terrible beyond endurance," in the phrase used by Thomas Schelling in the readings section of this chapter.

When resorting to coercion, states ordinarily communicate their intentions openly by word (a policy statement) or action (movement of troops) so that other nations and particularly the target nation are made aware of the gravity of the situation. Coercion is not always violent or illegitimate, nor does it always involve military action. Most people, for example, would view the United Nations' economic sanctions against the South African government in response to the latter's occupation of Namibia and, more recently, its continued adherence to apartheid, as completely justified. Similarly, nations can and do use coercion for humanitarian purposes, as in the case of U.S. curtailment of economic and military aid to regimes accused by the Carter administration of human rights violations.

More commonly, however, coercion is employed for the pure maximization of a state's interests. And the bulk of the data produced and analyzed by international relations scholars suggests that in the post-1945 world it is the superpowers who have employed coercion most frequently. Although their patterns and styles differ, both the United States and the Soviet Union have frequently resorted to coercion in one or another form to achieve their ends. *Force Without War* by Barry Blechman and Stephen Kaplan and Kaplan's later study, *The Diplomacy of Power*, provide detailed and comprehensive descriptions of this behavior.

In his analysis of 158 separate incidents of coercive Soviet behavior, Kaplan—whose study covered the period from 1951 until just before the Soviet invasion of Afghanistan in late 1979—uncovered a number of different purposes and tactics. He concluded that on only one occasion during the period of his study did the Soviet Union pursue coercive diplomacy for *expansionary* purposes, this in the form of a 1975 missile test in the Barents Sea intended as a "show of force" to the Norwegian government. By far the most common pattern of Soviet coercion is one involving the threat or use of direct military intervention to maintain Soviet control and promote communist orthodoxy in neighboring countries. The most prominent examples of this pattern include the 1953 use of direct military force in East Germany, the repression of the Hungarian revolution in 1956, and the occupation of Czechoslovakia in 1968. More recent examples from the period following Kaplan's study include the 1979 armed intervention in Afghanistan and the indirect but very public application of pressure on Poland in 1980-1981 in response to the rise of Solidarity, the Polish workers' movement, whose activities and demands were seen by the Soviets as threatening to their policies and control over the Polish state. Although the Afghan and Polish interventions occurred after Kaplan's study, each typifies the pattern he described.

In contrast to the postwar Soviet pattern, the United States has resorted to coercion more frequently in a broader range of geographic settings and for a more diverse set of goals. Blechman and Kaplan identified 215 such incidents in their study. Far more active than the Soviet Union in Third World conflicts, the United States' actions have exhibited a considerable variation in the intensity of the threat involved. These actions have ranged from demonstrations of support in the form of aid programs and policy statements for pro-Western governments in Greece and Italy in the 1940s and 1950s through the multilevel campaign waged by the Reagan administration in the 1980s against Nicaragua. In this last case, overt coercion in the form of direct anti-Nicaragua diplomatic efforts, a disinformation campaign, military aid to the contras, and economic sanctions—including the blocking of international loans and disruption of trade—were employed alongside covert action, including the authorized mining of harbors by the CIA and allegedly unauthorized private actions on behalf of the contras. (For further details on coercion by the superpowers, see the original studies of Blechman and Kaplan, which are cited in the bibliography at the end of this chapter.)

Similar tactics have been and are employed by less powerful states such as South Africa, Israel, and India. And although any state that resorts to this means of persuasion can be expected to argue its virtues—particularly as compared to war—over the past two decades new forms of international coercion have emerged, many of which are unpredictable and thus inherently destabilizing. The overall level of coercion has increased. Among the new forms of coercion are clandestine operations, state terrorism, and surrogate terrorism. We will explore these developments further in Chapter 9.

It would appear, then, that a new and more violent set of options has been added to the nation-state's foreign policy arsenal. Whether the coming years will witness a return to advancing state interests and solving disputes through diplomacy and bargaining or a continued increase in the use of coercive violence remains a mystery.

The Readings

The readings for this chapter include two classic examples of international relations theory, a widely cited data-based study, and two policy excerpts. We begin with an excerpt from Thomas Schelling's classic work, *Arms and Influence*. "The Diplomacy of Violence" contrasts the directness, if not the brutality, of military force with the more sophisticated notion of psychological coercion. The strength of this selection lies not only in its theoretical clarity but in the wealth of historical examples that Schelling uses to support his argument.

In the next selection, Anatol Rapaport, the brilliant game theorist, portrays the impasse in U.S.-Soviet negotiations on nuclear weapons as a classic example of the "prisoner's dilemma." In such a game, the author argues, a successful strategy requires both an understanding of the payoffs and choices of the "other side" and the application of "conscience."

Leng and Wheeler's more general article is also more data based. After reviewing the literature on bargaining with aggressors, Leng and Wheeler examine the ways parties to serious disputes have, in fact, managed both to avoid war and to maximize their own interests. Their finding—that a strategy that emphasizes reciprocity (a "reciprocating strategy") works better than one based on escalation (a bullying strategy) or other alternatives—also informs the policy opinion piece by Leng that appeared in the *Christian Science Monitor* of October 1982.

The Leng piece is helpful in two ways. First, it illustrates the relevance of theoretical findings from the international relations literature to the public discussion of policy. Second, it examines the "lessons" to be drawn from the Cuban missile crisis when we take into account not only this single incident but the larger context of U.S.-Soviet competition and relevant findings from the conflict and bargaining literature.

The final selection,"U.S. Diplomacy and the Search for Peace," by Undersecretary of State Michael H. Armacost, analyzes U.S. foreign policy by geographic region, with a particular emphasis on Central America. Armacost also provides a useful comment on American negotiating style.

5.1 ▬▬

THOMAS SCHELLING

The Diplomacy of Violence

The usual distinction between diplomacy and force is not merely in the instruments, words or bullets, but in the relation between adversaries—in the interplay of motives and the role of communication, understandings, compromise, and restraint. Diplomacy is bargaining; it seeks outcomes that, though not ideal for either party, are better for both than some of the alternatives. In diplomacy each party somewhat controls what the other wants, and can get more by compromise, exchange, or collaboration than by taking things in his own hands and ignoring the other's wishes. The bargaining can be polite or rude, entail threats as well as offers, assume a status quo or ignore all rights and privileges, and assume mistrust rather than trust. But whether polite or impolite, constructive or aggressive, respectful or vicious, whether it occurs among friends or antagonists and whether or not there is a basis for trust and goodwill, there must be some common interest, if only in the avoidance of mutual damage, and an awareness of the need to make the other party prefer an outcome acceptable to oneself.

With enough military force a country may not need to bargain. Some things a country wants it can take, and some things it has it can keep, by sheer strength, skill and ingenuity. It can do this *forcibly*, accommodating only to opposing strength, skill, and ingenuity and without trying to appeal to an enemy's wishes. Forcibly a country can repel and expel, penetrate and occupy, seize, exterminate, disarm and disable, confine, deny access, and directly frustrate intrusion or attack. It can, that is, if it has enough strength. "Enough" depends on how much an opponent has.

There is something else, though, that force can do. It is less military, less heroic, less impersonal, and less unilateral; it is uglier, and has received less attention in Western military strategy. In addition to seizing and holding, disarming and confining, penetrating and obstructing, and all that, military force can be used *to hurt*. In addition to taking and protecting things of value it can *destroy* value. In addition to weakening an enemy militarily it can cause an enemy plain suffering.

Pain and shock, loss and grief, privation and horror are always in some degree, sometimes in terrible degree, among the results of warfare; but in

---

traditional military science they are incidental, they are not the object. If violence can be done incidentally, though, it can also be done purposely. The power to hurt can be counted among the most impressive attributes of military force.

Hurting, unlike forcible seizure or self-defense, is not unconcerned with the interest of others. It is measured in the suffering it can cause and the victims' motivation to avoid it. Forcible action will work against weeds or floods as well as against armies, but suffering requires a victim that can feel pain or has something to lose. To inflict suffering gains nothing and saves nothing directly; it can only make people behave to avoid it. The only purpose, unless sport or revenge, must be to influence somebody's behavior, to coerce his decision or choice. To be coercive, violence has to be anticipated. And it has to be avoidable by accommodation. The power to hurt is bargaining power. To exploit it is diplomacy—vicious diplomacy, but diplomacy.

The Contrast of Brute Force with Coercion

There is a difference between taking what you want and making someone give it to you, between fending off assault and making someone afraid to assault you, between holding what people are trying to take and making them afraid to take it, between losing what someone can forcibly take and giving it up to avoid risk or damage. It is the difference between defense and deterrence, between brute force and intimidation, between conquest and blackmail, between action and threats. It is the difference between the unilateral, "undiplomatic" recourse to strength, and coercive diplomacy based on the power to hurt.

The contrasts are several. The purely "military" or "undiplomatic" recourse to forcible action is concerned with enemy strength, not enemy interests; the coercive use of the power to hurt, though, is the very exploitation of enemy wants and fears. And brute strength is usually measured relative to enemy strength, the one directly opposing the other, while the power to hurt is typically not reduced by the enemy's power to hurt in return. Opposing strengths may cancel each other, pain and grief do not. The willingness to hurt, the credibility of a threat, and the ability to exploit the power to hurt will indeed depend on how much the adversary can hurt in return; but there is little or nothing about an adversary's pain or grief that directly reduces one's own. Two sides cannot both overcome each other with superior strength; they may both be able to hurt each other. With strength they can dispute objects of value; with sheer violence they can destroy them.

And brute force succeeds when it is used, whereas the power to hurt is most successful when held in reserve. It is the *threat* of damage, or of more damage to come, that can make someone yield or comply. It is *latent* violence that can influence someone's choice—violence that can still be withheld or inflicted, or that a victim believes can be withheld or inflicted. The threat of pain tries to structure someone's motives, while brute force tries to over-come his strength. Unhappily, the power to hurt is often communicated by some performance of it. Whether it is sheer terroristic violence to induce an irrational response, or cool premeditated violence to persuade somebody that you mean it and may do it again, it is not the pain and damage itself but its influence on somebody's behavior that matters. It is the expectation of *more* violence that gets the wanted behavior, if the power to hurt can get it at all.

To exploit a capacity for hurting and inflicting damage one needs to know what an adversary treasures and what scares him and one needs the adversary to understand what behavior of his will cause the violence to be inflicted and what will cause it to be withheld. The victim has to know what is wanted, and he may have to be assured of what is not wanted. The pain and suffering have to appear *contingent* on his behavior; it is not alone the threat that is effective—the threat of pain or loss if he fails to comply—but the correspond-ing assurance, possibly an implicit one, that he can avoid the pain or loss if he does comply. The prospect of certain death may stun him, but it gives him no choice.

Coercion by threat of damage also requires that our interests and our opponent's not be absolutely opposed. If his pain were our greatest delight and our satisfaction his greatest woe, we would just proceed to hurt and to frustrate each other. It is when his pain gives us little or no satisfaction compared with what he can do for us, and the action or inaction that satisfies us costs him less than the pain we can cause, that there is room for coercion. Coercion requires finding a bargain, arranging for him to be better off doing what we want—worse off not doing what we want—when he takes the threatened penalty into account.

It is this capacity for pure damage, pure violence, that is usually associated with the most vicious labor disputes, with racial disorders, with civil uprisings and their suppression, with racketeering. It is also the power to hurt rather than brute force that we use in dealing with criminals; we hurt them afterward, or threaten to, for their misdeeds rather than protect ourselves with cordons of electric wires, masonry walls, and armed guards. Jail, of course, can be either forcible restraint or threatened privation; if the object is to keep criminals out of mischief by confinement, success is measured by how many of them are got-ten behind bars, but if the object is to *threaten* privation, success will be measured by how few have to be put behind bars and success then depends on the subject's understanding of the consequences. Pure damage is what a car threatens when it tries to hog the road or to keep its rightful share, or to go first through an intersection. A tank or a bulldozer can force its way regardless of others' wishes; the rest of us have to threaten damage, usually mutual damage, hoping the other driver values his car or his limbs enough to give way, hoping he sees us, and hoping he is in control of his own car. The threat of pure dam-age will not work against an unmanned vehicle.

This difference between coercion and brute force is as often in the intent as in the instrument. To hunt down Comanches and to exterminate them was brute force; to raid their villages to make them behave was coercive diplomacy, based on the power to hurt. The pain and loss to the Indians might have looked much the same one way as the other; the difference was one of purpose and effect. If Indians were killed because they were in the way, or somebody wanted their land, or the authorities despaired of making them behave and could not confine them and decided to exterminate them, that was pure unilateral force. If *some* Indians were killed to make *other* Indians behave, that was coercive violence—or intended to be, whether or not it was effective. The Germans at Verdun pereived themselves to be chewing up hundreds of thousands of French soldiers in a gruesome "meatgrinder." If the purpose was to eliminate a military obstacle—the French infantryman, viewed as a military "asset" rather than as a warm human being—the offensive at Verdun was a unilateral exercise of military force. If instead the object was to make the loss of young men—not of impersonal "effectives," but of sons, husbands, fathers, and the pride of French manhood—so anguishing as to be unendurable, to make surrender a welcome relief and to spoil the foretaste of an Allied victory, then it was an exercise in coercion, in applied violence, intended to offer relief upon accommodation. And of course, since any use of force tends to be brutal, thoughtless, vengeful, or plain obstinate, the motives themselves can be mixed and confused. The fact that heroism and brutality can be either coercive diplomacy or a contest in pure strength does not promise that the distinction will be made, and the strategies enlightened by the distinction, every time some vicious enterprise gets launched.

The contrast between brute force and coercion is illustrated by two alternative strategies attributed to Genghis Khan. Early in his career he pursued the war creed of the Mongols: the vanquished can never be the friends of the victors, their death is necessary for the victor's safety. This was the unilateral extermination of a menace or a liability. The turning point of his career, according to Lynn Montross, came later when he discovered how to use his power to hurt for diplomatic ends. "The great Khan, who was not inhibited by the usual mercies, conceived the plan of forcing captives— women, children, aged fathers, favorite sons—to march ahead of his army as the first potential victims of resistance." [1] Live captives have often proved more valuable than enemy dead; and the technique discovered by the Khan in his maturity remains contemporary. North Koreans and Chinese were reported to have quartered prisoners of war near strategic targets to inhibit bombing attacks by United Nations aircraft. Hostages represent the power to hurt in its purest form.

---

[1] Lynn Montross, *War Through the Ages*, 3d ed. (New York, Harper and Brothers, 1960), p. 146.

Thomas Schelling

Coercive Violence in Warfare

This distinction between the power to hurt and the power to seize or hold forcibly is important in modern war, both big war and little war, hypothetical war and real war. For many years the Greeks and the Turks on Cyprus could hurt each other indefinitely but neither could quite take or hold forcibly what they wanted or protect themselves from violence by physical means. The Jews in Palestine could not expel the British in the late 1940s but they could cause pain and fear and frustration through terrorism, and eventually influence somebody's decision. The brutal war in Algeria was more a contest in pure violence than in military strength; the question was who would first find the pain and degradation unendurable. The French troops preferred—indeed they continually tried—to make it a contest of strength, to pit military force against the nationalists' capacity for terror, to exterminate or disable the nationalists and to screen off the nationalists from the victims of their violence. But because in civil war terrorists commonly have access to victims by sheer physical propinquity, the victims and their properties could not be forcibly defended and in the end the French troops themselves resorted, unsuccessfully, to a war of pain.

Nobody believes that the Russians can take Hawaii from us, or New York, or Chicago, but nobody doubts that they might destroy people and buildings in Hawaii, Chicago, or New York. Whether the Russians can conquer West Germany in any meaningful sense is questionable; whether they can hurt it terribly is not doubted. That the United States can destroy a large part of Russia is universally taken for granted; that the United States can keep from being badly hurt, even devastated, in return, or can keep Western Europe from being devastated while itself destroying Russia, is at best arguable; and it is virtually out of the question that we could conquer Russia territorially and use its economic assets unless it were by threatening disaster and inducing compliance. It is the power to hurt, not military strength in the traditional sense, that inheres in our most impressive military capabilities at the present time. We have a Department of *Defense* but emphasize *retaliation*—"to return evil for evil" (synonyms: requital, reprisal, revenge, vengeance, retribution). And it is pain and violence, not force in the traditional sense, that inheres also in some of the least impressive military capabilities of the present time—the plastic bomb, the terrorist's bullet, the burnt crops, and the tortured farmer.

War appears to be, or threatens to be, not so much a contest of strength as one of endurance, nerve, obstinacy, and pain. It appears to be, and threatens to be, not so much a contest of military strength as a bargaining process—dirty, extortionate, and often quite reluctant bargaining on one side or both—nevertheless a bargaining process.

The difference cannot quite be expressed as one between the *use* of force and the *threat* of force. The actions involved in forcible accomplishment, on the one hand, and in fulfilling a threat, on the other, can be quite different.

Sometimes the most effective direct action inflicts enough cost or pain on the enemy to serve as a threat, sometimes not. The United States threatens the Soviet Union with virtual destruction of its society in the event of a surprise attack on the United States; a hundred million deaths are awesome as pure damage, but they are useless in stopping the Soviet attack—especially if the threat is to do it all afterward anyway. So it is worth while to keep the concepts distinct—to distinguish forcible action from the threat of pain—recognizing that some actions serve as both a means of forcible accomplishment and a means of inflicting pure damage, some do not. Hostages tend to entail almost pure pain and damage, as do all forms of reprisal after the fact. Some modes of self-defense may exact so little in blood or treasure as to entail negligible violence; and some forcible actions entail so much violence that their threat can be effective by itself.

The power to hurt, though it can usually accomplish nothing directly, is potentially more versatile than a straightforward capacity for forcible accomplishment. By force alone we cannot even lead a horse to water—we have to drag him—much less make him drink. Any affirmative action, any collaboration, almost anything but physical exclusion, expulsion, or extermination, requires that an opponent or a victim *do* something, even if only to stop or get out. The threat of pain and damage may make him want to do it, and anything he can do is potentially susceptible to inducement. Brute force can only accomplish what requires no collaboration. The principle is illustrated by a technique of unarmed combat: one can disable a man by various stunning, fracturing, or killing blows, but to take him to jail one has to exploit the man's own efforts. "Come-along" holds are those that threaten pain or disablement, giving relief as long as the victim complies, giving him the option of using his own legs to get to jail.

We have to keep in mind, though, that what is pure pain, or the threat of it, at one level of decision can be equivalent to brute force at another level. Churchill was worried, during the early bombing raids on London in 1940, that Londoners might panic. Against people the bombs were pure violence, to induce their undisciplined evasion; to Churchill and the government, the bombs were a cause of inefficiency, whether they spoiled transport and made people late to work or scared people and made them afraid to work. Churchill's decisions were not going to be coerced by the fear of a few casualties. Similarly on the battlefield: tactics that frighten soldiers so that they run, duck their heads, or lay down their arms and surrender represent coercion based on the power to hurt; to the top command, which is frustrated but not coerced, such tactics are part of the contest in military discipline and strength.

The fact that violence—pure pain and damage—can be used or threatened to coerce and to deter, to intimidate and to blackmail, to demoralize and to paralyze, in a conscious process of dirty bargaining, does not by any means imply that violence is not often wanton and meaningless or, even when purposive, in danger of getting out of hand. Ancient wars were often quite "total" for the loser, the men being put to death, the women sold as slaves, the boys castrated, the cattle slaughtered, and the buildings leveled, for the sake of revenge, justice, personal gain, or merely custom. If an enemy bombs a city, by design or by carelessness, we usually bomb his if we can. In the excitement and fatigue of warfare, revenge is one of the few satisfactions that can be savored; and justice can often be construed to demand the enemy's punishment, even if it is delivered with more enthusiasm than justice requires. When Jerusalem fell to the Crusaders in 1099 the ensuing slaughter was one of the bloodiest in military chronicles. "The men of the West literally waded in gore, their march to the church of the Holy Sepulcher being gruesomely likened to 'treading out the wine press'. . . ," reports Montross, who observes that these excesses usually came at the climax of the capture of a fortified post or city. "For long the assailants have endured more punishment than they were able to inflict; then once the walls are breached, pent up emotions find an outlet in murder, rape and plunder, which discipline is powerless to prevent." The same occurred when Tyre fell to Alexander after a painful siege, and the phenomenon was not unknown on Pacific islands in the Second World War. Pure violence, like fire, can be harnessed to a purpose; that does not mean that behind every holocaust is a shrewd intention successfully fulfilled.

But if the occurrence of violence does not always bespeak a shrewd purpose, the absence of pain and destruction is no sign that violence was idle. Violence is most purposive and most successful when it is threatened and not used. Successful threats are those that do not have to be carried out. By European standards, Denmark was virtually unharmed in the Second World War; it was violence that made the Danes submit. Withheld violence— successfully threatened violence—can look clean, even merciful. The fact that a kidnap victim is returned unharmed, against receipt of ample ransom, does not make kidnapping a nonviolent enterprise. The American victory at Mexico City in 1847 was a great success; with a minimum of brutality we traded a capital city for everything we wanted from the war. We did not even have to say what we could do to Mexico City and make the Mexican government understand what they had at stake. (They had undoubtedly got the message a month earlier, when Vera Cruz was being pounded into submission. After forty-eight hours of shellfire, the foreign consuls in that city approached General Scott's headquarters to ask for a truce so that women, children, and neutrals could evacuate the city. General Scott, "counting on such internal pressure to help bring about the city's surrender," refused their request and added that anyone, soldier or noncombatant, who attempted to leave the city would be fired upon.)[2]

Whether spoken or not, the threat is usually there. In earlier eras the etiquette was more permissive. When the Persians wanted to induce some

---

[2] Otis A. Singletary, *The Mexican War* (Chicago, University of Chicago Press, 1960), pp. 75-76.

Ionian cities to surrender and join them, without having to fight them, they instructed their ambassadors to

> make your proposals to them and promise that, if they abandon their allies, there will be no disagreeable consequences for them; we will not set fire to their houses or temples, or threaten them with any greater harshness than before this trouble occurred. If, however, they refuse, and insist upon fighting, then you must resort to threats, and say exactly what we will do to them; tell them, that is, that when they are beaten they will be sold as slaves, their boys will be made eunuchs, their girls carried off to Bactria, and their land confiscated.[3]

It sounds like Hitler talking to Schuschnigg. "I only need to give an order, and overnight all the ridiculous scarecrows on the frontier will vanish. . . . Then you will really experience something. . . . After the troops will follow the S.A. and the Legion. No one will be able to hinder the vengeance, not even myself."

Or Henry V before the gates of Harfleur:

> We may as bootless spend our vain command
> Upon the enraged soldiers in their spoil
> As send precepts to the leviathan
> To come ashore. Therefore, you men of Harfleur,
> Take pity of your town and of your people,
> Whiles yet my soldiers are in my command;
> Whiles yet the cool and temperate wind of grace
> O'erblows the filthy and contagious clouds
> Of heady murder, spoil and villainy.
> If not, why, in a moment look to see
> The blind and bloody soldier with foul hand
> Defile the locks of your shrill-shrieking daughters;
> Your fathers taken by the silver beard,
> And their most reverent heads dash'd to the walls,
> Your naked infants spitted upon pikes,
> Whiles the mad mothers with their howls confused
> Do break the clouds . . .
> What say you? will you yield, and this avoid,
> Or, guilty in defence, be thus destroy'd?
>
> (Act III, Scene iii)

Pure violence, nonmilitary violence, appears most conspicuously in relations between unequal countries, where there is no substantial military challenge and the outcome of military engagement is not in question. Hitler could make his threats contemptuously and brutally against Austria; he could make them, if he wished, in a more refined way against Denmark. It is noteworthy that it was Hitler, not his generals, who used this kind of language; proud military establishments do not like to think of themselves as extortionists. Their favorite job is to deliver victory, to dispose of opposing military force and to leave most

---

[3] Herodotus, *The Histories*, Aubrey de Selincourt, transl. (Baltimore, Penguin Books, 1954), p. 362.

of the civilian violence to politics and diplomacy. But if there is no room for doubt how a contest in strength will come out, it may be possible to bypass the military stage altogether and to proceed at once to the coercive bargaining.

A typical confrontation of unequal forces occurs at the *end* of a war, between victor and vanquished. Where Austria was vulnerable before a shot was fired, France was vulnerable after its military shield had collapsed in 1940. Surrender negotiations are the place where the threat of civil violence can come to the fore. Surrender negotiations are often so one-sided, or the potential violence so unmistakable, that bargaining succeeds and the violence remains in reserve. But the fact that most of the actual damage was done during the military stage of the war, prior to victory and defeat, does not mean that violence was idle in the aftermath, only that it was latent and the threat of it successful.

Indeed, victory is often but a prerequisite to the exploitation of the power to hurt. When Xenophon was fighting in Asia Minor under Persian leadership, it took military strength to disperse enemy soldiers and occupy their lands; but land was not what the victor wanted, nor was victory for its own sake.

> Next day the Persian leader burned the villages to the ground, not leaving a single house standing, so as to strike terror into the other tribes to show them what would happen if they did not give in. . . . He sent some of the prisoners into the hills and told them to say that if the inhabitants did not come down and settle in their houses to submit to him, he would burn up their villages too and destroy their crops, and they would die of hunger.[4]

Military victory was but the *price of admission*. The payoff depended upon the successful threat of violence.

Like the Persian leader, the Russians crushed Budapest in 1956 and cowed Poland and other neighboring countries. There was a lag of ten years between military victory and this show of violence, but the principle was the one explained by Xenophon. Military victory is often the prelude to violence, not the end of it, and the fact that successful violence is usually held in reserve should not deceive us about the role it plays.

What about pure violence during war itself, the infliction of pain and suffering as a military technique? Is the threat of pain involved only in the political use of victory, or is it a decisive technique of war itself?

Evidently between unequal powers it has been part of warfare. Colonial conquest has often been a matter of "punitive expeditions" rather than genuine military engagements. If the tribesmen escape into the bush you can burn their villages without them until they assent to receive what, in strikingly modern language, used to be known as the Queen's "protection." British air power was used punitively against Arabian tribesmen in the 1920s and 30s to coerce them into submission.

---

[4] Xenophon, *The Persian Expedition*, Rex Warner, transl. (Baltimore, Penguin Books, 1949), p. 272.

If enemy forces are not strong enough to oppose, or are unwilling to engage, there is no need to achieve victory as a prerequisite to getting on with a display of coercive violence. When Caesar was pacifying the tribes of Gaul he sometimes had to fight his way through their armed men in order to subdue them with a display of punitive violence, but sometimes he was virtually unopposed and could proceed straight to the punitive display. To his legions there was more valor in fighting their way to the seat of power; but, as governor of Gaul, Caesar could view enemy troops only as an obstacle to his political control, and that control was usually based on the power to inflict pain, grief, and privation. In fact, he preferred to keep several hundred hostages from the unreliable tribes, so that his threat of violence did not even depend on an expedition into the countryside.

Pure hurting, as a military tactic, appeared in some of the military actions against the plains Indians. In 1868, during the war with the Cheyennes, General Sheridan decided that his best hope was to attack the Indians in their winter camps. His reasoning was that the Indians could maraud as they pleased during the seasons when their ponies could subsist on grass, and in winter hide away in remote places. "To disabuse their minds from the idea that they were secure from punishment, and to strike at a period when they were helpless to move their stock and villages, a winter campaign was projected against the large bands hiding away in the Indian territory." [5]

These were not military engagements; they were punitive attacks on people. They were an effort to subdue by the use of violence, without a futile attempt to draw the enemy's military forces into decisive battle. They were "massive retaliation" on a diminutive scale, with local effects not unlike those of Hiroshima. The Indians themselves totally lacked organization and discipline, and typically could not afford enough ammunition for target practice and were no military match for the cavalry; their own rudimentary strategy was at best one of harassment and reprisal. Half a century of Indian fighting in the West left us a legacy of cavalry tactics; but it is hard to find a serious treatise on American strategy against the Indians or Indian strategy against the whites. The twentieth is not the first century in which "retaliation" has been part of our strategy, but it is the first in which we have systematically recognized it.

Hurting, as a strategy, showed up in the American Civil War, but as an episode, not as the central strategy. For the most part, the Civil War was a military engagement with each side's military force pitted against the other's. The Confederate forces hoped to lay waste enough Union territory to negotiate their independence, but hadn't enough capacity for such violence to make it work. The Union forces were intent on military victory, and it was mainly General Sherman's march through Georgia that showed a conscious and articulate use of violence. "If the people raise a howl against my barbarity and

---

[5] Paul I. Wellman, *Death on the Prairie* (New York, Macmillan 1934), p. 82.

cruelty, I will answer that war is war. . . . If they want peace, they and their relatives must stop the war," Sherman wrote. And one of his associates said, "Sherman is perfectly right. . . . The only possible way to end this unhappy and dreadful conflict . . . is to make it terrible beyond endurance." [6]

Making it "terrible beyond endurance" is what we associate with Algeria and Palestine, the crushing of Budapest and the tribal warfare in Central Africa. But in the great wars of the last hundred years it was usually military victory, not the hurting of the people, that was decisive; General Sherman's attempt to make war hell for the Southern people did not come to epitomize military strategy for the century to follow. To seek out and to destroy the enemy's military force, to achieve a crushing victory over enemy armies, was still the avowed purpose and the central aim of American strategy in both world wars. Military action was seen as an *alternative* to bargaining, not a *process* of bargaining.

The reason is not that civilized countries are so averse to hurting people that they prefer "purely military" wars. (Nor were all of the participants in these wars entirely civilized.) The reason is apparently that the technology and geography of warfare, at least for a war between anything like equal powers during the century ending in World War II, kept coercive violence from being decisive before military victory was achieved. Blockade indeed was aimed at the whole enemy nation, not concentrated on its military forces; the German civilians who died of influenza in the First World War were victims of violence directed at the whole country. It has never been quite clear whether blockade—of the South in the Civil War or of the Central Powers in both world wars, or submarine warfare against Britain—was expected to make war unendurable for the people or just to weaken the enemy forces by denying economic support. Both arguments were made, but there was no need to be clear about the purpose as long as either purpose was regarded as legitimate and either might be served. "Strategic bombing" of enemy homelands was also occasionally rationalized in terms of the pain and privation it could inflict on people and the civil damage it could do to the nation, as an effort to display either to the population or to the enemy leadership that surrender was better than persistence in view of the damage that could be done. It was also rationalized in more "military" terms, as a way of selectively denying war material to the troops or as a way of generally weakening the economy on which the military effort rested.

But as terrorism—as violence intended to coerce the enemy rather than to

---

[6] J. F. C. Fuller reproduces some of this correspondence and remarks, "For the nineteenth century this was a new conception, because it meant that the deciding factor in the war—the power to sue for peace—was transferred from government to people, and that peacemaking was a product of revolution. This was to carry the principle of democracy to its ultimate stage. . . ." *The Conduct of War: 1789-1961* (New Brunswick, Rutgers University Press, 1961), pp. 107-12.

weaken him militarily—blockade and strategic bombing by themselves were not quite up to the job in either world war in Europe. (They might have been sufficient in the war with Japan after straightforward military action had brought American aircraft into range.) Airplanes could not quite make punitive, coercive violence decisive in Europe, at least on a tolerable time schedule, and preclude the need to defeat or to destroy enemy forces as long as they had nothing but conventional explosives and incendiaries to carry. Hitler's V-1 buzz bomb and his V-2 rocket are fairly pure cases of weapons whose purpose was to intimidate, to hurt Britain itself rather than Allied military forces. What the V-2 needed was a punitive payload worth carrying, and the Germans did not have it. Some of the expectations in the 1920s and the 1930s that another major war would be one of pure civilian violence, of shock and terror from the skies, were not borne out by the available technology. The threat of punitive violence kept occupied countries quiescent; but the wars were won in Europe on the basis of brute strength and skill and not by intimidation, not by the threat of civilian violence but by the application of military force. Military victory was still the price of admission. Latent violence against people was reserved for the politics of surrender and occupation.

The great exception was the two atomic bombs on Japanese cities. These were weapons of terror and shock. They hurt, and promised more hurt, and that was their purpose. The few "small" weapons we had were undoubtedly of some direct military value, but their enormous advantage was in pure violence. In a military sense the United States could gain a little by destruction of two Japanese industrial cities; in a civilian sense, the Japanese could lose much. The bomb that hit Hiroshima was a threat aimed at all of Japan. The political target of the bomb was not the dead of Hiroshima or the factories they worked in, but the survivors in Tokyo. The two bombs were in the tradition of Sheridan against the Comanches and Sherman in Georgia. Whether in the end those two bombs saved lives or wasted them, Japanese lives or American lives; whether punitive coercive violence is uglier than straightforward military force or more civilized; whether terror is more or less humane than military destruction; we can at least perceive that the bombs on Hiroshima and Nagasaki represented violence against the country itself and not mainly an attack on Japan's material strength. The effect of the bombs, and their purpose, were not mainly the military destruction they accomplished but the pain and the shock and the promise of more. . . .

5.2 ▬▬▬

ANATOL RAPAPORT

Prisoner's Dilemma

Prisoner's dilemma is the best known example of a non-zero-sum game which illustrates the dramatic failure of zero-sum methods in the new context. The name of the game derives from an anecdote which was originally used to illustrate it. We shall use another illustration closer to the main theme of this book.

The players are two nations, A and B. Each has a range of defense policies, i.e., levels of armaments, deployment of weapon systems, etc. For simplicity we shall assume that only two policies are under consideration by each government, namely, Policy C: total disarmament; and Policy D: high level of armaments. To continue to keep the problem simple, we shall also assume that A and B are the only nations whose military potential needs to be considered, and that when both are fully armed a "balance of power" obtains, that is, each nation has reasonable assurance that the other will not attack it. When both countries are disarmed, we shall assume that each is likewise secure from attack. However, *unilateral* disarmament (we shall suppose) is highly disadvantageous to the disarmed nation, and advantageous to the nation that has remained armed (or, say, has rearmed while the other has remained disarmed).

Besides safety there are also costs to take into account. High levels of armament, it is generally conceded, are more costly than low levels. Thus, the degrees of safety in both the bilaterally armed and the bilaterally disarmed state being the same, we must assign a lower utility to the bilaterally armed than to the bilaterally disarmed state. Let us assign the value +5 to the latter state and the value of −5 to the former. Since being disarmed alone is worse than being armed (even if the other is) we shall assign −10 to this state. Similarly, the advantage of being the only armed nation shall be represented by +10. The resulting game is represented by Matrix 7.

	C	D
C	5, 5	−10, 10
D	10, −10	−5, −5

Matrix 7

Now the principal feature of this game is the fact that strategy D dominates strategy C for both players. On the face of it, therefore, we seem to be confronted with the simplest type of two-person game, namely, one in which each player has a clearly dominating strategy, one that is sure to be better than the other no matter what the other player does. In fact, if B is armed, this is the strongest of reasons for A to remain armed. If B disarms, A is still better off armed, because it is then the only armed one. In the case of the zero-sum game, the choice of a dominating strategy, if such exists, is the only rational choice. Observe, however, that in the game now before us, this is no longer the case. If both players choose the dominating strategy (remain armed), they both do worse than they would have done if they had both chosen the dominated strategy (to disarm).

An obvious way out of the dilemma is for the players to get together and to agree to disarm. But this raises a host of questions. For example, what does it mean to "agree"? The concept has not been used heretofore except in the context of agreeing to abide by the rules of the game. But here the meaning of "to agree" is clearly different. Agreement refers here not to something that occurs before the game (and so need not be considered again) but to something that takes place *during* the game. Is agreement a "move"? But games schematized in matrix form do not have "moves." Is an agreement a new rule set up while the game is progressing? Whatever the nature of this "agreement," the following question is interesting in its own right. What if the rules of the game explicitly prohibit communication (or the nature of the situation makes it impossible)? Can one speak of "agreement" in that case?

Can the Cooperative Choice Be Rationalized?

The dilemma results from a bifurcation of the idea of rationality. If one asks, "With which strategy am I better off?" the answer is unequivocally, "With strategy D." The choice of strategy C is dictated by collective interest. If one asks, "Where are we both better off?" the answer is, "With strategy C." Thus, strategy D is dictated by self-interest while strategy C is dictated by collective interest. Nevertheless, the choice between C and D is not quite a choice between altruism and selfishness. In choosing C, a player does not necessarily serve collective interest *at the expense* of his self-interest as does, say, a man who suffers discomforts or faces danger to promote the welfare of others. The motivation for choosing C is cooperation, not self-sacrifice. But the player who chooses C does not control the outcome by himself. The outcome depends on what the other player does. If the other chooses D, the attempt to induce cooperation fails. The defector benefits at the cooperator's expense, but it was not intended this way. The cooperator assumed that the other would cooperate, not defect. If he had cooperated, *both* would have benefited. Therefore the choice of C is not an act of self-sacrifice but rather an act of trust. But trust is not enough, because even convincing evidence that the other will choose C need not induce C. Not only must one be trusting; one must also be trustworthy; that is, one must resist the temptation to betray the other's trust.

Is it "rational" to be trusting and trustworthy? Here the common usage of the term "rational" sometimes intrudes and beclouds the issue. The usual sense of this question is, "Is it safe to trust people?" But put in this way, the question is clearly an empirical one, to be answered by examining the behavior of a given sample of people in given circumstances. It is not the justification of a policy on the basis of empirical evidence that makes the policy rational but rather the consistency of the policy with certain axiomatically stated principles. Clearly to be "trusting" in a prisoner's dilemma game means to assume that the other will not choose a dominating strategy, i.e., to deny "rationality" to the other. On the other hand to be "trustworthy" means to discard the dominating strategy in favor of a dominated one, which is not "rational."

To be sure, one could defend trustworthiness, at least in response to the other's trust, on the basis of insuring the other's trust the *next* time. This is clearly advantageous and is reflected in the business dictum "Honesty is the best policy." However, such pragmatic arguments do not apply if there is no next time, if the game is played only once. In this case, there is only one good reason to choose C, namely in order to remain at peace with one's conscience.

It appears that we have now brought in a concept totally alien to the notion of rational decision. The notion of conscience is sometimes gotten around by invoking the idea of "hidden utility." The man who chooses C, it is argued, must assign greater utilities to the associated outcomes than are indicated in the game matrix. (In other words, if we observe that someone chooses C, we conclude that the game he is playing is not prisoner's dilemma.) Such an argument cannot be refuted, because it reduces the question of motivation to a tautology. Whatever is chosen guarantees *ipso facto* the greater utility. But we have seen how such a reduction makes trivial the very notion of utility and with it of motivation. We learn nothing if we always redefine utilities in such a way that the choices come out "right." But we may learn a great deal if we observe how people choose when the motivations dictating the choices conflict, e.g., when desire for gain indicates one choice while other considerations prescribe another.

Whatever "conscience" is, considerations having to do with it are not instrumental. One does not obey one's conscience in order to gain some other end, but simply in order to appease it. In other words, obeying one's conscience is an end in itself, like escaping from pain.

Actually we encounter situations of this sort already in those decisions under risk where one must gamble on unique events. Suppose the decision-maker must choose between two acts, each involving a risky outcome, knowing that the situation will never recur. The prevailing opinion is that he should choose the risk with the greater expected gain. But why? If the situation were to be repeated many times, the choice could be rationalized on the grounds that the expected gains will in the long run become *actual* gains, so that the gambler will be simply choosing a larger gain over a smaller one (supposing that the utilities accruing successively can be added). But clearly this argument does not hold for the single case.

There is no getting around the fact that the decision-maker who chooses the gamble with the greater "expected value" cannot rationalize his choice on the basis of comparing the actual returns. What he compares are *expectations*, i.e., his own states of mind associated with each of the choices. If there is no long run, the expectation remains an expectation, that is, only a mental state like conscience. In the last analysis, one chooses the gamble with the greater expectation simply because "it is the right thing to do."

If the choice of strategy C in a *single* play of prisoner's dilemma can be rationalized at all, it must be rationalized on similar grounds. The player who chooses C does so because he feels it is the proper thing to do. He feels that he ought to behave as he would like the other to behave. He knows that if they both behave as he expects, both will benefit. I submit that these are pretty compelling reasons for choosing C. However, they are not strategic reasons. Indeed they contradict the "rational" strategic principle, which dictates D unconditionally.

███████ **5.3**

RUSSELL J. LENG
HUGH G. WHEELER

Influence Strategies, Success, and War

The *serious dispute*, that is, a dyadic conflict serious enough for one or both sides to threaten armed force but still short of all-out war, represents one of the most promising environments for studying internation conflict behavior. The bargaining that takes place is too important to be overshadowed by other matters; yet the level of violence has not reached the point where diplomacy has been cast aside in an armed struggle to vanquish the adversary. There are exceptions to be sure, but in most instances each side is engaged in an intense effort to influence the behavior of the other. The study that follows is an attempt to discover whether certain combinations of *influence strategies* are more or less likely to predict war, compromise, or a diplomatic victory for one side and a defeat for the other.

We assume that each party enters the dispute with preconceptions about which influence attempt combinations, or influence strategies, are most likely to succeed in attaining compliance with its demands. These preconceptions

From *Journal of Conflict Resolution*, Vol. 23 (December 1979), pages 699-680. Copyright © 1979 by Sage Publications, Inc. Reprinted by permission of Sage Publications, Inc.

result in initial influence strategies that may be reinforced or weakened to a greater or lesser extent by the feedback received from the responses of the other disputant to particular influence attempts. Considered from this perspective, conflict bargaining may be conceived of as a mutual learning-conditioning process. Each party is engaged in modifying its own strategies at the same time that it is attempting to influence the goals and behavior of the other (see Ikle and Leites, 1962).

We define an effective influence strategy as one that avoids either a diplomatic defeat or war. The ineffectiveness of an influence strategy that results in a diplomatic defeat, that is capitulation to (or the resistance to) the demands of the other party, is obvious enough. And if we can assume that the purpose of diplomatic bargaining is to reach agreement, then we can agree with Morgenthau (1978) that "diplomacy that ends in war has failed in its primary objective: the promotion of national interest by peaceful means." There are, of course, instances when at least one party to the dispute has no desire to avoid war, so that diplomacy is conducted with no intention of reaching agreement, but for what Ikle (1964) has referred to as "side-effects." We would argue, nonetheless, that these instances are exceptional, that most often a dispute that escalates to war represents a diplomatic failure for both sides. By the same token, we consider a compromise agreement as a partial success for both sides.

Let us propose that the failures have occurred in large part because of the influence strategies employed by national decision-makers in serious disputes, and because of the inability of these decision-makers to learn from negative feedback, in the form of the responses of the other party, in sufficient time to correct ineffective strategies. If these propositions are correct, then we ought to meet with some success in predicting the likely outcomes of serious dyadic disputes based on the influence strategies employed by the two participants. . . .

I. Four Influence Strategies

The subtlety of international diplomacy suggests an endless range of possible influence strategies, but a systematic examination of the propositions presented above requires the simplest possible classification of basic types. At the risk of erring on the side of oversimplification, we have chosen four basic types of influence strategies. We believe these are a reasonable representation of the most prominent types appearing in historical accounts of international diplomacy, as well as in experimental studies of conflict bargaining behavior. The four types are: *bullying, reciprocating, appeasing,* and *trial-and-error.* A description of each follows, along with a review of findings regarding the prevalence of the type and its relative effectiveness.

A Bullying Influence Strategy

In a purely rational context, one could assume that compliance with an influence attempt will be forthcoming if the inducements employed by the influencer are credible and if the punishments or rewards to be imposed outweigh the target's expected gains from noncompliance. A bullying strategy is based on escalating negative inducements. In its purest form, any response short of outright compliance is met with a more severe threat or punishment on each successive influence attempt-response sequence until the target has been induced to comply. . . .

Reciprocating

The universality of the norm of reciprocity has been widely noted (Masters, 1969; Gouldner, 1960), and its place in diplomacy is well established. Evidence of a "tit-for-tat" pattern has appeared in a number of empirical studies of internation conflict behavior and bargaining (Hopmann and Smith, 1977; Leng and Goodsell, 1974; North, 1967; North, Brody and Holsti, 1964; Gamson and Modigliani, 1971; Wilkenfeld et al., 1972). In controlled bargaining experiments, social psychologists (Esser and Komorita, 1975; Pruitt and Johnson, 1970; Chertkoff and Conley, 1967) have found that subjects tend to reciprocate the cooperative moves of their opponents.

There is also evidence that reciprocity can be a very effective influence strategy. Bargaining experiments with human subjects suggest that a reciprocating, or "firm-but-fair" approach is more effective than a bullying strategy (Esser and Komorita, 1975). By the same token, experiments with repeated plays of Prisoner's Dilemma games have indicated that a tit-for-tat strategy will produce a high degree of cooperation when the game is played with human subjects (Oskamp, 1971). This simple strategy also is remarkably effective as a programmed strategy against more complex programmed Prisoner's Dilemma strategies, as demonstrated in the results of the first round of a computer tournament of competing strategies for an iterated Prisoner's Dilemma game (Axelrod, 1978). . . .

Appeasing

An appeasing strategy is virtually the opposite of the bullying strategy. Anything short of outright compliance by the target results in more positive inducements. The assumption behind an appeasing strategy is that the adversary has finite demands that can be satisfied at a reasonable cost if one is willing to compromise. Needless to say, the approach has become infamous since Neville Chamberlain's Munich diplomacy.

Today few would argue the merits of an appeasing strategy, except perhaps when dealing with significantly weaker opponents who would not be likely to interpret concessions as a sign of weakness. Some of the bargaining experiments outside of international politics support the effectiveness of offering concessions to induce concessions (Esser and Komorita, 1975; Wall, 1977). And Leng (1977) found, in an events data study of twelve internation conflicts, that positive inducements were as effective as negative inducements in predicting to positive responses. None of these studies, however, focuses on an appeasing strategy per se. But, despite the folklore resulting largely from the Munich example, the prevalence and the alleged ineffectiveness of appeasing influence strategies are still a matter of conjecture. . . .

Trial-and-Error

Each of the first three influence strategies assumes that the actor holds definite assumptions about what is likely to motivate the target and has developed an influence strategy based on those assumptions. A trial-and-error influence strategy begins with no such assumptions. The actor simply adjusts his choices of inducements based on the target's response to the previous influence attempt. Inducements that produce positive responses are repeated; inducements that produce negative responses are not. In theory, the closest approximation to trial-and-error learning is probably Thorndike's (1931) "solution learning"; but Thorndike saw the subject as ultimately becoming conditioned by rewarding responses to behave in a *habitual* manner, which is more than is suggested here. We assume merely that national decision-makers normally hold strong preconceptions regarding what is most likely to motivate the target, but that there are cases where decision-makers find their previous experiences so ambiguous, or the current situation so unique to them, that they choose their inducements by trial-and-error until they hit on a pattern that appears to work.

Trial-and-error learning is an inefficient process in the simplest of circumstances, but it appears to be especially so when one considers the variety of possible types of influence attempts and responses, not to mention the opportunities for misperception, in international disputes. . . .

Taking the two actors together, and assuming that each remains faithful to his initial influence strategy, which of the four strategies is most likely to be successful? According to the logic of the decision rules, the predicted outcomes for pairs of intersecting influence strategies appear in Table 5-1.

Table 5-1 Influence Strategies and Predicted Outcomes

B's Influence Strategy	A's Influence Strategy			
	Bullying	Reciprocating	Appeasing	Trial-and-Error
Bullying	war	war	B wins	B wins or war
Reciprocating	war	compromise	B wins or compromise	compromise
Appeasing	A wins	A wins or compromise	compromise	A wins
Trial-and-error	A wins or war	compromise	B wins	compromise

For the conservative statesmen employing a minimax approach, the best strategy would be either reciprocating or trial-and-error. A bullying strategy presents the extremes of either a diplomatic victory or war; an appeasing strategy offers only the dubious advantage of avoiding war through accepting diplomatic defeat. (The situation could be a bit different, of course, if there is a good deal of asymmetry in either power or determination between the two players. War may well be an acceptable cost or risk for a strong and determined nation facing a weak and/or irresolute opponent.) It is also interesting to note that war is a likely outcome only when one or both sides employ a bullying strategy. These predictions can be stated as Hypotheses 1 and 2.

> *Hypothesis 1:* Serious dyadic disputes are most likely to end in war when one or both parties employ a predominantly bullying strategy.
> *Hypothesis 2:* Without prior knowledge of the strategy employed by the other disputant, either a *reciprocating* or *trial-and-error* influence strategy is the most effective means of avoiding a diplomatic defeat without going to war.

. . . Given the decision rules of the bullying and trial-and-error strategies, it appears more likely that it would be the trial-and-error strategist that would be conditioned to change by adopting an appeasing strategy, rather than the other way around. In sum, when we consider the logic of the four influence strategies, a reciprocating strategy would appear to be the best counter to a bullying adversary, assuming that the bully also wishes to avoid the onset of war.

This leads to our third hypothesis:

> *Hypothesis 3:* If one of the parties to a serious dispute employs a predominantly bullying influence strategy, then a reciprocating influence strategy provides the most effective means for the other side to avoid a diplomatic defeat without going to war.

II. Data Generation

The Cases

The association between influence strategies and war, and the validity of the three hypotheses, will be examined in twenty interstate conflicts occurring in this century. Nine of these cases are disputes that resulted in war. Most of these cases were randomly selected from an updated version of the Singer-Small (1972) list of interstate wars occurring between 1815 and 1965. The eleven nonwar cases were selected from an unpublished list of serious disputes compiled by Leng for the same time period. Given our attempt to stick to a random selection as closely as possible, we would make no claim that these are the twenty most important dyadic disputes occurring during this period, or even that the dyads chosen are the most important antagonists in a particular conflict. We deviated from a purely random selection of cases in two ways.

243

Table 5-2 Serious Dyadic Disputes

Dispute and Adversaries	Dates	War or Nonwar
First Moroccan Crisis France-Germany	3/31/1905- 3/31/1906	nonwar
Bosnian Crisis Austria-Serbia	9/16/1908- 3/31/1910	nonwar
Second Moroccan Crisis France-Germany	4/1/1911- 11/4/1911	nonwar
Pre-World War I Austria-Serbia	6/28/1914- 7/28/1914	war
Pre-World War I France-Germany	6/28/1914- 7/28/1914	war
Italo-Ethiopian War Italy-Ethiopia	12/5/1934- 10/3/1935	war
Occupation of Rhineland Germany-Britain	3/7/1936- 12/31/1936	nonwar
Anschluss, 1938 Germany-Austria	1/7/1938- 3/12/1938	nonwar
Munich Crisis Britain-Germany	2/20/1938- 9/29/1938	nonwar
Munich Crisis Germany-Czechoslovakia	2/20/1938- 9/29/1938	nonwar
Pre-World War II Britain-Germany	10/31/1938- 9/1/1938	war
1st Kashmir Dispute India-Pakistan	10/1/1947- 11/30/1948	war
Trieste Italy-Yugoslavia	8/29/1953- 10/5/1954	nonwar
Sinai War Britain-Egypt	7/26/1956- 10/31/1956	war
Berlin Crisis U.S.-USSR	7/25/1961- 11/30/1961	nonwar
Cuban Missile Crisis U.S.-USSR	8/22/1962- 11/20/1962	nonwar
Cyprus Dispute Greece-Turkey	11/30/1963- 8/30/1964	nonwar
2nd Kashmir War India-Pakistan	3/ /1964- 8/5/1965	war
Six Day War Israel-Egypt	4/7/1967- 6/5/1967	war
Bangladesh India-Pakistan	3/1/1971- 12/3/1971	war

First, we did not include cases drawn from the larger lists for which there were no available comprehensive narrative accounts. Second, certain disputes (the Pre-World War II cases, Berlin, and Cuba) were drawn together to provide a conflict-to-conflict comparison for another study. . . .

The list of cases appears in Table 5-2. . . .

Testing the Hypotheses

Turning now to our three hypotheses, we find the results for the first two to be relatively straightforward. Hypothesis 1 states that a serious dispute is most likely to end in war when at least one of the disputants employs a bullying strategy. Six of the ten cases in which bullying strategies were employed by at least one participant ended in war. In only one instance did war occur when neither side employed a bullying strategy. The results appear in Table 5-3.

The differences in outcomes are consistent with the hypothesis. Because the twenty disputes do not represent a truly random sample, we cannot justify use of statistical significance tests to make any inferences about a larger population. We can, however, use such tests to tell us whether the variables we have selected to test our hypothesis tell us anything about the distribution of our cases beyond mere chance (Winch and Campbell, 1969). Do our variables, in other words, discriminate among our cases sufficiently well that we can be confident that we have found systematic patterns in our data stronger than those that would be found by chance alone (by randomly assigning our cases to subsets, for example)? Statistical significance tests provide an objective answer to that question. Given the smaller number of cases compared, here and in subsequent tests, we have employed Fisher's Exact Test (see Bradley, 1968), a more conservative measure than, say, a chi-square. The differences appearing in Table 5-3 are significant at the $p = .01$ level.

The one case in which a war resulted when neither side met our criteria for a bullying influence strategy was Suez. Here there was no determined Egyptian strategy beyond the initial nationalization of the Canal. In one of the four bullying strategies that did not result in war—the Anschluss—a weak opponent employed an appeasing strategy that allowed the bully to achieve a

Table 5-3 Bullying Influence Strategies and War

Influence Strategy	Dispute Outcome		
	War	Nonwar	Total
Bullying	6	4	10
Other	1	9	10
Total	7	13	20

diplomatic victory and in another case—Germany and Czechoslovakia at Munich—the Czechs made no discernible effort to influence Germany directly, but Britain employed an appeasing strategy on their behalf. These outcomes are consistent with the predictions in Table 5-1, but the other two instances in which a bullying strategy fails to result in war are not. In both the Berlin Crisis of 1961 and the Cyprus dispute of 1964-1965, a bullying strategy is countered by a reciprocating strategy with the conflict ending in a compromise. These cases raise some interesting possibilities to which we will return in our discussion of Hypothesis 3.

Hypothesis 2 states that, without foreknowledge of the strategy to be employed by the other disputant, either a reciprocating or a trial-and-error strategy would be the most effective means of avoiding a diplomatic defeat without going to war. This appears to be borne out by the figures shown in Table 5-4. In the sample of twenty cases a trial-and-error strategy emerges as the *safest*, with a nonwar outcome occurring in all five disputes in which it is employed. A reciprocating strategy, on the other hand, produced four diplomatic victories, along with six compromises, but it also resulted in three wars.

If we collapse the possible outcomes into two categories, that is, either diplomatic victory or compromise on the one hand, or diplomatic defeat or war on the other, and compare the outcomes for each of the possible strategies taken two at a time, it is possible to calculate the statistical significance of the differences evident in Table 5-4. To save space, we have not reproduced each of the resulting two-by-two tables; however, the differences between either reciprocating and trial-and-error strategies and appeasing strategies are significant to at least the $p = .05$ level, as is the difference between the reciprocating strategy and the bullying strategy. The difference between the trial-and-error and bullying strategies is in the right direction but it barely misses being significant at the $p = .05$ level. There are no statistically significant differences in effectiveness between the two least successful strategies: bullying and appeasing. Nor is there any statistically significant difference between recipro-

Table 5-4 Influence Strategies and Outcomes

Strategy	Outcome				
	Diplomatic Victory	Compromise	Diplomatic Defeat	War	
Bullying	2	2	0	9	13
Reciprocating	4	6	0	3	13
Appeasing	0	0	5	1	6
Trial-and-error	0	4	1	0	5
	6	12	6	13	37

cating and trial-and-error, the two most effective strategies. It should be noted, though, that in the four disputes in which trial-and-error strategies were employed, one was a case where *each* party employed a trial-and-error strategy. Moreover, in no instance was a trial-and-error strategy employed against a bullying opponent. In short, the results indicate support for Hypothesis 2, although there are interesting differences between the reciprocating trial-and-error influence strategies.

Hypothesis 2, of course, did not consider the influence strategy employed by the other disputant. But what of the relative effectiveness of an influence strategy against a *particular* opposing strategy? This leads to the question posed by Hypothesis 3. What is the most effective strategy against a bullying adversary? The results of the study to this point underline the importance of that question. We have found that a bullying strategy is not only the strategy most likely to predict to war, but that it also ties with reciprocating for being the influence strategy most commonly employed in our sample of twenty disputes.

Based on [our research], a reciprocating strategy is the influence strategy most commonly used against a bullying opponent. Of the nine disputes in which one of the disputants employed a bullying strategy, the other countered with a reciprocating strategy four times, with a bullying strategy three times, and with an appeasing strategy in the other two cases. Only the reciprocating strategy shows any success, with two compromise outcomes and two wars. All three attempts to counter a bullying strategy with a bullying strategy resulted in war; the appeasing strategies produced one war and one diplomatic defeat.

But if we consider the logic of how a reciprocating strategy is supposed to work against a bullying opponent, [this initial conclusion] may be misleading. The strategy signals the reciprocator's resolve to respond in kind to the bully's coercive tactics, even if it should lead to war, but at the same time it signals the willingness of the reciprocator to initiate the mutual concessions necessary for a compromise resolution of the dispute. Presumably, the combination of tit-for-tat responses to the other disputant's inducements, coupled with one or two unilateral positive inducements, should encourage the bullying adversary to abandon his bullying strategy. If this is so, it is possible that the change could take place early enough in the dispute for the newly adopted strategy to replace the bullying strategy as the predominant strategy. . . . In other words, we may have ignored some cases of would-be bulliers who abandoned their bullying strategies early on in the dispute. With this in mind, we took a second look at all of those cases in which either side employed a reciprocating strategy. In each instance, employing the same coding rules we used earlier, we selected the predominant influence strategy employed by the other disputant *before* any unilateral positive inducement by the reciprocator. It was possible, of course, that besides adding cases we may have missed, we would also have to drop some of those [cases] as bullying strategies if they became predominantly

Table 5-5 Reciprocating Versus Bullying Strategies

Dispute	Outcome for Reciprocator
First Moroccan	diplomatic victory
Bosnia	diplomatic victory
Pre-W.W. II (GB-G)	war
Trieste	compromise
Berlin	compromise
Cuba	diplomatic victory
Cyprus	compromise
Bangladesh	war

bullying only *after* a positive inducement by a reciprocating opponent. This, by no means implausible, finding would suggest the opposite of the logic of our hypothesis. It would suggest that the unilateral positive initiative was interpreted as a sign of weakness that encouraged the adversary to take a tougher line.

Our inspection revealed that all four of the cases originally identified . . . continued to meet the criteria, and four new cases were added. The eight disputes, with the outcome for the nation employing the reciprocating strategy, appear in Table 5-5.

We can get a sense of the significance of the record of success in Table 5-5 by comparing the reciprocating strategy with other strategies used against bullying strategies. The striking difference, which is shown in Table 5-6 below, is significant at the $p = .05$ level, with an exact probability of .016.

The results in Table 5-6 support the general proposition that not only is a reciprocating influence strategy the most commonly used technique against a bullying opponent, but that it is likely to be the most effective too. The remaining question is "why?" It is impossible to answer that question on the

Table 5-6 Success Against Bullying Strategies

Strategy	Outcome		
	Victory or Compromise	Defeat or War	
Reciprocating	6	2	8
Others	0	5	5
	6	7	13

basis of the preceding analysis, but at least within the limits of this sample, we can suggest some plausible answers by taking a closer look at the particular cases.

A Closer Look at the Findings

Five of the six disputes in which a reciprocating strategy succeeded in reversing a bullying strategy appear to fall into one of two distinct classes, with the Cuban Missile Crisis somewhere on the borderline between the two. . . .

The advantage that a reciprocating strategy provides in allowing an adversary to find a face-saving way out of an escalating dispute appears to be a salient component of at least four (Morocco, Bosnia, Trieste, Cuba) of the six cases. This is consistent with the findings of social psychologists (Chertkoff and Baird, 1971; Lamm and Rosch, 1972; Brown, 1971) of the importance of face-saving—a willingness to sacrifice tangible values to avoid looking foolish or weak in public—in interpersonal bargaining. In the Moroccan and Cuban Crises this interpretation is also consistent with the case studies of Snyder and Diesing (1977), who classify the structures of these disputes as "called bluff," with the victorious party providing a modest degree of face-saving for an unequal compromise.

It is interesting to note too that in four of the six cases (Morocco, Bosnia, Trieste, and Cyprus) action by a third party played a principal role in encouraging the positive inducements that led to the deescalation of the dispute. This too is consistent with the face-saving hypothesis in that there is evidence (Pruitt and Johnson, 1970) that bargainers are likely to accept lower settlements if they are proposed by a third party, rather than by the adversary. In the cases at hand, we may be observing a two-step process in which the third party convinces one of the disputants to abandon a simple tit-for-tat strategy to offer unilateral positive inducements which are then seized by the disputant that has found itself in the weaker bargaining position.

Finally, we find a remarkable regularity to the reciprocating pattern observed in five of the six cases. Each of these began with a series of unyielding and threatening responses to the consistently negative inducements of the bullying adversary. These were followed by one or two unilateral positive inducements. Then the reciprocator returned to tit-for-tat responses to the bully's mix of cooperative and conflictive actions for the remainder of the dispute. Only in the First Moroccan Crisis did the reciprocating nation begin with a unilateral positive inducement—and the early initiative was unsuccessful. In the other five cases, the pattern is quite similar to the Prisoner's Dilemma strategy found most effective by Harford and Solomon (1967): initial noncooperation, then unconditional cooperation, followed by conditional cooperation. Presumably, the bullying disputant was made aware of the resolve of the reciprocating nation, which then—usually with the help and encouragement of a third party—offered a face-saving way out of the escalating conflict, followed by a "firm-but-fair" pattern of responding in kind to the bully's succeeding moves.

But, what of the two cases in which the reciprocating strategy failed to prevent war? The Pre-World War II crisis in 1939 between Britain and Germany, and Bangladesh are dramatically different types of disputes in a great many respects, but they share something in common in the absence of any real negotiating situation. Most historians are agreed that Germany was bent on war by the summer of 1939 and that it was too late for Britain to stop it by exhibiting the firmness that was lacking at Munich. In Bangladesh, the situation was somewhat different in that the demands, which the Indian government felt forced by circumstances to make, were conditions that the Pakistani government was powerless to meet. Instances like this are reminders that not every dispute can be settled, even temporarily, by even the best bargaining strategy....

References

Axelrod, R. (1978) "A report on the computer tournament for the iterated Prisoner's Dilemma: tit for tat wins the first round." Institute of Public Policy Studies Discussion Paper No. 128. Institute for Public Policy Studies, University of Michigan. (mimeo)

Bradley, J. V. (1968) Distribution-Free Statistical Tests. Englewood Cliffs, N.J.: Prentice-Hall.

Braver, S. L. and V. Rohrer (1978) "Superiority of vicarious over direct experience in interpersonal conflict resolution." J. of Conflict Resolution 22: 143-154.

Brown, B. R. (1971) "Saving face." Psychology Today 4: 55-59, 86.

Chertkoff, J. M. and S. L. Baird (1971) "Applicability of the big lie technique and the last clear chance doctrine to bargaining." J. of Personality and Social Psychology 20: 298-303.

Chertkoff, J. M. and M. Conley (1967) "Opening offer and frequency of concession as bargaining strategies." J. of Personality and Social Psychology 7: 181-184.

Esser, J. K. and S. Komorita (1975) "Reciprocity and concession making in bargaining." J. of Personality and Social Psychology 31: 864-872.

Gamson, W. and A. Modigliani (1971) Untangling the Cold War. Boston: Little, Brown.

Gouldner, A. W. (1960) "The norm of reciprocity: a preliminary statement." Amer. Soc. Rev. 25: 161-178.

Harford, T. and L. Solomon (1967) " 'Reformed sinner' and 'lapsed saint' strategies in the Prisoner's Dilemma game." J. of Conflict Resolution 11: 104-109.

Hopmann, P. T. and T. C. Smith (1977) "An application of a Richardson process model: Soviet-American interactions in the Test Ban Negotiations 1962-1963." J. of Conflict Resolution 22: 701-726.

Ikle, F. C. (1964) How Nations Negotiate. New York: Harper and Row.

_____ and N. Leites (1962) "Political negotiation as a process of modifying utilities." J. of Conflict Resolution 6: 19-28.

Lamm, H. and E. Rosch (1972) "Information and competitiveness of incentive structure as factors in two-person negotiation." European J. of Social Psychology 2: 459-465.

Leng, R. J. (1979) "Strategies of influence in interstate conflict: an examination of the realist prescription," in J. D. Singer (ed.) Correlates of War, II.

_____ (1975) "Coder's manual for identifying and describing international actions." Middlebury, Vt.: Middlebury College. (mimeo)

_____ and R. Goodsell (1974) "Behavioral indicators of war proneness in bilateral conflicts," in P. McGowan (ed.) Sage International Yearbook of Foreign Policy Studies, II. Beverly Hills: Sage Publications.

Masters, R. D. (1969) "World politics as a primitive political system," in J. Rosenau (ed.) International Politics and Foreign Policy. Englewood Cliffs, N.J.: Prentice-Hall.

Morgenthau, H. J. (1978) Politics Among Nations. New York: Alfred A. Knopf.

North, R. (1967) "Perception and action in the 1914 crisis." J. of Int. Affairs 27: 16-39.

_____ and R. Brody, and O. Holsti (1964) "Some empirical data on the conflict spiral." Peace Research Society (Int.) Papers 1: 1-14.

Oskamp, S. (1971) "Effects of programmed strategies on cooperation in the Prisoner's Dilemma and other mixed motive games." J. of Conflict Resolution 15: 225-259.

Pruitt, D. G. and D. F. Johnson (1970) "Mediation as an aid to face-saving in negotiation." J. of Personality and Social Psychology 14: 239-246.

Singer, J. and M. Small (1972) The Wages of War, 1816-1965. New York: John Wiley.

Snyder, G. H. and P. Diesing (1978) Conflict Among Nations. Princeton, N.J.: Princeton Univ. Press.

Thorndike, E. L. (1931) Human Learning. New York: Appleton-Century-Crofts.

Wall, J. A. (1977) "Operantly conditioning a negotiator's concession making." J. of Experimental Social Psychology: 431-440.

Wilkenfeld, J., V. L. Lussier, and D. Tahtinen (1972) "Conflict interactions in the Middle East, 1949-1967." J. of Conflict Resolution 16: 135-154.

Winch, R. F. and D. T. Campbell (1969) "Proof? No. Evidence? Yes. The significance of tests of significance." Amer. Sociologist: 140-143.

Michael H. Armacost

5.4 ▮▮▮▮

MICHAEL H. ARMACOST

U.S. Diplomacy and the Search for Peace

The Chinese ideograph for the word "crisis" has two characters; one means "danger," the other "opportunity." Without suggesting that we face a crisis overseas, I would like to focus this evening on some foreign policy opportunities. In making foreign policy, the trick is to stay ahead of events, to shape them in accordance with our objectives and values. Warding off dangers and capitalizing on opportunities are two sides of the same coin. The months ahead present us with some special opportunities for at least three reasons.

☐ For the first time since Vietnam, the United States has a president with a strong mandate for a second term. The Soviet Union has recently had a change of leadership, and we have resumed arms control discussions with the Soviets in Geneva. This conjunction of events alters the context for East-West relations.

☐ Second, we are in a better position than we have been for many years to take advantage of diplomatic opportunities. In Soviet parlance, "the correlation of forces" has been shifting in our favor. The sustained increases in our defense spending have begun to restore our position in the strategic balance. The resilience of our economy lends strength to our diplomacy. Our alliances are in solid shape. Our ideas—democracy and the free market—have renewed appeal even in the Third World.

Conversely, a new Soviet leadership faces a Soviet economy that resists modernization; Moscow's allies are restless; its adventure in Afghanistan is a psychological and material drain and complicates its relations with the nonaligned. The Soviet Union has little to offer the Third World save military hardware—scarcely a relevant response to the problems of drought and famine in Africa, debt in Latin America, or the desire for peace and reconciliation in the Middle East.

The Soviet Union remains a dangerous adversary, yet shares with us a vital interest in avoiding nuclear war. The resumption of arms negotiations in Geneva, along with the prospect of a meeting with Mr. Gorbachev, offers the promise of a renewed dialogue with the Soviets on the full range of issues of mutual concern. We should have no illusions: the U.S.S.R. remains a formidable military power with

An address before the Baltimore Council on Foreign Affairs, Baltimore, Maryland, April 24, 1985.

expansionist aims. Yet there is at least a possibility that the new Soviet leadership will recognize an interest in better external relations while it tries to address its systemic internal problems. We cannot presume on a long-term change in Soviet intentions; we can seek to engage Moscow in constructive, mutual efforts to improve our relationship.

☐ Third, there are signs of ferment and diplomatic movement in the Middle East, Central America, and southern Africa. In each of these areas, we are deeply engaged in negotiating processes; the American role is vitally important. The issues have long proved intractable and may remain so. Yet the benefits to us of a peaceful resolution of longstanding regional conflicts are self-evident.

We are in a strong position to pursue these opportunities. Our challenge is to turn our strength, vitality, and ideas into constructive accomplishments in the promotion of peace and the reduction of tensions.

Let me offer some observations on these regional negotiations and then discuss the factors on which the success of our negotiating efforts will depend.

The Middle East

Four times in the past 12 years the United States has successfully brokered peace arrangements in the Middle East. These included three Egyptian-Israeli agreements between 1974 and 1979 and a Syrian-Israeli agreement in 1974. Once again, we are being called upon by the states in the area to help restore momentum to the peace process.

We have a vital stake in peace between Israel and its neighbors. Conflict in the Middle East risks Great Power confrontation, the security of Israel, disruption of oil supplies, expanded political and military opportunities for the Soviet Union, and the growth of Islamic radicalism and other threats to friendly governments.

Conditions for accentuating the search for peace are more encouraging than they have been for some time.

☐ The Israeli Government is withdrawing from Lebanon and has offered to negotiate with Jordan without preconditions. Prime Minister Peres said in a March 31 interview, "We are prepared to negotiate unconditionally with a joint Jordanian-Palestinian delegation, a Jordanian delegation, or a Palestinian delegation in our efforts toward an immediate, peaceful solution or a solution in stages."

☐ King Hussein has defied intimidation from hostile states to work with Palestinians toward eventual negotiations with Israel.

☐ Egypt is reentering the mainstream of Arab politics, actively seeking to broaden the negotiating process and to improve its relations with Israel.

☐ Iraq has developed closer relations with moderate Arab neighbors and established full diplomatic relations with us.

These developments provide grounds for cautious optimism, but we must not blind ourselves to remaining difficulties. Continued reluctance by Arab leaders to negotiate directly with Israel, differences within governments in the region, the "cold peace" between Israel and Egypt, hesitations among the Palestinians, and Syria's ability to play a spoiler's role all are factors that complicate the effort to arrange direct negotiations, let alone achieve a successful outcome. It is scarcely surprising that many claim that Israel and its Arab neighbors, if left entirely to their own devices, could not conceivably resolve their differences. The corollary is the insistent request of many parties for active U.S. involvement. Only the United States, they maintain, possesses the influence and credibility to assume the role of honest broker.

Under the proper circumstances, we are prepared to assume a more active role. Indeed, for many months we have worked to create those circumstances.

- ☐ We sought to facilitate a negotiated and orderly Israeli withdrawal from Lebanon. That attempt foundered on Syrian intransigence and Lebanese disarray, but the Israelis are withdrawing, nonetheless.
- ☐ We have actively encouraged improved Egyptian-Israeli relations—an effort we think will bear fruit.
- ☐ We have urged Israel and Jordan to work in parallel to improve the "quality of life" of the Palestinians in the West Bank and Gaza as a positive step to build confidence and strengthen the forces of moderation.
- ☐ We have encouraged King Hussein's initiative with the Palestinians and supported his effort to move toward direct negotiations with Israel.
- ☐ We have urged other Arab states to play a more active and constructive role.

On February 11, King Hussein reached a framework agreement with Yasir Arafat which spoke of negotiations and a peaceful solution. This may prove to have been an important milestone *if* it facilitates Jordanian entry with appropriate Palestinian representation into direct negotiations with Israel. President Mubarak has also put forward ideas to push the peace process along. Dick Murphy, our able Assistant Secretary for Near Eastern and South African Affairs, is in the region now, exploring these and other ideas. The test of their utility is whether they facilitate or impede early and direct negotiations between Israel and Jordan, with Palestinian participation.

Once such negotiations are joined, the positions we will take will be those set forth in President Reagan's September 1, 1982, speech on the Middle East. Other parties will bring other negotiating positions. The place to negotiate is at the table. We will not accept attempts to change our position in advance of negotiations—and it is time the negotiating commenced. If not now, when? Hard choices must be made by all who desire peace. Aware of the difficulties, we are prepared to play our part, as others accept their own responsibilities.

Central America

Closer to home, vital interests in Central America have compelled us to take an active part in equally complex multilateral negotiations. Longstanding problems have ripened to a point where the states of the region recognize the need to find a comprehensive settlement. At the request of our friends in Central America, we have sought to help. While some argue that Nicaragua does not directly threaten us, the fact is that it does pose a challenge to important American security interests.

The basic problem is clear: Nicaragua, with encouragement and substantial support from the Soviet Union and Cuba, has sought to exploit the social, economic, and political difficulties faced by the Central American countries. Over the past 6 years, Nicaragua has established intimate ties with the Eastern bloc; it has undertaken an arms buildup that intimidates its neighbors and far exceeds its defense requirements; it supplies logistic support and the command structure for insurgents in El Salvador, it has supported armed struggle in Guatemala and Honduras and trained potential insurgents in Costa Rica.

If the problem is clear, so is our objective: to promote regional peace and stability by addressing the needs of our friends and the Nicaragua problem.

We have sought bipartisan support for a strategy with these components:

- [ ] A major effort to strengthen our friends by substantially increasing economic and security assistance while encouraging rapid growth and democratic political development;
- [ ] Support for the Contadora negotiating process to define political and security arrangements, on the basis of which the regimes and peoples of the region can develop their institutions and their economies;
- [ ] Direct dialogue with the parties involved in that process—including Nicaragua—in an effort to promote the Contadora process; and
- [ ] Encouragement of democratic reforms throughout the region, including support for the opposition within Nicaragua which is working for a ceasefire, dialogue, and reform on the basis of a democratic political program.

Over the past year, we have seen substantial progress in some areas, less in others. Our friends are significantly stronger. Democratic institutions have shown vitality under fire in Costa Rica, Honduras, and El Salvador. President Duarte has initiated impressive reforms, earned an expanded electoral mandate, and undertaken a process of dialogue and reconciliation with Salvadoran guerrilla insurgents. Democracy and dialogue in El Salvador stand in marked contrast to the Sandinista government's intransigent refusal to even talk with its democratic opposition, much less begin a genuine process of democratization.

Consonant with the Contadora agreement, the countries of the region have persevered in efforts to achieve a regional settlement. We have seen some progress. Agreement in principle has been reached on some provisions of a draft Contadora treaty providing for verification of eventual security arrangements. We and our Central American friends remain concerned that security arrangements, including withdrawal of foreign forces and achievement of military parity, must be implemented simultaneously and that compliance must be fully verified.

While the Contadora process progressed, we also talked directly with the Sandinistas in an effort to contribute to a Contadora settlement. Following their elections last November, however, the Sandinistas sought to use the talks to achieve a separate bilateral deal with us, rather than to engage in frank substantive exchanges to achieve a Contadora agreement. Consequently, we suspended those talks and tossed the ball back into the wider Contadora court.

We support the Contadora process because its objectives are compatible with our own concerns: ending the arms buildup in Nicaragua; removing Soviet, Cuban, and other foreign military personnel from Nicaragua; ending Sandinista support of the insurgency in El Salvador and other countries; and promoting political pluralism in Nicaragua in accordance with the Sandinista promises made to the OAS [Organization of American States] at the time of the revolution. The intense regional interest in achieving a settlement, the internal and external pressure on the Sandinistas, and international support for a settlement offer prospects for progress over the coming months.

It is in this context that the President's initiative of April 4 should be viewed. He called for a dialogue between the Nicaraguan regime and its internal opposition. He called for a cease-fire. He called for democracy in Nicaragua.

In making this proposal, the President is building on the consensus that some form of democratization is essential in all Central American countries. Democracy is a key element in the Contadora Document of Objectives and in the initial Contadora draft agreements. In supporting the President's call for dialogue, the Contadora countries and other Latin friends have recognized the fundamental importance of democratic pluralism and internal reconciliation. The president has also indicated that we are prepared to resume discussions with the Sandinistas in an effort to encourage that process.

A comprehensive and patient approach, with bipartisan support at home, can succeed. Both incentives and pressures on the Sandinistas are needed. The democratic opposition in Nicaragua deserves our support as an integral part of a broader regional strategy aimed at achieving a peaceful settlement. If the Sandinistas come to believe that they are home free, under no pressure to compromise with their neighbors, much less their internal opposition, then there will be no settlement, and there could be a dangerous deterioration of the regional situation. There is a wiser alternative open to us—and the President's peace plan of April 4 shows the way.

Southern Africa

The Reagan Administration's intense involvement in southern Africa since 1981 reflects its recognition of an opportunity to promote peaceful change in the region. We can derive satisfaction from the role we have played in working toward three key objectives:

- ☐ Promoting peace through the cessation of violence and the removal of foreign forces from the region;
- ☐ Bringing about the independence of Namibia under UN Security Council Resolution 435; and
- ☐ Promoting peaceful change in South Africa away from the loathsome apartheid system and toward a more just society.

Our involvement has already yielded benefits. We encouraged the Nkoinati accord between South Africa and Mozambique, and the Lusaka accord between Angola and South Africa. Both have helped diminish cross-border violence and made the point that peace can be negotiated. The recent completion of South African withdrawal from southern Angola should improve prospects for a broader regional settlement. With respect to Namibia, progress has been made in securing agreement on a set of constitutional principles, and the South African Government has reaffirmed its commitment to implement Resolution 435 once agreement is reached on the withdrawal of troops from Angola.

Our effort, from the outset, has been based, as in Central America, on a sober assessment of the regional realities and on an understanding that our role should be to encourage a regional peace process, not to impose one from outside. The African countries have welcomed our involvement.

The Angolan presentation of a Cuban troop withdrawal proposal last fall was a major, positive development, and as differences between Angola and South Africa have narrowed, we have intensified our role as broker. Last month, we tabled a "synthesis" proposal drawn from the positions of both sides in an effort to expedite agreement. Acceptance of a Cuban troop withdrawal formula would be a key element of a settlement package which must also include assurances of Angola's territorial integrity and the implementation of Resolution 435 in Namibia. Such a package would go a long way toward promoting regional stability. It would also pave the way for the Angolans themselves to achieve national reconciliation without outside interference.

The process of change is underway within South Africa as well. Its prospects are enhanced if there is stability in the region. We can and should help encourage that process in constructive and peaceful directions. The South African Government has taken some important steps toward reform, including extension of trade union rights, repeal of the mixed marriage and immorality laws, cessation of forced removals of black communities, and a pledge to move toward a common citizenship for all South Africans. While these steps do go to the heart of the doctrine of apartheid, there is still a long and difficult road which will have to be traveled in order to achieve a just society in South Africa. All Americans, and the world at large, find the doctrine of apartheid repugnant. It is our firm view that the process of peaceful change must continue, and dialogue among all groups in South Africa is essential for this purpose. We have made our views known to the South Africa Government. Our policy of constructive engagement is intended to encourage peaceful change.

American Negotiating Style

We Americans bring a peculiar blend of our own cultural values to the task of diplomacy. Whether bargains are struck between American companies, American unions, or American political parties, a measure of trust and confidence is usually assumed. We rely heavily upon persuasion. Splitting the difference is an honorable tradition. We tend to believe that if men of good will can sit down across a table from each other, even the most intractable problems can be overcome.

Yet we need a more multifaceted perspective if our multilateral regional negotiations are to have the success they deserve. Our recent experience in Central America, the Middle East, and South Africa suggests some lessons which would make our diplomacy more effective.

"The art of diplomacy," Henry Kissinger has said, "is not to outwit or dupe the other party but to persuade it either of the existence of convergent interests, or convince it that the persistence of impasse will result in serious penalties." Put another way, diplomatic progress requires inducements both positive and negative: carrots and sticks. Gestures of flexibility by the Sandinistas have materialized only in response to international and internal pressures—one of the reasons why the Nicaraguan democratic resistance deserves our support. We are strengthening our dialogue with Mozambique and Angola as a "carrot" to encourage their participation in the southern African search for peace. In the Middle East, our foreign assistance programs for Israel, Egypt, and others are complementary to our diplomatic efforts to nudge along the search for peace.

We should not expect immediate results when negotiating. Things normally take longer than one expects. We Americans are an impatient, can-do people. We believe that it is better to get immediately down to cases rather than to avoid the most contentious issues or delay a solution until conditions are ripe. We sometimes tire of problems before the potential for their resolution has matured. We are anxious to achieve results—not least because of the pressures of public and congressional opinion.

By contrast, the Soviets and their clients have no legislative pressures to worry about; they can take their time, and they know the advantages of patience and persistence when negotiating with us. We should recall the slow but steady progress toward resolution of regional conflicts in southern Africa, where there have been few negotiating deadlines and relatively little media attention. Indeed, we tend to overlook the value of the negotiating process itself. Active U.S. mediation—even if it does not produce quick results—puts us at the center of events and forces contending parties to take our interests into account. The very process of brokering is, moreover, an alternative to confrontation and violence, even if there is no rapid, binding resolution of underlying difficulties.

In dealing with tough regional problems, we should not allow others to abandon their own responsibilities, shifting the burdens onto our shoulders. Put another way, we should not let others assume we have a stronger stake in agreements than they do. Regional realities are such that any lasting resolution of conflicts in Central America, the Middle East, and southern Africa can be achieved only by the people who live there. But we can help. In Central America, we should continue to do all that we can to support and encourage Contadora; in southern Africa and the Middle East, likewise, we are encouraging the governments and groups to be flexible and imaginative.

We must learn to tolerate ambiguities. We have to face the fact that there are no easy answers or permanent fixes to issues as complex as the Middle East, southern Africa, or Central America. In Nicaragua, for example, we should recognize the utility of maintaining contact with the Sandinista government while at the same time supporting the freedom fighters. Similarly, we talk to the Angolan government (which we do not recognize) and maintain contact with UNITA [National Union for the Total Independence of Angola] (which is a legitimate indigenous opposition group) while maintaining formal relations with neither.

We must also recognize the need to live with complexity. No negotiation exists in isolation. At play are the global interests of the United States, the needs of our allies, the domestic realities of the parties directly involved. In southern Africa, a negotiation that ends violence between Mozambique and Pretoria is directly relevant to the pace of internal change in South Africa. Regional negotiations also represent an element of our wider strategy, including efforts to reduce Soviet influence. A reduction of Soviet influence in southeastern Africa sends a direct and unmistakable signal to other areas of the world, including Afghanistan, the Horn of Africa, Central America, and Southeast Asia, where Soviet and Soviet-backed power spread tension and instability in the last decade. Peace in southern Africa affects the vital economic interests of our key European allies; stability there assures continued access to strategic minerals and assures safe passage of commercial and military shipping along sensitive sea routes.

We must not let adversaries exploit our own political system to deprive us of flexibility and the tools needed for effective bargaining. We should not end up bargaining with ourselves. Our continued support for those in Nicaragua

259

struggling for democracy constitutes essential leverage for successful negotiations.

Public and congressional support are essential ingredients for successful negotiations in Central America, the Middle East, and southern Africa.

We should prize neither negotiations nor agreements for their own sake. Reliability and verification are indispensable elements. These are not merely technical issues; in the last analysis, states abide by agreements because they serve their interests and reflect accurately the balance of forces at a particular time. Openness and pluralism in the Nicaraguan political system would also strengthen a Contadora agreement by constructing an open environment which makes verification of security commitments much easier. Negotiations require a recognition of a common ground between the parties involved and an active desire on both sides for a resolution.

Finally, as I hope I have demonstrated, bipartisan cooperation is essential if our efforts to promote the peaceful resolution of regional conflicts are to bear fruit. We can scarcely serve as an effective broker in southern Africa if Congress imposes economic sanctions against Pretoria. More than 20 pieces of sanctions legislation have been introduced into the Congress during the current session. We oppose punitive disinvestment legislation, since we think this will impose economic hardship on the black majority we are seeking to help. It will exacerbate tensions, not promote racial harmony. Passage would jeopardize our effectiveness as a mediator in the region without promoting social and racial justice in South Africa.

Congressional votes on the Jackson plan and support for the democratic resistance in Nicaragua will affect our negotiating leverage in the Contadora process. Those who have negotiated with the Nicaraguans understand the consequences of removing pressure. If support for the resistance is rejected, Congress removes an inducement for Nicaragua to contemplate seriously a regional settlement.

We are already putting these lessons to use. I hope that you will find them useful as you watch our diplomatic moves over the next few months. You can be sure your government is pursuing every opportunity in the quest for peace. This is the American tradition in foreign policy. It is also our responsibility as a great power. But in our democracy, an active diplomatic role will require your support. Together we can do great things.

■■■■■ **5.5**

RUSSELL J. LENG

Misapplying Lessons from the Cuban Missile Crisis

Twenty years ago this month, America had its closest brush with nuclear war during the Cuban missile crisis. In the two decades since those 13 fearful days, it has become America's most popular model of how to manage a confrontation with the Soviets, and its "lessons" are especially popular with the Reagan administration.

For students of foreign policy generally, the dramatic neatness of the Cuban crisis makes it especially appealing: the sudden disclosure of the missiles, Kennedy's televised challenge to Khrushchev, and, above all, the textbook display of skillful coercive bargaining resulting in an American triumph. It has become the American foreign policy crisis par excellence.

For the Reagan administration, the Cuban missile crisis provides the case for maintaining strategic military superiority, for negotiating from strength. A more seductive "lesson" from the Cuban experience is the demonstration that if the United States only acts with sufficient resolve, the Soviets will submit to its will. It is time for us to seize the initiative, the President tells us. We should be willing to challenge the Soviets and then stick to our guns. "More nations have got themselves into trouble through retreat and appeasement than by sticking up for what they believe."

Paradoxically, the same people who readily accept such historical analogies, are likely to ignore systematic attempts to generalize from a large sample of cases. This is unfortunate, because a better understanding of the dynamics of inter-nation crisis behavior generally, as well as of Soviet-American bargaining over the three major crises since World War II (Berlin in 1948 and 1961, as well as Cuba), might help us avoid acting out the same drama with a tragically different outcome.

Quantitative analyses of the interactions of nation-states in crises occurring over the last century and a half, in fact, indicate a good deal of reciprocity in the bargaining of states relatively evenly matched in military capabilities. The three Soviet-American crises are no exception to this rule. Far from a pattern of one side bullying the other into submission, we find that threats, especially explicit threats of force—from either side—have most often been met in kind.

The most successful American bargaining tactics have been carrot-and-stick inducements combining promises of rewards with *deterrent* warnings

---

From the *Christian Science Monitor*, October 27, 1982. Reprinted by permission of the author.

stated with sufficient vagueness to allow the Soviets to avoid appearing to submit to American bullying. Even in the Cuban missile crisis, Kennedy's ultimatum to Khrushchev was tempered with a secret promise to remove US missiles in Turkey, as well as the promise to refrain from any future invasion of Cuba.

Despite these face-saving concessions, Cuba was an extremely costly defeat for the Soviets; they "blinked," as Dean Rusk put it. The metaphor may appeal to the John Wayne mentality of some in the Reagan administration, but the past performance records of nations finding themselves in successive crises offers a stern warning. Our findings indicate that when evenly matched nations find themselves in two or more successive crises, the *loser* of the previous crisis invariably bargains more aggressively in the next encounter. Since the winner is likely to attempt to repeat its successful exercise in coercive bargaining, it is not surprising that the likelihood of war increases with each successive encounter.

It is not hard to guess why the loser of the one crisis adopts a more belligerent stance in the next one. Among evenly matched powers, submitting to threats or ultimatums, especially in public view, exacts an unacceptable cost to the government's reputation for resolve. Kennedy realized this when he warned his associates against gloating over the outcome of the Cuban crisis, noting that "every setback has the seeds of its own reprisal, if the country is powerful enough." Thanks largely to the "lesson" of being outgunned in the Cuban crisis, the Soviets are now powerful enough.

The success of an exclusively coercive bargaining strategy is dependent on a symmetry in the resolve of the opposing sides. In a replay of the Cuban crisis, what is the likelihood of the opposite Soviet response and escalation to nuclear war? What if *both* sides adopt the approach suggested by Reagan? The situation could be tragically reminiscent of Russian-Austrian relations at the beginning of the century. Having suffered two embarrassing political defeats at the hands of the Austrians in the Balkans in 1908 and 1913, the Russians adopted a "never again" attitude that included an intensive program to achieve military parity and a determination to seize the initiative and force an Austrian retreat in the next crisis. The next crisis with Austria was in the summer of 1914 and it led to the Russian mobilization that preceded World War I.

President Reagan has warned that, because of their defeat in Cuba, the Soviets embarked on an arms buildup that has eliminated America's military advantage. Yet the President's belligerent rhetoric encourages another confrontation with the Soviets. If it comes, we can only hope that he is aware of the other "lessons" that the Soviets are likely to have drawn from their embarrassment in the Cuban missile crisis.

Discussion Questions

For these questions you will need access to a newspaper that provides consistent coverage of foreign affairs. We recommend either the *Christian Science Monitor*, the *New York Times*, or the *Washington Post*.

1. Identify and read all of the articles on foreign affairs that appear in your chosen source over a two-week period. Select from the articles that report on interactions involving the United States, and classify these interactions according to the following scheme:

    a. Actor—the nation-state that initiates (is the primary agent of) the action in the story.

    b. Target—the nation at which the action is "aimed."

    c. Type of action—choose from the following the type of action involved in the story and explain your choice: (1) diplomacy, (2) bargaining, or (3) coercion.

    d. Type of issue—choose one of the following as the issue involved in the story and explain your choice: (1) military affairs or military security, (2) regional or international economic affairs, (3) internal economic affairs, (4) other (please specify).

2. Summarize your classifications in chart form and then respond in writing to the following questions:

    a. Who are the major actors on the globe?

    b. Which nation or group appears to be the most frequent target?

    c. What type of actions predominates in foreign affairs?

    d. Which actors employ diplomacy most often?

    e. Which actors employ bargaining most often?

    f. Which actors employ coercion most often?

3. Explain why those states that appear to be the most frequent targets of foreign policy coercion attract this type of action. What foreign policy goals of the coercing states are furthered by such actions?

4. Select one of the interactions you have listed in response to question 1 above that appears to involve conflict. What would you recommend to decision makers as an appropriate bargaining strategy for resolving the conflict? Why?

For Further Reading

Classic Studies

Burton, John W. *Conflict and Communication: Their Use in International Relations.* New York: Macmillan, 1969. Burton is an important theorist of the British peace research community who has written extensively on the theory and practice of managing disputes short of using force. This book contains an outline of the basic elements of his "controlled communications" approach.

Carr, E. H. *The Twenty Years' Crisis*. New York: Harper & Row, 1964. This superb diplomatic history recounts European diplomatic efforts between 1919 and 1939, while offering a number of general propositions about dealing with aggressor nations.

Gamson, W., and A. Modigliani. *Untangling the Cold War*. Boston: Little, Brown, 1971. A sophisticated analysis of the interactive patterns of the two superpowers in the post-1945 world.

Iklé, Fred C. *How Nations Negotiate*. New York: Harper & Row, 1964. A standard text for many years for those involved in international diplomacy. Its analysis of successful bargaining strategies was of special interest during the early 1980s when Iklé was undersecretary of defense for policy.

Osgood, Charles E. *An Alternative to War or Surrender*. Urbana, Ill.: University of Illinois Press, 1962. This widely read work contains an explanation of Osgood's communication theory and of his argument that reciprocal actions to reduce tension between adversaries can both maximize a nation's interests and avoid war.

Schelling, Thomas. *The Strategy of Conflict*. Cambridge, Mass.: Harvard University Press, 1970. Along with the author's influential work, *Arms and Influence*, this volume describes and analyzes the various forms of influence, bargaining, and coercion in international affairs.

Singer, J. David. "Inter-Nation Influence: A Formal Model," *American Political Science Review* (June 1963). An important article describing the various relational patterns that may arise between states as they seek to influence one another's foreign policy positions.

More Recent Titles

Axelrod, Robert. *The Evolution of Cooperation*. New York: Basic Books, 1985. A succinct analysis of how persons and groups can engage in joint problem-solving efforts that enhance the potential outcomes for all parties.

Blechman, Barry, and Stephen Kaplan. *Force Without War*. Washington, D.C.: Brookings Institution, 1978. The definitive study of the use of force by the United States in the post-1945 world. The authors describe and analyze 215 incidents involving the use of force by the United States on behalf of its interests around the globe.

Center for the Study of Foreign Policy. *International Negotiation: Art and Science*. Washington, D.C.: Center for the Study of Foreign Policy, 1984. A useful collection of essays originally delivered at a major conference on negotiation convened by the U.S. State Department's Foreign Service Institute.

Craig, Gordon A., and Alexander L. George. *Force and Statecraft: Diplomatic Practices of Our Time*. New York: Oxford University Press, 1983. A relatively little-known but extremely useful volume that includes a description of the various techniques of persuasion and dialogue commonly used by foreign policy elites in the routine course of diplomacy.

Druckman, Daniel. *Negotiations: Social-Psychological Perspectives.* Beverly Hills, Calif.: Sage Publications, 1977. One of the first—and still the most helpful—analyses of the dynamics of international negotiation. It contains a long list of propositions about the conditions under which negotiation is most likely to be successful.

Fisher, Roger, with the assistance of William Ury. *International Mediation: A Guide for Practitioners.* New York: International Peace Academy, 1978. This is the intellectual predecessor to the popular and much less sophisticated *Getting to Yes.* In this volume, the authors pose a series of questions about processes, perceptions, and people and point out the major stumbling blocks to successful mediation and negotiation.

Kaplan, Stephen. *The Diplomacy of Power.* Washington, D.C.: Brookings Institution, 1981. A complement to the Blechman-Kaplan study, this book examines the use of coercion by the Soviet Union. Kaplan finds very low levels of Soviet intervention in the Third World but a much higher level of coercive diplomacy in areas bordering the Soviet Union.

Leng, Russell J. "When Will They Ever Learn? Coercive Bargaining in Recurrent Crises." *Journal of Conflict Resolution* (September 1983). The author investigates eighteen different disputes and finds an intriguing pattern. States use effective bargaining strategies if their prior crisis experiences involved a successful resolution, but they resort to coercive methods if the prior crisis was resolved unsuccessfully.

Zartman, I. William. *The 50% Solution.* New York: Anchor-Doubleday Books, 1980. A useful collection of essays on various diplomatic problems from interstate relations to bargaining with terrorists.

POWER IN INTERNATIONAL RELATIONS 6

Power has long been one of the central concepts in the study of international relations. It is, however, an elusive concept, one commonly employed in at least three different ways, each with its own distinct meaning. Power may be an attribute, a goal, or a relationship, and a clear understanding of how it is being used in the case at hand is essential.

One of the better known and more quotable definitions of politics is that offered by the political scientist Harold Lasswell. Lasswell defined politics as the means by which we decide "who gets what, when and how." In similar fashion, we can define *power* in its most general sense as the capability to do what, to whom, and under what conditions. As an attribute, power involves control over resources. As a goal, power relates to control over specific outcomes. Power as a relationship has to do with control over actors and events.

All three usages of the word *power* have been important to students and practitioners of international relations. Analysts and advisers since Machiavelli have recognized the importance of power as an attribute and have attempted to describe its components. Policy makers have often focused on power as a goal, viewing the maintenance and growth of national power and a willingness to use it in its many forms as the test of successful leadership. And citizens have long understood the central business of international politics to be the skillful and careful use of power (as a relationship) to advance national goals while preserving peace and order.

Among the most frequently asked questions about power—and the most difficult to answer—are the following:

1. What are the components of power?
2. What meaning does it have in international relations?
3. What is the relationship between power and other important aspects of international affairs?

To these we add two other questions of particular concern to us in this volume:

4. How does our theoretical understanding of power affect the way it is understood and employed by foreign policy decision makers?
5. How has the use of power by national leaders influenced our theoretical understanding of the concept?

Power as an Attribute

Scholarly efforts to define and measure power have produced everything from lengthy lists of national resources to equations that purport to yield a "power score" for each nation of the globe. A discussion of the "natural" components of power has been a common element in these analyses.

We can define the *natural components of power* as those attributes or endowments that a state possesses as a result of either the good fortune of nature or its social history. Such endowments include mineral resources, population—notably the size and characteristics thereof, and geographic advantages and disadvantages.

History has shown that larger states generally have greater resources and larger populations than smaller states and thus, in this sense at least, have been more powerful. This explains, in part, why national leaders have so often attempted to expand their state's territory. To gain control over additional resources is to increase national power.

Yet size alone is a potentially misleading indicator of power and has often been considered a mixed blessing. While large states can mobilize greater resources than their smaller neighbors, they also have a longer border to protect. Thus, size can present disadvantages even in an era of nuclear weaponry. Soviet analysts, for example, often express concern over their state's awkward security position, especially its 7,000-mile border, 3,500 miles of which adjoin their historical enemy, China.

Ironically, there are perhaps no clearer examples of the value of size—and its contribution to power—than the invasions of Russia by Napoleon in the nineteenth century and Hitler in the twentieth. In both cases, the sheer distance between Russia's European border and the Russian heartland, coupled with the severity of the Russian winter, proved decisive, contributing to the defeat of the invading forces and thus to national survival.

But there is often little a state can do to alter the power potential of its geographic resources. Most states that have relied heavily on geography have benefited from passive neighbors or quirks of physical geography. The political histories of the United States and Switzerland serve as classic examples of the defensive benefits (and power) of oceans and mountains. So, too, the historical rivalry of Argentina and Chile has been buffered by their 2,000-mile shared border astride the southern portion of the Andes Mountains.

Conversely, some "accidents" of geography have a negative impact on national power, contributing to weakness or difficulty in avoiding war. Had their national boundaries been drawn differently or had the most important veins of European ore deposits not been concentrated near their borders, Germany and France would not have been the two most war-prone states in the international system from 1870 to 1945. Similarly, if Poland or the Benelux states were as mountainous as Peru, their efforts to observe neutrality during two hundred years of European wars might have proven far more successful.

For all these reasons, then, efforts to analyze the contributions to national power of a state's geography must take into account not only the size of its territory, but also the location of its borders and any physical features that affect its ability to defend itself.

According to many analysts, geography waned in importance in the years after World War II. The experience of total war and the development of long-range strategic weapons systems seemed to render insignificant such national attributes as the length of coastlines or relationships with neighboring countries. But with the development of shorter range missile systems, a series of crises over resources such as food and oil, and a new era of East-West tension in the early 1980s, geography once again became a central focus of discussions of national power. Such renewed attention may be deserved. But, as will be noted later in this essay, too single-minded a focus on any one attribute of power could lead to an underemphasis on other attributes, with serious consequences for policy and policy makers.

A state's natural resources are another of the natural components of its power. The term *natural resources* often makes us think of raw materials, such as iron ore, mineral deposits, and petroleum. In the mercantile era of the sixteenth and seventeenth centuries, European explorers journeyed to the "new worlds" of the Americas, Africa, and Asia in search of precious metals. The major European powers fought a series of devastating wars during the eighteenth and nineteenth centuries, as each sought to enlarge or defend its colonial possessions and control access to vital natural resources in Europe itself. Japan's need for access to the raw materials of Southeast Asia was a major factor leading to the outbreak of World War II in the Pacific.

But mineral deposits are not the only raw materials of power. The fishing areas off the coasts of Peru and Iceland are so important to the economic vitality of both nations that both have been involved in confrontations with larger and more powerful states in efforts to protect their claims. The Peruvian navy forced some U.S. fishing vessels away from areas claimed by Peru in the late 1960s and early 1970s; Iceland engaged Great Britain in the more bloody "war of the fishes" at about the same time.

The size and social characteristics of a *population* is another natural component of national power. In earlier times, numbers were all-important. A large populace meant a large armed force and thus a militarily powerful state. But the development of advanced modern weapons and need for technical training to use them give a military advantage to nations with a highly educated rather than merely a large population. Too large a population can, in fact, be a handicap. In some Third World countries, too rapid a rate of population growth has placed excessive demands on a developing economy, eroding rather than promoting economic progress and national power.

The last natural component of a state's power is its *economic attributes*. These include its level of industrial development, technology, and agriculture. Each is critical not only to the modern state's economic power but also to its military strength. National leaders continually seek to enhance their country's economic power through diplomacy, commercial agreements, and through policies and programs designed to develop domestic natural resources.

Power as a Goal

Power as an attribute refers to a nation's resources. When we speak of power as an attribute, we are speaking of power as a means. But *power may also be a goal*, a central objective of a state's foreign policy. The pursuit of power causes leaders to adopt particular foreign policy stances designed to enhance national prestige or military power. Ordinarily, that pursuit will entail a willingness or resolve to employ the nation's resources (power as an attribute) in an effort to bring about some desired objective (power as a goal).

Japan's postwar experience is a useful illustration of the pursuit of power as a goal by national policy makers. Some forty years after its devastation in World War II, Japan has become an economic giant—despite greater population pressures and a larger disparity between its natural resources and its industrial needs than it faced during the 1930s. How? Largely, the answer lies in the decision of postwar Japanese leaders to develop the nation's technological expertise and to foster a work environment that would make efficient use of a highly trained work force. By using its human resources efficiently, Japan has been able to finance the purchase of essential imports—particularly oil and agricultural products—with money earned from massive exports of automobiles, electronic consumer goods, and high-technology machinery.

Political leaders often subscribe to what may initially appear to be a confusing set of propositions about power as a goal. The first is the belief that the more power (especially military and economic) a state possesses, the less it needs to employ that power to influence events. Those who carry big sticks are less likely to have to wield them. Yet leaders also seem to believe that they must repeatedly demonstrate their willingness to employ their power. Failure to do so, it is commonly argued, will undermine national "credibility."

The 1986 diplomatic and military hostilities between the United States and Libya over access to the Gulf of Sidra is a useful illustration of this type of thinking. On the one hand, the United States was unable to prevent Libya from claiming the gulf as an extension of its territorial waters. On the other hand, superior U.S. military power meant that Libya would be equally unable to prevent the United States from entering the gulf at will. U.S. power effectively guaranteed that the American claim would prevail, thus making military conflict pointless and unnecessary.

But when Libya responded by firing missiles at American vessels in the contested area, the forceful U.S. reaction involved the use of air and naval forces. While some might have claimed that the United States had been "forced" into making use of its superior power, the intensity of the U.S. response far exceeded that necessary for mere self-defense. The explanation was that, in the minds of U.S. policy makers, the Libyan actions jeopardized U.S. credibility. Shortly after the incident, Secretary of State George P. Shultz noted that one important outcome of the U.S. actions was that they demonstrated to others—notably Spain and other European nations—that the United States was prepared to defend as necessary its right of access to the Strait of Gibraltar (the gateway between the Atlantic Ocean and the Mediterranean Sea) and surrounding areas.

This seemingly ironic juxtaposition of beliefs is indicative of the psychological aspects of power. In the world of global politics, nations seek power (as a goal) by actions designed to persuade other nations that they already possess its attributes—economic strength and military might—and the will to use them.

Power as a Relationship

Power may be either an attribute or a goal. It may also be a relationship. When viewing power as a relationship, we should keep in mind three generalizations. The first is that, however extensive and prudently employed, *power is always relative in nature rather than absolute*, and it is very much affected by changing circumstances.

Consider, for example, the post-1945 rivalry between the United States and the Soviet Union. It is the two nations' vast superiority relative to all other nations that has given them their status as "superpowers." Yet, despite their military superiority vis-à-vis the rest of the world, the two nations have been locked in an arms race throughout much of the postwar period.

Why? The answer lies in the relative nature of power. The central issue is not so much "How much power do we have at our disposal?" as "How much power do we have compared to our rival?" In assessing nation A's power, the question to be asked is "What resources does nation A have at its disposal in relation to nation B, and how can it employ these resources to control nation B?"

At the same time, it should be emphasized that the possession of greater military power than one's rival is not, in itself, sufficient to ensure success. To be sure, superior military power is seldom a disadvantage. Research has shown that in conflicts between two states the militarily superior one emerges victorious about 80 percent of the time. Yet in the remaining cases, the "less powerful" nation wins, often because of the weaker power's greater willingness to absorb losses—a willingness motivated by belief in a cause. Even the largest and most powerful states have at various times been defeated on the battlefield by smaller and less powerful but highly motivated opponents. For examples, we need look no further than the bitter U.S. experience in Vietnam and the more recent Soviet intervention in Afghanistan.

The second generalization we could make—and one of the distinctive features of the contemporary international system—is that under some circumstances, *economic power may be superior to military power*. Economic power enabled the members of the Organization of Petroleum Exporting

Countries (OPEC) to bring the powerful but oil-dependent Western states to their industrial knees during the mid-seventies. The OPEC cartel's ability to control the price of the oil so vital to the West outweighed the West's far greater military power. Yet economic power, like military power, is relative and inherently fragile. We have seen this fragility during the 1980s as OPEC has been unable to retain its control of oil prices in the face of increased production by non-OPEC suppliers and worldwide energy conservation efforts.

To these two generalizations about power must be added a third. *The amount of power that can be brought to bear on a particular situation will vary.* Simply stated, the most powerful of nations will at times be unable to make use of all of its resources. Power, unlike money, is not a universally accepted or uniform commodity. Some of its components—a literate population, nuclear superiority—are irrelevant to some situations. The result is the "paradox of power" in which very powerful nations will sometimes find themselves unable to employ their power to advantage. For example, in the mid-1980s the United States, despite its great power, could not effect the release of American hostages held in Lebanon.

The fact that power is relative means that it is always subject to erosion as the result of external developments. As the article by Robert O. Keohane and Joseph S. Nye in the readings section of this chapter informs us, analysts talk about the vulnerability and sensitivity of power. *Sensitivity* refers to the magnitude of the impact of particular, unfavorable, and external developments on a nation's power. In evaluating nation A's sensitivity to certain actions by nation B, we ask how quickly the actions would have an adverse effect on nation A and what form those effects would take.

Vulnerability refers to situations in which the affected nation lacks the ability to counteract the effects of the external action. OPEC's success in the mid-1970s owed much to the inability, at least in the short run, of the major oil-consuming nations—the United States, Japan, and the countries of Western Europe—to respond effectively to a reduction in OPEC exports. Over the longer run, the West was able to greatly reduce its dependence on OPEC oil by implementing energy conservation programs, developing domestic oil supplies, increasing use of alternate forms of energy, and purchasing oil from non-OPEC sources. Nonetheless, this episode demonstrated the West's sensitivity and vulnerability to external actions that threatened its energy supplies.

The Readings

The use and meaning of power in the modern world of international affairs is a consistent theme of the readings in this chapter.

We begin with a selection by Jeffrey Hart in which he defines and then distinguishes among three critical views of the meaning and use of power. Hart makes a strong case for an approach that focuses on power as control over events and outcomes.

Our next selection, by Keohane and Nye, is one of the more influential recent additions to the literature on power. Keohane and Nye examine the special character of power in an interdependent world. They explore the importance of sensitivity and vulnerability and demonstrate that we need to think in terms other than military power if we wish to understand how states may be compelled to act against their own interests and in the interests of others.

The selection by Ulf Lindell and Stefan Persson examines the interesting problem of how to measure the power of "weak states." In discussing what they call the "paradox of weak state power," they note that systemic conditions, internal structures and dynamics, state policies, and even historical accidents can provide weak states with greater leverage than an objective calculation of their power might suggest. It is for such reasons, they point out, that weak states sometimes prevail in conflicts with larger and more powerful opponents or under what they describe as "asymmetric power conditions." Lindell and Persson's conclusion reminds us, however, that, in interactions between smaller nations and great powers, great powers are more likely to prevail.

The readings conclude with two policy excerpts, one by U.S. secretary of state George P. Shultz and the other by political scientist Robert Johansen. Shultz examines the conceptual and practical aspects of the use of power, emphasizing the concerns that preoccupy the United States as it seeks to employ its power wisely and effectively in pursuit of its foreign policy objectives. The careful reader will note the similarities of tone and substance in the Shultz and Hart pieces.

The Johansen article offers a contrasting perspective on power and its uses. Johansen notes that traditional approaches to the use of power fail to address the most pressing issues of our time, particularly the enhancement of global living conditions and a reduction in the potential for war and violence. Johansen suggests, therefore, that we need to develop a new perspective on power and its uses—the "human interest" perspective.

Jeffrey Hart

6.1 ▰▰▰

JEFFREY HART

Three Approaches to the Measurement
of Power in International Relations

There are three main approaches to the observation and measurement of
power: 1) control over resources, 2) control over actors, and 3) control over
events and outcomes. The control over events and outcomes approach emerges
as the best approach to the measurement of power in contemporary
international politics because: 1) it is the only approach which takes into
account the possibility of interdependence and collective action, 2) it is more
general than the other two approaches, and 3) it produces a type of analysis
which has both descriptive and normative advantages. I will discuss each of
these approaches at length and criticize them. I will argue that the third
approach is superior to the other two for the measurement of power in
contemporary international politics because it is better suited to situations in
which interdependence and collective action exist. It is also the most general
of the three approaches.

Power as Control over Resources

The control over resources approach is the most widely used and accepted
approach to the study of national power. Military expenditures, the size of
armed forces, gross national product, and population are frequently used as
indicators of national power in empirical studies. [Rudolph J.] Rummel and
others have shown that, across the set of all nations, these indicators tend to
rank states in a consistent manner. Even though there is a tendency toward
consistency, some scholars have suggested that the presence or absence of
inconsistency can be used to explain the behavior of nations. For example,
[Johan] Galtung and Rummel predict that nations which score high on some indicators but low on others will tend to behave in a hostile manner toward other
nations. In any case, the control over resources approach rests on assumptions
about how control over resources can be converted into control over actors or
events. . . .

The main difficulties with this approach are: 1) it is not always certain that
actors will be able to use resources which are nominally under their control; 2)
it is not always clear what types of resources should be included in a general

measure of power, and one suspects that for different types of conflicts different combinations of resources will be needed to explain the outcomes of conflicts; 3) some types of resources, such as the will to use force, are extremely difficult to measure; 4) the focus on national power precludes the consideration of the role of non-state actors in determining the outcome of conflicts; and 5) it is not clear how one is to deal with interdependence, coalitions, and collective action. To amplify this last point, suppose that one wishes to assess the power of a bloc or alliance of nations. Is the power of the bloc or the alliance equal to the sum of the national power scores of its members? Some theorists suggest that this is so, but others assert that nations, by joining alliances, lose their flexibility in dealing with others and thereby lose control. Thus, they argue that the power of an alliance is less than the sum of its members' power. Nevertheless, despite these objections, the control over resources approach is needed for a number of theoretical purposes, some of which will be mentioned in the concluding section of this article.

Power as Control over Actors

The control over actors approach is perhaps the most familiar one to political scientists in general, if not to students of international politics. Robert Dahl's definition of power as the ability of A to get B to do something which he would otherwise not do is a control over actors definition, and has not been greatly improved upon since its appearance in 1957.

One possible objection to Dahl's definition is that if A does not want B to do that "something," then his ability to get B to do it is not terribly useful, except insofar as the nonexercise of this power produces the desired results. Some people distinguish positive from negative power, where negative power is the ability to get someone to do the opposite of what you want. But I prefer to deal only with positive power, since the nonexercise of negative power can be interpreted as a form of positive power.

Another possible objection is that A may be able to get B to do a certain thing but not others. But in his original formulation, Dahl noted that power may be more or less limited in "scope." That is, power may be limited to a specific type of activity or domain of action. It is possible, therefore, for A to have power over B in one domain but not in another.

It also may be somewhat misleading to define power in a way which suggests a deterministic relationship between A's acts and B's behavior. A's acts may merely limit the range of alternative actions for B. The compromise position between these two extremes, the one chosen by Dahl in his original article, is that A's action affects the probability of B's action. This probability may be interpreted as the effect of A's actions on B's over a series of attempts to exercise power or as the effect of A's action on B's "mixed strategy" on one particular attempt which is not repeated. In either case, the probabilistic approach is compatible with the idea of limiting alternatives.

Power can be coercive or noncoercive. A can get B to do something which he would not have done by using threat or persuasion. The persuasive type of power is sometimes called "influence," to distinguish it from coercive power. Klaus Knorr calls noncoercive power "nonpower influence" to distinguish it from both power, which in his formulation must be based on coercion, *and* influence, which can be used to refer to either coercion or persuasion. He also argues, quite convincingly, that "nonpower influence" has been a neglected concept in the study of international politics. There is, of course, no consensus on the use of these terms. Therefore, I will assume that noncoercive power is a form of power since noncoercive power is consistent with Dahl's original definition.

There are clear and important examples of noncoercive power in international politics. Most of the power exercised in the recent conferences on population, food, and the law of the sea was noncoercive. Noncoercive power is exercised when for example, A supplies new information to B or A persuades B that their interests and goals are compatible. In this case, it may be questioned whether we can consider the change in B's behavior to be evidence of a power relationship. [Peter] Bachrach and [Morton] Baratz argue that there must be a conflict of interests in a power relationship. But a more satisfactory precondition, in my opinion, is that there be a perceived conflict of interests *prior to*, but not necessarily after, the exercise of power.

Finally, one may want to distinguish between intentional and unintentional power. That is, a change in B's behavior may result from his *anticipation* of a change in A's behavior, despite the fact that A had no intention of changing his behavior or producing the change in B's behavior. A may be pleased or displeased about the change, but it is clear that he did not intend to produce the change. This is a phenomenon which Knorr calls "silent power." An example of silent power in international politics is the eagerness of Burma to avoid any act which might seem offensive to the People's Republic of China. If there is a great deal of "silent power" in a particular relationship, it may be difficult to observe and measure power in general since silent power operates without any visible attempts to exercise power. Yet this is not the only disadvantage of the control over actors approach.

It is possible for the weaker actor, even in a highly asymmetrical power relationship, to exploit its weakness to gain power over the stronger actor. For example, the South Vietnamese regime could affect the bargaining position of the United States during the Indochina war by putting itself in danger. Similar techniques were used by the Nationalist Chinese in the battle over Quemoy and Matsu. The reason for the mutuality of power, even in asymmetric relationships, is that power is defined in terms of desired outcomes *for the more powerful actor*. If A has more power over B than vice versa, then B can still threaten noncompliance (at high cost, perhaps) in order to change A's behavior. B will succeed to the extent that the threat of noncompliance is credible and the compliance outcome is important to A.

This leads, as [John] Harsanyi first demonstrated, to the game theoretic notion of power as a function of the outcome of bargaining between two actors. The outcome of bargaining, in turn, depends on the expected utilities which the two actors assign to compliance and noncompliance outcomes as well as their relative abilities to escalate threats or offer inducements. If the actors are self-interested utility maximizers, and if both can escalate threats in a way which places the mutual noncompliance outcome on a line connecting the "no agreement" point with the Nash solution point (the point which maximizes the product of utilities) in utility space, then the result of bargaining will be the Nash solution. Thus, deviations from the Nash point can be used to indicate the degree of asymmetry in threat or inducement capabilities. Unfortunately, this approach requires a priori information about utilities, information which is only rarely available.

What game theory tells us is that power, seen as control over actors, is a rather complicated matter, involving both objective and subjective factors. Given the highly psychological nature of power relationships, is it ever possible to use available information to measure power?

A crude, but nevertheless serviceable, method is to set aside negative, noncoercive, unintentional, and silent power and to observe systematically actual attempts to exercise power (i.e. positive, coercive, and intentional power) and the results of these attempts. Strangely enough, this sort of investigation has been extremely rare in the study of international politics. Perhaps the best explored territory is the use of economic sanctions to pursue political goals.

Before I review this research, I would like to show how the use of economic sanctions fits into the more general framework of power as control over actors. Suppose nations A and B are engaged in a variety of economic exchanges—e.g. trade, investment, and aid. The ability of A to get B to do something which B does not want to do, using these exchanges as the basis for threats and inducements, depends on a variety of factors: 1) the relative value of these activities for A and B, 2) the availability of other types of exchanges and other possible partners, and 3) the availability of domestic substitutes for the exchange.

Let us focus on trade for the moment. Suppose that A trades with a large number of nations but receives only a small proportion of its imports from (and sends only a small proportion of its exports to) any particular nation (including B) while B's trade is highly concentrated in a few trading partners (including A). Suppose also that A imports and exports a wide variety of commodities while B tends to import manufactured or technological goods while exporting a limited variety of goods, most of which are unprocessed. Finally, suppose that A's trade makes up only a small proportion of its national product while B's trade makes up a large proportion of its product. Then doesn't it seem likely that A can get its way with B if it chooses to threaten the disruption of trade?

This is the assumption made by a number of "dependency" theorists, but there are several reasons why it might not be true: 1) B may have alternative trading partners which can absorb a high proportion of its exports and which can supply goods normally imported from A; 2) B can find substitutes for the goods imported from A at reasonable prices; and 3) B may be willing to absorb the losses caused by the disruption of trade as the cost of avoiding compliance with A's demands. Even when conditions are ideal for the exercise of economic power, therefore, the sanctioned nation may still refuse to comply with the demands of the sanctioners. Indeed, it may be considered more ignominious to bow to economic sanctions than to military force. Also, it appears that the use of sanctions often fails to produce the desired results because the imposition of sanctions increases the domestic support of the sanctioned government. There is also the possibility that the ill effects of sanctions can be shifted onto some innocent or powerless sector of society. Thus, the unequal internal impact of sanctions, increased domestic support, and national pride can enhance the willingness of governments to absorb losses.

Studies of actual attempts to exercise economic power show, almost universally, that such attempts are rare historically and rarely succeed. For example, Klaus Knorr concluded his study of the question by noting that:

> Coercively wielding economic power by means of trade reprisals or special trade advantages is rarely successful, because even states of great economic strength do not command a compelling degree of monopolist or monopsonist control in their foreign trade, and because the punishment that can be imposed by these means does not inflict enough pain, on the one hand, and tends to arouse the will to resist, on the other.

There are other methods of exercising economic power: e.g., 1) the raising of prices; 2) the use of import or export restrictions; 3) the curtailing of credit and/or the freezing of assets; 4) the dumping of currencies; 5) the reduction of foreign aid or investment; and 6) nationalization of foreign enterprises. Each of these methods has different effects on the nations involved, and the effects are not always anticipated. But the fact that they are used means that it is possible to observe attempts to exercise economic power. Whether attempts are successful depends on the initial goals of the actors and the outcomes. The direct observation of these phenomena should be an improvement over the use of measures of potential bilateral power (sometimes called "dependency") such as the ratio of bilateral trade to GNP, the ratio of bilateral trade to total trade, or measures of the commodity composition of trade. These indicators of "dependency" may be useful in defining the constraints to economic power and may help to explain variation in other variables, but they are no substitute for more direct measures of power.

I conclude, therefore, that it is possible to observe attempts to exercise economic power and to assess the success of these attempts if the initial goals of the actors can be discovered, and if negative, noncoercive, unintentional, and silent power are assumed to be relatively unimportant. A similar argument could be made for the exercise of noneconomic power. It may be feasible, then, to test the "conversion" theories advanced by those who favor the control over resources approach. That is, it may then be possible to test the hypothesis that nations with greater control over resources are able to exercise control over other actors more successfully than actors with less control over resources. If noneconomic power is like economic power, the hypothesis will be disconfirmed.

Besides the measurement problems discussed above, there are a number of other possible disadvantages to using the control over actors approach. Although it may be possible to include non-state actors in observations of attempts to exercise power, it is not a simple matter to determine the degree to which subnational, transnational, or supranational actors are independent of the national governments with which they are associated. When the European Community acts on an issue of interest to only one of its members is it acting as an independent agent or as an agent of the government in question? When a multinational corporation acts in cooperation with one government against another, does it act as a free agent or as the agent of the cooperating government? Also, it is not clear how one is to deal with collective action and coalitions, in general. The emphasis on bilateral power in the control over actors approach means that one must either disaggregate collective action into its bilateral components, or else treat coalitions (sets of actors) as if they were more or less the same as governmental actors. Disaggregation is difficult in situations in which collective action is possible but bilateral action is not. This seems particularly unfortunate since international politics may be increasingly oriented toward collective actions of this sort in the future. Finally, since control over other actors may be limited in scope to a particular activity, and since bilateral power in one domain may be quite different from that in another, it is not obvious how one is to reconcile these differences in an overall assessment of bilateral power. Whereas in the control over resources approach, there is a problem of aggregation across resources, here there is a problem of aggregation across types of activities. Nevertheless, there are a number of reasons why this approach should not be discarded altogether, some of which I will discuss after describing the third major approach to the measurement of power.

Power as Control over Events and Outcomes

This approach was first developed by James S. Coleman and is best articulated in his book, *The Mathematics of Collective Action*. It is based on a rational choice theory of power, in which the reasons for controlling resources or other actors arise out of the desire to achieve certain *outcomes*. Outcomes are social states which are the results of individual or collective action and which are mutually exclusive. Desired outcomes, or *goals*, can be defined as outcomes which produce a net increase in the actor's utility, where utility is simply a function of the actor's preferences over the set of outcomes.

Instead of making a direct connection between actions and outcomes,

Coleman provides for intermediate links between actions and *events* and between events and outcomes. Each event is associated with at least one outcome for each actor, and each outcome is associated with a net impact on utility. Events associated with more than one outcome in a probabilistic fashion will be associated with an *expected* utility, equal to the sum of expected net impacts on utility of each outcome. The focus on events, rather than outcomes, frees the analyst from having to identify all the possible, mutually exclusive outcomes of every action, and allows him to focus on events, of which there will be a smaller number and which may be associated with sets of outcomes which are not mutually exclusive. Also events will be more salient to the actors themselves than outcomes since people do not normally think about the consequences of their actions in terms of mutually exclusive social states.

Clearly, if one actor has total control over all events, then that actor has no need to control other actors. He can simply present them as a fait accompli. Similarly, although one expects to use resources to gain control over events, there is no a priori reason to believe that the degree of control over events is directly proportional to the degree of control over resources. Therefore, unless the actors regard control over other actors or resources as valuable in themselves, then the ability to control actors and resources will be considered secondary to the ability to control events.

If an actor does not have total control over all events, but only those events which are *consequential* to him, i.e. which produce net gains or losses in utility, then that actor also has no need to control other actors. But normally actors have only partial control over events which are consequential to them. Also, some events are likely to be consequential for more than one actor. Therefore, in general, *actors tend to share control over events which are mutually consequential.* A few examples of this shared control in international politics may be useful here. The United States and the Soviet Union have, individually, only partial control over the likelihood of a nuclear exchange. There is no foreseeable way in which either can obtain total control over this event (despite elaborate attempts to develop first-strike capabilities on both sides). Yet a nuclear exchange would have drastic consequences for both nations. Similarly, the industrialized nations have only partial control over the recovery of the world economy in a global recession, yet such recessions are consequential for all.

It is possible for actors to have control over events which are consequential for others, but not for themselves. For example, the United States excluded Venezuela and Ecuador from the recent Trade Act because of their membership in OPEC. This would have excluded the two countries from the benefits of preferential tariffs, while the consequences for the United States in terms of increased tariff revenues or future participation of the two countries in OPEC would not have been substantial. But this sort of situation may be rare, and it is interesting to note that the United States changed its policy after other Latin American governments came to the defense of Venezuela and Ecuador.

Thus, the most common form of control over events in contemporary international politics may be shared control over mutually consequential events—a condition which some scholars might call "interdependence." Since neither the control over actors nor the control over resources approaches are capable of dealing with interdependence, it would be extremely useful to have an approach which is. This is one of the major advantages of the control over events and outcomes approach. . . .

In sum, the control over events and outcomes approach, as exemplified by Coleman's theory, is extremely useful for measuring power in the context of interdependence and collective action. It allows one to derive insights about bilateral power and control over resources from estimates of control over and interest in events. Although there will be measurement problems connected with the application of this approach, data requirements are not as great as they are for conventional control over actors approaches, and analysis is richer, both descriptively and normatively, than that which is possible with the control over resources approach. Finally, its theoretical base, power derived from control over events and outcomes, is more general than the other two approaches.

Conclusions

Three approaches to the observation and measurement of power have been described and compared here: 1) control over resources; 2) control over actors; and 3) control over events and outcomes. The control over events and outcomes approach emerges as the best approach for the measurement of power in contemporary international politics, because: 1) it is the only approach which takes into account the possibility of interdependence among actors and of collective action; 2) it is more general than the other approaches; and 3) it produces a type of analysis which has both descriptive and normative advantages over the types of analysis which are associated with the other approaches. . . .

6.2 ■■■■■■

ROBERT O. KEOHANE
JOSEPH S. NYE

Power and Interdependence

Power has always been an elusive concept for statesmen and analysts of international politics; now it is even more slippery. The traditional view was that military power dominated other forms, and that states with the most military power controlled world affairs. But the resources that produce power capabilities have become more complex. In the eyes of one astute observer, "the postwar era has witnessed radical transformation in the elements, the uses, and the achievements of power." And Hans Morgenthau, author of the leading realist text on international politics, went so far in his reaction to the events of the early 1970s as to announce an historically unprecedented severing of the functional relationship between political, military, and economic power shown in the possession by militarily weak countries of "monopolistic or quasi-monopolistic control of raw materials essential to the operation of advanced economies."

Power can be thought of as the ability of an actor to get others to do something they otherwise would not do (and at an acceptable cost to the actor). Power can also be conceived in terms of control over outcomes. In either case, measurement is not simple. We can look at the initial power resources that give an actor a potential liability; or we can look at that actor's actual influence over patterns of outcomes. When we say that asymmetrical interdependence can be a source of power we are thinking of power as control over resources, or the *potential* to affect outcomes. A less dependent actor in a relationship often has a significant political resource, because changes in the relationship (which the actor may be able to initiate or threaten) will be less costly to that actor than to its partners. This advantage does not guarantee, however, that the political resources provided by favorable asymmetries in interdependence will lead to similar patterns of control over outcomes. There is rarely a one-to-one relationship between power measured by any type of resources and power measured by effects on outcomes. Political bargaining is the usual means of translating potential into effects, and a lot is often lost in the translation.

To understand the role of power in interdependence, we must distinguish between two dimensions, *sensitivity* and *vulnerability*. Sensitivity involves degrees of responsiveness within a policy framework—how quickly do changes in one country bring costly changes in another, and how great are the costly effects? It is measured not merely by the volume of flows across borders but also by the costly effects of changes in transactions on the societies or governments. Sensitivity interdependence is created by interactions within a framework of policies. Sensitivity assumes that the framework remains unchanged. The fact that a set of policies remains constant may reflect the difficulty in formulating new policies within a short time, or it may reflect a commitment to a certain pattern of domestic and international rules.

An example of sensitivity dependence is the way the United States, Japan, and Western Europe were affected by increased oil prices in 1971 and again in 1973-74 and 1975. In the absence of new policies, which could take many years or decades to implement, the sensitivity of these economies was a function of the greater costs of foreign oil and the proportion of petroleum they imported. The United States was less sensitive than Japan to petroleum price rises, because a smaller proportion of its petroleum requirements was accounted for by imports, but as rapid price increases and long lines at gasoline stations showed, the United States was indeed sensitive to the outside change. Another example of sensitivity interdependence is provided by the international monetary situation prior to August 15, 1971. Given the constraints on policy created by the rules of the International Monetary Fund (IMF), European governments were sensitive to changes in American monetary policy, and the United States was sensitive to European decisions whether or not to demand the conversion of dollars into gold.

Sensitivity interdependence can be social or political as well as economic. For example, there are social "contagion effects," such as the trivial but rapid spread of the fad of "streaking" from American to European society in 1974, or, more significant, the way in which the development of radical student movements during the late 1960s was reinforced by knowledge of each other's activities. The rapid growth of transnational communications has enhanced such sensitivity. Television, by vividly presenting starvation in South Asia to Europeans and Americans about to sit down to their dinners, is almost certain to increase attention to and concern about the issue in European and American societies. Sensitivity to such an issue may be reflected in demonstrations or other political action, even if no action is taken to alleviate the distress (and no economic sensitivity thereby results).

Using the word *interdependence*, however, to refer only to sensitivity obscures some of the most important political aspects of mutual dependence. We must also consider what the situation would be if the framework of policies could be changed. If more alternatives were available, and new and very different policies were possible, what would be the costs of adjusting to the outside change? In petroleum, for instance, what matters is not only the proportion of one's needs that is imported, but the alternatives to imported energy and the costs of pursuing those alternatives. Two countries, each importing 35 percent of their petroleum needs, may seem equally sensitive to price rises; but if one could shift to domestic sources at moderate cost, and the other had no such alternative, the second state would be more *vulnerable* than the first. The vulnerability dimension of interdependence rests on the relative availability and costliness of the alternatives that various actors face.

Under the Bretton Woods monetary regime during the late 1960s, both the United States and Great Britain were sensitive to decisions by foreign speculators or central banks to shift assets out of dollars or sterling, respectively. But the United States was less vulnerable than Britain because it had the option (which it exercised in August 1971) of changing the rules of the system at what it considered tolerable costs. The underlying capabilities of the United States reduced its vulnerability, and therefore made its sensitivity less serious politically.

In terms of the costs of dependence, sensitivity means liability to costly effects imposed from outside before policies are altered to try to change the situation. Vulnerability can be defined as an actor's liability to suffer costs imposed by external events even after policies have been altered. Since it is usually difficult to change policies quickly, immediate effects of external changes generally reflect sensitivity dependence. Vulnerability dependence can be measured only by the costliness of making effective adjustments to a changed environment over a period of time. . . .

Vulnerability is particularly important for understanding the political structure of interdependence relationships. In a sense, it focuses on which actors are "the definers of the *ceteris paribus* clause," or can set the rules of the game. Vulnerability is clearly more relevant than sensitivity, for example, in analyzing the politics of raw materials such as the supposed transformation of power after 1973. All too often, a high percentage of imports of a material is taken as an index of vulnerability, when by itself it merely suggests that sensitivity may be high. The key question for determining vulnerability is how effectively altered policies could bring into being sufficient quantities of this, or a comparable, raw material, and at what cost. The fact that the United States imports approximately 85 percent of its bauxite supply does not indicate American vulnerability to actions by bauxite exporters, until we know what it would cost (in time as well as money) to obtain substitutes.

Vulnerability applies to sociopolitical as well as politico-economic relationships. The vulnerability of societies to transnational radical movements in the late 1960s depended on their abilities to adjust national policies to deal with the change and reduce the costs of disruption. When Sweden criticized American policy in Vietnam, its vulnerability to a possible American suspension of cultural contacts would have depended on how it could adjust policy to the new situation. Could exchange professors and tourists be attracted from elsewhere?

Let us look again at the effects on the United States of a famine in South

Asia. The vulnerability of an American administration to domestic protests over its lack of a food aid policy would depend on the ease with which it could adjust policy (for instance, by shipping more grain to India) without incurring other high political or economic costs.

How does this distinction help us understand the relationship between interdependence and power? Clearly, it indicates that sensitivity interdependence will be less important than vulnerability interdependence in providing power resources to actors. If one actor can reduce its costs by altering its policy, either domestically or internationally, the sensitivity patterns will not be a good guide to power resources.

Consider trade in agricultural products between the United States and the Soviet Union from 1972 to 1975. Initially, the American economy was highly sensitive to Soviet grain purchases: prices of grain rose dramatically in the United States. The Soviet Union was also sensitive to the availability of surplus American stocks, since its absence could have internal political as well as economic implications. The vulnerability asymmetries, however, ran strongly in favor of the United States, since its alternatives to selling grain to the USSR (such as government storage, lower domestic prices, and more food aid abroad) were more attractive than the basic Soviet alternative to buying grain from the United States (slaughtering livestock and reducing meat consumption). Thus, as long as the United States government could retain coherent control of the policy—that is, as long as interest groups with a stake in expanded trade did not control it—agricultural trade could be used as a tool in political bargaining with the Soviet Union.

Vulnerability interdependence includes the strategic dimension that sensitivity interdependence omits, but this does not mean that sensitivity is politically unimportant. Rapidly rising sensitivity often leads to complaints about interdependence and political efforts to alter it, particularly in countries with pluralistic political systems. Textile and steel workers and manufacturers, oil consumers, and conservatives suspicious of radical movements originating abroad are all likely to demand government policies to protect their interests. Policymakers and policy analysts, however, must examine underlying patterns of vulnerability interdependence when they decide on strategies. What can they do, at what cost? And what can other actors do, at what cost, in response? Although patterns of sensitivity interdependence may explain where the shoe pinches or the wheel squeaks, coherent policy must be based on an analysis of actual and potential vulnerabilities. An attempt to manipulate asymmetrical sensitivity interdependence without regard for underlying patterns of vulnerability is likely to fail.

Manipulating economic or sociopolitical vulnerabilities, however, also bears risks. Strategies of manipulating interdependence are likely to lead to counterstrategies. It must always be kept in mind, furthermore, that military power dominates economic power in the sense that economic means alone are likely to be ineffective against the serious use of military force. Thus, even effective manipulation of asymmetrical interdependence within a nonmilitary area can create risks of military counteraction. When the United States exploited Japanese vulnerability to economic embargo in 1940-41, Japan countered by attacking Pearl Harbor and the Philippines. Yet military actions are usually very costly; and for many types of actions, these costs have risen steeply during the last thirty years. . . .

We conclude that a useful beginning in the political analysis of international interdependence can be made by thinking of asymmetrical interdependencies as sources of power among actors. Such a framework can be applied to relations between transnational actors (such as multinational corporations) and governments as well as interstate relations. Different types of interdependence lead to potential political influence, but under different constraints. Sensitivity interdependence can provide the basis for significant political influence only when the rules and norms in effect can be taken for granted, or when it would be prohibitively costly for dissatisfied states to change their policies quickly. If one set of rules puts an actor in a disadvantageous position, that actor will probably try to change those rules if it can do so at reasonable cost. Thus influence deriving from favorable asymmetries in sensitivity is very limited when the underlying asymmetries in vulnerability are unfavorable. Likewise, if a state chafes at its economic vulnerabilities, it may use military force to attempt to redress that situation as Japan did in 1941; or, it may subtly threaten to use force, as did the United States in 1975, when facing the possibility of future oil boycotts. But in many contemporary situations, the use of force is so costly, and its threat so difficult to make credible, that a military strategy is an act of desperation.

Yet this is not the whole story of power and interdependence. Just as important as understanding the way that manipulation of interdependence can be an instrument of power is an understanding of that instrument's limits. Asymmetrical interdependence by itself cannot explain bargaining outcomes, even in traditional relations among states. As we said earlier, power measured in terms of resources or potential may look different from power measured in terms of influence over outcomes. We must also look at the "translation" in the political bargaining process. One of the most important reasons for this is that the commitment of a weaker state may be much greater than that of its stronger partner. The more dependent actor may be (or appear to be) more willing to suffer. At the politico-military level, the United States' attempt to coerce North Vietnam provides an obvious example.

Yet the point holds even in more cooperative interstate relations. In the Canadian-American relationship, for example, the use or threat of force is virtually excluded from consideration by either side. The fact that Canada has less military strength than the United States is therefore not a major factor in the bargaining process. The Canadians can take advantage of their superior position on such economic issues as oil and natural gas exports without fearing military retaliation or threat by the United States. Moreover, other conditions of contemporary international interdependence tend to limit the abilities of statesmen to manipulate asymmetrical interdependence. In particular, the smaller state may have greater internal political unity than the larger one. Even though the more powerful state may be less dependent in aggregate terms, it may be more fragmented internally and its coherence reduced by conflicts of interest and difficulties of coordination within its own government. . . .

<hr style="border: 3px solid black; width: 30%; margin-left: auto; margin-right: 0;" /> **6.3**

ULF LINDELL
STEFAN PERSSON

The Paradox of Weak State Power: A Research and Literature Overview

Introduction

Some forty years ago, when the present international system was emerging, it was a widespread opinion that in the future the small countries would find themselves increasingly powerless and unimportant. The states about to become known as Superpowers were superior when it came to the resources which were considered crucial, and the power gap was predicted to widen during the decades to come.

However, "small states" or "weak states" have not always turned out to be as powerless as expected. They have certainly come to play a larger role than predicted by commentaries of the late 1940s.

Great Powers and even Superpowers have on occasion found small opponents very hard to defeat in outright war. In political interaction small states have also been known to hold their own vis-à-vis big allies or to play significant roles in multilateral negotiations. Recently, some of the smaller NATO members have had a say in the matter of nuclear arms deployments; and in the Conference on Security and Cooperation in Europe the contributions of the so-called NNA Group have been important. Developments like these make the subject area of "small state power" a current and interesting issue in today's world. The paradoxical nature of the phenomenon seems to give it the character of what Rosenau calls "a genuine puzzle"—one of the main platforms for scientific inquiry.

The paradox of relatively resourceless states being able to exercise substantial influence in international relations has from time to time been noted

Reprinted from "The Paradox of Weak State Power: A Research and Literature Overview," by Lindell and Persson, in *Cooperation and Conflict*, Vol. XXI (1986), published by Norwegian University Press (Universitetsfarlaget), Oslo.

in the literature. The subject received some attention in connection with the general interest in the situation and foreign policies of small states that seemed to prevail in the Nordic countries in the late 1960s and the early 1970s.

The weak state-powerful state relations have, however, also been dealt with in a number of more recent studies, some of which were written in other parts of Europe and in America. So, whereas one or two overviews of the small state field were done some fifteen years ago, we feel that it may be time to re-visit the subject area, and again take stock of the work that has been done. At that time (around 1970), it was often said that the field had not been studied sufficiently. A decade and a half later, similar verdicts can still be found:

> The literature on power asymmetry is amazingly barren. For the most part, it is limited to showing that the country with the greatest power (variously defined) does best in negotiation. The post hoc determinism in this view is inescapable. Much more interesting and much more useful would be a better understanding of possible behavior by the weaker party to improve its position.

This is an inventory of the propositions that have so far been produced concerning the ways in which small states can and do exercise influence over Great Powers and Superpowers. Which factors, conditions and strategies have been highlighted as possible explanations of this phenomenon?

While the primary aim of this review is to present a fairly comprehensive outline of these propositions, there is also, we believe, a certain need to be met by compiling an extensive bibliography in the general area of small states in international relations.

An important and contested aspect is, of course, how to define a "small" or "weak" state. This question is closely related to the classical problem of how to measure power. In the numerous attempts and suggestions that have been made, the criteria for the designation of Small (and Medium, Great, Super, etc.) Power status vary, as do the terminologies—the labels used to constitute a classification scheme of power status. Although the definition and criteria for selection cannot be entirely separated from the propositions about small state power to be discussed below, we will proceed to take a look at these without having "solved" the problem of definition. Our concept of small state is thus a wide or "inclusive" one. This means, of course, that we are dealing with a large and rather disparate group of countries.

One common way of discussing state power is in terms of *resources* or power bases. Another is to proceed from a *bargaining* perspective. It is our impression that the direction in which the more recent studies have been looking (e.g., discussions about interdependence, issue-specific and actor-specific power) have placed greater emphasis on the latter perspective.

The factors that have been singled out in the various propositions or statements about small state influence can, for the sake of order and overview, be divided into several types. They sometimes have the character of background conditions or general environment, and sometimes they are more "direct" causes like certain strategies and tactics.

The categories that we have chosen are both of the "power base" type and of an "alternatives of action" type. In the former we find: (a) the structure of the international system, (b) the state of the international system, (c) international norms, and (d) actors' qualities. These are systemic or resource-oriented factors that are more or less "given," i.e., impossible or very difficult for the small state to change. The second category consists of: (a) alignment policy, (b) exploitation of Great Power weaknesses, and (c) other diplomatic and negotiatory strategies or tactics. In these cases the actor can choose whether to pursue a certain line of action or not.

The "Power Base" Factors

The relevance of systemic factors in the small state context has been emphasized by Huldt, among others:

> It is obviously the case that small states' possibilities to act ... are dependent
> on the character of the international system in which they exist.

The Structure of the International System

In the literature a number of propositions can be found to the effect that the possibilities the small states have of exercising influence largely depend on whether the international system is hierarchical or hegemonical, and whether it is characterized by a balance of power or not. Most of them take the balance of power for granted, and proceed to distinguish between bipolar and multipolar systems. In the former case, a distinction is also made between "tight" and "loose" bipolarity.

If we, to begin with, look at the propositions concerning the effects of a balance of power system (i.e., a system in which two or more approximately equal Powers dominate), some say that this is beneficial for the small states. Branner, for instance, writes that "the position of the small state is strengthened when there is an equality of power in the international system." [Michael] Handel elaborates this theme:

> ... the more nearly equal the division of strength between the super
> powers, the greater the need to improve their relative positions, even the small
> increments of strength obtained by alliances with the nonaligned weak states.
> Under such circumstances the bargaining position of the weak states is
> strengthened and they can ask and obtain higher prices for their cooperation.

Robert Rothstein is representative of the opposite view:

> A functional balance of power system ... limits the ability of small
> powers to achieve their own goals.

Those analysts, who regard the matter of bipolarity versus multipolarity as a relevant factor, seem to agree that bipolarity is better for small state influence than is multipolarity. In addition, they tend to argue that the tighter the polarity, the better the conditions for successful small state influence. It has been said that the decreasing number of Great Powers since World War II has had this effect. When, on the other hand, the development during the last decade or so is discussed, it has been argued that:

> ... the tight bipolar system has gradually been tranformed into a loose bipolar system, and this has automatically weakened the bargaining position of many of the weak non-aligned states.

The only statement about the consequences of a hegemonical system that we have come across declares that in such a system the small state will find itself within the sphere of influence of the hegemonical Power, or at least run a serious risk of ending up in that situation—one of the worst possible cases in terms of possible small state influence.

The State of the International System

The second type of systemic factors focuses on the *state* of the system, primarily in the sense of the degree of tension and conflict. The salience of these factors is stressed by several researchers.

Most propositions in this area claim that tension in the system will lead to increased possibilities for the weaker states to exercise influence. Lower tension and/or increased cooperation between the dominating actors will thus tend to bring about worse conditions for the small countries' attempts to influence the bigger ones:

> War among the great powers is ... one situation in which small-power diplomacy may be observed to advantage.
> In the past, the influence of the Small Powers rose only when they were sought as allies on the eve of a Great Power conflict.
> ... whenever two great powers are locked in serious conflict they can spare little if any of their coercive strength to deal with minor offenders. ...
> Weak countries awake to their own interests and to conditions favorable to them do not fail to appreciate the advantages accruing to them, without their doing, whenever major powers are forced to concentrate on struggles among one another.
> ... an increase in the intensity of conflict between the dominating states leads to an increased status for the small states, since the lack of joint actions means that the individual great power instead—through benevolence—will try to reach a better relation and perhaps an alliance with smaller states.

Goldmann discusses four different hypotheses: the "neutralism," "deterrence," "coalition," and "polarization" hypotheses. Of these, all but the last mentioned is compatible with the quotations above.

The neutralism hypothesis holds that the higher the tension between the Superpowers, the greater the opportunity for smaller states to "play" or "match" the former against each other. The deterrence hypothesis argues that high tension prevents the Superpowers from using their massive resources out of fear of retaliation from the other Superpower, which conceivably can improve the position of the weaker states. One other consequence of such a development may be an increased frequency of international negotiations. Bjol suggests the following proposition:

> Most of the time international relations are not dominated by threats of war, but by negotiations, and in negotiations the weak have in periods of stability several means of furthering their interests.

Yet others have emphasized the importance of the existence of nuclear weapons in the arsenals of the Great Powers, which, paradoxically, are believed to have contributed to the possibilities of small state influence. Handel is among those who argue that the restrictions the Superpowers have set up for themselves have increased the small states' freedom of action.

Rothstein also notes that all-out war has become unlikely, and argues that this has entailed a shift of focus in world politics toward regional conflicts. The tendency to look upon regional conflicts as a considerable threat to world peace "accounts in some significant degree for the influence of many small states," he concludes.

According to the third line of reasoning, the so-called coalition hypothesis, a high degree of tension will lessen the Superpowers' inclination to form some kind of coalition or condominium, at least partly directed against the smaller states.

The polarization hypothesis, on the other hand, argues that increased tension in a system will mean worse conditions for small power influence. The idea is that high tension will make the Superpowers more anxious to tighten the control of their allies and other countries within their reach. In contrast to the first three hypotheses, this view will, as Goldmann writes, not consider détente between the Superpowers as any problem for the weak states.

It may be interesting to compare this view with the following statement by Olaf Palme, which seems closest to the coalition hypothesis:

> We are living in a time when the hegemony of the superpowers grows stronger and stronger and détente between them may mean a threat to the independence of the small nations.

Some of the propositions take a situation of cooperation as their point of departure and claim that such situations will make it harder for small states to be influential. Again, there are opposing views. Bjol, for instance writes that "it would seem as an integration system would be the most advantageous to the small state."

The most circumscribed view of the relation between tension and the conditions for small (neutral) state influence is perhaps the one given by Frei, suggesting that the correlation is not linear:

> Concerning the relation between the position of the neutrals and the degree of tension between the two powers in conflict, there seems to be a kind

of *optimal intensity of conflict*. Up to this level every increase in the tension means an improvement in the position of the neutrals. . . . If the intensity of conflict rises above this optimum, the favorable position of the neutrals will decline with the growing tension.

International Norms

We have found some other propositions which we refer to the systemic level, although they relate neither to the structure of nor the level of tension in the international system.

Goldmann, among others, has discussed the importance of international norms as "power base elements" for weak states. He argues that the importance of international norms is often underestimated, and that their significance seems to be increasing. As particularly essential Goldmann views the norms that restrict the right to use certain resources—primarily military force.

Scholars have also pointed out that "the continuing growth of an internationalist ethic" may be a factor of some importance in this c ntext. Other norms sometimes adduced as partial explanations (in addition to "the increasing disapproval of the use of naked force between states") are "the right of every nation to self-determination" and "the growing equality of states in international organization and international law." Rothstein writes that in today's world, the LDCs can hope to achieve more than before by acting in concert as an international pressure group, because of "the decline in the utility of force and the slow and tenuous evolution of democratic and moral norms."

It has also been suggested that the fact that international organization *per se* has come to play a greater role in international relations during the last few decades has been advantageous for the small states. It is a general view that the better the adherence to international law and other norms, the better are the possibilities for the small states to influence others.

On the whole, most of the above-mentioned factors can be viewed as background variables, as perhaps necessary but not sufficient conditions for the exercise of small state power.

Actors' Internal Qualities

The researchers who have dealt with the question of small state influence have also called attention to a number of factors related to the actors in the international system.

Some of the theoretical propositions regarding "internal qualities" point to the importance of geographical factors. It is, for example, suggested that a certain geographical position may increase the small state's possibilities of exercising influence. Ronfeldt claims that a large part of the strong positions of Iran and Cuba, in their relations with the US and the USSR during the 1970s, can be explained by the latters' perception of these countries' extremely important strategic position close to the border of the competing Superpower. A similar aspect is discussed by Sjöstedt, who writes that a small state's position may be strengthened if it is "located at the centre of an important network of international transactions."

Conditions within the small states that are said to be generally advantageous are, on the one hand, the material ones, e.g., natural resources and industrial and technological level, and, on the other, human resources. The latter refer, for example, to an ethnically homogeneous population and unity among the political elite regarding basic values. The ability to mobilize the will of the people is also seen as important, and most smaller states are said to have a relatively high capability in this respect.

Another factor is the reputation of the small state. Modelski, among others, argues that "a 'good' reputation is invaluable in the daily dealings of diplomacy." Sjöstedt also discusses what he calls "reputation power," and says that it is based on the fact that a country is known to be reliable and to have good judgement. It has, furthermore, been pointed out that a state can achieve a good reputation with positive effects on its ability to exercise influence through the creation of a "civilized political and social system."

One proposition attaches importance to the "organizational capabilities" of the small state, arguing that well working and adjustable political, public and military institutions may contribute to increasing the small state's possibilities of exercising influence.

Greater importance has been attached to the differences in "the foreign policy situation" of the Small Powers and the Superpowers. The most significant difference is said to be that the small state has fewer relations with other states and, therefore, is involved in fewer questions. Bjol points out that the foreign relations of the Superpowers are mostly multilateral ("by virtue of its global presence, the United States offers maximum hostage surface"), while the small states more often have bilateral relations. The following quotes illustrate how this is believed to be beneficial for the small states:

> ... the smaller state ... can take large-scale patterns of international politics for granted, since nothing it does can possibly affect them very much. Thus a country like Nationalist China is able to concentrate on a narrow range of vital interests and ignore almost everything else.
>
> Possibly the main advantage a small power's foreign minister has over his great-power colleague is that he is not obliged to adopt a position on every international issue that arises.
>
> ... assets of a weaker power eager to block policies of a larger one [include] ... "the asymmetry of attention" and the "greater cohesion of concentration" of the weaker government compared to the more powerful state. The latter has to disperse its attention over a huge number of chessboards and players and cannot always keep its own internal bureaucratic coalitions together.

According to these propositions, the small state does not have to take so many considerations into account when choosing its policy, since the effects of its actions are very limited in most cases. It is thereby possible for the small state, in comparison to greater powers, to reach a higher "intensity of interest" in the comparatively few questions it is involved in; i.e., the small state may be prepared to pay a higher price to reach its goal, which is considered to have positive effects on the influence it can exercise.

The small state's foreign policy decision-making process may also be of some interest in this context. For example, Ronfeldt argues that the possibilities a small state has of exercising influence may increase if its regime is highly centralized and stable. In other words, it is claimed that "authoritarian rule" and/or "continuity of decision-making" may have this effect:

> ... authoritarian personal rule helps prevent an outside power from playing upon bureaucratic or sectoral differences within a client-state. Conversely, where its ruler has been in power for a decade or more, he and his regime may gain considerable experience at playing upon bureaucratic politics within the foreign power in order to manipulate or lever a favorable response on some issue.

A similar aspect is discussed by Vital:

> ... the policy-makers [in the weak state] can themselves become personally familiar with the detail of the topics they are most concerned with. The influence of the bureaucracy is therefore much reduced and decisions are more apt to be taken without or despite its advice and with far less inhibition than might be the case in great powers.

In this context, the importance of credibility and unambiguous commitments is emphasized. For example, the fact that the small state's range of foreign policy alternatives is frequently limited by factors that it cannot influence has been seen as a possible source of strength and influence. Thus, it is suggested that a small state can increase its credibility by showing that it has no other alternative than to act in a certain way.

> It could even be argued that the apparently weaker actor frequently has the greater bargaining power, because its range of choice is—and is perceived to be—so limited that there is hardly any will involved and therefore no doubt about the nature of the commitment.

> Strong states tended to make more use of volitional means of gratifying and depriving—promise and threat—whereas weak states relied on nonvolitional means—predictions and warnings.

A small state's "bargaining power" depends, of course, on other factors, too. Some of these are related to individuals or groups, rather than to nations. For example, the small state's determination and ability to express its opinion clearly and unambiguously—to "demonstrate ... resolve clearly and convincingly" are regarded as essential qualities. Other similar "skills" that are considered favorable for the small state are: skills in formulating "suggestive solutions," "... sense of what is generally felt to be 'legitimate,'" and "sense of the right moment."

Concluding Remarks

In preparing our "inventory," we have made a number of assumptions about concepts and definitions. The value of the work to some extent depends on the viability of these assumptions. Basically, we have *simplified* the complicated concepts of power, influence, compellence, strategy, etc. Needless to say, the literature from which we have collected the "propositions" has not always treated these concepts and phenomena in the way we have, nor has it been uniform or homogeneous in this respect. Nevertheless we hope that our broad overview may still serve its purpose.

We have made three basic assumptions that deserve to be noted. We have assumed that it is both possible and meaningful to distinguish between: (i) exercise of influence and creation of security; (ii) active influence ("compellence") and passive deterrence, and finally (iii) influence due to a certain state's own qualities or actions and influence as a result of an adversary's inability or shortcomings.

The propositions were presented in two main groups, divided into four and three subcategories respectively. The first group of propositions—those which focus on "power bases"—has been regarded as statements about the effects of various basic conditions for the small states. We tend to think that the factors highlighted in the propositions classified as alternatives of choices of actions/policy, and particularly the ones that deal with what we have called "bargaining power," are more interesting.

Despite the intriguing character of the problem area we have been discussing, we must not blow it out of proportion. Important as power structures are, they are hardly, as Odell writes, all-determining. And when the weak state power phenomenon occurs, it may sometimes be the result of a certain inability or failure on behalf of the Great Power, rather than following from a small state manipulating or actively taking advantage of some weak point. The factors associated with the "impotence of the superpower" are surely inescapable complements to any explanation of the power of the weak, because, as Wilcox says:

> ... if you really want to understand international politics, what you have to understand first are constraints, not capacities.

Finally, we need perhaps to remind ourselves that the strongest states usually *are* the ones with the most influence. One of our sources of propositions, Michael Handel, puts it in the following way:

> ... all in all, the great powers are still more powerful than they are weak, and the weak states are characterized by their relative weakness, not strength. Weak states do not usually "twist the arms" of the big powers. ...

6.4 ■■■■■■

GEORGE P. SHULTZ

Power and Diplomacy in the 1980s

Over 20 years ago, President John Kennedy pledged that the United States would "pay any price, bear any burden, meet any hardship, support any friend, oppose any foe, in order to assure the survival and the success of liberty." We know now that the scope of that commitment is too broad—though the self-confidence and courage in those words were typically American and most admirable. More recently, another administration took the view that our fear of communism was "inordinate" and that there were very complicated social, economic, religious, and other factors at work in the world that we had little ability to affect. This, in my view, is a counsel of helplessness that substantially underestimates the United States and its ability to influence events.

Somewhere between these two poles lies the natural and sensible scope of American foreign policy. We know that we are not omnipotent and that we must set priorities. We cannot pay *any* price or bear *any* burden. We must discriminate; we must be prudent and careful; we must respond in ways appropriate to the challenge and engage our power only when very important strategic stakes are involved. Not every situation can be salvaged by American exertion even when important values or interests are at stake.

At the same time, we know from history that courage and vision and determination can change reality. We can affect events, and we all know it. The American people expect this of their leaders. And the future of the free world depends on it.

Americans, being a moral people, want their foreign policy to reflect the values we espouse as a nation. But Americans, being a practical people, also want their foreign policy to be effective. If we truly care about our values, we must be prepared to defend them and advance them. Thus we as a nation are perpetually asking ourselves how to reconcile our morality and our practical sense, how to pursue noble goals in a complex and imperfect world, how to relate our strength to our purposes—in sum, how to relate power and diplomacy.

We meet this evening amid the excitement of America's quadrennial exercise of self-renewal, in which we as a country reexamine ourselves and our international objectives. It is an unending process—almost as unending as the presidential campaign season. But there are some constants in our policy, such

An address before the Trilateral Commission, Washington, D.C., April 3, 1984.

as our alliance with the industrial democracies, as embodied in the distinguished gathering. This partnership—the cornerstone of our foreign policy for 35 years—itself reflects our ability to combine our moral commitment to democracy and our practical awareness of the crucial importance of maintaining the global balance of power. So I consider this an appropriate forum at which to share some thoughts on the relationship between power and diplomacy in the last two decades of the 20th century.

The World We Face

By the accident of history, the role of world leadership fell to the United States just at the moment when the old international order had been destroyed by two world wars but no new stable system had developed to replace it. A century ago, the international system was centered on Europe and consisted of only a few major players. Today, in terms of military strength, the dominant countries are two major powers that had been, in one sense or another, on the edge or outside European diplomacy. But economic power is now widely dispersed.

Power and Diplomacy

In this environment, our principal goal is what President Reagan has called "the most basic duty that any President and any people share—the duty to protect and strengthen the peace." History teaches, however, that peace is not achieved merely by wishing for it. Noble aspirations are not self-fulfilling. Our aim must always be to shape events and not be the victim of events. In this fast-moving and turbulent world, to sit in a reactive posture is to risk being overwhelmed or to allow others, who may not wish us well, to decide the world's future.

Americans have sometimes tended to think that power and diplomacy are two distinct alternatives. To take a very recent example, the Long commission report on the bombing of our Marine barracks in Beirut urged that we work harder to pursue what it spoke of as "diplomatic alternatives," as opposed to "military options." This reflects a fundamental misunderstanding—not only of our intensive diplomatic efforts throughout the period but of the relationship between power and diplomacy. Sometimes, regrettable as it may be, political conflict degenerates into a test of strength. It was precisely our military role in Lebanon that was problematical, not our diplomatic exertion. Our military role was hamstrung by legislative and other inhibitions; the Syrians were not interested in diplomatic compromise so long as the prospect of hegemony was not foreclosed. They could judge from our domestic debate that our staying power was limited.

In arms control, also, successful negotiation depends on the perception of a military balance. Only if the Soviet leaders see the West as determined to modernize its own forces will they see an incentive to negotiate agreements establishing equal, verifiable, and lower levels of armaments.

The lesson is that power and diplomacy are not alternatives. They must go together, or we will accomplish very little in this world.

The relationship between them is a complex one, and it presents us with both practical and moral issues. Let me address a few of those issues. One is the variety of the challenges we face. A second is the moral complexity of our response. A third is the problem of managing the process in a democracy.

The Range of Challenges

If we are to protect our interests, values, and allies, we must be engaged. And our power must be engaged.

It is often said that the lesson of Vietnam is that the United States should not engage in military conflict without a clear and precise military mission, solid public backing, and enough resources to finish the job. This is undeniably true. But does it mean there are no situations where a discrete assertion of power is needed or appropriate for limited purposes? Unlikely. Whether it is crisis management or power projection or a show of force or peacekeeping or a localized military action, there will always be instances that fall short of an all-out national commitment on the scale of World War II. The need to avoid no-win situations cannot mean that we turn automatically away from hard-to-win situations that call for prudent involvement. These will always involve risks; we will not always have the luxury of being able to choose the most advantageous circumstances. And our adversaries can be expected to play rough.

The Moral Issues

Of course, any use of force involves moral issues. American military power should be resorted to only if the stakes justify it, if other means are not available, and then only in a manner appropriate to the objective. But we cannot opt out of every contest. If we do, the world's future will be determined by others—most likely by those who are the most brutal, the most unscrupulous, and the most hostile to our deeply held principles.

Without being boastful or arrogant, the American people know that their country has been a powerful force for good in the world. We helped Europe and Asia—including defeated enemies—rebuild after the war, and we helped provide a security shield behind which they could build democracy and freedom as well as prosperity. Americans have often died and sacrificed for the freedom of others. We have provided around $165 billion in economic assistance for the developing world. We have played a vital facilitating role in the Middle East peace process, in the unfolding diplomacy of southern Africa, as well as in many other diplomatic efforts around the globe.

We have used our power for good and worthy ends. In Grenada, we helped restore self-determination to the people of Grenada, so that they could choose their own future. Some have tried to compare what we did in Grenada to the Soviet invasion of Afghanistan. We welcome such comparison. Contrast, for example, the prospects for free elections in the two countries. In Grenada, they will be held this year; in Afghanistan, when? Contrast the number of American combat troops now in Grenada 5 months after the operation with the number of Soviet troops in Afghanistan 55 months after their invasion. The number in Grenada is 0; the number in Afghanistan is over 100,000.

More often, the issue is not the direct use of American military power but military assistance to friends to help them defend themselves. Around the world, security support for friends is a way to prevent crises; it bolsters our friends so they can deter challenges. And it is a way of avoiding the involvement of American forces, because it is only when our friends' efforts in their own defense are being overwhelmed that we are faced with the agonizing decision whether to involve ourselves more directly. Security assistance is thus an essential tool of foreign policy. It is an instrument for deterring those who would impose their will by force and for making political solutions possible. It gets far less support in this country than it deserves.

Central America is a good example. The real moral question in Central America is not do we believe in military solutions, but do we believe in ourselves? Do we believe that our security and the security of our neighbors has moral validity? Do we have faith in our own democratic values? Do we believe that Marxist-Leninist solutions are antidemocratic and that we have a moral right to try to stop those who are trying to impose them by force? Sure, economic and social problems underlie many of these conflicts. But in El Salvador, the communist guerrillas are waging war directly against the economy, blowing up bridges and power stations, deliberately trying to wreck the country's economy.

The conflict in Central America is not a debate between social theorists; it is one of those situations I mentioned where the outcome of political competition will depend in large measure on the balance of military strength. In El Salvador, the United States is supporting moderates who believe in democracy and who are resisting the enemies of democracy on both the extreme right and the extreme left. If we withdrew our support, the moderates, caught in the crossfire, would be the first victims—as would be the cause of human rights and the prospects for economic development. And anyone who believes that military support for our friends isn't crucial to a just outcome is living in a dream world. And anyone who believes that military support can be effective when it's given on an uncertain installment plan is not facing reality.

Accountability Without Paralysis

The third issue I want to mention is the question of how this country, as a democracy, conducts itself in the face of such challenges.

Robert C. Johansen

Over the last 35 years, the evolution of the international system was bound to erode the predominant position the United States enjoyed immediately after World War II. But it seems to me that in this disorderly and dangerous new world, the loss of American predominance puts an even greater premium on consistency, determination, and coherence in the conduct of our foreign policy. We have less margin for error than we used to have.

If the purpose of our power is to prevent war, or injustice, then ideally we want to discourage such occurrences rather than have to use our power in a physical sense. But this can happen only if there is assurance that our power would be used if necessary.

A reputation for reliability becomes, then, a major asset—giving friends a sense of security and adversaries a sense of caution. A reputation for living up to our commitments can, in fact, make it less likely that pledges of support will have to be carried out. Crisis management is most successful when a favorable outcome is attained without firing a shot. Credibility is an intangible, but it is no less real. The same is true of a loss of credibility. A failure to support a friend always involves a price. Credibility, once lost, has to be reearned.

6.5

ROBERT C. JOHANSEN

The Threat to Survival

. . . [U]nprecedented problems that are global in scope increasingly exceed the capacity of traditional diplomatic practices and institutions to resolve. In general, our perception of foreign policy problems and opportunities has failed to stay abreast of rapidly changing world realities. This has meant that many policies have been growing increasingly unrealistic in the sense that they simply cannot achieve the ends sought. To oversimplify only slightly, the political leadership and attentive public apply essentially nineteenth-century diplomatic ideas to the solution of twenty-first-century problems, the technical and social origins of which are in the present. Nineteenth-century diplomatic ideas encourage (1) the continued emphasis on serving the national interest defined largely in terms of military power and sovereign control over a carefully defined piece of territory and segment of humanity; and (2) the assumption that the present system of competing national sovereignties either cannot or should not be fundamentally changed, and that it both can and will

From *The National Interest and the Human Interest: An Analysis of U.S. Foreign Policy* by Robert C. Johansen. Copyright © 1980 by Princeton University Press. Excerpt, pp. 4-14, reprinted with permission of Princeton University Press.

respond adequately to the foreseeable problems of national security, widespread poverty and resource shortages, severe ecological damage, and pervasive denial of human rights. Under the influence of old diplomatic habits and strong vested interests in the political and economic system inherited from the past, officials continue diplomacy as usual to confront newly emerging twenty-first century problems. For example, traditional diplomatic ideas and institutions persist even though their inadequacy is obvious for averting misuse of nuclear technology, the consequences of which cannot be confined to a carefully defined piece of territory, layer of the atmosphere, or segment of humanity. Traditional uses of military power and sovereign control, however sincerely and faithfully practiced, are impotent in the face of irresponsible behavior by a relatively small number of people who could affect millions of others in many countries for decades, centuries, or millennia to come.

A stark reality faces all inhabitants of the earth: through consequences resulting from major war or ecological imbalance, widespread suffering for millions of people and even eventual extinction of the human species are possibilities. Such statements have become commonplace, and thus they have lost their ring of urgency. Yet predicaments mount while time slips away, making remedial action more difficult and perhaps less likely. Even without major war or ecological collapse, existing political institutions prevent a billion of the world's people from having sufficient food, often resulting in permanent mental or physical disability, even though adequate nutrition is technically feasible. In brief, the decentralized structure of world power and authority, distributed among many sovereign states, perpetuates a relatively anarchic international system in which the danger of war, the shortage of food and other resources, and the presence of persistent ecological hazards threaten the survival of many people, if not, in the long run, of all human civilization. . . .

A reassessment is also useful because present goals and institutions make it increasingly difficult to implement our most cherished values and ethical principles. Indeed, the existing international structure of power in itself violates these principles. For example, the globe is presently divided into nation-states with power unsystematically and inequitably related to population. This means that the simple exercise of sovereignty by a superpower violates the principle of self-determination on a global basis. It is doubtful that any democratic society can long survive with its democratic principles intact if those principles are repeatedly denied in its own conduct. Yet in following the traditional approach to serving the national interest the U.S. government regularly carries out policies that affect millions of people outside its borders who have no control over the making of U.S. policies. When the United States pursues economic policies and consumption patterns that stimulate world inflation, thus decreasing the buying power of non-U.S. citizens, this is a modern, global equivalent of taxation without representation. Similarly, United States citizens are touched directly by the acts of other great powers, although we are unrepresented in their political processes. If other governments put radioactive substances in the atmosphere, American citizens suffer contamination without representation.

Even though he has kept his administration well within the guidelines of traditional diplomacy, President Jimmy Carter seemed to acknowledge part of the representation problem when he delivered a message to the "citizens of the world" immediately after his inaugural address: "I have chosen the occasion of my inauguration ... to speak not only to my own countrymen—which is traditional—but also to you, citizens of the world who did not participate in our election but who will nevertheless be affected by my decisions."

Rapidly changing technology and patterns of social interaction are making societies inseparable from one another, but the present pattern of international political participation remains relatively unchanged. As long as this system remains constant, it authorizes some people to make decisions that affect other people who are unrepresented in the decision-making process. As this incongruity between political institutions and social needs is allowed to deepen, self-government will be undermined in a national context because it will be unable to respond to citizens' needs. It will fail to take root and flourish in a global context because intra- and inter-societal inequities will not diminish, and severe inequities of wealth and power make it impossible to fulfill the democratic principle in which power must be widely shared. Democracy cannot indefinitely survive within a global political structure that prevents people from participating in decisions that affect their own lives.

Consider the capacity of present political institutions to fulfill a person's most basic need and right—adequate food. The world today faces—for the first time in its history—shortages in each of the four basic agricultural resources: land, water, energy, and fertilizer. No nation can isolate itself from these scarcities or their economic and political consequences. Japan imports more than half of its total cereal supplies. Egypt imports about 40 percent. The farmers of the European Economic Community import 80 percent of their high protein feed for livestock. Nearly all their petroleum is imported. The United States is the supplier of 85 percent of all soybeans on the entire world market, so when in 1973 it ordered an export embargo in order to curb price rises at home, numerous other people, with no opportunity to influence the U.S. decision, were adversely affected. In another example, when Thailand once restricted its rice exports, the action "wreaked havoc with efforts to prevent runaway food prices in other Southeast Asian countries."

Each year approximately one billion people suffer from malnutrition. Fifteen million children die annually before reaching age five because of insufficient food and infections that become lethal due to malnourishment. That is one quarter of all deaths in the world. Almost all children born to poor parents in the less developed countries suffer some degree of malnutrition at one time or another. In the early 1970s, experts estimated that an average of 10,000 people died weekly from lack of food.

Overpopulation is not the only source of this human tragedy. Because of the petroleum-based fertilizer shortages partially resulting from the oil embargo imposed by the Organization of Oil Exporting Countries (OPEC) in 1973-74, the United States suspended its usual fertilizer exports. This action contributed to a 1.5-million-ton fertilizer shortage in the less developed countries, which cost them 15 million tons in lost grain production in 1974. Yet, during the same year, people in the United States used on lawns, cemeteries, and golf courses about 3 million tons of fertilizer—twice the shortage in the poor countries. Obviously, no food grew from this U.S. usage. Moreover, for each pound of fertilizer applied to grain production in the nearly saturated soils of the United States, farmers could increase their yields by an average of only two to three pounds. But in nutrient-starved India, each pound of fertilizer could have yielded an additional production three times as large as the increment derived from U.S. use of the fertilizer. Thus, a slight decrease in U.S. productivity would have yielded a major increase in productivity for fertilizer-poor countries.

Of the total grain produced in the United States, much is fed to cattle, which are inefficient converters of grain into protein. Georg Borgstrom estimates that the world's cattle eat as much food as would be required to feed 8.7 billion people, or twice the world's present population. By including less meat and more grain in their diets, people in the rich countries could enable existing food supplies to extend to far more persons on the globe. In India, where the major source of protein is feed grains, direct and indirect consumption averages about 400 pounds of grain per person per year. In the United States, where much protein is eaten in the form of meat, eggs, or milk, the grain consumed directly or indirectly through production of meat is almost 2,000 pounds per person per year. Thus, the average North American consumes five times as many agricultural resources as the average person in India. U.S. average consumption extends by two to four times the quantity of protein that the human body can utilize. The remainder is excreted. If Americans were to reduce their meat consumption by only 10 percent, in one year 12 million tons of grain would be freed for human consumption. This amount would feed 60 million people for one year, enough to have prevented famine in parts of India and Bangladesh in 1974.

Sufficient resources exist to feed everyone *if* the resources are shared fairly. Many demographers believe this condition would also cause population growth to decline. However, past policies of food distribution have been governed by traditional diplomatic habits. As the former Secretary of Agriculture, Dr. Earl Butz once explained: "Food is power. Food is a weapon. It is now one of the principal tools in our negotiating kit." A CIA research study, written shortly before the World Food Conference in Rome in 1974, concluded that the world grain shortages in the future "could give the United States a measure of power it had never had before—possibly an economic and political dominance greater than that of the immediate post-World War II years." The report predicted that "in bad years . . . Washington would acquire virtual life-and-death power over the fate of the multitudes of the needy." (Without exaggeration, the hungry might view such a condition as starvation without representation.) The report warned that when societies became desperate the hungry but powerful nations (which possessed nuclear weapons) might engage in nuclear threats or in massive migration backed by force. They might even seek to induce climatic changes, such as "trying to melt the Arctic ice cap." Despite the exaggerated expression of alarm in the image of a rising tide of poor people engulfing the United States, the report accurately described the power of life and death that can be exerted by the world's largest food exporter.

More effectively than existing international organizations, a global food authority could maximize world production, bank grains for periods of drought or famine, ration and allocate fertilizer for optimal increases in production, encourage less consumption of grain by cattle, and decrease the use of food as a diplomatic weapon to gain political influence over other governments. Without increased global coordination of food policies, resentment, repression, and unnecessary human misery are likely to continue throughout the 1980s.

In summary, the decentralized and inequitable distribution of power among states perpetuates an international system in which the most powerful countries maintain privileged positions at the expense of the weak and poor societies. However, even the citizens of the great powers are unable to escape the consequences of other governments' policies that they have no authority to influence. This arrangement of power and authority denies further realization of global justice and basic human rights. Not only is the denial of justice undesirable in itself, it also contributes to the difficulty and detracts from the desirability of maintaining peace. Thus the present distribution of power threatens both the quality of life for a substantial number of coinhabitants of the globe and ultimately the survival of human civilization. Whether one wants to be politically prudent or morally sensitive or both, modern technology has now made it necessary to consider an alternative basis for making foreign policy decisions.

Discussion Questions

1. What do we mean when we discuss power as an attribute, as a goal, and as a relationship? What are the differences between these three conceptions of power? Which do you feel is the most important? Why?

2. The Lindell and Persson reading discusses various paradoxes of power, especially those having to do with smaller or weaker states. What are these paradoxes? What other important paradoxes of power are suggested by other readings in this chapter?

3. What are the major differences in the interpretations of power and its role in international affairs offered by Shultz and by Johansen? Which of the two interpretations do you believe ought to guide U.S. foreign policy? Why?

4. In the section entitled "Power as a Relationship," we offer several generalizations about how power works in contemporary international affairs. Identify recent international events that, in your judgment, either support or disprove each of these generalizations.

5. In their analysis of power in an interdependent world, Keohane and Nye define the concepts of sensitivity and vulnerability. Can you identify recent international events that illustrate each of these concepts?

For Further Reading

Classic Studies of Power

Claude, Inis, Jr. *Power and International Relations.* New York: Random House, 1962. One of the first works to develop a comprehensive theory of international politics based on the use of power.

Holsti, K. J. "The Concept of Power in the Study of International Relations." *Background* 7 (February 1964). One of the best-written early analyses of power that established the importance of power to the behavioral study of international relations.

Morgenthau, Hans. *Politics Among Nations: The Struggle for Power and Peace.* New York: Knopf, 1965. The first three chapters of Morgenthau's classic work are a synopsis of the realist view of power that has been so dominant in international relations.

Critical Interpretations of Power

Keohane, Robert O., and Joseph S. Nye. *Power and Interdependence.* Boston: Little, Brown, 1977. The first postrealist challenge to receive wide attention. Influential for both its critique of realism and the alternative approach advanced by the authors, it helped set the stage for future work on the international political economy.

Knorr, Klaus. *The Power of Nations: The Political Economy of International Relations.* New York: Basic Books, 1975. One of the first detailed analyses of the economic forms of power.

Nagel, Jack H. *The Descriptive Analysis of Power.* New Haven, Conn.: Yale University Press, 1975. A critique of the argument that power "causes" certain developments in international relations.

More Recent Analyses of Power

Baldwin, David A. "Power Analysis and World Politics: New Trends versus Old Tendencies," *World Politics* 31 (January 1979). The primary thesis of this article is that power is often discussed, measured, and even employed without full understanding of its attributes or purpose.

For Further Reading

Cline, Ray S. *World Power Assessment*. Washington, D.C.: Georgetown Center for Strategic and International Studies, 1975. A quantitative comparison of world military and economic power by an analyst whose thinking had some impact on the Reagan administration.

Hart, Jeffrey. "Three Approaches to the Measurement of Power in International Relations." *International Organization* 30 (Spring 1976). A widely cited study that compares and contrasts different approaches to power and its measurement.

DETERRENCE AND NATIONAL SECURITY 7

The strongest linkage between theory and policy in contemporary international affairs lies in the area of national security. Scholars and statesmen have in many instances played equally important roles in the formulation of national security policy.

In the United States the relationship between the scholarly and policy-making communities has been particularly close, with many individuals shuttling back and forth between academic posts and middle and upper management positions at the departments of state and defense and the Central Intelligence Agency.

Central to discussions of national security since World War II has been the debate over the role of nuclear weapons. At the heart of this debate has been the theory of nuclear deterrence and the policies derived from it. In its simplest sense, *deterrence* is a threat relationship in which nation A threatens nation B with unacceptable sanctions to dissuade nation B from undertaking actions that nation A seeks to prevent.

Mutual deterrence exists when the relationship involves threats by both nations A and B. *Nuclear deterrence* is deterrence predicated on the threatened use of nuclear weapons. While the theoretical requirements of deterrence are well known, disagreements concerning the specific characteristics of a credible threat or an adequate retaliatory force have been a continuing source of great contention for the past forty years.

Beyond deterrence lies compellence. While deterrence is a threat relationship in which the purpose of the threat is to persuade the other actor(s) *not* to undertake certain actions, *compellence* is a threat relationship in which nation A threatens nation B to induce (or compel) nation B to take some specific action. The requirements of compellence are far stricter than those for deterrence, for it is invariably far more difficult to compel another state to act against its will than to deter it from acting.

An understanding of the deterrence relationship in any specific case requires that we examine the following elements: (1) the specific actions to be deterred; (2) the manner in which the proposed threats are to be made and demonstrated; and (3) the various weapons systems and defense strategies required to yield a "credible" deterrent. This chapter discusses these three topics.

Deterrence and How It Works

The nature and meaning of deterrence have changed over time. Policy makers' and analysts' confidence in the prevailing doctrine of deterrence has varied with current military doctrine, the nature of the perceived threat, and the weapons systems available to ensure deterrence. In the 1980s, as our readings in this chapter make clear, new developments in each of these areas have in turn led to new, critical assessments of the nature, the functioning, and the future of deterrence.

The classic definition of deterrence has already been stated. Deterrence is a relationship in which nation A threatens nation B with unacceptable sanctions in order to convince nation B not to take (or to cease taking) actions that nation A seeks to prevent. The actions to be deterred may include an attack on nation A's territory or nation B's attempt to gain territory, new allies, or even prestige. In contemporary international affairs, deterrence relationships may involve the threatened use of either nuclear or non-nuclear forces.

There are, in fact, several types of deterrence. The U.S.-Soviet relationship over the past four decades is an example of strategic deterrence. *Strategic deterrence* exists when there is a direct confrontation between two states or groups of states in which each party employs explicit threats of war to deter the other from certain actions. In the U.S.-Soviet relationship nuclear weapons are central to the thinking of military planners on each side. Each possesses a nuclear arsenal sufficient to inflict unacceptable damage on the other. It is this capability that ensures the credibility of the threat, thus creating a deterrence relationship.

Clearly, however, there are some circumstances in which threats to retaliate directly against the other side are either inappropriate or lack credibility. U.S. and Soviet military strategists have, therefore, attempted to extend the notion of deterrence to situations other than those involving direct physical confrontation between these two nations—for example, guerrilla wars or Third World coups in which one or both sides have an interest in the outcome. In *extended deterrence,* it is the escalation potential of the military forces involved that constitutes the threat. In such cases the potential destructive power of nuclear weapons makes their utility as a deterrent obvious even to the casual observer.

Nonetheless, deterrence does not require nuclear weapons. Given the differences in military strength among "members of the nuclear club," it may be said that deterrence within this group of nations becomes not only a strategy for preventing war (strategic deterrence) but also a strategy for preserving the balance of power and maintaining regional and global peace (extended deterrence). Nations that lack nuclear weapons must rely on "conventional" forces. These nations deter potential invaders of their territory by threatening to retaliate by conventional means.

Each of these types of deterrence has the following components:

1. A clear sense on both sides of the actions that are to be prevented (deterred).

2. A communication of the threat by A to effect unacceptable damage. A intends for B to be fully aware of the threat.

3. The observation by B of actions and capabilities that make A's threat credible.

4. An interaction between the opponents as each assesses the other's intentions, capabilities, and credibility.

It must be understood that deterrence is a threat relationship. For the threats to be meaningful, nation B must perceive and react to them. As we noted above, deterrence is most usefully understood as a relationship. The mere possession of weapons of mass destruction does not mean that a nation understands the power and influence of the weapons and the way in which possession affects relations with other nations.

In the relationship between the United States and the Soviet Union, the priorities of the two powers have been similar. Each has sought, first and foremost, to deter the other from a direct attack. Second, each has sought to deter the other from attacking any member of their respective major alliances. Examples of such alliances are the North Atlantic Treaty Organization (NATO); the Australia, New Zealand, and United States alliance (ANZUS); the Warsaw Treaty Organization (WTO); or those allies to whom the United States and the Soviet Union are bound by bilateral security arrangements—for example, Japan and Cuba. Each side has also sought to deter encroachments by the other in regions where neither has formal allies. To realize these goals, the two nations have announced doctrines and developed forces intended to make credible their threatened response to both direct and indirect challenges.

But the superpowers' pursuit of extended deterrence has varied over time and seldom has involved clear threats to use their respective nuclear capabilities. More often they have in such instances signaled their credibility by supplying conventional weapons, economic assistance, military advisers, and diplomatic support to friends and clients around the globe. Thus, in Southeast Asia, Afghanistan, Central America, Sub-Saharan Africa, and the Middle East, the superpowers have provided support for client groups, while avoiding actions that might lead to direct confrontations between U.S. and Soviet forces. As we will see later, the observance of this mutually self-imposed constraint has made it more difficult for either nation to employ extended deterrence. However, it has also reduced the risk of nuclear confrontation and probably contributed to the credibility of the strategic deterrence relationship between the superpowers.

Although threats involving the use of conventional weapons may seem less frightening than threats to employ nuclear weapons, they can nonetheless be effective. Thus, rivals often parade (literally) their conventional arms capabilities for potential foes to see. Further, in most cases, leaders make reasonably clear proclamations about which areas and interests they will defend. As the selection by Paul Huth and Bruce Russett in this chapter illustrates, knowing exactly when a state will defend and not defend an interest may be as essential to successful deterrence as knowing the firepower of your foe.

The Logic of the Nuclear Era: Deterrence and the Choice of Weapons

Until the dawn of the atomic age, deterrence was based primarily on a nation's demonstrated ability to defend its territory and the willingness and capability to punish rivals who challenged its interests. The advent of nuclear weapons, however, has changed the meaning of "strategic forces," for today's nuclear strategic forces are useful only as deterrents. More than one scholar has noted that before nuclear weapons the purpose of military arsenals was to win wars, but that in the post-Hiroshima age their purpose is to prevent wars. While once the winners could kill the losers, now the losers can also kill the winners. This fundamental change requires a new approach to strategic doctrine.

For the two superpowers that emerged from World War II, the distinctive logic of deterrence in the nuclear age was shaped by three major concerns: (1) a fear of further armed conflict in the wake of the devastation wrought by World War II; (2) the realization of the destructive potential of atomic weapons; and (3) a growing suspicion and fear of each other's beliefs, intentions, and actions. In seeking to cope with this new reality, the two sides by 1949 (after the Soviet Union obtained nuclear weapons) had gradually adopted a strategy in which deterrence came to mean more than the ability to defend one's homeland or to punish a foe. By the end of the 1950s, both countries recognized that their ability to defend themselves against nuclear attack was severely limited. This awareness was and still is basic to the theory of nuclear deterrence. And this theory, when translated into policy terms, led to a search for "survivable" nuclear forces, forces that could inflict unacceptable damage on an aggressor even in the event of surprise attack.

For both parties, the implications of this logic are clear: the key to the success of A's effort to prevent war rests only in part on A's own decisions and actions. It resides as well in B's belief that an attack on A will inevitably result in unacceptable costs. Ironically, then, in today's world the current Soviet and American leaders each hold part of the key to the other's security. Both Soviet and American citizens are dependent not only upon the rationality of their own leadership, but on that of their potential opponent's as well. The success of the U.S.-Soviet deterrent relationship, therefore, rests on a precariously balanced set of policy doctrines and new weapons systems developed in accordance with the peculiar logic of deterrence.

Although an examination of the various doctrines and weapons systems that have developed during the more than forty-year history of the nuclear era is beyond the scope of this short commentary, we can highlight some of the major points. The reality of the past four decades is that doctrine and weapons have had an interactive and self-reinforcing evolution, but we will discuss them separately, beginning with weapons systems.

The nuclear arms competition between the United States and the Soviet Union began in earnest after the dropping of the Hiroshima and Nagasaki bombs. As is indicated in Table 7.1, the evolution of nuclear weapons has involved a series of "races" for ever more powerful explosives and ways in which to deliver them. As the data clearly shows, the U.S. "won" most of these races but was generally able to maintain its edge for only a few years before the Soviets caught up. Always, in fact, the side which was behind has within a short period of time "caught up." Overall superiority, however, clearly rested with the United States in the first two decades, 1945-1965, of the nuclear era. Until the late 1950s, the Soviet Union was incapable of inflicting unacceptable damage on the continental United States. Since the mid-1960s, a rough parity of destructive sufficiency has existed; both sides have had the capability of destroying the other regardless of which one might strike first.

Until the late 1970s the deterrent forces of the two sides were distinctive in form. The U.S. force had three major elements: land-based missiles (ICBMS), submarine-based missiles (SLBMS), and a strategic bomber force. This Strategic Triad was in part the product of superior U.S. technology, but it also reflected an American emphasis on survivability as one of the keys to deterrence. The Soviets, on the other hand, placed much heavier emphasis (about 65 percent of their nuclear force) on land-based ICBMS, many in hardened silos, in the belief that their numbers and the relative invulnerability of the silos would deter a U.S. attack.

Table 7-1 Superpower Nuclear Competition

United States	Innovation	Soviet Union
1945	Fission explosion	1949
1948	Intercontinental bomber	1955
1952	Fusion explosion	1953
1958	Test of ICBM	1957
1960	Operational ICBM	1959
1960	Operational SLBM	1963
1962	Solid propellant ICBM	1968
1966	Multiple warhead (MRV)	1968
1972	Anti-ballistic missile system (ABM)	1968
1970	Multiple independently targetable reentry vehicle (MIRV)	1975
1982	Long-range cruise missiles	198?
1983	Neutron bomb	198?

Throughout this period, both sides attempted to ensure the survivability of their deterrent force by a variety of strategies, such as increasing the number of warheads and delivery vehicles, hardening their missile launching sites, dispersing missiles to different locations. and developing mobile launching systems. Most experts and policy makers agree that throughout this period a certain balance of terror existed between the superpowers. The Soviets tended to have more launchers and larger warheads, while the United States' missiles were more accurate. This particular mix of deterrent forces resulted in a relatively stable form of deterrence. Each side had certain tactical advantages over the other but not enough to risk a preemptive strike. Over time, each nation also developed a retaliatory (second-strike) capability sufficient to dissuade the other side from launching a first strike regardless of the circumstances.

The 1980s witnessed changes in each superpower's satisfaction with the existing strategic balance. The Soviets sought to remedy what was in their minds a substantial imbalance of forces by building more submarine launchers and modernizing their ICBM force. As part of the latter program, the Soviets began deployment of a new generation of weapons, medium- and shorter-range mobile systems, such as the SS-17, SS-18, SS-19, and SS-20 systems.

Fearing that the Soviets now sought superiority, especially in Europe, U.S. policy makers countered by deploying new medium-range missiles, the Pershing II and ground-launched cruise missiles (GLCMs), and began research on space-based missile defense systems (the strategic defense initiative or SDI to its proponents, Star Wars to its detractors).

The strategic effect of these deployments was to reduce the time each side had to determine during a crisis whether a nuclear strike by the other was imminent or underway. The resulting "launch on warning" situation, as it has been called, is regarded by most analysts as dangerous and potentially destabilizing. The recognition of the dangers inherent in this situation, along with the growth of peace movements in Europe and a desire to improve the overall U.S.-Soviet relationship, contributed to the agreement in late 1987 on the U.S.-Soviet INF treaty banning intermediate-range nuclear forces—including mobile systems.

Developments in Europe in the early 1980s and the subsequent INF accord made political issues of the dramatic growth of U.S. strategic forces *and* the evolution of U.S. strategic thinking. Initially, the Reagan administration suggested the purpose of its extensive defense buildup was to strengthen the credibility of the U.S. deterrent. Relevant trends in Soviet weapons acquisitions were cited to bolster the argument. It seems clear, however, that President Ronald Reagan also wished to alter traditional thinking about the role of nuclear weapons and deterrence. Viewing reliance on the doctrine of mutual assured destruction (MAD), which involves the threat of massive destruction of population centers, as immoral, he saw SDI as a very attractive alternative. In addition, at least some proponents of SDI, including Reagan and his first secretary of defense, Caspar Weinberger, were also thinking in terms of a war-fighting strategy (the outlines of which may be found in the article by Colin S. Gray and Keith Payne in this chapter). Such a strategy represented a fundamental shift in post-1945 strategic thinking.

The Logic of the Nuclear Era: Strategic Doctrines

If the logic of deterrence is in part determined by the nature of the available weapons, so is it also shaped by prevailing strategic doctrines. In the case of the United States, these doctrines have taken a variety of forms over time.

The first coherent U.S. doctrine was *massive retaliation*. As popularized in the 1950s by U.S. secretary of state John Foster Dulles, massive retaliation involved the threat to unleash the entire U.S. strategic nuclear force in the event of any unacceptable Soviet behavior. The problem with massive retaliation as a doctrine soon became clear. The credibility of the threat involved was dependent not only upon U.S. superiority in nuclear weapons and, more importantly, a willingness to employ them under a very wide range of circumstances, but also upon the Soviet Union's inability to mount an effective attack upon the United States. Once the Soviet Union became capable of launching such an attack, the credibility of American threats was greatly diminished.

Dissatisfied with massive retaliation, strategists in the late 1950s developed a new doctrine, *flexible response*, initially adopted by the Kennedy administration. Under flexible response, aggressive actions by the Soviets were to be met with equivalent, or slightly more than equivalent, responses. Deterrence then was to be maximized by providing policy makers with a wider range of possible responses, thus increasing the credibility of the threat.

In the early 1960s, both massive retaliation and flexible response were replaced by yet another strategic doctrine, *assured destruction*, or, as it quickly became known by proponents and opponents alike, *mutual assured destruction*, or *MAD*. Mutual assured destruction called for both sides to target each other's population centers. With both sides having a recognizable second-strike capability, the two nations were thus assured that, regardless of who attacked first, both sides would be destroyed. In the logic of MAD, there would be no attack because the result would be self-destruction. In effect, MAD holds the populations of both superpowers hostage.

A continuing issue under all three doctrines—massive retaliation, flexible response, and MAD—was targeting. In the jargon of the nuclear era, the alternatives are *countervalue targeting*, or targeting aimed at population and industrial centers, and *counterforce targeting*, or targeting aimed at weapons and military installations. From 1962 until 1979, the official declaratory policy of the United States called for countervalue targeting. Proponents of countervalue targeting, such as Robert McNamara, secretary of defense from

1961 to 1967, had argued successfully against counterforce targeting by noting that it would call into question the survivability of each side's second-strike forces, thus weakening deterrence. Nonetheless, as we have subsequently learned, the Single Integrated Operational Plan (SIOP), the actual targeting plan for United States strategic forces, had throughout this period employed a counterforce targeting strategy, U.S. declaratory policy notwithstanding. Since 1979 both declaratory and actual targeting policy have involved a mix of counterforce and countervalue targeting. As both sides' destructive capabilities grew to unprecedented levels, a harsh and ironic set of realities became apparent. First, the competition in weapons development had led to something more than the original objective of deterrence. It now also promised the destruction of both the United States and the Soviet Union if deterrence failed.

Second, because the risks of MAD were too high, and because the destructive capabilities of the weapons on which it rested were so great as virtually to preclude their use, both sides felt compelled to seek new, less powerful but more accurate weapons. And with the search for new weapons came a quest for new doctrine. Thus, in the early 1980s the once-discarded concept of limited (or theater) nuclear war was once again being openly discussed. Deterrent policy had moved from mutual assured destruction to nuclear utilization target selection—or—as the title of the article by Spurgeon M. Keeny, Jr., and Wolfgang K. H. Panofsky so aptly indicates, from MAD to NUTS!

Third, in such a context, the United States and the Soviet Union find arms control agreements beneficial to their security in direct proportion to the extent to which they enhance deterrence. Thus the SALT I and SALT II treaties (the second unratified by the United States but nonetheless observed by both sides until late 1986) appeared helpful to both superpowers, because each agreement established some quantitative limits on force levels. But, as critics note, this approach to arms control has neither slowed the arms race nor reduced the risk of war. Nor, they argue, will it accomplish either until a serious reduction in missile numbers and control of the qualitative aspects of nuclear weapons—range, destructive capability, and launch type—become the goals of superpower arms control discussions. Until then, the arms control process may, in fact, sustain the arms race.

Finally, whereas deterrence was originally developed as a theoretical framework for understanding the implications of nuclear weapons for national security policy, it may in some sense have now become the strategy itself. For the United States this may be best illustrated by the comments of former secretary of state Alexander Haig, reprinted here. Concerns about the stability of the deterrence relationship, as well as the ever-increasing power of nuclear weapons, have led more than one scholar to ask the fearful question: Will deterrence survive this century, and therefore, by implication, will we?

The Readings

The readings that follow quite clearly illustrate the interconnections between deterrence policy and theory and the available choices in weaponry. The fundamental assumptions of deterrence theory and the effectiveness of the deterrent provided by different weapons systems and deployment strategies are debated in contrasting articles. Gray and Payne argue that deterrence will be improved by choosing counterforce nuclear targeting options and adopting a military posture that makes it possible to fight a nuclear war. This NUTS approach requires, in addition to continued improvements in the range, accuracy, and precision of offensive weapons, improvements in ballistic missile and air defense to increase the survivability of offensive systems. In direct contrast, Keeny and Panofsky claim that such strategies are destabilizing and illusory. They assert that the technological improvements in the destructive powers of the weapons themselves doom attempts to break out of the assured destruction stalemate. In their view it will always be a MAD world.

The arguments advanced by Gray and Payne are similar to those underlying the Reagan administration's arms control and defense policies. Keeny and Panofsky's argument is representative of the mainstream strategic arms community's challenge to the Reagan administration's policies and is also, as both sets of authors make clear, much closer to the prevailing scholarly position of the past forty years.

The next selection, by Huth and Russett, reminds us of the importance of the larger political and military context of any deterrence relationship. Their data-based examination of the conditions under which national leaders "make good" on their threats to extend deterrence empirically tests a number of the assumptions discussed in this chapter. Their analysis reveals that close ties are the best predictor of whether nation A will, in fact, carry out a threat aimed at deterring action by nation B against nation C. Their findings also suggest that nuclear weapons are of marginal value in extending deterrence to third parties. This selection provides a real-world test of some of the important predictions of deterrence theory.

Finally, the diametrically opposed policy statements by former secretary of state Alexander Haig and political scientist James Stegenga illustrate the diversity of uses to which theory can be put. It is important to note that the Haig speech was specifically intended by the Reagan administration to reinforce the importance of deterrence to U.S. defense policy and to a stable world order. When Haig made the statement, the United States was under heavy criticism in Europe for the scheduled deployment of Pershing II and ground-launched cruise missiles (GLCMs). At the same time, in the United States, a proposed nuclear freeze was being debated on the floor of Congress. In the face of division abroad and dissension at home, the administration sought both to elucidate its theory of defense and to provide a rallying point for allies and those who sought peace in a world beset by weapons of mass destruction.

315

Introduction

The concluding piece, by Stegenga, challenges the Haig argument. Stegenga questions the reliability and morality of deterrence as a strategy and the costs of both its "successful" continuance and—in his view—its probable failure. Underlying his concern is the possibility that the technology of nuclear weaponry has reduced, if not fatally weakened, the ability of the nation-state and the nation-state system to provide international security.

Interestingly, a year after Haig's speech, President Reagan gave public utterance to his own doubts about the deterrence "solution." Addressing the disquieted audience that had reacted to a lack of progress in arms control, the deployment of still more missiles in Europe, and requests for additional increases in defense expenditures, Reagan enunciated his vision of a strategic defense initiative. In a politically adept, vintage Reagan speech, the president expressed his pride in American technology and his hope for the future while confessing his doubts about deterrence. He proposed a technological fix, a defensive shield to intercept and destroy ballistic missiles before they could reach U.S. soil or that of its allies.

While the scientific merits of the president's proposal have been subjected to much criticism, it is clear that the hope of finding a technological fix to the problem of nuclear weapons is likely to be with us for some time. Along with the seemingly inevitable emergence of more powerful weapons and continuing efforts at arms control, this hope seems likely to shape the development of U.S. national security policy for many years to come.

■■■■■■ **7.1**

COLIN S. GRAY
KEITH PAYNE

Victory Is Possible

Nuclear war is possible. But unlike Armageddon, the apocalyptic war prophesied to end history, nuclear war can have a wide range of possible outcomes. Many commentators and senior U.S. government officials consider it a nonsurvivable event. The popularity of this view in Washington has such a pervasive and malign effect upon American defense planning that it is rapidly becoming a self-fulfilling prophecy for the United States.

Recognition that war at any level can be won or lost, and that the distinction between winning and losing would not be trivial, is essential for intelligent defense planning. Moreover, nuclear war can occur regardless of the quality of U.S. military posture and the content of American strategic theory. If it does, deterrence, crisis management, and escalation control might play a negligible role. Through an inability to communicate or through Soviet disinterest in receiving and acting upon American messages, the United States might not even have the option to surrender and thus might have to fight the war as best it can. Furthermore, the West needs to devise ways in which it can employ strategic nuclear forces coercively, while minimizing the potentially paralyzing impact of self-deterrence.

If American nuclear power is to support U.S. foreign policy objectives, the United States must possess the ability to wage nuclear war rationally. This requirement is inherent in the geography of East-West relations, in the persisting deficiencies in Western conventional and theater nuclear forces, and in the distinction between the objectives of a revolutionary and status quo power.

U.S. strategic planning should exploit Soviet fears insofar as is feasible from the Soviet perspective; take full account of likely Soviet responses and the willingness of Americans to accept those responses; and provide for the protection of American territory. Such planning would enhance the prospect for effective deterrence and survival during a war. Only recently has U.S. nuclear targeting policy been based on careful study of the Soviet Union as a distinct political culture, but the U.S. defense community continues to resist many of the policy implications of Soviet responses to U.S. weapons programs. In addition, the U.S. government simply does not recognize the validity of

Reprinted with permission from *Foreign Policy* 39 (Summer 1980). Copyright © 1980 by The Carnegie Endowment for International Peace.

attempting to relate its freedom of offensive nuclear action and the credibility of its offensive nuclear threat to the protection of American territory.

Critics of such strategic planning are vulnerable in two crucial respects. They do not, and cannot, offer policy prescriptions that will insure that the United States is never confronted with the stark choice between fighting a nuclear war or surrendering, and they do not offer a concept of deterrence that meets the extended responsibilities of U.S. strategic nuclear forces. No matter how elegant the deterrence theory, a question that cannot be avoided is what happens if deterrence mechanisms fail? Theorists whose concept of deterrence is limited to massive retaliation after Soviet attack would have nothing of interest to say to a president facing conventional defeat in the Persian Gulf or in Western Europe. Their strategic environment exists only in peacetime. They can recommend very limited, symbolic options but have no theory of how a large-scale Soviet response is to be deterred.

Because many believe that homeland defense will lead to a steeper arms race and destabilize the strategic balance, the U.S. defense community has endorsed a posture that maximizes the prospect for self-deterrence. Yet the credibility of the extended U.S. deterrent depends on the Soviet belief that a U.S. president would risk nuclear escalation on behalf of foreign commitments.

In the late 1960s the United States endorsed the concept of strategic parity without thinking through what that would mean for the credibility of America's nuclear umbrella. A condition of parity or essential equivalence is incompatible with extended deterrent duties because of the self-deterrence inherent in such a strategic context. However, the practical implications of parity may be less dire in some areas of U.S. vital interest. Western Europe, for example, is so important an American interest that Soviet leaders could be more impressed by the character and duration of the U.S. commitment than by the details of the strategic balance.

A Threat to Commit Suicide

Ironically, it is commonplace to assert that war-survival theories affront the crucial test of political and moral acceptability. Surely no one can be comfortable with the claim that a strategy that would kill millions of Soviet citizens and would invite a strategic response that could kill tens of millions of U.S. citizens would be politically and morally acceptable. However, it is worth recalling the six guidelines for the use of force provided by the "just war" doctrine of the Catholic Church: Force can be used in a just cause; with a right intent; with a reasonable chance of success; in order that, if successful, its use offers a better future than would have been the case had it not been employed; to a degree proportional to the goals sought, or to the evil combated; and with the determination to spare noncombatants, when there is a reasonable chance of doing so.

These guidelines carry a message for U.S. policy. Specifically, as long as nuclear threat is a part of the U.S. diplomatic arsenal and provided that threat reflects real operational intentions—it is not a total bluff—U.S. defense planners are obliged to think through the probable course of a nuclear war. They must also have at least some idea of the intended relationship between force applied and the likelihood that political goals will be achieved—that is, a strategy.

Current American strategic policy is not compatible with at least three of the six just-war guidelines. The policy contains no definition of success aside from denying victory to the enemy, no promise that the successful use of nuclear power would insure a better future than surrender, and no sense of proportion because central war strategy in operational terms is not guided by political goals. In short, U.S. nuclear strategy is immoral.

Those who believe that a central nuclear war cannot be waged for political purposes because the destruction inflicted and suffered would dwarf the importance of any political goals can construct a coherent and logical policy position. They argue that nuclear war will be the end of history for the states involved, and that a threat to initiate nuclear war is a threat to commit suicide and thus lacks credibility. However, they acknowledge that nuclear weapons cannot be abolished. They maintain that even incredible threats may deter, provided the affront in question is sufficiently serious, because miscalculation by an adversary could have terminal consequences; because genuinely irrational behavior is always possible; and because the conflict could become uncontrollable.

In the 1970s the U.S. defense community rejected this theory of deterrence. Successive strategic targeting reviews appeared to move U.S. policy further and further from the declaratory doctrine of mutual assured destruction adopted by former Secretary of Defense Robert S. McNamara. Yet U.S. defense planners have not thoroughly studied the problems of nuclear war nor thought through the meaning of strategy in relation to nuclear war. The U.S. defense community has always tended to regard strategic nuclear war not as war but as a holocaust. Former Secretary of Defense James R. Schlesinger apparently adopted limited nuclear options (LNOs)—strikes employing anywhere from a handful to several dozen warheads—as a compromise between the optimists of the minimum deterrence school and the pessimists of the so-called war-fighting persuasion. By definition, LNOs apply only to the initial stages of a war. But what happens once LNOs have been exhausted? If the Soviets retaliated after U.S. LNOs, the United States would face the dilemma of escalating further or conciliating.

Deterrence may fail to be restored during war for several reasons: The enemy may not grant, in operational practice, the concept of intrawar deterrence and simply wage the war as it is able; and command, control, and communications may be degraded so rapidly that strategic decicisions are precluded and both sides execute their war plans. Somewhat belatedly, the U.S. defense community has come to understand that flexibility in targeting and

LNOs do not constitute a strategy and cannot compensate for inadequate strategic nuclear forces.

LNOs are the tactics of the strong, not of a country entering a period of strategic inferiority, as the United States is now. LNOs would be operationally viable only if the United States had a plausible theory of how it could control and dominate later escalation.

The fundamental inadequacy of flexible targeting, as presented in the 1970s, is that it neglected to take proper account of the fact that the United States would be initiating a process of competitive escalation that it had no basis for assuming could be concluded on satisfactory terms. Flexible targeting was an adjunct to plans that had no persuasive vision of how the application of force would promote the attainment of political objectives.

War Aims

U.S. strategic targeting doctrine must have a unity of political purpose from the first to the last strikes. Strategic flexibility, unless wedded to a plausible theory of how to win a war or at least insure an acceptable end to a war, does not offer the United States an adequate bargaining position before or during a conflict and is an invitation to defeat. Small, preplanned strikes can only be of use if the United States enjoys strategic superiority—the ability to wage a nuclear war at any level of violence with a reasonable prospect of defeating the Soviet Union and of recovering sufficiently to insure a satisfactory postwar world order.

However, the U.S. government does not yet appear ready to plan seriously for the actual conduct of nuclear war should deterrence fail, in spite of the fact that such a policy should strengthen deterrence. Assured-destruction reasoning is proclaimed officially to be insufficient in itself as a strategic doctrine. However, a Soviet assured-destruction capability continues to exist as a result of the enduring official U.S. disinterest in strategic defense, with potentially paralyzing implications for the United States. No matter how well designed and articulated, targeting plans that allow an enemy to inflict in retaliation whatever damage it wishes on American society are likely to prove unusable.

Four interdependent areas of strategic policy—strategy, weapons development and procurement, arms control, and defense doctrine—are currently treated separately. Theoretically, strategy should determine the evolution of the other three areas. In practice, it never has. Most of what has been portrayed as war-fighting strategy is nothing of the kind. Instead, it is an extension of the American theory of deterrence into war itself. To advocate LNOs and targeting flexibility and selectivity is not the same as to advocate a war-fighting, war-survival strategy.

Strategists do not find the idea of nuclear war fighting attractive. Instead, they believe that an ability to wage and survive war is vital for the effectiveness of deterrence; there can be no such thing as an adequate deterrent posture unrelated to probable wartime effectiveness; victory or defeat in nuclear war is possible, and such a war may have to be waged to that point; and, the clearer the vision of successful war termination, the more likely war can be waged intelligently at earlier stages.

There should be no misunderstanding the fact that the primary interest of U.S. strategy is deterrence. However, American strategic forces do not exist solely for the purpose of deterring a Soviet nuclear threat or attack against the United States itself. Instead, they are intended to support U.S. foreign policy, as reflected, for example, in the commitment to preserve Western Europe against aggression. Such a function requires American strategic forces that would enable a president to initiate strategic nuclear use for coercive, though politically defensive, purposes.

U.S. strategy, typically, has proceeded from the bottom up. Such targeting does not involve any conception of the war as a whole, nor of how the war might be concluded on favorable terms. The U.S. defense community cannot plan intelligently for lower levels of combat, unless it has an acceptable idea of where they might lead.

Most analyses of flexible targeting options assume virtually perfect stability at the highest levels of conflict. Advocates of flexible targeting assert that a U.S. LNO would signal the beginning of an escalation process that the Soviets would wish to avoid in light of the American threat to Soviet urban-industrial areas. Yet it seems inconsistent to argue that the U.S. threat of assured destruction would deter the Soviets from engaging in escalation following an LNO but that U.S. leaders could initiate the process despite the Soviet threat. What could be the basis of such relative U.S. resolve and Soviet vacillation in the face of strategic parity or Soviet superiority?

Moreover, the desired deterrent effect would probably depend upon the Soviet analysis of the entire nuclear campaign. In other words, Soviet leaders would be less impressed by American willingness to launch an LNO than they would be by a plausible American victory strategy. Such a theory would have to envisage the demise of the Soviet state. The United States should plan to defeat the Soviet Union and to do so at a cost that would not prohibit U.S. recovery. Washington should identify war aims that in the last resort would contemplate the destruction of Soviet political authority and the emergence of a postwar world order compatible with Western values.

The most frightening threat to the Soviet Union would be the destruction or serious impairment of its political system. Thus, the United States should be able to destroy key leadership cadres, their means of communication, and some of the instruments of domestic control. The USSR, with its gross overcentralization of authority, epitomized by its vast bureaucracy in Moscow, should be highly vulnerable to such an attack. The Soviet Union might cease to function if its security agency, the KGB, were severely crippled. If the Moscow bureaucracy could be eliminated, damaged, or isolated, the USSR might disintegrate into anarchy, hence the extensive civil defense preparations intended to insure the survival of the Soviet leadership. Judicious U.S. targeting and weapon procurement policies might be able to deny the USSR the assurance of political survival.

Once the defeat of the Soviet state is established as a war aim, defense professionals should attempt to identify an optimum targeting plan for the accomplishment of that goal. For example, Soviet political control of its territory in Central Asia and in the Far East could be weakened by discriminate nuclear targeting. The same applies to Transcaucasia and Eastern Europe.

The Ultimate Penalty

Despite a succession of U.S. targeting reviews, Soviet leaders, looking to the mid-1980s, may well anticipate the ability to wage World War III successfully. The continuing trend in the East-West military balance allows Soviet military planners to design a theory of military victory that is not implausible and that may stir hopes among Soviet political leaders that they might reap many of the rewards of military success even without having to fight. The Soviets may anticipate that U.S. self-deterrence could discourage Washington from punishing Soviet society. Even if the United States were to launch a large-scale second strike against Soviet military and economic targets, the resulting damage should be bearable to the Soviet Union given the stakes of the conflict and the fact that the Soviets would control regions abroad that could contribute to its recovery.

In the late 1960s the United States identified the destruction of the 20-25 per cent of the population and 50-75 per cent of industrial capacity as the ultimate penalty it had to be able to inflict on the USSR. In the 1970s the United States shifted its attention to the Soviet recovery economy. The Soviet theory of victory depends on the requirement that the Soviet Union survive and recover rapidly from a nuclear conflict. However, the U.S. government does not completely understand the details of the Soviet recovery economy, and the concept has lost popularity as a result. Highly complex modeling of the Soviet economy cannot disguise the fact that the available evidence is too rudimentary to permit any confidence in the analysis. With an inadequate data base it should require little imagination to foresee how difficult it is to determine targeting priorities in relation to the importance of different economic targets for recovery.

Schlesinger's advocacy of essential equivalence called for a U.S. ability to match military damage for military damage. But American strategic development since the early 1970s has not been sufficient to maintain the American end of that balance. Because the U.S. defense community has refused to recognize the importance of the possibility that a nuclear war could be won or lost, it has neglected to think beyond a punitive sequence of targeting options.

American nuclear strategy is not intended to defeat the Soviet Union or insure the survival of the United States in any carefully calculated manner. Instead, it is intended to insure that the Soviet Union is punished increasingly severely. American targeting philosophy today is only a superficial improvement over that prevalent in the late 1960s, primarily because U.S. defense planners do not consider anticipated damage to the United States to be relevant to the integrity of their offensive war plans. The strategic case for ballistic missile defense and civil defense has not been considered on its merits for a decade.

In the late 1970s the United States targeted a range of Soviet economic entities that were important either to war-supporting industry or to economic recovery. The rationale for this targeting scheme was, and remains, fragile. War-supporting industry is important only for a war of considerable duration or for a period of post-war defense mobilization.

Moreover, although recovery from war is an integral part of a Soviet theory of victory, it is less important than the achievement of military success. If the USSR is able to win the war, it should have sufficient military force in reserve to compel the surviving world economy to contribute to Soviet recovery. Thus, the current trend is to move away from targeting the recovery economy.

To date, the U.S. government has declined to transcend what amounts to a deterrence-through-punishment approach to strategic war planning. Moreover, the strategic targeting reviews of the 1970s did not address the question of self-deterrence adequately. The United States has no ballistic missile defense and effectively no civil defense, while U.S. air defense is capable of guarding American air space only in peacetime. The Pentagon has sought to compensate for a lack of relative military muscle through more imaginative strategic targeting. Review after review has attempted to identify more effective ways in which the USSR could be hurt. Schlesinger above all sought essential equivalence through a more flexible set of targeting options without calling for extensive new U.S. strategic capabilities. Indeed, he went to some pains to separate the question of targeting design from procurement issues.

The United States should identify nuclear targeting options that could help restore deterrence, yet would destroy the Soviet state and enhance the likelihood of U.S. survival if fully implemented. The first priority of such a targeting scheme would be Soviet military power of all kinds, and the second would be the political, military, and economic control structure of the USSR. Successful strikes against military and political control targets would reduce the Soviet ability to project military power abroad and to sustain political authority at home. However, it would not be in the interest of the United States actually to implement an offensive nuclear strategy no matter how frightening in Soviet perspective, if the U.S. homeland were totally naked to Soviet retaliation.

Striking the USSR should entail targeting the relocation bunkers of the top political and bureaucratic leadership, including those of the KGB; key communication centers of the Communist party, the military, and the government; and many of the economic, political, and military records. Even limited destruction of some of these targets and substantial isolation of many of the key personnel who survive could have revolutionary consequences for the country.

The Armageddon Syndrome

The strategic questions that remain incompletely answered are in some ways more difficult than the practical problems of targeting the political control structure. Is it sensible to destroy the government of the enemy, thus eliminating the option of negotiating an end to the war? In the unlikely event that the United States identifies all of the key relocation bunkers for the central political leadership, who would then conduct the Soviet war effort and to what ends? Since after a large-scale counter-control strike the surviving Soviet leadership would have little else to fear, could this targeting option be anything other than a threat?

The U.S. defense community today believes that the political control structure of the USSR is among the most important targets for U.S. strategic forces. However, just how important such targeting might be for deterrence or damage limitation has not been determined. Current American understanding of exactly how the control structure functions is less than perfect. But that is a technical matter that can in principle be solved through more research. The issue of whether the Soviet control structure should actually be struck is more problematic.

Strategists cannot offer painless conflicts or guarantee that their preferred posture and doctrine promise a greatly superior deterrence posture to current American schemes. But, they can claim that an intelligent U.S. offensive strategy, wedded to homeland defenses, should reduce U.S. casualties to approximately 20 million, which should render U.S. strategic threats more credible. If the United States developed the targeting plans and procured the weapons necessary to hold the Soviet political, bureaucratic, and military leadership at risk, that should serve as the functional equivalent in Soviet perspective of the assured-destruction effect of the late 1960s. However, the U.S. targeting community has not determined how it would organize this targeting option.

A combination of counterforce offensive targeting, civil defense, and ballistic missile and air defense should hold U.S. casualties down to a level compatible with national survival and recovery. The actual number would depend on several factors, some of which the United States could control (the level of U.S. homeland defenses); some of which it could influence (the weight and character of the Soviet attack); and some of which might evade anybody's ability to control or influence (for example, the weather). What can be assured is a choice between a defense program that insures the survival of the vast majority of Americans with relative confidence and one that deliberately permits the Soviet Union to wreak whatever level of damage it chooses.

No matter how grave the Soviet offense, a U.S. president cannot credibly threaten and should not launch a strategic nuclear strike if expected U.S. casualties are likely to involve 100 million or more American citizens. There is a difference between a doctrine that can offer little rational guidance should deterrence fail and a doctrine that a president might employ responsibly for identified political purposes. Existing evidence on the probable consequences of nuclear exchanges suggests that there should be a role for strategy in nuclear war. To ignore the possibility that strategy can be applied to nuclear war is to insure by choice a nuclear apocalypse if deterrence fails. The current U.S. deterrence posture is fundamentally flawed because it does not provide for the protection of American territory.

Nuclear war is unlikely to be an essentially meaningless, terminal event. Instead it is likely to be waged to coerce the Soviet Union to give up some recent gain. Thus, a president must have the ability not merely to end a war, but to end it favorably. The United States would need to be able to persuade desperate and determined Soviet leaders that it has the capability, and the determination, to wage nuclear war at ever higher levels of violence until an acceptable outcome is achieved. For deterrence to function during a war each side would have to calculate whether an improved outcome is possible through further escalation.

An adequate U.S. deterrent posture is one that denies the Soviet Union any plausible hope of success at any level of strategic conflict; offers a likely prospect of Soviet defeat; and offers a reasonable chance of limiting damage to the United States. Such a deterrence posture is often criticized as contributing to the arms race and causing strategic instability, because it would stimulate new Soviet deployments. However, during the 1970s the Soviet Union showed that its weapon development and deployment decisions are not dictated by American actions. Western understanding of what determines Soviet defense procurement is less than perfect, but it is now obvious that Soviet weapon decisions cannot be explained with reference to any simple action-reaction model of arms-race dynamics. In addition, highly survivable U.S. strategic forces should insure strategic stability by denying the Soviets an attractive first-strike target set.

An Armageddon syndrome lurks behind most concepts of nuclear strategy. It amounts either to the belief that because the United States could lose as many as 20 million people, it should not save the 80 million or more who otherwise would be at risk, or to a disbelief in the serious possibility that 200 million Americans could survive a nuclear war.

There is little satisfaction in advocating an operational nuclear doctrine that could result in the deaths of 20 million or more people in an unconstrained nuclear war. However, as long as the United States relies on nuclear threats to deter an increasingly powerful Soviet Union, it is inconceivable that the U.S. defense community can continue to divorce its thinking on deterrence from its planning for the efficient conduct of war and defense of the country. Prudence in the latter should enhance the former.

7.2 ▬▬▬

SPURGEON M. KEENY, JR.
WOLFGANG K. H. PANOFSKY

MAD Versus NUTS:
Can Doctrine or Weaponry Remedy the Mutual Hostage Relationship of the Superpowers?

Since World War II there has been a continuing debate on military doctrine concerning the actual utility of nuclear weapons in war. This debate, irrespective of the merits of the divergent points of view, tends to create the perception that the outcome and scale of a nuclear conflict could be controlled by the doctrine or the types of nuclear weapons employed. Is this the case?

We believe not. In reality, the unprecedented risks of nuclear conflict are largely independent of doctrine or its application. The principal danger of doctrines that are directed at limiting nuclear conflicts is that they might be believed and form the basis for action without appreciation of the physical facts and uncertainties of nuclear conflict. The failure of policymakers to understand the truly revolutionary nature of nuclear weapons as instruments of war and the staggering size of the nuclear stockpiles of the United States and the Soviet Union could have catastrophic consequences for the entire world.

Military planners and strategic thinkers for 35 years have sought ways to apply the tremendous power of nuclear weapons against target systems that might contribute to the winning of a future war. In fact, as long as the United States held a virtual nuclear monopoly, the targeting of atomic weapons was looked upon essentially as a more effective extension of the strategic bombing concepts of World War II. With the advent in the mid-1950s of a substantial Soviet nuclear capability, including multimegaton thermonuclear weapons, it was soon apparent that the populations and societies of both the United States and the Soviet Union were mutual hostages. A portion of the nuclear stockpile of either side could inflict on the other as many as 100 million fatalities and destroy it as a functioning society. Thus, although the rhetoric of declaratory strategic doctrine has changed over the years, mutual deterrence has in fact

From *Foreign Affairs* (Winter 1981/82). Copyright © 1981 by the Council on Foreign Relations, Inc. Reprinted with permission.

remained the central fact of the strategic relationship of the two superpowers and of the NATO and Warsaw Pact alliances.

Most observers would agree that a major conflict between the two hostile blocs on a worldwide scale during this period may well have been prevented by the specter of catastrophic nuclear war. At the same time, few would argue that this state of mutual deterrence is a very reassuring foundation on which to build world peace. In the 1960s the perception of the basic strategic relationship of mutual deterrence came to be characterized as "Mutual Assured Destruction," which critics were quick to note had the acronym of MAD. The notion of MAD has been frequently attacked not only as militarily unacceptable but also as immoral since it holds the entire civilian populations of both countries as hostages.

As an alternative to MAD, critics and strategic innovators have over the years sought to develop various war-fighting targeting doctrines that would somehow retain the use of nuclear weapons on the battlefield or even in controlled strategic war scenarios, while sparing the general civilian population from the devastating consequences of nuclear war. Other critics have found an alternative in a defense-oriented military posture designed to defend the civilian population against the consequences of nuclear war.

These concepts are clearly interrelated since such a defense-oriented strategy would also make a nuclear war-fighting doctrine more credible. But both alternatives depend on the solution of staggering technical problems. A defense-oriented military posture requires a nearly impenetrable air and missile defense over a large portion of the population. And any attempt to have a controlled war-fighting capability during a nuclear exchange places tremendous requirements not only on decisions made under incredible pressure by men in senior positions of responsibility but on the technical performance of command, control, communications and intelligence functions—called in professional circles "C³I" and which for the sake of simplicity we shall hereafter describe as "control mechanisms." It is not sufficient as the basis for defense policy to assert that science will "somehow" find solutions to critical technical problems on which the policy is dependent, when technical solutions are nowhere in sight.

In considering these doctrinal issues, it should be recognized that there tends to be a very major gap between declaratory policy and actual implementation expressed as targeting doctrine. Whatever the declaratory policy might be, those responsible for the strategic forces must generate real target lists and develop procedures under which various combinations of targets could be attacked. In consequence, the perceived need to attack every listed target, even after absorbing the worst imaginable first strike from the adversary, creates procurement "requirements," even though the military or economic importance of many of the targets is small.

In fact, it is not at all clear in the real world of war planning whether declaratory doctrine has generated requirements or whether the availability of weapons for targeting has created doctrine. With an estimated 30,000 warheads at the disposal of the United States, including more than 10,000 avowed to be strategic in character, it is necessary to target redundantly all urban areas and economic targets and to cover a wide range of military targets in order to frame uses for the stockpile. And, once one tries to deal with elusive mobile and secondary military targets, one can always make a case for requirements for more weapons and for more specialized weapon designs.

These doctrinal considerations, combined with the superabundance of nuclear weapons, have led to a conceptual approach to nuclear war which can be described as Nuclear Utilization Target Selection. For convenience, and not in any spirit of trading epithets, we have chosen the acronym of NUTS to characterize the various doctrines that seek to utilize nuclear weapons against specific targets in a complex of nuclear war-fighting situations intended to be limited, as well as the management over an extended period of a general nuclear war between the superpowers.

While some elements of NUTS may be involved in extending the credibility of our nuclear deterrent, this consideration in no way changes the fact that mutual assured destruction, or MAD, is inherent in the existence of large numbers of nuclear weapons in the real world. In promulgating the doctrine of "countervailing strategy" in the summer of 1980, President Carter's Secretary of Defense Harold Brown called for a buildup of nuclear war-fighting capability in order to provide greater deterrence by demonstrating the ability of the United States to respond in a credible fashion without having to escalate immediately to all-out nuclear war. He was very careful, however, to note that he thought that it was "very likely" that the use of nuclear weapons by the superpowers at any level would escalate into general nuclear war. This situation is not peculiar to present force structures or technologies; and, regardless of future technical developments, it will persist as long as substantial nuclear weapon stockpiles remain.

Despite its possible contribution to the deterrence of nuclear war, the NUTS approach to military doctrine and planning can very easily become a serious danger in itself. The availability of increasing numbers of nuclear weapons in a variety of designs and delivery packages at all levels of the military establishment inevitably encourages the illusion that somehow nuclear weapons can be applied in selected circumstances without unleashing a catastrophic series of consequences. As we shall see in more detail below, the recent uninformed debate on the virtue of the so-called neutron bomb as a selective device to deal with tank attacks is a depressing case in point. NUTS creates its own endless pressure for expanded nuclear stockpiles with increasing danger of accidents, accidental use, diversions to terrorists, etc. But more fundamentally, it tends to obscure the fact that the nuclear world is in fact MAD.

The NUTS approach to nuclear war-fighting will not eliminate the essential MAD character of nuclear war for two basic reasons, which are rooted in the nature of nuclear weapons and the practical limits of technology. First, the destructive power of nuclear weapons, individually and most certainly in the large numbers discussed for even specialized application, is so great that the collateral effects on persons and property would be enormous and, in scenarios which are seriously discussed, would be hard to distinguish from the onset of general nuclear war. But more fundamentally, it does not seem possible, even in the most specialized utilization of nuclear weapons, to envisage any situation where escalation to general nuclear war would probably not occur given the dynamics of the situation and the limits of the control mechanisms that could be made available to manage a limited nuclear war. In the case of a protracted general nuclear war, the control problem becomes completely unmanageable. Finally, there does not appear to be any prospect for the foreseeable future that technology will provide a secure shield behind which the citizens of the two superpowers can safely observe the course of a limited nuclear war on other people's territory.

The thesis that we live in an inherently MAD world rests ultimately on the technical conclusion that effective protection of the population against large-scale nuclear attack is not possible. This pessimistic technical assessment, which follows inexorably from the devastating power of nuclear weapons, is dramatically illustrated by the fundamental difference between air defense against conventional and nuclear attack. Against bombers carrying conventional bombs, an air defense system destroying only 10 percent of the incoming bombers per sortie would, as a practical matter, defeat sustained air raids such as the ones during World War II. After ten attacks against such a defense, the bomber force would be reduced to less than one-third of its initial size, a very high price to pay given the limited damage from conventional weapons even when over 90 percent of the bombers penetrate. In contrast, against a bomber attack with nuclear bombs, an air defense capable of destroying even 90 percent of the incoming bombers on each sortie would be totally inadequate since the damage produced by the penetrating 10 percent of the bombers would be devastating against urban targets.

When one extends this air defense analogy to ballistic missile defenses intended to protect population and industry against large numbers of nuclear missiles, it becomes clear that such a defense would have to be almost leakproof since the penetration of even a single warhead would cause great destruction to a soft target. In fact, such a ballistic missile defense would have to be not only almost leakproof but also nationwide in coverage since the attacker could always choose the centers of population or industry he wished to target. The attacker has the further advantage that he can not only choose his targets but also decide what fraction of his total resources to expend against any particular target. Thus, an effective defense would have to be extremely heavy across the entire defended territory, not at just a few priority targets. The technical problem of providing an almost leakproof missile defense is further compounded by the many technical measures the attacking force can employ to interfere with the defense by blinding or confusing its radars or other sensors and overwhelming the system's traffic-handling capacity with decoys.

When these general arguments are reduced to specific analysis, the conclusion is inescapable that effective protection of the population or industry of either of the superpowers against missile attack by the other is unattainable with present ABM (anti-ballistic missile) defense technology, since even the most elaborate systems could be penetrated by the other side at far less cost. This conclusion is not altered by prospective improvements in the components of present systems or by the introduction of new concepts such as lasers or particle beams into system design.

These conclusions, which address the inability of ballistic missile defense to eliminate the MAD character of the strategic relationship, do not necessarily apply to defense of very hard point targets, such as missile silos or shelters for mobile missiles. The defense of these hardened military targets does offer a more attractive technical opportunity since only the immediate vicinity of the hardened site needs to be defended and the survival of only a fraction of the defended silos is necessary to serve as a deterrent. Thus, the technical requirements for the system are much less stringent than for population or industrial defense and a much higher leakage rate can be tolerated. When these general remarks are translated into specific analysis which takes into account the many options available to the offense, hard site defense still does not look particularly attractive. Moreover, such a defense, even if partially successful, would not prevent the serious collateral fallout effects from the attack on the population discussed above. Nevertheless, the fact that these systems are technically feasible, and are advocated by some as effective, tends to confuse the public on the broader issue of the feasibility of urban defense against ballistic missiles.

The United States has a substantial research and development effort on ballistic missile defenses of land-based ICBMs as a possible approach to increase survivability of this leg of the strategic triad. The only program under serious consideration that could be deployed in this decade is the so-called LOAD (Low Altitude Defense) system. This system, which would utilize very small hardened radars and small missiles with small nuclear warheads, is designed to intercept at very close range those attacking missiles that might detonate close enough to the defended ICBM to destroy it. This last ditch defense is possible with nuclear weapons since the defended target is extremely hard and can tolerate nuclear detonations if they are not too close. While such a system for the defense of hard sites is technically feasible, there has been serious question as to whether it would be cost-effective in defending the MX in fixed Titan or Minuteman silos since the system could be overwhelmed relatively easily. In the case of the defense of a mobile MX in a multiple shelter system, the economics of the exchange ratios are substantially improved if the location of the mobile MX and mobile defense system are in fact unknown to the attacker; however, there are serious questions whether the presence of radiating radar systems might not actually compromise the location of the MX during an attack.

Looking further into the future, the U.S. research program is considering a much more sophisticated "layered" system for hard site defense. The outer layer would involve an extremely complex system using infrared sensors that would be launched on warning of a Soviet attack to identify and track incoming warheads. Based on this information, many interceptors, each carrying multiple, infrared-homing rockets with non-nuclear warheads, would be launched against the cloud of incoming warheads and attack them well outside the atmosphere. The warheads that leaked through this outer exoatmospheric layer would then be engaged by a close-in layer along the lines of the LOAD last ditch system described above.

It has been suggested that the outer layer exoatmospheric system might evolve into an effective area defense for population and industry. Actually, there are many rather fundamental technical questions that will take some time to answer about the ability of such a system to work at all against a deter-mined adversary in the time frame needed to deploy it. For example, such a system would probably be defeated by properly designed decoys or blinded by nuclear explosions and, above all, may well be far too complex for even prospective control capabilities to operate. Whatever the value of these types of systems for hard site defense to support the MAD role of the deterrent, it is clear that the system holds no promise for population or industry defense and simply illustrates the technical difficulty of dealing with that problem.

While the government struggles with the much less demanding problem whether it is possible to design a plausible, cost-effective defense of hardened ICBM silos, the public is bombarded with recurring reports that some new technological "breakthrough" will suddenly generate an "impenetrable um-brella" which would obviate the MAD strategic relationship. Such irresponsible reports usually rehash claims for "directed energy" weapons which are based on the propagation of extremely energetic beams of either light (lasers) or atomic particles propagated at the speed of light to the target. Some of the pro-posals are technically infeasible, but in all cases one must remember that for ur-ban defense only a system with country-wide coverage and extraordinarily effective performance would have an impact on the MAD condition. To constitute a ballistic missile defense system, directed energy devices would have to be integrated with detection and tracking devices for the incoming warheads, an extremely effective and fast data-handling system, the necessary power supplies for the extraordinarily high demand of energy to feed the directed energy weapons, and would have to be very precisely oriented to score a direct hit to destroy the target—as opposed to nuclear warheads that would only have to get in the general vicinity to destroy the target.

There are fundamental considerations that severely limit the application of directed energy weapons to ballistic missile defense. Particle beams do not penetrate the atmosphere. Thus, if such a system were ground-based, it would have to bore a hole through the atmosphere and then the beam would have to be focused through that hole in a subsequent pulse. All analyses have indicated that it is physically impossible to accomplish this feat stably. Among other things, laser systems suffer from the fact that they can only operate in good weather since clouds interfere with the beam.

These problems involving the atmosphere could be avoided by basing the system in space. Moreover, a space-based system has the desirable feature of potentially being able to attack missiles during the vulnerable launch phase before the reentry vehicles are dispersed. However, space-based systems involve putting a very complex system with a large power requirement into orbit. Analysis indicates that a comprehensive defensive system of this type would require over a hundred satellites, which in turn would need literally thousands of space shuttle sorties to assemble. It has been estimated that such a system would cost several hundred billion dollars. Even if the control mechanisms were available to operate such a system, there are serious questions as to the vulnerability of the satellites to physical attack and to various measures that would interfere with the system's operation. In short, no responsible analysis has indicated that for at least the next two decades such "death ray weapons" have any bearing on the ABM problem or that there is any prospect that they would subsequently change the MAD character of our world.

Defense against aircraft further illustrates the inherently MAD nature of today's world. Although the Soviets have made enormous investments in air defense, the airborne component of the U.S. strategic triad has not had its damage potential substantially reduced. Most analyses indicate that a large fraction of the "aging" B-52 fleet would penetrate present Soviet defenses, with the aid of electronic countermeasures and defense suppression by missiles. It is true that the ability of B-52s to penetrate will gradually be impaired as the Soviets deploy "look down" radar planes similar to the much publicized AWACS (Airborne Warning and Control System). However, these systems will not be effective against the air-launched cruise missiles whose deployment on B-52s will begin shortly; their ability to penetrate will not be endangered until a totally new generation of Soviet air defenses enters the picture. At that time, one can foresee major improvements in the ability of both bombers and cruise missiles to penetrate through a number of techniques, in particular the so-called "stealth" technology which will reduce by a large factor the visibility of both airplanes and cruise missiles to radar.

In short, there is little question that in the defense-offense race between air defenses and the airborne leg of the triad, the offense will retain its enormous damage potential. For its part, the United States does not now have a significant air defense, and the limited buildup proposed in President Reagan's program would have little effect on the ability of the Soviets to deliver nuclear weapons by aircraft against this country. Consequently, the "mutual hostage" relationship between the two countries will continue, even if only the airborne component of the triad is considered.

It is sometimes asserted that civil defense could provide an escape from the consequences of the MAD world and make even a general nuclear war between the superpowers winnable. This assertion is coupled with a continuing controversy as to the actual effectiveness of civil defense and the scope of the present Soviet civil defense program. Much of this debate reflects the complete failure of some civil defense advocates to comprehend the actual consequences of nuclear war. There is no question that civil defense could save lives and that the Soviet effort in this field is substantially greater than that of the United States. Yet all analyses have made it abundantly clear that to have a significant impact in a general nuclear war, civil defense would have to involve a much greater effort than now practiced on either side and that no amount of effort would protect a large portion of the population or the ability of either nation to continue as a functioning society.

There is evidence that the Soviets have carried out a shelter program which could provide fallout and some blast protection for about ten percent of the urban population. The only way even to attempt to protect the bulk of the population would be complete evacuation of the entire urban population to the countryside. Although to our knowledge there has never been an actual urban evacuation exercise in the Soviet Union, true believers in the effectiveness of Soviet civil defense point to the alleged existence of detailed evacuation plans for all Soviet cities. Yet, when examined in detail, there are major questions as to the practicality of such evacuation plans.

The U.S. Arms Control and Disarmament Agency has calculated, using a reasonable model and assuming normal targeting practices, that even with the general evacuation of all citizens and full use of shelters, in a general war there would still be at least 25 million Soviet fatalities. Such estimates obviously depend on the model chosen: some have been lower but others by the Defense Department have been considerably higher. The time for such an all-out evacuation would be at least a week. This action would guarantee unambiguous strategic warning and provide ample time for the other side to generate its strategic forces to full alert, which would result in a substantially greater retaliatory strike than would be expected from normal day-to-day alert. If the retaliatory strike were ground burst to maximize fallout, fatalities could rise to 40 to 50 million; and if part of the reserve of nuclear weapons were targeted against the evacuated population, some 70 to 85 million could be killed. Until recently little has been said about the hopeless fate of the vast number of fallout casualties in the absence of organized medical care or what would become of the survivors with the almost complete destruction of the economic base and urban housing.

Finally, there is no evidence that the Soviets are carrying out industrial hardening or are decentralizing their industry, which remains more centralized than U.S. industry. This is not surprising since there is nothing they can do that would materially change the inherent vulnerability of urban society in a MAD world.

In sum, we are fated to live in a MAD world. This is inherent in the tremendous power of nuclear weapons, the size of nuclear stockpiles, the collateral damage associated with the use of nuclear weapons against military targets, the technical limitations on strategic area defense, and the uncertainties involved in efforts to control the escalation of nuclear war. There is no reason to believe that this situation will change for the foreseeable future since the problem is far too profound and the pace of technical military development far too slow to overcome the fundamental technical considerations that underlie the mutual hostage relationship of the superpowers.

What is clear above all is that the profusion of proposed NUTS approaches has not offered an escape from the MAD world, but rather constitutes a major danger in encouraging the illusion that limited or controlled nuclear war can be waged free from the grim realities of a MAD world. The principal hope at this time will not be found in seeking NUTS doctrines that ignore the MAD realities but rather in recognizing the nuclear world for what it is and seeking to make it more stable and less dangerous.

7.3

PAUL HUTH
BRUCE RUSSETT

What Makes Deterrence Work?
Cases from 1900 to 1980

Extended Deterrence of Overt Threats

The use of military force to achieve foreign-policy objectives is an enduring feature of international politics. Force, or the threat of force, may be used either to change the status quo or to maintain it. Threatening the use of force to maintain the status quo often takes the form of deterrence, defined by Patrick Morgan as "the threat to use force in response as a way of preventing the first use of force by someone else." Deterrence sometimes succeeds and sometimes fails. Failures are attested to by numerous international wars of history. In the nuclear age, a failure could cost us our lives. The conditions of successful deterrence thus require thorough logical and empirical analysis.

Deterrence may seek to prevent an attack on oneself, or an attack on some other party—in international politics, an ally, a client state, or a friendly neutral. Deterrence as practiced by major powers is most commonly deterrence

From *World Politics* 36, no. 4 (July 1984). Copyright © 1984 by Princeton University Press. Excerpts reprinted with permission of Princeton University Press.

of an attack on another party. This is known as "extended deterrence." For the United States since 1945, it has meant deterrence of attack on American allies in Western Europe, Asia, and the Middle East. It is a more precarious and demanding task than that of deterring a frontal attack on oneself. "Extended deterrence" will be the focus of this article. . . .

In this article we shall lay out an expected-utility model of deterrence and test that model on a set of cases of extended, immediate deterrence from the period 1900 to 1980. We shall conclude that successful deterrence is very much more than just a matter of having a favorable military balance, and very much a matter of the nature and extent of ties between the defender state and the state it wishes to protect. . . .

The problem, then, is one of immediate deterrence. We will employ Morgan's criteria to identify the relevant cases:

1. The officials in a state (which we shall call the "attacker") are considering attacking a state ("protégé") that is formally allied to or deemed important by a third state ("defender").

2. Key officials in the defender state realize this.

3. Recognizing that an attack is a distinct possibility, the officials of the defender state, either explicitly or by movement of military forces, threaten the use of retaliatory force in an effort to prevent the attack.

The threats of the attacker and defender states must be overt and clearly entail the use of military force, and the target of the attack (protégé) must be clearly identifiable. We are concerned only with the period before substantial interstate violence begins. Subsequently the defender's task becomes one of compellence—stopping an action already undertaken—which is more demanding than deterrence. . . .

An Expected-Utility Model

Deterrence can be viewed as a game of strategic interaction, in which a "rational" opponent assesses the potential costs and benefits of its actions based upon expectations regarding the likely behavior of its adversary. By this view, a deterrent threat is effective to the extent it can product cost-benefit calculations on the part of the potential attacker in which the expected utility of an attack would be less than the expected utility of foregoing the attack. The expected gains from an attack must be so small, or the expected losses so substantial, that abstaining from attack will produce a more favorable outcome (greater gains or, more likely, smaller losses). . . .

Most attention in analyzing deterrent situations is usually given to the balance of military capabilities between attacker and defender. The attacker must assess whether it has sufficient military power to win a war with the defender, and at what cost. . . .

Deterrence is a much more complex problem than simply weighing military balances, however. As [Alexander] George and [Richard] Smoke point out, "the requirements for implementing deterrence are much less a matter of acquiring, proving possession of, or using raw military capabilities than a matter of demonstrating concern, motivation and commitment." This is especially true in the case of deterrence of attack on a third party, since the costs of failing to meet an attack on the third party are rarely as great as the costs of failing to defend one's home territory. Bargaining power is a product of resolve as well as of capability, and resolve is in turn a function of the interests at stake and of "inherent" resolve (that is, risk-proneness). Presumably (again, other things being equal) the willingness to run risks or pay costs to defend a protégé will be greater the greater the objective or intrinsic value of the protégé, perhaps as measured by wealth, population, or strategic importance. But that value may not be very helpful in analyzing a deterrent situation, since the greater the value of the protégé, the higher the costs and the greater the risks the attacker will presumably be willing to accept in order to acquire it. The "objective" value of the protégé thus appears on both sides of the equation.

Motivation, commitment, and resolve are in some part a matter of the "psychology" of the decision-maker. Some decision-makers seem to be determined, others irresolute. Or, in decision-making terms, some may be risk-acceptant (Hitler in 1938) and others risk-averse (Chamberlain). An attacker (whatever his own attitude toward risk) must try to assess the behavior of the defender in previous international crises, if they are relevant. Ideally one would look at the behavior of the particular decision-maker(s) in charge of the defender state; lacking that example one might look at the behavior of previous decision-makers in charge of the state.

What conclusions can be drawn from such considerations? The obvious one would follow from an assumption that risk-acceptance or risk-aversion are inherent to a decision-maker (or state). If he was unwilling to take the risk of fighting the last time, the odds may be that he will be risk-averse once again. An alternative assumption, however, would be that attitudes toward risk-taking are determined more by political context than by personality or "character." Context may be determined so randomly (for example, variations in the intrinsic importance of the protégé in each case) that past behavior will provide little or no guidance for predicting future behavior. Or it may operate perversely, leading to an opposite prediction. For example, Chamberlain's acquiescence in the dismemberment of Czechoslovakia may have made him less willing to acquiesce in the case of Poland a year later. Some research suggests that the defender's previous behavior does not systematically predict either way subsequent behavior, but we still must take it into account in our analysis. Certainly the "need" to demonstrate resolve (to avoid falling dominoes) was a key rationalization for America's experience in Vietnam and throughout the post-Munich era.

Motivation and resolve are also affected by aspects of the relationship between the defender and its protégé. Resolve may be communicated by establishing a formal military alliance between the two—and once established, it may serve to strengthen a defender's resolve by raising the stakes it has to lose by failing to honor its alliance commitment (weakening its credibility the next time it is challenged). Motivation may be strengthened by a variety of economic, political, and military ties between defender and protégé, such as trade, investment in the protégé's economy, economic assistance or military equipment and advisers to the protégé from the defender, and a host of less tangible forms of political or cultural affinity. Again, holding other elements of the calculation constant, the defender should be more willing to take risks in defense of a third party the more tangible and intangible interests there are at stake. The immediate role of tangible interests like trade and investment is obvious. Additionally, they, and other less tangible ties, may widen the defender's image of itself, providing an emotional stake in the wellbeing of politically or culturally related peoples. There also is some evidence from systematic comparative analyses to this effect.

Cases and Hypotheses

We shall test hypotheses about conditions favoring deterrence on a set of historical cases of attempted deterrence of attack on third parties. The cases include all those we were able to identify in the international system in the period since 1900. [See Table 7-2.] We limited ourselves to that period because reliable information on earlier cases is too difficult to acquire, and because even with reliable data the utility of some of the measures (the significance, for instance, of certain military forces) shifts as one moves into earlier historical epochs. Even so, we were able to identify fifty-four relevant cases including examples from both the nuclear and prenuclear eras. Thus we can test whether nuclear weapons make a difference. . . .

We have attempted to identify the conditions under which deterrence will succeed or fail. Thus for explaining the attacker's decision we simply code that decision as "attack the protégé" (0) or "no attack" (1). A military attack is defined as a government-sanctioned engagement of its regular armed forces in combat with the regular armed forces of the protégé and/or its defender, resulting in more than 250 fatalities. Once this level of combat and casualty has been reached, subsequent events become a matter of "intrawar" deterrence. We also include as "attacks" (failures of deterrence) instances in which the attacker gained its principal goals even though fatalities were minimal (e.g., Czechoslovakia in 1938, case no. 25; Cyprus in 1964, no. 44; Goa, no. 39), and instances in which the attacker occupied territory of the protégé for several years.

We have also analyzed the cases in which deterrence failed: can we explain the defender's decision whether or not to fight? Attackers often misjudge the defenders' resolve. As [Richard Ned] Lebow remarked, describing his results, "Perhaps our most striking finding is the extent to which crisis strategies in the cases we studied were based on unrealistic assessments of how

Table 7-2 Deterrence Cases, 1900-1980

Cases of Attempted Deterrence

Case	Year(s)	Attacker	Protégé	Defender	Outcome
1	1902/3	Germany	Venezuela	United States	Success
2	1904	Russia	Korea	Japan	Failure
3	1905/6	Germany	Morocco	France	Success
4	1905/6	Germany	France	Britain	Success
5	1908	Turkey	Persia	Russia	Success
6	1908/9	Russia/Serbia	Austria-Hungary	Germany	Success
7	1908/9	Austria-Hungary/Germany	Serbia	Russia	Failure
8	1911	Italy	Tripoli	Turkey	Failure
9	1911	Germany	Morocco	France	Success
10	1911	Germany	France	Britain	Success
11	1912	Serbia	Albania	Austria-Hungary	Success
12	1912	Austria-Hungary	Serbia	Russia	Success
13	1912	Russia-Serbia	Austria-Hungary	Germany	Success
14	1913	Rumania	Bulgaria	Russia	Success
15	1913	Bulgaria	Greece	Serbia	Failure
16	1913	Serbia	Albania	Austria-Hungary	Success
17	1914	Austria-Hungary/Germany	Serbia	Russia	Failure
18	1914	Russia/Serbia	Austria-Hungary	Germany	Failure
19	1914	Germany/Austria-Hungary	Russia	France	Failure
20	1914	Germany	Belgium	Britain	Failure
21	1920	Soviet Union	Iran	Britain	Failure
22	1927	Yugoslavia	Albania	Italy	Success
23	1935	Italy	Ethiopia	Britain	Failure
24	1936	Japan	Outer Mongolia	Soviet Union	Success

25	1938	Germany	Czechoslovakia	Britain/France	Failure
26	1938/39	Italy	Tunisia	France	Success
27	1939	Japan	Outer Mongolia	Soviet Union	Failure
28	1939	Germany	Poland	Britain/France	Failure
29	1940	Soviet Union	Finland	Germany	Success
30	1946	Soviet Union	Iran	United States	Success
31	1947	Soviet Union	Turkey	United States	Success
32	1948/49	Soviet Union	W. Berlin/W. Germany	United States	Success
33	1950	United States	North Korea	China	Failure
34	1954/55	China	Taiwan/Islands	United States	Success
35	1957	Turkey/United States	Syria	Soviet Union	Success
36	1957	Egypt/Syria/Soviet Union	Turkey	United States	Success
37	1958	China	Taiwan/Islands	United States	Success
38	1961	Iraq	Kuwait	Britain	Success
39	1961	India	Goa	Portugal	Failure
40	1961	Soviet Union	W. Berlin/W. Germany	United States	Success
41	1962	India	Nepal	China	Success
42	1962	North Vietnam	Thailand	United States	Success
43	1963/64	Indonesia	Malaysia	Britain	Failure
44	1964	Turkey	Cyprus	Greece	Failure
45	1964/65	North Vietnam	South Vietnam	United States	Failure
46	1965	India	Pakistan	China	Failure
47	1966/67	Turkey	Cyprus	Greece	Failure
48	1967	Israel	Syria	Egypt	Failure
49	1970	Syria	Jordan	Israel	Success
50	1973	Soviet Union	Israel	United States	Success
51	1974	Turkey	Cyprus	Greece	Failure
52	1975	Morocco	Western Sahara	Spain	Success
53	1976/77	Guatemala	Belize	Britain	Success
54	1978/79	Tanzania	Uganda	Libya	Failure

(table continues)

Table 7-2 (continued)

Cases of Failed Deterrence

Case	Year(s)	Attacker	Protégé	Defender	Does defender Intervene?
2	1904	Russia	Korea	Japan	Yes
7	1908/9	Austria-Hungary	Serbia	Russia	No
8	1911	Italy	Tripoli	Turkey	Yes
14	1913	Bulgaria	Greece	Serbia	Yes
17	1914	Austria-Hungary/Germany	Serbia	Russia/France	Yes
18	1914	Russia/Serbia	Austria-Hungary	Germany	Yes
19	1914	Germany/Austria-Hungary	Russia	France	Yes
20	1914	Germany	Belgium	Britain	Yes
21	1920	Soviet Union	Iran	Britain	Yes
23	1935	Italy	Ethiopia	Britain	No
25	1938/39	Germany	Czechoslovakia	Britain/France	No
27	1939	Japan	Outer Mongolia	Soviet Union	Yes
28	1939	Germany	Poland	Britain/France	Yes
33	1950	United States	North Korea	China	Yes
39	1961	India	Goa	Portugal	No
43	1963/64	Indonesia	Malaysia	Britain	Yes
44	1964	Turkey	Cyprus	Greece	No
45	1964/65	North Vietnam	South Vietnam	United States	Yes
46	1965	India	Pakistan	China	No
47	1966/67	Turkey	Cyprus	Greece	No
48	1967	Israel	Syria	Egypt	Yes
51	1974	Turkey	Cyprus	Greece	No
54	1978/79	Tanzania	Uganda	Libya	Yes

adversaries would respond when challenged. In every instance brinkmanship was predicated upon the belief that the adversary (defender) in question would back down when challenged.". . .

Our general hypothesis is that an expected-utility model will provide a better-than-chance explanation of defenders' and attackers' decisions. But much more important than that, we wish to test various hypotheses about which elements of an expected-utility analysis provide the most powerful explanations. Our hypotheses, tapping aspects of the variables in the model, come under three general categories: those emphasizing relative power, those concerning the role of past behavior in signaling current intentions, and those stressing the contextual importance of communitarian ties between states. By including variables of all three types in our equations we can test their relative explanatory power. The hypotheses and independent variables are as follows:

1. The relative balance of military capabilities will help explain the results.

1a. Attacker will be more likely to fight (deterrence to fail) to the degree that attacker's *overall* ("strategic") military and economic capabilities (a measure of military *potential*) exceed those of defender.

1b. Attacker will be more likely to fight to the degree that attacker's *overall existing* military forces exceed those of defender.

1c. Attacker will be more likely to fight to the degree that attacker's *potential local* (in the area of the protégé) military capabilities exceed those of defender.

1d. Attacker will be more likely to fight to the degree that attacker's *existing local* military capabilities exceed those of defender.

1e. Attacker will be less likely to fight if defender is known to possess nuclear weapons.

To measure overall military and economic capabilities (military potential) we used the composite national capabilities index developed by the Correlates of War Project. This index measures three theoretically distinct dimensions of national capabilities: military, industrial, and demographic. The military dimension includes each state's military personnel and military expenditures (weighted equally) for each year. (This is the measure we use for existing military capabilities for hypotheses 1b and 1d.) The industrial dimension consists of each state's production of ingot steel and industrial fuel consumption and measures the potential of a state to support a military effort. The demographic dimension includes each state's population and urban population and indicates the state's potential to increase its power by drawing on its civilian population during extended war. In the index of military potential for hypotheses 1a and 1c the three dimensions are weighted equally.

For local capabilities the military dimension is adjusted to reflect the impact of distance. If both defender and attacker share a border, or share one with the protégé, then no adjustment is made. Otherwise the indices of military capabilities are adjusted for the distances between the attacker's and defender's loci of power and the protégé, and for the principal military transport capabilities of the day (expressed in travel days). Ideally it might have been desirable to measure actual locally available military forces (divisions, gunboats, etc.) but that would have required a level of information not easily accessible, and in any case still would not have evaded decisions about forces that, although not immediately on the scene, could be brought in within a "reasonable" time. The procedure we did use seems less arbitrary, and adequate to the purpose. In all cases the power of the protégé is added to that of the defender. As noted earlier, military capability should affect both one's own utilities and one's subjective probability that the other will fight.

Reciprocal hypotheses apply to the behavior of the defender in those cases in which the potential attacker has actually attacked:

1f. Defender will be more likely to fight to the degree that defender's overall military potential exceeds attacker's.

1g. Defender will be more likely to fight to the degree that defender's overall existing military capabilities exceed attacker's.

1h. Defender will be more likely to fight to the degree that defender's potential local military capabilities exceed attacker's.

1i. Defender will be more likely to fight to the degree that defender's existing local military capabilities exceed attacker's.

1j. Defender will be more likely to fight if defender possesses nuclear weapons. This hypothesis cannot really be tested because there were only three instances in which an attacker pressed an attack against a nuclear-armed defender.

2. The second set of hypotheses concerns the effect of the defender state's previous behavior in deterrent situations (if any are applicable). This variable measures the extent to which the defender has a record of strongly supporting a threatened protégé and suggests the likelihood that the defender will fight (its degree of risk-proneness).

2a. Attacker will be more likely to fight if defender has not fought in the past when its protégé was attacked.

2b. Attacker will be less likely to fight if defender has not fought in the past. This is the alternative hypothesis, suggesting that a defender who earlier demonstrated "weakness" will be less likely to do so again.

In the statistical analysis, we assigned a series of "dummy variables" to three different possibilities: whether the defender had fought on behalf of a protégé in the past, whether it had not fought, and whether it had a record of successful deterrence. In all of these cases a "no" could indicate either the opposite historical experience or simply no relevant experience. (For example, a success would be coded 1 for the last dummy variable and a 0 for either no past experience or a failure.) We tested the hypotheses by examining the defender's behavior in the most recent past case of attempted deterrence.

Similary, we have corresponding hypotheses to explain the behavior of the defender if attack occurred.

2c. Defender will be more likely to fight if it has fought in the past.

2d. Defender will be more likely to fight if it has not fought in the past.

3. Third, we have a set of hypotheses concerning the effect of ties between the defender and protégé, with more or stronger ties raising the value of the protégé to the defender and thus raising the probability that the defender will fight rather than allow the protégé to be overcome.

3a. Attacker will be less likely to fight if defender was linked to protégé by a formal military alliance prior to the emergence of the immediate deterrence situation.

For our purposes a military alliance was defined as a written agreement, bilateral or multilateral, between sovereign states. Both defense pacts and (rare) ententes were coded as 1, and the absence of either as 0. Five cases in this study were instances in which the threatened protégé was a colony. Although a formal military alliance between sovereign states could not, by definition, exist in those cases, we assumed that there exists an unwritten but internationally recognized alliance between a colony and its metropole. Thus we treated a colonial relationship as one of formal military commitment.

The corresponding hypothesis for the defender is:

3b. Defender will be more likely to fight if it was linked to the protégé by a formal military alliance prior to the emergence of the immediate deterrence situation.

Two similar hypotheses apply to the role of economic linkages:

3c. Attacker will be less likely to fight the stronger the economic linkages between defender and protégé.

3d. Defender will be more likely to fight the stronger the economic linkages between defender and protégé.

We measured economic linkage as the protégé's share of defender's total merchandise exports and imports. These figures were calculated as the average level over a two- to three-year period, depending on the availability of data prior to the outbreak of the dispute. This variable attempts to estimate the extent to which the defender has developed an important and direct material interest in its relationship with the protégé. Exports to the protégé represent the interests of those firms and industries selling abroad; imports suggest commodities for which the defender's economy may be "dependent" on reliable supplies of goods of a known quality or at favorable prices. Norming the volume of trade by the size of the defender's economy is thus appropriate. Although the decision-makers of the attacker are unlikely to calculate the exact amount of the defender's trade accounted for by the protégé, they are likely to be aware of the general level of commercial activity between the two states. Greater refinement for measuring this variable might result from analyzing exports and imports separately, but the high correlation between the two prevents their separation in statistical analysis. Data on the defender's private foreign investment in the protégé would be desirable but are not available for enough of the cases.

Two further parallel hypotheses apply to political-military linkages:

3e. Attacker will be less likely to fight the stronger the political-military linkages between defender and protégé.

3f. Defender will be more likely to fight the stronger the political-military linkages between defender and protégé.

Finally, we have two further hypotheses about power that apply only to the defender's decision whether or not to fight if an attack does materialize. The defender must decide on the basis of the protégé's value; this includes both values as reflected in linkages and "intrinsic" value as represented by the protégé's strategic, military, or industrial potential. The utility of "peace" under circumstances in which the protégé is lost will depend in some degree on that intrinsic value. We tapped this in two ways. One was to use the measures earlier employed for potential military capability (the composite national capabilities index) and existing military capability, and to calculate the ratio of the protégé's capability on each to that of the defender. As a partial measure of the protégé's strategic importance to the defender we also included a dummy variable for whether they shared a common border. Both defender and attacker will have to take these considerations into account in estimating the defender's utility for not fighting, and thus into account in deriving subjective probabilities for each other's actions. The relevant hypotheses therefore are:

1k. Defender will be more likely to fight the greater the ratio of protégé's existing or potential military capability to its own.

1l. Defender will be more likely to fight if its territory borders directly on that of protégé. . . .

Conditions Affecting Deterrence:
Some Empirical Results

We analyzed the data through probit analysis, which is analagous to multiple regression analysis for situations in which the dependent variable is dichotomous (yes-no, 1-0). Table 7-3 gives the results of the best (most powerful explanatory) equation. It employs the best (most powerful) indicator for each of the theoretical concepts specified earlier. . . .

We measured political-military linkages by the amount of military assistance provided by the defender to the protégé—specifically the percentage share of major weapons systems (aircraft, ships, missiles, armored equipment) imported by the protégé from the defender. Because available data were incomplete and imprecise we coded this variable on a four-point scale rather than on strict percentages: 0-25 per cent = 1, 26-50 per cent = 2, 51-75 per cent = 3, 76-100 percent = 4.

The first point to be made about these results is the fact that a majority (78 per cent) of the outcomes are correctly predicted by the model. No social science model can explain every case, and this rate compares very well with chance, or with the simple prediction that deterrence will always work. (It did in 57 percent of the cases.) It also is a very robust result in terms of consistency when various cases are added to or deleted from our set, as, for example, in earlier analyses before events such as August 1914 were "unpacked" into discrete cases or before our list of cases had been thoroughly checked for appropriate inclusion by historians and other authorities. The results from all these analyses are very robust in that the proportion of correct predictions remains very stable; the same three variables (trade, military assistance, and local military balance) consistently make significant contributions to the equations, and only these variables consistently do so. Finally, our findings here compare well with the results derived from a set of expected utilities computed by Bruce Bueno de Mesquita for *The War Trap* and kindly provided to us by that author. Of the forty-nine cases for which Bueno de Mesquita has data, his model correctly predicts 71 per cent and ours, 76 per cent. Bueno de Mesquita has since revised his method of computing expected utilities. By that new method, his results would give correct predictions for 72 per cent of the eighteen cases to which those data apply, and we correctly predict 83 per cent of those cases.

But our model here, in addition to showing substantial credibility for our expected-utility model in the aggregate, provides a means of disaggregating components of the model to show which variables are the most effective predictors to deterrence success. Turning to look at the individual variables, the equation shows strong effects for economic linkage (the share of defender's trade with the protégé, hypothesis 3c), arms transfers from defender to protégé (hypothesis 3c), and the military balance, in the variant of existing local capabilities (hypothesis 1d), and a negative effect for military alliance (hypothesis 3a). Military assistance and the local military balance are of about equal importance and are significant at the level of .98 or above, and trade is at the .95 level. Trade and military assistance testify to the importance of economic and political linkages: deterrence is more likely to be effective the greater the defender's visible and symbolic stake in the protégé.

The presence of a negative relation between alliance and successful deterrence is a surprise, just the opposite of the standard hypothesis (hypothesis 3a). The relationship is not very strong, but nevertheless is strong enough to require explanation. An attacker may threaten a protégé that is formally allied to the defender, fully realizing that the risks are very high precisely because of the formal alliance relationship. In such a situation, the potential attacker has made a firm decision to force the opponent to back down or to go to war. Successful deterrence is therefore much more difficult to achieve. Russia in July of 1914 (case no. 18) was determined to protect Serbia against Austria-Hungary in order to avoid the humiliation of Bosnia in 1908-1909 and realized the risks of a confrontation with Germany in doing so. Similarly, Hitler in September of 1939 (case no. 28) pressed ahead with the attack against Poland, accepting the possibility that Britain and France would declare war.

It is also important to note the variables that do not enter into the equation. For example, the defender's past behavior in crises seems to make no systematic difference. Neither do the other kinds of military power indicators, such as power potential or overall ("strategic") military superiority by the defender (hypotheses 1a-1c), make a significant contribution. We also tried a dummy variable for either local or overall military superiority on the basis that *either* might suffice to deter an attack, but found that effort made no greater contribution to our results.

One other power variable—defender's possession of nuclear weapons— also is absent, perhaps surprisingly, from these results. We cannot entirely dismiss a possible effect for nuclear weapons, because that dummy variable did approach (at .88) our cutoff level for statistical significance, and it does appear at an acceptable significance level if the case of Vietnam (no. 45) is deleted from the analysis. Although the Vietnam case does not fit our analysis very well (and will be discussed below) it is not so deviant that it should be dropped as an "outlier" from the statistical examination. We do not delete this case but merely point out here that this result at least is sensitive to the treatment of Vietnam. The effect of nuclear weapons is nonetheless marginal, not one on which to put much weight. Moreover, the possession of nuclear weapons is sometimes irrelevant (spurious), as in the British successful effort to deter Guatemalan seizure of Belize (case no. 53).

With probit analysis it is possible to compute the change in probability that the "1" value of the dependent variable will be achieved for a given change in any one of the dependent variables while holding the other independent variables constant. This is the more readily interpretable measure of the impact of each independent variable, better than the probit coefficients at the top of Table 7-3. The lower half of Table 7-3 shows those impacts. We see that if the protégé takes 25 per cent or less of its arms imports from the defender the probability of successful deterrence is just .28, but if the proportion of military imports from the defender exceeds 75 per cent, the probability of successful deterrence rises to .79. Similarly, with no trade between defender and protégé the chances of successful deterrence are just about even, but if as much as 6 per cent of the defender's trade is with its protégé, the chances of effective deterrence rise to about seven out of eight. Trade and arms sales can be considered relatively susceptible to policy manipulation by the defender, perhaps more so than are relative power bases. Local military superiority likewise shows a wide range of effect, from a 26 per cent chance of successful deterrence even if defender and pawn have only a tenth of the attacker's power, to a very high probability if together they have a ten-to-one advantage.

The importance of local but not overall capabilities, coupled with the absence of much explanatory power for nuclear weapons, has profound import for contemporary superpower deterrence. It suggests that rhetoric about "windows of vulnerability" is off the mark. Local military capabilities (of the

Table 7-3 Conditions Promoting Effective Deterrence

Success = −1.57 + .18 *Trade* + .60 *Arms* + .16 *Local Military Balance* − 1.02 *Alliance*
    (− 2.93) (1.94)   (2.84)   (2.35)   (−1.93)

		Predicted	
		Failure	Success
Actual	Failure	18	5
	Success	7	24

Contributions to Probability of Success

	Value	Probability of Success
Trade	0%	.49
	1%	.56
	2%	.63
	4%	.76
	6%	.86
Arms	0-25%	.28
	26-50%	.35
	51-75%	.38
	76-100%	.79
Local military balance	0.1	.26
	0.5	.28
	1.0	.32
	2	.37
	3	.43
	5	.56
	10	.83
Alliance	Yes	.39
	No	.77

Note: Percentage of predictions correct = 78; R^2 = .31; N = 54.

defender and protégé combined) seem to have more to do with successful deterrence than do strategic ones, and both may be less important than having a dense network of political and economic bonds between defender and protégé. Israel, for instance, arguably is better protected by its own local, conventional military strength (possibly augmented by that of the United States) than it would be by American strategic superiority (now declined) or by its own overt possession of nuclear weapons. It also, in terms of our results, is better protected by its dense network of political and economic linkages with the United States than it would be by a formal military pact (e.g., in the Yom Kippur war of 1973, case no. 50).

Certainly the mere fact of a military alliance between defender and protégé makes no positive contribution by itself, as the existence of more tangible interests does. Just as the formal alliances provided little deterrence for Czechoslovakia and Poland, they did not suffice either for various "protégés" who had them in 1914 (although the alliance system did insure that war, once begun, would cascade to include most of the great powers). Insofar as United States foreign policy decision-makers continued to fight the Vietnam War for almost a decade in order to preserve the credibility of America's "pledged word," they may have missed the real point. The operative ties that drew the United States in were not those of the formal commitment represented by the SEATO pact, but rather the close links of economic and military assistance, and political commitment, to the South Vietnamese government. Moreover, our results indicate that the effect of honoring that commitment was not central to the credibility of American deterrent threats in the face of subsequent challenges: the defender's past behavior against a threat does not predict whether the defender will be able to succeed in deterring a later attack.

Mention of the Vietnam War is important because it does not fit standard theories of deterrence. The United States had nuclear weapons, overwhelming total superiority over Vietnam, and clear local military superiority if its forces were fully engaged, and it provided virtually all of South Vietnam's military capabilities. Up to that point the United States had no record of having failed to come to an attacked protégé's defense, and, indeed, it had come to South Korea's defense in 1950 even without having first made any prior deterrent threat.

Substantively and theoretically, the Vietnam case shows the limitations of many extant theories of deterrence. Those we have tapped here would not have predicted the true outcome. The reason lies in the element of a full expected-utility model of deterrence that we have not been able to incorporate in this empirical test—the value of "peace" to the would-be deterree was not sufficiently high. That is, the government of North Vietnam valued very highly its campaign to eliminate the vestiges of colonial rule in all of Vietnam and to reunify the nation. To that end it was prepared to suffer great costs rather than be deterred. Its goals in the war far exceeded those of the Americans and sustained them despite the latter's apparent advantages. If American deterrence of North Vietnamese intervention in South Vietnam epitomizes the limitations of our empirical test, the successful earlier American deterrence of North Vietnamese intervention into Thailand (case no. 42) exemplifies the strength of our model. All the conditions that applied there applied in the subsequent case—except for much more important goals held by the North Vietnamese.

Two other cases where our model erroneously predicted successful deterrence are those of Austria-Hungary against Serbia, and Germany against Belgium. (Cases nos. 17 and 20. We correctly predicted the other two 1914 results.) The events of "the guns of August" illustrate what can go wrong in a deterrence crisis—the limits of any "rational" model. The complex array of alliance commitments and quasicommitments of the many powers made it unusually difficult to predict behavior. Mobilization plans made it virtually impossible to make a military threat, or even to take defensive measures, without provoking the other side. Shifting power relationships made the value of continued peace uncertain, and few expected the costs of war to be as catastrophic as they proved to be.

What Happens After Deterrence Fails?
Empirical Results

Predicting the attacker's decision whether to press ahead or to be deterred is important, but so too is the matter of what happens after deterrence fails. The attacker's move is known, and the defender has to make a choice: whether to allow its bluff to be called or to resist the attacker's move against the protégé. The defender must decide whether it will lose more by going to war or by not resisting. Table 7-4 shows the results of our analysis of the cases in which a defender faced this choice.

Our equation correctly predicted eighteen of the twenty-three decisions (78 per cent). This record is the same as that obtained when predicting whether deterrence would or would not succeed, and it compares favorably with the success rate using data from Bueno de Mesquita's *War Trap* (80 per cent success for us in the twenty cases for which his data are available, and 50 per cent success using his method).

In fifteen out of the twenty-three cases the defender chose to fight. A decision to fight is more likely where the protégé's military capability is fairly substantial compared with the defender's own capability (hypothesis 1k). That is, the defender will fight to retain a "big" protégé. To fail to do so would be too costly, materially as well as perhaps to its reputation. The value of "peace" without trying to defend the protégé would be too low, even as compared with the costs of war. The cutoff point comes fairly quickly with increments to power. By the time the protégé's existing military power (protégé power) reaches even 10 per cent of its defender's the probability the defender will fight becomes better than two to one, and by 4 per cent the probability virtually reaches unity. Sharing a common border with the protégé did not, however, significantly increase the probability that the defender would fight (hypothesis 1l).

In this exercise too, the defender's past behavior proved to have no power in predicting whether it would fight on the subsequent occasion. However, the existence of a formal military alliance does contribute substantially to a defender's decision to fight (hypothesis 3b). Without an alliance the chances

Table 7-4 Conditions Promoting Defender Resistance

Fight = −.50 + 3.91 *Protégé Power* + 1.37 *Alliance*
        (−1.11)   (1.36)   (1.87)

		Predicted	
		Not Fight	Fight
Actual	Not Fight	6	2
	Fight	3	12

Contributions to Probability of Resistance		
	Value	Probability of Resistance
Protégé Power	5%	.61
	10%	.69
	20%	.81
	30%	.89
	40%	.95
Alliance	No	.69
	Yes	.97

Note: Percentage of predictions correct = 78; R^2 = .29; N = 23.

the defender would fight were only about two in three; with an alliance, virtually unity. We predicted all but two of the eight instances in which a defender was not willing to use military force on behalf of a protégé. One of those cases dealt with the Indian seizure of Goa (no. 39). Despite the fact that Goa was juridically part of Portugal, and thus protected by a formal bond even stronger than a mere alliance, the Indians took Goa without resistance. Doubtless they were emboldened by their own overwhelming local military superiority, and by their knowledge that the Portuguese empire was moribund and unable to offer effective resistance. The other such case is Czechoslovakia in 1938, when Hitler correctly assessed the relatively greater importance of his own local military capabilities as compared with the substantial overall capabilities of his opponent and—more crucially—the absence of his opponents' political will to honor the alliance between France and Czechoslovakia.

Perhaps more important, we correctly identified twelve of the fifteen cases in which the defender *did* fight. Very often these cases, in which large-scale violence did transpire, had very costly consequences that all parties would have done better to avoid. The most notable of those for which our model did not predict resistance by the defender were Russia over Serbia and Britain over

Belgium in 1914. Our earlier comments about decision-making in 1914 are apropos. Also, in both the Russian and British decisions the absence of a formal military alliance is deceptive. Russia was deeply committed to maintaining Serbia's independence, and Britain was drawn into World War I as much to prevent Germany from defeating France and dominating the continent as it was by the catalyst of the invasion of Belgium.

Note that the influences associated with a defender's decision to fight once deterrence has failed are not the same as those associated with successful deterrence. Only formal alliance plays a role in both—and in opposite directions. An alliance made it more likely that the defender would fight if deterrence failed but was negatively associated with the success of deterrence. A military alliance not backed up by more tangible linkages—linkages that perhaps give the defender some control to prevent adventurism by a protégé—thus may *increase* the danger that a defender will be drawn into war. Local military superiority clearly made a contribution to effective deterrence, but, in the defender's decision to fight, military power was relevant only in the sense that the defender was more likely to fight on behalf of a protégé with substantial existing military strength. Trade ties and arms transfers, which were important for deterrence, did not appear in the second analysis.

Perhaps there is a serious and potentially dangerous mismatch between attacker's and defender's calculations. But that is not a necessary conclusion from our results. Since deterrence usually succeeds where the defender and protégé have close economic and political ties, it may well be that the attacker is correct in assuming that the defender will fight on behalf of such a protégé, and thus it rarely presses its challenge to a full military attack. (For example, where the protégé accounts for 6 per cent or more of the defender's trade, deterrence almost always is successful.) In cases where those ties are weaker the attacker is more likely to press forward, and other influences predominate. Another consideration, contained in our analysis of the defender's calculation, is missed entirely in the one for the attacker. Sometimes a war, even with the high probability of intervention by the defender, may look like a reasonable option to a rationally calculating attacker. The attacker may expect to win the war at a tolerable cost. Such a reasonable calculation could even apply if the attacker believed it might very well lose, if the other options looked worse. North Vietnam's decision to push ahead with its attempt to unify the Vietnamese nation may be a case in point.

Conclusion

We have developed and tested an expected-utility model of deterrence and its immediate consequences. Writing about the deterrence literature, Lawrence Freeman has judged that "much of what is offered today as a profound and new insight was said yesterday." We may not have offered striking new insights, but we have uncovered some notable empirical findings that help discriminate among alleged insights. We have produced these results without analyzing the process of bargaining and threat that goes on during a deterrence crisis. Very likely, additional explanatory power could be found by such analysis, perhaps especially by looking at the ways bargaining may serve to call attention to the very elements of capability and interest we have identified in this macro-level analysis.

For deterrence attempts, we found that in our sample success was most often associated with close economic and political-military ties between the defender and its protégé. Local military superiority for the defender and its protégé helped bolster deterrence, but a military alliance was associated with deterrence failure. Only a marginal contribution was made by the possession of nuclear weapons. Other elements of national power and the history of the defender's earlier deterrence behavior played no significant role. Existence of a formal military alliance played no positive role, and, if not backed up by more tangible ties, actually worked against the success of deterrence. We want to caution the reader that these findings apply only to cases of immediate deterrence; that is, to instances in which an overt military threat from a potential attacker has already become manifest. Perhaps this kind of case understates the value of military strength in general deterrence. If military power were overwhelming, possibly no aggressor would ever rise to the level of making the overt challenge that characterizes these cases. But in the world of the Cold War, for example, United States military power has never been so dominant as to prevent the ten challenges we have listed here.

The problem of immediate deterrence touches on many of the most dangerous opportunities for the outbreak of war. These are portentous occasions, and our conclusions have important implications for policy, especially in an era when overwhelming military superiority is not available to either superpower. Our conclusions suggest that a definition of deterrence as primarily sensitive to strict calculation of military capability is both mistaken and profoundly dangerous. A quest for strategic nuclear superiority is unlikely to be the most effective means for providing security to America's friends and allies in a crisis, or to America itself. Nor does success in deterrence follow merely from establishing a record of "standing firm" in the past. Insofar as military strength is critical, local military forces—in some combination of forces of defender and local protégé—are likely to prove more effective than overall or "strategic" forces. Finally, an important contribution to effective deterrence may emerge from achievement of a goal that is usually sought for other purposes—maintaining and strengthening the ties of mutual interest among nation-states in an open global economic system.

██████ **7.4**

ALEXANDER HAIG

Peace and Deterrence

It is a melancholy fact of the modern age that man has conceived a means capable of his own destruction. For 37 years mankind has had to live with the terrible burden of nuclear weapons. From the dawn of the nuclear age, these weapons have been the source of grave concern to our peoples and the focus of continuous public debate. Every successive president of the United States has shared these concerns. Every Administration has had to engage itself in this debate.

It is right that each succeeding generation should question anew the manner in which its leaders exercise such awesome responsibilities. It is right that each new Administration should have to confront the awful dilemmas posed by the possession of nuclear weapons. It is right that our nuclear strategy should be exposed to continuous examination.

Strategy of Nuclear Deterrence

In debating these issues, we should not allow the complexity of the problems and the gravity of the stakes to blind us to the common ground upon which we all stand. No one has ever advocated nuclear war. No responsible voice has ever sought to minimize its horrors.

On the contrary, from the earliest days of the postwar era, America's leaders have recognized that the only nuclear strategy consistent with our values and our survival—our physical existence and what makes life worth living—is the strategy of deterrence. The massive destructive power of these weapons precludes their serving any lesser purpose. The catastrophic consequences of another world war—with or without nuclear weapons—make deterrence of conflict our highest objective and our only rational military strategy for the modern age.

Thus, since the close of World War II, American and Western strategy has assigned a single function to nuclear weapons: the prevention of war and the preservation of peace. At the heart of this deterrence strategy is the requirement that the risk of engaging in war must be made to outweigh any possible benefits of aggression. The cost of aggression must not be confined to the victims of aggression.

An address before Georgetown University's Center for Strategic and International Studies, Washington, D.C., April 6, 1982.

This strategy of deterrence has won the consistent approval of Western peoples. It has enjoyed the bipartisan support of the American Congress. It has secured the unanimous endorsement of every successive allied government.

Deterrence has been supported because deterrence works. Nuclear deterrence and collective defense have preserved peace in Europe, the crucible of two global wars in this century. Clearly, neither improvement in the nature of man nor strengthening of the international order has made war less frequent or less brutal. Millions have died since 1945 in over 130 international and civil wars. Yet nuclear deterrence has prevented a conflict between the two superpowers, a conflict which even without nuclear weapons would be the most destructive in mankind's history.

Requirements for Western Strategy

The simple possession of nuclear weapons does not guarantee deterrence. Throughout history societies have risked their total destruction if the prize of victory was sufficiently great or the consequences of submission sufficiently grave. War and, in particular, nuclear war can be deterred, but only if we are able to deny an aggressor military advantage from his action and thus insure his awareness that he cannot prevail in any conflict with us. Deterrence, in short, requires the maintenance of a secure military balance, one which cannot be overturned through surprise attack or sudden technological breakthrough. The quality and credibility of deterrence must be measured against these criteria. Successive administrations have understood this fact and stressed the importance of the overall balance. This Administration can do no less.

The strategy of deterrence, in its essentials, has endured. But the requirements for maintaining a secure capability to deter in all circumstances have evolved. In the early days of unquestioned American nuclear superiority the task of posing an unacceptable risk to an aggressor was not difficult. The threat of massive retaliation was fully credible as long as the Soviet Union could not respond in kind. As the Soviet Union's nuclear arsenal grew, however, this threat began to lose credibility.

To sustain the credibility of Western deterrence, the concept of flexible response was elaborated and formally adopted by the United States and its NATO partners in 1967. Henceforth, it was agreed that NATO would meet aggression initially at whatever level it was launched, while preserving the flexibility to escalate the conflict, if necessary, to secure the cessation of aggression and the withdrawal of the aggressor. The purpose of this strategy is not just to conduct conflict successfully if it is forced upon us but, more importantly, to prevent the outbreak of conflict in the first place.

Flexible response is not premised upon the view that nuclear war can be controlled. Every successive allied and American government has been convinced that nuclear war, once initiated, could escape such control. They have, therefore, agreed upon a strategy which retains the deterrent effect of a possible nuclear response, without making such a step in any sense automatic.

The alliance based its implementation of flexible response upon a spectrum of forces, each of which plays an indispensable role in assuring the credibility of a Western strategy of deterrence. At one end of the spectrum are America's strategic forces, our heavy bombers, intercontinental missiles, and ballistic missile submarines. Since NATO's inception, these forces have been the ultimate guarantee of Western security, a role which they will retain in the future.

At the other end of the spectrum are the alliance's conventional forces, including U.S. forces in Europe. These forces must be strong enough to defeat all but the most massive and persistent conventional aggression. They must be resistant and durable enough to give political leaders time to measure the gravity of the threat, to confront the inherently daunting prospects of nuclear escalation, and to seek through diplomacy the cessation of conflict and restoration of any lost Western territory. The vital role which conventional forces play in deterrence is too often neglected, particularly by those most vocal in their concern over reliance upon nuclear weapons. A strengthened conventional posture both strengthens the deterrent effect of nuclear forces and reduces the prospect of their ever being used.

Linking together strategic and conventional forces are theater nuclear forces, that is NATO's nuclear systems based in Europe. These systems are concrete evidence of the nature of the American commitment. They are a concrete manifestation of NATO's willingness to resort to nuclear weapons if necessary to preserve the freedom and independence of its members. Further, the presence of nuclear weapons in Europe insures that the Soviet Union will never believe that it can divide the United States from its allies or wage a limited war with limited risks against any NATO member.

The strategy of flexible response and the forces that sustain its credibility reflect more than simply the prevailing military balance. Western strategy also reflects the political and geographical reality of an alliance of 15 independent nations, the most powerful of which is separated from all but one by 4,000 miles of ocean.

Deterrence is consequently more than a military strategy. It is the essential political bargain which binds together the Western coalition. Twice in this century, America has been unable to remain aloof from European conflict but unable to intervene in time to prevent the devastation of Western Europe. In a nuclear age neither we nor our allies can afford to see this pattern repeated a third time. We have, therefore, chosen a strategy which engages American power in the defense of Europe at the outset and gives substance to the principle that the security of the alliance is indivisible.

Alexander Haig

The Task Ahead

During the past decade the Soviet Union has mounted a sustained buildup across the range of its nuclear forces designed to undermine the credibility of the Western strategy. Soviet modernization efforts have far outstripped those of the West. The development and deployment of Soviet intercontinental ballistic missiles now pose a serious and increasing threat to a large part of our land-based ICBM [intercontinental ballistic missile] force. A new generation of Soviet intermediate-range missiles is targeted upon our European allies.

In the last 10 years, the Soviets introduced an unprecedented array of new strategic and intermediate-range systems into their arsenals, including the SS-17, SS-18, and SS-19 ICBMs, the Backfire bomber, the Typhoon submarine and several new types of submarine-launched missiles, and the SS-20 intermediate-range missile. In contrast, during this same period, the United States exercised restraint, introducing only the Trident missile and submarine and the slower air-breathing cruise missile.

In order to deal with the resulting imbalances, President Reagan has adopted a defense posture and recommended programs to the U.S. Congress designed to maintain deterrence, rectify the imbalances, and thereby support the Western strategy I have just outlined. His bold strategic modernization program, announced last October, is designed to insure the maintenance of a secure and reliable capability to deny any adversary advantage from any form of aggression, even a surprise attack.

The President's decision, in his first weeks in office, to go ahead with the production and deployment of the Pershing II and ground-launched cruise missiles, in accordance with NATO's decision of December 1979, represents an effort to reinforce the linkage between our strategic forces in the United States and NATO's conventional and nuclear forces in Europe. A response to the massive buildup of Soviet SS-20s targeted on Western Europe, this NATO decision was taken to insure that the Soviet Union will never launch aggression in the belief that its own territory can remain immune from attack or that European security can ever be decoupled from that of the United States. . . .

Let us remember, first and foremost, that we are trying to deter the Soviet Union, not ourselves. The dynamic nature of the Soviet nuclear buildup demonstrates that the Soviet leaders do not believe in the concept of "sufficiency." They are not likely to be deterred by a strategy or a force based upon it.

Let us also recall that nuclear deterrence must work not just in times of peace and moments of calm. Deterrence faces its true test at the time of maximum tension, even in the midst of actual conflict. In such extreme circumstances, when the stakes on the table may already be immense, when Soviet leaders may feel the very existence of their regime is threatened, who can say whether or not they would run massive risks if they believed that in the end the Soviet state would prevail?

Deterrence thus does not rest on a static comparison of the number or size of nuclear weapons. Rather, deterrence depends upon our capability, even after suffering a massive nuclear blow, to prevent an aggressor from securing a military advantage and prevailing in a conflict. Only if we maintain such a capability can we deter such a blow. Deterrence, in consequence, rests upon a military balance measured not in warhead numbers but in a complex interaction of capabilities and vulnerabilities.

The Military Balance, Crisis Management, and the Conduct of American Diplomacy

The state of the military balance and its impact upon the deterrent value of American forces cast a shadow over every significant geopolitical decision. It affects on a day-to-day basis the conduct of American diplomacy. It influences the management of international crises and the terms upon which they are resolved.

The search for national interest and national security is a principal preoccupation of the leaders of every nation on the globe. Their decisions and their foreign policies are profoundly affected by their perception of the military balance between the United States and the Soviet Union and the consequent capacity of either to help provide for their security or to threaten that security.

More important still, perceptions of the military balance also affect the psychological attitude of both American and Soviet leaders, as they respond to events around the globe. For the foreseeable future the relationship between the United States and the Soviet Union will be one in which our differences outnumber our points of convergence. Our objective must be to restrain this competition, to keep it below the level of force, while protecting our interests and those of our allies. Our ability to secure these objectives will be crucially influenced by the state of the strategic balance. Every judgment we make and every judgment the Soviet leadership makes will be shaded by it.

Arms Control and Nuclear Deterrence

In no area of diplomacy does the military balance have greater effect than in arms control. Arms control can reinforce deterrence and stabilize a military balance at lower levels of risk and effort. Arms control cannot, however, either provide or restore a balance we are unwilling to maintain through our defense efforts.

Just as the only justifiable nuclear strategy is one of deterrence, so the overriding objective for arms control is reducing the risk of war. The essential purpose to arms control is not to save money, although it may do so. Its purpose is not to generate good feelings or improve international relationships, although it may have that effect as well. Arms control's central purpose must be to reinforce the military balance, upon which deterrence depends, at reduced levels of weapons and risk.

In the area of strategic arms, as well, there is little prospect the Soviet Union will ever agree to equal limits at lower levels unless first persuaded that the United States is otherwise determined to maintain equality at higher levels. It is, for instance, unrealistic to believe that the Soviet Union will agree to reduce the most threatening element of its force structure, its heavy, multiwarheaded intercontinental missiles unless it is persuaded that otherwise the United States will respond by deploying comparable systems itself.

For many opposed to reliance on nuclear weapons—even for defense or deterrence—the issue is a moral one. For those who first elaborated the strategy of deterrence, and for those who seek to maintain its effect, this issue is also preeminently moral. A familiar argument is that, in a nuclear age, we must choose between our values and our existence. If nuclear weapons offer the only deterrent to nuclear blackmail, some would argue we should submit rather than pose the risk of nuclear conflict. This choice, however, is a false one. By maintaining the military balance and sustaining deterrence, we protect the essential values of Western civilization—democratic government, personal liberty, and religious freedom—and preserve the peace. In failing to maintain deterrence, we would risk our freedoms, while actually increasing the likelihood of also suffering nuclear devastation.

Americans have always been conscious of the dilemmas posed by the nuclear weapon. From the moment that science unleashed the atom, our instinct and policy have been to control it. Those who direct America's defense policies today share completely the desire of people everywhere to end the nuclear arms race and to begin to achieve substantial reductions in nuclear disarmament.

Confronted by the dire perils of such weapons, America has responded in a manner that best preserves both security and peace, that protects our society and our values, and that offers hope without illusion. The strategy of deterrence has kept the peace for over 30 years. It has provided the basis for arms control efforts. And it offers the best chance to control and to reduce the dangers that we face.

Deterrence is not automatic. It cannot be had on the cheap. Our ability to sustain it depends upon our ability to maintain the military balance now being threatened by the Soviet buildup. If we are to reinforce deterrence through arms control and arms reduction, we must convince the Soviets that their efforts to undermine the deterrent effect of our forces cannot and will not succeed.

The control and reduction of nuclear weapons, based on deterrence, is the only effective intellectual, political, and moral response to nuclear weapons. The stakes are too great and the consequences of error too catastrophic to exchange deterrence for a leap into the unknown. The incentives for real arms control exist, and we have both the means and the duty to apply them.

Let us be clear about our objectives in the nuclear era. We seek to reduce the risk of war and to establish a stable military balance at lower levels of risk and effort. By doing so today, we may be able to build a sense of mutual confidence and cooperation, offering the basis for even more ambitious steps tomorrow. But above all, we shall be pursuing the "highest possibility" for peace.

███████ **7.5**

JAMES A. STEGENGA

Deterrence: Reckless Prudence

Should we buy more or less of gadget A? Should we reduce deployment B by a few percentage points or not? Most current articles on defense policy stay at the level of asking such questions as these. What is missing in nearly all of the contributions to the debate is an examination of some fundamental assumptions and implications of the cornerstone of American defense policies, nuclear deterrence: hoping and confidently expecting to persuade the Soviet Union not to attack us by threatening thermonuclear counterattack. Most public officials, writers, and ordinary folk deem deterrence to be reliable and proper. Deterrence is widely accepted as one of the few "givens" in contemporary affairs.

But if a principal function of the intellectual is—almost by definition—to subject society's "given" operating assumptions to continuous scrutiny, then surely few topics are more in need of this ongoing critical examination than deterrence doctrine.

According to this doctrine, the government in Moscow can be counted on to behave like a rational individual. It will value survival more than any other goal. It will be well-informed. It will carefully calculate all the consequences and all the pros and cons of each option in every crisis. It will be sensible. And it will cautiously adopt limited objectives in the international arena so as not to incur American wrath and revenge.

Flawed Mortals

But the Soviet government is run by a collection of people. And most of what we know about both human behavior and governmental decision-making should make us skeptical about the rosy picture the confident proponents of deterrence paint.

Reprinted from *Air University Review* (January-February 1977). Reprinted by permission of *Air University Review*.

People can be ·counted on to behave rationally only part of the time, nonrationally and even irrationally the rest. Frequently throughout history they have held some things more dear than "mere" survival—honor and glory come to mind. To some extent people are also usually captive of habit or ideology or public opinion. And they may be poorly informed, especially about secrecy-shrouded military capabilities and intentions. They are clearly capable of evil and folly, error and accident, misperception and delusion, incompetence and passion.

The problem may be compounded when such decisions are made by small groups of people rather than by single individuals. What psychologist Irving Janis calls "groupthink" sets in, with all the members of the group so anxious to get along with each other, maintain their power positions, appease the group leader, and push the interests of their respective bureaucracies that they suspend the critical thinking required for rational decision-making.

The problem is certainly further aggravated in a crisis situation when time pressures, poorer information, fear, exhaustion, higher risks, and a tendency toward belligerent machismo all cause a deterioration in the already low level of rationality we can expect from the flawed mortals hovering over the buttons.

Can we really count on the Soviet system always to work so well, producing wise leadership groups that will behave so rationally on into the 1980s and beyond even in the gravest crises? Most of us know too much history to have that kind of confidence in the performance of any political system, per-haps especially highly personalistic authoritarian regimes lacking institutional-ized controls on executive discretion. Paradoxically, those in our society most critical and suspicious of the Soviet government—call them conservatives or hawks—who ought to have the gravest doubts about Kremlin dependability are, nonetheless, the staunchest and most confident supporters of deterrence doctrines and attendant weapon systems and budgets.

"But," someone is sure to say, "deterrence has worked pretty well these past thirty years, hasn't it?" Can we really be sure, though? Perhaps, like the fellow standing on the corner waving his arms and blowing a whistle who had managed to convince himself that he was thereby successfully keeping the elephants from attacking, we have convinced ourselves that the only reason the Russians have not conquered Europe is because we have frightened them into restraint. They, of course, have likewise managed to convince themselves that the only reason their system has not been overthrown by angry Westerners is that they have frightened us into abandoning such goals. Historians may well conclude that neither side ever had the intentions the other feared and thought it had discouraged with threats of nuclear retaliation.

And, anyway, even if it could somehow be proved that nuclear deterrence has kept the peace for the past thirty years, these same historians would be quick to point out that thirty years is not a very long time, that devices for keeping the peace in other times have worked as long only to fail later.

It ought to be clear to all of us that deterrence—really a form of applied psychology—is historically, psychologically, and politically naive to a danger-ous degree, our confidence in it quite unwarranted. One of these days—if, alas, the balloon goes up—I suspect the survivors will say: "Of course deterrence was bound to fail; how silly that we ever had any faith in it!"

Ethical Doubts

Since government policies also ought to be judged on ethical as well as practical grounds, we should look, too, at some of the more troublesome ethical implications of nuclear deterrence policies.

Our government openly and unabashedly contemplates the deliberate killing of tens of millions of people, most of them noncombatants. In the authoritarian countries of Eastern Europe and Asia against which the United States would retaliate, the people we hold hostage have so little to say about their governments' decisions that they could hardly be deemed culpable of aggression and thus deserving of annihilation. And in neighboring countries not even parties to the quarrel, the citizens and ecological support systems would notwithstanding suffer permanent radioactive poisoning. Could this undis-criminating genocidal and ecological destruction even conceivably be deemed justifiable vengeance? For that matter, is vengeance of any kind consistent with our deepest moral convictions?

Second, if decisions to retaliate must be virtually automatic and instanta-neous, how can the decisions of our President and his associates possibly be based on moral choice which requires time-consuming reflection and consider-ation of alternatives, as well as—under our democratic system—at least some role for public opinion?

Finally, might society's values that deterrence is designed to protect be endangered by the nuclear deterrent itself? Can a constitutional polity governed by elected civilians endure even as military men and military thinking gain in political influence during a time of continuous national insecurity? Can a traditionally liberal and humane society survive as such even as its people and their leaders become calloused by their acceptance of nuclear holocaust as an instrument of national policy? And, if deterrence fails (as it has, of course, countless times throughout history), whatever Americans survive the catastrophe will surely not enjoy the blessings of liberty and democracy during the extended, harsh recuperative period. Of what moral character is a means which itself endangers or surrenders the end?

Beyond Nation States

If deterrence, then, is not only unreliable but also morally bankrupt, what shall we do, now that we realize our predicament? Or, you might say, "OK, suppose nuclear deterrence *is* dangerous and repugnant; what alternative do you suggest?" Well, less reliance on threats and other negative sanctions and more reliance on positive incentives would be a start; people ordinarily seem to react better to offers of mutually beneficial deals than to scare tactics. We are now betting our lives that the Soviet leaders are ordinary and sensible enough to be dependable custodians of nuclear weapons and advanced delivery systems. Presumably, they are thus likewise sensible enough to be manipulable with inducements. So let us have less self-righteousness and more détente, arms control, expanded trade, and improved diplomacy—the usual liberal approaches that have finally caught on even with conservative administrations. Shifting our emphasis increasingly away from negative and toward positive approaches may help. Developing and relying increasingly on programs with a positive cast and moving the violent tools back into their proper place of final resort would be an improvement over the present threat system in global relations. Such a shift of emphasis would also, of course, result in more ethically agreeable policies.

But maybe one day soon we will have to concede that there is no way to reconcile continued national sovereignties on the one hand and the nuclear weapons that have rendered governments unable to perform their key function of protecting their citizens on the other. Just as gunpowder, revolutionary ideals, and industrial commerce spelled doom for the feudal system of castles and moats 400 years ago, thermonuclear weapons and ICBMs may force the replacement of obsolescent national states and governments. If deterrence is no defense, perhaps there is none to be found. The whole effort to "improve" deterrence may be just as doomed as were the efforts that I suppose were made by sixteenth century defense intellectuals and military planners to "improve" their moats and castle walls to protect against threats that they could not quite see were undermining the entire social and political order. We are probably now living in the transition period between the age of nation states and whatever era is around the corner.

Discussion Questions

1. At their summit meeting in Iceland in October of 1986, President Ronald Reagan and General Secretary Mikhail Gorbachev discussed possible reductions of 30 percent or more in each side's offensive missile capability. If such a recommendation were to become reality, what would happen to deterrence?

2. The Huth and Russett article discusses a number of historical illustrations of deterrence. What examples would you add to this list in light of international events of the past decade?

3. James Stegenga offers a moral attack on deterrence. What are the strengths and weaknesses of his argument? Should arguments like his be more influential in setting national defense policy in the United States? Why?

4. What nuclear weapons strategies would you advocate for preserving

national and global security through the year 2000? If your strategy is substantially different from the one we now have, how do you suggest that the transition to your strategy be made?

5. In your estimate, will deterrence last out the century? How and why?

6. What are the assumptions that underlie the president's strategic defense initiative? What would be its impact on deterrence?

7. What are the implications of counterforce and countervalue targeting for (a) the operation of deterrence and (b) arms control strategies? How does the possibility of counterforce targeting alter a nation's retaliatory force needs?

For Further Reading

History of Strategy

Freedman, Lawrence. *The Evolution of Nuclear Strategy*. New York: St. Martin's Press, 1981. Reviews the major concepts of deterrence and provides a comprehensive historical context.

Kaplan, Fred. *The Wizards of Armageddon*. New York: Simon & Schuster, 1983. A history of strategic doctrine that focuses on the personalities of the developers of American strategic doctrine.

Thinking About Deterrence

Rapoport, Anatol. *Strategy and Conscience*. New York: Schocken Books, 1964. The classic formal analysis of deterrence that presents the game theory tools used to analyze military strategy in a form suitable for beginning students.

Russett, Bruce. *The Prisoners of Insecurity*. New York: W. H. Freeman, 1983. An excellent and up-to-date guide to important contemporary strategic issues in the tradition of Schelling and Rapoport.

Schelling, Thomas. *Arms and Influence*. New Haven: Yale University Press, 1966. A classic account of the major concepts in strategic thought.

Weapons

Cochran, Thomas, William Arkin, and Milton Hoenig. *Nuclear Weapons Databook. Volume 1: U.S. Nuclear Forces and Capabilities*. Cambridge, Mass.: Ballinger, 1984. An encyclopedic description of U.S. nuclear weapons.

Cockburn, Andrew. *The Threat: Inside the Soviet Military Machine*. New York: Random House, 1983. A critical assessment of Soviet military forces that challenges the Reagan administration's frequently stated belief in the superiority of Soviet conventional and nuclear strength.

U.S. Department of Defense. *Soviet Military Power*. Washington, D.C.: Government Printing Office. An annual governmental publication that presents the official U.S. view of Soviet military strength.

The Effects of Nuclear War

Katz, Arthur M. *Life After Nuclear War*. Cambridge, Mass.: Ballinger, 1982. A comprehensive and empirically based analysis of the social and economic effects of a moderate nuclear attack on the United States.

Office of Technology Assessment. *The Effects of Nuclear War*. Totowa, N.J.: Rowman & Allanheld, 1979. An official U.S. government report, compiled at the request of the Senate Foreign Relations Committee, that examines the consequences of a range of nuclear exchanges.

Nuclear Ethics

Hardin, Russell, et al., eds. *Nuclear Deterrence: Ethics and Strategy*. Chicago, Ill.: University of Chicago Press, 1985. Contains an interesting dialogue between ethicists and strategists on questions of deterrence, arms control, no first use, and disarmament.

National Conference of Catholic Bishops. *The Challenge of Peace: God's Promise and Our Response: A Pastoral Letter on War and Peace*. Washington, D.C.: U.S. Catholic Conference, 1983. This controversial statement by the U.S. Catholic bishops has had a major impact on the arms control and deterrence debate during the 1980s.

Nye, Joseph. *Nuclear Ethics*. New York: Free Press, 1986. A former assistant secretary of state, Nye argues that deterrence can work and can be justified within a just war tradition.

Walzer, Michael. *Just and Unjust Wars*. New York: Basic Books, 1977. A provocative analysis of deterrence within the just war tradition.

The Future

Dyson, F. *Weapons and Hope*. New York: Harper & Row, 1984. An analysis of the nuclear dilemma that places the problem within a historical context. The author looks to changes in that context for solutions while arguing that the genie cannot be placed back in the bottle.

The Strategic Defense Initiative

Long, Franklin A., Donald Hafner, and Jeffrey Boutwell, eds. *Weapons in Space*. New York: W. W. Norton, 1986. A rich collection of essays by a number of individuals involved in discussions of strategic doctrine and weapons in the past several decades. Includes a section on ballistic missile defense technologies and another on the policy implications of SDI.

Union of Concerned Scientists. *Empty Promise: The Growing Case Against Star Wars*, 1986. A set of essays that take strong issue with SDI on technical, military, and political grounds. The Union of Concerned Scientists has opposed SDI since its inception. One of the best available critiques of SDI.

PROCESSES OF CONFLICT, PEACE, AND GLOBAL PARTICIPATION

ALLIANCES AND THE
SEARCH FOR SECURITY **8**

I n Chapter 2 we discussed the rules that guide national decision makers in international relations. We also pointed out that, within these rules, a number of central concepts and theories have emerged as general explanations for how nations interact. Predominant among these has been balance of power theory. In practice, nations seek to construct a balance of power vis-à-vis actual or perceived rivals by forging alliances with other nations.

In fact, one of the most intriguing trends of the modern era has been the extent to which nations have chosen to ally themselves with other nations in an attempt to establish the power balance necessary to their own security. In this chapter we will be examining alliances and the issues that surround them: why states form alliances, what factors seem to determine the character and success of alliances, and what differences alliances make—both to international politics and to the states themselves.

Alliance Formation

An *alliance* is a formal agreement between two or more states, the purpose of which is to advance certain shared foreign policy objectives, the most prominent of which is security. When two states are involved, the resulting treaty is often called a mutual security agreement. In the early stages of the Cold War, 1947-1954, the United States entered into a number of major alliances and mutual security agreements. The alliances created four new regional organizations: the Organization of American States or OAS (Latin America, 1947); the North Atlantic Treaty Organization, better known as NATO (Western Europe, 1949); ANZUS (Australia and New Zealand, 1951); and the Southeast Asia Treaty Organization or SEATO (Southeast Asia, 1954). The mutual security agreements were mostly bilateral. The most noteworthy were those with Japan (1951), the Philippines (1951), South Korea (1953), and Taiwan (1954).

What were U.S. objectives in entering into these agreements? Was the primary purpose to defend the United States against the Soviet Union or perhaps to defend the other nations involved? For how long are such agreements likely to serve the interests of the parties? These kinds of questions dominate the scholarly literature and policy discussions on alliances.

States form alliances for a number of reasons. As observers since Thucydides have noted, *a common perception of threat* and the resulting *mutual fear* are the primary reasons states decide to ally themselves with other states. More is involved, however, than merely obtaining assistance in the event of attack. Membership in an alliance also involves a reciprocal commitment to assist other members of the alliance should they be attacked. States join alliances to receive help or to help states they wish to protect. Thus, the decision to join an alliance involves determining not only whom you would like to have fighting on your behalf but also whom you are willing to defend. In making this decision, leaders must carefully determine where their nation's vital interests lie.

Some analysts claim that alliances are formed for different reasons during relatively peaceful times than during periods of international tension. In times of crisis, the decision to join an existing alliance—or form a new one—may be heavily influenced by an *immediate threat to national security*. National leaders are planning for a potential war and are doing their utmost to ensure that, if war does occur, they will prevail. Under these conditions, alliances can be seen as "latent war communities." Many observers have viewed the extensive network of alliances forged by both the United States and the Soviet Union after World War II as exercises of precisely this sort.

But national security considerations are not the only reasons nations enter into alliances. Consider the agreement between Syria and Egypt in the late 1950s that resulted in the creation of the United Arab Republic (U.A.R.). There were military reasons for such an alliance, to be sure, but a major objective was *to enhance the international status* of the two parties involved. Egypt and Syria believed that the U.A.R. would provide some of this status. So, too, smaller states sometimes ally themselves with a larger and more powerful state nearly half a globe away to gain prestige in the international community.

Finally, states enter into alliances for the simple reason that the *benefits of doing so exceed those of nonparticipation* or "going it alone." This calculation of the marginal utility of aligning oneself with other nations is, however, one that national leaders continually reassess. In the United States, for example, discussions of the U.S. commitment to NATO often prompt questions such as "Is the defense of Europe still in our vital interest in an age of nuclear weaponry?" Similarly, many Europeans today are inclined to ask whether the presence of U.S. forces in Europe represents an obstacle to peace between Eastern and Western Europe. Although similar in content, the two queries reflect quite different perspectives concerning the relative costs and benefits of the NATO alliance.

Alliance Effectiveness and Longevity

Issues such as national security, international status, and calculations of marginal utility not only induce states to form alliances, they also play a role in determining the longevity and effectiveness of alliances. States that enter into alliances in response to a perceived threat to their national security are likely to retain their alliance membership as long as the original threat remains. The durability of NATO and the Warsaw Pact—the 1955 alliance between the Soviet Union and its Eastern European allies—is probably best explained in such terms.

There are four major factors that contribute to an effective alliance. The first is a *common objective,* clearly defined and agreed upon. In the absence of a shared interest, there is little reason to form an alliance. Similarly, if the original interest that motivated alliance formation and membership disappears, the alliance itself is likely to crumble.

The second factor contributing to an effective alliance is a clear under-standing of the *causus foederis,* that is, the conditions under which the alliance becomes operational and its members will actually come to the aid of their partners. If the conditions under which alliance members can expect aid from their partners—or are required to offer it—are unclear, the alliance's effectiveness will suffer.

A third factor that contributes to the effectiveness of alliances is the *technical means of cooperation.* Effective alliances specify not only the enemy and the conditions under which the alliance becomes operational but also the development of operational plans. Depending on the nature of the alliance, the weapons systems available, and the theater of operations, these plans may involve little more than a promise to use nuclear weapons in the case of an all-out attack. More likely, however, they will take the form of a detailed plan providing for a joint command structure and the integrated use of the troops and weapon systems supplied by each member.

The fourth requirement of an effective alliance is a *penalty for noncooperation* that assures members of aid from their partners if attacked. This is a particularly crucial requirement. If there is any uncertainty that aid will be provided by the other alliance members to a member who is attacked, and if this uncertainty is detected by potential enemies, the effectiveness of the alliance as a deterrent will be greatly diminished.

In addition to these four major factors, several other characteristics affect the longevity of alliances. Foremost among these is *size.* Although it does not appear that political leaders ordinarily take size into account when deciding whether to join or form an alliance, research findings suggest that for any given alliance there is a minimum and maximum number of participants that is conducive to survival. The optimal number of participants is always the minimum number required to achieve the intended objectives—for example, defense or status enhancement. The reason for this is that the benefits accruing to each individual participant decline with every additional member above the required minimum. In short, when an alliance has too many participants, there are not enough pieces of the political, military, and economic pie to go around.

A second factor contributing to alliance longevity is *the relative ease*

*with which the benefits of alliance membership in one area "spill over"
into others.* One reason for the continuing cohesion of NATO and the Warsaw
Pact is that the concerns of each group have shifted over time from military security narrowly defined to security broadly defined and then to security-
related matters. Thus, during the OPEC oil embargo of the mid-1970s, NATO
members consulted closely with one another about contingency plans for
dealing with further decreases in oil supplies. Although not directly attributable
to the existence of NATO, the breadth and pervasiveness of Western Europe's
economic links to the United States also tend to strengthen ties among alliance
members. A similar pattern can be observed in scientific research, space
exploration, and weather prediction—all of which NATO members have come
to consider security-related matters.

A third factor in a successful alliance is *a high level of participation by
all members in the working of the alliance and the communication
associated with (or resulting from) such a participation.* In alliances whose
members are of unequal size and power, unequal levels of participation can become a major problem. The tendency, of course, is for the larger, more
powerful state—which often has the most to lose if the alliance fails—to
dominate the alliance. History shows that in such cases the larger state often realizes its worst fears. The alliance does fail, largely because the major state's attempts to dominate the alliance drive its partners away.

As important as all of these factors are, they should not obscure the two
basic reasons that lead states to form or join alliances in the first place and then
to retain their membership. First, nations enter into alliances for purposes of
national security, doing so when they believe taking on one or more partners
will enhance the security of their nation in a way that "going it alone" cannot.
Second, nations ally themselves with others who share common interests and
goals, and they will retain their membership in such alliances as long as the resulting gains outweigh the costs.

What Differences Do Alliances Make?

Both in the literature and among policy makers, there is a widespread
belief that alliances are valuable because they contribute to the preservation of
peace and the enhancement of the security of their members. The prevalence
of this point of view makes it important to ask whether it is accurate. In
addition, we might well ask whether alliance formation has other consequences
for the conduct of international affairs.

Do alliances keep peace? The evidence is unclear. Studies that examine
the strength of the relationship between alliances and war do not yield
definitive findings. In the nineteenth century, alliances proved to be a
moderate deterrent to war—that is, they helped to preserve the peace. In the
twentieth century, however, the formation of alliances appears to be moderately related to the occurrence of war.

But as the essay by Randolph M. Siverson and Michael R. Tennefoss in this chapter suggests, this is not all we know about alliances. We know, for example, which types of alliances are more likely to become involved in war. Generally speaking, alliances that include both powerful and less powerful states are less likely to become involved in war than alliances composed only of less powerful states. In fact, participation in alliances by powerful states appears both to deter attacks on weaker states and to discourage weaker states from initiating wars.

As for the benefits of alliance membership to individual states, the literature suggests several possible conclusions. First, the belief that joining an alliance will ensure a state's receiving assistance from others if attacked is clearly borne out by the historical data. States that are members of an alliance receive help 75 percent of the time when attacked; states with no formal ties receive assistance less than 20 percent of the time.

Second, somewhat to the chagrin of policy makers, alliance membership contributes little toward winning a war. Other factors such as the relative power of the nations involved, their respective willingness to endure losses, and the characteristics of the nation that initiated the war are better predictors of victory. Although the differences between the probabilities of defeat are small, it is useful to note that, when a state is attacked by another state, its chances of losing the war are nearly 70 percent if it has allies, but greater than 80 percent if it has none.

Analyses of alliances contain another interesting finding. While it may seem logical that a state that finds itself under attack would immediately seek allies, the historical data for the period 1815-1965 suggests otherwise. Of the 177 alliances created during this period, only 8 were established at the outbreak of a war or within a three-month time span immediately preceding the war. It would seem, then, that (a) alliances are rarely born in a time of great and immediate tension, and (b) policy makers lay their plans for defense in a clear and formal way long before hostilities occur.

In addition to their observed effects on war, alliances have other consequences for international relations. Together with the growth of regional economic and trade organizations (for example, the European Community) and international governmental organizations (for example, the International Monetary Fund), alliances have greatly contributed to the increasing interdependence of nations in the postwar period. Among states of equal power, the result is usually increased interdependence in economic and security matters. When allied states are of dramatically unequal power, the weaker members become extremely dependent on the stronger ones. While the relationship between equal powers can be marked by friction, dependent relationships often produce much higher levels of conflict. Moreover, alliances involving dependent states are often associated with increased repression within the weaker state.

In the post-1945 world, alliances may, thus far, have prevented war between the two superpower blocs. Yet alliance membership has also served as a mechanism by which dominant members have exercised control over their weaker partners. Thus, the Soviet Union has, on several occasions, intervened directly in the internal affairs of its partners to maintain or restore its control over them. In 1956 the Soviets crushed a major revolt in Hungary as well as the precursor of a similar disturbance in Poland. In August of 1961 they erected the infamous Berlin wall, literally overnight, to halt the massive defections of East German citizens to the West when that migration threatened the economic stability of East Berlin. In 1968 Soviet-led Warsaw Pact forces invaded Czechoslovakia to topple the regime of Alexander Dubchek, whose liberal socialist reforms ran counter to Soviet orthodoxy. More recently, during the 1980-1981 unrest in Poland the Soviets applied indirect pressure—including the implied threat of Warsaw Pact intervention—to "encourage" the Polish government to put its own house in order and to repress the dissident political movement, Solidarity.

Nor does this exhaust the list of superpower interventions. Within the past two decades, both superpowers have been involved, directly or indirectly, in devastating regional conflicts in Southeast Asia and the Middle East. Both have sided with different factions in African civil wars. Today, as in the past, the chief beneficiaries of alliances are the major powers and their closest allies. And today's extensive network of complex and multifaceted international commitments has made more problematic the future of smaller nations that have chosen not to join alliances or are totally dependent for their security on alliance membership.

The Readings

The scholarly literature on alliances is extensive. One of the premier analysts in this area since the 1960s has been Bruce Russett, the coauthor of our first article. Russett and Harvey Starr examine the difficult issue of who pays for and who benefits from the enhanced security provided by an alliance relationship.

In "Power, Alliance, and the Escalation of International Conflict, 1815-1965," Siverson and Tennefoss analyze some 250 international conflicts that occurred over a 150-year period. They explore the relationship among relative power, alliance behavior, and the likelihood of war. The article, from which we have deleted most of the more complex data analysis, illustrates how the analysis of historical data can both advance our theoretical understanding and provide guidelines for policy formulation.

The third essay, by Immanuel Wallerstein, combines theory, historical analysis, and a discussion of policy. Wallerstein first proposes a theory of how alliances deteriorate to the point that former allies become competitors, then he examines the process he calls the "hegemonic decline" of U.S. global influence. Finally, he speculates on the consequences of this decline for the United States and other nations. As in his other writings, Wallerstein is very much concerned with the economic repercussions of these developments.

We conclude the readings section with two policy excerpts, both seminal statements of the U.S. perspective on alliances during the 1980s. In the first, "The Atlantic Alliance and the American National Interest," former U.S. ambassador to the United Nations Jeane J. Kirkpatrick offers a well-developed analysis of the sources of the recent strains and pressures on NATO, a forty-year-old defense coalition among friends. Her perspective on NATO's difficulties and her proposed responses represent the traditional American view of the alliance. Like Russett and Starr, she proposes that problems are inherent in all alliance relationships, but that gains will ordinarily outweigh the costs. When they do not, states can be expected to terminate their membership. Whether we should, therefore, be anticipating the demise of NATO is likely to be an important issue for many years.

In a speech entitled "On Alliance Responsibility," Secretary of State George P. Shultz responds to the February 1985 decision of New Zealand, a member of the ANZUS alliance, to refuse port to the USS *Buchanan*. Shultz first outlines the U.S. perspective on the purposes of an alliance and emphasizes the shared responsibilities by alliance members. In Shultz's view, the New Zealand government's decision to bar U.S. ships carrying nuclear weapons from docking in New Zealand ports was effectively a decision to opt out of its ANZUS commitment.

There are, of course, alternative explanations. In announcing his government's decision, Prime Minister David Lange of New Zealand argued that New Zealand merely wished not to be defended by nuclear weapons nor to bear the risks associated with allowing such weapons within its territorial waters. Taken at face value, Lange's explanation suggests that New Zealand and the United States disagreed on the technical means of cooperation rather than on the virtues of the ANZUS pact. What New Zealand saw as an issue of national sovereignty was perceived by the United States not only as a challenge to the viability of ANZUS but also as a threat to the larger system of U.S. alliances.

8.1 ■■■■

BRUCE RUSSETT
HARVEY STARR

Alliances and the Price of Primacy

Alliances and Collective Goods

Both the United States and the Soviet Union have tried to ease their defense burdens by acquiring numerous allies. Formal alliances may have many purposes, of which the pursuit of military security is but one. A state may ally with another in order to achieve direct "side-payments" such as territorial concessions or economic assistance. Or a state may seek arms shipments in return for alliance with a larger power, in order better to restrain its own populace instead of for reasons of international politics. Even alliances concluded with external threats in mind may pursue security in either or both of two ways. A state may take on an ally in order to augment its own power, hoping that the new ally's army, when combined with its own forces, will be enough to deter or defeat a prospective opponent. This is perhaps the most common consideration in classic military alliances. In other cases, however— and these seem especially common for the United States in the post-World War II period—the alliance serves to extend an umbrella from the strong power to cover weak allies. In the long run and with more immediate military considerations in mind, the large state may consider the smaller one important to its security even though the small one's armed forces are weak. Thus the individual Scandinavian or Low Country allies make little increment to NATO military power, but the United States hopes to add its strength to theirs and so deter any communist attack on them.

Contemporary American alliances, and perhaps also those of Russia, serve either or both of the last two purposes for the great power. America and the Soviet Union are overwhelmingly suppliers, not recipients, of economic and military assistance in their respective alliances (Russia after World War II was a partial exception), so most side-payments are unimportant to them except as they use them to entice smaller states into alliance. What the superpowers seek is to augment their own military strength with that of their allies or to extend the deterrent umbrella. But insofar as the first is important, both superpowers

---

By Bruce M. Russett with Harvey Starr, reprinted from Bruce M. Russett, *What Price Vigilance?* (New Haven, Connecticut: Yale University Press, 1965). Copyright © 1965 by Yale University Press. Reprinted by permission of the publisher.

regard most of their alliances as by no means the successes for which they had hoped. The Soviets long have had good reason to question the reliability of their allies in any actual combat with Western troops. Even now one wonders whether Hungarian and Czechoslovak troops—especially if they were not fighting West German forces—would constitute a net gain or a loss to the communist side in a war. Conceivably they could pin down nearly as many Soviet troops to insure their allegiance as they would add to the collective strength.

The Western side may not have many worries of this sort, but United States military and political spokesmen have long complained that their allies provide less than a fair share contribution to the joint defense. A well-known analyst of American foreign policy exemplifies this very widely held view: "Two decades after a war from which they have long since recovered economically, they show few signs of fulfilling the original postwar expectation that they would assume the major burden of their own defense in return for an American guarantee." In all of its multilateral alliances—NATO, SEATO, and the Rio Pact—the United States devotes a much larger proportion of its national income to defense than does *any* other alliance member. This becomes a matter of acrimony, especially at NATO, when members' contributions are reviewed. Apparently the Soviet Union has the same problem, since it devotes a larger proportion of its income to military purposes than does any other member of the Warsaw Pact. And Russians too seem to feel that their allies are freeloading.

The problem is a basic one in alliances among states which, though juridically equal, are very unequal in power. If the bigger power hopes simultaneously to extend its umbrella to protect the smaller ally and to gain the ally's resources as an increment to its own, the two goals come into conflict. For so long as the smaller state is neither coerced by the big one nor offered special incentives, and unless the threat to the small state is very grave indeed—as in actual wartime—the small nation is likely to regard the big country's armed forces as a substitute for its own. The small country will feel able to relax its own efforts because it has obtained great power protection. Thus the big power's success in extending its umbrella works against its other goals of using the alliance to enhance its own military strength. The small power's effort will vary inversely with its confidence in the big power's guarantee and the disparity in size between the two.

This matter of alliance burden-sharing is an aspect of a wider concern among economists with the theory of "public" or "collective" goods, produced by organizations whose function is to advance the common interests of members. The theory, and the evidence for it, are important in any understanding of alliance behavior. It was originally set forth by Paul Samuelson, was further developed by John Head, and has recently been applied to alliances and other small groups in important studies by Mancur Olson and Richard Zeckhauser.

Public, or collective, goods are defined by two properties. One is that of "external economy" or "nonexclusiveness." External economies are benefits that are made equally available to all members of a group; it is not possible or economically feasible to exclude nonpurchasers from the benefits. The other is called "nonrivalness" or "jointness" of supply, meaning that each individual's consumption leads to no subtraction from the supply available to others; this implies that the additional or marginal cost to others, if a good is provided for one, is small or actually zero. These properties are conceptually distinct, and both are required to identify a public good. "Private" goods lack both of these properties; "mixed" goods may have some degree of both or of one and not the other.

At the *national* level, deterrence is virtually a pure public good. Under most circumstances an attack upon any one part of the country will meet with as strong a response as an attack on any part of the nation. It is neither militarily nor politically feasible to exclude Mississippi or California from the deterrent umbrella that covers the entire United States. And once the deterrent force is provided for any 49 states, inclusion of the 50th in no way diminishes the security provided to the others. In a military *alliance*, the collective good aspect remains very strong but is somewhat mixed. Nonexclusiveness is not necessarily met, because of a nation's will or ability to regulate the credibility of deterrence. As Ypersele notes, "It is partly an awareness of this possibility which had led France to start building its own deterrence." The great power may indeed want to limit the credibility of its assurances, since they carry a risk of involvement in major war for the sake of allies' objectives that to it may be trivial. Even with resolute will and high capability, the amount of "automatic" security provided by the United States in NATO, for instance, will not be the same for its allies as for itself nor the same for all allies. It will unavoidably be influenced by such factors as geographic proximity and the web of almost intangible political, social, and economic ties between the big power and the states it would protect. Consider, for example, the differences between Canada and Turkey, the least and probably the most exposed to Soviet ground forces, and respectively probably with the strongest and weakest intangible ties to the United States.

Let us nevertheless assume for the moment that deterrence is the only function of a military alliance and that the deterrence provided by any one member for itself becomes entirely a public good for all other members. (Both these assumptions will be relaxed below.) The biggest power will buy a lot of deterrence, much more than any of the small powers would buy for itself given the same tastes and costs the big power has. Because in the alliance they get this deterrence free from the big power, they also will buy much less for themselves than they would do in the absence of an alliance. But how much will they buy? Will smaller nations all make approximately the same proportionate contribution to collective deterrence (but a much smaller proportionate contribution than the big power), less increasingly in proportion to their smallness, or in fact none at all?

Olson and Zeckhauser show, in a technical argument that need not be repeated here, that under reasonable assumptions the larger the nation the more disproportionate the share of the total military cost it will bear. In small groups this effect may be mitigated because freeloaders can be spotted, and their laggardness may be highlighted by publicity about members' contributions (for example, the NATO annual review and press releases showing the defense budgets of all members). Thus the larger the group the greater the proclivity for "exploitation" of the big members by the small ones. Some form of group coordination and/or organization may provide social incentives for smaller states' contributions, but short of actual coercion (and the theory is meant to apply only to voluntary groups) some disproportionality will remain. There are even cases where the small powers will provide nothing.

> In some small groups each of the members, or at least one of them, will find that his personal gain from having the collective good exceeds the total costs of providing some amount of that collective good; there are members who would be better off if the collective good were provided, even if they had to pay the entire cost of providing it themselves, than they would be if it were not provided.

In such small groups (which Olson labels "privileged") where it is worthwhile for some member to provide all the good, the others may indeed not buy any.

But as we have noted, even if the purpose of military expenditures were only to provide deterrence against external threats, in a real-world alliance only a portion of the security obtained for itself by the large country can be extended to its allies, due to problems of credibility. As said above, the characteristics of a pure public good are rarely met in situations of alliance, and thus the smaller countries will have to buy some measure of security for themselves. Because the security provided by the big country is only partly a public good for its allies, the total derived from the big power alone may be less than the ally would have provided if it were not in alliance. Thus the ally is induced to supplement this automatic security. This supplement is also a partial public good, and "the smallest allies will, in turn, benefit from the additional security provided by the medium-sized countries" all along the line. Therefore the smallest countries will incur minuscule (but probably greater than zero) military expenditures. The big countries also get *some* very modest benefit from the supplement provided by the small, and hence everyone's expenditures are reduced by the alliance, but for the small nations not by as much as if deterrence were a pure public good. In a narrow economic evaluation, the big power must ask itself whether the increment to its own security provided by its allies' efforts is greater than the additional cost (for instance, in maintaining foreign air and missile bases or a "tripwire" presence) it incurs because of the alliance.

If we relax the assumption that military expenditures only provide deterrence, other reasons for military spending by small allies become apparent. *Defense* or damage-limiting capability if deterrence fails, even in the purely national setting, is less clearly a public good than is deterrence. There will be questions about which cities to defend with ABMs or, in West Germany, whether to draw the line of battle at the East German border, at the Rhine, or somewhere between. In an alliance these choices are all the harder, and each ally is almost sure to give priority to its own defense at the expense of others. Defense does not meet either criterion (nonrivalness or nonexclusiveness) for a public good. For these reasons few nations will rely entirely on the deterrence and defense forces provided by alliance with a larger power but will supplement as private goods from their own resources whatever is provided by the alliance. Great concern about defense, however, implies a failure of the alliance to provide for its members a high level of confidence in the pact's deterrent capability. In wartime or periods of acute threat, defense may become a "superior good" defined as something for which an amount at least equal to all income increments will be spent.

Furthermore, there will usually be some private returns from military expenditures, benefits that have nothing to do with defense or deterrence. Overseas colonies are explicitly excluded from the NATO umbrella, and colonial powers must themselves provide for their security. Ground forces may be needed to maintain internal security or to restrain rebellious colonies. Some kinds of military research and development offer potential civilian benefits. French and British leaders have often been unwilling to cut themselves off from large areas of technological advance as the price for forgoing certain kinds of weapons development. For the same reasons nations in alliance will be reluctant to specialize too heavily according to the principle of comparative advantage—for instance, supplying infantry but giving up military R & D.

The analytical distinction among the functions of military expenditure, cast in terms of collective and other goods, is important because of the prediction that to the degree the alliance provides a collective good, the smaller allies will lack incentive to raise armed forces of their own and instead will rely largely upon the greater power member(s). Thus the failure of smaller NATO and Warsaw allies to match their protectors' proportionate exertions could be explained in very general rather than ad hoc terms. It would be seen as a "normal" consequence of alliance rather than a lack of ideological fervor or, as has sometimes been alleged, a common European preference to shirk burdens and rely upon others wherever possible.

In addition to refuting that kind of pejorative argument, the applicability of the theory would indicate a measure of the success of NATO (or Warsaw) in meeting at least one of the aims of its superpower originator—to extend the umbrella of deterrence so that other nations will have confidence in the will and ability of the superpowers to resist or avenge attack on its clients. The *failure of burden-sharing* would thus indicate the *success of deterrence,* and the initial hope of American policy to obtain a high degree of both would be fundamentally contradictory. We will therefore look at the relative applicability of the collective goods theory at different points in time, associating changes with the evolution of strategy and political cooperation. Also, we can compare the NATO and Warsaw Pact experience with that of other multilateral alliances in the post-World War II era. Various alliances are affected in different ways by big power dominance, and the alliances serve a different mix of functions. By comparing the distribution of burdens actually borne with that predicted by the theory of collective goods, we can better understand what these functions are in each case. Where some or all members spend more than predicted, we have three possible explanations to weigh:

1. They lack confidence in the resolve of their protector (the nonexclusiveness criterion is not met) or in his ability.

2. They seek private goods (e.g. internal security, research and development, control of colonies) from military spending.

3. They are coerced by the big power into spending more than they would (the alliance is not a voluntary organization).

Finally, we will be able to make a general assessment of the value of alliances to the United States and of the degree to which, if at all, it is reasonable to hope that a significant reduction in American military burdens will be made possible by our allies' contributions. . . .

Alliances and the Goals of American Policy

From a theoretical viewpoint, both the power of the theory of collective goods and its limitations are impressive. Occasionally it works quite well and in so doing illuminates the purposes of an alliance. In other instances it predicts less well or not at all. It should not be taken as a universal key to alliance burden-sharing, as some writers have implied. But the theory's failures, as well as its successes, help to show what are the goals of particular alliances and of particular states. Used carefully it has a very wide potential for explicating international problems. Proponents of collective security might benefit from considering how rarely the conditions for true joint action against a rule-violator are likely to occur. The collective goods problem permeates all of international relations because of the low level of organization or coercion present in the international system.

The theory tells us enough about what one can reasonably expect from various kinds of alliances to offer considerable guidance to Americans. In forming or retaining an alliance with other states and providing them with deterrence, a great power such as the United States must expect that its allies will continue to contribute something to their own military security but less than they would spend in the absence of the alliance. (Unless, perhaps, lacking alliance the small nation would find any military effort within its power to be hopelessly inadequate and hence resort to some sort of unarmed neutrality.) Therefore, the total amount of military spending by states in the alliance will be *less* than would occur without the alliance. If the American goals are to bring other nations under its deterrent shield so as to protect them either more effectively or at less cost to them—allowing them, for instance, to use more scarce resources for development—then it should so judge the alliance's success.

If, however, the United States goal is to save money for itself by in part substituting allies for its own military expenditures, the evaluation is more difficult. America must balance the (small) increment to its own security that will be provided by the collective good portion of the new ally's spending against the additional costs the United States will incur in whatever extra military forces it needs to give security to the ally. Probably neither of these will be great, and by this criterion the net gain or loss from the alliance is not likely to be great.

But neither of these criteria allow for the overall economic and political value of the small ally, beyond its immediate military contribution of forces-in-being. If, in the absence of alliance, the small ally could not or would not spend enough to protect itself, then it is only necessary that the net cost of putting the ally under the great power's umbrella not exceed the additional expenditures for American security that would be required if an opposing power or alliance gained control of the small state. From that perspective, the alliance is much more likely to appear as a benefit to the United States. Insofar as a big power chooses wisely, concentrating on states of high intrinsic value that would not or could not defend themselves adequately alone, the big power will be better off for having accepted the commitment. In any event, a great power such as America or Russia must still expect to spend a greater share of its resources for military security than will small powers. That is the price of primacy.

In evaluating NATO, the verbal balance sheet might look like this: NATO was born when Western perceptions (whether accurate or not) of a communist threat were sharply rising. If one accepts the assumption that some NATO countries would have lost their independence without the American guarantee, then America's acquisition of new allies in 1949 almost certainly kept United States military expenditures from rising much faster and farther than in fact they did. But once the alliance was well established and its forces were built up to meet Europe's security needs reasonably well, it was surely erroneous to hope that American spending could be reduced relative to theirs. Only full political union, making everyone's deterrent spending truly a public good for everyone else, could accomplish that.

Given a constant level of threat to any small nonaligned nation, conclusion of an alliance with it is unlikely to permit any relaxation of United States military expenditures. Any efforts to establish new alliances, as for example in Southeast Asia (unlikely as that may seem in the current domestic and international political climate), should take these facts into account. Finally, efforts to reduce American defense spending by shifting burdens to our current allies are very unlikely to succeed. To extract a very much larger contribution from others we would have to cut our own by so much as really to diminish our allies' sense of security.

RANDOLPH M. SIVERSON
MICHAEL R. TENNEFOSS

Power, Alliance, and the Escalation of International Conflict, 1815-1965

Despite the advent of an empirical revolution, research and theory in the study of international conflict are frequently contradictory and sometimes inchoate. This is nowhere clearer than in the body of research and theory that attempts to relate the distribution of power between and among nations to the onset of international conflict and war. In general, there are two opposing views of the relationship between power distribution and war. The first is known as balance of power theory: it argues that equal power leads to an equilibrium in which the chances of war are reduced because no nation can by itself prevail over its equals. The second view is that power equality leads to war, whereas inequality of power leads to peace because preponderant powers, through their position, are able to influence outcomes without resorting to war. In essence, these two theoretical positions make directly opposite predictions about the effects of power relationships on the outbreak of war.

The goal of this research is to explore the linkage between power relationships and the outbreak of war. Further, we will consider the role of alliances as they may interact with power relationships in the escalation of conflicts to war.

Power Relationships and War

A fundamental assertion of balance-of-power thought is that large-scale conflict between nations will be avoided when their power is approximately equal, and, conversely, will be more likely between nations that diverge in their power. This assertion is based on the assumption, frequently hidden, that in a conflict between any two nations there is a direct relationship between power and victory and, other considerations aside, the more powerful nation will prevail. Further, rational decision makers are assumed to be able to reach this same conclusion and to have reasonably accurate information on relative power relationships. Hence these decision makers will avoid initiating or escalating conflicts with nations that are equal to or more powerful than their own nation. This assumption leads to the hypothesis that it will be the stronger nation which

From *American Political Science Review*, Vol. 29 (1984). Copyright © 1984 by American Political Science Association. Reprinted with permission.

initiates and escalates conflicts (Organski & Kugler, 1980). In essence, then, the balance-of-power view leads to the expectation of relative peace when nations are roughly equal in power, but the possibility of serious conflict when they are unequal in power. There is, however, a notable alternative point of view.

Organski (1968) argues that it is precisely when power is equal between nations that war is most likely. He reasons that in situations of conflict and unequal power, the strongest nation need not employ war to achieve its aim because weaker nations will not be able to resist its power. According to Organski's argument, when nations have nearly equal power, each will believe it has a chance of winning, thus making war more likely; conversely, when one nation is significantly more powerful, peace is more likely. Although several empirical studies appear to sustain Organski's hypothesis (Garnham, 1976a, b; Organski & Kugler, 1980; Singer, Bremer, & Stuckey, 1972; Weede, 1976), a recent review of this research argues that the findings are heavily influenced by research designs that variously 1) include data not closely connected to the theory; 2) reduce the variance in the independent variables measuring power; 3) exclude cases of potential power disparity by using only conflicts between contiguous nations; or 4) analyze a restricted range of cases (Siverson & Sullivan, 1983).

Unfortunately, direct comparisons of the effects of different patterns of power distribution on war have been few (Organski & Kugler, 1980), perhaps because power relationships are correctly seen as an important component of the balance of power, whereas the balance of power is incorrectly thought to be a phenomenon of the system level alone (Waltz, 1979). Although some of the literature conceptualizes the balance of power as a purely systemic phenomenon, it is also true that numerous traditional and contemporary versions of the balance of power devote major attention to dyadic relationships (Craig & George, 1983; Wight, 1946). Moreover, as Singer (1980) has noted, there are likely to be significant parallels between systemic properties and dyadic relationships: "Most of a system's properties rest upon and can be inferred from the relationships among its components." Thus, in many respects the system level may be seen as an aggregation of dyadic relationships. Our approach to the problem will be at the level of the dyad. This will not only permit an analysis that is free of any problems of the ecological fallacy (Sullivan & Siverson, 1981), but will also permit comparison of the balance of power to Organski's theory of "power preponderance."

Power in international politics is not only a property of the individual nation, but also of nations aggregated in alliances. In particular, alliances are thought to be especially important in adjusting power relationships in the balance of power. For example, in writing about conflict strategy in the balance-of-power system, George and Smoke (1974) note: "The usual object was to insure that one had as many great powers on one's own side as were numbered among the likely opponents. Accordingly, to be diplomatically isolated—without apparent allies—was to have one's deterrent capabilities undermined, and to isolate one's opponent was the prerequisite of going to war against him." It is the realization that a nation in isolation is in danger which is hypothesized to lead national decision makers into a search for allies to counterbalance their opponent's strength (Kaplan, 1957). In general, the effect accorded alliances in the balance of power is very similar to that of individual power; that is, when alliances are equal, relative peace will ensue, but when one alliance has greater power, war becomes possible.

A different view of alliances is developed by Organski and Kugler (1980) in their conception of the power preponderance approach. In general, they argue that alliances have little or no impact upon the onset of war. For example, in their comparison of the power-preponderance and balance-of-power theories, Organski and Kugler denigrate the role of alliances as a method of adjusting or redistributing power. They argue that "alliances are simply not a realistic method of preventing threatening changes in the distribution of world power, given the skewness of relations between the great and the lesser nations, and also among the half-dozen great powers themselves." Moreover, according to their view, even if alliances made a difference, they would be in-effective because "alliances cannot easily be made or unmade." They then conclude: "The assumption that underlies much of the balance of power model, namely, that the dictates of power considerations are sufficiently strong to guide the behavior of countries in making or breaking alliances, is not true." The results of their data analysis indicate that alliances play a relatively small role in the onset of war.

From the above review it may be seen that there is little agreement about the effects of power relationships and alliances upon the outbreak of war. In the next section we show how several new aspects of our analysis allow an as-sessment of how, individually and jointly, power relationships and alliances affect the escalation of international conflicts to the military activities typically associated with war.

The Approach and the Data

Our approach to analyzing the linkages between power relationships, alliance, and war differs in several important ways from those of other re-searchers. The most significant difference is that our dependent variable is not war alone; rather, we focus on a range of conflict measured on a three-point scale, the highest point of which corresponds to war. Our definition of conflict is similar to that of Bloomfield and Leiss, who view it not as a single incident of hostile activity, but as a series of phases of violent or nonviolent behavior.

> Within each phase exist factors—conditions, perceptions, or events—that generate pressures. Some of these pressures tend toward violence and some tend away from violence. . . . Within each phase the factors interact in such a way as to push the conflict ultimately across a series of thresholds toward or away from violence. . . . Violence-producing factors and those tending away

from violent outcomes in fact have their interaction during phases. . . . The event of transition is itself a product of forces that have been at work throughout the phases (emphasis in original deleted).

From our perspective, power relationships and alliances constitute important factors which are hypothesized to have various effects upon whether a conflict will enter a new, more violent phase, or, alternatively will be settled without recourse to violence. Conflicts hence consist of various thresholds, the crossing of any one of which indicates a highly significant change in conflictual activity. Our research is directed toward understanding to what extent power and alliances affect the possibility that a conflict will cross a threshold, especially the threshold associated with the mutual use of organized military activity. In a very direct way, this method of observing conflict measures the extent to which conflicts escalate.

Specifically, we are interested in three levels of conflict:

1) *Threat*. An explicit verbal statement threatening overt military action, directed at a target nation or nations.

2) *Unreciprocated military action*. Military action taken by one state against an unresponsive target state. This action may involve physical violence, but it may also include acts that are not necessarily violent, such as a naval blockade.

3) *Reciprocated military action*. Military action taken by one nation that provokes a target state to engage the initiator in military combat. This category includes qualifying international wars.

Unlike studies that use only war as a dependent variable, the use of conflict measured on a three-point index allows us to evaluate not just the outbreak of very violent conflict, but also *the relative tendencies* of conficts to reach this severe level.

Beside allowing the observation of escalation, the use of the three-point scale of conflict for measuring the dependent variable has another subtle, but significant advantage. In a rigorous analysis of the logic of the research designs used in the study of war, Most and Starr (1982) argue persuasively against the adoption of an approach that has only war as the dependent variable. A consequence of research designs in which war is the dependent variable is that numerous researchers:

often in effect focus on conflicts that are reported to have occurred— "successful" occurrences of the dependent war variable—and work backward. Using a design or case selection procedure that is appropriate only for probing possible necessary relationships, they proceed to examine questions of sufficiency and utilize statistical techniques that are appropriate for such queries. They fail to match the cases they consider with the questions that they ask and the methods that they employ.

Most and Starr conclude that "an understanding of the conditions that are sufficient for war logically entails the inclusion of both 'war' and 'peace' as the dependent variable." For an appropriate test of the balance of power, such an approach is vital. As we have noted above, the balance of power is in part a theory of why wars do not occur. If we were to explore this idea in the way most recent researchers have, it would entail correlating the wars that took place with the extent to which, for example, power was equal or unequal. It would not, however, tell us anything about the extent, if any, to which power equality mitigated against conflicts escalating into wars, which is precisely the prediction of balance-of-power theory. By using the three-point scale, we are able to observe conflicts that did *not* become wars.

Our approach also differs from previous research on war in three other ways. First, the only nations for which data are collected are the initial two participants in a conflict; this reflects our central interest in the outbreak of conflict rather than its subsequent spread. Research that has sought to link alliances with variables such as the nation-months of war (Singer & Small, 1968) may be measuring the war-spreading effects of alliances rather than their impact upon the onset of war (Siverson & King, 1979). Our focus upon only the two initial actors will avoid this problem and permit us to assess the effects of alliances upon the onset of war. A second difference is that we identify one of the initial two participants as the initiator and the other as the target. Because power and alliances are hypothesized by the balance of power to deter nations from initiating conflicts against nations with specific power and alliance attributes, the data cannot really be tested without distinguishing between the two opponents. It should be noted, however, that the initiator of a conflict is not necessarily the aggressor, but rather the nation that made the initial overt threat. Finally, we examine only the effects of alliances that include at least one major power, because if alliances are supposed to augment a nation's power, then the effects of alliance should be most clearly evident in those cases where the incremental increase in power is the greatest. Such would be the case with a major power ally.

Although the procedures used to create our data set are discussed at length elsewhere (Siverson & Tennefoss, 1982), we believe it is useful to describe them briefly. The data set was created by locating international conflicts in numerous studies of European and international history and then categorizing these conflicts according to their level of hostility on the three-point scale discussed above. To be included in the data set, a conflict must meet two criteria: first, both participants had to be recognized as nation states, and second, at least one of the participants must have been a major power. Table 8-1 lists the major powers and dates of inclusion as such. This list is similar but not identical to other lists of the major powers (Singer & Small, 1972). (A list of minor powers appears in Silverson & Tennefoss, 1982.)

Three points need to be made about the relationship between our index of conflict and the data measured by it. First, empirically the index constitutes a monotonic ordinal scale. It is monotonic in the sense we assume that every case of unreciprocated military action was previously at the threat level, and that every case of unreciprocated military action passed through the two previous

Table 8-1 Nation-states Classified as Major Powers and Time Periods of Classifications, 1816-1965

Austria-Hungary	1816-1918
France	1816-1940
	1945-1965
Great Britain	1816-1965
Prussia/Germany	1816-1918
	1923-1945
West Germany	1955-1965
Russia	1816-1917
	1922-1965
Sardinia/Italy	1860-1943
Japan	1895-1945
United States	1899-1965
China	1950-1965

levels of conflict. In some cases this passage was very brief, whereas in others it was drawn out. In those instances in which events unfolded relatively slowly, our decision to treat the situation as either one case or more than one case was governed largely by the historical descriptions in our sources. Second, as defined by Singer and Small (1972), wars are coded as reciprocated military actions rather than as a separate category of conflict. As noted above, we sought an index that had clearly visible thresholds of substantive import. To move from a threat to the actual use of military force, for example, involves a clear and unmistakable shift in the type and nature of a conflict. Similarly, when one actor uses violence, the other must make a choice about the nature of his response. Once both actors choose to use force, however, the thresholds are not so clearly delimited, and escalation proceeds not so much in terms of violations of thresholds as it does in changes in the actual severity or spread of the conflict. Although we may characterize the highest level of hostility as war, it is necessary to recognize that this category is closer to Garnham's (1976b) "lethal dyads" than to Singer's and Small's (1972) wars, even though many of the latter are included in our data.

Third, our data base contains only instances of conflictual activity; at a minimum, all cases involve threatening behavior by at least one antagonist. Therefore we cannot, nor is it our intention to, draw inferences about the conditions for the initiation of conflicts. Our interest is in exploring the effects of power and alliances on the escalation of conflict to mutual military action. We start from the assumption that a serious dispute is already taking place and then examine the influence of power relationships and alliance on the escalation of hostilities. Threat, our lowest level of conflict, serves as the base

Table 8-2 International Conflict by Time Periods

Conflict Level	1815-1914		1915-1965		Total
	N	%	N	%	
1	42	42.8	73	46.2	115
2	28	28.6	50	31.6	78
3	28	28.6	35	22.1	63
Total	98		158		256

from which we start our analysis; events must at least have reached that threshold to be studied.

We have claimed several virtues for our approach, but candor compels our recognition of at least two limitations. Had resources been available, it would have been desirable to locate all conflicts taking place between nations; that is, to have included also those involving only minor powers. As it is, the exclusion of solely minor power conflicts will impose a limit on our ability to draw inferences about the effects of power. A second problem is that our measurement of power is dichotomous, and thus our ability to explore fully the relationships between major powers is limited. For this reason alone, our analysis must be seen as tentative rather than conclusive. Nonetheless, the strength of our results should in some degree compensate for these two limitations.

Our data set contains a total of 256 conflicts. Table 8-2 breaks down these cases according to their conflict level and when they occurred. It may be noted that the relative proportion of cases at each level of conflict does not vary greatly across time periods.

Data Analysis

Let us begin by examining the effect of the power relationship in a dyad on the tendency for conflicts to escalate to the highest level of our scale, reciprocated military action. Table 8-3 gives the results of cross-tabulating the conflict data by the power of the initiator and the target. In these data several interesting patterns are immediately apparent. Generally, differences in power had a substantial effect on the level of the conflict, but in different ways. First, among major powers, where presumably power was roughly equal, 61.7% of the conflicts never moved beyond the lowest level, and only relatively few (19.8%) involved mutual military action. Second, in instances in which major powers initiated conflicts with minor powers, a much higher proportion (27%) escalated to the highest level. Both of these patterns are generally in accord with what might be expected from balance-of-power theory. However,

Table 8-3 Antagonists' Power Relationship and Conflict

Initiator's Power	Major				Minor	
Target's Power	Major		Minor		Major	
Conflict Level	N	%	N	%	N	%
1	50	61.7	48	38.1	17	34.7
2	15	18.5	44	34.9	19	38.7
3	16	19.8	34	27.0	13	26.5
Total	81		126		49	

$X^2 = 14.31$
$df = 4$
$p < .01$
$N = 256$

balance-of-power theory not only asserts the conditions for conflict, but also implies who will initiate it. What is apparently not in complete accord with the ideas of the balance of power is the number and level of conflicts initiated by minor powers against major powers; minor powers initiated 49 conflicts (19.1%) with major powers, and a substantial proportion (26.5%) of these escalated to the highest level. Because the balance-of-power theory predicts that it is the stronger nation which will initiate conflicts, these data are somewhat anomalous. As we have noted, however, alliances are often seen as a method of increasing a nation's strength, and hence we need to explore the possibility that the minor powers initiating conflict with major powers had major power allies. With such support, they might feel confident in their actions. We examine this possibility, but first we look at the individual effect of alliances on conflict.

Table 8-4 reports conflict data in terms of whether or not the initiator and target had at least one major power ally. In large part, the data are strikingly consistent with balance-of-power theory. In those cases in which both nations had a major power ally, there was a pronounced tendency for the conflicts to remain at the lowest level (58.3%). Conflicts arose, but in general they were not pursued to higher levels. However, we find that the largest proportion of cases (35.6%) escalated to the highest level when the initiator had a major power ally and the target did not; in fact, these cases not only constitute the highest proportion of those escalating, they also represent the largest concentration of cases ($N = 26$) at the highest level. Such a pattern in the data is, of course, completely consistent with the balance-of-power idea that alliances can be used to gain the necessary strength to initiate conflicts. When neither nation had a major power ally, we also found that relatively few conflicts escalated to reciprocated military activity, even though a rather large percentage involved only one nation engaging in military activity.

Table 8-4 Antagonists' Major Power Ally Status and Conflict

Did initiator have a major power ally?	Yes				No			
Did target have a major power ally?	Yes		No		Yes		No	
Conflict level	N	%	N	%	N	%	N	%
1	49	58.3	26	35.6	28	43.9	22	37.9
2	20	23.8	21	28.5	13	31.7	24	41.4
3	15	17.8	26	35.6	10	24.4	12	20.6
Total	84		73		41		58	

$X^2 = 14.45$
$df = 6$
$p < .05$
$N = 256$

A pattern inconsistent with the balance of power is apparent in those instances in which the initiator did not have a major power ally and the target did. Although the overall number of cases is relatively small, their existence and the proportion that escalated (24.4%) suggest that achieving deterrence in the balance of power is probably not just a matter of major power alliances.

We now consider the joint effects of alliances and power relationships. The three parts of Table 8-5 display the results of considering the conflict data with the power status and alliance status of the initiator and target. From the balance of power perspective, the relationships are, to say the least, perplexing. In conflicts between major powers, the presence of a major power ally does not make any significant difference in the level of the conflict. This finding tends to support both Organski's view that wars begin when nations are equal in power and Organski and Kugler's finding that allies do not make a substantial difference in the onset of war between major powers.

When major powers initiated conflict with minor powers, a very different pattern may readily be seen. Although allied major powers initiated no small amount of conflict with allied minor powers, only a modest number of the conflicts went to the highest level (16.7%), and the majority of conflicts (52.8%) remained at the lowest level; the pattern is similar to the major power versus major power cases discussed above. However, when allied major powers initiated conflicts with nonallied minor powers, the results were clearly lethal. Fully 42.4% of these conflicts moved to the highest level, whereas only 26.8% remained at the lowest level. Equally telling is the overall lack of data in those instances in which a nonallied major power initiated conflict with an allied minor power. One may be tempted to dismiss the lack of data as merely a consequence of the fact that because major powers are alliance-prone (Job, 1976; Siverson & Duncan, 1976), there were relatively few instances in which they did not have a major power ally. However, such an explanation does not hold because an examination of the last column of data, containing conflicts in which neither the major power nor minor power had an ally, shows a significant amount of conflict. A more plausible explanation for the lack of data is the protective effect of a major power ally. For minor powers, a major power ally was evidently able to provide the augmentation of national strength necessary to achieve deterrence. In sum, the relationship between a major power initiator and a minor power target is very heavily influenced by whether or not these nations have a major power ally.

Above we promised to consider further the cases in which minor powers initiated conflicts against major powers. We suggested that the surprising high frequency with which these cases appeared could be consistent with balance of power theory if the minor powers had major powers to support them. The third section of Table 8-5 shows that just the opposite is true. Among these data no allied minor power initiated a conflict with a major power that eventuated at the highest level. In fact, once again there is a significant lack of data. One possible explanation for this is that major powers protected their minor power allies so well that the latter did not have the need to engage in much conflict themselves; however, data on conflicts initiated by major powers against allied minor powers seem to indicate that this is not the case (Table 8-5, second section). A more probable explanation would be that major powers very effectively control their minor power allies and refuse to allow them to initiate conflicts that are potentially too costly for the major power. Recent research by Weede (1983) details such control and describes the accompanying erosion of the minor powers' sovereignty as part of the heavy price of peace.

If data are relatively sparse for allied minor power initiators, they are surprisingly abundant for nonallied minor power initiators. Clearly under some circumstances minor powers lacking a major power ally are willing to initiate conflicts with major powers. We will return to this point below.

Interactions Among Variables

An important problem which our analysis thus far has not directly considered is the extent to which the effects of 1) alliances with major powers, and 2) power status, jointly or independently influence the escalation of conflict. The exploration of this relationship is essential for determining to what extent alliances and power status are themselves responsible for escalating conflicts, and to what extent they interact to do the same.

A useful method of investigating this relationship is through log-linear modeling, a relatively recent development that constitutes a significant advance in the analysis of multiway contingency tables of the sort we use. Relying upon the definition of interaction based upon cross-product ratios of

Table 8-5 Antagonists' Alliance Status, Power Status, and Conflict

Initiator has major power ally?	Yes				No			
Target has major power ally?	Yes		No		Yes		No	
Conflict level	*N*	%	*N*	%	*N*	%	*N*	%
Major versus major conflict								
1	23	60.5	10	71.4	9	64.3	8	53.3
2	6	15.8	2	14.3	3	21.4	4	26.6
3	9	23.7	2	14.3	2	13.3	3	20.0
$X^2 = 2.02$								
$df = 6$								
$p < .80$								
$N = 81$								
Major versus minor conflict								
1	19	52.8	15	26.8	2	67.0	12	38.7
2	11	30.5	17	30.4	0		16	51.6
3	6	16.7	24	42.4	1	33.3	3	9.6
$X^2 = 18.74$								
$df = 6$								
$p < 0.02$								
$N = 126$								
Minor versus major conflict								
1	7	70.0	1	33.0	7	29.2	2	16.6
2	3	30.0	2	67.0	10	41.7	4	33.3
3	0		0		7	29.2	6	50.0
$X^2 = 11.86$								
$df = 6$								
$p < 0.07$								
$N = 49$								

expected cell frequencies, log-linear modeling permits the simultaneous examination of mutual variation among qualitative variables. Thus we are able to engage in the direct assessment of interaction among variables in contingency tables, and by using this technique we can determine whether the effects of alliance and power status on conflict are independent or interactive.

The data in Table 8-5 were analyzed using the log-linear modeling program BMD P3F (Dixon & Brown, 1979). The resulting partial and marginal associations are presented in Table 8-6. The results indicate four significant second order interactions conflict and the target's alliance status [*CT*], power

Table 8-6 Partial and Marginal Association for Selected Variables, 1815-1965

Effect	DF	Partials		Marginals	
		X^2	p	X^2	p
C	2	15.31	<.01		
P	2	32.98	<.01		
T	1	.13	.72		
I	1	12.37	<.01		
CP	4	11.25	.02	13.56	<.01
CT	2	4.71	.09	7.05	.03
CI	2	2.59	.27	3.39	.18
PT	2	38.46	<.01	30.58	<.01
PI	2	39.49	<.01	30.08	<.01
TI	1	12.68	<.01	3.29	.07
CPT	4	4.26	.37	3.27	.51
CPI	4	10.67	.03	11.47	.02
CTI	2	.54	.76	3.28	.19
PTI	2	4.07	.13	2.17	.34
CPTI	4	5.04	.28		

C = Conflict level
P = Power status
I = Major power alliance status of initiator
T = Major power alliance status of target

status and the target's alliance status [PT], power status and the initiator's alliance status [PI] and the target's and initiator's alliance status [TI], and one significant third order interaction (conflict, power status, and the initiator's alliance status [CPI]), and no significant fourth order interaction. It is noteworthy that neither the second order interaction between the level of conflict and the initiator's major power alliance status ([CI]), nor the third order interaction, which further incorporates the target's major power alliance status ([CTI]), is significant. In other words, *when the log-linear models are fitted, relationships that earlier appeared to be important wash out.*

Our attempt to determine which variables and combinations of variables can best account for the distribution of cases in Table 8-5 will be governed by two main considerations: first, although a model could conceivably be constructed around all the significant parameters in Table 8-6, the demands of parsimony dictate otherwise. Instead we are required to construct that model with the fewest possible parameters. Second, in log-linear modeling there is, strictly speaking, no dependent variable, only cell probabilities affected by the variables. Because we are interested in the effects of independent variables on the escalation of conflict, our modeling should center on how power and alliance variables affect the distribution of conflict ([C]).

Table 8-7 lists the 13 models we considered. We began with a very simple model specifying that conflict [C] values were influenced by power status ([P]), the major power alliance status of the initiator ([I]), and the major power alliance status of the target ([T]). The resulting Model 1, [CT] [CI] [CP], however, yields a very poor fit ($X^2 = 95.3$, $df = 21$, $p < 0.001$). We then tested three other models having as a base this same four variable combination plus in each model one different second order interaction. As Table 8-7 indicates, the addition of [PT] or [PI] or [TI] to Model 1 did nothing to improve the fit of Models 2, 3, or 4, respectively. Model 5, which includes the third order interaction [PTI], does not fit well either, but it does produce the first observable probability value.

Model 6 introduces the third order interaction [CPI], which through nesting also includes both [CP] and [CI] as well as [PI]. The resulting model produces a very strong fit between the model's expected values and the data ($X^2 = 9.6$, $df = 10$, $p = 0.48$). Although the fit of Model 6 is quite good, there are reasons why we need to look beyond this model; quite simply, the fit is "too good." In model building of this type, one is interested in using the fewest possible variables to get the best fit between the model and the data. However, Knoke and Burke (1980) and Bishop, Feinberg, and Holland (1975) both warn of fits that are "too good." Although it is not clear exactly what specifications determine whether or not a fit is "too good," Knoke and Burke suggest that models with probabilities between 0.10 and 0.35 should be the most useful; Model 6 exceeds the upper threshold. Our second reason for looking beyond Model 6 is its size and complexity. It encompasses nine individual second and third order interactions and leaves only 10 degrees of freedom. In an effort to

Table 8-7 Models of the Data in Table 8-5

Model	DF	X^2	p
1. [CT] [CI] [CP]	21	95.3	<.001
2. [CT] [CI] [CP] [PT]	19	66.7	<.001
3. [CT] [CI] [CP] [PI]	19	65.7	<.001
4. [CT] [CI] [CP] [TI]	20	92.4	<.001
5. [CT] [CI] [CP] [TPI]	14	22.2	.07
6. [CT] [CPI] [PTI]	10	9.6	.48
7. [CPI] [PTI]	12	15.4	.22
8. [PT] [TI] [CT] [CPI]	12	12.9	.38
9. [PT] [TI] [CT] [CP] [PI]	18	26.9	.08
10. [TI] [CT] [CPI]	14	51.3	<.001
11. [PT] [CT] [CPI]	13	25.5	<.02
12. [PT] [TI] [CPI]	14	17.6	.23
13. [CP] [CI] [PI] [PT] [TI] [CT]	16	24.3	.08

produce a more parsimonious model, we deleted [CT] from Model 6. The resulting model, Model 7, has a significantly worse fit than Model 6.

Next we deleted [PTI] from Model 6, producing Model 8. This model has seven interactions, including three nested second order relationships. The model offers a good (but not too good) fit between the expected values and the data ($X^2 = 12.19$; $df = 12$; $p = 0.38$). Given our interest in conflict, the main interactions of interest are [CT] and the third order interaction [CPI]. Although still complex, this model is less complex than Model 6. Although Model 8 contains an additional two degrees of freedom, the X^2 value is only 3.3 greater than in Model 6, and the difference between Models 6 and 8 is not significant at the $p = 0.10$ level. However, its fit of $p = .38$ is still marginally "too good."

We next tried four variations of Model 8, with mixed success. Model 9 removes the third order interaction [CPI] and fits poorly. Model 10 reintroduces [CPI] but drops [PT]; it fares even worse than Model 9. Model 11 replaces [TI] with [PT] and does slightly better, but still provides an inadequate fit. Model 12 replaces [CT] with [TI] and produces a much more reasonable fit ($X^2 = 17.6$; $df = 14$; $p = .23$), in fact better than the more complex Model 7 we passed by above. Finally, Model 13 reintroduces [CT] and breaks [CPI] into its three nested second order interactions; it, too, yields a poor fit.

We chose to accept Model 12 ([PT], [TI], [CPI]) over Model 8 for two reasons. First, Model 8 slightly exceeds the suggested upper threshold for a model that fits well. More important, Model 12 is more parsimonious than Model 8, incorporating as it does one fewer second order interaction. Also, although Model 12 has an additional two degrees of freedom, the difference between the fit of the two models ($X^2 = 4.7$; $df = 2$; $p < .05$) is not statistically significant.

In Model 12, we are accepting a model in which the data in Table 8-5 may be accounted for by the interactions [PT], [TI], and [CPI]. Although this one set of relationships was selected, it should be noted that each of the other possible candidates for selection, that is, Models 6, 7, and 8, also contain [CPI]. Hence, the evidence strongly suggests that the variation in conflict may be accounted for by the interaction between power status and the initiator's alliance status. The relationship encompassed in [CPI] can be reconstructed from Table 8-5, and we report it as Table 8-8.

There are two direct implications of the [CPI] relationship shown in Table 8-8, and both lead to a slightly different view of the data in Table 8-5. First, the strength of the [CPI] relationship suggests that the target's alliance status is not necessary to account for the distribution of the cases. Put differently, the strength of [CPI] offers considerable support for the balance-of-power interpretation of international conflict, because it confirms that strong nations tend to initiate conflicts that escalate. More precisely, of the 63 cases of reciprocated military action, 41 (65%) were initiated by major powers with a major power ally. Nonetheless, it is also evident that the relationship is only modest in the case of conflicts between major powers; the most significant effects of the [CPI]

Table 8-8 Conflict, Power Status, and the Initiator's Alliance Status [*CPI*]

Power status of initiator	Major				Minor	
Power status of target	Major		Minor		Major	
Initiator had major power ally?	Yes	No	Yes	No	Yes	No
Conflict level	N %	N %	N %	N %	N %	N %
1	33 63.4	17 58.6	34 36.9	14 41.2	8 61.5	9 25.0
2	8 15.4	7 24.1	28 30.4	16 47.0	5 38.5	14 38.9
3	11 21.2	5 17.2	30 32.6	4 11.8	0	13 36.1
Total	52	29	92	34	13	36

$X^2 = 29.72$
$df = 10$
$p = <0.01$

relationship are to be found in conflicts initiated by allied major powers and nonallied minor powers.

Conclusion

This research has been directed at evaluating the relative ability of theories of power equality and power preponderance to account for the escalation of international conflict. In this effort we have examined not only the effects of power, but also the augmentation of power furnished by an alliance with a major power. Although the data are not in all respects clearcut, we are persuaded that the balance of power provides a better means of accounting for the escalation of conflict than do the ideas contained in Organski's theory of power preponderance. Our conclusion, however, is not without its difficulties, not the least of which is the behavior of nonallied minor powers. Before dealing with this issue, we will draw together several findings from our data analysis which we believe sustain the predictions of balance-of-power theory.

The most important evidence in favor of the balance of power is the strong tendency for conflicts to be initiated by allied major powers and for those conflicts then to escalate to reciprocated military action. As noted above, the substantial majority of conflicts at the highest level take place when allied major powers acted as the initiator. To be sure, the effect is at its weakest in conflict between major powers, but even then it is not absent. Our interpretation of the data is that for the major powers, alliances are of less significance than basic national capabilities. However, it must be noted that in conflicts between major powers these capabilities were apparently sufficiently inhibiting that the large majority of the conflicts did not escalate. Organski's theory, in which nations of relatively equal capability are the ones that are likely to go to war, finds little support in the pronounced disinclination of the major powers to escalate conflicts. What is clear from the data is the almost unequivocal support for the balance of power to be found in the behavior of major powers with a major power ally toward minor powers, particularly toward those minor powers with a major power ally. Put simply, our conclusion is that equality of national power, supplemented by major power alliances for those nations that are weak, tends to restrain the likelihood that a conflict will escalate.

Despite this conclusion, there remain the 13 interesting cases in which a nonallied minor power initiated a conflict with a major power which escalated to reciprocal military action. Although these conflicts are not numerous enough to undermine our conclusion, they stand in sufficient contrast to the other cases and the balance of power to merit attention. Although it is clear that most relatively cohesive nations will fight if national existence is directly in question, these cases do not appear to be of that character. These conflicts were initiated by the minor power. An inspection of the cases indicates that they fall into one of three broad groups: first, several constituted attempts on the part of newly emerging nations (especially Italy) to remove or reduce the already established interests or presence of a great power. If one adopts a perceptual perspective on the evaluation of power, it is possible to argue that the emergence of nationalism in a nation may lead its population and decision makers to overestimate their power (Wright, 1965). Such errors in power estimates might well result in conflict with stronger nations, particularly if the minor power lacked a major power ally to "correct" its perceptions. This relative inability to assess a situation correctly may have been significant in a second group of conflicts which took place over borders. A notable example of such a conflict was the second Schleswig-Holstein War. This conflict was initiated by Denmark against Prussia. The Danes were willing to initiate the conflict because they anticipated support from England, even though there was no alliance or even clear indication that such support would be forthcoming (Taylor, 1954). It proved to be a monumental misjudgment. East (1973) suggests that minor powers are prone to make such mistakes, which appear to be rash or even reckless, because they have relatively poor information-processing capabilities about the world around them. Finally, there were a number of conflicts that took place at a considerable distance from the home territory of the major power. These may be related to Boulding's (1962) concept of the "loss-of-strength gradient." If it is true, as Boulding suggests, that power degrades with distance, then it might be that at the scene of the conflict, the major power was actually less able to bring its strength to bear than was the minor power. Even if power does not become reduced over distance (Wohlstetter, 1968), the minor power may perceive the major power as relatively weak. These comments are speculative; it is only clear that conflicts such as these might profitably be the subject for further research.

The main finding of this research is that the balance of power offers a reasonable explanation for the escalation of conflict to reciprocated military action. Several studies have, however, rejected similar hypotheses derived from the balance of power. As noted above, a recent review of several of those studies (Siverson & Sullivan, 1983) argues that their research designs were such that a subtle but strong bias against the balance of power was present. However, another study has also rejected the balance of power in favor of a more powerful explanation. In *The War Trap* (1981), Bueno de Mesquita presents an explicit comparison of his theory of expected utility with the idea that the "strong attack the weak," a hypothesis that he states is consistent with the balance of power. His finding was that although there was a fairly general overall tendency for the strong to attack the weak ($Q = .81$ for the period 1816-1974), the results obtained from expected utility were better ($Q = .94$). Moreover, Bueno de Mesquita shows that although the balance of power does slightly better ($Q = .98$) than expected utility ($Q = .97$) in the nineteenth century, the results for the balance of power in the twentieth century are, to say the least, miserable ($Q = .52$) when compared to expected utility ($Q = .91$).

Notwithstanding the strong results from the expected utility model, it must be noted that in carrying out his analysis of the "strong attack the weak" hypothesis, Bueno de Mesquita relied only upon composite national capability scores to determine who was the stronger and did not include the capability-augmenting effects of alliances in his measurements. Yet Bueno de Mesquita clearly recognizes the traditional capability augmenting effect attributed to alliances in the balance-of-power approach. Unfortunately, a full comparison of the results obtained from our analysis with those of Bueno de Mesquita is limited by at least two factors. First, the data sets, although similar in some respects, are significantly different. For instance, 1) our data do not include any conflicts between minor powers, whereas such data are used by Bueno de Mesquita; 2) our category of "reciprocal military actions" is not equivalent to his wars; and 3) *The War Trap* uses data as recent as 1974, whereas our data stop at 1965. Second, although the results in the present analysis were obtained from only two independent variables, the expected utility model required significantly more information, including a variable that measured the presumed decay of power over distance. Hence, whether or not expected utility does better than the balance of power remains a task that will at least require a simultaneous test on one data set.

Our comments on the respective merits of these two approaches, however, must be tempered by two *considerations*. First, there are shortcomings in our own design. In the present study, power is measured in a rather crude way. If we had at hand more precise data on national *capabilities* for the major powers, it could be that the findings would diverge from those presented here. We also lack data on conflicts between minor powers. The introduction of these data could also cause a revision of the findings. Second, the point of the comparison is not to suggest that Bueno de Mesquita's analysis is wrong and ours correct. At a minimum, the differences in the data sets alone preclude any such inference. What we would like to suggest is that the ideas of the balance of power may be worth further attention, and that efforts to pronounce them useless may be premature.

The findings here are highly informative. The deterrent effect of alliances, although limited to minor powers, is a significant finding not uncovered in other research (Russett, 1963; Singer & Small, 1974). The extent to which a major power controls its minor power allies is noted by Weede (1983) for the bipolar era; our data make it clear that it goes considerably beyond the post-World War II era in its generality.

Finally, and most important, it is evident that for conflicts initiated by major powers, alliances are an important explanatory factor in accounting for escalation. In a thoughtful evaluation of several books on war, Gochman (1976), after noting a number of shortcomings with their proposed explanations of war, hypothesized that "factors ... immediate to the conflict, such as alliance associations or the relative capabilities of the antagonists, will have the greatest impact on the escalation, duration and outcome of violence." This research suggests that his hypothesis is accurate.

References

Bishop, Y., Feinberg, S., & Holland, P. *Discrete multivariate statistics.* Cambridge, Mass.: MIT Press, 1975.

Bloomfield, L. P., and Leiss, A. C. *Controlling small wars.* New York: Knopf, 1969.

Boulding, K. *Conflict and defense.* New York: Harper and Row, 1962.

Bueno de Mesquita, B. *The war trap.* New Haven, Conn.: Yale University Press, 1981.

Craig, A., & George, A. *Statecraft.* New York: Oxford University Press, 1983.

Dixon, W. J., & Brown, M. B. *BMDP-79: Biomedical computer programs, P-Series.* Los Angeles: University of California Press, 1979.

East, M. Size and foreign policy behavior, *World Politics*, 1973, *25*, 556-576.

Feinberg, S. *The analysis of cross-classified categorical data.* Cambridge, Mass.: MIT Press, 1977.

Garnham, D. Dyadic international war, 1816-1955, *Western Political Quarterly*, 1976, *29*, 231-242. (a)

Garnham, D. Power parity and lethal international violence, 1969-1973, *Journal of Conflict Resolution*, 1976, *20*, 379-394. (b)

George, A., & Smoke, R. *Deterrence in American foreign policy.* New York: Columbia University Press, 1974.

Gochman, C. Studies in international violence: five easy pieces? *Journal of Conflict Resolution*, 1976, *20*, 539-560.

Job, B. Membership in inter-nation alliances, 1815-1965. In D. A. Zinnes & J. V. Gillespie (Eds.), *Mathematical models in international relations*. New York: Praeger, 1976.

Knoke, D., & Burke, P. J. *Log-linear models*. Sage University paper series, 07-20. Beverly Hills, Calif.: Sage, 1980.

Mark, A. Why big nations lose small wars: The politics of asymmetric conflict, *World Politics*, 1975, *27*, 175-200.

Most, B. A., & Starr, H. Case selection, conceptualizations and basic logic in the study of war," *American Journal of Political Science*, 1982, *26*, 834-856.

Organski, A. F. K. *World politics* (2nd ed.). New York: Knopf, 1968.

Organski, A. F. K., & J. Kugler. *The war ledger*. Chicago: University of Chicago Press, 1980.

Rosen, S. War Power and the Willingness to Suffer. In B. M. Russett (Ed.), *War, peace and numbers*. Beverly Hills, Calif.: Sage, 1972.

Russett, B. M. The calculus of deterrence, *Journal of Conflict Resolution*, 1963, *7*, 97-109.

Sabrosky, A. N. The utility of interstate alliances. Presented at the annual meeting of the International Studies Association, 1975.

Singer, J. D. Accounting for international war: the state of the discipline, *Annual Review of Sociology*, 1980, *6*, 349-367.

Singer, J. D., Bremer, S., and Stuckey, J. Capability distribution, uncertainty and major power war, 1820-1965. In B. Russett (Ed.), *War, peace and numbers*. Beverly Hills, Calif.: Sage, 1972.

Singer, J. D., & Small, M. Alliance aggregations and the onset of war, 1815-1945. In J. D. Singer (Ed.), *Qualitative international politics: insights and evidence*. New York: Free Press, 1968.

Singer, J. D., & Small, M. Foreign policy indicators: predictors of war in history and in the state of the world message, *Policy Sciences*, 1974, *5*, 271-296.

Singer, J. D., & Small, M. *The wages of war*. New York: Wiley, 1972.

Siverson, R. M., & Duncan, G. Stochastic models of international alliance initiation. In D. A. Zinnes & J. V. Gillespie (Eds.), *Mathematical models of international relations*. New York: Praeger, 1976.

Siverson, R. M., & King, J. Alliances and the expansion of war, 1815-1965. In J. D. Singer & M. Wallace (Eds.), *To augur well*. Beverly Hills, Calif.: Sage, 1979.

Siverson, R. M., & Sullivan, M. P. The distribution of power and the onset of war," *Journal of Conflict Resolution*, 1983, *27*, 473-494.

Siverson, R. M., & Tennefoss, M. R. Interstate conflicts: 1815-1965, *International Interactions*, 1982, *9*, 147-178.

Sullivan, M. P., & Siverson, R. Theories of war: Problems and prospects. In P. T. Hoppman, D. A. Zinnes, & J. D. Singer, *Cumulation in international relations research*. Monograph series, *World Affairs*, 1918, *18*, 9-38.

Taylor, A. J. P. *The struggle for mastery in Europe: 1848-1918*. Oxford: Clarendon Press, 1954.

Waltz, K. *Theory of international politics*. Reading, Mass.: Addison-Wesley, 1979.

Weede, E. Extended deterrence by superpower alliance, *Journal of Conflict Resolution*, 1983, *27*, 231-254.

Weede, E. Overwhelming preponderance as a pacifying condition among contiguous Asian dyads, 1950-1969, *Journal of Conflict Resolution*, 1976, *20*, 395-411.

Wholstetter, A. Theory and opposed system design, *Journal of Conflict Resolution*, 1968, *20*, 302-331.

Wight, M. *Power politics*. London: Royal Institute of International Affairs, 1946.

Wright, Q. A *study of war* (2nd ed.). Chicago: University of Chicago Press, 1965.

8.3 ■■■■

IMMANUEL WALLERSTEIN

Friends as Foes

The year 1980 marks the midpoint in a global process: the steady erosion of the hegemonic position of the United States in the world economy. The political keystone of this hegemony has been a strong alliance with Western Europe and Japan. Until 1967 the United States dominated the world military arena and political economy—including the markets of other industrialized countries—and Western Europe and Japan followed U.S. leadership willingly and completely. By 1990 the former allies will have parted company with the United States.

This process is not fortuitous, mysterious, or reversible. Roughly comparable declines in the capitalist world-economy have taken place twice before: Great Britain from 1873 to 1896; and, although this is less well-known, the United Provinces (the modern-day Netherlands) from 1650 to 1672. In each case, a nation of unquestioned supremacy fell to the lesser status of a very powerful state defending very central economic interests in the world-economy,

Reprinted with permission from *Foreign Policy* 40 (Fall 1980). Copyright © by the Carnegie Endowment for International Peace.

but nonetheless one state amid several. And, in each case, in the decades following the loss of hegemony, the former predominant power continued to decline as a center of political-military strength and of high-profit enterprise, to the advantage of other states within the world-economy.

Such cyclical patterns—the rise and decline of hegemonic powers and the more frequent expansion and stagnation of the world-economy—exist within the framework of long-term secular trends that have been leading to a systemic crisis that transcends the immediate difficulties of the moment. These trends, characteristic of a capitalist world-economy, may be seen in the constant development of the division of labor in the world-economy as a whole and in the continued development of the interstate system.

For 400 years the development of the division of labor has involved a steady increase in the degree to which production has been mechanized, land and labor made into commodities purchasable on the market, and social relations regulated by contracts rather than by customary rules. This secular division of labor has proceeded in a step-like fashion that alternates 20-30 year periods of expansion with similar periods of contraction (sometimes called Kondratieff cycles, or A-phases and B-phases). Each A-phase of expansion has culminated in a major blockage of the world accumulation process, resulting in stagnation. And each B-phase of stagnation has been overcome by the further concentration of capital, the launching of new product cycles, the expansion of outer boundaries of the world economy, and the expansion of effective demand—in short, by the spreading and deepening of the capitalist world-economy and the further polarization of distribution as measured globally and not within individual states.

The development of the interstate system has involved the elaboration and institutionalization of power in each of the member states, within the constraints of interstate rules that have become increasingly explicit. As the roles of the state machineries have become more prominent, the state has become even more the focus of antisystemic forces—social movements opposed to the basic mode of operation of the world-system—that have sought power in the name of socialist and nationalist ideologies. The strengthening of capitalist forces and the development of the world-economy itself have bred these antisystemic forces, whose own strength has increased significantly in the twentieth century.

A Mature Liberalism

This is the context within which the United States became the political center of global economic forces between 1945 and 1967. During that great postwar boom, despite the paranoia of American leaders and the constant clamor about national danger, there was no serious opposition in the world to U.S. hegemony. In the late 1950s, it was the communist world (with de-Stalinization) and not the West that was undergoing political crisis. The Soviet

Union was easily contained; indeed, it was struggling to hold its own politically and economically, while it sought to rebuild militarily. Western Europe and Japan, the main beneficiaries of a massive creation of global effective demand via U.S. economic aid and military support, operated as virtual client states during the 1950s. Decolonization in Asia and Africa went smoothly, largely to the political advantage of the United States. And at home, the anticommunist political repression of the 1940s and 1950s (from President Truman's loyalty oaths to McCarthyism) seemed to stifle the dangerous social tensions of earlier periods.

The one major exception to complete U.S. hegemony was China, where the accession to power of the Communist party represented an effective overthrow of foreign domination and a radical alteration of China's position in the world-system.

For the most part, a generalized, self-congratulatory contentment pervaded the United States during the Kennedy administration, evincing the liberalism of a mature hegemonic power and encouraging the growth of its offshoots—the Peace Corps, civil rights, and détente.

This liberal self-confidence explains the tremendous psychological shock experienced by U.S. political and business leaders in response to the events of 1967-1968: the currency and gold crises that marked the fall of the U.S. dollar from its pedestal; the Tet offensive against South Vietnam that revealed that a small Third World people could hold U.S. military power in check; the student-worker rebellions—such as those at Columbia University and in France—that showed that internal struggles within Western states were once again on the agenda.

In retrospect, the sudden explosions of 1967-1968 should not have been so surprising. The economic reconstruction of Western Europe and Japan created centers of competition with U.S.-based firms and contributed to the global overexpansion of world production. By concentrating on the military sphere, the Soviet Union had increased its military strength relative to that of the United States. At the same time, direct U.S. military intervention had severe financial and economic consequences for the United States. The steady decolonization of the world could not possibly remain a controlled and formal process; it would inevitably become more radical and spread to the Western industrialized, or core, countries themselves (to the "Third World within"). And the liberalism of the mature hegemonic power would retreat once its largess was rejected by oppressed groups asserting demands on their own terms.

All of a sudden, in 1967 the United States found itself in a B-period, a period of decelerated growth. In the world economy, the most significant result of this period of relative economic stagnation has been a striking decline in the competitiveness of U.S.-based production organizations compared with those located in Japan and Western Europe, excluding Great Britain. This relative decline is evident upon comparing growth rates, standards of living, capital investments as a percentage of gross national product, growth in productivity, capital-labor ratios, share in the world market, and research and development expenditures. The decline is also reflected in the relative strengths of currencies and in the rates of inflation and unemployment.

A second striking result of this B-phase has been the relocation of industry. On a world scale, this relocation involved the rise of the newly industrializing countries and the opening of free trade zones—the creation of the so-called new international division of labor. In general, the bargaining power of large semiperipheral countries such as Brazil and countries with key commodities such as the Organization of Petroleum Exporting Countries (OPEC) bloc has been greatly strengthened.

Acquiescence or Collusion

With respect to the changing world-economy, it is the OPEC price rises that have caught everyone's attention and that politicians and the press have transformed from consequence into cause. Two things should be noted about the oil price rises. First, they began in 1973, not in 1963 or 1953. The oil-producing countries did not suddenly become avaricious. Rather, in 1973 oil price rises became, for the first time, economically and politically possible, in large part because the global rise of industrial production entailed a vast increase in demand for current energy production. This overproduction in turn promoted competition among the core powers, thereby limiting their economic and military bargaining power. OPEC simply capitalized on this situation.

Second, the oil price rises met little opposition from the core states. This cannot be written off to political lassitude resulting from economic stagnation. There probably also existed U.S. acquiescence, even collusion. It is hard otherwise to account for the crucial support in 1973 for this policy by the Saudi and Iranian governments, without which there would have been no OPEC price rise. James Akins, former U.S. ambassador to Saudi Arabia, reported that the Saudis went along with the price rise only when they could not persuade the United States to put pressure on Iranian price demands.

The United States could have seen two short-run advantages in the 1973 oil price rise: a competitive boost relative to Western Europe and Japan because of their greater dependence in 1973 on imported oil; and the creation of financial bases for the shah and to a lesser extent the Saudis so they could serve as proconsuls for the United States, relieving in part the U.S. political and financial burden.

There are also long-run advantages for the core powers collectively in the oil price rises—advantages that probably outweigh any disruptive effects. In a situation of global stagnation, one key problem concerns possibilities for new industrial complexes of high-profit growth. One such complex could involve new energy sources and energy-saving devices. The first advantage, then, is that the higher cost of petroleum created a major incentive for this kind of complex. Former Secretary of State Henry Kissinger after all

403

did talk of a floor for petroleum prices and not of a ceiling.

The second major advantage is that inflation itself can in fact lead to a considerable decline in the real wage bill of the core countries, redistributing surplus to owners in a form that is far more manageable than the bread lines of 1933.

German Chancellor Helmut Schmidt has spoken of the struggle for the world product, emphasizing only interstate allocations. This might better be called the world class struggle in which reallocations are being made within as well as between states. For example, if the oil-producing states have gained considerably in the last decade, it is scarcely the large oil multinationals that have lost. It is, rather, the middle and lower strata in both core and peripheral countries.

The decline of U.S. hegemony has had major effects on the interstate system as well. Alliances that emerged after World War II are collapsing. The Sino-Soviet split, begun in the 1950s but consecrated in the 1960s, did not necessarily serve the interests of the United States as a global power. The split made it impossible to consolidate stability through a political deal with the USSR and muddied irremediably ideological waters. And when the United States came to terms with China, Western Europe and Japan could not simply maintain their old alliance with the United States, but were forced to reconsider all the options.

The Sino-Soviet split was liberating for national movements in the Third World. The split closed the books on the Communist International and forced liberation groups to move where they were under pressure to move anyway— to action that was autonomous of the world alliance system. Despite U.S.-Soviet détente, a de facto U.S.-Chinese alliance, and socialist wars in Southeast Asia, the 1970s saw a steady acceleration of revolutionary movements (southern Africa, Central America and the Caribbean, and the Middle East) rather than the reverse.

The West-West Conflict

The most difficult issues, however, that confront U.S. policy makers in the coming decades are neither East-West issues (notwithstanding Afghanistan) nor North-South issues (notwithstanding Iran). Rather they are West-West issues that are based on the great economic and therefore political threat of the two significant U.S. rivals, Western Europe and Japan. President Carter's handling of the crises in Afghanistan and Iran as well as his decision to develop the MX missile could be viewed as attempts to maintain U.S. political leadership in the West and regain economic supremacy via ideological pressure on U.S. allies. Indeed, the effort to constrain U.S. allies bids fair to become the priority concern of U.S. foreign policy.

What are the real problems facing the United States in this growing West-West conflict? There is the immediate problem of fending off the worst aspects of the economic decline of the 1980s. There is the more important, long-run concern of trying to profit maximally from the probable renewed economic expansion of the 1990s.

Because there will have to be major contraction in some centers of world production, the basic issue for the 1980s is who will export unemployment to whom. Thus far inflation has masked this issue, at least politically; but should a dramatic fall in world prices occur, minimizing the resultant economic damage will become a matter of survival for regimes throughout the West.

In the short run, the United States has two major mechanisms at its disposal. It can prop up technologically doomed industries (the Chrysler handout), which reduces unemployment in one sector at the expense of others and also diminishes the capital available for investment in industries that will make America competitive in the 1990s. In addition, it can increase military expenditures, also at the expense of long-run development.

For the 1990s the basic policy issue is who will gain the competitive edge in the new technologies of microelectronics, biotechnology, and energy resources. Success will be determined by an interlocking triplet of research and development innovations; reduction of real costs of production; and increased access to markets for the older sectors of production—formerly high-profit sectors, now medium-profit sectors—such as electronics, automobiles, and even computers.

What is happening today in industries such as steel, automobiles, and electronics is a double process. First, West European and Japanese firms are undercutting U.S.-based firms, even in the U.S. home market. Second, production processes are being broken up. Large parts of production chains are being moved to semiperipheral countries, including socialist countries, and the chains themselves are more likely to end in Western Europe and Japan rather than in the United States.

The structural causes of this massive shift in production centers outside the United States—a shift that is likely to accelerate sharply in the 1980s—are twofold. On the one hand, given larger and older U.S. industrial hardware, there are the higher costs of amortization of the overall plant. On the other, there is the higher U.S. wage bill. The real difference between U.S. costs of production and those of Western Europe and Japan does not lie in the wages paid a skilled mechanic. The political bargaining strength of workers is basically the same in all parts of the West. The real difference in costs—paid in part directly by companies, in part indirectly through government expenditures—lies in the salaries of the well-to-do middle stratum (i.e., professionals and executives).

It is not that the individual incomes of U.S. executives or professionals exceed those of their allied counterparts. In many cases, the opposite is true. Rather, it is that in the United States the well-to-do middle stratum is a significantly larger percentage of the total population. Hence, the social bill of the U.S. middle class is dramatically higher, and it is impossible for either the government or the large corporations to do anything about it.

An attack on these expenditures of a magnitude sufficient enough to make U.S.-based industry cost competitive again would entail higher political costs than anyone dares pay, especially because American political structures are heavily dominated by precisely those people whose incomes would have to be cut. It is therefore far easier for a multinational corporation to consider shifting its sites of production and research and eventually even its headquarters than to try to reduce costs directly. This has already begun to occur.

The process of disinvestment in the old industries will affect the research and development expenditures on the new ones by reducing both the U.S. tax and profit bases of U.S.-based companies. The markets for the new industries will be located primarily in the core countries themselves, but the markets for the older industries will be more worldwide. It will be important for producers to find fresh markets—zones whose expansion depends upon the products of these older industries. Such zones encompass the semiperipheral countries that are industrializing and that, even if they have their own plants and production sites, will need advanced machinery and hardware. The European Economic Community countries are up front in this effort in terms of their economic partnership with developing countries covered by the Lomé Convention. The largest likely market of the 1980s and, to an even greater extent, of the 1990s will comprise the socialist countries. Behind the Sino-Soviet controversy lies a struggle to be this market in the most advantageous way possible. This is called catching up or modernizing.

European-Soviet Cooperation

Within this economic reality—this B-phase of stagnation—lie the bases for the realignment of alliances in the interstate system. In a sense, China jumped the gun by its dramatic and successful attempt to make an arrangement with the United States. It is no accident that this diplomatic turnabout was done with Richard Nixon, who represented those U.S. forces whose deep anticommunist ideology was not tightly linked to a commitment to a North Atlantic Treaty Organization alliance structure.

Japan, no doubt miffed by its exclusion from the very first diplomatic steps, quickly allowed its true interests to prevail in the Sino-Japanese reconciliation. Because of the strong, complementary economic interests of the two countries and the fundamental link of civilization (still a major factor in policy making), the reconciliation is even more important than the joint U.S.-Chinese Shanghai communiqué.

If the United States has moved in the direction of China, it is because such movement makes geopolitical, strategic sense. And given that during the 1970s the economic fruits of détente with the Soviet Union were clearly being garnered by Western Europe rather than by the United States, these strategic considerations seemed worth the risk.

In terms of the political economy of the world-system, Western Europe and the USSR have much to offer each other, both positively and negatively. Were the two sides to move slowly toward a de facto structure of cooperation that need not involve anything affirmative in the sphere of military alliances, the USSR could obtain the capital equipment it needs to improve its long-term relative position in the world-economy, thus meeting the most pressing demand of its own cadres. Of course, the Soviet Union would also thereby obtain security against any dangers (real or imagined) implied by the U.S.-Chinese structure of cooperation.

In conjunction with Western Europe—and probably not without it—the Soviet Union could also effectuate a significant breakthrough in economic links with the Middle East. This presumes that the USSR and Western Europe would be able to complete the Camp David process by an arrangement between Israel and the Palestine Liberation Organization. In addition, a Middle East agreement might partially defuse the Soviet Union's greatest internal danger point, the potentially higher consciousness of the central Asian Moslem peoples.

Moreover, an arrangement of this sort between the Soviet Union and Western Europe—in which the German Social Democratic Party would have to play a large part—could also discourage the revolt of Eastern Europe against the USSR. The uprisings in Prague during spring 1968 threatened the USSR in two ways. The idea of liberalization might spread eastward, particularly to the Ukraine. And Czechoslovakia might move out of the Soviet orbit, especially in economic terms, and into that of West Germany. In the context of West European-Soviet cooperation, the latter fear would become less relevant.

Such an arrangement could look equally attractive to Western Europe. The Soviet market would be opened in some meaningful sense to Western Europe-based industries. The resources of the Soviet Union would become available, at least over a crucial 20-30 year period. And the USSR and East European countries could serve as geographically convenient and politically constrained reservoirs of relatively cheap labor for participation in Western Europe's claims of production.

Furthermore, a solution to the East European question from the Soviet perspective is also a solution from the viewpoint of Western Europe. Cooperation would permit the reintegration of Europe—culturally, economically, and eventually politically—a development that has up to now been barred by Soviet military strength. In particular, cooperation would permit, at a minimum, the two Germanies to move closer together.

An amicable, working relationship with the Soviet Union would even have political advantages for Western Europe. Just as the USSR might not gain a breakthrough in the Middle East without Western Europe, so might the reverse be true. In addition, by guaranteeing a relatively strong position to West European firms during the difficult years of the 1980s, a structure of cooperation would insure the continuance of the high degree of social peace that Western Europe is currently enjoying. On the ideological front, it would also contain in part the USSR.

Immanuel Wallerstein

A New Hegemony?

Needless to say, the ideological sentiments on both sides remain very strong—but not unswerving. In the case of West Germany, ideological commitments have not changed, but their role has: In the 1950s and 1960s, West Germany's economic interests were served by emphasizing ideological commitments, whereas in the 1970s and the 1980s, these same economic interests are being advanced by playing down political beliefs.

Should this kind of realignment come about, the most indecisive power will be Great Britain, which faces difficulty no matter which way it turns. But in any West-West split, Britain will probably have to stay with the United States, if only because in the very important geopolitical struggle over southern Africa, British and American interests are closely linked. And in a world in which British markets are declining everywhere, southern Africa might be one of the last secure trading partners.

In this picture of potential realignments, what happens to the North-South struggle? At one level, a realignment of the Northern powers along the lines suggested would create incredible ideological confusion in the South. At another level, it might lead to an ideological clarification. The process of disintegration of the world system, brought about by the cumulative strength of the world's antisystemic forces, cannot be controlled by the United States or the Soviet Union. Revolutions in, say, Honduras, Tunisia, Kenya, or Thailand are not primarily a function of geopolitical arrangements among the great powers. What realignments may bring about is a greater disillusionment among these revolutionary movements regarding the efficacy of achieving power via the control of individual state structures. After a century of detour, the emphasis may return to the importance of creating real worldwide intermovement links—ones that would cut across North-South and East-West boundaries. This is what is meant by ideological clarification.

And this is why even if the world economy takes a major upturn in the 1990s and even if Western Europe begins to play the role of a new ascending hegemonic power, the world is not entering merely another cyclical moment of the present system. It is in this sense that the underlying, long-run systemic crisis of world capitalism may be more meaningful over the next 50 years. In the middle run, world capitalism will seem to recuperate; in the long run, it will be transformed fundamentally.

In the short run, however, the biggest traumas will be felt by the United States. Americans have spent the past 30 years getting used to the benefits of a hegemonic position, and they will have to spend the next 30 getting used to life without them. For the majority of the world, it may not make that big a difference. For that majority, the real question is not which nation is hegemonic in the present world-system, but whether and how that world-system will be transformed.

GEORGE P. SHULTZ

On Alliance Responsibility

On February 4 of this year, New Zealand rejected an American request for a visit by the *U.S.S. Buchanan,* a conventionally powered destroyer that was to participate in an ANZUS [Australia, New Zealand, United States security treaty] naval exercise. The Government of New Zealand rejected the request because the United States would neither confirm nor deny the presence of nuclear weapons aboard the ship.

New Zealand's decision followed months of quiet consultations between our two countries, in which we explored an amicable solution. We pointed out that port access for our ships in accordance with our worldwide policy of neither confirming nor denying the presence of nuclear weapons aboard ships was an essential element of the ANZUS security relationship. The implication of New Zealand's decision was that no American ship that could not be identified as unambiguously non-nuclear-armed could ever call in that nation again. Without access to ports, we could not fulfill our treaty obligations either in peacetime or in a crisis.

Our policy of neither confirming nor denying the presence of nuclear weapons aboard our naval vessels is essential: it prevents adversaries from identifying our most capable ships, thereby enhancing targeting difficulties and reinforcing deterrence.

We did not challenge New Zealand's right to choose its own policy. Indeed, several allied, friendly, and neutral countries have special policies regarding nuclear weapons but, nevertheless, permit ship visits. No other ally, however, refuses to permit port visits on the basis of our "neither confirm nor deny" policy as New Zealand has. And if New Zealand's objective was to enhance Pacific security and reduce the nuclear danger, it has acted against its own interest: by adding a new element of risk and uncertainty, New Zealand has weakened regional stability, one of the most important links in the efforts to prevent nuclear war. And the erosion of Western unity only weakens the Western position and the chances for success in arms control.

When New Zealand decided to reject the *Buchanan,* it also decided, in effect, that the basic operational elements of the ANZUS treaty would not apply to it. In a sense, New Zealand walked off the job—the job of working with each other to defend our common security. This made inevitable the

---

An address before the East-West Center and the Pacific and Asian Affairs Council, Honolulu, Hawaii, July 17, 1985.

cancellation or restructuring of a number of military exercises and exchanges with New Zealand, including the naval exercise in which the *Buchanan* was to have participated.

We have left the door open, however. The President said on February 7: "It's our deepest hope that New Zealand will restore the traditional cooperation that has existed between our two countries. Allies must work together as partners to meet their shared responsibilities." We have not sought, nor do we seek, to punish New Zealand. New Zealand remains a friend. We hope that our current differences will eventually be overcome and that further actions which exacerbate our differences can be avoided.

Our differences with New Zealand are specific and immediate; yet they raise the most basic questions about alliances and about alliance responsibilities in the modern world: What is the purpose of our alliances? What qualities are unique to an alliance of democracies? How do we manage our alliances in a new era in furtherance of our common purpose?

The Goal of Our Alliances

After the end of the Second World War, the Western democracies that had united, together with the Soviet Union, to defeat Hitler soon found themselves faced with another threat to peace and freedom. The Soviet Union took advantage of the temporary weakness of nations struggling to recover from the war; it sought to expand its power and control in Europe and Asia. The West responded by uniting in common defense of its values and of world peace. In 1949, the United States, Canada, and the nations of Western Europe signed the North Atlantic Treaty. A year later, after the communist invasion of South Korea, this web of alliances was extended to East Asia and the Pacific, where the United States entered into alliances with Japan, Australia and New Zealand, the Philippines, and, later, Korea and Thailand. And in recent years we have strengthened our strategic cooperation with Israel.

The goal of our alliances 35 years ago was to deter aggression against the alliance partners and preserve the peace, particularly against threats from the Soviet Union and its proxies. Soviet power and its expansionist aims were then clear to all. Today they should be even clearer, in light of the massive Soviet military buildup of the past two decades, the Soviet invasion of Afghanistan, and efforts to extend the reach of Soviet power in Africa, Asia, and Central America. The purpose of our alliances, therefore, remains the same today: to deter aggression and to preserve peace by making it clear, beyond a shadow of a doubt, that allied nations will resist, repel, and punish the aggressor.

And something else that was true 35 years ago is also true today: it is not enough for allies to agree that when war starts they will come to each other's aid. Words and agreements alone will not deter war. Allies must work together to ensure that we have the capability to fight and win such a war—and that our adversaries know it. That is the real deterrent.

The Unique Qualities of Democratic Alliances

If the goal of our alliances is clear, we cannot achieve that goal unless we understand, equally clearly, the special characteristics of an alliance of democracies.

For our postwar alliance system is unique. Throughout history there have been many alliances; but never before has there been so enduring a partnership between so many nations committed to democracy. Today, our key alliances are democratic alliances; they are not agreements between rulers or governing elites but between peoples. The commitments made abroad must be approved and supported by our peoples through their selected representatives.

This unique quality is a continuing source of strength. Bonds among peoples who share fundamental values can survive periodic changes of leadership where other kinds of alliances might have collapsed. The democracies are united not only by strategic interest but also by moral bonds, which add a special intimacy and completeness to our cooperation. As Portugal's President Eanes recently said of his own nation's participation in the defense of the values and fundamental principles of the NATO alliance: "Dignified by its reunion with democratic countries, Portugal now shares, with no hesitation, the historical ideals and essential objectives of the Treaty of Washington."

Yet alliances among peoples, as opposed to rulers, also present special problems and place greater demands on all partners.

Deterring aggression is never an easy task. But for democracies, there is a special difficulty. A democracy at peace would much rather focus on the more immediate and tangible social benefits to its people than on the potential danger that exists beyond the horizon. Indeed, we sometimes take for granted that security itself is a vital part of our public welfare. The painful lessons of this century have, unfortunately, not quite rid us of the temptation to avoid burdensome precautions.

A democracy at peace, therefore, finds it hard to prepare for war in order to deter war. But it is a delusion to think that sacrifices can be safely deferred and that others will pick up the slack. The reality is that the collective deterrence of allies provides the umbrella of security under which nations can advance the well-being of their people.

When even one partner shirks its responsibilities, the health and unity of the entire alliance are placed in jeopardy. All the allies face the same kind of domestic problems; all would prefer to use their resources in other ways that offer more immediate and tangible benefits to their peoples; and all would rather avoid the political complications that may be brought on by fulfilling alliance commitments. If one partner is unwilling to make these sacrifices, others will wonder why they should carry their share of the burden. The result may be the gradual erosion of popular commitment to the common cause.

George P. Shultz

Shared Responsibilities

What, then, specifically, are the "shared responsibilities" of which President Reagan spoke?

The first and most basic responsibility is that each of us has a share in maintaining the overall deterrent strength of the alliance. For the United States, that means restoring our own strength, in both conventional and nuclear arms. It means helping our allies, as best we can, to maintain their strength, both economically and militarily. It means consulting and planning so that collective efforts are directed effectively toward common goals. Finally, and most importantly, it means making clear, through both words and actions, that we are resolutely committed to the defense of our allies, that we have the will to act in the defense of our common ideals and our security.

Our allies, of course, have an equally grave responsibility to help maintain the deterrent strength of the alliance. They must make the necessary effort to ensure their own security—and particularly in the area of conventional defense. Joint military exercises and intelligence cooperation are also essential. They need not possess their own nuclear deterrent; but if they undermine ours, as New Zealand has, they weaken their own national security. Commitments cannot be met selectively by one nation without eroding the security of all and undermining popular support for the alliance.

In the modern world, keeping the peace and preventing nuclear war involves more than maintaining an adequate deterrent, however. We also share a responsibility to seek a more constructive relationship with our adversaries. Our allies have every right to expect the United States to manage relations with the Soviet Union responsibly. As nuclear superpowers, the United States and the Soviet Union share a special responsibility to seek to reduce the danger of nuclear war. Our allies can expect us to make reasonable proposals and to explore every promising avenue at the bargaining table in pursuit of arms reduction. We will do so, in our own interest as well as in the interest of the free world. We consult with our allies at every stage of the negotiating process, and together with our allies we seek to put forward the most flexible positions consistent with alliance security.

Our allies also have a responsibility in this regard. A principal Soviet aim throughout the postwar period has been to divide the alliance. Instead of pursuing arms negotiations seriously in the quest for an equal and stable strategic balance, the Soviets have often tried to develop and exploit differences among the allies, leaving us to negotiate among ourselves while they sit back and wait for unilateral concessions that they need not reciprocate.

Our unity is essential to the success of East-West negotiations. The Soviets must understand that their efforts to divide the alliance will not work. The Atlantic allies made this point loudly and clearly when we went ahead with the alliance INF [intermediate-range nuclear forces] decision in the face of the biggest Soviet propaganda campaign ever. We must continue to be firm. The

412

Soviets must see that only through negotiations can they achieve limits on our forces, and only if they are prepared to make concessions to match our own.

The value of unity is also relevant to the current discussion of the Strategic Defense Initiative, or SDI. President Reagan bears a responsibility to do all he can to protect the world from the nuclear danger. That is why he is pursuing research into strategic defenses, which, if they prove feasible, can diminish the threat of a first strike and hasten the day when nuclear arsenals can be reduced.

Soviet propaganda on SDI is both cynical and hypocritical. The Soviets are heavily involved in strategic defense and have been for years. Over the last two decades, they have spent roughly as much on strategic defense as on their massive offensive nuclear forces. They have deployed around Moscow the world's only operational antiballistic missile system. Their large phased-array radar near Krasnoyarsk in Siberia is a violation of the ABM Treaty. Since the 1960s the Soviets have pursued research in advanced technologies for strategic weapons, including high-energy lasers, particle-beam weapons, radio frequency weapons, and kinetic energy weapons. These are the same types of technologies that the United States is now looking into in our SDI program. Not surprisingly, the Soviets proposed to stop our research while continuing theirs.

We should not be led astray by such self-serving propaganda. Last month's NATO ministerial in Lisbon showed solid support for the U.S. position in Geneva. If we want Geneva to succeed, we must continue to ensure that the Soviets are given no reason to hope that they can divide us over SDI.

Mutual Confidence and Broader Cooperation

The shared responsibilities in a democratic alliance are broader and deeper than deterrence of a military threat. Such a partnership depends on a bond of mutual confidence and mutual support across the broad range of our relations.

Many challenges to common interests, after all, lie outside the purview of formal treaties. Yet cooperation in meeting these challenges is important not only to protect the interests of individual allies but also to bolster the mutual confidence that underpins the entire alliance system. We cannot allow the enemies of our way of life to attack each ally one by one in the hope that we will be divided and thus incapable of a coordinated response.

That is precisely one of the hopes of the international terrorist network. In Western Europe, terrorists and their sponsors have tried to weaken the fabric of the NATO alliance by sowing fear and wreaking destruction on the peoples of the NATO countries. In the Middle East, terrorists and their sponsors count on disunity to prevent effective sanctions against those who harbor terrorism. In the recent hijacking of TWA Flight #847, the terrorists hoped to cause strains in the close and enduring friendship between the United States and Israel. In Asia, when North Korean terrorists bombed and murdered South Korean Government officials in Rangoon, they sought, among other things, to weaken

South Korea's ties to its treaty ally, the United States.

These murderous efforts to divide us, to sow confusion and fear among our peoples, have not succeeded and will not succeed. But we must do more than just hold the line. We must fight back. We must realize that we are under a continuing attack. We must cooperate to deter and dramatically raise the costs to both the terrorists and those who support them and offer safe haven to them.

Our alliance treaties state that an attack on one ally is an attack on all. When these treaties were signed, we were preparing to defend ourselves against traditional kinds of threats. Let there be no mistake: the threat posed by terrorism is no less real, no less a form of warfare, no less a direct attack on the interests of the democratic alliance. No nation can take refuge in silence or inaction. No nation can afford to define its interests so narrowly as to imagine it is not affected. No nation will be spared.

And terrorism is only one issue where cooperation outside the formal alliance is essential. The fight against international narcotics smuggling—which is clearly linked to terrorism—also requires cooperation. We in the Western Hemisphere see all too well the efforts of Cuba and Nicaragua in the narcotics field. None of us can ignore this problem. To one degree or another, all of us are weakened by the plague of narcotics. At both the Bonn summit and at ASEAN [Association of South East Asian Nations], we and our partners issued statements affirming our heightened determination to cooperate in the fight against narcotics trafficking and the terrorists who so often profit by it.

The same imperative of cooperation applies to economic issues. Economic matters are often the source of the most contentious disagreements among allies. Domestic concerns weigh heavily on many economic decisions, as well they should. Yet protectionism, for example, is destructive for all of us. We cannot afford to let economic disagreements undermine the political unity that ensures our common security—the security that underpins our common prosperity. Our divisions can only becloud our common future, and bring comfort only to our adversaries.

On regional issues, as well, we owe it to each other to be supportive when an ally's vital interests are threatened, even when treaty obligations are not involved. Thailand, for instance, today faces the threat of Vietnamese aggression in Cambodia. We provide direct aid to Thailand to help the Thai people defend their security interests. But beyond that, we must also be sensitive to Thailand's concerns and its understanding of the best way to deal with the Cambodian situation and the problems of Vietnamese aggression. Similarly, we owe the Republic of Korea support and understanding in its efforts to engage North Korea in a direct and responsible dialogue.

A few years ago, in the South Atlantic, the United States confronted a dilemma: both Argentina and Britain are friends. American interests, narrowly conceived, might have called for taking a neutral position. Our NATO obligations do not require us to support our European allies outside the North Atlantic region. Nevertheless, we supported the principle that such disputes should not be settled by force. We were right to do so, and we were right to help our NATO partner, Britain, uphold that principle.

We feel that similarly important interests of ours are at stake today in Central America. The Nicaraguan communists, with Cuban and Soviet support, are trying to consolidate a totalitarian state on the Central American mainland. They have tried to undermine their neighbors by supporting communist guerrillas and terrorists. We do not ask our allies to help us actively resist communist aggression in our hemisphere. But we have every reason to expect that they will not undermine our own efforts in a region so vital to us. Allies are free to differ on many political issues. But comity and the preservation of mutual confidence call for understanding of the concerns of those most affected.

The Spirit of Alliance Unity

Before we entered the war against Hitler, Franklin Roosevelt explained the lend-lease program by a simple analogy. When you see a neighbor's house on fire, he said, you lend him your garden hose. You don't ask him to pay you back. You know he'll do it when he can. That is the spirit of mutual support that must guide us.

So far, we and all our allies have done an outstanding job. Our alliances are working. They have confounded the skeptics and those who, at every stage, complained of disarray. For 35 years, our global alliance system has kept the peace and preserved our freedom in Europe and in most of Asia. For 35 years, nations and peoples with diverse cultures and histories, with different needs and national aspirations—and sometimes with differing views of the proper tactics for managing the many international challenges—have, nevertheless, remained committed to partnership in defense of what we hold dear.

We have preserved the deterrent strength upon which both our security and our freedoms depend. We have worked to reduce nuclear arsenals and enhance our conventional deterrent even while realizing that, for the moment, at least, the nuclear deterrent is essential for the security of all of us in the Atlantic and Pacific.

Of course, we face problems. How could free and sovereign peoples not occasionally disagree? But those who would have the United States withdraw from its commitments take a dangerously short-sighted view of our interests. A world in which the United States had withdrawn from its worldwide alliances, or from any part of the alliance structure, would be a grim world indeed. The arguments for isolationism or unilateralism should have been dashed long, long ago. The global equilibrium would be that much more precarious. Nor is it a serious option for our allies: the aggression we see in many parts of the world has shown that there is no defense in isolation. For any of us, to retreat from this collective security system—in a world of new dangers—would be foolish.

Those who would have us ignore or paper over allied disagreements,

415

however, are equally short-sighted. Alliances such as ours must be carefully tended if they are to flourish. All sides must be conscious of the price that is paid when solidarity is weakened. Governments must lead and educate their peoples. All sides must take care to prevent the erosion of the spirit of unity among their peoples—the unity that is the essential foundation of our common freedom.

As President Reagan said at the United Nations last September: "Every alliance involves burdens and obligations, but these are far less than the risks and sacrifices that would result if the peace-loving nations were divided and neglectful of their common security."

American support for alliances, therefore, is not part of some sentimental attachment to the past, nor a mindless devotion to continuity. We support our alliances, first of all, because they work. Experience shows that we can overcome our differences if we make a real effort to do so. And we support our alliances, most of all, because of the values and ideals they are meant to defend. May America and America's allies always remain faithful to the global cause of freedom and democracy, security, and peace.

8.5 ▬▬▬

JEANE J. KIRKPATRICK

The Atlantic Alliance
and the American National Interest

There is a widespread, growing sense on both sides of the Atlantic that we have come once again to one of those periodic times of decision: will we continue as we are, working in and through the existing framework, or is it time for new departures? Articles on the "crisis" of the alliance have become a staple of editorial pages in the United States and in Europe. In the European press, these articles often criticize U.S. policies and question whether our policies and our rhetoric do not make the world a more dangerous place—for Europeans. In the United States, European shortcomings are less emphasized than questions about whether it makes any sense at all for the United States to go on investing so many people and so much money in the NATO enterprise.

Not all issues that are hotly discussed in the media and on debating platforms make their way onto legislative calendars. Some simply die. But widespread public interest in an important subject, if not necessarily a harbinger of official changes to come, at least gives notice of that possibility.

An address before the National Committee on American Foreign Policy, New York City, April 30, 1984.

The relationship of the United States and Europe is an example of an issue in which there is informal, unofficial discussion and little or no formal or official action. I should like to emphasize that there is now no discussion in the U.S. Government of restructuring NATO, withdrawing American troops, or changing American strategic doctrine. Certainly no such discussion occurs at authoritative levels. Nonetheless, the discussion persists and spreads, the op-ed pieces multiply, and more and more influential persons join the dialogue. Have we reached a point like that about which John Quincy Adams said: "I do not recollect any change in policy, but there has been a great change in circumstances"?

How important are the changed circumstances which confront the Atlantic alliance 35 years after its founding? How basic? How threatening or liberating? Is this relationship among the nations of the Atlantic alliance still necessary and, if so, to whom and for what?

Departure from Traditional U.S. Attitudes

Certain facts—known to persons present—need, nonetheless, to be mentioned to set the questions and discussion in context. First, the fact that, from the U.S. perspective, the alliance represented a sharp departure from traditional U.S. attitudes and behavior. In his memoirs, President Harry Truman wrote:

> On April 4, 1949, I stood by Secretary of State Dean Acheson as he signed his name, on behalf of the United States, to a treaty which was the first peacetime military alliance concluded by the United States since the adoption of the Constitution.

Signing the North Atlantic Treaty was, as Truman noted, "one more step in the evolution of U.S. foreign policy, along with the United Nations Charter, the Greek-Turkish Aid Program, and the Marshall Plan." It was also a specific violation of the nation's traditional policy of refusing permanent alliances.

Americans had never been comfortable with the notion that our fate is bound up with the fate of foreign powers. As everyone who is familiar with American history is aware, the Founding Fathers of the United States took pains not to become drawn into what they considered the net of European entanglements, rivalries, and power politics. This view is, of course, summarized in George Washington's warning of September 1796:

> Europe has a set of primary interests which to us have no, or a very remote relation, hence she must be engaged in frequent controversies the causes of which are centrally foreign to our concern.

This policy of noninvolvement in European politics was supplemented in 1823 by another famous American declaration which also distinguished our interests from those of Europe's. The Monroe Doctrine extended the protection of the young United States beyond its continental limits for the first time to the whole of the Western Hemisphere and declared that, at the risk of war, the

United States would thereafter resist the creation of new European empires in the Western Hemisphere. This step was not prompted by a desire to become involved in international diplomacy. To the contrary, it was seen as a prudent measure which would protect the United States and the other American republics against the rivalries and conflicts characteristic of European politics of the era, including, of course, the politics of Russia. These attitudes persisted past World War II.

The identification of our security with countries beyond our borders, beyond the Atlantic, remained unsettling to Americans. The comments of the late Senator Robert A. Taft of Ohio, who warned against ratification of the North Atlantic Treaty, manifested these traditional American concerns. Addressing the U.S. Senate in 1949, Taft said:

> By executing a treaty of this kind, we put ourselves at the mercy of the foreign policies of 11 other nations, and do so for a period of 20 years. . . . The Monroe Doctrine left us free to determine the merits of each dispute which might arise and to judge the justice and the wisdom of war in the light of the circumstances at the time. The present treaty obligates us to go to war if certain facts occur.

Although there was a growing sense of global interdependence in the postwar United States, we still approached international commitments with caution and only with the expectation that they would be temporary in duration. The founding fathers of the alliance did not intend to establish a permanent security system. Rather, they hoped to allow the war-weakened democracies of Western Europe a security framework within which they could take refuge from Soviet threats and subversion until, with massive American aid, they repaired their devastated economies and rebuilt their defenses, thereby impairing the Soviets' ability to challenge their security.

Response to the Soviet Threat

The second point I desire to emphasize is again well known; yet more and more often its importance is underestimated with the passage of time. It is that the alliance was forged as a direct response to the actual, imminent danger to Western Europe of Soviet subversion and aggression. No amount of historical revisionism can explain away facts of Soviet expansion into Europe. Truman described these to the Congress in a speech to a joint session on March 17, 1948:

> Since the close of the hostilities, the Soviet Union and its agents have destroyed the independence and democratic character of a whole series of nations in eastern and central Europe.
>
> It is this ruthless course of action, and the clear design to extend it to the remaining free nations of Europe, that have brought about the critical situation in Europe today.
>
> The tragic death of the Republic of Czechoslovakia has sent a shock throughout the civilized world. Now pressure is being brought to bear on

Finland, to the hazard of the entire Scandinavian peninsula. Greece is under direct military attack from rebels actively supported by her Communist-dominated neighbors. In Italy, a determined and aggressive effort is being made by a Communist minority to take control of that country. The methods vary, but the pattern is all too clear.

The ensuing decades of European peace, stability, and economic development have so transformed the security and well-being of Europe that it is easy to forget the reality of destabilization, intimidation, and outright aggression in the late 1940s. The Soviet threat to which the alliance was a response constituted a large part of the "Red Scare" of the times. Events in Poland, Hungary, Finland, and Czechoslovakia dramatized the character as well as the reality of the danger confronting Greece and Italy and the prospects for democracies in Europe.

Perception of Repeated Crises

The third point that I desire to underscore is that despite, or perhaps because of, its duration and patent success, the alliance has repeatedly, even chronically, been perceived as undergoing some sort of crisis which threatened to transform if not destroy it.

We err if we think that the alliance, having once enjoyed a golden age of nearly uniform judgments on all things important, has now lapsed into a progressively problematic relationship. In his *Fire in the Ashes,* published in 1953, Theodore White wrote of the passing of a period marked by great closeness and constructive cooperation and the entry into a period of new problems and new misunderstandings that challenge whether we can deal with these misunderstandings at all.

The same sense that the solutions to the problems of the postwar Soviet threat to Europe were being overtaken by events was expressed by Arthur Schlesinger's comments in *The Kennedy Years:*

> By 1960 the economic dependence on the United States had largely disappeared. Western Europe had been growing twice as fast as America for a decade; it had been drawing gold reserves from America; it had been outproducing America in coal. Americans were flocking across the Atlantic to learn the secrets of the economic miracle. And, at the same time, the military dependence had taken new and perplexing forms. If the prospect of a Soviet invasion of Western Europe had ever been real, few Europeans believed it any longer. Moreover, the Soviet nuclear achievement, putting the United States for the first time in its history under the threat of devastating attack, had devalued the American deterrent in European eyes. These developments meant that the conditions which had given rise to the Marshall Plan and NATO were substantially gone. The new Europe would not be content to remain an economic or military satellite of America. The problem now was to work out the next phase in the Atlantic relationship.

Hans Morgenthau expressed the same concern that basic premises and characteristics of the alliance could not remain unchanged in a rapidly changing world. He wrote in 1962:

> NATO was created as, and is still today officially considered to be, the shield that protects Western Europe from a Soviet attack on land. Yet it has never been clear how NATO could perform that function with the forces actually at its disposal or how it could have performed that function even with the much larger forces which its official spokesmen from time to time declared to be indispensable. Nor has it been clear how such a military organization, top-heavy as it is with collective agencies for the making of decisions, would operate effectively in case of war.
>
> These are some of the doubts which arise from within NATO itself. There are others which concern the relations between NATO and the overall political and military purposes of the Western alliance and, more particularly, of the United States. What is the place of NATO within the overall military strategy of the United States? What functions could NATO perform for the European communities and a more closely integrated Atlantic community? What impact is the impending diffusion of nuclear weapons likely to have upon the policies and the very existence of NATO? And what of the probable replacement of the manned bomber and bases supporting it by long-distance missiles? These are some of the questions which the Western governments should have raised long ago and answered.

That was 22 years ago. Today the search for definitive answers to those questions and others continues. Henry Kissinger has recently advised us that the problems facing the alliance today may require "a remedy that is fundamental, even radical." He suggests that the time may have arrived for Europe to assume the responsibility for its own defense against conventional attack, time to draw down or withdraw entirely the 300,000 U.S. troops in Germany. Recently, James Schlesinger and Helmut Schmidt had a widely reported public dialogue in which they, too, questioned the validity of using long-established NATO security arrangements to face the challenges of today. And perhaps the most basic question of all has been raised by *La Stampa's* Arrigo Levi: "Can one generation's experiences be bequeathed to the next?"

The fact is that there has never been a time in the 35-year life of NATO when everyone has been entirely satisfied with its performance. We have disagreed as to the nature of the Soviet threat and anguished over how to deal with it. We have disagreed about policies outside the area of the alliance. Diversity of the interests and views of the members in matters outside the treaty area has resulted in some dramatic conflicts inside the alliance. It is hard to remember, retrospectively, the passion associated with the Suez crisis of 1956, with European colonization, and with France's withdrawal from NATO in 1966. Yet even a casual review of alliance history reveals disagreements so frequent and so widespread that they have sometimes obscured the fact that we have continued to share a general sense of the reality of a potential Soviet threat to the security of Western Europe and a belief that the Atlantic alliance is the best available option for protection from that threat. The permanence of the debate is instructive. It compels us to examine the reasons for the longevity of the alliance in defiance of the doubts and challenges that have plagued it and the chronic problems of divisive democracies trying in peacetime to make and maintain common policies with regard to a potential military threat.

Flexibility and Strain

The problems are to a significant degree a consequence and a reflection of its success. The persistence of the alliance over the three-and-one-half decades demonstrates that it is a much more flexible instrument than it is usually conceived as being. Established as a framework for the participation of the United States in the defense of Europe, it has been a colossal success. Many things have changed since 1949. But most important is the reality of two generations of peace and prosperity in Western Europe, which has not. The relative cohesion among European states that have fought one another for centuries is, itself, a remarkable occurrence. Its effect on the security and stability of Europe is also remarkable. There has not even been a significant European centered East-West confrontation since the last Berlin crisis in 1962. And within this relative stability, the economies and cultures of all alliance members have flourished.

Indeed, European stability has been so uninterrupted it now seems unremarkable and is frequently viewed with indifference. A decade ago, the late Raymond Aron labeled this development "the routinization of the Atlantic Alliance," by which he meant that the alliance "... no longer arouses enthusiasm or hostility." Aron suggested that while "we may imagine a system that is better, we cannot dismiss as of marginal importance NATO's protection of Western European security against Soviet attack and subversion. Whatever the feasible alternatives to Atlantic security arrangements are, there is no evidence that they could hope to fulfill their basic purposes as successfully as the current arrangement has done."

However, it is never clear that what is will continue to be or even that what is successful will survive. It is not necessary to be a Hegelian or a Marxist to be impressed with the tendency of solutions to become problems, requiring new solutions. Obviously, there are strains within the alliance. Some of these are deeply rooted.

The United States and its partners share certain characteristics of democracies that create problems for maintaining permanent military alliances. The dynamics of electoral politics predispose democracies to focus on short-range problems and short-range solutions. Moreover, democracies, reflecting as they do the concerns of ordinary citizens, are in their very nature predisposed to seek and to expect peace, not war; to resent military expenditures; and to evade long-range planning. The very fact of four decades of peace in Europe makes the need for maintaining the alliance less plausible.

There are also the geopolitical realities, in which the American tradition of isolationism and universalism are alike based. "An island continent," Walter Lippmann called us, "separated by two oceans from Europe and Asia, separated, too, by history and demography: Most Americans came here seeking relief from their former conditions and are in some sense ambivalent about permanent involvement in the affairs of other nations." Geographic realities give the Western Hemisphere irreducible importance to America, and the westward course of American destiny links us to the Pacific states. We cannot transcend nor ignore these realities.

My good friend Larry Eagleburger [former Under Secretary of State for Political Affairs], whose departure from public service impoverishes us all, recently predicted what he perceived as "the shift of the center of gravity of U.S. foreign policy from the transatlantic relationship toward the Pacific Basin and particularly Japan." Besides the growing importance of Pacific states in the world economy, he cites the Europeans having "become so concerned with their own problems that it has tended to make it ever more difficult to get Western Europe to look outside its borders" as the reason underlying this perceived shift.

Certainly, the U.S. involvement with the nations of the Pacific is longstanding. We have been going west throughout our history. Our trade with that region has surpassed that with Europe and is growing at a faster rate.

There is also the special relationship with our hemisphere and the other nations of the Americas. Geography, demography, and history alike link our security and destiny with the Americas.

Beyond geography, there is, of course, history and identity. The United States has historical and demographic ties to the Pacific, Africa, and Latin America but strongest historical and demographic ties to Europe.

Indeed, one could say that the Atlantic community is as old as the European discovery of America. We are part of what is called Western civilization. That Greco-Roman, Judeo-Christian approach to life defines us just as surely as it defines Europe. We are the heirs of the liberal democratic tradition born of the efforts of Englishmen and other Europeans to make just government dependent on the consent of the governed. To be an American means to be part of that civilization. It does not mean that we are European. It does not mean we are Eurocentric. But we share a civilization with Europe, a heritage, an identity that defines our destiny at the same time it links our destiny to Europe. This sense of identification reinforced those who sought successfully to involve the United States in World Wars I and II. And there are less readily categorized ways in which our national interest links us to Europe.

Hans Morgenthau, writing in 1951, explained how U.S. national interests led us to participate in the politics of the Old World.

> Since a threat to our national interest in the Western Hemisphere can only come from outside it—historically from Europe—we have always striven to prevent the development of conditions in Europe which would be

conducive to a European nation's interfering in the affairs of the Western Hemisphere or contemplating a direct attack upon the United States. These conditions would be most likely to arise if a European nation, its predominance unchallenged within Europe, could look across the sea for conquest without fear of being menaced at the center of its power; that is, in Europe itself.

It is for that reason that the United States has consistently pursued policies aiming at the maintenance of the balance of power in Europe. It has opposed whatever European nation—be it Great Britain, France, Germany, or Russia—was likely to gain ascendancy over its European competitors which would have jeopardized the hemispheric predominance and eventually the very independence of the United States. Conversely, it has supported whatever European nation appeared capable of restoring the balance of power by offering successful resistance to the would-be conqueror.

A balance of power? A would-be conqueror? Revisionists affirm these concerns were ever illusory and join a larger chorus of voices that question their contemporary realism.

Realities and Expectations

Two questions, each important, must be addressed. One concerns reality. Does the Soviet threat to the peace, national independence, and freedom of Western Europe, which stimulated NATO's formation, still exist? The answer seems to me to be found in the sponsorship by the Soviet Union of subversion, coups, insurgency, invasion, incorporation in other continents, and the new unilateral vulnerabilities created for Western Europe by Soviet deployment of new generations of missiles targeted on Western Europe. *Le Monde* last week commented in an editorial on *"le style Tchernenko."*

> The observers who have been wondering if the new Soviet leadership installed last February would harden the policy followed previously have now new evidence. Events of the last days in Afghanistan confirm the warnings of the leaders of Afghanistan's resistance: Moscow has mounted a new form of combat much more massive and brutal, devoid of any of the subtleties which Andropov demonstrated.

Afghanistan is not Europe. The rulers of the Soviet Union are capable of differentiated response. But their continued boycott of the INF [intermediate-range nuclear forces] talks, the demand for superiority present in the adamant insistence on removal of Euromissiles, seems to underscore many other indications that Soviet hegemony over Western Europe remains a realistic concern. The most powerful argument for the persistence of the alliance is the persistence of the threat of peace, national independence, and freedom which stimulated its formation in the first place, a threat symbolized today in the SS-20s and their various cousins.

Freedom from fear is not tantamount to freedom from danger, Lawrence Martin has reminded us, adding:

It is the difficult task of Western strategists . . . to preserve the real safety of their nations in an environment of conflict which the nations would rather ignore and a price in money, and in blood, which the peoples would, quite reasonably, rather not pay.

Between threat and threat perception lies the whole subjective world with its well-known possibilities for deceit, exaggeration, hopes, fears, and illusions concerning both self and others. There lies, too, the domain of value and choice.

The objective persistence of threat does not guarantee the persistence of its perception and constant perception does not guarantee constant response.

The Europe of the late 1940s was vulnerable and felt vulnerable. The recent experience with conquest and despotism had left a clear, deeply felt, widely held sense of the superiority of freedom, the horror of subjection. The United States of the late 1940s enjoyed clear military and economic superiority and, felt the confidence, community and purpose born of victory over tyrants. The confidence was so strong that, to this day, no revisionists have arisen seriously to question whether World War II was a necessary war, whether the stakes were as high as then perceived, whether the devastation of war was justified at all.

In neither Europe nor America is there today quite the same clarity and confidence about the choices and stakes: about the problem to which the alliance is the solution or about the solution.

At the most radical level, some Europeans doubt today the moral difference between "the superpowers." John Vinocur wrote in yesterday's *New York Times Magazine* of certain German intellectuals who speak of "America as aggressor; America as polluter, nuclear terrorist and profiteer; America as-the-force-keeping-us-from-the-way-we-want-to-be." (Of course, he also described in the same piece, the dramatic turnaround with regard to the United States of French intellectuals.)

The transformations of time have dimmed old visions, eroded old ties, and created at the same time new possibilities. The rulers of East Germany have reinforced the wall but also seem to have understood that the personal ties among Germans lead not to satiation but to the desire for more. The longing to break barriers between the Germanies reinforces the fear of nuclear war in this frontline state, creating a state of mind called neutralism—much as the sense of unnecessary vulnerability and unappreciated solidarity feeds American isolationist impulses.

Accompanying these ongoing mutual reevaluations of moral and political character, strategy and tactics are also widely discussed. Should Europe risk becoming a battlefield in a war between superpowers? Should Americans continue to expose themselves to nuclear war to protect Western Europe?

The evidence suggests that in no country of Western Europe a majority holds that their interests would be better served outside of the NATO security guarantee. On the contrary, I believe that in many cases media coverage of constructive debates over the relative merits of NATO defense modifications has magnified radical perceptions and prescriptions. When the die was cast, Europeans and Americans alike decided the issue of deployment in favor of an allied response to a new European vulnerability.

Some Europeans like to believe that the American stake in Western Europe is so great that the United States necessarily be involved in an attack on a NATO nation.

Some Americans, thinking radically, doubt that this is necessarily the case—providing we had neither troops nor missiles in Europe. Some Americans insist that European and American defense is divisible.

It is as tempting and mistaken to exaggerate distrust, dislocation in U.S.-European relations as it is to ignore them.

Dissatisfaction with the alliance's tactics, plans, and structures surely is rooted in changing economic and military facts and relations which must be continually updated.

But much of the current "crisis mongering" is surely rooted less in changed objective realities than in changed expectations. We have overloaded the alliance with expectations which it was never intended to bear; then, because it does not meet these new expectations, we are surprised and view this instrument as deficient. The image of frictionless relations between allies is almost exactly analogous to the image of the frictionless marriage or the perfectly ordered house. These exist only in fantasy. The fact is that the relations between the United States and its NATO allies today are very good and very strong. They are based on common values, deeply related common institutions and legal systems, and a very great deal of mutual respect on the part of most significant figures in all of the societies—not just governments but societies.

The debate over the alliance security strategies was not begun with the installation of Soviet SS-20s. It will not end when deployment of INF is completed. For many the idea that the United States would consider an attack upon Western Europe as an attack upon itself has always seemed hard to accept. We would hope that for now the absence of any authoritative discussion of reducing the level of U.S. troop strength in Europe, the rejection of proposals to renounce first-use of nuclear weapons in Europe, the improvement of theater nuclear defenses, and, of course, the continued expressions of unshakeable support from Washington for U.S. commitments to European security would allow European fears to subside. But questions will and, of course, should continue. And new developments will require new modifications. The emergence of chemical weapons promises to raise new questions about the nuclear threshold to illuminate Europe's commitment to a nuclear defense, to illuminate, as well, U.S. vulnerabilities deriving from any strategy that foresees "going nuclear" as an early response.

Doubtless, too, there will be new demands for and against restructuring decisionmaking within the alliance. Italian Foreign Minister Colombo suggested in a recent speech a new "Euro-American friendship pact, and also periodic meetings between foreign ministers to coordinate their respective views . . ." and provide continuity in discussions among NATO governments.

The instrumentalities necessary for adaptation to changing realities exist. Power in the alliance is shared, as former German Chancellor Helmut Schmidt noted 2 years ago during the controversy over NATO modifications: ". . . the voice of the Europeans is strong enough to be heard if they so desire. There are fifteen members in the Alliance, thirteen of which are Europeans. Why don't they speak if they want to be heard?"

They do want to be heard. They do speak. The NATO system can and will respond.

Doubtless, too, there will be U.S. frustrations with the alliance which will doubtless persist. In the U.S. Government, we chafe today over European failure to understand an emphasis with our problems outside Europe. Larry Eagleburger, a staunch and warm supporter of the alliance, expressed his disappointment that, in a year after the Falklands, the Europeans could not restrain harsh criticism over the Grenada landing in which we moved in careful concert with the nations of the Caribbean: "At the very least could not our friends have suspended judgment until the emerging situation became clearer?"

It is not a perfect marriage; no counselor can make it one. We have and will continue to have distinct interests and shared ones as well. "Who profits most from the Alliance—Europe or America?" Aron asked a decade ago.

The fact that the question was not easily answered then and is not easily answered today illuminates the foundations of the alliance. This pattern of cooperation and alliance among the nations of the Atlantic area will survive generational change because it is bound on more than nostalgia. It will survive new important economic ties to the Pacific because it is bound together by more than shared economic interests. It will survive disappointments and misunderstandings because the leaders of the democracies understand, finally, that all our nations, and all their freedoms, depend finally but immediately on the civilization that sustains us all.

There is no perfect alliance. There are no perfect friends, and as James Reston commented concerning this debate on NATO defense improvements: "There is no perfect security. There is only the struggle. With friends at our side doing the best we can."

The American government and the people it serves have every intention of continuing that struggle, side-by-side with our European friends.

Discussion Questions

1. What factors motivate states to form alliances? Are there other factors that motivate states to remain in alliances, even when the original

reasons have disappeared?

2. Are the benefits from participation in alliances equal for all states? In what ways? Explain your answer.

3. Why have alliances been such a common feature of international affairs throughout history? Do you believe this trend will continue through the present century? Why or why not?

4. In his speech, "On Alliance Responsibility," Secretary of State Shultz chastises New Zealand for refusing harbor to a U.S. destroyer. If you were the head of the New Zealand government, how would you respond to the secretary's statements about your government's responsibilities as an alliance member?

5. How does the existence of alliances make a difference in the affairs of nations?

For Further Reading

Classic Studies

Deutsch, Karl W., and J. David Singer, "Multipolar Power Systems and International Stability." *World Politics* 16, no. 3 (April 1964). A detailed analysis of the multipolar system and its impact on the occurrence of peace and war.

Kissinger, Henry A. *A World Restored.* New York: Grosset and Dunlap, 1964. This famous study by the even more famous scholar turned practitioner analyzes the nineteenth-century multipolar system that Kissinger maintained was a near-perfect mechanism for preventing war.

Liska, George F. *Nations in Alliance: The Limits of Interdependence.* Baltimore: Johns Hopkins University Press, 1962. A basic work on the study of alliances.

Olson, Mancur, Jr. *The Logic of Collective Action.* Cambridge, Mass.: Harvard University Press, 1965. Still considered the classic work on the theory of collective action.

Riker, William. *The Theory of Political Coalitions.* New Haven: Yale University Press, 1962. A complex and widely cited study that examines the conditions under which coalitions and alliances are formed.

Rosencrance, Richard N. "Bipolarity, Multipolarity and the Future," *Journal of Conflict Resolution* 21. no. 1 (September 1968). A useful comparison of the two major balance of power models viewed in their contemporary settings.

Rothstein, Robert L. *Alliances and Small Powers.* New York: Columbia University Press, 1968. A useful though not well-known volume on the differential benefits of alliance participation.

More Recent Studies

Bueno de Mesquita, Bruce. *The War Trap*. New Haven: Yale University Press, 1981. One of the major scholarly books of the 1980s, although a methodologically difficult work for most college students. By comparing the actual occurrence of war with expected utility calculations, the author concludes, among other things, that the linkage between war and the existence of a balance of power system is much weaker than was previously thought.

Bueno de Mesquita, Bruce, and J. David Singer. "Alliances, Capabilities, and War: A Review and Synthesis," in Cornelius Cotter, ed. *Political Science Annual*, Vol. 4. Indianapolis: Bobbs-Merrill, 1973. An important summary of social science research findings on alliances and their impact on war. Contains a particularly detailed overview of the Correlates of War project.

Groennings, Sven, E. W. Kelley, and Michael Leiserson, eds. *The Study of Coalition Behavior*. New York: Holt, Rinehart and Winston, 1970. This useful collection of essays by a number of the most respected scholars in the field discusses coalitions, balance of power systems, and alliances.

Singer, J. David, Stuart Bremer, and John Stuckey, "Capability Distribution, Uncertainty and Major Power War, 1820-1965," in Bruce M. Russett, ed. *Peace, War and Numbers*. Beverly Hills, Calif.: Sage Publications, 1972. A major but somewhat inconclusive study of the impact of the distribution of power on the likelihood of war. The authors find that during the nineteenth century greater concentrations of power were associated with conflict while the opposite has been true during the twentieth century.

CONFLICT AND VIOLENCE IN THE INTERNATIONAL SYSTEM 9

Almost twenty-five centuries ago, Croesus, the king of Lydia, threatened with invasion by Cyrus the Persian, spoke of the true meaning of war. As the story was retold by Herodotus, Croesus said, "No one is so senseless as to choose of his own free will war rather than peace, since in peace the sons bury their fathers, but in war the fathers bury their sons." Long before the clash between Lydia and Persia, and long since, scholars and statesmen have recognized the enduring problems of conflict and violence in the international system. We focus in this chapter on these two enduring phenomena of international politics, their sources, their various forms, and their consequences. We will have cause to contemplate the true meaning of Karl von Clausewitz's celebrated dictum that "War is nothing more than the continuation of politics by other means."

Sources and Types of Conflict

In discussing power in Chapter 6 we noted that politics may be usefully conceived as centering around questions of "who gets what, when and how," as Harold Lasswell put it. We also said that power may be understood as the capability to do what, to whom and under what conditions. Within this framework, conflict may be seen as the result of the incompatibility of structures and interests that produce alternative responses to these basic political questions. *Conflict* is thus defined as a situation in which two or more parties have an incompatibility of goals, values, or interests such that any resolution will make at least one of the parties worse off. In this respect conflict is a ubiquitous phenomenon, a common feature of all domestic and international political systems.

Nonetheless, there is more than one type of conflict. In international relations, social scientists often distinguish between two types of conflict—structural and perceptual. The difference between the two lies in their sources.

Structural conflicts arise from situations in which there is a fundamental incompatibility of goals, interests, or values, with the result that if A gets what it wants, B *cannot* get what it wants. A structural conflict is a *conflict of interests* that can be understood quite readily by outside observers once the situation is described for them. A conflict between a colonial power seeking to preserve its empire in the face of its colonial subjects' demands for independence is a structural conflict. Clearly the colonial power's goal, to maintain control over its colonies, is fundamentally incompatible with the independence of those colonies.

Resource scarcities—or shortages of basic needs such as food, water, and shelter—are the most common source of structural conflict. Another is the need for territory. The most familiar contemporary example of a structural conflict based on conflicting territorial claims is the longstanding Israeli-Palestinian conflict. Israel may exist as a sovereign state on its current territory only if there is no Palestinian state on that territory. If the Palestinians were to be granted statehood within the territory they define as their homeland, the current state of Israel, which occupies that territory, could not continue to exist. The conflict does not arise from a misunderstanding of the other party's position but rather from mutually exclusive claims to the same territory. Each side can attain its desired ends only if the other "loses."

Perceptual conflicts arise when A believes that B is an actual or potential source of harm to one or more of A's vital interests or primary values. The most common sources of perceptual conflict in international relations are "misunderstandings" that arise out of ideological, historical, religious, nationalist, racial, or ethnic differences.

While such conflicts are quite real to the actors involved, they will often be perceived by outside observers as irrational or unnecessary, or, at the very least, as effectively complicating structural conflict. Thus, from a realist perspective, the "real" or "structural" conflict between the United States and the Soviet Union involves not ideology but the struggle for power. To realists, the real issue in such a rivalry lies in the relative power positions of the two parties. All other issues are perceptual, the product of the two actors' competing ideological beliefs rather than more "objective" considerations.

How an analyst views the sources of a conflict is apt to have a significant effect on policy recommendations. Consider, for example, the question of whether the continuing Soviet assistance to the Sandinista regime in Nicaragua means that that regime represents a de facto Soviet "beachhead" in the Western Hemisphere. Analysts who view U.S.- Soviet differences as structural would answer this question very differently than would those who define the underlying issues in perceptual terms.

While the analytical distinction between structural and perceptual conflicts is clear, serious structural conflicts that continue over time will inevitably develop a perceptual dimension. The objective interests of the parties to the conflict will become entwined with differences in race, ethnicity, ideology, or religion, and with the hostility that such differences may evoke. These will in turn serve to sustain the objective differences and exacerbate the conflict. Thus, in the Arab-Israeli conflict (as in any structural conflict) perceptual differences have over time taken on a life of their own and become important factors in sustaining the conflict.

Conflict Situations and Conflict Behaviors

It is necessary to distinguish among situations that produce conflict, the factors that structure it, and the behaviors of the parties involved. Thus, upon examining the Arab-Israeli conflict, we can describe the objective problem as that arising from competing claims to the same territory. The result is a conflict situation.

We next must determine whether the conflict is manifest, latent, or suppressed. *Manifest conflicts* are those that have produced clear behavioral evidence—violent acts, threats, or demands—of the existence of conflict. A *latent conflict* is one in which an objective conflict can be identified, although there may not yet be clear behavioral evidence of that conflict. *Suppressed conflicts* are similar to latent conflicts in that conflict behavior has not yet emerged—because the more powerful of the parties involved has threatened to respond to such behavior with overwhelming force. For example, a repressive state may successfully suppress many forms of protest—riots, strikes, or revolution—without the necessity of taking action, because its citizens recognize and fear its capacity for harsh and repressive violence.

Thus, conflict evokes a variety of responses. Not all of these need be destructive. Often, in fact, conflict may be simultaneously associated with both constructive and destructive behavior. To be sure, conflict often results in violence, war, and terrorism. It may, however, also produce *competition,* a form of behavior in which the two parties pursue the same or similar goals while subscribing to an agreed-upon set of rules. Consider the case of two runners competing in a race. The scarce value is finishing first, because only one runner can be first. The contest can be defined as a competition if the two runners observe a mutually agreed-upon set of rules—for example, that neither will seek to win except by simply running faster.

In a similar fashion, the United States and the Soviet Union engaged for many years in a worldwide competition to demonstrate the superiority of their systems of government. The "weapons" involved in this competition were foreign assistance programs and models for development. The objective was to obtain the allegiance of as many as possible of the newly emergent nations of the Third World.

Indeed, the two nations extended their competition to the track itself and have regularly met in many athletic events, with both sides seeking to demonstrate through athletic victories the superiority of their systems. Thus, even the most powerful of nations locked in a global conflict may find nondestructive outlets for their rivalry. Most conflict behavior in the international arena, in fact, is of the nondestructive variety.

As we are all aware, however, international conflict can also result in destructive behavior. We may distinguish here between two types of destructive behavior—violent and nonviolent.

The responses available to nations engaged in conflict are numerous.

431

These include notes of diplomatic protest, the recall of ambassadors, public denunciations, economic sanctions, and the breaking of diplomatic relations. Also included in this category, as long as the party involved stops short of actual action, are threats to use force, impose a blockade, occupy territory, retaliate in some unspecified way, or declare war.

Conflict behavior crosses the line from nonviolent to violent when it involves acts of physical harm. We may measure the intensity of such acts by noting the "destructiveness" of the instrument chosen—that is, by counting the deaths. We can measure a violent act's magnitude by noting the level and duration of commitment of forces, resources, and time—that is, by determining the number of troops and the duration of the conflict. We can then compare the relative magnitude and intensity of violent acts and conflicts in general.

The Correlates of War Project described in Melvin Small and J. David Singer's *Resort to Arms* has measured the magnitude and intensity of wars and civil wars for the period 1816-1980. The violent acts range from relatively low-level acts—such as terrorist attacks, shelling, hostage taking, and seizures of small amounts of territory—to armed attacks, bombing raids, seizures of significant amounts of territory, and, of course, war.

War

War is the best-known and most widely studied form of international conflict. Nonetheless, there is disagreement about its definition. While we all have an intuitive sense that we "know" what war is, the term is not always used consistently. Perhaps the simplest approach is to define *war* as armed violence between two or more sovereign states. This is, in fact, the central notion in most legal definitions of war.

As straightforward as this concept may seem, its application to reality is fraught with ambiguity. Should our definition require that the participating states issue a formal declaration of war? If so, must they actually engage in hostilities, for how long, and with what severity and intensity? Consider, for example, the Vietnam War, a major military conflict—in terms of duration and casualties. It lasted more than twenty years and produced over 10 million civilian and military casualties. Despite its magnitude, however, the Vietnam War was never considered—by the U.S. government, at least—a conflict between two sovereign states. The United States never formally recognized the government of the Democratic Republic of (North) Vietnam, nor did it ever issue a declaration of war.

The questions involved here are not purely academic. The ways they are posed and answered may have profound implications. In the case of the Vietnam War, the dispute over the true nature of that conflict and the American role in it were intimately bound up with views of the constitutional division of responsibilities between the executive and the Congress. One result of that dispute was the passage of the War Powers Act (1973), which was intended to limit the president's use of U.S. military forces in the absence of a formal declaration of war. This, in turn, prompted President Richard Nixon and his successors to express concern that this congressional attempt to limit the "unbridled" use of American power represented an undue restriction on the chief executive's powers as commander-in-chief.

The Vietnam example is instructive in other ways. The emphasis on guerrilla tactics, the widespread use of chemical defoliants, and the frequent bombing of civilian areas typical of that conflict reflect recent changes in the context of international relations and the technology of war. As a result of these changes, not only is war potentially more deadly and destructive today than ever before, but the distinctions between war and peace have been irrevocably blurred.

The conditions under which nations choose or stumble into war have not necessarily changed, however. In any analysis of the causes of war it is important to distinguish among *causes*, which is to say the objectives involved (for example, territory, political unification, revenge, the honoring of commitments, liberation, or access to resources), the *dynamics* that led to the establishment of such objectives, and the *circumstances* leading to the actual outbreak of hostilities. While social scientists have not yet developed a satisfactory theory of the causes of war, there has been much progress in identifying the associated factors or correlates. Of particular note is the Correlates of War Project mentioned earlier. In any case, war remains a troubling phenomenon. The data compiled by Melvin Small and J. David Singer for the Correlates of War Project testifies to the frequency and deadliness of war, declared and otherwise, in the twentieth century. The reading in this chapter by R. J. Rummel places this state of affairs in perspective by reminding us that war is not the leading cause of death in this century. Yet the prospect of war is not to be taken lightly in the nuclear age.

Terrorism and Low-Intensity Conflict

Nation-states may use a variety of forms of violence short of war to further their interests, and they have done so increasingly in the past decade. A conflict in which such tactics are employed is called a *low-intensity conflict,* which can be defined as the use of violence short of full-scale war by state agents against other members of the international system. The tactics of low-intensity conflict include terrorism, bombing raids, sabotage, mining of sea lanes and harbors, and a disturbing range of other alternatives.

Not all international conflicts involve the nation-state. Political violence involving nonstate actors has long been a common feature of international affairs, and such conflicts are often fraught with escalation potential. Often, the participants will seek assistance from foreign governments in the form of a safe haven, a base from which to operate freely; advisers; training; access to arms; or actual military support. Similarly, states that are the targets of such attacks are likely to seek outside aid with the result that the conflict involved can easily spill over into the international arena or even escalate into full-blown war.

In the contemporary world, for example, the African National Congress (ANC), which seeks to end apartheid in South Africa and establish a government based on majority rule, has long maintained bases in Zimbabwe and other "front-line states" that border South Africa. In response, the South African government's policy has been to bomb such bases and pursue ANC forces into the territory of neighboring states that allow the ANC to operate within their borders. Similarly, the use of bases in Honduras by the "contras" who—beginning in 1981—sought to overthrow the Sandinista regime in Nicaragua produced great tension between these two countries. The possibilities of war are ever present under such conditions.

Disputes may spill over into the international realm even in the absence of any direct involvement by outside states in another's "domestic" dispute. Sometimes an outsider's concern for the plight of one of the parties to the dispute is all that is required to trigger a conflagration. Thus the assassination of the Archduke Ferdinand of Austria by Serbian nationalists in June 1914 set in motion the series of events that led to World War I. The principals in the assassination had no foreign connections and received no outside assistance, and the assassination itself in no way directly affected the interests of states other than Austria. For these reasons, the rise of terrorism in recent years and particularly its increasing use by nation-states constitute a disturbing trend.

The images that we normally associate with terrorism are those of a masked gunman holding hostage some terrified airline passengers or the aftermath of a bombing on a crowded city street. Clearly such forms of terrorism have existed for some years and are of increasing significance as potential sources of international conflict. The nonstate actors involved in sponsoring such actions have the potential to cause great damage, both physically and politically. They can and do threaten and take the lives of significant numbers of people each year. More than three thousand people have perished from these forms of terrorism in the past decade, making terrorism a security problem of great concern to many who fear a replay of the World War I precedent. Thus, leaders of many states have begun to seek ways to combat terrorism and reduce the threat it poses to the continued stability of the international system.

However, we cannot and should not assume that all states are equally opposed to all forms of terrorism and other uses of violence short of war. In the past few decades, a growing awareness of the unsuitability of weapons of mass destruction for many purposes has led to an increased interest in various forms of low-intensity conflict as a policy tool. To be sure, this is not an altogether new phenomenon. Throughout history states have sought less costly and "safer" methods short of full-scale war for dealing with conflict. Thus, the attitudes of any given state toward particular conflict behaviors are likely to be a function of the context, the actor, and the target involved. To understand why states are willing both to engage in and to assist others to engage in low-intensity conflict, it is necessary first to examine the nature of violence and terrorism as political instrument.

If political violence is an act involving physical harm, and low-intensity conflict involves political violence that falls short of war, *terrorism* is a special form of low-intensity violence that involves the purposeful threat or use of violence for political purposes. Terrorism may be undertaken by individuals or groups, acting in opposition to *or on behalf of* established governmental authority. In all cases, the distinguishing feature of terrorism is the intent to influence a specific target group rather than the victim, who may or may not be a party to the immediate dispute. Terrorism is then a coercive political strategy that employs the threat of violence and pain as its chief instrument.

An important aspect of the way terrorism differs from "ordinary" political violence is that with terrorism the act or the threat of the act of violence is but the first step. Terrorism is purposeful behavior designed to influence the behavior of targeted individuals or groups beyond the immediate victims. Terrorists' objectives are to change policies, decisions, or the allocation of resources—all of which lie well outside the immediate circumstances of the act itself. The violence that is terrorism seeks to influence the behavior of others, not merely—or even chiefly—to eliminate victims. The violence of other low-intensity conflict behaviors is direct—the destruction of a particular target, elimination of retaliatory capability, or assassination.

The behavior of nation-states involved in low-intensity conflict takes three major forms: coercive diplomacy, covert action, and the use of surrogates. The aim of *coercive diplomacy* is to make noncompliance with a particular demand painful. While the existence of the threat is openly communicated, the precise nature of the threat may be implicit and the form of retaliation is quite often left unstated. Coercive diplomacy is overt behavior. The parties to the conflict are fully aware of the existence of the threat.

The Soviet Union employed coercive diplomacy in the Polish crisis of 1980-1981. Faced with what it considered an unacceptable challenge to "orthodoxy" in the form of the rise of the Polish workers' union, Solidarity, the Soviet Union embarked on a campaign of intimidation that involved Soviet troop maneuvers on the Polish border, amphibious landings on the Polish coast, a military alert, and explicit warnings to the Polish military to take control of the situation before outside intervention became necessary. When the Polish military responded as directed and effectively dismantled Solidarity, the threat of Soviet intervention disappeared.

Similarly, the Christmas bombing of Hanoi in 1972 is an example of the use of coercive diplomacy by the United States. When peace negotiations between the United States and North Vietnam stalled in late 1972—largely because of the South Vietnamese government's opposition to the proposed terms, which had been worked out between Secretary of State Henry Kissinger and representatives of the North Vietnamese government—President Nixon ordered saturation bombing of Hanoi. The bombing was intended as a demonstration of U.S. determination to achieve its policy objectives in Southeast Asia. It demonstrated to the South Vietnamese that the United States did not intend to abandon South Vietnam in the face of continued aggression by the North. To the North Vietnamese, the bombing carried the implicit threat of further U.S. action if they did not return to the bargaining table, even though it was the South Vietnamese who had first rejected the agreement. Shortly thereafter, presumably in response to the bombings, both the North and the South Vietnamese returned to the negotiating table, and the Paris peace accords were signed in January 1973.

Covert action, the second form of state behavior common to low-intensity conflicts, is of two varieties. *Clandestine state violence* is a form of covert action that involves direct participation by state agents in acts of violence. *State-sponsored violence* is a form of covert action in which groups or individuals not directly associated with the state are employed to undertake violent actions at the direction of the sponsoring state.

In either case, the intelligence agencies of the sponsoring state usually play a major role in initiating, coordinating, or carrying out the actions involved. The target may be either national elites or the larger society. The objective may be direct intimidation of government officials through bombings, armed attacks, assassinations, and coup attempts or the destabilization of the target society and a consequent collapse of the government and a change in national leadership. While the existence of a threat will ordinarily be obvious, the sponsoring state will usually try to deny any connection with the actions.

Both clandestine violence and state-sponsored violence were employed by the United States in its campaign against Nicaragua that began in 1981. Agents of the Central Intelligence Agency mined Nicaraguan harbors and assisted the Nicaraguan rebels. At the same time an elaborate support network, at first covert and later quite open, was established to assist a third party, the contras, in their effort to overthrow the Sandinista regime.

The third form of low-intensity conflict behavior by states involves the *use of surrogates.* Such behavior involves assisting another state or an insurgent organization to engage in violence that might otherwise be beyond its capabilities. Surrogates, unlike third parties who participate in state-sponsored violence, do not take their marching orders directly from the party providing assistance. Rather, that party merely "supports" their general activities.

Such activities are of two major types. *State-supported behaviors* involve particular actions taken by third parties that are supported, after the fact, by the interested state. *State acquiescence* is given by states that do not explicitly support but fail to condemn or openly oppose terrorism or other violent behaviors of third parties. The assistance provided by the United States to the "freedom fighters" in Angola and Afghanistan is an example of the use of surrogates. The recipients of this assistance have their own agenda and strategy. The United States merely supplies weapons and material support. Likewise, the guerrilla training provided to various Palestinian groups by the Soviet Union during the 1960s and 1970s and the subsequent Soviet failure to halt that assistance when it became clear that it was contributing to the recipients' ability to conduct terrorism are recent examples of state acquiescence.

Some Final Comments on International Violence

In discussing the many forms of international political violence we have concentrated on behavior that is deliberately and consciously calculated to cause harm. We have in effect focused on purposeful actions and their perpetrators. If, however, we examine all types of violence from the standpoint of the victims, it becomes clear that purposeful actions are not the only types of actions that cause physical harm. What might be the toll of violence if we were to examine all forms of violence—purposeful or not—that cause the deaths of victims?

This raises the problem of structural violence. *Structural violence* is violence resulting from choices made by policy makers or even entire societies—choices that lead to large numbers of deaths because of the way scarce resources are employed. Some scholars have suggested that structural violence occurs whenever people become victims because of the structure of their political and social environment. Of course, determining whether people are victims of their political and social environment is a difficult and controversial task.

It is, nonetheless, a task that has attracted the attention of at least one group of scholars. Researchers at the Stockholm International Peace Research Institute have estimated the magnitude of structural violence in a dramatic way, using the concept of "excess deaths." Defining *excess deaths* as those deaths that would not have occurred if all countries possessed a health care system as advanced as that of Sweden and defining success at its most basic level—namely, keeping the population alive, they have developed a simple formula that challenges conventional notions of the extent and costs of political violence. The formula may be expressed as:

$$\frac{\text{Population of country n}}{\text{Life expectancy in country n}} - \frac{\text{The population of country n}}{\text{Life expectancy in Sweden}}$$

Applying the formula to real-world data results in an estimate of 12 million to 13 million excess deaths worldwide in 1978. To put it another way, using 53,000 as the number of deaths resulting from the bombing of Hiroshima in August 1945, the total number of excess deaths worldwide in 1978 was equivalent to the dropping of 236 nuclear bombs or one bomb every one and one-third days of the year.

Thus, we can see that political violence is an even larger problem than most of us might ever imagine. To be sure, many will object to a definition of violence so broad that it requires no conscious attempt to cause harm. For the victims this is, of course, irrelevant. What is more important is that such a perspective can help us, the survivors, become more aware of the many different forms that violence assumes and thereby combat it more effectively.

The Readings

With the advent of nuclear weapons, the ever-present risk of war between the superpowers has become a major concern of contemporary scholars, policy makers, and citizens. In the first selection in this chapter, Jack S. Levy analyzes historical trends in the occurrence of war between great powers, with particular attention to the hypothesis that such wars have become less frequent but more serious. In so doing he illustrates some of the concerns raised elsewhere in this chapter. He finds that the frequency of great-power war decreased from the sixteenth through the nineteenth centuries, only to increase slightly during this century.

In the second selection Harvey Starr and Benjamin Most analyze recent Third World conflicts. In a search for more general lessons, they examine the forms, levels, locales, participants, and the overall effects of these conflicts and develop a clear, operational definition of war. They conclude that both domestic problems and external threats play a significant role in the origins of Third World conflicts. Woven into their analysis is a comparison of their findings with those of other major studies of war by social scientists over the past fifty years.

The third selection, by Andrew Mack, examines an intriguing aspect of international conflict: how militarily more powerful nations are sometimes defeated by weaker powers. In his analysis of "asymmetric conflict," Mack concludes that a key factor in such outcomes is the larger power's loss of the political capability to wage war. Mack's findings serve to remind us of the wisdom of Clausewitz's dictum that war is not simply a question of guns and ammunition but is an extension of politics.

In his short but provocative piece, "War Isn't This Century's Biggest Killer," R. J. Rummel focuses on other sources of violence in the international system and reminds us of the importance of our definitions in any attempt to identify the leading sources of international and domestic violence. While some will argue with Rummel's calculations and the sources of his data, few will challenge the importance of the issues he raises.

We conclude this chapter with two policy selections. George P. Shultz examines an issue of concern to him throughout his tenure as secretary of state, namely the problems that low-intensity warfare poses for policy makers. Shultz suggests a strategy for confronting such challenges short of all-out war and argues, as he has on other occasions, that the United Nations Charter's provision for the right of self-defense encompasses armed response to terrorist activities. The second policy selection by one of the editors of this volume critiques both the intellectual basis and the effectiveness of the policies and rhetoric of the Reagan administration with respect to terrorism. While Shultz is concerned that the U.S. failure to confront terrorism directly will result in disaster, Stohl worries that the methods recommended by Shultz will themselves lead to grave difficulties.

9.1 ■■■■■

JACK S. LEVY

Historical Trends in Great Power War, 1495-1975

It is widely believed that the probability of a war between the super-powers is diminishing but that its potential destructiveness is increasing. Our argument is that this phenomenon, if it exists, is not simply a product of the nuclear age but also a manifestation of long-term historical trends in war that have been underway for many centuries. While the future is a matter of conjecture, the question of past historical trends is eminently suitable for rigorous and systematic empirical research. The aim of this study is to test the hypothesis that war between the Great Powers has been decreasing in frequency but increasing in seriousness over the past several centuries.

These "Great Power wars" are of enormous importance for international politics. They have generally been history's most destructive conflicts and have had the greatest impact on the stability of the international system. For the most part, the interaction of the Great Powers determines the structure and evolution of the system and serves as the basis for most of our theories of international politics. This question of historical trends in Great Power war is more than one of simple historical curiosity, however, for the occurrence of another Great Power war might very well bring an end to contemporary civilization. The Great Power wars of the past provide a rich source of historical data and in many respects provide the best empirical referents for a hypothetical superpower war of the future. While theory provides the best grounds for predictions about the future, in the absence of theory an empirically confirmed explanation of historical trends may be quite useful, particularly if the factors contributing toward the trend show no signs of abating.

Our task requires the definition and identification of the powers and the modern Great Power system, specification of criteria for the identification of their wars, measurement of the wars along several key dimensions, and selection of appropriate methods of analysis given the question under consideration and the nature of the data.

From *International Studies Quarterly,* Vol. 26, No. 2 (June 1982). Reprinted with permission of the International Studies Association.

The Modern Great Power System

A Great Power can be defined generally as a state which plays a major role in international politics with respect to security-related issues. Operational indicators of Great Power status include the following: possession of a high level of power capabilities, which provides for reasonable self-sufficiency in security matters and permits the conduct of offensive as well as defensive military operations; participation in international congresses and conferences; de facto identification as a Great Power by an international conference or organization; admission to a formal or informal organization of Powers; participation in Great Power guarantees, territorial compensation, or partitions; and, generally, treatment as a relative equal by other Great Powers (for example, protocol, alliances, negotiations, and so forth).

The modern Great Power security system originated in early modern Europe and has gradually evolved into a truly global system. It is the late fifteenth century in general and 1495 in particular (formation of the League of Venice in response to the French invasion of Italy) that defines the origins of the system. This point marks the fusion of several distinct historical processes: the internal centralization of power within territorial states, the decline of the universal secular authority of the Pope and Holy Roman Emperor, the coalescence of the major territorial states of Europe into an interdependent system of power relations, and the emergence of a global world economy centered in Europe and sustained by sea power. This is consistent with a diverse body of literature on the origins of the modern system. The theoretical criteria noted above are applied to the historical literature, and the resulting Great Power system is presented in Table 9-1.

Table 9-1   The Modern Great Power System

France	1495-1975
England/Great Britain	1495-1975
Austrian Hapsburgs/Austria-Hungary	1495-1519; 1556-1918
Spain	1495-1519; 1556-1808
Ottoman Empire	1495-1699
United Hapsburgs	1519-1556
Netherlands	1609-1713
Sweden	1617-1721
Russia/Soviet Union	1721-1975
Prussia/Germany/West Germany	1740-1975
Italy	1861-1943
United States	1898-1975
Japan	1905-1945
China	1949-1975

Jack S. Levy

Table 9-2 Great Power Wars

War	Dates[a]
War of the League of Venice	1495-1497
Neapolitan War	1502-1504
War of the Holy League	1511-1514
Austro-Turkish War	1512-1519
Second Milanese War	1515-1515
First War of Charles V	1521-1526
Ottoman War	1521-1531
Second War of Charles V	1526-1529
Ottoman War	1532-1535
Third War of Charles V	1536-1538
Ottoman War	1537-1547
Fourth War of Charles V	1542-1544
Siege of Boulogne	1544-1546
Arundel's Rebellion	1549-1550
Ottoman War	1551-1556
Fifth War of Charles V	1552-1556
Austro-Turkish War	1556-1562
Franco-Spanish War	1556-1559
Scottish War	1559-1560 (1560)
Spanish-Turkish War	1559-1564
First Huguenot War	1562-1564
Austro-Turkish War	1565-1568
Spanish-Turkish War	1569-1580
Austro-Turkish War	1576-1583
War of the Armada	1585-1604
War of the Three Henries	1589-1598
Austro-Turkish War	1593-1606
Spanish-Turkish War	1610-1614
Spanish-Turkish War	1618-1619
Thirty Years War—Bohemian Period	1618-1625 (1621)
Thirty Years War—Danish Period	1625-1630
Thirty Years War—Swedish Period	1630-1635
Thirty Years War—Swedish-French Period	1635-1648
Franco-Spanish War	1648-1659
Anglo-Dutch Naval War	1652-1654
Great Northern War	1654-1660
English-Spanish War	1656-1659
Ottoman War	1657-1664 (1661)
Anglo-Dutch Naval War	1665-1667
Revolutionary War	1667-1668
Dutch War of Louis XIV	1672-1678
Ottoman War	1682-1699
Franco-Spanish War	1683-1684

442

Table 9-2   (continued)

War of the League of Augsburg	1688-1697
Second Northern War	1700-1721 (1715)
War of the Spanish Succession	1701-1713
War of the Quadruple Alliance	1718-1720
British-Spanish War	1726-1729
War of the Polish Succession	1733-1738
War of the Austrian Succession	1739-1748
Seven Years War	1755-1763
War of the Bavarian Succession	1778-1779
War of the American Revolution	1778-1784
French Revolutionary Wars	1792-1802
Napoleonic Wars	1803-1815
Crimean War	1854-1856
War of Italian Unification	1859-1859
Austro-Prussian War	1866-1866
Franco-Prussian War	1870-1871
World War I	1914-1918
Russian Civil War	1918-1921
Russo-Japanese War	1939-1939
World War II	1939-1945
Korean War	1950-1953

[a] For wars which do not begin as Great Power wars, the date of intervention of the second Power is given in parentheses.

Great Power War:
Conceptualization, Identification, and Measurement

A Great Power war is an armed conflict between the organized military forces of two or more Great Powers, operationally defined as involving at least 1000 battle deaths, or an annual average of 1000, among the Powers. Civil, imperial, and colonial wars do not satisfy the definition and are excluded. For the identification of wars prior to 1815, the Wright, Sorokin, and Woods and Baltzly data-sets are used, and any Great Power war included in at least two of the three is included here. For the post-1815 period, the Singer-Small compilation is used with minor modifications based on our criteria. The resulting compilation of Great Power wars is given in Table 9-2.

In order to test the hypothesis that Great Power wars have become less frequent but more serious, we analyze war in terms of several key dimensions in addition to *frequency*. The *duration* of war refers to its total elapsed time (measured in years). The *extent* of war refers to the number of participating Great Powers. The *magnitude* of war, reflecting a joint spatial and temporal dimension and combining the extent and duration indicators, is the total nation-years of war for all participating Powers. The human destructiveness or *severity* of war is measured by the number of battle-connected deaths. Whereas the severity of war refers to loss of life in absolute terms, the *intensity* of war reflects the human destructiveness in relative terms and is the ratio of battle deaths to European population. The *concentration* of war in space and time is another important dimension and is the ratio of battle deaths to nation-years of war. The 64 Great Powers wars since 1495 are measured along these dimensions using data from the Wright, Sorokin, and Singer-Small compilations. . . .

Our first question is whether Great Power wars are becoming more or less frequent over time. There is little doubt about the answer. . . . There has been a continuous decline in the number of Great Power wars in each century from the sixteenth to the nineteenth, with a very slight increase in the twentieth century. Over 75% of the Great Power wars occur in the first half of the 480-year system (prior to 1735), while less than 25% occur in the last 240 years. An examination of the data based on a five-year period of aggregation demonstrates that only 25% of the half-decades since 1815 have witnessed the initiation of Great Power war, compared to nearly 60% in the previous three centuries. The relative absence of Great Power war in the nineteenth century (except for the 1850-1875 period) is quite striking, particularly in contrast with the relatively high frequency of Great Power war in earlier periods (ranging up to nine in one 25-year period in the sixteenth century). The average frequency of Great Power war in the twentieth century is only a fourth of its average frequency in the sixteenth century.

Having established that Great Power war has been declining in frequency, let us now ask our second question: Given that a Great Power war occurs, is it getting more or less serious in terms of the dimensions of duration, extent, magnitude, severity, intensity, and concentration? . . . [My analysis indicates] that over the last five centuries Great Power wars have become increasingly serious in every respect but duration. While the *duration* of Great Power wars has remained basically constant since the late fifteenth century, the *extent* of Great Power wars has increased sharply. . . . [T]he number of Powers participating in Great Power war has been increasing by approximately .006 per year (regardless of whether a war actually occurs) or by over one Power every two centuries. The significance of this is evident when one considers that the average number of Powers participating in a single Great Power war is only 3.2 (and the median only 2.5). In more substantive terms, an analysis [of the data] . . . would suggest the following: Prior to the Thirty Years War, no conflict involved more than four Powers and most wars involved two Powers; from the early seventeenth century to the early nineteenth century, the number of warring Powers varied from one to six, the median being four; no war in the nineteenth century involved more than three Powers, but the two World Wars in the twentieth century involved seven and eight Powers, respectively. Furthermore, the proportion of Great Power wars which involve a large number of Powers is much higher in recent times than previously. Since

Vienna, for example, two-thirds of these wars have involved three or more Powers, whereas previously this ratio was less than half. Thus the proportion of conflicts which expand into larger wars involving several Powers has been increasing over time.

The *magnitude* of Great Power war has also been increasing but less than half as fast as its extent. . . . [Data] suggests that the magnitude of war has been increasing by over two nation-years each century (compared to a mean of 16, median of 11). This is not statistically significant, however, given the large variance in magnitude. Great Power wars have also become increasingly destructive in terms of all of the fatality-based indicators. . . .

The *severity* of Great Power war has been increasing at an average rate of .62% each year. At this rate, the average number of battle deaths in a Great Power war has doubled every 110 years or so. The *intensity* of war has increased nearly as rapidly (.46% per year), doubling every 150 years. The most pronounced trend in Great Power war . . . is its increasing *concentration* over time. The number of battle deaths has increased at a rate of .67% per year, doubling every 100 years. An examination of the scattergrams of the data would clearly reveal that these upward trends are not simply the product of the enormous destructiveness of two World Wars, but would hold true without them.

Interpretation of the Historical Trends

The preceding data analysis leaves little doubt regarding historical changes in wars between the Great Powers over the last five hundred years. Great Power wars have been rapidly diminishing in frequency but increasing in extent, severity, intensity, concentration, and (to a certain degree) magnitude. That is, Great Power wars have involved an increasing number of belligerent Powers, and nation-years of war, and have become increasingly violent in terms of absolute and per capita battle deaths and their relative number per nation-year of war. Of the important dimensions of Great Power war defined here, only its frequency has diminished and only its duration has been relatively constant over time. The hypothesis that Great Power wars have become less frequent but more serious or destructive is confirmed beyond any reasonable doubt.

The description of historical trends is easier than their explanation, however. Before it could be fully accepted, such an explanation would itself have to be tested against the historical evidence. This would require the operationalization and measurement of the explanatory variables (and plausible control variables as well) in as systematic a manner as we have dealt with the dependent variable. This is an enormous task lying far beyond the scope of this study. Having rigorously and systematically described longitudinal trends in Great Power wars, we can here only hypothesize about their theoretical explanations, by identifying the important variables and

445

suggesting plausible theoretical linkages.

Of all the trends, perhaps most puzzling is the relatively unchanging duration of Great Power war. We might have expected that improvements in communications and logistics would have increased the speed of military operations on the battlefield and that innovations in military technology and the increasing destructiveness of military conflict would have increased the costs of war; both would presumably force an earlier termination of the hostilities. Obviously, there are other variables which counteract this tendency. While the costs of war have become much greater, the gradual industrialization of basically agricultural societies has increased their economic capacity to sustain a war and accept the costs. We might also hypothesize that, in spite of the enormous changes in military technology, the defense has managed to keep up with the offense, so that it takes equally long to obtain a decisive advantage on the battlefield. Finally, the increasing organizational momentum and incrementalism generated by a larger and more firmly entrenched bureaucracy, and the increasing political insecurity of elites (deriving from the decline of dynastic legitimacy) in conjunction with increasing nationalist pressures, both make it ever more difficult to withdraw from a costly but inconclusive war.

Equally interesting is the fact that an ever-increasing number (and proportion) of Great Powers have been participating in these wars. We might hypothesize that this derives in part from the increasing interdependence of the modern Great Power security system. As the Great Powers evolved from dynastic to nation-states, their "national interests," as well as their capabilities to project power in defense of their interests, tended to expand and their commercial relationships also became closer. The Great Powers came increasingly to perceive their own strategic and economic interests as dependent on power relationships in the system as a whole, and were increasingly likely to intervene in external wars to maintain a "balance of power" or their own influence and prestige. Hence the extent (and also the magnitude) of Great Power war has increased over time.

Let us now consider the increasing destructiveness of war in terms of severity, intensity, and concentration. The most obvious explanation, of course, is *technological:* the major changes not only in the destructive power of weapons, but also in their range, accuracy, volume of fire, mobility, and penetrability, and the speed and efficiency of military transport and communications systems. In addition, there has been an increasing economic capacity to produce a larger quantity of weapons and support systems. Much of the increased capacity for violence over the past centuries can be traced to the changes in production and transport generated by the industrial revolution; the mechanization of war at the beginning of the twentieth century; the development of airpower a few decades later; and (in terms of potential destruction for the future) the development of nuclear weapons and global delivery systems by the second half of this century.

446

Technological innovation alone, however, cannot fully explain the increasing destructiveness of Great Power wars in the last five centuries. There are several interrelated political, socioeconomic, and cultural factors contributing to the gradual emergence of total war. Let us briefly consider these in approximate chronological sequence. First was the increasing *rationalization* of military power under the state, beginning in the late fifteenth century and intensifying after the legal codification of the existing sovereign state system at Westphalia. The wars for the personal honor, vengeance, and enrichment of kings and nobles in [the] Middle Ages (which may have contributed to their frequent but limited nature) were increasingly replaced by the "rational" use of force as an efficient instrument of policy for the achievement of political objectives, first by dynastic/territorial political systems and ultimately by nation-states. The seriousness of the wars grew proportionally with the expansion of these political objectives, from personal gain, to the territorial aggrandizement of the state, to the national ambitions of an entire people.

Reinforcing this was the increasing *centralization* of political power within the state. This began with the gradual subordination of feudal interests to centralized state authority in the early sixteenth century, and intensified in the late seventeenth century with the development of an administrative and financial system capable of supporting a military establishment and providing the logistical basis for an expanded military effort.

Contributing further to the power of states and their ability to make war was the *commercialization* of war beginning in the early seventeenth century. There was an increasingly symbiotic relationship between the state and the commercial classes. Commerce generated the wealth necessary to sustain war and war in turn became a means of expanding commerce. In the mercantilist conception, commerce was a continuation of war (with an admixture of other means) and war was a continuation of commerce. The merchants' enthusiasm for war diminished somewhat as this mercantilist system was replaced by free trade in the late eighteenth century, but the link was hardly broken and subsequent economic progress contributed further to the state's capacity for war.

This period also marked the emerging *popularization* of war: the rise of nationalism and popular ideology, the institution of conscripted manpower, and the creation of the "nation in arms." Each of these phenomena contributed to the enhancement of the military power of the state.

The state's ability to utilize these expanding resources was furthered by the *professionalization* of military power in the late nineteenth century. This refers to the development of a peacetime military establishment directed by a new professional military elite that was independent of the aristocracy, headed by a general staff system, run according to new principles of scientific management, and supported by a system of military academies. These developments not only increased the efficiency of the conduct of war; they also enhanced the legitimacy of the military profession and contributed to the trends towards militarism, the acceptance of the values of the military subculture as the dominant values of society. At the same time, the earlier moral and cultural restraints on war associated with the Christian and Humanist traditions were gradually eroded by the materialism and individualism of industrial society.

These trends culminated in World War II with what Millis calls the *scientific revolution* in war: the harnessing, for the first time, of the entire scientific, engineering, and technological capacities of the nation directly for the conduct of the war. This mobilization of the intellectual as well as material and social resources of the nation for the purposes of enhancing military power continues now in peacetime. These political, social and cultural developments, in conjunction with technological innovation, have been largely responsible for the increasing destructiveness of war.

Let us consider some plausible explanations for the declining frequency of Great Power war. It can generally be argued that the potential benefits of Great Power war have not kept up with their rising human and economic costs. Warfare has involved enormous increases in casualties and human suffering, the physical destruction of industrial infrastructure, and opportunity costs for society deriving from increasing costs of weapons systems, manpower, and logistics. The greater tendency toward external intervention in Great Power war (described above) further raises the costs or reduces the potential benefits from war, whether by adding the military burden of an additional enemy or by necessitating the sharing of the gains with an ally. The declining legitimacy of Great Power war has increased its diplomatic and domestic political costs. Finally, the changing bases of national power and the declining value of territorial conquest have reduced the potential benefits of Great Power war, as has the increasing congruence between state and ethnic boundaries (at least for the Great Powers). These increasing costs of Great Power war relative to its perceived benefits have reduced its utility as a rational instrument of state policy and largely account for its declining frequency.

As noted earlier, these statements should be interpreted as hypotheses to be tested rather than empirically confirmed theoretical generalizations. The existing literature on the evolution of war provides an ample reservoir of information from which data can be extracted to test these hypotheses. It should be recognized, however, that such a task would involve some very difficult analytical and methodological problems.

We have established empirically that, over the last five centuries, wars between the Great Powers have become less frequent but more serious in terms of their extent, severity, intensity, concentration, and (to a certain degree) magnitude. We have also suggested some hypotheses to account for these trends, but these hypotheses have yet to be empirically confirmed. The "big" question of course, is whether there will be Great Power wars in the future, and if so, what will they be like? An extrapolation from past historical trends into the future would provide one possible answer to this question. Prediction in international relations presents major problems, however, particularly in the absence of an empirically confirmed explanation of past trends, and in an age in which the international system has undergone some fundamental transformations.

What is ultimately necessary for prediction is a *theory* of the causes and escalation of Great Power war and an analysis of how each of the variables and interrelationships of the theory has been affected by recent transformations of the international system. In this way we could generate a theory of Great Power war in the nuclear age, and therefore a basis for making predictions about the future.

■■■■ **9.2**

HARVEY STARR
BENJAMIN A. MOST

Patterns of Conflict: Quantitative Analysis and the Comparative Lessons of Third World Wars

The focus of this chapter is the lessons that can be drawn from quantitative comparative analyses of the trends, patterns, and relationships in recent Third World conflicts. Each Third World conflict provides its own lessons—lessons idiosyncratic to the special circumstances and conditions of that conflict. It is possible, however, to identify a set of factors, or variables, that are applicable to a wider sampling of such conflicts. The population of Third World conflicts may be summarized, or modeled, in terms of these variables to describe the aggregate lessons of wars in the Third World that have occurred in the post-1945 period.

In this chapter we will be taking such an aggregate, or comparative, perspective on the lessons of conflict. We wish to employ the basic notions of a comparative approach by comparing and contrasting across a number of cases and looking for patterns of similarities. This will permit us to make more general statements concerning conflict in the international system—statements that not only point out similarities but also permit us to identify significant differences. By creating a statistical baseline, we will have a starting point from which to judge the lessons presented in the following case studies and understand how unique or "normal" each case actually is.

We must make clear that the following discussion is intended to be a descriptive general introduction to the patterns of post-World War II conflict. Focusing on violent conflict in the Third World by no means implies that

Reprinted, by permission of the publisher, from *The Lessons of Recent Wars in the Third World*, Vol. 1 edited by Robert E. Harkavy and Stephanie G. Newman (Lexington, Mass.: Lexington Books, D. C. Heath and Company, Copyright © 1985, D. C. Heath and Company).

actual and potential violent conflict in other areas of the world is insignificant. However, the great preponderance of violence in the contemporary international system has erupted in Third World areas—either as internal violence or as cross-border war. This leads us to a second use of *context* in the discussion of patterns of Third World conflict. In addition to a general context of lessons to aid in the understanding and utility of case studies, the patterns discussed here provide an important context for each state or any international actor in the system. Simply, each nation-state is embedded in an international system that constrains its possible and probable behavior. Violent conflict in the Third World constitutes at least one important element in the environment of states in other areas of the world. Insofar as it has the actual or potential capability of affecting those other states, Third World conflict constitutes a phenomenon that other states (as well as Third World states) must understand and may need to take into account in their foreign policy formulation and execution.

In this chapter, we will specifically be looking at the forms, levels, locales, and overall effects of Third World conflict. These variables will have an impact on the parties and forces involved, the strategies they follow, the possibility of outside intervention, the expansion of the war, and the like. In turn, these questions of strategy, intervention, and expansion will affect questions of war termination, military and political payoffs, and costs.

Before moving to the analyses, we will provide a brief consideration of the validity of the quantitative comparative approach and its utility for drawing lessons that are policy-relevant.

The Validity and Utility of the Comparative Approach

Consider for a moment just what we mean by the term *lesson*. In our view, the word is most commonly connected with the drawing of inferences or the making of generalizations; something has happened, presumably for some reason, which we believe we can specify, and we wish to generalize to other possible future occurrences. Sometimes we wish to avoid the reappearance of the event altogether; in other instances, we want to alter the outcome should similar situations develop in the future, or we may wish to understand why an occurrence turned out the way it did, so that we can reproduce that result in the future. We might want to understand what has happened so that we can better learn to anticipate or recognize problems while they are still in their early phases of development or to understand the effects of previous policies.

Other lessons might be sought; this listing is by no means exhaustive. The point is that efforts to specify or delineate lessons seem closely related to the drawing of inferences and the making of generalizations from the study of a number of cases of conflict in the Third World. To do this, however, we must determine what evidence, analyzed in what ways or developed using what types of research designs and approaches provides an adequate basis for drawing inferences. Should one, for example, use historical or experiential evidence from a single case—or would one be better advised to be as systematic as possible, specifying each step in the analysis, developing quantitative data, and assessing them across large numbers of cases or within a given case across time?

No one way of proceeding is always appropriate; analysts and interpreters need to figure out what they want to say and select the methods appropriate to those ends. Such methods should be seen as tools, and the question we must ask continually is whether they are useful or not useful given the task at hand.

If *lessons* means (in a minimal sense) learning the relationships between variables in one case to be able to understand those relationships in another case, one must compare cases. Using theoretical or conceptual frameworks, a small set of "important" variables is selected for such comparison. This is necessary because it would be impossible to compare cases if the totality (if one could indeed construct such a thing) of those cases was used; each case is truly unique. For a number of reasons relating to the logic of research design, efforts to draw lessons seem likely to be best advanced by studies that utilize a variant of two basic comparative research designs: cross-sectional and time-series. The former involves looking across a large number of cases at one point in time; the latter involves looking at a single case across a large number of time points. In both cases, one is comparing cases on a theoretically selected set of variables, a set much smaller than that used in a case study.

One can perhaps begin to understand the reasoning behind these research designs by noting, first, that each datum, "fact," or variable can be defined on three dimensions: it is only one of many possible variables; it is selected from a particular polity or case; and it is drawn from a specific point in time. Taken together, these three dimensions may be understood to define a hypothetical cube that encompasses all of the "facts" in the world (see Figure 9-1, a).

In parts b, c, and d of Figure 9-1, three different ways of "slicing" reality are demonstrated. A case study approach focuses on the relationships among a large number of variables in one case at a single point in time. A cross-sectional (or synchronic) design focuses on the relationships among variables in a large number of cases at a single point in time. Finally, a time-series (or diachronic) design focuses on the relationships that hold through a large number of points in time in a single case.

To summarize a lengthy and complex set of arguments found in the literature, the case study approach, as a rule, is likely to produce complete explanations and yield lessons that have a demonstrated applicability to only one case and an unspecified generalizability across space and through time. . . . The output of a case study is generally difficult to evaluate (because of the generally low degree of explicitness) and is likely to yield findings that are difficult to explain to decision makers because of their complexity and detail. To the extent that proponents of case studies stress that the unique and idiosyncratic nature of the world dictates their approach, they implicitly embrace the comparative perspective when they attempt to apply the lessons learned in a

Figure 9-1 Models for Research Design: (a) hypothetical cube encompassing all of the "facts" in the world; (b) case study approach—one entity, one point in time, many variables; (c) cross-sectional design—one to N entities analyzed simultaneously, one point in time, few variables; (d) time-series design—one entity, up to an infinite number of time points *J*, few variables.

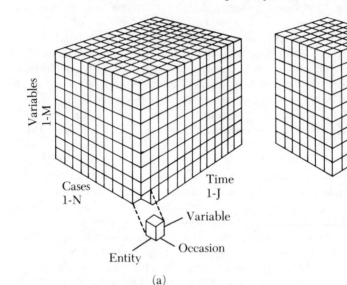

(a)   (b)

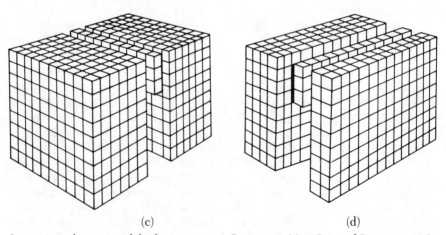

(c)   (d)

Source: An earlier version of this figure appears in Benjamin A. Most, *Points of Departure: An Introduction to the Systematic Study of Public Policy* (Cambridge, Mass.: Schenkman, forthcoming). That figure, in turn, is based on a figure in John V. Gillespie, "An Introduction to Macro-Cross National Research," in John V. Gillespie and Betty Nesvold, eds., *Macro-Quantitative Analysis* (Beverly Hills, Calif.: Sage, 1971).

case study to current problems; this necessarily involves making at least implicit comparisons. Thus, they reason like comparativists but adopt none of the systematic rigor and precision of the comparative approach.

The cross-sectional design, in contrast, is capable of producing relatively simple and partial (that is, somewhat inaccurate) explanations that have some demonstrated generality and the potential for greater generalizability across additional cases. Because analysts who use the cross-sectional design tend to be more explicit about their initial assumptions, biases, and expectations, about how they operationalize their concepts, about how they select and manipulate their data and weigh their evidence, and about the predictions they wish to make and the evidence that would refute those predictions, readers will be better able to evaluate the quality of their work. While this type of comparative design thus has certain advantages, it is by no means a cure-all. It limits one to static views and correlational findings. The results from the analysis may or may not be generalizable to different points in time.

The attributes of the time-series design are somewhat similar to those of the cross-sectional approach insofar as it, too, is likely to yield simple and partial explanations. In this instance, however, the demonstrated generality is through time within a given case; the likely potential for further generalizability is to more time points in that case. Time-series research has the potential for yielding dynamic findings. Unfortunately, the time-series approach leaves unexplored the question of whether or not the lessons are generalizable across space to other cases. It is therefore less well suited than the cross-sectional design for isolating patterns and tendencies that hold across a number of cases.

Analysts typically compensate for limitations in the cross-sectional and time-series designs by selecting independent and dependent variables from different time slices, or by executing a "comparative statics" design in which separate cross-sectional analyses are conducted on several slices of time. Although this solves many of the problems of each approach, there is no assurance that the comparative method will necessarily enable the investigator to identify cause and effect. However, it is logically impossible to identify cause-and-effect relationships and to sort out genuine linkages from those that are the result of happenstance unless one adopts an explicitly comparative approach. The case study method alone will not and cannot suffice. The comparative method is logically necessary—though admittedly not sufficient— for drawing the types of lessons in which we are often interested.

Patterns and Trends in Third World Conflicts

Forms of Conflict

Few concepts in the study of international relations and foreign policy are neat and precise. The concepts of violent conflict and war are not exceptions.

Conceptualizations, measurement criteria, and operational indicators vary markedly across different war data sets and from one research project to another.

Some of these distinctions are reflected in the major studies that have focused on wars since the Napoleonic period. Quincy Wright stressed the "legalist" notion that war was a special state of international law that took place between legally similar entities (that is, states) and that was bounded by such legal activities as declarations of war, peace treaties, declarations of neutrality, and the like. Lewis F. Richardson, another pioneer in the systematic study of war, based his study on "deadliness." His primary criterion was death caused by violence, from one death up to magnitudes of deadliness in the 6.5 to 7.5 range (3,162,278 to 31,622,777 deaths). The Correlates of War Project has primarily used criteria that tap the large-scale, organized quality of war, combining aspects of both Wright's and Richardson's approaches. Wars must have at least one state taking part (interstate wars require at least one state on each side) and must cause at least 1000 battle deaths.

Studies that have investigated only the post-World War II period have used less stringent criteria for war. Istvan Kende, for example, uses the following guidelines: (1) there must be activities of regular armed forces on at least one side; (2) there must be a certain degree of organization and organized fighting on both sides; and (3) there must be a certain continuity between armed clashes. Events-data sets for all or some of the postwar systems have also attempted to categorize conflictual interactions. The Conflict and Peace Data Bank (COPDAB), for example, has created a fifteen-point cooperation-conflict scale, using events in the three "most conflictual" categories to create a conflict data set.

Although these studies make many distinctions, and could be compared in a variety of ways, one primary distinction is between interstate war and other forms such as civil war, colonial war, or extrasystemic war. Until World War II, when most observers thought of war, it was of the type called "interstate" (Correlates of War), "balance of power" (Wright), "border" (Kende), or "international" (Azar). Indeed, before World War II, this was the predominant form of violent international conflict. Wright's war data for 1900-1941 show that 80 percent were interstate wars.

Since World War II, however, that trend has been reversed. Kende's study of armed conflicts during the 1945-1976 period (120 such events are reported) indicates that only 15 percent of them were interstate, while the remaining 85 percent were some form of internal war. Thus, in contrast to earlier trends, most contemporary wars are being fought either between colonial powers and rebel groups or *within* the territory of a single state. Increasingly since World War II, moreover, we have seen the legal trappings of war being dropped; that is, wars have been fought without any declaration of the state of hostilities.

Although most of the legal aspect of war has been dispensed with, however, the somatic consequences of war—people dying—have continued to characterize war in this era. Indeed, two different compilations of casualties caused by post-1945 civil/internal wars indicate that the loss of life has been quite large. The Correlates of War Project, using a rigorous and highly specified set of criteria for inclusion, identify thirty civil wars between 1945 and 1980. These thirty conflicts lasted a total of 1,268 months, with an average duration of 3.5 years. It is not surprising that such protracted conflict would produce more than 3,830,000 battle-related deaths (an average of 127,700 deaths per civil war). Ruth Leger Sivard presents a list of wars between 1945 and 1983 from which eighty-six cases of civil war, civil strife, and colonial wars of independence can be identified. Sivard estimates a total of more than 11,750,000 military and civilian deaths resulting from these violent conflicts during this period. This staggering total averages out to more than 136,700 per case (not greatly discrepant from the Correlates of War average for military-related deaths). In line with past analyses of civil and international war, the civil wars of the contemporary era have tended to be long and deadly.

Two additional patterns discovered by Kende should also be noted. Focusing on three categories of war—internal antiregime, internal tribal, and border wars, all of which are coded as having occurred with or without foreign intervention—Kende observes that the principal form of conflict during the 1945-1976 era was internal antiregime with foreign participation. Somewhat surprisingly, however, internal tribal wars accounted for 30 percent of the conflicts between 1967 and 1976, up from 15.5 percent during the 1945-1970 period. Thus, many of the challenges to Third World governments seem *not* to be arising directly from foreign sources, although outside elements may play a role. Rather, threats increasingly appear to result from internal tribal and ethnic cleavages. Because of the heterogeneous nature of many Third World states—such as Lebanon—it seems fair to presume that this trend will continue.

The pattern that Kende observes in connection with the sources of foreign intervention in Third World conflict is also of interest. In the last ten years, Western involvement has dropped, but there has been more Third World and Socialist participation in the world's internal conflicts (again, Lebanon and Central America are good examples). It is no longer a matter of having a few excolonial powers ceasing to intervene. Rather, the trend indicates that regional intervention is increasing in frequency. In Africa, for instance, local armies have increased in size to the point where external use is now plausible (for example, the Tanzanian activity in Uganda). Although they are still small compared to the armies of other regions and as a ratio of population, the use of these local armies as a foreign policy tool for intervention is now an option.

The trend of regional intervention also highlights the changing roles of the United Nations and regional organizations in the management of local conflict. Recent research has indicated that referrals of conflicts to both the United Nations and regional organizations fell to a low point in the mid-1970s but rose again in 1980 to a level comparable to that of the early 1960s. However, the rates of success in "managing" conflicts for the United Nations (10 percent) and regional organizations (15 percent) in 1980 were the lowest for the entire 1945-1980 period.

It is also important to note that changes in the form of Third World conflicts have been accompanied in many instances by alterations in the nature of conflicts that are being waged. Put simply, the internal conflict that now characterizes most of the fighting in the Third World is highly politicized. This politicization derives from the fact that it is revolutionary conflict that challenges governments. This challenge may be motivated by ideological, political, economic, or ethnic goals. What we have, however, are governments being challenged by nonstate actors who wish to seize power (often wanting to change the entire institutional structure of the governing system) or to break off part of the state into a separate political entity. This challenge to governments is the heart of the growing politicization of conflict. Wars are fought to win the support of people and/or to alienate the people from the existing government. One can see this especially in Lebanon and Central America, but it is also apparent in the Spanish Sahara and the Horn of Africa.

Political factors, then, very often take precedence over strictly military ones. Revolutionary forms of war, such as guerrilla warfare (or violence such as terrorism), predominate. For a variety of reasons, they have become internationalized—for example, through proxy wars of the superpowers, through what Pierre Hassner has called "international civil war" (supporting those rebelling against one's opponent), or through "holy alliance" (supporting the governments of friends against their rebels). One very basic lesson that emerges from all of this should therefore be clear: A very different type of conflict has evolved in the post-World War II era. A related set of lessons seems implicit in the fact that the need for international organization has apparently increased at the same time that there has been a trend toward decay of the post-World War II conflict management regime. The increasing incidence of internal war in the Third World poses the familiar question of whether or not outside parties should intervene, and on which side. This, in turn, relates to questions of the role and activity of international organizations dedicated to order and conflict resolution.

Reviewing the outcomes of conflict, however, one lesson may be that it is still difficult to topple governments, especially if there is outside intervention to support the government. Looking at the Correlates of War civil war list, and removing the four cases that are still ongoing, governments have won in seventeen of twenty-six cases (65.4 percent); the opposition has won in nine cases (34.6 percent). In the eight cases in which there was intervention on the government's side, the government won six times (75 percent).

Thus, the international context within which states must act will be made much more complex by the changing forms of international conflict. Most Third World conflicts, internal in form, create ambiguity regarding the policy responses of outside powers (and often produce strange bedfellows, as in the Biafran war or even in the more traditional interstate war between Iraq and

Iran). Policy responses of specific states become entangled with the increasingly complicated issues of international law and the responses of international organizations. Internal war directly impinges on questions of the recognition of governments, the identification of the "legitimate" or "legal" government, more general issues of identification of the parties to conflict and their standing as legal international actors, legal strictures against intervention in the internal affairs of sovereign states, and equally explicit norms regarding the rights of self-determination and autonomy.

The United States and the Soviet Union, as superpowers with extensive alliance systems, spheres of interest, and, by definition, global concerns, will be more affected than most states by this complexity. How should states deal with aggression? What is aggression in this context, particularly given the ambiguity of the UN definition of aggression (Resolution on the Definition of Aggression, December 14, 1974, UNGA Res. 3314 [XXIX]) and its inability to handle internal conflict? Closely related to aggression is the question of whether or not the superpowers, especially the United States, should support the governments of friends and allies. Which ones require such support? Which ones deserve it? The internal nature of Third World conflict makes discrimination in the support of allies both more crucial and more difficult. The lessons of such conflicts force policymakers to confront the same questions of priorities that George Kennan posed a quarter of a century ago: Which areas of the world are of central interest to American policy and warrant possible intervention?

In sum, the changing nature of the forms of international conflict in the Third World creates a more ambiguous and complex environment for the foreign policy of states. The next two sections present variations on this theme, concerning the increase or decrease of international violence and the location of that violence.

Increase and Decrease in International Violence

Because of the evolution in the dominant forms of international conflict, some observers have claimed that the world is more warlike since World War II, while others claim it is less so. For the latter group, this appears to be so because of the growing infrequency of cross-border international wars. The former group points to both the increasing number of internal wars and the enormous loss of life since 1945: the total figure for Correlates of War international war and civil war is 7,205,000 battle deaths; Sivard claims a world total of 16 [million] military and civilian deaths.

What have the longer-run and short-run trends been in international conflict? A number of researchers, including Wright, Richardson, and the Correlates of War Project, have found cycles of international violence; that is, aggregating the amount of international violence in the system as a whole, alternating periods of peace and war have been found. The war-peace cycles discovered have usually been in the twenty- to thirty-year range. These studies have investigated the international system since the Napoleonic wars, although Wright's data cover the period from 1480 to 1965. The cyclical nature of the occurrence of war does not seem to have demonstrated any long-term increase or decrease in international conflict.

Richardson, using a variety of statistical and mathematical techniques, found that wars are distributed randomly in time, and he uncovered no evidence that war was becoming either more or less frequent. The Correlates of War Project, with a different set of wars but covering approximately the same time period (1816-1965, later updated to 1980), also found that interstate war was neither waxing nor waning; no trend could be discovered. This research did, however, find that extra-systemic war, between states and nonstate actors, was increasing during this period. Kende's first study seemed to support such a finding in the postwar period. His findings indicated that there was an increase, but mostly in internal war with outside intervention, not in the classic interstate border war.

Table 9-3 shows the steady increase in the average number of armed conflicts occurring during four-year time periods. The average rises from 6.3 in 1945-1948 to over 20 during 1965-1968. Kende's original study, which stopped in 1968, indicated an upward trend since World War II. However, as Kende's later study indicates, this trend began to reverse itself at the end of the 1960s, as the last two time periods in Table 9-3 show. The average number of wars for 1973-1976 is approximately the same as the average for the whole 1945-1976 period. Thus, instead of finding a major upward trend, it appears that we have another cycle. This finding is supported by the COPDAB data set, which reveals an average of twenty-five conflicts per year during the 1965-1970 period. This falls to an average of fourteen for 1971-1975 and fifteen for 1976-1979.

One possible lesson of this pattern in the rate of warfare during the 1945-

Table 9-3 Average Number of Wars, 1945-1976

Time Period	Average Number of Armed Conflicts
1945-1948	6.3
1949-1952	6.6
1953-1956	8.3
1957-1960	9.6
1961-1964	13.3
1965-1968	20.1
1969-1972	17.1
1973-1976	11.1

Source: Istvan Kende, "Twenty-Five Years of Local Wars," *Journal of Peace Research* 8 (1971): 5-27; and "Wars of Ten Years (1967-1976)," *Journal of Peace Research* 15 (1978): p. 228.

1980 period is that, *contrary* to allegations that the Soviet Union has increasingly supported revolutionary movements, that it has done so with increasing (some seem to assume "invariable") success, and *despite* the dramatic increase in the number of nations in the international system that could be involved in war and the general trend toward "nationalism," *there has not been an uninterrupted trend* in the overall rate of warfare.

The increase and decrease in the frequency of international conflict since World War II is closely related to both the change in the forms of conflict and the change in the location of and participants to conflict. Although the states are not faced with an ever more conflictual world, they must try to understand where and why and how international conflict is taking place and the prospects for the continuation of such trends.

Location of and Parties to Conflict

Before World War II, the majority of wars took place in Europe (or close by) and were fought by European powers. This reflects the Eurocentricity of an international system dominated by European technology and colonization. Yet a simple but striking fact is that since the end of World War II, very little violent conflict has taken place in Europe. War has taken place almost entirely on the territory of Asian, African, and Latin American countries. The arena of war has been the Third World, with the occurrence of internal wars that have been internationalized by external intervention.

As shown in Table 9-4, part A, only 5 of Kende's 120 armed conflicts (4 percent) during the 1945-1976 period occurred in Europe. For that period, the Middle East and Asia led the world in violent conflict (with 30 percent and 29 percent, respectively). The Third World as the arena for conflict is also confirmed by analyses using nation-years of war rather than simple frequency. As a measure of intensity, nation-years tap[s] the length of conflict and the number of states involved. Europe still contributed the fewest nation-years of war from 1945 to 1976, with only 3.8 percent. Using this measure, Asia ranked first, with 40.7 percent, and Africa moved into second place, with 25.5 percent. This reflects the short, sharp interstate wars in the Middle East in contrast to the many protracted, internal anticolonial and guerrilla wars of Asia and Africa.

One of the more important trends to note is the increasing occurrence of armed conflict in Africa. Part A of Table 9-4 also indicates the distribution of wars over the 1967-1976 period. The largest rise during this period was in Africa, with 17.5 percent during the whole 1945-1976 period but 28.6 percent during the last ten years of that period. This is particularly evident when using the nation-years measure of intensity of conflict; Africa accounts for 35 percent of nation-years of war over the 1967-1976 period. This appears to be related to the aforementioned increase in tribal/ethnic-based antiregime activity, but it is also at least partially a result of the conflict directed against white-dominated

Table 9-4   Distribution of International Conflicts in the Postwar System

A. Geographic Distribution of Wars

	Number of Wars		Nation-Years of War	
	1945-1976	1967-1976	1945-1976	1967-1976
Europe	5 (4.0%)	1 (0.02%)	3.8%	4.7%
Asia	35 (29.0%)	12 (24.5%)	40.7%	33.9%
Middle East	36 (30.0%)	17 (34.7%)	19.4%	17.4%
Africa	21 (17.5%)	14 (28.6%)	25.5%	35.0%
Latin America	23 (19.0%)	5 (10.2%)	10.7%	9.0%

B. COPDAB Data on Interventions

Intervening Parties	1965-1970	1971-1975	1976-1979	Total
Developed West	58	21	2	81
Third World	8	21	13	42
Communist states	3	1	8	12

C. Locations of Terrorist Incidents, 1968-1975

Location	Number of Incidents
Atlantic community	572 (49.0%)
Middle East	159 (13.6%)
Asia	102 (8.7%)
East Europe	18 (1.5%)
Latin America	282 (24.0%)
Africa	37 (3.2%)

Sources: Part A: Istvan Kende, "Wars of Ten Years (1967-1976)," *Journal of Peace Research* 15 (1978): 229. Part B: William Eckhardt and Edward Azar, "Major World Conflicts and Interventions, 1945 to 1975," *International Interactions* 5 (1978): 75-109. Part C: Edward Mickolus, "Trends in Transnational Terrorism," in M. H. Livingston, ed., *International Terrorism in the Contemporary World* (Westport, Conn.: Greenwood Press, 1978).

rule in the former Portuguese colonies, Rhodesia and South Africa. In addition, the tacit U.S.-Soviet agreement not to intervene in Africa appears to have broken down, beginning with Soviet activities in Angola. This latter point, as well as the multiethnic nature of most African states and the increasing willingness by regional powers to intervene, indicates that Africa should continue to see high levels of violent conflict.

As noted, many internal conflicts were fought with some external intervention. Kende observes that for the whole 1945-1976 period, 38 percent of the armed conflicts were fought with foreign participation; for the 1967-1976 period, 40 percent were fought with foreign participation. The Center for

Defense Information study notes that foreign combat troops were involved in eight (20 percent) of the forty violent conflicts occurring in 1983. Kende's data and the COPDAB data agree that the Western powers were the major interveners until the early 1970s. Kende's first study had the United States as the most frequent intervener (in twenty-six of ninety-seven armed conflicts), followed by Britain with nineteen and France with twelve. The COPDAB data in part B of Table 9-4 also indicate that the developed West was the major intervention force during the 1965-1970 period.

Both Kende and COPDAB also demonstrate that Western intervention has decreased. Kende notes that, from 1945 to 1966, developed capitalist countries intervened forty-four times, whereas the Third World and Socialist countries each had three interventions. In the 1967-1976 period, the Western interventions numbered only twenty, compared to fourteen from Third World countries and three from Socialist countries. The COPDAB data in part B also indicate that Third World interventions matched Western activity in the 1971-1975 period, and both Third World and Communist activity surpassed Western interventions during 1976-1979. For 1983, six of the eight interventions involving combat troops identified by the Center for Defense Information came from Socialist countries (for example, Vietnam in Cambodia), one such intervention was Third World (Syria in Lebanon), and one was Western (United States). Eckhardt and Azar note simply: "The era of Western imperialism in terms of military intervention would seem to have come to an end." Although we may not want to go that far, there has certainly been a change in the nature of interventionary states. This, too, makes for a more complex international environment.

We have noted that intervention on behalf of the government appears to favor that side in civil conflict, but there are still many confounding factors in predicting the outcomes of conflict involving Third World states (either internal or cross-border wars). One lesson of the postwar period is that simple preponderance in military capability does not ensure victory. As Andrew Mack has pointed out, large, developed states fighting local wars are caught in an asymmetry that militates against success; just because they are large and their survival is not threatened, they cannot mobilize the will or the resources needed to defeat a smaller opponent whose survival *is* at stake. This model of power as the willingness to suffer was most clearly demonstrated in the Vietnam conflict. North Vietnam was willing to suffer—to not be defeated—in order to win. The losses accepted were considerably beyond those that forced states to concede in other modern wars.

The location of contemporary conflict is clearly of importance, both for theory and for policy. A brief discussion of some of the reasons for this distribution may highlight reasons for its continuance. First, there is the general opportunity for the occurrence of these forms of conflict. There are presently more than 160 states in the system, most of them Third World states that have attained independence since 1945 and very few of which are internally homogeneous. Various subcultural cleavages tear at the fabric of these societies. At the same time, most of these states are less developed and are struggling to improve economically and create the infrastructure of the modern state. The challenges and problems they face are enormous, creating much internal turmoil and instability. In addition, they are states without the habit and precedent of peaceful change. Many lack mechanisms for a regular or peaceful change of government or transfer of political power. Many, such as in the Horn of Africa or the Spanish Sahara, have also inherited border conflicts as a result of the artificial boundaries drawn by the colonial powers, which both exacerbate tribal or ethnic cleavages and provide further opportunities for internal and external conflict. Finally, such vulnerable states exist in a world where two superpowers espouse conflicting ideologies and economic and governmental systems and where a call for aid will be heard by one and the other will move to aid the opponent, whether government or challenger. All of these factors tend to reinforce the patterns of Third World conflict described here.

Internal problems also make many states targets for external "penetration," to use [James N.] Rosenau's term. The growing economic and ecological interdependence of the system makes such penetration more likely. Conflict and intervention are possible consequences of the sensitivity and vulnerability that come with interdependence. The relationship between internal conflict and the internationalization of conflict could also be reversed, however. Government leaders, recognizing the problems sketched out here, could try various strategies at "nation-building"—the drawing together of diverse peoples into one group with nationalist feelings of group identity. Early nation-builders, such as Sukarno, Nkrumah, and Nasser, often used the existence of external opponents as a means to attempt to bring about internal cohesion. The possible relationship between external threat and internal unity has been developed by sociologists such as [Georg] Simmel and [Lewis A.] Coser. Conditions for the success of such a strategy are not easy or automatic. This strategy may lead to external intervention in one's affairs or to interstate conflicts. Idi Amin's miscalculations regarding Tanzania led to a war that looked very much like a standard interstate war. However, the Tanzanian goal was simply to remove Amin and aid his internal opponents, so it could also be classified as external intervention. The point in this example, however, was how external enemies were used for internal purposes (on the part of Amin) and how this strategy could lead to international conflict.

Another lesson concerning terrorism may be found by investigating the location of transnational terrorist activity and other forms of armed violence. Part C of Table 9-4 shows the geographic distribution of 1,170 transnational terrorist incidents studied by Mickolus. Note that the West (the Atlantic community) serves as the location for most of the activity, while Africa has the least. Transnational terrorism appears to occur where other forms of international violence do not appear. The reasons for this provide a useful contrast between war—especially the various forms of internal, guerrilla war—and terrorism.

Clearly, if one is at war to overthrow a specific government, then terrorism (the "weapon of the weakest") is not necessary for its purposes of propaganda, highlighting a cause, or discomforting the government. Where there is internal war, there is no need for terrorism. If, however, the government is so strong that internal war is out of the question, then the terrorist weapon is more appropriate. The states of the Atlantic community, which, for a variety of reasons, have not experienced war, have thus been the location of terrorist activity. More important, these states are also democracies. If "terrorism is theater," as suggested by Brian Jenkins, then terrorists require media that will focus attention on their acts. The free mass media of democracy provide the best environment for terrorist activities; the figures reported for Eastern Europe, for example, comprise only 1.5 percent of the total terrorist activities identified by Mickolus.

Although there are some similarities between terrorism and guerrilla war activities, this comparison of location highlights the great differences between the two forms of violence and the very different lessons each provides. The character of the states and situations in which each form occurs says much about the utility and purposes of each. There are also clues here to the manner in which states could or should respond to these forms of conflict in the international environment.

Contagion and Diffusion: Do Dominoes Fall?

Returning to the question of the opportunity for conflict, it should be noted that research on the relationship between borders and war has indicated that small nations' numbers of borders are correlated with their war involvements. More important, perhaps, is the consistent finding across several data sets, samples of nations, and time frames that countries with warring states on their borders, in contrast to countries whose neighbors are at peace, are significantly more likely to experience conflicts of their own. Although additional investigations are in progress, the preliminary evidence suggests—as many U.S. national security policymakers have argued—that some types of "first" wars, under at least certain conditions, do have a potential for destabilizing nations and areas beyond the arena in which the conflict initially erupts.

The increase in the number of states, especially in Africa but throughout the Third World, the resulting increase in the aggregate number of international frontiers, and the concomitant expansion in the number of nations that could trigger diffusion processes or be affected by them, suggest a likely continuation of these trends. The populations that can initiate or receive the "war disease" is growing. For a variety of reasons, both external (for example, numbers of borders and dependent status) and internal (for example, ethnic or tribal divisions and low degrees of government institutionalization), more and more of that population seems vulnerable to catching the disease.

This does not mean that Communism will spread from one nation to another in the Third World, as some analysts and observers have contended. Work on diffusion and contagion has focused to date on the spread of war occurrences, not on the outcomes of the wars. Thus, it does not really demonstrate that "dominoes" actually "fall." Nevertheless, the lesson from this work is that there is at least some validity to one aspect of the domino theory. If the analyses to date are correct, one consequence of war is more war. Thus, the outbreak of conflict in one nation or between one pair of nations should indeed alert decision makers to the possibility that other, neighboring nations could soon experience similar events.

Conclusion

We have presented a number of patterns and trends derived from cross-sectional studies employing different data sets of war and violent conflict since 1945. The description of the international system presented here, which derives from an analysis of the total population of conflicts identified by these data sets, indicates that there are still decision makers, states, and nonstate actors willing to use violence to achieve their goals.

Although most of these conflicts are internal, the utility of violence between states is also quite evident—producing, according to Correlates of War data, over three million battle casualties in the post-World War II era (with the Iraq-Iran war being the most prominent contemporary example). The data indicate that organized violence continues to destroy large numbers of human beings and that this violence is occurring in the Third World. It has demonstrated a tendency to diffuse across space, so that the occurrence of violent conflict is dangerous to neighboring states as well (even if the conflict is internal or civil). This is in line with identified short-term trends indicating an increase in violence between states and nonstate actors.

The patterns and trends outlined here also indicate that conflict in the Third World is highly politicized and largely internal, with revolutionary conflict subjected to intervention from external sources. The pool of possible sites for conflict and possible interveners is extensive, drawing upon most of the global system, not just Western "imperialists." The internal nature of these Third World conflicts muddies up and makes much more complex the interpretation of the guidelines offered by traditional views of security, by international law concerning behavior during war, and by norms concerning intervention in the internal affairs of sovereign states (at a time when it appears that the international conflict management regime is in decline). Although Quincy Wright attempted to define war as a special legal situation between two actors of equal legal status, contemporary conflict often deals with actors of unequal legal status and raises issues of sovereignty and intervention in internal affairs.

Although this brief conclusion summarizes the major points developed in this chapter, a number of other generalizations could be presented. Our point is simply that such a characterization of the contemporary system (and the two contexts discussed at the beginning of the chapter) could be developed only by a systematic survey of the total universe of conflict as identified in the various data sets. As noted, whereas the case studies presented later in this volume will provide rich detail on each particular conflict, we have attempted here to provide a broader context within which to place those studies.

███████ **9.3**

ANDREW MACK

Why Big Nations Lose Small Wars: The Politics of Asymmetric Conflict

A cursory examination of the history of imperialist expansion in the late nineteenth and early twentieth century reveals one thing very clearly: Third-World resistance, where it existed, was crushed with speedy efficiency. In terms of conventional military thinking such successes were not unexpected. Indeed, together with the Allied experience in the first and second World Wars, they served to reinforce and to rigidify the pervasive notion that superiority in military capability (conventionally defined) will mean victory in war. However, the history of a number of conflicts in the period following World War II showed that military and technological superiority may be a highly unreliable guide to the outcome of wars. In Indochina (1946-54), Indonesia (1947-49), Algeria, Cyprus, Aden, Morocco, and Tunisia, local nationalist forces gained their objectives in armed confrontations with industrial powers which possessed an overwhelming superiority in conventional military capability. These wars were not exclusively a colonial phenomenon, as was demonstrated by the failure of the United States to defeat its opponents in Vietnam. . . .

The purpose of this paper is to attempt to provide a "pre-theoretical perspective" within which the *outcome* of such "asymmetric conflicts" may be explained. In the field of conflict research, the study of the outcome and the conduct of wars, as against that of their *etiology*, has received remarkably little attention. The outcome of "asymmetric conflicts" as described in this paper has been almost totally neglected. . . .

For students of strategy the importance of these wars lies in the fact that the simplistic but once prevalent assumption—that conventional military

From *World Politics* 27, no. 2 (January 1975). Copyright © 1975 by Princeton University Press.

superiority necessarily prevails in war—has been destroyed. What is also interesting is that although the metropolitan powers did not *win* militarily, neither were they *defeated* militarily. Indeed the military defeat of the metropolis itself was impossible since the insurgents lacked an invasion capability. In every case, success for the insurgents arose not from a military victory on the ground—though military successes may have been a contributory cause—but rather from the progressive attrition of their opponents' *political* capability to wage war. In such asymmetric conflicts, insurgents may gain political victory from a situation of military stalemate *or even defeat.*

The most recent and obvious example of this type of conflict is the American war in Vietnam, which has brought home several important lessons. First, it has provided the most obvious demonstration of the falsity of the assumptions that underlie the "capability" conception of power. Not only does superiority in military force (conventionally defined) not guarantee victory; it may, under certain circumstances, be positively counter-productive. Second, the Vietnam conflict has demonstrated how, under certain conditions, the theatre of war extends well beyond the battlefield to encompass the policy and social institutions of the external power. The Vietnam war may be seen as having been fought on two fronts—one bloody and indecisive in the forests and mountains of Indochina, the other essentially nonviolent—but ultimately more decisive—within the polity and social institutions of the United States. The nature of the relationship between these two conflicts—which are in fact different facets of the same conflict—is critical to an understanding of the outcome of the war. However, the American experience was in no sense unique, except to Americans. In 1954 the Vietminh destroyed the French forces which were mustered at Dien Bien Phu in a classic set piece battle. The direct military costs to the French have been much exaggerated; only 3 per cent of the total French forces in Indochina were involved. The psychological effects—like those of the Tet offensive some fourteen years later—were shattering, however. The Vietminh did not of course defeat France militarily. They lacked not only the capability but also any interest in attempting such a move. Dien Bien Phu, however, had the effect of destroying the *political* capability ("will" in the language of classical strategy) of the French Government to mobilize further troops and to continue the struggle—this despite the fact that the greater part of the financial costs of the war were being borne by the United States. Third, the Vietnam war, which for the Vietnamese revolutionaries has now lasted over a quarter of a century, has emphasized the enormous importance which guerrilla strategists place on "protracted warfare." This is articulated most clearly in Mao Tse-tung's works, but it is also found in the military writings of General Giap and Truong Chinh and in the works of the leading African guerrilla strategists, Cabral and Mondlane. The certainty of eventual victory which is the result of intensive political mobilization by the guerrilla leadership is the key to what [Steven] Rosen sees as a critical factor in such conflicts—namely, the willingness to absorb costs. [E. L.] Katzenbach has

noted of Mao's strategic theory that it is based on the premise that "if the totality of the population can be made to resist surrender, this resistance can be
turned into a war of attrition which will eventually and inevitably be
victorious. Or, as Henry Kissinger more succinctly observed in 1969: "The
guerrilla wins if he does not lose."

Above all, Vietnam has been a reminder that in war the ultimate aim must
be to affect the will of the enemy. Most strategic theorists would of course con-
cur with this view. But in practice, and at the risk of oversimplification, it may
be noted that it is a prevalent military belief that if an opponent's military capability to wage war can be destroyed, his "will" to continue the struggle is irrelevant since the means to that end are no longer available. It is not surprising
that this should be a prevalent belief in modern industrial societies: strategic
doctrine tends to mold itself to available technology, as critics of strategic
weapons deployment have forcefully pointed out. Neither is it surprising that
guerrilla strategists should see strategy in very different terms. Lacking the
technological capability or the basic resources to destroy the external enemy's
military capability, they must of necessity aim to destroy his political
capability. If the external power's "will" to continue the struggle is destroyed,
then its military capability—no matter how powerful—is totally irrelevant.
One aim of this paper is to show how and why, in certain types of conflict, conventional military superiority is not merely useless, but may actually be
counter-productive. The implications for those military systems which rely
almost wholly on industrial power and advanced technology need hardly be
spelled out.

As I have noted above, in none of the asymmetric conflicts did the local
insurgents have the capability to invade their metropolitan opponents' homeland. It *necessarily* follows that insurgents can only achieve their ends if their
opponents' *political* capability to wage war is destroyed. This is true whether
the insurgents are revolutionaries or right-wing nationalists, whether they rely
on guerrilla warfare, urban terrorism, or even nonviolence. The destruction of
the external power's forces in the field places no *material* obstacle in its path
which will prevent it from simply mobilizing more forces at home and
dispatching them to the battlefront. The constraints on mobilization are
political, not material. In none of the conflicts noted was more than a fraction
of the total *potential* military resources of the metropolitan power in fact
mobilized. The U.S. war in Vietnam has by any measure had the greatest
impact on international and American domestic politics of any conflict since
World War II, but the maximum number of U.S. troops in Vietnam at the peak
of the ground war in 1968 amounted to less than one quarter of one per cent of
the American population. The political constraints operating against full
mobilization of the metropolitan forces arise as a consequence of the conflicts
in the metropolis—both within the political elite and in the wider society—
which the war, *by its very nature*, will inevitably tend to generate. To
paraphrase Clausewitz, politics may become the continuation of war by other

467

means. Therefore the military struggle on the ground must be evaluated not in terms of the narrow calculus of military tactics, but in terms of its political impact in the metropolis: "Battles and campaigns are amenable to analysis as rather self-contained contests of military power. . . . By contrast, the final outcome of wars depends on a much wider range of factors, many of them highly elusive—such as the war's impact on domestic politics. . . ." The significance of particular battles does not lie in their outcome as "self-contained contests of military power." Thus, although the United States could contend that the 1968 Tet offensive marked a dramatic defeat for the revolutionary forces in terms of the macabre military calculus of "body counts," the offensive was in fact a major strategic defeat for the U.S., marking the turning point in the war. The impact of Tet on American domestic politics led directly to the incumbent president's decision not to stand for another term of office. And, for the first time, military requests for more resources (a further 200,000 men) were refused *despite the fact* that the military situation had worsened. . . .

Why are asymmetries in structure important, and what do we in fact mean by "asymmetry" in this context? We must first note that the *relationship* between the belligerents is *asymmetric*. The insurgents can pose no direct threat to the survival of the external power because, as already noted, they lack an invasion capability. On the other hand, the metropolitan power poses not simply the threat of invasion, but the reality of occupation. This fact is so obvious that its implications have been ignored. It means, crudely speaking, that for the insurgents the war is "total," while for the external power it is necessarily "limited." Full mobilization of the total military resources of the external power is simply not politically possible. (One might conceive of cases where this is not the case—as in a popularly backed "holy war" for example— but such possibilities are of no relevance to the present discussion.) Not only is full mobilization impossible politically, it is not thought to be in the least *necessary*. The asymmetry in conventional military capability is so great and the confidence that military might will prevail is so pervasive that expectation of victory is one of the hallmarks of the initial endeavor.

The fact that one belligerent possesses an invasion capability and the other does not is a function of the differences in level of industrial and technological capability of the two sides. The asymmetric *relationship* is thus a function of the asymmetry in "resource power."

Some strategic implications of symmetric and asymmetric conflict relations may now be spelled out. The insurgents, faced with occupation by a hostile external power, are able to capitalize on those powerful forces to which political scientists have given the label "nationalism." What this means essentially is that disparate and sometimes conflicting national groups may find a common unity—a national interest—in opposing a common enemy. In that case the cohesion generated is only *indirectly* a consequence of the asymmetry in resource power: its social and psychological bonds are to be found in the common hostility felt toward the external enemy. . . .

It is my contention that the process of political attrition of the metropolitan power's capability to continue to wage war is *not* the consequence of errors of generalship, though these may well occur. Rather, it is a function of the *structure* of the conflict, of the nature of the conflictual relationship between the belligerents. Where the war is perceived as "limited"—because the opponent is "weak" and can pose no direct threat—the prosecution of the war does not take automatic primacy over other goals pursued by factions within the governments, or bureaucracies or other groups pursuing interests which compete for state resources. In a situation of total war, the prosecution of the war *does* take automatic primacy above all other goals. Controversies over "guns or butter" are not only conceivable in a Vietnam-type conflict, but inevitable. In a total-war situation they would be inconceivable: guns would get *automatic* priority. In contrast to the total-war situation, the protagonists of a limited war have to compete for resources—human, economic, and political—with protagonists of other interests—governmental, bureaucratic, "interest groups," and so forth. Clearly, if the war is terminated quickly and certain benefits are believed to be accruing from victory (as in the case of the mini-wars of colonial expansion) the *potential* for divisive domestic conflict on the war issue will not be realized. But this is simply another way of stating that if the insurgents are to win, they must not lose.

In his highly prophetic paper published in 1969 ["The Vietnam Negotiations"], Henry Kissinger observed of America's war in Vietnam: "We fought a military war; our opponents fought a political one. We sought physical attrition; our opponents aimed for our psychological exhaustion. In the process, we lost sight of one of the cardinal maxims of guerrilla warfare: the guerrilla wins if he does not lose. The conventional army loses if it does not win."

In order to avoid defeat, the insurgents must retain a minimum degree of invulnerability. In order to *win*, they must be able to impose a steady accumulation of "costs" on their opponent. They must not only be undefeated; they must be *seen* to be undefeated. Strategically, the insurgents' aim must be to provoke the external power into escalating its forces on the ground. This *in itself* will incur economic and political costs in the metropolis. Such a process of escalation did in fact mark the history of the conflicts in Indochina, Algeria, Portuguese Africa, Vietnam, and the current conflict in Ulster. The *direct* costs the insurgents impose on the external power will be the normal costs of war—troops killed and matériel destroyed. But the aim of the insurgents is not the destruction of the military capability of their opponents as an *end in itself*. To attempt such a strategy would be lunatic for a small Third-World power facing a major industrial power. Direct costs become of strategic importance when, and only when, they are translated into indirect costs. These are psychological and political: their objective is to amplify the "contradictions in the enemy's camp."

In the metropolis, a war with no visible payoff against an opponent who poses no direct threat will come under increasing criticism as battle casualties rise and economic costs escalate. Obviously there will still be groups in the metropolis whose ideological commitments will lead them to continue to support the government's war policy; others (munitions manufacturers, for example) may support the war because they have more material interests at stake. But if the war escalates dramatically, as it did in Algeria and Vietnam, it makes a definite impact on the economic and political resources which might otherwise have been allocated to, say, public welfare projects. Tax increases may be necessary to cover the costs of the war, a draft system may have to be introduced, and inflation will be an almost certain by-product. Such costs are seen as part of the "necessary price" when the security of the nation is directly threatened. When this is not the case, the basis for consensus disappears. In a limited war, it is not at all clear to those groups whose interests are adversely affected why such sacrifices are necessary.

But that is only part of the story. Just as important is the fact that the necessity for the sacrifices involved in fighting and risking death will appear less obvious to the conscripts and even the professional soldiers when the survival of the nation is not directly at stake. American soldiers fought well in the second World War, but the last years in Vietnam were marked by troop mutinies, widespread drug addiction, high levels of desertion, and even the murders of over-zealous officers intent on sending their men out on dangerous patrols. This in fact led to a strong feeling among some senior U.S. army officers that it was necessary to get out of Vietnam before morale collapsed completely. It is impossible to explain such a dramatic deterioration of morale within the army and the massive opposition to the draft without reference to the *type* of war being fought.

There is also the question of the morality of the war. When the survival of the nation is not directly threatened, and when the obvious asymmetry in conventional military power bestows an underdog status on the insurgent side, the morality of the war is more easily questioned. It is instructive to note that during World War II the deliberate Allied attempt to terrorize the working-class populations of Dresden and other German cities generated no moral outrage in Britain. This despite the fact that the thousand-bomber raids were designed to create fire storms so devastating in effect that more people died in one night of bombing over Dresden than perished in the Hiroshima holocaust. On the other hand, the aerial bombardment of civilian localities in Vietnam, the use of herbicides and defoliants, napalm, and anti-personnel weapons have been all met with widespread controversy and protest. One should not deduce from this that the British public was more callous to the effects of human suffering than was the American. Moral outrage is in large part a function of the interests perceived to be at stake in the conflict. Where survival is the issue, the propensity to question and protest the morality of the means used to defeat the enemy is markedly attenuated.

As the war drags on and the costs steadily escalate without the "light at the end of the tunnel" becoming more visible, the divisions generated within the metropolis become *in themselves* one of the political costs of the war. The government—or, more precisely, that faction of the government which is committed to the war—will continue to argue that prosecuting the war *is* in the national interest, that vital security interests *are* at stake, that the international credibility and prestige of the nation is at issue, and so forth. Whether or not these claims bear any relationship to reality—whether they are wholly true or wholly false—is quite immaterial. What counts in the long run is what the opponents of the war believe to be at stake and how much political capital they can muster.

Finally, another word about "contradiction." Mao and Giap have repeatedly emphasized that the principal contradiction which the imperialist army must confront on the ground derives from the fact that forces dispersed to control territory become spread so thinly that they are vulnerable to attack. If forces are concentrated to overcome this weakness, other areas are left unguarded. For the external power to overcome this contradiction requires a massive increase in metropolitan forces; but this immediately increases the domestic costs of the war. On the other hand, if the imperialists wish to pacify the opposition at home by withdrawing some of their forces, the contradiction on the battlefronts is sharpened. Any attempt to resolve one contradiction will magnify the other. The guerrilla strategists understand perfectly that the war they fight takes place on two fronts and the conflict must be perceived as an integrated whole. From this perspective, those who oppose the war in the metropolis act *objectively*—regardless of their subjective political philosophies—as a strategic resource for the insurgents. Governments are well aware of this, since it is they who have to confront the political constraints. Yet government accusations that those opposed to the war are "aiding the enemy" are contemptuously rejected. They are nevertheless objectively correct. From this perspective we can also see why the slogan "imperialism is a paper tiger" is by no means inaccurate. It is not that the material resources of the metropolitan power are in themselves underestimated by the revolutionaries; rather, there is an acute awareness that the political constraints on their maximum deployment are as real as if those resources did not exist, and that these constraints become more rather than less powerful as the war escalates. . . .

Summary

The initial problem was one of explaining how the militarily powerful could be defeated in armed confrontation with the militarily weak. This was not just idle speculation; in a number of critically important conflicts in the post-World War II epoch, industrial powers *have* failed to gain their objectives in wars fought on foreign soil against local nationalist forces. In all of these cases the superiority in conventional military capability of the external power was overwhelming. In a sense, these wars may be seen as a replay of the mini-wars of colonial conquest which took place in the late nineteenth and early twentieth centuries, but with a critical difference. In the earlier era, the industrial powers used minimal force to achieve rapid success, whereas in the post-World War II conflicts, the same industrial powers confronted the same Third-World countries with massive forces and lost.

In explaining the successes of the "weaker" party, I pointed out that an obvious minimal requirement for victory was that the insurgents should not lose. They achieved this by refusing to confront the industrial powers on their own terms and by resorting instead to "unconventional" forms of warfare—guerrilla war, urban terrorism, or even nonviolent action. However, I did not examine this aspect of the problem in any detail. I took the fact that the insurgents did not lose as a "given" when I inquired into the more interesting problem—namely, how did they *win?* I noted that one of the key asymmetries which characterized the relationships of the belligerents was that, as a consequence of the asymmetry in wealth and economic and technological development, the insurgents lacked the physical capability to attack the metropolitan power. It thus followed *logically* that the metropolitan power could not be defeated militarily. In turn, victory for the insurgents could only come about as a consequence of the destruction of the external power's *political* capability to wage war. The historical evidence of the outcome of the post-World War II conflicts confirms the logic of the argument.

As a next step, I examined the dynamics of the process of political attrition, arguing that the asymmetries which characterized the conflict provided the basis, not only for the initial restraints on mobilization of military forces, but also for the emergence of internal divisions as the war dragged on and costs accumulated. The fact that the war was by definition "limited" also provided the basis for a sustained moral critique of the military means employed—from torture to napalm—while reducing the willingness of troops to risk their lives in combat and of the domestic population to make economic sacrifices. However, the process of attrition was not seen as arising primarily from a steady across-the-board increment of "war weariness," as some writers have suggested; still less was it seen as a process of conversion at the top whereby the political leadership was gradually persuaded of the immorality or undesirability of its policies. The controversies *themselves* became one of the costs of the war. Time is a resource in politics, and the bitter hostilities such wars generate may come to dominate political debate to the detriment of the pursuit of other objectives. Provided the insurgents can maintain a steady imposition of "costs" on their metropolitan opponent, the balance of political forces in the external power will *inevitably* shift in favor of the anti-war factions. Although the main discussion dealt essentially with domestic constraints, I also recognized that *international* constraints were often of great importance in asymmetric conflicts. However, whereas the mechanisms giving rise to internal constraints could be identified, it was impossible to say anything in the abstract about external constraints.

Having outlined in fairly general terms the conditions under which the process of political attrition might be expected to manifest itself in practice, I then briefly examined the countervailing forces. I noted that the nature of the polity of the external power might either inhibit or facilitate the generation of domestic conflict. But I also argued that internal divisions were primarily a function of the conflict *relationship* and not of differences in the political structure of the metropolis. Finally, I noted that the salience of the interest which the external power—or rather factions within it—had in pursuing the war would also affect the process of political attrition.

███████ **9.4**

R. J. RUMMEL

War Isn't This Century's Biggest Killer

Our century is noted for its bloody wars. World War I saw nine million people killed in battle, an incredible record that was surpassed within a few decades by the 15 million battle deaths of World War II. Even the numbers killed in 20th-century revolutions and civil wars have set historical records. In total, about 35,654,000 people have died in this century's international and domestic wars, revolutions, and violent conflicts.

Yet, even more unbelievable than these vast numbers killed in war is a shocking fact. The number of people killed by totalitarian or extreme authoritarian governments already far exceeds that for all wars, civil and international. Indeed, this number already approximates the number that might be killed in a nuclear war.

[Table 9-5] provides the relevant totals and classifies them by type of government (definitions provided by Freedom House, a New York-based human-rights group) and war. By "killed" is meant the direct or indirect killing by government officials, or government acquiescence in the killing by others. Excluded from the totals are those people executed for what are conventionally considered criminal acts (murder, rape, spying, treason, and the like). Those included in the totals were killed apart from the pursuit of any continuing military action or campaign, or as part of any conflict. The Jews that Hitler slaughtered during World War II are counted, since their merciless and systematic extermination was unrelated to and actually conflicted with Hitler's pursuit of the war.

Underestimation Possible

The totals in the table are based on a nation-by-nation assessment and are minimum figures that may underestimate the true total by 10% or more.

R. J. Rummel

Table 9-5 Twentieth Century Killed, by Cause

Cause	Totals (in millions)	Averages per 10,000 population
Government	119.4	349
Communist	95.2	477
Other non-free	20.3	495
Partially free	3.1	48
Free	.8	22
War	35.7	22
International	29.7	17
Civil	6.0	26

Note: All figures are rounded.

Source: Various historical materials.

Moreover, they do not even include the 1921-1922 Soviet famine and the 1958-1961 Chinese famine, which caused about four million and 27 million deaths, respectively. The Soviet famine was mainly due to the imposition of a command agricultural economy and forced requisitions of food by the government; the latter was wholly caused by Mao's destructive collectivization of agriculture.

However, the table does include the Soviet government's planned starvation of the Ukraine that was begun in 1932 as a way of destroying Ukrainian nationalism and breaking peasant opposition to collectivization. As many as 10 million may have been starved to death or succumbed to famine-related diseases; I estimate eight million died. Had these people all been shot, the Soviet government's moral responsibility would have been no greater.

The table lists 831,000 people killed by free democratic governments, a fact that should startle most readers. This figure includes the French massacres in Algeria before and during the Algerian War (36,000 killed, at a minimum), and those Eastern Europeans killed by the Soviets after the Western democracies forcibly repatriated them during and after World War II.

It is appalling that the democracies, particularly Britain and the U.S., turned over to Soviet authorities more than 2,250,000 Soviet citizens, prisoners of war, and Russian exiles (who were not Soviet citizens) found in the Allied zones of occupation in Europe. Most of these people were terrified of returning and refused to cooperate; often whole families preferred suicide. An estimated 795,000 of those repatriated were executed or died in or traveling to slave-labor camps.

If a government is to be held responsible for those prisoners who die in freight cars or in camps from privation, surely those democratic governments that turned helpless people over to totalitarian rulers with foreknowledge of

474

their peril also should be held responsible.

It is sad that hundreds of thousands of people can be killed by governments with hardly an international murmur, while a war killing several thousand people can cause an immediate world outcry and global reaction. Contrast the international focus on the relatively minor 1982 war between Britain and Argentina with the widescale lack of interest in Burundi's killing or acquiescence in the killing of some 100,000 Hutu in 1972, of Indonesia slaughtering a likely 600,000 people it accused of being "communists" in 1965, and of Pakistan's eventual killing of from one million to three million Bengalis in 1971.

A most noteworthy example of this double standard is the Vietnam War. The international community was outraged at the U.S. efforts to prevent North Vietnam from taking over South Vietnam and ultimately Laos and Cambodia. "Stop the killing" was the cry, and eventually the pressure of foreign and domestic opposition forced an American withdrawal. The overall number killed in the Vietnam War on all sides was about 1.2 million people.

South Vietnam was eventually conquered by the North, and Cambodia was taken over by the communist Khmer Rouge, who in trying to recreate a primitive communist agricultural society slaughtered from one million to three million Cambodians. If we take two million as the best estimate, then in four years the government of this small nation of seven million alone killed 64% more people than died in the 10-year Vietnam War. Overall, the best estimate of those killed by the victorious communists in Vietnam, Laos and Cambodia is 2,270,000. And the killing still goes on.

To view this double standard from another perspective, both world wars cost 24 million battle deaths. But from 1918 to 1953, the Soviet government executed, slaughtered, starved, beat or tortured to death, or otherwise killed some 39.5 million of its own people (estimates vary from between 20 million and 83 million). In China under Mao Tse-tung, the communist government eliminated, as an average figure between estimates, 45 million people. The number killed in just these two nations is about 84.5 million, or a lethality of 252% more than both world wars together. Yet, have the world community and intellectuals generally shown anything like the same horror or outrage over these Soviet and Chinese megakillings as has been directed at the much less deadly world wars?

However, as large as the number of people killed by communist governments is, it is nearly the same as for other non-free governments. This is due to the massacres and widescale killing in the very small country of East Timor, where since 1975 Indonesia has eliminated (aside from the guerrilla war and associated violence) an estimated 100,000 Timorans out of a population of 600,000. Omitting this country alone would reduce the average killed by noncommunist, non-free governments to 397 per 10,000, or significantly less than the 477 per 10,000 for communist countries.

In any case, we can still see from the table that the more freedom in a nation, the fewer people killed by government. Freedom serves as a brake on a governing elite's power over life and death.

Deadliest Scourge

This principle appeared to be violated in the two special cases mentioned above. One was the French government's mass killings in the colony of Algeria. There the Algerians were considered second-class citizens and lacked the right to vote in French elections. In the other case, the Allied democracies acted during and just after wartime, under a regime of strict secrecy, to turn over foreigners to the Soviet Union. These foreigners, of course, had no rights as citizens that would protect them in the democracies. In no case have I found a democratic government carrying out massacres, genocide and mass executions of its own citizens; nor have I found a case where such a government's policies have knowingly and directly resulted in the large-scale deaths of its people through privation, torture, beatings and the like.

Absolutist governments (those that Freedom House would classify as not free) are not only many times deadlier than war, but are themselves the major factor causing war and other forms of violent conflict. They are a major cause of militarism. Indeed, absolutism, not war, is mankind's deadliest scourge of all.

In light of all this, the peaceful, nonviolent fostering of civil liberties and political rights must be made mankind's highest humanitarian goal. Not simply to give the greatest number the greatest happiness, not simply to obey the moral imperative of individual rights, but because freedom preserves peace and life.

9.5 ▬▬▬

GEORGE P. SHULTZ

Low-Intensity Warfare: The Challenge of Ambiguity

I commend the Department of Defense, the National Defense University, and Secretary Weinberger for convening this conference. It comes at an important time, for it addresses one of the most pressing problems in U.S. foreign and defense policy today.

The problem of low-intensity warfare requires us to confront a host of political, military, intellectual, legal, and moral questions. The label, indeed,

An address before the Low-Intensity Warfare Conference, National Defense University, Washington, D.C., January 15, 1986.

may be misleading. When they are shooting at you or trying to blow you up, it's pretty high intensity. Nor is low-intensity warfare the same as limited war.

No, it's a more complicated set of new and unconventional challenges to our policy. It is the scourge of terrorism worldwide; the struggle for Nicaragua between the democratic resistance and the communist regime; it is the insurgencies against the Soviet and Cuban intervention in Angola and Ethiopia; the civil war and terrorism in Lebanon; our rescue of Grenada; and the Cambodian resistance against the Vietnamese occupation. It is the heroic struggle of the Afghan people against Soviet aggression and occupation. It is a matrix of different kinds of challenges, varying in scope and scale. If they have a single feature in common, it is their ambiguity: the fact that they throw us off balance, that we grope for appropriate means to respond, and that we as a society even debate sometimes over the need to respond.

The ironic fact is, these new and elusive challenges have proliferated, in part, *because* of our success in deterring nuclear and conventional war. Our adversaries know they cannot prevail against us in either type of war. So they have done the logical thing: they have turned to other methods. Low-intensity warfare is their answer to our conventional and nuclear strength—a flanking maneuver, in military terms. They hope that the legal and moral complexities of these kinds of challenges will ensnare us in our own scruples and exploit our humane inhibitions against applying force to defend our interests. Ambiguous warfare has exposed a chink in our armor.

The Nicaraguan communists, for instance, have done all they can to hide their true ambitions. Some were fooled by this. The Nicaraguans used progressive rhetoric to obscure their totalitarian goals. They imported Cuban experts to construct a totalitarian state, but, at first, only a small number, so as to not attract attention. Then, as the numbers rose, we were told the Cubans were teachers or construction workers (who happen to handle guns quite well, as we learned in Grenada). Now we are told they aren't really organized troops, just advisers—who seem to wander into combat. We warned against the Nicaraguans' import of MiGs and other advanced weapons; so they have brought in powerful weapons below that threshold, like Hind helicopters. They have committed aggression against their neighbors and provided arms to terrorists like the M-19 group in Colombia, but cynically used the International Court of Justice to accuse *us* of aggression because we joined with El Salvador in its defense.

These tactics obviously play on the moral scruples that discipline our power, on the American people's antipathy to violence and desire for peace. Well, the truth—which most of us here long recognized—is now gaining wider and wider acceptance. A consensus is emerging in Congress that the Sandinistas are not reformers—or even Sandinistas—but Leninists who seek a monopoly of power at home and subversion of their democratic neighbors—and who must be stopped.

But look at the time the Nicaraguan communists have gained to consolidate their tyranny. Years in which we have been consumed in acrimonious internal debate have been used by them to tighten their grip and heighten the danger to the whole region.

In Grenada, the tactics were similar. Documents we captured when our forces landed there 2 years ago reveal how ambiguity and deception were employed as tools of power. The construction of an airport whose true aim was to serve as a Soviet/Cuban base was, we were told, for civilian purposes to aid the local economy. And if we had not intervened when we did, that "civilian" airport might have been in service today, as a transit point for sending more Cuban mercenaries to Angola or more Libyan arms to Nicaragua or more terrorists to our hemisphere.

In southern Africa, of course, the problems are not solely the result of communist subversion. There is the profound problem of South Africa's internal policies and Namibia's right to independence. But there *is* a serious East-West dimension which we, because of the Clark amendment, prevented ourselves from gappling with for 10 years: this is the extraordinary Soviet and Cuban military intervention in Angola, in which we have just seen a massive escalation in the last year and a half. Some will argue that this threat is not serious enough to warrant a response from us, or that we'll be on the wrong side, or that *we* would be escalating. This illustrates the seeming ambiguity of such geopolitical challenges to Western interests. But what would it mean globally, or for Africa, if Soviet/Cuban military intervention—and escalation—became the arbiter of local or regional political conflicts?

Terrorism, of course, is the most striking example of ambiguous warfare. Terrorist acts are a form of criminality, waged by surprise against unarmed men, women, and children in cold blood. Terrorist attacks are sometimes the random, senseless acts of zealots; more often, they are systematic and calculated attempts to achieve political ends. Despite the horror they inflict and the widespread recognition that their acts are criminal, few terrorists are caught, and fewer still are punished to the full extent they deserve. They know we abhor the loss of innocent lives; so they live and train in the midst of their women and children. And we debate among ourselves over the appropriate targets or the foreign policy consequences of a punitive blow. Terrorism is the newest strategy of the enemies of freedom—and it's all too effective.

We are right to be reluctant to unsheath our sword. But we cannot let the ambiguities of the terrorist threat reduce us to total impotence. A policy filled with so many qualifications and conditions that they all could never be met would amount to a policy of paralysis. It would amount to an admission that, with all our weaponry and power, we are helpless to defend our citizens, our interests, and our values. This I simply do not accept.

So we must meet this challenge of low-intensity conflict and ambiguous warfare. We have no choice.

The Intellectual Challenge of Ambiguous Warfare

Our first task, it seems to me, is to come to grips with the problem intellectually.

For various reasons, at least in this century, we Americans have been uncomfortable with conflicts involving limited uses of force for limited ends. Nor have we had to confront systematic terrorism here at home, as Israel has for almost four decades. We have, sometimes, been slow in confronting dangers from abroad, waiting until a limited or ambiguous challenge has escalated into one of global dimensions. Today, we are faced with demands that we be absolutely certain of the need to act before doing so; that we act openly, swiftly, and conclusively; and that we support only those whose aims and conduct we approve in every way.

We know, today, that such simple clarity in the use of power is often elusive in the modern world. We have seen and we will continue to see a wide range of ambiguous threats in the shadow area between major war and millennial peace. Americans must understand, and I believe most Americans do understand, that a number of small challenges, year after year, can add up to a more serious challenge to our interests. The time to act, to help our friends by adding our strength to the equation, is not when the threat is at the doorstep, when the stakes are highest and the needed resources enormous. We must be prepared to commit our political, economic, and, if necessary, military power when the threat is still manageable and when its prudent use can prevent the threat from growing. We have far less margin for error today than we did even 30 years ago. We cannot afford to be complacent about events around the world in the expectation that, in the end, we will have the strength to overcome any challenge. We do not have the luxury of waiting until all the ambiguities have disappeared.

This is the essence of statesmanship—to see a danger when it is not self-evident; to educate our people to the stakes involved; then to fashion a sensible response and rally support.

Our intellectual challenge is especially to understand the need for prudent, limited, proportionate uses of our military power, whether as a means of crisis management, power projection, peacekeeping, localized military action, support for friends, or responding to terrorism—*and* to coordinate our power with our political and diplomatic objectives. Such discreet uses of power for limited purposes will always involve risks. But the risks of inaction will, in many circumstances, be greater.

Our political analysis must be clear sighted. Allies and friends may object to our action—or say they object. But this cannot be decisive. Striking against terrorism in the Middle East, for example, is bound to be controversial. But the worst thing we could do to our moderate friends in the region is to demonstrate that extremist policies succeed and that the United States is impotent to deal with such challenges. If we are to be a factor in the region—if we want

479

countries to take risks for peace relying on our support—then we had better show that our power is an effective counterweight to extremism.

Among other things, this has to include the military supply relationships we have long had with our friends in the Arab world. This is tangible backing for their security in a dangerous period and an important factor for regional stability.

And we must show staying power. Americans are a nation of problem-solvers, and that is a mark of our greatness. Yet many of the problems we face are not susceptible to a quick fix. Few threats can be dealt with as rapidly as Grenada. Most will require perseverance and a longer term commitment. The struggle against terrorism will not be ended by a few dramatic actions. The safeguarding of fragile democracies and vulnerable allies against subversion and covert aggression, in Central America or elsewhere, will require more than brief and quickly completed uses of American power.

Our objective in these situations will always be to prevail. Sometimes, as in the case of Grenada, success will take the form of a total military victory and the removal of foreign troops. In other cases, success will consist of denying victory to the adversary so that political solutions become possible.

We must avoid no-win situations, but we must also have the stomach to confront the harder-to-win situations that call for prudent involvement, even when the results are slow in coming. Steadfastness and endurance are the keys to success; our adversaries notice when we are impatient, uncomfortable, or vacillating. Thus we lose our leverage, and we *make* the problem more prolonged and more difficult to resolve.

The Political, Legal, and Moral Challenges

Unfortunately, in the wake of Vietnam, our endurance against any kind of challenge has been open to question.

Recent decades have left a legacy of contention between the executive and legislative branches and a web of restrictions on executive action embedded in our laws. The result has been a loss of coherence and recurring uncertainty in the minds of friend and foe about the constancy of the United States. The War Powers Resolution sets arbitrary 60-day deadlines that practically invite an adversary to wait us out, that invariably sends signals that the United States, despite all our power, may be "short of breath." That description—"short of breath"—was offered by a Syrian, 2 years ago, who watched our congressional debates and concluded that we lacked staying power; this undercut the prospects for successful negotiation. The rationale of our diplomacy—that the May 17 agreement was the way to bring Israeli withdrawal—was itself undercut when Israel pulled back. This problem can recur as we seek to meet other challenges.

We must tackle this political dilemma head on. Recently, a legislator criticized us for not consulting with the Congress before our interception of the airliner carrying terrorists who had killed an American. But if we delayed acting in order to consult, the terrorists would surely have escaped. I have no doubt that the American people want to see their president acting flexibly, effectively, and decisively against the terrorist menace to defend our citizens. Surely there can be accountability without paralysis.

The fact is, we will never face a specific threat that does not involve some hard choices that are difficult for a democracy. The simple, tragic truth about many low-intensity challenges is that the "rules of the game" are often blurred, at best. Terrorists do not abide by the Geneva convention. They place a premium on the defenselessness and helplessness of their victims. The more heinous the crime, the more attention terrorists attract to their "cause."

The same is true of communist guerrillas, whose fundamental tenet is that the goal of seizing power justifies any method that comes to hand—urban terrorism or waging war on the civilian economy, as in El Salvador. They believe, as Castro once said, that history will absolve them. In the Philippines, the communist guerrillas are men of extraordinary brutality; they have been compared to the Cambodian communists, and this is not a wild comparison.

In the wake of the recent attacks at the Rome and Vienna airports, we have heard it asserted that military action to retaliate or preempt terrorism is contrary to international law. Some have suggested that even to contemplate using force against terrorism is to lower ourselves to the barbaric level of the terrorists. I want to take this issue head on.

Unlike terrorists and communist guerrillas, we do not believe the end justifies the means. We believe in the rule of law. This nation has long been a champion of international law, the peaceful settlement of disputes, and the UN Charter as a code of conduct for the world community.

But the Charter's restrictions on the use or threat of force in international relations include a specific exception for the right of self-defense. It is absurd to argue that international law prohibits us from capturing terrorists in international waters or airspace; from attacking them on the soil of other nations, even for the purpose of rescuing hostages; or from using force against states that support, train, and harbor terrorists or guerrillas. International law requires no such result. A nation attacked by terrorists is permitted to use force to prevent or preempt future attacks, to seize terrorists, or to rescue its citizens when no other means is available. The law requires that such actions be necessary and proportionate. But this nation has consistently affirmed the right of states to use force in exercise of their right of individual or collective self-defense.

The UN Charter is not a suicide pact. The law is a weapon on our side, and it is up to us to use it to its maximum extent. Cooperation in law enforcement, international agreements against hijacking and terrorism, extraditing and prosecuting terrorists when captured—these are indispensable tools. But we can go further.

There should be no confusion about the status of nations that sponsor terrorism against Americans and American property. There is substantial legal authority for the view that a state which supports terrorist or subversive attacks against another state, or which supports or encourages terrorist planning and other activities within its own territory, is responsible for such attacks. Such conduct can amount to an ongoing armed aggression against the other state under international law. As the president said last week:

> By providing material support to terrorist groups which attack U.S. citizens, Libya has engaged in armed aggression against the United States under established principles of international law, just as if [it] had used its own armed forces.

Think about the practical and strategic implications of allowing a state to evade responsibility for the acts of its terrorist surrogates: a nation like Qadhafi's Libya would acquire immunity while carrying on the secret or ambiguous warfare which poses such a threat today to the security and well-being of free nations. And to let ourselves be deterred by Qadhafi's threats from doing what is needed to stop him will only establish in his mind, and in the minds of other fanatics, that the scheme has worked. State-supported terror will increase through our submission to it, not from our active resistance.

The future will be grim, indeed, if we permit this. The potential gravity of terrorist acts is certain to increase as terrorists obtain the means to use weapons far more destructive and harmful than guns, grenades, and bombs. In fact, state support will probably be the single most important factor in enabling terrorists to acquire such weapons, which may well include nuclear devices small enough for terrorists to assemble but devastating enough to destroy a government's leadership and a nation's morale. We must use the law to preserve civilized order, not to shield those who would wage war against it.

The armed ideologues of the world may believe that our devotion to international law will immobilize us at home. As we have shown in response to Nicaragua's hypocritical suit in the World Court, we will not permit our enemies—who despise the rule of law as a "bourgeois" notion—to use *our* devotion to law and morality as a weapon against us. When the United States defends its citizens abroad or helps its friends and allies defend themselves against subversion and tyranny, we are not suspending our legal and moral principles. On the contrary, we are strengthening the basis of international stability, justice, and the rule of law.

Our morality must be a source of strength, not paralysis. We cannot walk away from every situation that poses a moral dilemma. The use of force at *any* level involves moral issues. We should use our military power only if the stakes justify it, if other means are not available, and then only in a manner appropriate to a clear objective. We cannot wait for absolute certainty and clarity. If we do, the world's future will be determined by others—most likely by those who are the most brutal, the most unscrupulous, and the most hostile to everything we believe in.

A Strategy for Ambiguous Warfare

Thus, the United States needs an active strategy for dealing with ambiguous warfare. We must be better prepared intellectually and psychologically as a nation; we must be better prepared organizationally as a government. Many important steps have been taken. But more needs to be done.

First of all, our policy against ambiguous warfare must be *un*ambiguous. It must be clearly and unequivocally the policy of the United States to fight back—to resist challenges, to defend our interests, and to support those who put their own lives on the line in a common cause. We must be clear in our own minds that we cannot shrink from challenges.

For this, there must be public understanding and congressional support. That is why, again, I applaud you for holding this conference—not only for probing deeper into the problem but for contributing to the body of public knowledge and education.

In fact, we are much farther along as a nation in this regard than we were a few short years ago. Unfortunately, much of what we learned, we learned the hard way. Public discussion and debate about the problem must continue—not to magnify our hesitations but to crystallize a national consensus.

Second, we must make the fullest use of all the nonmilitary weapons in our arsenal. Strengthening the collaboration of governments, developing new legal tools and methods of international sanctions, working to resolve conflicts through diplomacy, taking defensive measures to reduce our vulnerability—all this we must keep doing.

Our programs of security and economic assistance to friends are essential. In this era of budgetary stringency, I want to record an urgent plea on behalf of security assistance. As the president has said, "Dollar for dollar, security assistance contributes as much to global security as our own defense budget." In El Salvador, we see how the wise provision of sufficient economic and military assistance obviates the need to consider any direct involvement of American forces. And we must extend moral or humanitarian or other kinds of support to those resisting totalitarianism or aggression. Our ideals and our interests coincide.

We must also strengthen our intelligence capabilities—not only intelligence collection and intelligence cooperation with allies but also our means for covert action. In this regard, it is imperative that we stop leaks. There is no disagreement within this Administration that unauthorized disclosure of military or intelligence information is a crime. Since time immemorial, governments—including democratic governments—have conducted sensitive activities in secret, and the democracies only court disaster if they throw away this instrument through indiscipline.

One of the cliches one hears these days is that covert operations leak, so why try to do things covertly? First of all, I think we can keep things secret if we try harder. Second, other countries working with us often have good reasons not to want publicity, and unacknowledged programs afford them some protection, even if there are leaks in the press. It can mean the difference between success and failure for our effort. In addition, unacknowledged programs mean a less open challenge to the other side, affording more of a chance for political solutions. Covert action is not an end in itself, but it should have a place in our foreign policy.

Finally, there is the military dimension of our strategy. Just as we turned to our men and women in uniform when new conventional and nuclear threats emerged, we are turning to you now for the new weapons, new doctrines, and new tactics that this new method of warfare requires.

I have no doubt that we have the physical resources and capability to succeed. To combat terrorism we have created the Delta Forces; we have created the Special Operations Forces for a multitude of tasks; the Army is forming new light divisions; the Marines are developing new capabilities; the Air Force and Army are developing new concepts and doctrines. The courage and skill of our armed forces have been proven time and again—most recently in Grenada and in the capture of the *Achille Lauro* hijackers.

But the challenge we face continues. I am confident you will know what is required to ensure coordination and effectiveness. I do know we will need the closest coordination between our military power and our political objectives—because I, as secretary of state, know full well that power and diplomacy must go together. We need to re-learn how to keep our military options and preparations secret. There may be an important new role for our military in the area of covert operations.

Cap [Secretary of Defense Caspar Weinberger] and I discuss these issues and these challenges frequently, and we will be working together, in full agreement on the urgency of the problem.

Prospects

So, in conclusion, I can tell you that your topic is a prime challenge we will face, at least through the remainder of this century. The future of peace and freedom may well depend on how effectively we meet it.

I have no doubt we can succeed. We have learned much in recent years—about terrorism, about Soviet-backed insurgencies, and about how to use American power prudently. Our armed forces are better equipped, both physically and psychologically.

The American people are today more confident in themselves, in their nation, and in the rightness of their principles, and this will be a source of enormous strength in the future. And we draw strength from the newly democratic nations which have joined our ranks and look to us for leadership.

With the necessary will, hard work, and a degree of wisdom, we will prevail over this challenge, as we have prevailed over so many others in our proud history.

9.6 ███████

MICHAEL S. STOHL

Terrorism—What Should We Do?

The Reagan Administration came to office as the hostages of the 1979-81 Teheran American Embassy takeover were released from captivity. Mr. Reagan, who attained the presidency in part by promising to make America stand tall again, pledged that never again would the United States allow terrorists to humiliate it. Concurrently, Alexander Haig, the new Secretary of State, to further distance the Reagan Administration from the weakness that they had portrayed in their predecessors, suggested that terrorism was the main threat to human rights in the world and that the Soviet Union, through policies of aiding, abetting and funding international terrorists, was primarily responsible for international terrorism. The Administration from the outset indicated that it would work to relieve the threat of terrorism to the West by serving warning to international terrorist groups, and those states that supported them, that the United States would henceforth stand tall.

Terrorist attacks against United States military, diplomatic and private citizens have continued in the past four and a half years, with much greater loss of life than in the Carter years, but the United States has not yet made good on the President's retaliation and retribution promises. This has not stopped the President or his senior administrative officials from continuing their threats and posturing on the retaliation theme. As recently as the aftermath of this summer's TWA hijacking, in which again the President did not unleash the American forces he has so often threatened, Mr. Reagan emerged from a screening of Sylvester Stallone's *Rambo* and foolishly quipped that now he knew what he would do next time.

In the past year, Secretary of State Shultz has emerged as the most public and forceful of those calling for retribution and retaliation. Shultz has stressed that the law-abiding nations of the world must put an end to the barbarism that is terrorism, as it threatens the very foundations of civilized life. On October 25, 1984, the Secretary, in an address at the Park Avenue Synagogue in New York, enunciated what has become known as the "Shultz Doctrine":

> We must reach a consensus in this country that our responses should go beyond passive defense to consider means of active prevention, preemption, and retaliation. Our goal must be to prevent and deter future terrorist acts,

From *This World*, Vol. 12 (Fall 1985), pages 29-43. Copyright © 1985 by The Rockford Institute. Reprinted by permission of the publisher.

and experience has taught us over the years that one of the best deterrents to terrorism is the certainty that swift and sure measures will be taken against those who engage in it. We should take steps toward carrying out such measures.

In the months since Shultz went public the United States has had a number of opportunities to employ his doctrine but has failed to do so. Secretary Shultz was worried that by not responding to terrorists and allowing ourselves to be hamstrung by confusion and indecisiveness, the United States would thereby become "the Hamlet of nations, worrying endlessly over whether and how to respond." In fact, the Secretary, to continue his Shakespearean metaphor, has cast himself as Iago and advises the United States to become the Othello of nations, counseling a policy of "preemptive retaliation" [sic] which would slay the Desdemona of international law and the civilized behavior that the Secretary sees the terrorists as threatening. Far more important than the question of which is the proper Shakespearean metaphor, the Secretary's policy call is misguided because it subverts the very standards of behavior it seeks to protect and, at the same time, it is unlikely that it will produce the results he seeks while making the world a far more dangerous place to live in.

We now know that while Reagan Administration declaratory policy was for swift retribution and retaliation, and publicly nothing appeared to be occurring, the wheels of covert action were spinning. Preemptive retribution was turned on the Hizballah and its leaders as the United States became involved with Lebanese intelligence operatives through a C.I.A. operation to train and support several counterterrorist units for strikes against suspected terrorists before they could attack U.S. facilities in the Middle East. On March 8, 1985, members of one of these units, reportedly acting without C.I.A. authorization, hired others in Lebanon to detonate a car bomb outside the Beirut home of a militant Shiite leader believed to be behind attacks on U.S. installations. More than 80 persons were killed and 200 were wounded, while the target escaped injury. The Administration claimed it bore no responsibility for the actions, but to the victims and the Shiite community, the United States was clearly identified with the perpetrators and therefore the action. Beyond the questionable morality of the action, by aligning itself with parties of dubious merit the Administration showed itself to be both morally deficient and once again incompetent. The results must be seen as another failure for Mr. Shultz. You cannot terrorize any but innocent civilians by such shows of incompetence. The fanatics will not be deterred under such circumstances—they will believe only that God is on their side and their hatred will be fueled for further actions, as the TWA hijacking in the aftermath of the action bears witness. In October 1984, Mr. Shultz stated that "Our Challenge is to forge policies that keep faith with our principles." On this and other grounds the Reagan Administration policy on counterterrorism has been a failure.

Reagan Administration policy on terrorism has been a failure because the

Administration has failed to learn many of the lessons that our experience with terrorism over the past two decades should have taught.

1. These lessons begin with understanding that the type of terrorists that have caused the greatest consternation have not been simple lone psychopaths or merely agents operating at the instigation of Moscow. The terrorists with the greatest success and the longest durability have been connected to serious longstanding political causes, supported or at least tolerated, whether we approve or not, by populations they declare themselves as representing. The terrorism, once it begins, will not disappear until the basic problems which underlie it are settled or until a military solution is imposed and a constant iron fist employed. In the Middle East and elsewhere this gives little cause for hope. The Israelis, whom Mr. Shultz so approvingly cited in the speech giving rise to his doctrine—despite a policy of counterterror and retribution—have not eliminated the threat of terrorism from their territory.

2. The Administration has failed to distinguish the type of terrorism that it is confronting with a policy of preemptive retaliation or retribution. Is the policy meant to deter state terrorism, state-sponsored terrorism, insurgent terrorism that is state-supported or simply any terrorism wherever it occurs and whomever is responsible? When states are involved we can threaten to employ economic sanctions, isolate them diplomatically, recall ambassadors, and even request the closing of their embassies. Should we employ either preemptive or reactive retaliation we should find ourselves engaged in war, an outcome momentous enough that the credibility of the deterrent threat does not appear to be operative. If we are, on the other hand, confronting terrorists that are not operating on what is for them friendly ground, our options are much more likely to lead us to a "normal" law enforcement response which seeks the cooperation and assistance of friendly governments.

3. All first year students of diplomacy are aware that policy makers in coercive bargaining situations should never threaten to do that which they are either "unwilling" or "incapable" of acting upon if their bluff is called. The Secretary of State may be trying to convince the world that the United States is willing, but failure to act on those occasions when it would have appeared from his rhetoric that he "should," simply undermines the credibility of the policy. To claim that the United States did not have enough information to act, further undercuts the credibility and weakens our overall position. The policy as it is now stated simply leaves too many ambiguities: How bad will it have to be before retaliation will be carried out? Does the policy invite groups to try and find out, given the previous inaction? Who should we attack? How will we know? How many innocent lives lost is an acceptable number? What will be gained by retaliation? Will we deter terrorism or will we simply feel better to have acted?

4. Statesmen, even the United States' President and Secretary of State, cannot define or make policy on the basis of personal frustration. They must not define a United States' policy on terrorism because they feel that their

honor or their manhood is threatened by the continued affronts that terrorist attacks may be taken to imply. While we may empathize with the difficulties and frustrations this may cause individuals as private citizens, statesmen cannot be allowed that luxury.

5. There are no simple solutions to terrorism. We cannot prevent all possible acts of terrorism from occurring, whether at home or abroad. We can, however, reduce the likelihood of both domestic and international terrorists' success and the ability of terrorists to manipulate events in those areas under United States control, at embassies, military bases, and at airports in countries with whom we have friendly relations. The problem from the Administration standpoint is that there isn't much news value in events that don't happen, and quite often the public is skeptical of reports about the success of prevention. The public must be educated during the quiet periods to understand that it is unlikely that all terrorism can be eliminated, and that when events occur it does not mean that the United States is weak. Weakness comes from declaring that something must be done and not doing it, and from declaring that failing to prevent all terrorism is a sign of weakness. Terrorism will continue to occur. We can reduce its frequency and its cost by paying a price for increased security, but its threat will still be present.

6. Finally, the Administration has failed to understand that its policies in one arena have impact on other parts of the international system. Counterterrorism policy does not occur in a vacuum. The Administration's failure to prevent the continued occurrence of terrorism must be coupled with their own policies in other spheres of international relations which serve to undermine both their moral authority and their political credibility. An Administration which is consciously vocal in its condemnation of state terrorism and state terrorists would do well to consider what neutrals—as well as friends—think of policies which proclaim guerrilla forces as "freedom fighters" and "the moral equivalent of our founding fathers." How can an Administration that sends millions of dollars to forces who, were they carrying out their actions against regimes that we supported rather than opposed, would be defined by this Administration as terrorists, hope to convince others that we oppose terrorism and respect the rule of law? How will we build cooperation and respect for an international law with respect to terrorism which we find inconvenient to uphold? As long as we appear to claim the right as a superpower to stand above the law, we will not gain the international support we need to reduce the threat of terrorism. We cannot hope to defeat our terrorist adversaries if we implement policies by which we become what in our adversaries we condemn.

Discussion Questions

1. Compare the operational definitions of war employed by Levy and by Starr and Most, and list the differences between them. What effects, if any,

might these definitional differences have had on the authors' results?

2. Obtain and examine either the Sivard or the Small and Singer volumes listed in the readings section. Select one or more of the armed conflicts for which your source contains data, and research these conflicts in more detail. Prepare a brief report on the origins, contributing factors, and specifics of the armed conflict you have chosen. Devote particular attention to ways the conflict might have been prevented and the likely long-term consequences if it had been.

3. Select a current armed conflict that falls short of full-scale war, and determine whether, in your opinion, it involves state terrorism. If it does, what type or types of state terrorism? How likely does it appear this conflict will escalate to a full-scale war? Why or why not?

4. For one week, scan a major newspaper for reports on "terrorism," and classify the amount of reportage devoted to state terrorism as opposed to nonstate terrorism. Do you believe the relative amounts of coverage are a reasonable indicator of the importance and frequency of the two types of terrorism?

5. Secretary of State Schultz argues for a forceful response to terrorists, and Stohl argues that such a response will lead to further difficulties. What is the basis of each of their arguments?

6. The Swedish researchers employ a formula for excess deaths based on life expectancy. Devise an alternate formula for measuring such deaths. How does the total number of annual excess deaths, derived from your formula, compare to the total derived from the Swedish formula? To the total number of annual deaths directly caused by violence?

7. Compare the Rummel, Levy, and Starr and Most tables of violence. What regions of the world appear to have experienced the most violence? The least? How does this compare to your expectations?

For Further Reading

The Classics on War

Herodotus. *The Histories.* Aubrey de Selincourt, trans. Harmondsworth: Penguin, 1954. The first book of history, it recounts the relations between Greece and Persia and the war between them from 490 to 478 B.C.

Thucydides. *The Peloponnesian War.* Rex Warner, trans. Harmondsworth: Penguin, 1972. Considered the first book of international relations, it recounts the causes and consequences of the war between Athens and Sparta.

Von Clausewitz, Karl. *On War.* M. Howard and P. Paret, eds. and trans. Princeton, N.J.: Princeton University Press, 1986. Clausewitz's masterpiece, an analysis of the use of force in international politics, explores all aspects of the utility and consequences of war between states.

The Modern Classics

Richardson, Lewis Fry. *Statistics of Deadly Quarrels*. Pittsburgh: Quadrangle, 1960. Published posthumously, this volume reprints articles written over more than a quarter century. They represent some of the very earliest efforts to apply the tools of mathematical and statistical analysis to the study of war and its causes.

Sorokin, Pitrim. *Social and Cultural Dynamics*, Vol. 3: *Fluctuations of Social Relationships, War and Revolution*. New York: American Books, 1937. The third volume of Sorokin's massive modern classic investigates social dynamics from antiquity to modern times and the impact of those dynamics on the changing nature of war.

Wright, Quincy. *A Study of War*. Chicago: University of Chicago Press, 1942. This classic study of the causes of modern war is filled with interesting charts, tables, and historical facts.

Modern Compendiums

Beer, Francis. *Peace Against War*. San Francisco: W. H. Freeman, 1981. An analysis of war as a social disease, this book brings together much contemporary knowledge of the correlates of war and their consequences.

Sivard, Ruth L. *World Military and Social Expenditures, 1987*. Washington, D.C.: World Priorities, Inc., 1987. This annual compendium contains a range of statistical data not easily obtainable from other sources, including a comprehensive table on wars and war-related deaths.

Small, Melvin, and J. David Singer. *Resort to Arms: International and Civil Wars 1816-1980*. Beverly Hills: Sage Publications, 1982. The most comprehensive compilation of the attributes of international and civil wars yet published, an outgrowth of the Correlates of War Project.

Stohl, Michael, and George A. Lopez, eds. *Government Violence and Repression: An Agenda for Research*. Westport, Conn.: Greenwood Press, 1986. This collection examines the various contours of state violence, coercion, and terror, particularly for purposes of internal control. Several of the essays also examine the use of state and surrogate terror as a foreign policy tool.

Stohl, Michael, and George A. Lopez, eds. *Terrible Beyond Endurance: The Foreign Policy of State Terror*. Westport, Conn.: Greenwood Press, 1988. This volume focuses on state and surrogate terror as foreign policy; it also contains case studies of state terror policy as employed by the United States, the Soviet Union, South Africa, Israel, and Central American states.

Zimmerman, Charles, and Milton Leitenberg. "Hiroshima Lives On," *Mazingira: The World Forum for Environment and Development* No. 9 (1979), 60-65. An article that reports on the Stockholm International Peace Research Institute's study of excess deaths discussed in the chapter introduction.

PRESERVING PEACE
AND BUILDING ORDER
10

T hroughout this volume we have discussed the critical concepts and theories of international relations and how they inform citizens' and policy makers' understanding of their world. Some readings have illustrated how these theories have been translated into actual policy. Other readings have examined how the theory or the policy becomes actualized in practice.

In this chapter, in which we examine the urgent topic of preserving peace and building a humane global order, we note that systematic scholarship concerning the causes of peace is difficult to find. Over the years, international relations scholars have focused about 95 percent of their attention on the question of what causes war. There is, therefore, a limited amount of scholarly material available on keeping the peace.

On a second and more positive note, however, we do have some knowledge of the conditions for preserving peace and building order. Most of this knowledge emerges not from theory, but from case studies (some would call them policy analyses) of attempts to end conflict. In addition, there have been a number of attempts to "prescribe" methods by which international peace can be preserved. Our readings in this chapter are, therefore, of these two types rather than empirical scholarly studies.

Students of the peace process have been primarily interested in international law and organizations, as well as in the viability of various modes of dispute settlement among states. More recently, the scope of inquiry has expanded to include the design of new norms and institutions that would preserve peace in a more humane global order. The objective of such a global order is to provide a framework for international peace coupled with reasonable levels of global economic development, respect for cultural and human rights, and ecological balance.

In our discussion, we will be considering two critical questions:

1. What conditions have emerged since 1945 to give actors involved in serious disputes the means and incentives to solve their differences without resort to military force?

2. What new norms and institutions are necessary to build peace and sustain a more peaceful global order?

We will examine these questions at three levels—the level of the international system, of the nation-state, and of the citizen.

The International System

The Role of International Law

Any inquiry into existing means for preserving international peace moves quickly to the areas of international law and international organization. *International law* is usually defined as that evolving body of recognized customs, treaties, relevant national laws, and international court rulings that deal with the rights and duties of states in their relations with one another. As illustrated by Figure 10-1, the several sources of international law can be viewed as potentially overlapping and reinforcing. A "law" or precedent that is derived from and consistent with international legal custom, existing treaties, and national laws is clearly stronger than one derived solely from any one of these sources.

Thus, in confronting Iran over that nation's seizure of U.S. embassy personnel in the Tehran hostage incident of 1979-1981, the United States received virtually unanimous support from the World Court and from the United Nations' member states, including the communist bloc. The principle and practice of diplomatic inviolability was law, and the seizure of U.S. diplomats isolated Iran in the international community. (Ironically, the principle of diplomatic inviolability was first urged by Cyrus of Persia more than two millennia ago.)

Figure 10-1   The Sources of International Law

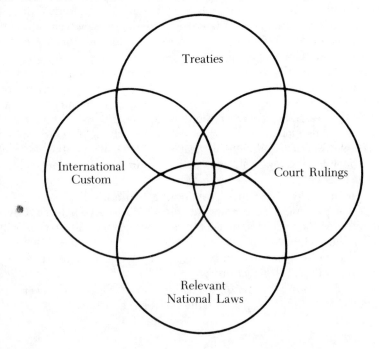

So too, the United States faced the condemnation of much of the globe when it chose to mine Nicaraguan harbors in the early 1980s and then defied a subsequent World Court ruling on the issue. Most other nations viewed the U.S. position as being in violation of international law, notwithstanding U.S. statements regarding the "national security threat" posed by the Sandinista regime.

Possibly no other topic in international relations sparks as much cynicism as that of international law, especially in the United States. As the article by Francis Anthony Boyle suggests, American foreign policy decision makers have often viewed international politics and international law as incompatible. In this respect, the American view of international politics has traditionally reflected a Hobbesian rather than a Grotian perspective. (Both approaches are discussed in Chapter 1.)

Nonetheless, international law plays a major role in contemporary international politics. Its development has closely paralleled major political and social changes in the international system. The now considerable body of law governing the use of the oceans, for example, was developed in response to conflict over trade routes and fishing rights. It was motivated not by some utopian dream but by highly practical concerns. If nations were to trade and to fish without conflict in a complex world, all parties would benefit from having rules and following them. So, too, as new technologies made war ever more destructive, states have sought under the rubric of law to develop means other than war for settling disputes and for regulating the more terrible aspects of war.

As international law has developed in response to political change, so too have states attempted to use existing law to define the acceptable parameters of international political behavior. Viewed in this manner, international law represents an important set of guidelines for foreign policy decision making. In the Cuban missile crisis, for example, the blockade option (carefully labeled for purposes of international law a "quarantine") was more attractive than a surgical air strike. Under international law the latter would almost certainly have been viewed as a clear affront to Cuban sovereignty and as far in excess of any actions permissible to the United States under its right to self-defense. A naval quarantine, by contrast, was an effective means for stopping the flow of materials to Cuba without directly attacking either Cuba or the Soviet Union. It represented a forceful challenge, but one that allowed a negotiated settlement of the dispute—while leaving the door open for escalation later.

One of the ways international law has contributed to the preservation of peace is by providing guidelines that, when observed, lead to predictable behavior in a number of contentious issue areas. These include international organizations, international business, commercial transactions, and travel—areas governed by a substantial body of rules known as *public international law*. That body of law, which pertains to the practices of nations as legal entities, today applies to such problems as the treatment of aliens, human rights, the recognition of states and governments, as well as the use of airspace, outer space, and the seas.

The last of these has been, within the past several decades, the focus of a major international effort to develop a systematic body of rules that would reduce the possibility of armed conflict over the use of the sea. Beginning in 1958, a series of international conferences and continuing efforts by the UN and other international agencies led to the eventual codification of international law governing the seas. Although portions of the laboriously developed treaty were subsequently rejected by the Reagan administration, this effort is illustrative of the potential for developing international law that contributes to the preservation of international peace and the building of world order.

This is not to intimate that law is a perfect tool for international peacemaking. It is likely, in fact, that as international politics become less predictable and more volatile, law will be subjected to ever greater pressure by states seeking to circumvent it in an effort to maximize their short-term advantages. On the other hand, it is impossible to envision a workable international system without international law.

International Organizations

Like international law, *international organizations* are vital to the functioning of a working international system. Such organizations are quite numerous. They include the United Nations, its "family" of allied organizations, and the more than two hundred other international governmental organizations established by states to deal with a specific task or issue—for example, the International Telecommunications Union (ITU) and the World Health Organization (WHO).

Much scientific, social, and economic progress has resulted from the work of international organizations since World War II. Among analysts and policy makers, there is little question that a number of conflicts have been averted by the efforts of such agencies. The exact number or cost of wars prevented must be left to speculation. For this reason the real value of much of the work done by these agencies often goes unrecognized.

One of the most valuable ways international organizations have contributed to reducing international violence has been the establishment of peacekeeping forces during and after hostilities. The efforts of the United Nations and such regional groups as the Organization of African Unity (OAU), the Arab League, and the Organization of American States (OAS) are especially noteworthy. The establishment of the United Nations Emergency Force (UNEF) in the wake of the Suez crisis in 1956 allowed the four belligerent parties to remove their forces from the area without further hostilities. The force remained for eleven years, during which there was no resumption of the fighting between Egypt and Israel.

Likewise, the United Nations Force in Cyprus (UNFICYP), by occupying a buffer zone between Turkish and Greek forces, dramatically reduced the level of violence on that island and the potential for violence between Greece and Turkey. The Arab League, the OAS, and the OAU have each performed a similar role in regional disputes and have engaged in other peacemaking functions such as fact-finding missions, mediation, and providing a public forum for the disputants. Some of these efforts are discussed in the articles by Carolyn Stephenson and Ernst B. Haas included in the readings.

Haas, who examines the evolution of the UN's peacekeeping authority in some detail, concludes that UN peacekeeping efforts did not so much fail—as has been often said—as that the norms of its members concerning the appropriate means of regulating conflict changed. Thus, his conclusions lend support to the notion that international organizations can play a viable role in the peacekeeping enterprise.

New Peacekeeping Mechanisms: Some Suggestions

In examining the prospects for preserving peace and building a viable world order, we should consider not only existing mechanisms but also possible alternatives. Although today's forms of violence represent an unprecedented challenge to global order, it is also true that the relative success and the experience of the past four decades—in forging viable international law, effective international organization, and new strategies of conflict management—ought to instruct us on where and how to use these new mechanisms.

Consider, for example, the difficult problems of insurgent and state terrorism. We know both are condemned by existing international law and that some nations have been unable to control these forms of violence. We also know that today the two types of terrorism are often related to one another in many places around the globe.

One possible solution, therefore, is simply to suggest that states take existing laws more seriously. This, indeed, might be helpful in some instances. But, by and large, this strategy has proven inadequate in the absence of effective means for deterring and punishing such forms of violence and dealing with their causes. Thus, new mechanisms are needed.

The form of these new mechanisms can only be suggested. As an example, we provide recommendations for dealing with one aspect of international conflict—terrorism. None of these is wholly original. All have previously appeared in one or more proposals or policy recommendations offered by various members of the scholarly and policy communities in recent years. Together, however, they provide a useful illustration of how we might devise new mechanisms for dealing with one of the most troubling and problematic forms of international violence.

495

Recommendation 1. *The establishment of an international criminal court, either as a separate entity or an adjunct to the World Court.*
Originally proposed in the early 1950s, this tribunal would be empowered to hear cases brought by nongovernmental actors as well as states. It would have jurisdiction over cases brought against individuals, such as hijackers and assassins. Thus, the new court could deal with cases in which a national government is reluctant to bring a terrorist to trial for fear that the officials involved might become the next target of the terror group. Such a court might also be empowered to bring charges, filed by citizens of a state, against a former head of state—the Shah of Iran, Somoza, or Marcos, for example—for certain kinds of offenses, such as violations of the Universal Declaration of Human Rights.

Recommendation 2. *The creation of a mechanism for expanding dialogue between state actors and nongovernmental actors, including representatives of clearly identifiable ethnic and minority groups through their increased participation in regional and international organizations.*
The proposed arrangement provides a means for airing grievances by enhancing the international status—and thus the visibility—of ethnic minorities, stateless people, and refugees. Making them a part of the system gives them a stake in maintaining it and avoiding behavior that would lead to ostracism.
Although controversial, such a strategy has been successfully employed in several cases involving domestic or international terrorism. The number of terrorist acts committed by Yassir Arafat's Palestine Liberation Organization (PLO), particularly those involving attacks on Americans and West Europeans, declined dramatically in the mid-1970s after the United Nations recognized the PLO as a bona fide representative of stateless Palestinians and granted them observer status in the UN General Assembly. Similarly, the terrorist acts of Basque separatists (ETA) in Spain declined in number and severity after a new Spanish government in the 1980s initiated a dialogue regarding Basque rights.

Recommendation 3. *The establishment of a grievance and mediation agency to act as a low-level intervenor in disputes and to provide a means of redress against state or insurgent terror.*
This proposed agency is similar to one called for during the original UN Charter conference over forty years ago. It is today an even more attractive proposal because of the growth in number and expertise of international lawyers and practitioners with experience mediating cross-cultural conflict. The success of U.S. agencies such as the Community Relations Service and the Federal Mediation and Conciliation Service, which have helped to lower the level of domestic racial and social violence over the past three decades, suggest that the proposed agency would be highly effective. Had such an agency

existed on the international level, it might, for example, have brought a more rapid resolution of the U.S.-Iranian hostage crisis.

In fact, the functions proposed for this agency are already being performed by a number of groups, such as regional commissions on human rights violations, and individuals such as the Anglican Church's "special envoy" and skilled mediator, Terry Waite. Before his own abduction in Lebanon in 1987, Waite secured the release of a number of hostages of terrorist groups in that strife-ridden area.

Recommendation 4. *The creation of a UN high commission and high commissioner for human rights.*

The proposed agency is modeled on the successful UN High Commission and High Commissioner for Refugees. Given the existence of a well-established structural precedent, the prospects for creating an international actor "with clout" to deal with state terror and gross violations of human rights rest on the member states' willingness to acknowledge the existence of state terror and provide a means for holding leaders accountable. Such a commission might have investigated the crimes of the Shah of Iran or of Somoza in Nicaragua and might have changed the course of U.S.-Iranian or U.S.-Nicaraguan relations.

These, then, are some examples of possible mechanisms for dealing more effectively with the grievances that encourage insurgencies and governmental terrorism. Together they represent one way we might make use of international law and organizations to preserve international peace. As the nature of conflict changes, so too must our response. But success will come not only from the adaptation of existing law but also from a clear vision of its place, purpose, and limits in the international system.

The Role of States

The nation-state can play a significant role in preserving regional and even international peace and prosperity. Perhaps the best modern example is that of the Scandinavian countries, which have enjoyed peaceful relations with one another since the beginning of this century. Unfortunately, such examples are relatively rare.

We know from our discussion in Chapter 5 that individual states can and have employed bargaining strategies to discourage the use of force, particularly by rival states. However, bargaining at a systemic level, when conducted by states of unequal power, may turn coercive and lead to escalating violence. Further, such bargaining is basically a unilateral response to specific circumstances that does little to prevent future conflict or contribute to its management.

Nonetheless, we can discern from a study of the international system some useful principles of behavior that, if adopted by states, would contribute to peacekeeping. But here, too, existing practices are inadequate to deal with the current levels of violence, let alone the challenges that lie ahead. Are there some guiding principles, as yet only partially tested in practice, that states might employ when assessing their policy options? We believe there are.

One of these concerns the norms governing the pursuit of "the national interest." Throughout the 1980s, many states, including the United States, have seen fit to define and pursue their national interests in ways that directly contradicted existing international law and world opinion. During this decade we have witnessed the Soviet Union's bloody intervention in Afghanistan, continuing Syrian aid to insurgents and international terrorists, and the U.S. mining of Nicaraguan harbors followed by U.S. claims that the World Court lacked jurisdiction to hear the case brought by Nicaragua in response to such actions. These cases illustrate that nations continue to place their national interest above the broader global or human interest.

Although we view this pursuit of national interest as a hindrance to world peace, we recognize that simply denouncing these policies is not likely to dissuade supporters of this strategy. We would like, therefore, to propose alternative strategies that, properly pursued, can and will enhance both the national interest—defined in a way consistent with the best American values— and the larger global interest. Two recent examples illustrate our argument.

The first strategy is the much-maligned policy on human rights of the Carter administration. Although portrayed as "soft" by critics who claimed it was "developed in the heart rather than the head," the Carter emphasis on human rights was, in fact, derived from a conviction that there were many areas in the world where such an emphasis was not only pragmatic but in keeping with American values. It was in this context that the Carter administration made the improvement of human rights a cornerstone of its foreign policy. Among the results of this effort were the Panama Canal treaty—which returned ownership of the canal to the country in which it is located—and the suspension of foreign aid to a number of regimes known to be consistent abusers of human rights.

These efforts were in many cases successful. While the short-term impact was to alienate some "friendly" nations, such as Guatemala and Brazil, the long-term results have been consistent with the original policy objectives. In Latin America, for example, governments in the 1980s are, on the whole, more democratic and less repressive than their 1970s counterparts. The emergence of such governments better serves U.S. national interests than a continuation of their more repressive predecessors, no matter how "friendly" to U.S. interests. Thus, we conclude, adopting a longer-term and broader view of the national interest is one way states can both advance their own interests and contribute to the peaceful development of world order.

A second strategy is to adopt the "lose to win" strategy discussed in Chapter 5. As we indicated there, such a strategy involves the sacrifice of possible short-term gains for the achievement of longer-term goals. It is, typically, an option most relevant to larger, more powerful states (such as the United States) engaged in bargaining with smaller ones. The larger state has the choice of either maximizing its "winnings" now or deliberately taking some short-term "losses" in the interest of nurturing a long-term relationship. The essence of the strategy is to ensure that all the parties involved in a negotiation come away with "something" so that they will willingly participate in future negotiations.

Examples of the application—and misapplication—of such a strategy abound. One recent example that illustrates both is the law of the sea conference.

The law of the sea conference was a series of conferences conducted over a period of years and involving as many as 140 nations. The purpose of the conference was to develop and codify a law of the sea that would be acceptable to all nations. The negotiations involved numerous compromises by all of the major powers—including the United States, the Soviet Union, and important European states—and ultimately produced a draft treaty, the text of which was a living example of the application of a "lose in order to win" strategy.

Many analysts were disappointed, therefore, when the Reagan administration subsequently rejected the full text of the final treaty because it would limit certain U.S. offshore mineral exploration rights and require the United States to share its marine mining technology with other nations. In so doing, the Reagan administration, unlike the four previous administrations that had participated in the law of the sea conference, chose to value the shorter-term interests of a single U.S. industry over the longer-term gains to be derived from acceptance of an agreement that had been painstakingly negotiated over many years. The result was the destruction of prospects for finalizing a truly monumental international achievement—the development of a law of the sea.

The Role of the Individual

What can individuals do to preserve the peace and promote world order? The answer depends in part on whether we are discussing political elites, who clearly are in a position to act on such issues, or ordinary citizens. As we will discuss in Chapter 11, ordinary citizens are playing an increasingly important role in the conduct of international affairs. Here, however, we would like to focus on what can be and has been done by political elites willing to take the initiative in dealing with troubling and controversial issues.

It should be noted that efforts of political elites take place at a time when the ethos of multilateralism at the nation-state level has given way to a manifest unilateralism even as dramatic initiatives by private citizens and nongovernmental elites have become a more prominent feature of international affairs. The contrast here is neither accidental nor ironic. The retreat from efforts to negotiate binding multinational agreements is a clear sign of withdrawal from participation in forging international peace efforts at the nation-state level. But this has occurred at the same time that elites—both governmental and nongovernmental—and broad-based citizen groups have increasingly involved themselves in efforts to draw nations closer together. The former trend may very well have inspired the latter.

The unilateral peace proposal championed by an individual head of state and offered as a means of ending a specific conflict is among the most dramatic and effective individual initiatives on behalf of peace. Such initiatives have in recent years become a common feature of international affairs. Egyptian president Anwar Sadat's dramatic visit to Israel in the 1970s and the subsequent initiative by Jimmy Carter that led to the Camp David accords are prime examples of this approach.

In the mid-1980s we witnessed a similar effort by President Oscar Arias Sánchez of Costa Rica, whose five-nation peace plan advanced prospects for peace in Central America. As of early 1988, his initiative, which he boldly championed in the international arena, had not produced immediate peace. But it had led to the opening of a dialogue between the Sandinista government of Nicaragua and the U.S.-supported insurgency movement, the contras, as well as a proposed schedule for demilitarization and disengagement. For his efforts, President Arias was awarded the 1987 Nobel Peace Prize.

A second area in which individual leaders can play a significant role is in the development of a treaty to limit the production and distribution of conventional arms. Such an effort is a vital first step toward the reduction of state terrorism and international conflict generally. Like the ultimately successful nineteenth-century effort to halt the slave trade, a treaty on conventional arms would almost surely require the cooperation of governmental elites, private industrialists, and individual traders. Without the cooperation of all three, the necessary enforcement measures—the patrol of shipping lanes, the isolation of pariah states, and effective mechanisms for punishing violators—would be impossible. Today's large network of arms suppliers and the trade in conventional arms in which they specialize are major threats to world peace that require the attention of international leaders.

A third area in which individual efforts have the potential to produce significant results is in the development of the "hard" technologies of peace. We do not refer here to programs such as the Strategic Defense Initiative that appear to be totally dependent on a "technological fix." Rather, we are proposing that increased attention be given to the development of devices that might enhance the security of smaller states.

The development of new electronic sensory devices, for example, played a major role in facilitating an Israeli-Egyptian settlement in the Sinai. The installation of such sensors in the Sinai made it possible for Israel to return that territory to Egypt without endangering its own national security. Thus the new technology made it possible for Israel to accede to one of Egypt's preconditions for the recognition of Israel and thus to the eventual settlement formalized at Camp David. Here, then, is an example of a way that, by encouraging the development of technology, political leaders can contribute to the preservation of peace.

As we will note in the chapter that follows, such efforts need not be the exclusive prerogative of national elites. There is a role here too for individual citizens and citizens' groups. The efforts of the latter, in particular, have become increasingly significant in the past decade.

The central point of this chapter is simply that the process of making peace, much like the process of making war, must be envisioned, planned, and undertaken with full vigor in order to succeed. The achievement of international peace will require no small measure of cooperation and social, as well as technological invention, including a recognition that the development of new modes of peacemaking is itself a valuable contribution to international relations. And it requires that nations realize that the gains associated with nonmilitary solutions to their disputes may outweigh those resulting from a resort to violence. Finding new ways to preserve international peace and to build world order is the major challenge of contemporary international relations.

The Readings

Our first excerpt is from a longer piece by Stephenson in which she reviews the literature on modes of conflict reduction and resolution. In the material reprinted here, she examines several techniques for resolving conflict and evaluates their effectiveness. Her discussion of the role of state and nonstate actors is especially helpful in an era when private efforts increasingly parallel public diplomacy.

The second selection, from Boyle's *World Politics and International Law*, argues for a U.S. foreign policy based on principles of international law and organization rather than on a realist conception of power politics. The utility of this reading is that it presents both an argument for law as an aspect of the international system and as a viable strategy for a state's survival in that system.

The third article, Ernst B. Haas's "Regime Decay: Conflict Management and International Organizations, 1945-81," is a systematic analysis of UN efforts to manage conflict. Haas points out that these efforts have passed through several distinct phases and have declined in effectiveness in recent years. This decline, he notes, reflects less the failure of the UN as an organization than it does a loss of faith in the norms of collective security. The responsibility for the decline of collective efforts to manage conflict, he argues, rests especially with those nation-states and national leaders who found it convenient to abandon the norm in pursuit of short-term gains.

Haas's study sets the stage for the policy selections that follow. In the first of these, Assistant Secretary of State for International Organization Affairs Gregory J. Newell sets forth the major reservations about the role of the UN shared by the U.S. government (and much of the American public as well) throughout the 1980s. Newell's perspective clearly contrasts with that of Haas.

In the final selection, Robert C. Johansen challenges both the facts and the spirit of Newell's assertions. Utilizing Haas's findings, Johansen demonstrates that unilateralism has dominated recent U.S. policies, but at considerable cost. He brings into full view the tensions between power politics and the approach to world law and order advocated by Boyle as he critiques U.S. policy's Machiavellian character. Over the long run, U.S. interests would be better served, Johansen asserts, by efforts to support the rule of international law and the organizational structures that embody that law.

CAROLYN STEPHENSON

Alternative Methods for International Security: A Review of the Literature

The primary purpose of this essay is to identify and review the literature which helps us to conceptualize alternative approaches to international security, and to ask what questions this literature opens and what questions it neglects. Although it will be important at some stage to examine systematically all of the peace research and international relations literature in this context, that is beyond the scope of this article, which is to review literature that proposes, investigates, or evaluates less violent methods for national and international security.

What is meant by alternative international security systems? In the broadest sense, an international security system is a group of methods which serve as alternatives to each other for the resolution or regulation of disputes which threaten the security of nations. By resolution or regulation of disputes is meant the settlement of conflict with mutual agreement or the reduction of the level of violence in those conflicts where agreement may not be forthcoming. By security of nations is meant the psychological, economic, socio-political, and military security (freedom from attack and fear of attack) of the *group of individuals* which comprises the *nation*. Individual methods include, among others, fact-finding, discussion, mediation, conciliation, arbitration, world or regional adjudication, strikes, sabotage, economic pressure, guerilla warfare, tank warfare, and nuclear warfare. These available methods are alternatives because they form a range from which combinations are chosen, and not because they are necessarily mutually exclusive (although this may be the case). Individual methods are chosen and grouped to form comprehensive policies in both national and international policy-making. Some of the groups of methods include nonviolent civilian defense, regional organization, world government, international peacekeeping forces, economic cartels, conventional military power, and nuclear deterrence. Insofar as groups of security methods are applied with reference to their effects on one another and the various conflicts they address, they may be regarded as security *systems*.

In this respect, a military system is one of several alternative combinations of security measures. Military security is not discussed in this article for two reasons: 1) it is widely known, discussed, and practiced, and 2) there

From *Peace and Change: A Journal of Peace Research*, Vol. VII, No. 4 (Fall 1981). Reprinted by permission of the publisher.

is a need for knowledge and development of less-violent methods. Accordingly, the methods emphasized in this essay are not only legitimate alternatives in the search for security, but are also alternatives to the war system.

Alternative approaches to security can be categorized in two complementary clusters. The first can be termed a world law/world government/international organization cluster, and the second can be termed a nonviolent conflict resolution cluster. The first literature cluster includes: 1) world law, 2) world government and world federalism, 3) international organization (including regionalism, globalism, functionalism, alliances and collective security), and 4) the United Nations system, and especially the World Court and U.N. peacekeeping forces. The second cluster includes both direct methods of conflict resolution such as nonviolent civilian defense and third-party methods including mediation, conciliation, and arbitration. These two clusters in the literature are complementary and overlap considerably, but they can be distinguished in at least three respects: the first emphasizes *structure* whereas the second emphasizes *process;* the first places a somewhat greater stress on centralized institutions whereas the second stresses decentralization; and the second evinces a greater commitment to the philosophy of nonviolence than does the first. . . .

Nonviolent Methods of Conflict Resolution and Regulation

The second literature cluster to be examined includes both work on the traditional methods of peaceful settlement and work on less traditional processes for the nonviolent resolution or regulation of potentially violent conflict. Three dichotomies characterize this literature, although they are often unstated and unclear. They are differences between: 1) those processes which have as their goal the resolution of conflict and those which are oriented to the regulation or management of it; 2) the processes based on principled nonviolence versus pragmatic nonviolence; and 3) those processes which apply some form of nonviolent coercion and those which eschew coercion in the interest of conversion or reconciliation. Other dichotomies characterize nonviolent methods of conflict resolution: direct and third party, official and unofficial (or governmental and nongovernmental), individual and group, domestic and international. This article excludes individual and domestic conflict resolution processes. Distinctions are difficult because various emphases may characterize the work of any single author or group and all have evolved concurrently. Even the classic example of Mohandas Gandhi encompasses most of these differences. While these distinctions are expressed as dichotomies for the sake of conceptual clarity, it should be clear that each is in fact conceived of as a continuum.

Table 10-1 is an attempt to conceptualize the types of nonviolent methods for the resolution of international conflict which are discussed in the literature, and to give examples of structures or situations within which they have been used.

Methods are listed down the center line according to whether they involve two parties directly resolving a conflict or whether there is a third-party intervention, while examples of the practice of this method by official govern-

Table 10-1 Nonviolent Methods for the Resolution of International Conflict

Governmental/ Intergovernmental		Nongovernmental
Direct		
German government-sponsored noncoopera-tion to French/Belgian occupation of Ruhr (1923)	non-violent civilian defense	Czech resistance, 1968-69
Diplomacy Sadat Feb. 1971 peace initiative	negotiation	international labor-business
G.R.I.T.	"confidence-building" measures	Quaker international service work
Third-Party		
	workshops-seminars	Burton: controlled communication Doob: Fermeda workshop Kelman: interaction approach
"shuttle diplomacy" (US) Algeria (US/Iran) U.N. Sec-Gen. (Congo) Inter-American Peace Committee of OAS	mediation conciliation	journalists (US-USSR-Cuba) International Committee of the Red Cross Quakers (India/Pakistan)
	arbitration	American Arbitration Association
International Court of Justice European Court of Human Rights	judicial decision	
International Peace Academy	peacekeeping	World Peace Brigade

mental or unofficial nongovernmental groups or individuals are listed on the sides. Methods will be discussed in the order listed, an order in which authority provides an internal structure. As one moves down the list, one moves away from control by parties themselves and approximately toward the increasing authority of the third party. Most of those practicing in this area would agree that it is desirable to move toward the greatest degree of control by the parties themselves.

One additional set of process alternatives which, while coercive, exhibit less direct violence than warfare, is the set of economic and other sanctions provided for in Article 41 of the U.N. Charter, including "complete or partial interruption of economic relations and of rail, sea, air, postal, telegraphic, radio, and other means of communication, and the severance of diplomatic relations." Although these are clearly coercive and involve threat rather than exchange or integrative power, they may be less violent than war itself, and thus they may be a useful transitional strategy to more peaceful settlement of disputes. Wallensteen examines the operation of economic sanctions, and Boulding relates economic conflict to general conflict theory. The literature on these methods is vast, crosses the disciplines of political science, economics, and history, and is beyond the purview of this article. Clearly, it requires a comprehensive review in order to be integrated into a general understanding of alternative international security systems. . . .

Not only intergovernmental organizations, but also nation-states and nongovernmental organizations, have been involved in mediation or conciliation. Bailey mentions the Soviet Union's sponsorship of the Tashkent meeting in January 1966, United States use of good offices on the Cyprus question in November/December 1967, and various countries' suggestions in the U.S./Vietnam question. Other examples include U.S. "shuttle diplomacy" in the Middle East and Algeria's role in the crisis between the United States and Iran. In some cases it may not be entirely clear whether a mediator is in fact representing an international organization or a nation-state. As Jacobson puts it, "They may discreetly bring the pressure of their governments to bear on a solution." This point may be illustrated by two case studies of crises in which Ellsworth Bunker played an important role, the Yemen Crisis in 1963 and the Dominican Crisis in 1965.

Private individuals and non-governmental organizations have acted as mediators. Allison has discussed the message-carrying function of correspondents and others during the Cuban missile crisis. Two non-governmental organizations have played roles as mediators in a fairly large number of international crises. The International Committee of the Red Cross is an all-Swiss organization which grew out of the effort to help the wounded in the Italian war of succession in 1859. In carrying out its purpose of providing humanitarian protection and assistance to individuals in "man-made disasters," it has used primarily *ad hoc* diplomacy and has sometimes carried information or established communication between parties, and even contributed to conflict resolution. Because it has not wished to jeopardize its humanitarian role, the ICRC has been extremely reticent about discussing its role and has deemphasized the conflict resolution aspects of that role. Pictet and especially Forsythe have reviewed the ICRC role.

The Society of Friends (Quakers) has been more self-consciously involved in conflict resolution. Warren analyzed his own role in attempting to further communication and conciliation between East and West German policy-makers. Byrd and Yarrow have described a variety of Quaker efforts, including food assistance in Europe after wars, international affairs seminars and conciliation efforts in a number of crises. Yarrow points out that humanitarian action *is* conciliation as well as being the opening to conciliation work between the parties. Yarrow notes the importance of developing credibility, salience, respect and continuity in conciliation work. Among the methods he discusses are listening, message-carrying, correcting misperceptions, and sometimes suggesting solutions. Yarrow's comments in this journal remind one of the similarity between methods of conciliation and the "active-listening" role described in the literature on psychological counseling and parent-effectiveness training. While Yarrow is modest about Quaker efforts, he does point out assets of a non-governmental third-party, including especially the flexibility to talk to unrecognized parties in the dispute.

Young sees the following resources and capabilities as required for successful third-party intervention: impartiality, independence, salience, respect, continuity, knowledge of politico-military affairs, diplomatic skill, initiative, and physical resources and the ability to mobilize them. Arguing that non-governmental organizations lack most of these, Young is skeptical of the value of their intervention, although he concedes the value of such impartiality and independence as they may have. Schelling has also stressed the importance of saliency in the solution of bargaining problems. Kenneth Boulding suggests that a mediator has three functions: to bring together the parties, to suggest or support a salient solution, by means of widening the agenda or other means, and to introduce a new element through outside pressure such as public opinion. Boulding points out that "messages between the parties have to pass through an intense emotional field in which they are likely to be distorted," while the conciliator is outside the field created by the conflict, and so can transmit messages without such extreme distortion.

Boulding, like Wehr, Young, and Jackson, finds the transfer of processes from one conflict arena to another to be helpful. Jackson cites parallels between industrial and international conflicts, including power, balance of power, group survival or vital interest, the status questions, as well as a growing realization of the costs of conflict, and strong emotional overtones. Wehr discusses conflict regulation literatures from a number of areas, including labor, community, family, and environmental dispute regulation, and the sociology of nonvi-olence. His annotated bibliography is a valuable source for further research. A Ford Foundation report on new approaches to conflict resolution examines a variety of approaches from different countries, ranging from neighborhood courts and *ombudsmen*, to arbitration on automobile and medical malpractice suits, to conciliation on family, landlord-tenant, social insurance, labor-management, and consumer problems, and then to the reform of institutions. The Foundation program has been important in a number of action-research projects. While most of these deal with conflict resolution at the individual level, they should at least be examined for relevance to the international system. . . .

International peacekeeping is a category different from the above; its purpose is more regulation than resolution of conflict. The U.N. peacekeeping literature has been discussed above in relationship to international structure. Another type of peacekeeping not discussed above is that of unarmed peacekeeping forces. This follows along the lines of Gandhi's *shanti sena* and its peacemaking/development teams in India. Walker, a founding member of the World Peace Brigade, gives a detailed account of nonviolence in Africa which includes the transnational development of the Brigade. It was founded in Beirut, Lebanon on 1 January 1962 to: 1) "organize, train and keep available a Brigade for nonviolent action" in conflict situations and against war and weapons of mass destruction, 2) "revolutionize the concept of revolution itself by infusing into the methods of resisting injustice the qualities which insure the preservation of human life and dignity," and 3) join people in their "struggle for national liberation and social reconstruction." Based on components from Gandhian movements, Western anti-war groups, local social justice campaigns, and independence movements, it was an attempt to internationalize and institutionalize diverse nonviolence movements. The conflict among nonviolence theorists between the primacy of the goals of reconciliation (through mediation), which stresses impartiality, and confrontation, which stresses partisan support of one side of a struggle, appears to have been built into the concept of the World Peace Brigade. Walker cites lack of organization and the fact that national rather than international action was more appropriate in this context, as the reasons for the loss of momentum for WPB in 1964. WPB is now being reorganized as Peace Brigades International. . . .

Conclusions

It is becoming increasingly clear from the literature that strategies which utilize positive sanctions are more likely to lead to peace than those which utilize negative sanctions. Hopmann's findings, in an examination of the partial test ban negotiations, suggest "that greater belligerency in foreign policy, and especially when tied by threats to negotiations, seems to detract from agreement." Milstein found, in looking at Arab-Israeli situations, that the violent actions of each side tended to be reactions to the other's violent actions rather than to changes in power base. Leng and Wheeler found that a reciprocating strategy is the best means to avoid diplomatic defeat without resort to war. Wallace tested the *realpolitik* dictum "if you want peace, prepare for war," and found that data show that this does not hold, but that on the contrary, if nations prepare for war, they get war. Naroll's study of deterrence through history reaches the same conclusions.

What, then, does the literature tell us about the alternatives to military force in the search for security and the conditions under which these alternatives may work? First, as Kenneth Boulding has said, "The biggest problem in developing the institutions of conflict control is that of catching conflicts young." He recommends "an international organization for the detection of young conflict processes." The use of fact-finding, including the development of data banks for this purpose, is mentioned in Bailey's UNITAR report. Newcombe's tensionometer is intended to measure tension levels between nations to predict war. Singer and Wallace have constructed early warning indicators from the correlates of war project. Hammarskjold's "preventive diplomacy" was a step toward developing a U.N. role in settling conflicts at an early stage.

Second, crises have life cycles with distinguishable phases, and differing scope and intensity, and there are some stages at which third-party intervention is more likely to have a significant effect. Young suggests study of crisis life cycles with a view to determining this. Burton argues that nations are only willing to solve conflicts when the disparity between costs and values is such that there are political pressures to end the conflict. Mitchell claims that the stage of crisis where controlled communication is welcomed and has the most impact is when attitudes are already becoming less rigid and the situation is more "fluid and uncertain." There are some hypotheses about kinds of conflicts in which various kinds of third parties are likely to be most useful. Fisher claims that a third party is less useful in economic or power conflicts than in ideological or value conflicts. Yarrow indicates that conciliation is "most appropriate in conflicts which arise primarily over differences in perception." This is consonant with Coser's statement that the main function of the mediator is to divest conflict situations of unrealistic elements or, as Boulding puts it, to reduce the distortion in the emotional field between the parties.

Third, nations are not likely to accept mechanisms which involve *authority* for a third party on matters of sufficient importance to warrant their consideration of the war alternative. Most of those who write on peacekeeping forces agree that they are useful only at the lower end of the war spectrum. Their role appears to be conflict regulating rather than resolving. Arbitrators appear to have a role in the international system mainly with respect to issues that are not of fundamental concern to nation-states. Peacekeeping, arbitration, and adjudication seem to be *status-quo* oriented.

Fourth, the literature leads us to believe that third-party intervention may only be appropriate in situations where there is a balance between the parties. Schmid argues that third-party intervention will not work in asymmetrical situations, that any peace obtained in that way would be a master-slave peace.

Curle maintains that in an unbalanced relationship mediation and conciliation are not appropriate, because confrontation is required. Where there is a low awareness of the conflict, education is an appropriate strategy to raise the level of awareness to a point of confrontation. At a point of higher awareness, various strategies of confrontation are appropriate to enable the underdogs to reach the point where they can negotiate on the basis of equality. When there is balance and awareness of the conflict, he considers mediation, conciliation and bargaining to be appropriate means to a settlement. Thus nonviolent action is a technique which is useful to the underdog in a situation of inequality for the purpose of attaining equality. It is also appropriate as defense against invasion and occupation, as well as to resist or overthrow an existing regime.

Fifth, the literature tells us that conflict is more easily resolved if one can move from a zero-sum to a positive-sum game. Burton notes that the trends in behavioral science and practice are away from coercive methods of conflict resolution and away from treating conflict as zero-sum. Boulding puts it quite clearly:

> When there seem to be abundant opportunities for increasing the pie, the problem of sharing it falls into the background. Furthermore, in a rich society, the importance of economic conflict is lessened, simply because of the decline in the marginal significance of redistributed income. A conflict about bread is going to be more severe than one about caviar.

Thus we have returned to our restatement of Russett's hypotheses about the conditions of peace in the OECD system: a high and growing amount of wealth, a relative degree of equality, and some autonomy.

Sixth, there appears to be a further requirement which has been the direct focus of this literature review: there is a need for a coordinated and accepted system of mechanisms for the resolution of disputes. Whether as a combination of *ad hoc* methods, or institutionalized in the form of a U.N. body, an independent commission, or as conflict resolution expertise in the relevant departments of each government, a full range of such mechanisms is necessary. Burton prefers the last of these, on the ground that this implies the least central coercion. This may be the most likely for nation-states to accept as well. Whatever the mechanisms, it is clear that there is now a body of specialized techniques, which require research, training and experience, available to nation-states as alternatives to military techniques. These alternative methods for international security may be the invention needed to replace the war system. . . .

■■■■■■ **10.2**

FRANCIS ANTHONY BOYLE

A New Philosophy for American Foreign Policy

The Alternative of International Law and Organizations

One viable alternative to power politics as a basis for the conduct of international relations by the United States can be found in the principles of international law and the procedures of international organizations for the peaceful settlement of international disputes. Adherence to the rules of international law is consistent with American national security interests whether considered expansively in terms of furthering world public order or parochially in terms of satisfying selfish policy goals. The classic Machiavellian dichotomy between the "is" and the "ought to be" does not hold true for American foreign policy decision making. That which is expedient and that which is just coincide and reinforce each other.

This situation exists because the United States is the outstanding example of a status quo power in the post-World War II system of international relations. By virtue of its victory in that war, the preservation of the resulting political, economic, and military status quo is to American advantage. America's national security interests are best served by obedience to international law as a policy for itself as well as other states because such conformity upholds the status quo. To the degree a state enjoys the benefits of the existing configuration of international relations, the greater should be its commitment to upholding international law and to the creation of effective international organizations for the peaceful settlement of disputes.

Phenomenologically, law is the instrument par excellence for the peaceful preservation and transformation of any political or economic status quo, whether domestic or international. By its very nature, the international legal order represents an attempt by advantaged international actors to legitimate (i.e., to impart a moral value content to) preexisting and proposed power relationships. A fundamental transformation in the international balance of power produced by systemic warfare results in the creation of new international law and organizations, which in turn endow these new power relationships with a connotation of moral value. Conversely, a change of international moral values (e.g., self-determination of peoples) produces new international law and organizations (e.g., U.N. General Assembly resolutions and committees

From Francis Anthony Boyle, *World Politics and International Law*. Pages 171-182. Copyright © 1985 Duke University Press. Reprinted with permission.

to promote decolonization), which in turn transform the existing international balance of power (e.g., the creation of a plethora of new states). Throughout this dialectical process, the rules of international law and the institutions of international organizations play the key role of intermediating agent between power and politics, on the one hand, and values and morality, on the other.

For these reasons, this author has emphatically rejected the reigning international legal positivist doctrine that there actually exists some radical phenomenological dichotomy between politics, law, and morality. . . . I have argued instead that there persists a process of dynamic interaction between international politics and international law, whereby the former continuously is and becomes the latter and vice versa. From such a "functionalist" perspective, moral value considerations are yet another element of this dialectical process that constitutes the essence of international political relations.

Because of their inherent propensity for successfully performing such a mediative role for the entire international system, international law and organizations can function as superlative instruments for the peaceful preservation and transformation of the international political and economic status quo even among international actors striving to realize their different and at times diametrically opposed national interests and moral values. International law enunciates those rules which the actors in the international system have found to constitute the least common denominator for that which is both essential and valuable for international life. And that which is both essential and valuable for international life becomes embodied in the rules of international law.

The principles of international law and the existence of international organizations for the peaceful settlement of disputes create a median way between the idealism of human values and aspirations and the reality of disparate power and economic conditions for all states in the international system. There is no realistic alternative for any state on the face of this planet to protect its vital national interests and to promote its cherished national values with due respect for the right of all other states to do the same. Whatever the defects of the contemporary international legal order might be, its improvement is far preferable to the pursuit of Machiavellian power politics, the threat and use of force, and nuclear war. The U.S. government must become the first to re-recognize the critical relevance of international law and organizations for the continued preservation of world peace.

The Relevance of International Law to Crisis Management Decision Making

One corollary to this thesis is that in time of international crisis, the government of a leading status quo state such as the United States should not rely upon dubious international legal principles such as retaliation, retorsion, reprisal, military intervention, counter-intervention, humanitarian intervention, self-help, etc. as a basis for its conduct of crisis management decision making. These alleged principles of customary international law are relics of nineteenth century "gunboat diplomacy" that were inflicted by the world's major imperial powers upon militarily inferior international actors and coveted colonial territories, but which have now been almost universally discredited in the post-U.N. Charter era. Nevertheless, in the late twentieth century, the validity of some of these principles is still stubbornly insisted upon by the great powers and their allies. Yet because of the fundamental transformation in the nature of the international system that has occurred since the mid-nineteenth century, it is precisely these status quo states that should be working most assiduously towards the complete extinction of such retrogressive principles from the recognized corpus of public international law and the established patterns of interstate behavior. When major status quo powers threaten or use force for reasons not explicitly sanctioned by contemporary standards of international law that have been formally accepted by all states of the world community, they undermine the integrity of that very international legal order which they have constructed to protect their vital national interests in the first place. Consequently, those states that currently reap and possess the major benefits of international relations should not unwittingly endeavor to lose them through resort to or encouragement of illegitimate violence and coercion by themselves and others.

In the modern world of international relations, the only legitimate justifications and procedures for the perpetration of violence and coercion by one state against another are those set forth in the U.N. Charter. The Charter alone contains those rules which have been consented to by the virtual unanimity of the international community that has voluntarily joined the United Nations Organization. Therefore, in times of international crisis, a major status quo power such as the United States must in good faith exercise its own threats or use of transnational force in strict accordance with the exact conditions prescribed by the United Nations Charter. These include and are limited to the right of individual and collective self-defense in the event of an "armed attack" as prescribed by article 51; "enforcement action" by the U.N. Security Council as specified in chapter 7; "enforcement action" by the appropriate regional organizations acting with the authorization of the Security Council as required by article 53 and specified in chapter 8; and the so-called peacekeeping operations organized under the jurisdiction of the Security Council pursuant to chapter 6, or under the auspices of the U.N. General Assembly in accordance with the Uniting for Peace Resolution, or by the relevant regional organizations acting in conformity with their proper constitutional procedures and subject to the overall supervision of the U.N. Security Council as specified in chapter 8 and articles 24 and 25.

For a leading status quo power such as the United States to threaten or use force on the basis of alleged justifications derived from antiquated and oppressive principles of customary international law ruthlessly practiced in a relatively primitive and essentially colonialist era of international relations risks generating a tremendous degree of political, economic, and military opposition from both the intended victim and all those states that share in common with it a history of repeated victimization by means of the same set of transparent pretexts for imperialistic intervention, occupation, and exploitation. Such a neo-imperialist policy also risks either nonexistent or minimal support from, or else outright opposition by, America's allied major status quo states acting in sympathy with such victims because the former have finally realized the need to eliminate the last vestiges of their own imperial behavior from the contemporary system of international relations after having experienced its pernicious consequences for themselves. It therefore lies within the vital national interest of a leading status quo power such as the United States for its crisis management decision makers to adopt and firmly adhere to an almost irrefutable presumption against any threat or use of force that does not squarely fit within the extremely few and severely restricted justifications and procedures for transnational violence and coercion set forth in the United Nations Charter. Thus, rather than relying upon doctrinal relics of the colonial past, or inventing novel international legal artifices (e.g., Kennedy's "quarantine" of Cuba), American foreign policy decision makers must restore the Charter as the fundamental operative premise for both the management of international crises and the overall conduct of its international affairs.

The Asymmetries of International Law and Politics

The continued invocation of these outmoded and dangerous principles of customary international law purporting to justify transnational violence and coercion by the government of a leading status quo power such as the United States demonstrates its subliminal attachment to an interconnected set of formal legal propositions. These principles are: (1) that the rules of international law should operate in a perfectly symmetrical manner upon equal and independent sovereign states in their mutual relations; and (2) that the normal condition of strict reciprocity in legal obligations between equal and independent sovereign states generally counsels derogation from a fundamental norm of international law by the government of one state in the event of a prior violation directly affecting it by another sovereign. These basic assumptions of equality, symmetry, and reciprocity in state behavior usually serve their intended purpose of facilitating the routine of day-to-day international relations. But in times of severe international crises, they can quickly prove to be totally dysfunctional for the purpose of crisis management decision making.

Admittedly, it is an elementary principle of international law that all states must be treated as equal and independent since each is sovereign within its own territorial domain. Even though this precept drastically departs from the glaring political, military, and economic inequalities of international life, the doctrine propounding the sovereign equality of states is essential to the preservation of world peace. It impedes the strong from inflicting unbridled depredation on the weak and thus forestalls a cataclysmic struggle among the strong over the division and conquest of the weak.

Nevertheless, although all states are, by definition, equal under international law, they do not all benefit equally from the rules of international law. The major status quo powers in today's world obtain comparatively greater benefits from the current international legal order because, in the aftermath of the Second World War, they possessed the overwhelming degree of political, military, and economic power requisite to promulgate and impose rules designed to operate to their distinct advantage. Thus, the international legal order is an inherently asymmetrical system. It functions to the proportionate advantage of states to the degree they benefit from the existing political, military, and economic status quo. And leading status quo powers such as the United States have the greatest stakes in upholding the integrity of the extant international legal order.

It follows, then, that a violation of an international legal rule by a minor state against a leading status quo power must not be treated by the latter as a sufficient condition for the responsive use of transnational violence and coercion (e.g., retaliation, retorsion, reprisal, intervention, self-help, etc.) in order to protect, assert, or enforce its alleged rights. If the victim of the violation enjoys a greater relative advantage than the violator in the maintenance of the status quo and thus the preservation of the international legal order, the government of the victim state must consider the long-term detrimental effects its arguably unjustifiable counterviolation will inflict on the stability of the entire international system. As a general proposition I should like to suggest that the damage to both its own national security interests and to the international legal, political, and economic status quo resulting from a counterviolation of international law by a leading status quo power almost invariably far outweighs any harm to either that might arise from both the original violation of international law by a minor state together with the supposed harm that might occur from the great power victim not unilaterally prosecuting its rights through illegitimate transnational violence and coercion. In this sense, then, a leading status quo power would be wise to follow Socrates' advice that it is better to suffer injustice than it is to inflict injustice, in the event of an offense perpetrated upon it by a minor state. This conclusion recommends that major status quo states such as the United States rely exclusively on the panoply of rules, techniques, and institutions afforded by the contemporary international legal order for the peaceful settlement of their disputes with minor states.

This recommendation is further strengthened by the observation that the international legal order simultaneously consists of elements and processes of both distributive justice and rectificatory justice as classically defined by Aristotle in book 5 of *The Nicomachean Ethics.* It is fundamentally unfair, transparently hypocritical, and ultimately self-defeating for a major status quo state in conflict with a minor adversary to insist upon its alleged right to rectificatory justice by means of retaliation, retorsion, reprisal, intervention, or self-help when the distributive elements and processes of the international system—whether pertaining to political power, economic wealth, or military might—are already overwhelmingly apportioned and inexorably operating to the former's distinct advantage. In a system of unequally distributed power, it becomes foolish for decision makers in a major status quo state stubbornly to insist upon fulfillment of the punctilio of rectificatory justice in regard to their claims, while at the same time they blithely ignore the claims of a distributive (and rectificatory) nature advanced by a minor adversary. . . . Exclusive reliance upon a rectificatory and positivistic approach to international law and organizations by the United States government throughout the Iranian hostages crisis produced a series of unmitigated disasters for American foreign policy, undermined the integrity of the international legal order, and set back the cause of world peace. . . .

10.3 ∎

ERNST B. HAAS

Regime Decay: Conflict Management and International Organizations, 1945-1981

If no less an expert than the Secretary-General of the United Nations, Javier Perez de Cuellar, declares that the United Nations "often finds itself unable to take decisive action to resolve conflicts and its resolutions are increasingly defied or ignored by those who feel themselves strong enough to do so," we might reasonably think that general disillusionment with the organization is fully justified. The Arab-Israeli conflict, South African repression and aggression, Cyprus, unrest in Southeast Asia, and the Kashmir dispute have been on the UN agenda almost since its inception. Nor have the conditions underlying these conflicts—arms races, insecurity, racial discrimination, demand for scarce resources, and mutually incompatible claims for national self-determination—been improved by collective action.

Yet it would be erroneous to claim that "the United Nations has failed" just because the record in the 1970s might show some marked change over the previous twenty-five years. Before correcting the error, however, the particulars of the decline must be admitted. First, the record of the United Nations and of the Organization of American States (OAS) in abating, isolating, and settling disputes among its members, as well as in stopping hostilities, has

Reprinted from *International Organization* Vol. 37: #2 by permission of The MIT Press, Cambridge, Massachusetts. Copyright © 1983 by the MIT Press.

worsened sharply since 1970. Second, that decline has not been compensated for by a proportional improvement in the success of the conflict management activities of the Arab League and the Organization of African Unity. Third, recent efforts to manage conflicts in Timor, Lebanon, Cambodia, Angola, Namibia, the Falkland Islands, and the Shatt-el-Arab have been characterized more by rhetorical posturing than by efforts to maintain or restore peace. Fourth, instead of routinized mediation and peacekeeping activities, large public conferences have become the preferred way of managing conflict. Finally, the major powers no longer exercise leadership in conflict management, the role of secretariats has declined, and financial and political disagreements militate against the mounting of operations to keep the peace and supervise truce agreements.

Is Collective Conflict Management a Failed Regime?

The common impression that collective conflict management has failed derives from the mistaken notion that the United Nations and the regional organizations are autonomous entities, set up to coerce or cajole states into substituting cooperation for conflict. Indeed, the very idea that cooperation is the opposite of conflict is a misconception in which professional analysts as well as the lay public widely indulge. The United Nations or the OAS cannot "fail," but their members can behave in such a fashion toward one another as to give life to the principles, norms, rules, and procedures enshrined in these organizations—or they can fail to do so.

These organizations were created to moderate conflict. (It bears repeating that conflict among states was and is taken as a given; conflict is, after all, almost a synonym for politics.) They were designed to reduce "collective insecurity dilemmas" stemming from their members' antagonistic striving for individual security. While they stress concerted action by some or all members as the desirable method for managing conflict, this is a long way from institutionalizing "cooperation" as a principle of behavior to substitute for managed conflict. To insist that the success of the United Nations must mean the victory of cooperation over conflict is to interpret world politics as an all-or-nothing game.

Collective conflict management is an aspect of foreign policy; it does not replace foreign policy. Diplomacy and action in the United Nations or a regional organization provide another way of implementing foreign policy. Far from transcending the objectives that states consider to be their national interests, conflict management organizations are forums for realizing these interests when action outside the organizations is either not possible or not desired. Action by the organizations never monopolizes the possibilities open to states; action outside them is usually possible and sometimes preferred. It is, of course, true that many in 1945 expected that the cumulative channeling of national objectives into these organizations would eventually lead to the institutionalized resolution of all interstate conflict by means of routinized procedures. Bilateral conflict would be moderated as the techniques of third-party intercession became accepted and the organizations might thus develop into autonomous agencies. Freed from continuing dependence on their member governments they would become actors on the international stage in their own right and thus properly become the targets of judgments of success and failure, much like autonomous bureaucratic agencies at the national level. We know this did not happen; we wish to know what occurred instead. That inquiry necessitates the substitution of the notion of "regime" for the more familiar "organization."

Regimes are often confused with organizations, with the international system, and with international order. They are none of these things. (When I later continue the practice of anthropomorphizing the United Nations the reader should recall that this is verbal shorthand for saying "the members of the regime did such and such.") Deterrence, strategic bargaining, military balances, unrequited aspirations for national self-determination, the fear of communist or capitalist encirclement—all of these are aspects of the international system and ingredients of foreign policy. The desire for peace and justice, an end to racism and the persecution of minorities, and the reduction of armaments—these constitute designs for a world order, a normatively better future. Though regimes may contribute to a new order or confirm the patterns inherent in the system they are none of these things; rather, they are man-made arrangements to manage conflict that originates in the system. Thus regimes ought not to be credited with maintaining international equilibrium, redistributing resources, dampening ideological fervor, or providing justice. Member states do these things or, more often, fail to do them. States interact within regimes to realize national interests; in the process they may accomplish outcomes related to systems maintenance or world order but regimes are not designed to produce such outcomes. Analysts focus studies of conflict management at the microlevel, the level of behavior. The association of the regime with the system and with world order implies projective judgments at the macrolevel. It is the microperspective which is our major concern here.

An international regime is a set of principles, explicit or implicit, norms, rules, and decision-making procedures around which the expectations of actors converge in order to coordinate actors' behavior with respect to an issue of concern to them all—in this case, the management of interstate conflict. Principles are beliefs of fact, causation, and rectitude. Norms are standards of behavior defined in terms of rights and obligations. Rules are specific prescriptions and prohibitions with respect to actors' behavior. Procedures are the prevailing practices for making and implementing collective choices. Analysts agree that these definitions tell us something about the manner in which states come to terms with complex interdependence in such fields as trade, money, health, and the protection of the environment. Whether we can say that regimes for conflict management exist is, however, a matter of controversy. Collective security, after all, is the issue-area least likely to be enshrined in a regime. The reason for this is clear: compared to other aspects of interdependence, collective insecurity as a matter of definition contains fewer shared objectives and more salient occasions for unilateral assertion. Why, then, discuss conflict management as if it were a regime?

The Argument

I intend to show that talk of the "failure of the United Nations" and of other entities as "organizations" is misleading and inaccurate. Failure as compared to what? Is there more intolerable conflict today as compared to 1950 or 1970? Are noninstitutionalized modes of managing conflict more successful than they were? I argue that "decay" is a more appropriate image for describing what has happened. Decay implies the gradual disintegration of a previously routinized pattern of conduct. If the concept of regime has been reasonably successful in describing such processes in other issue-areas, we ought to make the attempt to show its utility in the field of collective insecurity and its management. If the concept proves useful in this, the most demanding of issue-areas, its utility in other arenas of world politics will be all the more persuasive. Seen in this light, collective conflict management provides the limiting case for determining the overall applicability of the regime concept. It might give us a tool for describing the growth, stability, decay, or death of complex routines of behavior that cut across international organizations and take in only a portion of the total mandate of each organization.

My argument, futhermore, seeks to demonstrate just how decay came about. This requires a historical and statistical description of the effectiveness and the coherence of the regime, assuming, of course, that the existence of a regime can be demonstrated successfully. *Effectiveness* consists of the ability of member states to use the routines enshrined in principles, norms, rules, and procedures to moderate successfully the conflicts referred to the organizations; it also involves the stability to persuade members to refer the bulk of their disputes to the organizations instead of seeking unilateral or bilateral solutions. Effectiveness thus consists of a wide scope of activity matched with high success in management. The *coherence* of a regime consists of the mutual complementarity of its principles, norms, rules, and procedures—the support these components give one another. Effectiveness captures performance and behavior; coherence captures the institutional routines that are designed to channel behavior.

Given the well-known lag between behavior and institutions we cannot expect to map the life of the regime as if there were a perfect covariation between effectiveness and coherence. If the concept has any utility, however, we can expect that movement will be roughly in the same direction. This allows us to posit four possibilities in observing the "life" of regimes. Regime "growth" occurs when effectiveness and coherence increase in tandem. "Stability" prevails if the initial level of performance remains steady and is matched by an unchanging adjustment between the components. "Death" occurs when scope declines even though the regime may remain successful with respect to the remaining disputes referred to it and even though the coherence remains the same; of course success and coherence may also decline. "Decay," finally, is the situation in which both effectiveness and coherence decline but not necessarily in such a fashion that scope, success, and mutual complementarity of regime components covary perfectly.

My final task is to explain why decay occurred after a period of growth and after a decade of seeming stability. I shall examine several hypotheses, which are far from mutually exclusive.

1. Decline in effectiveness and coherence is due to the waning hegemony of the United States in world politics; earlier success was associated with active American leadership.

2. Decline in effectiveness and coherence in the United Nations is due to the increase in the number of voting blocs and the fragmentation of common interests and consensus among them. Winning coalitions on issues that earlier commanded big majorities can no longer be formed.

3. Winning coalitions and a wide consensus were associated with the predominance of the Cold War and decolonization as metaissues. The decline in salience of the metaissues implies a fragmentation of concern with conflict.

4. The remaining metaissues create an incentive for resolving conflicts in regional organizations rather than in the United Nations in order to isolate conflicts from global infection.

Effectiveness of the Regime

The UN Charter's Principles, Norms, Rules, and Procedures

Three principles of the regime are explicitly stated in the UN Charter. One affirms the notion of collective security (Art. 1); the second reaffirms the sovereign equality of the members (Art. 2 [1]); the third reaffirms that treaties are binding (Arts. 2 [2] and 25). A fourth principle is implicit in this regime as in all others: the benefits accruing to the members are expected to be roughly reciprocal even though sacrifices made in furthering the explicit principles need not be.

What, then, are the norms? The Charter recognizes several rights of the members. All peace-loving states able and willing to abide by the principles are entitled to membership (Art. 4). Disputes "essentially within the domestic jurisdiction" of a member are exempt from the principles and other norms (Art. 2 [7]). The right of self-defense remains unimpaired (Art. 51). Regional security arrangements outside the United Nations are permissible (Art. 52 [1]). The obligations of members specify the types of behaviors required to meet the principle of collective security. Thus "all Members shall settle their international disputes by peaceful means. . ." (Art. 2 [3]); "all Members shall refrain in their international relations from the threat or use of force . . ." (Art. 2 [4]); and "all Members shall give the United Nations every assistance in any action it takes. . ." (Art. 2 [5]). Finally, the recognized superiority of the Security Council in the management of conflicts (Art. 24) implies a particular right for its permanent members and an obligation for all others to abide by the inequality.

Norms are specifications of behaviors required to make principles real. Rules specify behaviors required to make norms real. The UN Charter lists these in the enumeration of the powers of its main organs; the same is true of decision-making procedures. Both can also be phrased as "obligations of the members," an expression I avoid only because it is cumbersome. The rules provide for the creation of a Military Staff Committee to aid the Security Council in mounting enforcement actions and for the duty of the membership to aid in their execution (Arts. 26, 47, 48). The details of how the peaceful settlement of disputes is to be carried out are enumerated in Articles 33 through 38. The Security Council determines whether armed attacks or acts of aggression have taken place (Arts. 39, 40). It also decides whether and what type of enforcement measures shall be taken (Arts. 41, 42, 48, 49). Member states are obliged to earmark military forces for such operations (Arts. 43-45). The General Assembly is to initiate studies and inquiries to determine whether situations exist that warrant the triggering of the conflict management rules (Arts. 13, 14). It also has the rights to concern itself with collective security when a specific dispute is not on the Security Council agenda, to call threats to peace to the Council's attention, and to be kept informed by the Council (Arts. 10, 11, 12). Regional arrangements are to be coordinated with UN plans (Arts. 52 [2-3], 53, 54). The Security Council is to enforce awards of the International Court of Justice (Art. 94). And the members are to hold Charter review conferences (Art. 109). The General Assembly approves the budget, assesses the annual contributions of the members, and suspends members for failure to pay them (Arts. 17 [3], 19).

Decision-making procedures tell us how the rules can be triggered. The General Assembly's resolutions are only recommendations (Arts. 11, 12, 35 [3]). Important recommendations require a two-thirds majority, less important ones a simple majority (Art. 18). The General Assembly can suspend or expel members (Arts. 5, 6) and establish subsidiary organs (Art. 22). The Security Council's oligarchic membership is specified in Art. 23 (as amended) and its restrictive voting procedures in Art. 27 (as amended). States not members of the Council are to be represented in discussions concerning conflicts in which they are involved (Arts. 31, 32). The Security Council can block amendments to the Charter (Art. 108), applications for membership (Art. 4 [2]), and the election of the Secretary-General (Art. 97); authority for initiating action on membership, amendments, and electing the Secretary-

General is vested in the General Assembly. Finally, the Secretary-General has the right to call threatening conflicts to the attention of the members (Arts. 12 [2], 99).

So much for the formal components of the regime, as instituted in 1945. Are these principles, norms, rules, and procedures mutually supportive and coherent? The norms do support the principles (if we overlook the fact that the principle of sovereign equality is not perfectly served by enshrining the oligarchy of the five permanent members as a norm). However, the norms are not mutually supportive in every way because there are two major escape clauses. The norm of individual and collective self-defense, when coupled to the voting procedure in the Security Council and the status of regional arrangements, contradicts the norms that are to govern state behavior. The domestic jurisdiction clause throws in doubt the type of conflict that is to be managed in the regime. Nevertheless, rules and procedures do serve the norms with a high degree of consistency. Thus, while the fit among the parts of the regime is not perfect, it is good enough to warrant the continuation of our inquiry. . . .

Correlates of Decay: The United Nations

To the extent that interpretations can be offered without looking at specific disputes and without allowing for situations specific to certain eras— such as the personality of secretaries-general or the overall turbulence of the global system—success for the United Nations over its entire history has ten characteristics.

1. The most intense disputes are the most likely to be managed. Insignificant and very low-intensity disputes can be marginally influenced. Disputes in the intermediate levels of intensity seem to be the most difficult to manage.

2. Unfortunately, the findings for intense disputes do not match the performance of the United Nations with respect to the seriousness of the fighting. Only 45 percent of the cases involving active warfare were managed, though the United Nations' impact tended to be moderate or great. Success comes more readily when the fighting is very limited, though then the impact is usually slight. It also seems clear that cases which did not involve fighting were not taken very seriously.

3. However, the most contagious disputes are the ones most frequently influenced by the United Nations, very often with great success. Disputes that the neighbors of the main contending parties are about to enter actively are the most difficult to manage, whereas it seems relatively simple to score some minimal impact on purely bilateral disputes.

4. Decolonization disputes are most readily managed, Cold War disputes very rarely (and then with minimal impact), while disputes not related to the metaissues show a very indifferent rate of success.

5. Cold War alignments complicate the management of conflict considerably.

6. Disputes involving the superpowers are very rarely managed with success, but cases pitting the weakest UN members against each other do not fare so well either. Disputes involving middle powers such as Argentina, Mexico, Egypt, Pakistan, the Netherlands, Belgium, and Spain yield most easily to UN action.

7. Strong decisions bring results. However, the failure to make a decision does not necessarily imply the failure of conflict management.

8. Energetic measures to enforce a truce and to separate the contestants bring results, overwhelmingly with great success. But small-scale mediation and conciliation also pay off over half of the time. However, we must recall that many of the instances of "no operation" were such as to make field missions inappropriate or impossible.

9. Weak powers make poor leaders but more powerful states do not do much better. When the superpowers happen to exercise their leadership together, of course, they are usually successful. The single most effective mode of leadership is the initiative of the Secretary-General, acting either alone or in concert with one of the larger states.

10. No effective action is possible without a wide or very wide consensus among the members.

Figure 10-2   Eventual Resolution of Failed UN and Nonreferred Disputes (N=154), in Percent

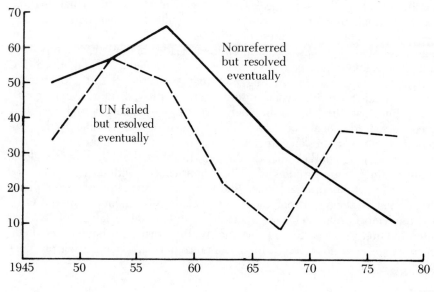

There is an appreciable difference between situations in which a major impact was scored and those in which a marginal one was scored. Major impact is correlated with active warfare, decolonization issues (until 1965), disputes involving super and large powers (until 1970), strong decisions, large operations, and the leadership of the Secretary-General. These add up to a very restrictive profile of disputes on which the United Nations had a major impact. Much more versatility, however, is suggested by the cases in which we observe only minor impact. Instances of marginal effectiveness are spread over a wide spectrum of dispute attributes and modes of management. If the membership is sufficiently concerned, it appears, the United Nations may still make a limited difference in a wide variety of circumstances even though the members will tend not to use it in decisively abating, isolating, or settling their disputes.

Can the United Nations' decline in success and scope since 1970 be correlated with any of the variables for describing salience? . . . While decay cannot be explained exclusively in terms of the changing salience of conflict, it appears as if a decline in salience induces the members to tolerate conflict rather than to manage it.

Conclusion

The aggregate success scored by most international organizations in managing conflicts has declined steadily after 1970. Success diminished with the advent of disputes among small and middle powers that did not relate to decolonization and the Cold War; the domination of the procedure by small and middle powers who are nonaligned with respect to the Cold War; the increasing average intensity of disputes; and the increasing incidence of disputes of local significance. These aspects of the international environment in which the conflicts arose, in turn, resulted in behaviors characterized by the reluctance of most organizations to adopt substantively meaningful decisions; the absence of prominent leadership by the superpowers; and the decline of leadership by the Secretary-General. Put slightly differently, the historical record suggests that collective efforts to manage conflict tend to thrive when disputes are perceived to threaten *global* peace but that they languish when disputes are scattered and relatively unconnected to global concerns. The corollary of this finding is the tendency on the part of some regional organizations to be increasingly effective in managing conflicts that do threaten to infect the region with a global ailment. Since some disputes of global significance continue to be referred to the United Nations and since states apparently are unwilling to have the United Nations confront them energetically, the members of the OAU and the Arab League seek to compensate by upgrading regional activity. This interpretation is strengthened by the finding that the number of high-intensity disputes not referred to any organization has declined sharply since 1975.

Coherence of the Regime

Change in Regime Coherence

Such are the facts of recent history. They suggest that the actors on the stage of world politics have learned little; or, perhaps, they have learned to manage conflict without needing an effective regime. After all, the sharp rise in international disputes since 1975 (after many ups and downs since 1945) has led neither to nuclear nor to a big conventional war. Before coming to any such conclusion, however, we have to show what happened to the regime during the process of decay. This requires us to summarize changes in principles, norms, rules, and procedures in such a way as to throw into relief the differences in pattern between the relatively successful initial twenty-five years and the more recent era of relative failure. And this leads us to a crucial question: why did improvements in regime coherence mapped during the first period not lead to their stabilization in the second?

Principles may change for a number of reasons, such as the appearance of a large number of new actors whose beliefs about causation and rectitude differ from the original membership's because of the emergence of new demands and of different expectations of behavior. If these demands and expectations prevail and agreement on new principles can be achieved, the regime "grows." If, however, the old and the new actors cannot agree, the regime "dies." Evidence of the death of a regime includes the withdrawal of large numbers of members or of a few important members, nonpayment of contributions, systematic absence from meetings, or consistent violations of norms by most of the members. The United Nations is not often plagued by such behavior. In all formal ways, the regime continues to exist and its scope remains wide. But it neither grew nor stabilized after 1970; the attributes of decay become crucial for understanding. Decay must be studied by looking at the changing coherence of norms, rules, and procedures in relation to principles. Norms may require adaptation for two reasons. It may become apparent that the initial fit between norms and principles was poor and that norms must be adjusted to serve principles better. In addition, the initial coherence among norms may have been deficient. The same is also true of rules and procedures. Each component may suffer from poor adjustment to the next "higher" component or with respect to the other rules and procedures. Moreover, the lack of fit may occur because of initial design flaws or because the next higher component is changing. Rules and procedures may require adaptation because norms are changing or even if norms remain constant.

Thus the coherence of a regime increases if norms that were initially poorly adjusted to one another are later made more mutually supportive; it decreases if norms are progressively permitted to contradict one another. Unless new norms improve the principles, a change in norms undermines the regime. Coherence decreases when the new norms tend to make the principle of collective security more problematic.

Regime Components and the United Nations

The subsequent discussion focuses on changes in the United Nations and neglects the regional organizations. We have seen that, despite the original regime norms, the regionals were progressively detached from UN procedures. Their development as separate entities further underlines the decay of the original regime.

Mapping changes in regime components is a tedious business, justified only if we take seriously our commitment as students of regimes to the concepts we have developed for these studies. There is no justification for using the terms unless we take the trouble to demonstrate what they can tell us about historical events. Nevertheless, we ought not to expect a perfect match between changes in regime components and the ups and downs in regime effectiveness. Principles, norms, rules, and procedures do not change even in five-year increments. Earlier changes are rarely repealed in later periods; they linger on as new changes are superimposed on them.

If we isolate certain features of UN practice, the historical record breaks down into four eras, though they overlap a bit. The features of interest are the overall pattern of polarity in world politics; the salience of the Cold War in world politics and the alignments among states that show up in UN behavior as a result; leadership exercised by the Cold War superpowers in the United Nations; and the consensus among the other members they are able to mobilize. The combination of these four features gives us eras I shall label "the concert" (1945-47 and occasionally thereafter), "permissive enforcement with balancing" (1948-55), "permissive engagement" (1956-70), and—despite my best efforts to find a pattern—a rather chaotic period of "no pattern" at all since 1970. The initial period of "the concert" corresponds to the regime components found in the UN Charter, which I have described earlier. Changes in components, therefore, must be analyzed with the concert as the baseline. In the terminology used by Mark Zacher, the trajectory of the regime ran from a principle of consensus to one of competition. While that competition in turn corresponded to a discernible pattern for over twenty years, my evidence suggests that this is no longer the case. . . .

Why Did the Regime Decay?

Before we consider the explanatory persuasiveness of the hypotheses advanced in the introduction, a prior question requires an answer: did the decline in effectiveness match the decline in coherence and did it match an increase in the ability of states to manage their conflicts peacefully outside the regime? Table 10-2 contrasts the success of the United Nations with the success

Table 10-2 Comparison of Scope, Success, Coherence, by Era

	% of Disputes Wholly or Partly Managed (N = 202)		Did UN Success Improve over Previous Period?	Did Regime Coherence Change over Previous Period?
	UN	Nonreferred		
1945-50	65	50	—	—
1951-55	33	57	No	Improvement
1956-50	69	67	Yes	Further improvement
1961-65	44	50	No	Stable
1966-70	64	33	Yes	Stable
1971-75	42	22	No	Decline
1976-81	42	10	No	Further decline

achieved by the parties in managing nonreferred disputes. We would have to find an inverse temporal relationship between the two columns in order to conclude that the world is about as well off without the United Nations. Table 10-2 also contrasts, era by era, changes in coherence with declining success. Even though the matching is not perfect the movement is in the predicted direction.

The United Nations lagged behind bilateral and extraorganizational success in managing conflict during the height of the Cold War and during the period of declining permissive engagement; it performed better than the extraorganizational efforts of states in five out of seven periods, including the most recent decade. There is no dominantly inverse relationship. This finding provides further evidence that obituaries for the United Nations are premature. Why did improvements in coherence not always correspond to improved performance? The same two five-year periods impair the perfect match. Improvements in coherence in 1951-55 were achieved in defiance of the Soviet Union, whose policy was also responsible for preventing additional success in conflict management; this situation was reversed in the next period, because the Soviets accommodated themselves to the regime's changes. In 1961-65 the previous improvements in coherence were stabilized but performance declined anyway. By 1970, effectivenss and regime coherence were moving in tandem—downward. Clearly there is a lag between institutional innovation and stability and the behavior of states with respect to conflict management.

Declining American Hegemony?

One popular explanation for the decay of the United Nations is the so-called "declining hegemony" thesis. Hegemony may be conceived as the national capability to advance long-range visions of world order (such as the

527

notion of collective security and other UN principles) by working with the preponderant resources available to the hegemon for the success of institutions charged with that task. In addition a hegemon would be expected to make side payments to reluctant coalition partners unwilling to follow the hegemon's lead spontaneously; and the hegemon is expected to forego its own short-range interests in favor of the final goal. Table 10-3 shows that the capability of the United States, in terms of overall economic and military power, eroded as the United Nations decayed. That, however, is not enough to prove that there was a causal connection between the two trends.

It is undeniable that the success of the United Nations until the early 1960s was due in large measure to American leadership, pressure, and support. Most institutional innovations were initiated by the United States or its close allies, the bulk of UN conflict management policy and procedures was consistent with American interests, and the United States offered side payments in the form of shouldering annually up to 33 percent of the organization's regular budget and sometimes as much as 50 percent of the technical assistance and humanitarian relief funds. Why, then, is the declining hegemony argument inconclusive? Some relevant consideration can be gleaned from Figure 10-3.

The United States began to declare its reluctance to make these side payments in 1962, with the insistence that peacekeeping expenses be paid by all members in proportion to their share of the regular budget contributions. It became more strident in 1965, with the insistence that the American contribution to the regular budget be kept to 25 percent annually. However, UN

Table 10-3 Indicators of U.S. Power Capability: Ratio of U.S. to World Total

	1950	1960	1970	1976	1978
National income[a]		.45	.39	.31	.29
Crude petroleum production	.53	.33	.21	.14	.14
Crude steel production	.45	.26	.20	.17	.16
Iron ore production	.42	.19	.13	.10	.09
Wheat production	.17	.15	.12	.14	.10
International financial reserves	.49	.21	.16	.07	.05
Military expenditures	.32	.48	.35	.27	.25
Exports	.18	.16	.14	.11	.11
Foreign aid[b]		.58	.45	.32	.29

[a] Only market economy countries.
[b] Only members of OECD, Development Assistance Committee.

Source: Updated from Stephen D. Krasner, "American Policy and Global Economic Stability," in William P. Avery and David P. Rapkin, eds., *America in a Changing World Political Economy* (New York: Longman, 1982), Table 2.2.

Figure 10-3 Indicators of U.S. Satisfaction with the United Nations, in Percent

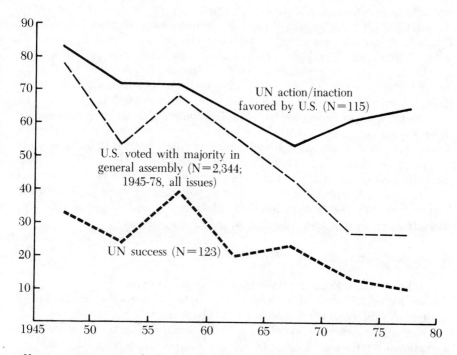

effectiveness *improved* after 1965, albeit not for long. Figure 10-3 also shows that the support the United States could garner in the General Assembly declined sharply after 1960; however, this occurred too soon to be consistent with the hypothesis and the same is true of the data summarizing U.S. support of and satisfaction with UN decisions. True, the divergence between UN decisions and U.S. preferences grew after 1960; but U.S. satisfaction never fell below 54 percent and *rose* again after 1965, even though overall UN effectiveness declined. This was not a bad showing for a fading hegemon.

The niggardliness of the United States with respect to financial contributions can hardly be blamed on a declining economic position, since the sums in question are paltry. Moreover, the U.S. contribution to the UN Emergency Force in the Sinai remained at 37 percent per year until 1967 (from a high of 47% in 1957). The United States paid between one half and one third of the Congo force's expenses every year between 1960 and 1964. Contributions to the force in Cyprus hovered around 40 percent per year until 1971; they rose to 50 percent for the period 1973-78. On the other hand, the expenses for the three UN forces separating Israel from the Arabs since 1974 have been borne by the regular UN budget, a signal victory for the American position. In short, when it suited American interests there was a willingness to pay for UN operations in excess of the declared ceiling on contributions.

One source of the mismatch between overall declining hegemony and the continuing U.S. role in the United Nations may be in the confounding of hegemony with influence. My data on leadership clearly show that the United States no longer tried very hard to impose its conflict management preferences after 1955, though Dag Hammarskjold largely assumed those preferences for the United States for another six years. Furthermore, after 1965 the United States had to resort to the veto to defend its interests. Was this inevitable? If the failure to exercise consistent leadership is to be associated with declining overall hegemony, it happened much too soon. Declining influence probably resulted from the appointment in the 1970s of a number of permanent representatives (Moynihan, Young, Kirkpatrick) chosen less for their abilities to build supporting coalitions than to propound America's displeasure with the Third World majority's economic and racial demands or to demonstrate America's support for national self-determination. It is quite possible that more diplomatically conservative representatives (Scranton, McHenry) could, if given the time, have reasserted American influence in building coalitions.

Unstable Alignments, Shattered Consensus

The notion of declining American influence is entirely compatible with a second hypothesis about the decay of the United Nations. As the number of voting blocs increases the simple distinction between U.S. and Soviet allies loses its salience as a constraint on behavior. It also means that, as there are more sets of national interests to be brought under a single hat, consensus comes about with greater difficulty. Therefore, winning coalitions have become more difficult to build.

This hypothesis also assumes that the early successes of the United Nations are largely explicable in terms of the importance of alignments. While effective conflict management could not be expected in situations pitting the opposing Cold War coalitions against one another, conflict management was quite possible when a member of one alignment faced a nonaligned antagonist. Moreover, this hypothesis suggests that UN effectiveness would remain respectable as long as the parties to dispute are superpowers, large powers, or smaller states under the diplomatic and military influence of a superpower. Nonaligned small states, however, escape these constraints. The increasing numbers would thus complicate conflict management because they are not reliable coalition partners and do not necessarily share the objectives of other states sufficiently to be part of a stable consensus.

Figure 10-4 gives considerable support to this explanation. It shows that while the main nonimplementers of UN decisions were until 1970 the members of Cold War alignments, this is no longer true. Now the nonaligned middle and smaller powers are the culprits. The curve confirms that in the most recent periods the earlier explanatory power of alignments in predicting UN involve-

Figure 10-4 Nonimplementers of Substantive UN Decisions (N=50), in Percent

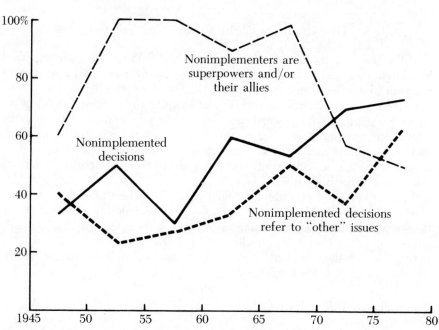

ment *and* UN success no longer holds. The diplomatic and military texture of the world has perhaps grown too complex for effective collective security practices.

The Decline of Metaissues

This explanation is, in turn, entirely consistent with another hypothesis: regime effectiveness and coherence are associated with a small number of metaissues around which consensus could be built. Once these metaissues lose their relevance and if no new overarching concern develops, conflict management becomes less effective.

Figure 10-4 also confirms this hypothesis. Decay is associated with the advent of nonaligned smaller states as the main antagonists; so is the increasing incidence of issues other than decolonization and the Cold War. The successes scored by the United Nations before 1970 were heavily concentrated on managing conflicts associated with colonial liberation movements. Now, few remain and they are recalcitrant cases. On the other hand, civil wars among rival movements in new countries, though perhaps supported by other states, cannot be considered as cases of decolonization. Global conflict may be increasing, but the issues over which countries disagree no longer fit the earlier categories. The regime has become the victim of the trend.

The Attempt to Achieve Regional Isolation

The decay of the United Nations and of the OAS has been accompanied by a slight increase in the effectiveness of the Arab League and a temporary spurt in the effectiveness of the OAU. These developments have been associated with an increase in disputes that threaten the intervention of distant and even extraregional powers and a spreading of the dispute beyond the immediate antagonists and their neighbors. This pattern suggests that, in Africa and in the Middle East, states are making an attempt to manage their conflicts in such a manner as to head off foreign intervention on a large scale, though not always successfully. It is unlikely, in view of the earlier histories of the OAU and the League, that the attempt would be made if the United Nations were perceived as an effective forum for guaranteeing isolation of disputes. Hence the decay of the United Nations with respect to consensus, the unstable alignment pattern, and the decline of metaissues are consistent with the hypothesis that these regional organizations now seek to compensate for the deficiencies of global arrangements.

Tolerance of Unresolved Conflict

These four hypotheses imply that the members of the regime display a far more tolerant attitude toward the nonresolution of conflict than the original principles and norms of the regime might have suggested, a situation predictable from the confirmation of the hypotheses. The principle of collective security is the principle of "all for one"; each state's insecurity is potentially of concern to all states. The decay of the regime demonstrates that belief in this principle has weakened during the almost forty years that have elapsed since World War II. Tolerance for the nonresolution of many conflicts, or acceptance of a certain permanent amount of conflict, is but the corollary of this weakened belief. Does regime decay therefore mean that states have become indifferent to conflict and its collective management, that they have learned nothing since 1965?

The conclusion that nothing has been learned can be justified only if we assume that the purpose of the regime was to create a new international order of peace, to transform the international system of sovereign states into a supranational system ruled by the superpowers and a few large states, and to turn the United Nations and the regional entities into a single autonomous organization charged with enforcing that supranationalism. Even if, in 1945, it was hoped that the regime would prevent (or at least limit) the use of force in all of international relations, this hope was soon scaled down to the expectation of limiting only those conflicts that, because of their potential destructiveness, threaten the system of independent states. The regime was soon turned into the instrument for tripling the number of sovereign entities. Many of them were and are motivated by the same fear of collective insecurity that elicited the creation of the regime. The old system was reenforced, not transcended, and given the principles of the regime no new order could come from the old. No autonomous organizations developed in the field of conflict management because the members did not wish them to develop. We cannot blame the United Nations or its members for not learning an institutional lesson that calls for moral perfectibility as the metaprinciple of the evolution of international relations.

The toleration of relatively low levels of conflict, however, is itself a lesson that has been learned. No conflict that threatens the system of independent states has emerged since 1945. Even the Cold War was managed, at least until now. Governments in the 1970s have learned to tolerate a level of conflict that does not threaten the system as a whole, while the United Nations and regional organizations continue to be effective in abating many conflicts and settling a few. Regime decay is not incompatible with learning lessons at another level of consciousness. The toleration of conflict that remains diffused, confined to weak states, and removed to the periphery of politics and geography may be a second-best solution to the problem of war. But it is better than making every conflict a matter of principle. Rousseau's metaphor of the staghunt retains all of its evocative power: hunting hares separately may not be as good as hunting a stag through collective effort, but it beats starving to death.

■■■■■■■ **10.4**

GREGORY J. NEWELL

The UN at Forty: Realism and Reappraisal

Forty years have now passed under the UN system, but events in the world at large have not taken the course that the founders envisioned. It never was plausible that the major powers among the victorious allies could cooperatively police the world and unitedly suppress all aggression. None now hold the belief that mere membership in the United Nations (or League of Nations) could banish conflict. The cause was oversold; disappointment was inevitable.

In his January 31, 1985, testimony before the Senate Foreign Relations Committee, Secretary Shultz expressed a legitimate and longstanding aspiration when he surveyed our past, our present, and a hoped-for future state of foreign relations.

An address before the Concord Century Club, Concord, California, June 25, 1985.

> This is an auspicious moment. . . . It is, for many reasons, a time of great
> promise and opportunity for the United States in world affairs.
> [T]oday . . . I would like to step back a bit and look at the present
> situation in . . . the perspective of the intellectual currents of our time, and the
> perspective of America's ideals and . . . the world's future. . . .
> [The year] 1945 . . . marked a major turning point. An international
> system that had lasted for more than a century had broken down under the
> weight of two world wars and a great depression. An international order
> centered on Europe and dominated by Europe was replaced . . . by a new
> arrangement—a world dominated by two new superpowers, torn by ideologi-
> cal conflict, and overshadowed by nuclear weapons that made a new world
> war potentially suicidal. At the same time, an integrated international
> economic system . . . based on the dollar and on . . . the freest possible flow of
> trade . . . replaced the unbridled economic nationalism that had helped
> undermine international peace between the wars.

It was in San Francisco in 1945 that an important step was taken—one
among many—marking the participation of virtually all then-independent
nations in the contemplated new international order, an order envisioned by so
many with so much hope.

But *Time* magazine, in its January 28, 1985, issue surveying foreign policy
challenges facing the United States in 1985, would overlook that event entirely.
The article explicitly recalled that 1985 is a year filled with symbolic
anniversaries. The year 1985, *Time* reported, is the 10th anniversary of the fall
of Saigon; the 30th of the Austrian State Treaty; the 40th of Yalta; the 40th of
V-E Day. It did not seem relevant to *Time*—even in an explicit discussion of
our nation's present foreign policy resources and problems—to mention or
recall the 40th anniversary of the founding of the United Nations.

Some of the "compromises" the great powers effected 40 years ago clearly
rewarded the Soviets but proved disappointing to those in the West who have,
since then, come to value freedom all the more. To this day, some suggest, the
Polish people may reasonably be aggrieved that the great powers seemed to assume the prerogative at Yalta of consigning that country to Soviet domination.
On the other hand, as some argue, what the Yalta agreement called for, on paper, was the holding of free elections. In today's Poland, at least, I think we
could predict the outcome of any such election. Many of the deplorable failures
of the postwar international order trace their origins to a persistent unrealism in
perspective; others, to the failure of participants to implement the magnifi-
cently idealistic accords and understanding at that time.

President Reagan has again declared—now and for all the future we can
see—that the United States remains committed to the ideals that led our
predecessors to create the United Nations 40 years ago. The Reagan Administration is justly proud of the continuity of its connection with the best of the
hard-won—blood-won—insights gained from the World War II years. We
sense that the time has come again for the United States to renew its historic
role in multilateral international relations—based on more realistic aspirations.

We now view prospects for some genuine achievements—based on a greater respect for realism.

All that is fundamental to the UN Charter, of lasting worth, still finds widespread support in the United States and has earned acclaim from all leaders of the United States. At a luncheon in connection with the UN's Special Session on Disarmament, President Reagan underscored the continuing commitment of the American people to the principles of the UN Charter, now 40 years old.

[I]t is a privilege ... to express this country's continued commitment to the principles on which the United Nations was founded some [40] years ago.

This body was born out of the brutality and chaos of a terrible war, a war that had engulfed the planet with a ferocity of destruction such as mankind had never known before. ... I ... remember the UN's first days and our hopes at that time that this would be a forum for all mankind, replacing armed conflict with debate. We hoped that when necessary, it could do what had to be done to prevent aggression. ...

I recall the inspiration of [President Roosevelt's] declaration with Winston Churchill of the Four Freedoms at a time when the freedom-loving people of the world were sorely in need of inspiration. In every real way, this, an institution dedicated to peace, was his dream. I can assure you today, however imperfect the reality may be, Americans still dream that dream. ...

Our countrymen can be proud that from the first day, the UN has had from the United States the utmost moral, political and ... financial support.

The President concluded that:

[The UN] institution has not become the panacea for all of mankind's problems as some expected. Nevertheless, it has been and can be a force for great good. While it hasn't solved every problem or prevented every conflict, there have been shining accomplishments. More than a few are alive and live decently because of this institution.

Perhaps now we have a more mature view of the United Nations. While recognizing its limitations, we don't overlook its real potential and the opportunities, opportunities that for the sake of humanity we cannot afford to waste.

President Reagan's pragmatic, realistic, and constructive approach has guided his first 4 years as President. This approach will continue. It will guide us through fundamental changes taking place in our world. An essentially Western world view prevailed 40 years ago. It no longer does. We have seen a transition to global perspectives—reflecting the reality that newly organized sovereign states govern whole continents where before a colonial foreign office did. It will, however, advance the welfare of no newly independent Third World nation if the influence of Whitehall or the Quai d'Orsay is replaced by a much more hurtful one coming from the Kremlin.

Our choice—and we have made a choice—is not only to support the United Nations but to emphasize the seriousness of our commitment. We are insisting that this cooperative venture fulfill the best of the hopes of its founders (and of those who later elected to join), i.e., that it not accept lethargy and the seeming degeneration of UN institutions as inevitable.

It is important to recognize that it is not in the Security Council and General Assembly that we most frequently find occasion to cooperate usefully. Occasions for cooperation more often arise, rather, in the UN's technical, development, and humanitarian agencies. Here, particularly, we find the vitality of the UN system; here, naturally, we seek the fruits of practical, realistic, cooperative, and beneficial efforts.

Some spokesmen in the Third World, to the delight of the Soviet Union (which did not earlier—and does now—support authentic multilateralism), pushed considerably too far in some UN organizations, seeking to create, with international endorsement, a statist and socialist "new international economic order" and a stifling "new world information and communications order." The scene of many of these demands was UNESCO [UN Educational, Cultural and Scientific Organization]. The experience of guiding the withdrawal of the United States from UNESCO during the past year and a half has been a sobering but instructive one. I have spoken often in the past months of the state of affairs that comes to exist when a UN system organization strays too far from the ideals and aspirations that animated the founders convened in San Francisco 40 years ago. But now, possibly, the lessons of our recent experience have largely been learned. Our present policy toward UN system organizations—a realistic one, genuinely supportive, seeking to help the specialized and technical organizations of the United Nations discharge their useful and much needed functions—is now more widely understood and respected.

Rather than recite herein any history of the development of our present policy toward UN system organizations, I desire to examine the new role we are prepared to play in the UN system. A realistic role, more precisely defined, we do support; in this work we share. It thus becomes important to recognize what role the United Nations itself has been created to serve.

The UN's Role

The United Nations was not, is not, cannot be a world government. It has neither legislative, executive, nor judicial competence in any usual sense. It is not sovereign—though its member states are. It is, moreover, neither a federation nor a confederation. New York City, the "capital" of the United Nations, cannot rightly be seen as analogous to Washington, New Delhi, Brasilia, or Ottawa—or even to Brussels, the "capital" of the European Community. The conference at San Francisco 40 years ago that brought the United Nations into being was not even remotely comparable or analogous in purpose to the Constitutional Convention in Philadelphia. The political organs of the United Nations—the General Assembly and the Security Council—represent, rather, an institutionalization of previously episodic international "conferencing." It is as if the Congress of Vienna, say, or the Conference of

Berlin were made permanent and perpetual. The titles and designations we all use reflect this: we speak of "Permanent Representatives" to the United Nations.

In candor, I am obliged to say the U.S. participation in the UN General Assembly gives us only limited advantages, contrary to the overblown rhetoric of its early domestic advocates. During the last 40 years, practical men and women recognized reality rather more readily than government officials did. But during the years of the Reagan Administration, our conduct in the UN system has been given an official injection of realism. We assumed for ourselves (and expected others to assume) a posture in which one said and did consistent things. We assumed the responsibility to conduct the affairs of the United States in a manner consistent with its undeniable great power status. The language of bilateral and multilateral diplomacy—as conducted by the United States—became more realistic and more responsible at the same time. Now we do protect our values and assert our views within the UN system. We have seen the system strengthened as various parties adopted a more realistic and precisely defined posture.

To repeat, the UN's proper role is not that of a world government—it is that of a meeting place for sovereign states, an available means for effecting useful and needed cooperation between nations without superseding their prerogatives as sovereigns to declare the several courses that independent nations will take to protect their peoples and secure their well-being.

There are some critics who make the mistake of asserting that the United Nations somehow has a vast power to do great harm to us and our system of government. It only repeats a truism to note that the UN General Assembly is not an authentic legislature. Nobody, acting realistically, assumes it to be such. There is a growing peril, however, that some parts and pieces of the UN system will come to think of themselves as regulatory agencies under conditions in which they cannot be held in check by the exercise of either a judicial or legislative power. The perils inherent in creating a multitude of international regulatory agencies are quite obvious to one who does have faith in the principle of separation of powers.

Again, it merely states the obvious to note that the reputation of the United Nations in the United States has not worn well over the last two decades. In some ways, this is not the fault of the United Nations. Some want of candor was our own; some disrespect for honest observation had its origins in our own press and public life. We would now do better to "use the United Nations for what it can do," not "abuse it for what it can't."

Our plan now should be to:

☐ Categorically deny that the quasi-parliamentary UN organs are jurisdictionally competent to regulate business internationally (in the same way that a domestic administrative agency could do) or to legislate for the world—if they were, we could not accept the implications of repeated lopsided UN votes taking positions opposed to our own, considering the real influence and significance of the United States in world affairs.

☐ Insist that concerned responsibility for the disposition of UN funds become more consonant with the sacrifices entailed in collecting them—to retain (or regain) credibility, UN member states must appreciate the importance of restraining runaway growth in unprioritized expenditures. The beginning point for needed reform is maintenance of a zero net growth policy and acute inquiry into the level of UN personnel compensation.

☐ Integrate multilateral and bilateral diplomacy—bilateral diplomacy should be reflected in multilateral forums. The United Nations should be seen as an additional forum in which the execution of U.S. foreign policy vis-à-vis other sovereign states is to be seriously advanced.

☐ View our participation in the United Nations as only one part of an integrated diplomatic effort—our participation in the United Nations, if it were to continue to function as it often did in the past (largely detached from our bilateral diplomacy), would then demand deemphasis even more. Yes, the United Nations is a "deliberative" body—but it is, in that regard, one that is more like a political party convention:

— A party platform is not law.

— Various specialized international organs serving technical, development, and humanitarian ends offer greater potential for needed cooperation. They are not dependent on the historic conception of a single, quasi-parliamentary UN organization, unitary and political in nature.

Some Abiding Problems

It is commonly known that we have found three systemic problems in the UN system. Their presence in UNESCO occasioned our recent withdrawal there. They are:

☐ Extraneous politicization;
☐ Advancement of statist theories; and
☐ Mismanagement and excessive budget growth.

Politicization

We seek to improve and maintain the integrity and competence of the UN agencies that contribute to mankind's well-being. We insist that they not be manipulated to serve only narrow political causes having nothing to do with their mandates. Through the insertion of such issues into the agenda, debates, resolutions, and work programs of the UN technical agencies, we have witnessed extraneous politicization of their work. In association therewith, we have seen rhetoric replace reason and confrontation win out over compromise.

We do not quarrel with the right of UN members to air political grievances; but we do not accept the practice of transferring political questions from the General Assembly (where they do belong) to the specialized agencies (where they do not). Their work is thereby disrupted, their useful potential is sacrificed, and unending conflict is created.

Statist Theories

We seek, further, to emphasize the primacy of individual rights over the demands of the state. Too often, doctrines of economic determinism take hold and serve as an excuse for enhancing and centralizing the power of the state. The result is a suppression of the personal liberties, energies, and talents that are essential for economic development. We believe that real development will be found in contributions to the well-being and sense of achievement experienced by each individual. The process of development is fulfilled when every person in a society has an opportunity to realize their fullest potential. We have seen in our own history how a free people working in a free market has created prosperity. But—as foreign visitors to the United States remarked at the beginning of the 19th century— a developing nation also prospers from the presence of free associations of individuals working together in voluntary and productive endeavors of every kind.

We believe that the UN system fails when (and because) it places the state in such a prominent position—when it thus denigrates the role of the market economy and the private sector. The crucial flaw in this approach is, frankly, that it shows only minimal concern for individual initiative, creativity, and liberty. The solutions now commonly accepted in the developing world— widespread government involvement, stifling economic controls, collective regimentation of agriculture, restriction of private initiative—have not prompted development; they have discouraged it. This is not surprising. The single most important element in development is the cultivation of human freedom. This can unleash creativity and initiative.

What we do find surprising is that many UN members, despite decades of failure by controlled economies—and notwithstanding the obvious quality of that failure—cling to solutions that history has discredited. Too often, they ritually condemn proven solutions—solutions associated with freedom that have, in fact, brought prosperity. I adhere to the President's view that "societies that achieved the most spectacular, broad-based economic progress in the shortest period of time have not been ... the most rigidly controlled. What has united them all was their belief in the magic of the marketplace."

The improving economic performance of many non-European nations shows this. There are many modern and prosperous societies whose cultures and past traditions are far removed from those of the European West. Hong Kong, South Korea, Singapore, and Taiwan come to mind.

In these matters, as in others, we believe we can offer constructive alternatives. We will be as patient in urging their adoption as we are sincere in hoping that they might be accepted—for they do hold the key to advancement, reconciliation, and development. Within the UN system, we will not shrink from urging that freedom and individual incentive—not a pervasive government presence—can create the climate in which economic development will flourish. We do understand that different cultures value cooperation differently. Still—whatever the unit of production may be—all will function more efficiently when price signals generated in a free market are taken seriously.

The United States desires to have the specialized agencies function as they were intended to function, e.g., that they deal realistically with concrete problems of trade and development in the developing world. Too often, agencies have veered off that course in recent years and have, instead, offered a platform for polemical North-South confrontation.

Mismanagement and Budget Growth

The UN system has been characterized by undisciplined budget growth, by excessive salaries, and by inflated pensions. To state this is to reiterate history, not ideology. The UN's assessed budget has grown in the last 10 years from $270 million to $794 million—a more than threefold increase. No government can justify to its citizens such large increases in multilateral programs while its own domestic programs are being significantly reduced. It is axiomatic that such rapid growth in programs spawns inefficiencies and redundancies. After the substantial program growth of recent years, the time has come for sober reflection on the priorities, benefits, and costs of the UN system.

Within the last 3 years, I have held private consultations with some 130 other nations. They revealed general agreement on the need for reductions in the rate of growth of UN expenditures and a need to examine proliferation of duplicative and questionably useful activities. The need now is to convert these private views into public action.

Our budget initiative is having an appreciable impact in bringing sound management to the specialized and technical agencies. The Reagan Administration believed that runaway UN budget growth was so advanced that only an abrupt halt within the entire system could curtail further excessive growth. As that goal is achieved, we might, joined by other major donors, become more sympathetic to requests for sound future plans coming from well-managed agencies.

Conclusion

During the past 3 years, the policy priorities we have followed in relation to multilateral affairs have:

- ☐ Focused our attention on renewed constructive leadership by the United States in UN system organizations;
- ☐ Sought, with some notable success, to persuade member states to use budget restraint and implement sound management practices;
- ☐ Emphasized an enhanced role for the private sector in international organization affairs;
- ☐ Promoted heightened attention to evaluation and analysis of programs and performance; and
- ☐ Sought to minimize the extraneous politicization of debates and proceedings in the UN's specialized and technical agencies.

We entertain the hope that much of great worth in the world of international relations will forthwith be based realistically on shared contributions to the common means we have adopted under UN auspices to promote the well-being of our several commonwealths. On the foundation of 40 years—through which sound girders still run—we can together promote the humane ideals of the UN's founders.

We trust, also, that greater security can be found, premised upon realistic and workable principles of comity and sovereignty, such that men and women will be free and will be permitted to live in peace. Profound new initiatives are under way, not least in the Western defense capabilities that guarantee all else.

And where is the United Nations in all this? Not in the center in any political sense; it is very much at the center, however, as it relates to the work rightly carried out within the several specialized and technical agencies headquartered in Geneva, Rome, Vienna, Montreal, Nairobi, and, of course, New York. The specialized and technical agencies within the UN system can become focal points for the organization of workable international cooperation in the important technical details of moving the mails, facilitating international air traffic, protecting us all against communicable disease, and preserving a healthy and viable natural environment, to mention only a few. Here is where the often unsung heroes of the UN system build and produce.

At Turtle Bay on the East River, however, we often heard a different story (or at least we did in the distant past). Apropos those operations, acute lay observers of foreign relations—and professional diplomats, too—have grown increasingly pessimistic.

- ☐ [Former UN Secretary General] Kurt Waldheim noted in *Foreign Affairs* last year that the United Nations "threatens to become increasingly irrelevant in the real world."
- ☐ [*New York Times* reporter] Flora Lewis, writing a major piece on "A U.N. Charter Review" in the *New York Times* on September 21, 1984,

added her plaintive cry that Third World delegates are not doing a healthy thing when they "log-roll the adoption of extremist resolutions that can achieve nothing" and that the United Nations suffers from "functional ineffectiveness and bureaucratic sterility."

☐ Harold Stassen, the Governor of Minnesota over 40 years ago, perennial presidential candidate, one "present at the creation" of the United Nations—still dreaming of its fancied glories, too—now admits, according to a report in the *New York Times* on January 25, 1985, that the United Nations is "deteriorating."

Any sober assessment of U.S. relations to the United Nations, in light of present realities, suggests to virtually all careful and experienced observers that a moderate and realistic stance must be adopted if the United Nations is to survive.

I can assure you that the Reagan Administration understands and appreciates the benefits that international cooperation has brought to our world during these 40 years. We are quite aware that the humanitarian, technical, and development agencies within the UN system have made significant contributions to the welfare of all member states—and continue to do so.

As they age, however, UN agencies have, on occasion, come to suffer from system-wide flaws. These flaws all too often have undermined the effectiveness of UN agencies as instruments of international cooperation. Now we would like to take ourselves—all of us—off the easy path. We are attempting to arrest the deterioration we have encountered. Our purpose, simply stated, is to make the UN system work. We wish to:

☐ Produce genuine economic and social development;
☐ Facilitate the sharing of useful information; and
☐ Promote real progress in reaching the humanitarian and technical objectives the UN system was founded to further.

A simple verse penned by the German poet, Friedrich Rückert—which is here translated with some liberty—well illustrates our present peril:

At forty years, the mountain has been climbed.
We then stand still and backward look without a laugh. . . .
Look back again! One can hear, anew inspired,
And put to use the trusty walking staff.
So, the mountain's peak is past; a broad plain lies ahead.
The challenge of a hard ascent is now not forced.
On that seductive walk none need be led;
And now, to take an upward path, one is not coerced.
But if you take the downward route, that of effort saved,
You come, with slow steps, heedless, to the grave.

Even though the benefits of workable, restrained, and authentic multilateral cooperation between sovereign states are appreciated in the United States, all of us are aware, too, that any celebration of a 40th anniversary—at least to the extent that the analogy to human life suggests itself—must caution constant reappraisal of one's course. Passing years urge patience, not hubris. President Reagan, at Cancun, modestly and soberly defined our basic position. "The program," he said, "... rests on a coherent view of what's essential to development—namely political freedom and economic opportunity." Not without great effort and dedication will either be achieved—now or at any time.

We retain the confidence given us by this nation's most abiding convictions—those shared by Washington, Jefferson, Lincoln, and the two Roosevelts. With that confidence, and with enduring conviction, the United States continues to support its own historic ideals in the "UN at 40." For us, this is a significant anniversary.

■■■■■■ **10.5**

ROBERT C. JOHANSEN

The Reagan Administration and the UN

Recent U.S. Policies Toward the United Nations

Whereas the major purpose of the United Nations is to serve the world community, the Reagan administration has instead sought to make the United Nations, in the words of former U.N. Ambassador Jeane Kirkpatrick, "a hospitable place for the American national interest." When the organization has refused to endorse Washington's agenda, administration officials have responded with loud condemnations of the U.N. system and selective withdrawal from it. The Reagan administration has accused the United Nations of straying far from its original goals, arguing that it has been hijacked by the Soviet Union and Third World leftists. Even the Security Council, according to Charles Lichenstein, former deputy U.S. ambassador to the United Nations, "has become the captive of a Soviet/Third World working majority and of that bloc's political agenda: anti-Israel, anti-West, anti-U.S." The administration has further charged that the United Nations undermines freedom, democracy, capitalism, human rights, and peace in the world. Indeed, officials like Ambassador Lichenstein seem to share the opinion of Heritage Foundation research director Burton Yale Pines—that "a world without the United Nations would be a better world."

In the administration's views, the United Nations, as it now operates, exacerbates conflict rather than fulfills its primary mission as a global

From "The Reagan Administration and the U.N., The Cost of Unilateralism," *World Policy Journal* III, 4 (Fall 1986).

peacemaker. Pressure from the Soviet Union and its allies breeds a polarization that leads to bloc voting—often without regard for an issue's merits—and deference to "narrow, selfish national interests." The Soviet-Third World "bloc" has produced a United Nations "perverted by politicization."

The Soviet Union is seen as so irresponsible that its performance at the United Nations, particularly its courtship of Third World countries, is causing the organization to fail. According to this view, the United Nations' "fatal flaw" lies in the expectation that the "Soviets and their clients and satellites subscribe to the fundamental principles of the U.N. Charter." It is "an illusion," Ambassador Lichenstein says, to think that Soviet leaders believe "that conflicts should be settled peacefully, without recourse to force, . . . that individual human rights should be protected and enhanced, . . . [and] that the autonomy of all nations should be respected." Because a majority of U.N. members are not democratic, the Reagan administration argues that the United Nations cannot function as a protector of human rights or a guardian of international peace.

An even more fundamental criticism is leveled against the United Nations' constitutional structure and the principle of one vote for each country in the General Assembly. U.S. officials would prefer a system that reflects U.S. military power, economic prowess, and financial contributions to the world body. Frustrated by its inability to control U.N. actions, the United States is in fact cutting back its financial contributions in an attempt to exert greater leverage over U.N. policies, U.N. voting procedures, and the voting preferences of other members. White House officials and members of Congress have frequently complained that, although the United States contributes 25 percent of the U.N. budget, it only receives one vote. Herbert Okun, the deputy chief U.S. delegate, has called this "tantamount to taxation without representation." Now, as a result of the Kassebaum amendment, the annual U.S. assessed contribution cannot exceed 20 percent of the annual budgets of U.N. agencies unless, among other conditions, the organization adopts a system of weighted voting on budgetary matters.

The Reagan administration is also using economic leverage in its bilateral relations with other countries to give the United States more influence within the United Nations. The White House has in certain instances made U.S. foreign aid conditional on a pro-U.S. voting record on the East River. U.N. Ambassador Jeane Kirkpatrick recommended "penalties for opposing our views" and "rewards for cooperating." Her successor, Vernon Walters, has reaffirmed that aid will be reduced for countries who do not vote with the United States. Any concern about the merits of particular issues or any acknowledgment of U.N. accomplishments is lost amid the administration's widespread criticisms.

U.S. officials have attacked the United Nations in order to justify unilateral policies that flout world opinion and Charter principles. In this broadly representative organization, the world's mightiest nation is frequently reminded that might does not make right—so it turns to bilateral diplomacy.

By operating outside the United Nations, U.S. officials are better able to dominate negotiations, avoid embarrassing criticism, and exclude the Soviet Union from international settlements.

To discredit the United Nations, Washington accuses it of bloc voting and the use of double standards designed to inflict diplomatic losses on Washington. But U.S. officials greatly exaggerate the significance of these problems. U.N. records do not show bloc voting, as Washington claims, but the growth of more complex voting patterns and the end of the pro-U.S. majority that existed throughout the United Nations' first two decades. From the United Nations' founding until 1970, Washington never lacked a majority on important issues and never exercised its veto in the Security Council. Moscow, on the other hand, used its veto 105 times in the same period. But the pattern has now been reversed; in the 1980-86 period, the United States vetoed 27 resolutions, while the Soviet Union vetoed only 4 (see Table 10-4). In General Assembly actions between 1975 and 1980 the United States still voted with the majority, or abstained, more often than it was outvoted. But by 1983, the United States voted with the majority only one-third as often as it had in 1977 and 1978.

Often when the United States perceives itself to be the victim of bloc voting, it has itself disregarded Charter principles and world opinion. Former U.S. Ambassador to the United Nations Donald McHenry blames U.S. isolation on a "go-it-alone" approach and an American foreign policy that is "out of step with the rest of the world." The United States does not want a strong vote in support of U.N. principles; it wants a bloc vote for U.S. positions. But voting patterns should be measured against the values embodied in the Charter, not against the president's definition of U.S. national interests, particularly when his definition is out of touch with the imperatives of international cooperation.

Not only have repeated U.S. unilateral actions isolated the United States, they have also encouraged anti-Americanism. The effort to coerce U.N. members into aligning themselves with the United States is demeaning and an affront to the principle of self-determination. It is also ineffective. The United

Table 10-4 U.S. and Soviet Vetoes in the Security Council

	United States	Soviet Union
1946-1950	0	47
1951-1955	0	30
1956-1960	0	15
1961-1965	0	11
1966-1970	1	2
1971-1975	11	4
1976-1980	10	4
1981-1985	20	2

States finds itself voting with some of its adversaries as often as with its closer friends. The Soviet Union and the United States vote on the same side of issues, for example, nearly as often as the United States and Jordan do; Zimbabwe, until recently the largest recipient of U.S. aid programs in sub-Saharan Africa, votes with the United States less often than Libya does. Poland votes more like the United States than Mexico does, Grenada more so than Britain, and Iran more so than India.

Despite Washington's claims to the contrary, the nonaligned group at the United Nations is hardly a monolith. Indeed, Third World countries have neither consistently supported the Soviet Union nor flatly opposed the United States, as the following examples illustrate:

☐ After Soviet military forces moved into Afghanistan in 1979, the General Assembly "strongly deplore[d] the ... armed intervention" and called for "immediate, unconditional and total withdrawal of the foreign troops." The Assembly has continued to condemn the Soviet military presence in Afghanistan with an increasing majority each year. The Assembly has also supported inquiries into U.S. charges that the Soviet Union waged illegal chemical war in Afghanistan. And when the Security Council condemned the downing of the Korean airliner in 1983, only Poland voted with the Soviet Union against the resolution.

☐ Radical states and communist governments besides the Soviet Union have also been criticized when Charter principles were clearly violated. After Vietnamese troops invaded Kampuchea in 1979, the General Assembly called for their "immediate withdrawal" and an end to "all acts or threats of aggression and all forms of interference in the internal affairs" of states of Southeast Asia. The General Assembly also rejected the Cuban effort to designate Puerto Rico as a U.S. colonial territory. And after Iranian militants took U.S. diplomats hostage in 1979, the Security Council and the International Court of Justice unanimously called for their release.

☐ Nonaligned countries have also generally opposed the aggressive use of force by other countries of the Third World. Unlike the United States, which ignored Charter principles in its support of the pro-Western King Hassan II, nonaligned countries rebuked Morocco's invasion of the Western Sahara. The General Assembly condemned Indonesia in 1975 for its seizure of East Timor. Nonaligned states were joined by many Western nations in upholding the principle of nonaggression; the United States, on the other hand, at first abstained and later voted with Indonesia against U.N. resolutions defending the rights of the Timorese people to self-determination.

In 25 key resolutions on war-peace issues from 1970 to 1986, U.N. majorities consistently upheld the Charter ban on the aggressive use of force. In contrast to what the Reagan administration would have us believe, Third

World countries have generally offered consistent support for the prohibition of aggressive use of force. They understand that it is in their interest—and in the interest of humanity generally—to resist the misuse of force.

It is against this record that one must evaluate the Reagan administration's claim that U.N. condemnation of the U.S. invasion of Grenada in 1983 exemplifies the anti-American bias of the United Nations. The General Assembly called the U.S. military intervention a "flagrant violation of international law and the independence, sovereignty, and territorial integrity of the state." But the many countries that condemned the U.S. invasion, including most of America's allies, did so not out of baseless hostility but in deference to the Charter principle prohibiting the aggressive use of force and out of concern that the U.S. action would establish a dangerous precedent for conflict resolution.

An objective analysis of voting records shows that the United States is among the *least* principled of all U.N. members on issues pertaining to the use of force. Washington defends the use of force by itself and its allies, while condemning most uses of force by its adversaries. In this regard, its record is no better than Moscow's.

The question of U.N. bias has pointedly arisen over the General Assembly's treatment of Israel and, to a lesser extent, South Africa. When these two countries violate the ban on aggressive use of force, they draw frequent, harshly worded criticisms seldom voiced against other states. Despite the Assembly's rhetorical excesses and insufficient attention to violence against Israelis, U.N. resolutions usually do apply appropriate Charter norms to the misuse of force by these two countries. Washington's acquiescence in or active support for many Israeli and South African policies that arguably contravene the ban on aggression is responsible for much of the animosity expressed against Washington on the East River. Resolution of the deep-seated conflicts involving Jerusalem and Pretoria would clear the clouded picture many Americans have of the United Nations. In addition, the world community would be more tolerant of the U.S. government if it consistently supported Charter norms and refused political support and denied arms sales to countries violating these principles.

Furthermore, just as U.S. officials distort the record to suggest an anti-U.S. bias, so do they twist reality when they charge that the Soviet presence in the United Nations condemns the organization to failure. To be sure, the Soviet Union is jealous of its sovereignty and treats the organization as an instrument to advance its own interests—but if this distinguishes Moscow from Washington, the difference is one of degree rather than of kind. Not infrequently, Soviet leaders have supported multilateral efforts—especially when they have protected state sovereignty, advanced self-determination, or diminished the prospect of war with the West.

And although Moscow has opposed Washington on numerous issues, the two often see eye to eye. Both are interested in maintaining their superpower privileges in the United Nations, including the right to veto resolutions in the Security Council. Neither wishes to make General Assembly resolutions legally binding, to allow the Secretary General much freedom of action in peacekeeping, to give priority to multilateral rather than bilateral negotiations on nuclear arms control, or to compromise the unrestricted passage of military vessels on the high seas. Both resist Third World efforts to claim Antarctica as the common heritage of all nations. If Moscow is irresponsible in such matters, then Washington is too.

On certain key issues, in fact, the Soviet Union has recently shown greater regard for U.N. principles. It has, for instance, acknowledged a growing need for the organization to function as a restraint on East-West conflict. Although both superpowers have opposed the French proposal, supported by more than 120 other nations, to create an international satellite monitoring agency to verify military deployments and arms agreements, the Soviet Union has recently moved closer than the United States to accepting multilateral monitoring of arms agreements. Moscow has also begun to appear more responsible on space and arms control issues, as reflected by its support for U.N. efforts to prevent the militarization of space and to initiate a nuclear freeze. Although the United States has opposed Soviet-supported resolutions on these and other issues, such initiatives could, if pursued, eventually lead to agreements that prohibit the first use of nuclear weapons, ban military weapons from space, halt nuclear weapons tests, freeze deployments of intermediate and intercontinental nuclear weapons, and condemn state terrorism and attempts by one government to overthrow another.

The complaint that the United States is underrepresented in the United Nations does not reflect a desire for more democratic procedures so much as an interest in exerting greater U.S. influence over global political processes. U.S. criticism of the one-country/one-vote principle in the General Assembly exaggerates its shortcomings, and U.S. counterproposals indicate that Washington prefers a voting formula more advantageous to itself.

The current constitutional structure of the United Nations provides more than equitable representation for the United States. It guarantees the United States a permanent seat on the Security Council, whose decisions, unlike those of the General Assembly, are binding. Moreover, the United States can single-handedly veto any Security Council resolution. Although being the largest financial contributor to the organization does not give Washington extra votes in the Assembly, little of real substance can happen in the U.N. system without U.S. cooperation and resources. On decisions of consequence negotiators are especially attentive to U.S. preferences. Washington also exerts considerable influence on the United Nations through those member states that hope to receive economic and military assistance from the United States. Thus, even within the existing voting arrangement, the United States is the single most influential member of the United Nations, and has been since its founding.

Is the United States paying too much of the U.N. budget? When the

United Nations was founded, the United States paid 40 percent of the total. The assessment declined to 33 percent in 1954. More recently, the U.N. Committee on Contributions, of which the United States is a member, has decided that no contributor shall pay less than 0.1 percent or more than 25 percent of the total budget. As a result, the United States contributes less than the 28 percent it would if it were assessed strictly on the basis of national income. On a per capita basis, U.S. contributions amount to approximately $0.85 annually. By this measure citizens in 18 countries pay more than the United States, 9 of them Third World nations.

The United States also enjoys unique benefits from the U.N. budget. Almost half of the United Nations' budget is spent in this country—an amount that is twice the U.S. contribution. Moreover, all the member nations have delegations in New York; at least $700 million per year flows into New York's economy from the United Nations and the diplomatic community.

Although Congress has adopted legislation mandating a cut in the U.S. contribution unless the United States is granted greater leverage over money matters, there is no basis in international law or democratic theory to justify this demand. Rather, in its unilateral reduction of payments to 20 percent of the U.N. budget, the United States is violating its treaty obligations. Many countries agree that the U.N. budget should be trimmed—and a U.N. committee is currently examining the problem—but they oppose Washington's unilateral reduction. All 12 members of the European Common Market have protested to Washington, and Secretary General Javier Pérez de Cuéllar has declared that the U.S. action places "the very operation of the United Nations ... in jeopardy."

The United Nations is a political institution, not a stockholders' meeting where the number of shares one owns determines voting power. It is no more justifiable to give the United States the most votes because it contributes the most money than to give a U.S. citizen in the 50 percent tax bracket 5 votes for every 1 cast by someone in the 10 percent bracket. To make voting proportional to financial contribution means that the United States would, for example, have roughly 70 votes to India's 1. To base voting power upon wealth or material power would make voting less democratic rather than more.

Complaints of bloc voting, an anti-U.S. bias, and an incongruity between the money that countries contribute to the U.N. budget and the votes that they wield in the General Assembly obscure the deeper reason for U.S. displeasure with the United Nations. The United States can maintain its globally disproportionate share of wealth and power only through an international system governed by minority rule—that is, by a U.S.-led minority of states. Officials believe that internationalism dilutes U.S. influence: in fact it is U.S. unilateralism, which many allies and other nations oppose, that ultimately diminishes U.S. power.

Broadly representative international institutions call into question the legitimacy of what has been, since World War II, essentially a U.S.-dominated world order. President Reagan thus complains that "the body established to serve the goals of the U.N. Charter is increasingly becoming instead a body whose members are dedicated to the goals of the majority." And Ambassador Kirkpatrick speaks of "an uncomfortable . . . U.N. consensus which the United States alone regularly opposes," leading her to complain, "we have been virtually powerless in the United Nations for more than a decade"—even though the United States in fact remains the single most influential member in the United Nations.

If certain U.S. policies do not enjoy widespread support in the world community, it is not because the United Nations has become "perverted by politicization," as Jeane Kirkpatrick charges. Rather, it is because the United States has moved outside the circle of multilateral consensus and conducted its foreign relations with hardly a nod toward Charter principles, much to the consternation of other member states. Consider the following examples:

- [ ] No West European ally voted with the United States against the General Assembly resolution deploring the U.S. invasion of Grenada. Similarly, most European and Latin American allies expressed reservations about Washington's shelling of Lebanon in 1984 and bombing of Libya in 1986.
- [ ] The United States has refused to pursue negotiations in earnest that could lead to a peaceful settlement of the Central America conflict. It has thwarted the Contadora negotiating effort initiated by Mexico, Venezuela, Colombia, and Panama, has rejected the rulings of the International Court of Justice condemning U.S. support of the contras, and has ignored Nicaraguan proposals for a multinational force to patrol borders and for a ban on all foreign bases and military personnel throughout the region.
- [ ] The General Assembly strongly endorsed ratification of the SALT II treaty after Washington and Moscow negotiated and signed it. But the United States moved outside this international consensus, first by refusing to ratify the treaty and then by engaging in a destabilizing game—pledging to abide by the treaty while at the same time threatening to withdraw from it.
- [ ] The General Assembly—by an overwhelming majority—called for a freeze on the development and deployment of additional nuclear weapons, but the United States vigorously opposed the idea and pushed its allies to vote against such a moratorium. The administration continues to reject the U.N.-endorsed, universally supported idea of a comprehensive ban on testing nuclear explosives.
- [ ] U.S. plans to militarize outer space violate a long-standing international practice of not deploying weapons in space and contradict the U.N. outer space treaty of 1967. The General Assembly has urged consideration of ways to prevent the militarization of outer space and

negotiations to conclude an agreement averting an arms race in space. More than 140 nations—including most of America's West European allies—have favored such a step, with the United States casting the sole negative vote. . . .

Reviving Internationalism

It is our fate to live in an era where our security increasingly depends upon the security and common sense of others. In such a world, the United States needs to rediscover its best internationalist traditions and revamp them to meet the country's changing security needs. Neither the Cold War internationalism of Truman and Kennedy nor the idealistic internationalism of Wilson will do. What is needed is an internationalism that integrates reliance on the United Nations and other global institutions into day-to-day U.S. policy-making.

As America's relative power further declines in the years ahead, U.S. ability to control events and determine its own security fate will inevitably decline as well. U.S. leaders must begin trying to put into place reliable global checks and balances on other countries' behavior, which will increasingly impinge on U.S. well-being. Even today, as we have seen, U.S. security interests, particularly in the Third World, are better protected through the United Nations with U.S. support than by the United States acting alone without the United Nations. And without a stronger U.N. collective security system, it is difficult to see how we will be able to achieve meaningful and lasting arms reductions and effective nuclear nonproliferation—let alone rid the planet of nuclear weapons.

A growing number of governments have come to recognize the need for the United Nations to play an increased role in promoting common security. Middle-range powers, like Australia, Canada, and Sweden, have long supported a stronger United Nations. A U.N. voting majority, including many nonaligned Third World countries, has also consistently supported Charter norms governing the use of force. And some have begun looking to world institutions for protection against great-power intervention—consider, for example, Nicaragua's submission of its dispute with Washington to the World Court. Even the Soviet Union under Gorbachev has become more receptive to the collective-security functions of the organization, such as international monitoring and peacekeeping. Moscow has accepted IAEA inspection of its civilian nuclear reactors, has for the first time supported the renewal of the UNIFIL peacekeeping force in Lebanon, and has sought U.N. cooperation for the control of international terrorism. All this suggests a modest but nonetheless real opening for internationalism.

What is sadly missing is the support of the United States. Despite the mistrust and hostility the Reagan administration has engendered, much of the world still looks to Washington for leadership on global issues. If a post-Reagan administration would encourage this new internationalist mood, the "atmosphere of ambivalence" that has surrounded the United Nations could give way to a new atmosphere of seriousness. The U.N. system could evolve into the cornerstone of world security that many of its founders envisioned. On the other hand, if Washington fails to take the multilateral path, this opportunity for internationalism, which may not be repeated, will be lost. And the United States will face a more hostile world at a time when its influence has declined and its security has become more vulnerable to outside events. Despite all its current shortcomings, then, the United Nations is still America's best hope for a more durable peace.

Discussion Questions

1. Prepare a list of the various policy options available to the international community for dealing with a state that has just invaded its neighbor. Describe each of the options and estimate their prospects for success.

2. How, in your judgment, do participation in the United Nations and respect for international law enhance or detract from the foreign policy interests of the United States?

3. Much of the editors' commentary and some of the readings in this chapter suggest that the "realist" approach to international politics has outlived its usefulness. Are there areas of international relations in which you believe such an approach is still relevant? If so, what would be the response of critics of realism to this assertion, and how would you respond to their arguments?

4. Several proposals for coping with the problem of terrorism are presented in the introduction to this chapter. State and insurgent terrorism, however, are but two of many vexing global problems. Select some other specific global issue—such as pollution, uses of outer space, or refugee problems—and develop a similar set of proposals for dealing with it.

For Further Reading

Studies on International Peacekeeping

Bailey, Sydney Dawson. *Peaceful Settlement of International Disputes: Some Proposals for Research.* New York: United Nations Institute for Training and Research, 1971. A short but engaging analysis in which the author examines UN peacekeeping operations of the 1960s against the background of the emerging literature in the field of peace research.

Doob, Leonard W., et al., ed. *Resolving Conflict in Africa: The Fermeda Workshop.* New Haven, Conn.: Yale University Press, 1970. Examines the successes and failures of the controlled communication workshop used by Doob and his colleagues in the Ethiopian-Somalian conflict.

Fisher, Roger, with William Ury. *International Mediation: A Working Guide—Ideas for the Practitioner.* New York: International Peace Academy, 1978. A practical volume that lists and examines the queries that good mediators must ask of themselves and of the mediation process. Fisher and Ury's popular paperback, *Getting to Yes,* was derived from this work.

International Peace Academy. *The Peacekeeper's Handbook.* New York: International Peace Academy, 1978. This unique field manual for peacekeeping forces based in civilian areas is derived from successful UN peacekeeping field operations in the Middle East.

Mitchell, C. R. *Peacemaking and the Consultant's Role.* London: Nichols, 1981. A thoughtful overview of the problems associated with independent fact finding, negotiation, and mediation of disputes. Reflects both the author's experience and the scholarly literature on dispute resolution.

Morris, Michael A., and Victor Millan, eds. *Controlling Latin American Conflicts: Ten Approaches.* Boulder, Colo.: Westview Press, 1983. A timely analysis of the successes and options for resolving conflicts in Latin America. The analysis of the Falklands/Malvinas war and the chapter on confidence-building measures are especially useful.

Rubin, Jeffrey Z., ed. *Dynamics of Third Party Intervention: Kissinger in the Middle East.* New York: Praeger, 1981. A balanced account and assessment of Kissinger's theoretical and practical initiatives, including shuttle diplomacy. On balance, few of the contributors believe that shuttle diplomacy can be effective over the long term.

Touval, Saadia. *The Peace Brokers: Mediators in the Arab-Israeli Conflict, 1948-1979.* Princeton, N.J.: Princeton University Press, 1982. An exceptional comparative history that examines the successes and failures of the efforts of Ralph Bunche, Gunnar Jarring, and Henry Kissinger to mediate a Middle East peace.

Wiseman, Henry, ed. *Peacekeeping: Appraisals and Proposals.* New York: Pergamon, 1983. A detailed assessment of UN, regional, and national peacekeeping experiences throughout the sixties and seventies.

_____ and Alastair M. Taylor. *From Rhodesia to Zimbabwe: The Politics of Transition.* New York: Pergamon, 1981. A fine microanalysis of the making of peace in this area of Africa from the Lancaster agreement to the inauguration of the present government.

Yarrow, C. H. Mike. *Quaker Experiences in International Conciliation.* New Haven: Yale University Press, 1978. Probably the only detailed account of the real contribution of nongovernmental religious groups to various phases of the peacemaking process. Its special focus is the work of the American Friends Service Committee in the Middle East and Africa.

International Law

Akehurst, Michael. *A Modern Introduction to International Law.* 5th ed. London: Allen and Unwin, 1984. One of the most widely read shorter sources on public international law, this work reflects a spirited British approach to the subject.

Boyle, Francis Anthony. *World Politics and International Law*. Durham, N.C.: Duke University Press, 1985. In this unusual book the author works through a detailed critique of power politics models and narrow legal thinking about international law to outline a new basis for U.S. foreign policy based on principles of international law.

Falk, Richard, et al. *International Law: A Contemporary Perspective*. Boulder, Colo.: Westview Press, 1985. A large compilation of some of the classic scholarly articles in international law, mixed with some newer articles that address relevant issue such as human rights and environmental protection.

Weston, Burns, et al. *International Law and World Order: A Problem Oriented Case Book*. New York: West Publishing, 1982. The strongest international law text available, this book is for those interested in both the solid legal issues and in the political dynamics of using law to build a better world order.

International Organizations

Bennett, A. LeRoy. *International Organizations: Principles and Issues*. Englewood Cliffs, N.J.: Prentice-Hall, 1977. A solid analysis of the UN family of organizations and the political, economic, and social problems they address.

Jacobson, Harold K. *Networks of Interdependence: International Organizations and the Global Political System*. 2d ed. New York: Knopf, 1984. A sophisticated treatment of the diverse array of transnational institutions.

Young, Oran R. *The Intermediaries: Third Parties in International Crises*. Princeton, N.J.: Princeton University Press, 1967. A comparative analysis of peacekeeping efforts of UN secretaries-general during the first two decades of the UN.

CONCLUSION

THE SEARCH FOR CONVERGENCE IN
THEORIES, POLICIES, AND PRACTICE 11

T hroughout this volume, in the commentaries and the readings, there is a consistent theme. That theme concerns the linkage between theory, policy, and practice in international relations. Theory affects policy, which affects practice, which in turn affects theory. As you come to the end of this book, this description of the intertwined dynamic of theory, policy, and practice may appear all too familiar and straightforward. Have international affairs not always been this way? How could there not be a clear linkage between theory, policy, and practice in the real world of international relations? If such is your reaction, we have accomplished much of this book's purpose.

Next, we summarize briefly the nature of this interaction and reflect upon possible future developments.

The Interaction of Theory, Policy, and Practice

The linkage between theory, policy, and practice can be represented diagrammatically, as in Figure 1-1 in Chapter 1. That relationship is dynamic, a never-ending cycle of interaction. Change in one of these areas inevitably leads to change in the others. What, then, is the current status of the relationship between international relations theory and practice in the areas we have examined in this volume? What, in short, is the relationship between what we know and what we do?

A complete answer to this question lies beyond the scope of an introductory text. However, the preceding chapters have examined the links between theory and policy. Among the issues arising from that examination are the following:

The Future of the Nation-State

The number of nation-states has more than tripled since 1945 to over 150, while the number and types of international organizations have proliferated. As a result, the current international system is far more complex than its Westphalian ancestor of 1648. Some theorists argue that effective global management of such a complex system requires a new form of international governance, one with the scope and authority to deal effectively with problems on a global scale. If this is the case, what will be the future role of the nation-state?

Decision Making, Politics, and the International Arena

Theory tells us that good decision making requires avoiding common pitfalls such as ethnocentrism, groupthink, and perceptual blinders. Yet human nature and political pressures tempt leaders to surround themselves with advisers who subscribe to their own worldview. How, in a world where the risks of faulty foreign policy making are greater than ever before, can we ensure that leaders consider all of the information required for sound decisions, especially during crisis?

Understanding the International Political Economy

Increasingly, theorists and policy makers agree on the importance of the relationship between politics and economics, especially in the areas of international trade, economic development, and resource distribution. Yet theorists offer us not one but several competing models in each of these areas. Each model in turn has a distinctive set of implications for policy and practice. How then can we identify the model whose associated policies will result in the greatest economic benefits to the largest number of people?

Quick Fixes Versus Long-term Solutions

International relations theory and a serious reading of history tell us that the best long-term solutions to international problems are almost always those arrived at through hard-nosed diplomacy and serious bargaining. In practice, however, leaders of larger nations are tempted to solve problems quickly by co-ercion—a temptation to which they have proven increasingly susceptible in recent decades. How can leaders be encouraged to make increased use of bargaining and diplomacy in resolving international disputes?

The Management of Power

The use of power is an enduring concern of international relations theorists and practitioners alike. How is the nature of power—as an attribute and as a relationship—likely to change in the coming years? How should power be used by leaders in the practice of international relations?

Finding a Substitute for Deterrence

The theory of deterrence, in its various forms, has been not only a preoccupation of theorists and policy makers throughout the postwar era but also the underlying logic of national security policy for both of the superpowers. Yet, given the destructive power of modern strategic weapons, deterrence represents a precarious foundation for international peace. When pressed to its logical conclusion, deterrence threatens not only the opponent but the user with destruction. How, then, can we devise a new theoretical foundation for preventing nuclear holocaust, one that provides the benefits of deterrence without its associated risks in the event of failure or abuse?

Encouraging Cooperation

Theory tells us that the behavior of nation-states is characterized by both conflict and cooperation. Alliances represent a form of cooperation in which some nation-states band together in order to be secure from violent conflict with other nation-states. How can we structure the international system to maximize the incentives for cooperation between nation-states and reduce the potential for conflict?

The Issue of State Violence

In an age of increasingly destructive and costly weaponry, nation-states are more and more tempted to use various forms of low-intensity violence, including terrorism, in pursuit of policy objectives. How can we reduce the incentives for pursuing such destabilizing policies?

Preserving International Peace

While we might wish otherwise, we have seen that existing international law and international peacekeeping organizations have only limited value as means of preserving international peace. The variety of forms of international conflict has grown steadily in recent years. The critical question in international relations is, What new mechanisms, rules, and procedures might we devise to resolve international conflict?

A look to the future of international relations inspires more questions than answers. One question concerns how theory might help us grapple with unresolved issues such as these.

The Changing Role of the Theorist

It is extremely unlikely that theory's contribution will be a full-blown general theory of international relations—one that would, for example, enable the policy maker to predict the outcome of a given policy decision much as the theory of gravity enables the physicist to predict the velocity of a falling object.

This is not to say that the systematic study of international relations cannot produce results of value to the policy maker. Rather, theorists can, and should, help policy makers to refine their operating assumptions, to define more clearly their basic concepts and worldviews, to place contemporary dilemmas in historical context, and to determine both the internal consistency and external validity of policies and policy proposals. Theorists can help, too, with policy evaluation, with the determination of whether a given policy accomplishes its intended objectives. In these and other ways, theory can, as we have argued throughout this volume, illuminate the world of policy.

In recent years there has been a resurgence of interest in the application of normative theory to policy in international relations. Normative theory asks, How should a nation act in a given case on the basis of moral criteria? Are actions dictated by the national interest different from those dictated by the general human interest? And if so, which set of interests should predominate? Properly applied, normative theory can give the policy maker new sets of standards with which to evaluate policy options and may even encourage the devising of new ones when existing options fail to satisfy moral criteria.

The importance of such questions can be seen in the debate over the appropriate U.S. response to famine in Ethiopia during the 1980s. Throughout this debate those who adhere to a "realist" perspective have opposed a major relief effort by the United States. Their argument has essentially been that assisting the current Marxist regime in Ethiopia is counter to U.S. interests. Given that that regime is hostile to the United States, that it was in many respects responsible for the famine, and that it could be expected to benefit from any aid provided by outside sources, the provision of such aid would, these individuals argued, be harmful to U.S. interests. Thus, although claiming that neither they nor anyone else really wanted to witness the mass starvation of innocent Ethiopians, they have called for a minimal relief effort.

This view has been strongly opposed by the argument that the United States was morally required to do whatever was necessary to prevent mass starvation in Ethiopia, the ideological slant of the current regime notwithstanding. This view was especially championed by those theorists and policy makers who, having adopted a "world order" perspective, considered the management of international issues, such as world hunger, the very substance of international relations. In the end, this point of view largely carried the day, prompting a major effort by various official international relief agencies and, subsequently, by a variety of individuals—including international celebrities—and ad hoc groups. Ultimately, the volume of the U.S. response was generous, in spite of the controversy surrounding the relief effort.

New Directions in Policy

Several trends in the realm of policy merit watching. One of these is the extent to which national policy makers are increasingly confronted with problems that do not respect national boundaries and that therefore often require international cooperation to solve.

When desert locusts ravaged large agricultural regions of the East African nations in the 1950s and 1960s, for example, the affected nations responded by creating the Desert Locust Control Organization. Similarly, the nations of Europe have created a series of regional economic organizations in the years since the close of World War II, most notably the European Common Market. The massive flow of refugees from Southeast Asia in the 1970s and from Central America in the 1980s has been managed by a broad coalition of actors including a number of nation-states, the United Nations High Commission for Refugees, and a variety of private church and relief organizations.

A second potentially significant trend has been the emergence of what is known as "Track II Diplomacy." Thus far largely restricted to the advanced industrial democracies, Track II diplomacy is diplomacy that results from the increasingly frequent efforts by an ever more mobile and informed citizenry to become involved in foreign affairs. Whereas before the 1960s international contacts involving citizens of more than one state were primarily prompted by athletic or cultural interests, there are today a number of citizen groups whose main interests lie with one or more issues of international policy.

The impact of these groups in framing the context for the public debate on particular issues should not be minimized. Not long after the Reagan administration began supplying military aid to the contras in Central America, for example, a variety of U.S.-based citizen groups were formed to monitor events in Central America, provide economic and humanitarian aid to Nicaragua, and report to the public on contra activities. From their efforts has emerged a portrait of contra activities quite different from that offered by the administration.

Among the groups involved in this effort were Witness for Peace and the Washington Office on Latin America. One of the activities sponsored by the first of these groups was the sending of American citizens into the area of hostilities along the Nicaraguan-Honduran border; another was to collect food and medicine to be distributed in Nicaragua. These activities, combined with the lobbying efforts of various groups, including the Washington Office on Latin America, meant that the administration was unable to monopolize the flow of information from Nicaragua and served, in the opinion of many observers, to place constraints on the use of American military force in the region.

Nor have relations between the superpowers been untouched by Track II diplomacy. Some six months prior to the unproductive October 1986 summit conference in Iceland, a group of U.S. and Soviet physicians traveled to Sweden to receive the Nobel Peace Prize. They were members of a group known as International Physicians Against Nuclear War, founded by a handful of U.S. and Soviet doctors who had come to know one another during their medical training and who shared the belief that the threat of nuclear war represented a major medical problem of our era.

For over a decade these physicians have lobbied the governments of both superpowers on behalf of a reduction in nuclear armaments and conducted a massive public education effort. Despite a membership that currently exceeds 60,000 doctors from all over the globe, these professionals and national citizens have certainly not brought a halt to the arms race. They have, however, kept the issue of arms control alive, even during low points in official U.S.-Soviet relations. Thus, it seems reasonable to suggest that these physicians, and other professional and citizen groups, have contributed to keeping the problem of nuclear armaments from becoming even more unmanageable than it might have been had the national leaders involved been left to their own devices.

The Track II efforts recounted here are but two of many that might have been mentioned. Similar efforts have emerged in response to many other issues of global significance, including the eradication of disease in Africa and continuing efforts to push for worldwide reform in human rights. And citizen exchange programs, "sister city" efforts, and international teleconferencing programs demonstrate that the "affairs of nations" are slowly, but surely, becoming the affairs of global citizens. Such activities have today become an increasingly common feature of international relations practice in a world where practice, policy, and theory continue to evolve and interact.

Discussion Questions

1. Of all the issues raised in this book, which do you consider the most crucial to international relations? Why?

2. Imagine that you are a foreign policy adviser to a major presidential contender. Your first assignment is to prepare a memo entitled, "Five significant findings from international relations and their implications for policy." Write that memo.

3. International relations theory is often criticized for being too distant from the "real world problems" of starvation, war, refugees, and economic development. Do you agree with this criticism? Why or why not?

For Further Reading

Alger, Chadwick F. "International Relations." *The International Encyclopedia of the Social Sciences*. New York: Macmillan, 1968. A useful overview of the origins of international relations and its potential value.

Beitz, Charles R. *Political Theory and International Relations*. Princeton, N.J.: Princeton University Press, 1979.

Beitz, Charles R. et al., eds. *International Ethics: A Philosophy and Public Affairs Reader*. Princeton, N.J.: Princeton University Press, 1985. Two volumes by one of today's premier theorists whose primary concern is with the application of normative and ethical theory to international politics. The recent edited volume represents the current "state of the art" in this area.

Bobrow, Davis. "On the Relevance Potential of Different Products." *World Politics 1972.* The article sketches various ways international relations research can contribute to policy thinking short of building general theories.

Dougherty, James E., and Robert L. Pfaltzgraff, Jr. *Contending Theories of International Relations: A Comprehensive Survey.* 2d ed. New York: Harper and Row, 1981. Although now almost a decade old, this work is still considered the most comprehensive survey of the critical concepts and theories of international relations.

Lyons, G. M. "Expanding the Study of International Relations: The French Connection." *World Politics* (October 1982).

———. "The Study of International Relations in Great Britain: Further Connections." *World Politics* (July 1986). Two pieces that review major research developments in France and Great Britain and compare research trends in these two countries with those in the United States.

Maghoori, Ray, and Bennett Ramberg, eds. *Globalism vs. Realism: International Relations Third Debate.* Boulder, Colo.: Westview Press, 1982. A collection of essays that assesses a major debate in the international relations literature: the interdependence perspective of the 1970s versus the realist perspective of the 1960s.

Mansbach, Richard, and John Vasquez. *In Search of Theory: A New Paradigm for Global Politics.* New York: Columbia University Press, 1981. A critique of the dominant realist and power politics perspectives coupled with a plea for an issues-based approach to the study of international affairs.

McClelland, Charles A. "International Relations: Wisdom or Science?" in James N. Rosenau, ed. *International Politics and Foreign Policy: A Reader.* New York: The Free Press, 1969. An important article that examines international relations' potential for becoming a more scientific discipline.

Puchala, Donald J., and Stuart I. Fagen, "International Politics in the 1970s: The Search for a Perspective." *International Organization* (Spring 1974). An overview of recent trends in international relations research and patterns of international politics.

Starr, Harvey. "The Quantitative International Relations Scholar as Surfer: Riding the Fourth Wave." *Journal of Conflict Resolution* (June 1974). A review of the early 1970s literature that examines the potential of several new lines of inquiry, particularly peace research.

Young, Oran. "The Perils of Odysseus." *World Politics 1972.* Young suggests that Richardson's theories of arms races and selected aspects of game theory are the only products of international relations research that are true theories in the scientific sense.

INDEX

Index

Index

Oppenheimer, J. Robert, 29, 31
Organization for Economic Cooperation and Development (OECD), 154, 161
Organization for European Economic Cooperation (OEEC), 154
Organization of African Unity (OAU), 494, 495, 517, 524, 532
Organization of American States (OAS), 367, 494, 495, 516, 517, 532
Organization of Petroleum Exporting Countries (OPEC), 37, 151, 161, 271-272, 280, 303, 370, 403
Organizational process model, 108, 113-116
Ottoman Empire, 17

Pacific basin countries
  U.S. relations, 422
  See also specific countries
Pahlavi (shah of Iran), 497
Pakistan, 61, 140, 475, 523
Palestine, 228, 234, 430, 437
Palestine Liberation Organization (PLO), 56, 134, 407, 496
Palme, Olaf, 291
Panama, 550
Panama Canal treaty, 67, 68, 498
Panofsky, Wolfgang K.H., 314, 315, 326-334
Pax Americana, 23, 34
Payne, Keith, 313, 315, 317-326
Peace. *See* International peace
Peace Brigades International, 508
Peace Corps, 402
Pearl Harbor, 67, 79-80, 88, 91, 112, 118, 126, 130, 286
Peloponnesian War, 34, 84, 91
Penetrated political systems, 11, 157
Perception
  affective dimension, 67-68
  bureaucratic politics model, 108, 121-127
  cognitive dimension, 66-67
  context in which incoming data are received, 79-80
  evaluative dimension, 68-69
  expectations' influence on, 76-77
  fitting incoming data into existing theories, 75-76, 82-83
  group cohesiveness effect. *See* Groupthink
  individual's development of concepts, 77-79
  moral reexamination of foreign policy, 139-147
  organizational process model, 108, 113-116

overestimation of coherency of another's policies, 80, 81
overestimation of hostility, 80
perceptual conflict, 430
as policy determinant, 66-69, 74, 17-108, 132
rational policy model, 108-110
realism, effect on political morality, 133-139
recognition of other's perception of data, 81-82
reliance on foreign office statements, 80-81
World War I. *See* 1914 crisis
Peres, Shimon, 135, 253
Pérez de Cuéllar, Javier, 516, 549
Pershing II missile, 312, 315, 356
Persia, 230-231, 429
Persson, Stefan, 273, 287-295
Peru, 45, 57, 61, 269
Philippines, 139, 140, 367, 410
Pines, Burton Yale, 543
Point Four Program, 154
Poland, 268, 534, 546
  Soviet repression, 144, 221, 232, 372, 419, 435
  World War II events, 83, 336, 345, 348
Polarization hypothesis, 291
Policy determinants
  crises as, 73
  factors summarized, 65-66
  perceptions as. *See* Perception
  process as, 69-70
  theory, policy, and practice interaction, 558
  wider political environment as, 71-72
Political economy. *See* International political economy
Politics
  definition, 267, 429
  See also International politics
Politics Among Nations (Morgenthau), 133
Population
  global growth, 20
  as indicator of power, 269, 293
Portugal, 350, 411
Postman, Leo, 75
Poverty, percentage of U.S. population, 61
Power
  assessment of contemporary policies, 273, 300-304
  as attribute, 268-270, 274-275
  definition and uses of, 267, 272-273, 281, 429
  diplomacy relationship, 55-56, 273, 296-300

Index

Union of Soviet Socialist Republics
(U.S.S.R.). *See* Soviet Union
UNITA (National Union for the Total
Independence of Angola), 259
United Arab Republic, 368
United Kingdom, 27, 91, 269, 378, 474, 546
alliances, 33, 396, 408
bargaining strategy, 219, 246, 250
coercive violence, 228, 232
economic development, 6, 167-169, 171
economic performance, 197
Falklands/Malvinas war, 67, 72, 220, 414-
415, 475
international economics, role, 161, 208
nuclear capability, 18
percent ownership of world wealth, 61
perception of Nazi aggressiveness, 65, 76,
77, 81-83, 88, 94
power position, 284, 346, 400
See also 1914 crisis
United Nations (UN), 8, 18, 152, 457, 494
alignment and consensus problems, 530-
532, 545-547
budget mismanagement, 538, 540
economic sanctions against South Africa,
221
new international economic order, 161-
162
peacekeeping effectiveness, decline, 455-
456, 501, 516-517,
519-520, 522-533
peacekeeping forces, 494-495, 504
peacekeeping role, 9, 18, 504
politicization criticism, 538-539
role reassessment, 517-519, 536-538, 541-
542
statist theories criticized, 539-540
U.S. commitment to, 501-502, 533-536,
541-543
U.S. economic support, 528-530, 544, 548-
549
U.S. policies criticized, 502, 543-552
United Nations Charter, 513, 520-522
United Nations Conference on Trade and
Development (UNCTAD), 161
United Nations Educational, Cultural and
Scientific Organization (UNESCO),
536, 538
United Nations Emergency Force, 494
United Nations Force in Cyprus, 495
United Nations high commission for human
rights (proposed), 497
United Nations High Commission for
Refugees, 497, 561
United Nations International Children's
Emergency Fund (UNICEF), 18

United States
coercive behavior, 221-222, 435-436
domestic stability, 36
economic exploitation policies, 23, 61, 62
fertilizer use, 303
food consumption, 303
gross national product, 61
percent ownership of world wealth, 61
percent of population in poverty, 61
percent of world exports, 158, 187, 194
percent of world GNP, 158
percent of world reserve currency, 158
power position, 32-33, 38-40, 280, 284,
285
strength of belief system, 37-38
UN economic support, 528-530, 544, 548-
549
U.S./Soviet strategic stability, 33, 34, 39,
53-54
See also specific countries and issues
Uruguay, 57

V-1 bomb, 235
V-2 rocket, 235
Venezuela, 147, 280, 550
Vietnam, 159, 348, 475
aggression in Cambodia, 55, 414, 461, 477,
546
Vietnam War, 165, 298, 432-433, 475, 506
asymmetrical power relationship, 271,
276, 286, 346, 348, 351,
402, 461, 465-470
coercive diplomacy, 435-436
policy-making determinants, 65, 71, 105,
122, 142
Viner, Jacob, 180
Vinocur, John, 424
Violence. *See* Conflict and violence;
Terrorism; War
Volcker, Paul, 309
Volkswagen, 160
Voluntary export limits, 153
Vulnerability interdependence, 273, 282-287

Waite, Terry, 497
Waldheim, Kurt, 541
Wallerstein, Immanuel, 372, 400-408
Walters, Vernon, 544
Waltz, Kenneth N., 34
War
casualty figures, 455, 457, 464, 473, 475
causes, 433
coercive violence, 228-235
commercialization of, 447
definitions, 432, 443, 454, 464
European stability, 53, 421, 459

580